ADA FROM
BEGINNING

INTERNATIONAL COMPUTER SCIENCE SERIES

Consulting Editors   A D McGettrick   University of Strathclyde
J van Leeuwen   University of Utrecht

OTHER TITLES IN THE SERIES

Software Engineering (2nd Edn.)   *I Sommerville*

A Structured Approach to FORTRAN 77 Programming   *T M R Ellis*

Handbook of Algorithms and Data Structures   *G H Gonnet*

Microcomputers in Engineering and Science   *J F Craine and G R Martin*

UNIX for Super-Users   *E Foxley*

Software Specification Techniques   *N Gehani and A D McGettrick (eds.)*

Data Communications for Programmers   *M Purser*

Local Area Network Design   *A Hopper, S Temple and R C Williamson*

Prolog Programming for Artificial Intelligence   *I Bratko*

Modula-2: Discipline & Design   *A H J Sale*

Introduction to Expert Systems   *P Jackson*

PROLOG   *F Giannesini, H Kanoui, R Pasero and M van Caneghem*

Programming Language Translation: A Practical Approach   *P D Terry*

System Simulation: Programming Styles and Languages   *W Kreutzer*

Data Abstraction in Programming Languages   *J M Bishop*

The UNIX System V Environment   *S R Bourne*

The Craft of Software Engineering   *A Macro and J Buxton*

An Introduction to Programming with Modula-2   *P D Terry*

Parallel Programming   *R H Perrott*

Software Development with Ada   *I Sommerville and R Morrison*

The Specification of Computer Programs   *W M Turski and T S E Maibaum*

ADA FROM THE BEGINNING

Jan Skansholm

Chalmers University of Technology

Translated by
Shirley Booth

ADDISON-WESLEY
PUBLISHING
COMPANY

Wokingham, England · Reading, Massachusetts · Menlo Park, California
New York · Don Mills, Ontario · Amsterdam · Bonn
Sydney · Singapore · Tokyo · Madrid · San Juan

The programs presented in this book have been included for their instructional value. They have been tested with care but are not guaranteed for any particular purpose. The publisher does not offer any warranties or representations, nor does it accept any liabilities with respect to the programs.

Cover design by Crayon Design of Henley-on-Thames
and printed by the Riverside Printing Co (Reading) Ltd
Typeset by Columns of Reading
Printed in Great Britain by Adlard & Son Ltd, Letchworth, Herts

First printed 1988.

British Library Cataloguing in Publication Data
Skansholm, Jan
    Ada from the beginning.
    1. Ada (Computer program language)
    I. Title   II. Ada från början. *English*
    005.13'3   QA76.73.A15

    ISBN 0-201-17522-3

Library of Congress Cataloging in Publication Data
Skansholm, Jan, 1949-
    Ada from the beginning.
    Translation of: Ada från början.
    Includes index.
    1. Ada (Computer program language)   I. Title.
QA76.73.A35S4913   1988   005.13'3   87-26902
ISBN 0-201-17522-3

Preface

This book is intended for use alongside an introductory course on programming. In contrast to most other books on Ada, it assumes no previous experience of programming. The book could also be of use to students who have programmed in other languages (such as Basic, Pascal or Fortran) and who want a 'soft' introduction to Ada.

The principal aim of the book is to teach the basics of writing computer programs; thus the fundamentals of good programming are emphasized. Throughout the book, aspects such as devising algorithms, making specifications, abstracting and representing data, constructing abstract data types, dividing a program into subprograms, concealing inessential details, developing a program in modules, and the general structure of a program are discussed. In particular, numerous examples are presented in which the technique of top-down design (also called stepwise refinement), is used to construct algorithms expressible as computer programs.

It is impossible to learn how to program simply by studying how to devise a program. To write programs in a real programming language and run them in a computer is also essential. The second aim of this book, therefore, is to provide a grounding in the programming language Ada. At present it is more common to use Pascal or Basic as a first programming language, but there is much to be said in favour of starting with Ada.

Ada is a modern language with a wide range of uses. It is suitable for both technical and administrative applications. In addition, Ada is a standardized language with strong international support. For most other languages there are different versions and dialects on different computers; there is only one version of Ada. The name Ada is protected as a brand name. Any implementation of Ada must be validated before it can use the name, i.e. it must go through a battery of tests to check that the Ada standard is adhered to.

Ada is built on the experience of the common conventional languages, such as Fortran, Algol, Pascal, COBOL and Basic. The fundamental constructs in Ada are similar to the corresponding constructs in Pascal. For this reason, someone who has learned Ada as a first language will have little difficulty in learning to write programs in other languages.

Even if the fundamental principles of designing a computer program are the most important part of a first programming course, it is undeniable that a programmer's way of thinking is influenced by the first language met. It is important, therefore, that this first language is a 'good' language. It should support the basic principles of programming and encourage good structure. Ada supports the design of programs based on algorithms, and Ada's types make data abstraction and the representation of data objects possible. Furthermore, the packages in Ada make modular program development a reality.

Ada is a language with wide possibilities, offering the student the opportunity for continued development within the language. When the time comes to go on and study more advanced programming, he or she can still use Ada; all the required programming concepts are to be found in the language. With Ada as a first language, there is no need, as there is when a simple first language is learned, to study special dialects and supplements, or go over to another language altogether in order to progress.

The fact that Ada is equipped with all these possibilities does not mean it is a 'hard' language. Compare it with Pascal, for example; thanks to its more refined structure, Ada is in many respects simpler for the beginner to learn and handle.

This book deals with most of the language, except for parallel programming. The basics of Ada, for example control statements, different data types and subprograms, are dealt with in the early chapters. In the later chapters, the more advanced constructs of the language are dealt with, such as packages, handling exceptions, dynamic data structures, files and generic program units.

No student should try to learn all versions of a construct in the language in one go. Instead, a spiral technique is recommended, so that learning takes place on several levels. The first priority is to acquire an overview of the basic features of the language and what they can be used for. Then the simplest versions of all the constructs can be learned. When these simpler features are thoroughly understood, and have been used successfully, then a further level can be taken on, in which the more complicated constructs are studied.

This book is written to enable such spiral learning to be applied. In Chapter 2 there is a broad overview of the basic language constructs in Ada, and a number of simple examples demonstrate how these constructs can be used for developing a program. There is a system of reserved sections; the symbol, ■, marks the start of such a section and □ marks the end. On a first reading, such a section can be omitted. Only when the contents of the first read-through are thoroughly understood should the reserved sections be returned to and studied.

The precise description of Ada is to be found in a special reference manual.[†] It is not intended as a textbook and is therefore rather hard to read, even for an experienced programmer. If Ada is to be used for advanced programming, the manual should be available, but the beginner and 'ordinary' programmer can manage without it.

Four appendices in this book are taken directly from Ada's reference manual. Appendix A1 gives the specification of the package TEXT_IO which is used for reading and writing text. Appendix A3 gives the specification of the package STANDARD, including the basic operators in Ada and a description of the type CHARACTER. Appendices A4 and A5 describe the packages SEQUENTIAL_IO and DIRECT_IO, which contain the resources for file handling.

Solutions to selected exercises are presented at the end of the book. Readers wishing to obtain a complete set of solutions may do so by writing directly to: Dr Jan Skansholm, Department of Computer Science, Chalmers University of Technology, 41296 Gothenburg, Sweden.

All the program examples in the book have been tested using the Verdix validated Ada compiler, version 5.1b, under the UNIX 4.2 operating system on a VAX 11/780 computer.

Finally, I would like to thank my colleagues at the Department of Computer Science of Chalmers University of Technology for their valuable suggestions regarding the content and form of this book. In particular, I wish to thank Erland Holmström and Hans Lindström.

Jan Skansholm

Gothenburg, Sweden

October 1987

[†] *Reference Manual for the Ada Programming Language*. 1983. ANSI/MIL-STD-1815A-1983. Washington, D.C.: US Department of Defense.

Contents

Preface   v

Chapter 1   An introduction to computers and programming
             languages   1

       1.1   A brief history   2
       1.2   A computer's structure and operation   4
       1.3   How the program gets into the computer   8
       1.4   Programming languages   14

Chapter 2   Program design   21

       2.1   Specifications and algorithms   22
       2.2   Top-down design   26
       2.3   Simple programming examples   30
             2.3.1   Simple output   30
             2.3.2   Reading and writing numbers   31
             2.3.3   Writing an invoice   36
             2.3.4   Drawing outsize letters   46
             2.3.5   Comparing numbers   55
             2.3.6   Calculating a selling price   59
             2.3.7   Producing tables   61
             2.3.8   How long before I'm a millionaire?   62
             Exercises   65

Chapter 3   The basics of Ada   69

       3.1   Standard types   70
             3.1.1   The numeric types INTEGER and FLOAT   71
             3.1.2   The type CHARACTER   78

3.1.3   The text type STRING   82
3.1.4   The logical type BOOLEAN   90
3.2   Identifiers   92
3.3   Literals   93
3.4   Expressions   96
3.4.1   Numeric expressions   97
3.4.2   Boolean expressions   106
3.4.3   Operator precedence   110
3.5   Variables and constants   111
3.6   Errors in programs   114
Exercises   120

Chapter 4   Control statements   125

4.1   Sequential program structure   126
4.2   Assignment statements   127
4.3   Selection: the **if** statement   128
4.4   Selection: the **case** statement   131
4.5   Iteration: the **loop** statement   136
4.5.1   Simple **loop** statement   137
4.5.2   The **loop** statement with **for**   138
4.5.3   The **loop** statement with **while**   142
4.6   **Exit** statement   147
4.7   Nested **loop** statements   148
4.8   Interactive input   150
Exercises   156

Chapter 5   Types   161

5.1   Data abstraction   162
5.2   Integer types   165
5.3   Real types   168
5.4   Enumeration types   172
5.5   The tools for input and output   176
5.6   Subtypes   182
5.7   Array types   187
5.7.1   Constrained array types   187
5.7.2   Array aggregates   194
5.7.3   Unconstrained array types   196
5.7.4   Assignment and comparison   199
5.7.5   Attributes   201
5.7.6   Catenating arrays   202
5.8   Searching and sorting   203
Exercises   210

Chapter 6   Subprograms   215

  6.1   Functions   216
  6.2   Procedures   235
  6.3   Parameter association   239
  6.4   Top-down design with subprograms   249
  6.5   The scope of a declaration   267
  6.6   Overloaded subprograms   270
  6.7   Named parameter association   273
  6.8   Recursive subprograms   277
  6.9   Functions as operators   288
        Exercises   290

Chapter 7   Data structures   297

  7.1   Multidimensional array types   298
        7.1.1   Constrained array types   298
        7.1.2   Matrices and unconstrained arrays   310
  7.2   Arrays of arrays   314
  7.3   Record types   319
  7.4   Arrays of records   327
        Exercises   334

Chapter 8   Packages   341

  8.1   Package specification   342
  8.2   The Ada programming environment   344
  8.3   Using packages   346
  8.4   Package bodies   349
  8.5   Different categories of packages   351
  8.6   Packages of types and constants   351
  8.7   Packages with memory   352
  8.8   Abstract data types   359
  8.9   Private types   372
        Exercises   376

Chapter 9   Input and output   381

  9.1   Output at the terminal   382
        9.1.1   Page and line structure   382
        9.1.2   Output of characters and text   388
        9.1.3   Output of integers   389
        9.1.4   Output of floating point numbers   391

9.1.5   Output of values of enumeration type   393
9.2   Input from the terminal   395
9.2.1   Page and line structure   395
9.2.2   Input of characters and text   405
9.2.3   Input of integers   407
9.2.4   Input of floating point numbers   408
9.2.5   Input of values of enumeration type   409
9.3   Text files   410
Exercises   426

Chapter 10   Exceptions   431

10.1   Predefined exceptions   432
10.2   Declaring exceptions   433
10.3   Handling exceptions   434
10.4   Errors arising during input and output   445
Exercises   448

Chapter 11   Dynamic data structures   451

11.1   Pointers and dynamic objects   452
11.2   Linked lists   457
11.2.1   Building up a list   458
11.2.2   Running through a list   461
11.2.3   Putting elements into a list and removing
         them   462
11.2.4   Linked lists and recursion   464
11.3   Doubly linked lists   465
11.4   Stacks and queues   469
11.5   Trees   476
Exercises   485

Chapter 12   Files   491

12.1   Sequential files   492
12.2   Sorted files   499
12.3   Direct files   513
Exercises   518

Chapter 13   **Generic units**   523

    13.1   Definitions and instances   524
    13.2   Generic parameters   529
        13.2.1   Value parameters   529
        13.2.2   Type parameters   531
        13.2.3   Subprogram parameters   536
        Exercises   544

APPENDICES

A1   The package TEXT_IO   549

A2   The package BASIC_NUM_IO   555

A3   The package STANDARD   557

A4   The package SEQUENTIAL_IO   562

A5   The package DIRECT_IO   564

Solutions to selected exercises   567

Index   609

Chapter 1
An introduction to computers and programming languages

1.1 A brief history
1.2 A computer's structure and operation

1.3 How the program gets into the computer
1.4 Programming languages

This first chapter presents a short history of the developments that have led to the computers of today. There is an introduction on how computers are constructed, their most important components, and what they do. The role of the program is explained in Section 1.3, together with how a program is translated and how the computer makes it work. Finally, an overview is presented of the most important common programming languages and their historical development.

1.1   A brief history

Computers are found everywhere in modern society and, for better or worse, we are becoming more and more dependent on them. Most large administrative systems, such as those dealing with wages, bank accounts, inventory control and sales, are now computerized. The computer is an indispensable work tool for the engineer who needs to make calculations of many kinds. In fact, some calculations would be impossible without some help from a computer. Computers have also come to play a greater and greater role as components in engineering systems, as a result of developments in the field of microelectronics, where it has become possible to manufacture powerful electronic units in large quantities and at low cost. Computers can be found as components in everything from kitchen stoves and sewing machines to space shuttles and satellites. Furthermore, in recent years, developments in personal computers have brought computers nearer to the man in the street.

It could be said that the development that led to today's computer started in the seventeenth century when the French mathematician Blaise Pascal (whose name was given to the programming language **Pascal**) built, using a number of cogwheels, a mechanical machine that could both add and subtract. Subsequent mechanical calculating machines had certain practical uses.

As we shall see, the basic idea behind computers is that their work is controlled by a **program**. The first hint of a program in connection with mechanical equipment came at the start of the nineteenth century with an automatic weaving loom, built by the Frenchman Joseph Jacquard. A number of hole-punched metal cards controlled the action of the loom and how the various threads were woven together.

In the 1820s, the English mathematician Charles Babbage combined both these ideas – mechanical calculators and the use of punched cards – to control machines, in what became known as his 'difference engine'. This was intended to be used for solving polynomial equations, but the project was abandoned because it was impossible to make the necessary components accurately. Later he designed a more advanced machine called an 'analytical engine'. This was not constructed in his lifetime, but the work had significance for further developments. Charles Babbage had an assistant called Augusta Ada Lovelace, daughter of the poet, Lord Byron. The programming language **Ada** has been named after her. Some consider her to be the first programmer because she had ideas about the control of Babbage's analytical engine and helped him develop the instructions for calculating with it.

The development of mechanical calculators continued, principally in the USA. In the 1880s, Hermann Hollerith, who worked for the American Census Bureau, constructed an electrically operated tabulator that used punched cards. The machine was utilized in the census of 1890 and, as a result, the census was completed in record time. Hollerith formed his own company which continued to manufacture and market similar machines. In fact, this was one of the companies that formed the basis of the famous IBM, International Business Machines, founded in the 1920s.

In 1936, the mathematician Howard Aiken designed a machine in which Babbage's ideas could be put into practice using more modern technology. The project was supported by IBM and gave rise to the first electromechanical computer, Mark I, in 1944. It was never particularly efficient but it received a lot of publicity.

A couple of years later another research group built a more powerful machine called ENIAC. The work had been initiated by the American Department of Defense, and the machine was intended for military calculations. ENIAC consisted of several thousand electronic valves, tubes and relays, and filled an entire room. It was programmed by connecting and reconnecting the electronic circuits – work that was both difficult and time-consuming.

The mathematician John von Neumann, who was a consultant to the group behind ENIAC, went on to develop an idea based on storing the program in a memory within the computer. This was a very important advance and today's computers are built on the same principle.

A milestone was reached with the first delivery of a computer to a civil customer in 1951. The machine was called UNIVAC and was a further development of ENIAC.

It is common to talk about **generations** of computers. In the first generation, during the 1950s, electronic valves were used. By the end of the decade a new stage of development was reached when transistors began to be used instead. It then became possible to build computers that were smaller, faster, cheaper and more reliable than before. Such computers are said to belong to the second generation.

Further improvements became possible at the end of the 1960s and during the 1970s, when the manufacture of electronic components could take advantage of integrated circuit technology and LSI (large scale integration). That gave the third generation computers.

The technology developed even more during the 1970s. VLSI technology (very large scale integration) started to be used. It became possible to include an increasing number of functions on a single 'chip'. For example, all the central functions of a computer could be put onto one chip, known as a microprocessor. This development means that today powerful, small and relatively cheap computers can be made. These are referred to as fourth generation computers. This is the stage we are at today, even if there is discussion of a fifth generation in some quarters. The rapid development of increasingly powerful electronic components is still in progress.

Generations of computers

- First generation: 1950s, valves.
- Second generation: 1950s, 1960s, transistors.
- Third generation: 1970s, LSI circuits.
- Fourth generation: 1970s, 1980s, VLSI circuits.
- Fifth generation: 1980s, improved technology.

1.2   A computer's structure and operation

A computer can be described as a 'machine' that can store and process information. A simplified representation of what apparently happens when a computer program is run is shown in Figure 1.1.

This shows that a computer can be seen as a unit into which certain data can be fed – the input. The computer manipulates these data and produces the output. The input and output data can take different forms – electric signals, light or sound. To start with, the computer may be thought of as communicating with people, and then it is natural that the input and output should take the form of written text. But computers are also used in many other situations where communication is not primarily with people, in manufacturing processes, for example, or as components of engineering systems such as aeroplanes and cars. Here the input

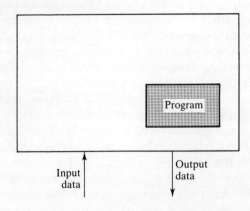

Figure 1.1

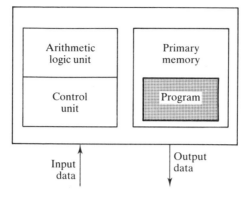

Figure 1.2

generally consists of signals from monitoring devices that feed information to the computer about the current state of the system, for instance temperature or speed. The output from the computer might be control signals to relays or motors, perhaps to change the flow of fuel or initiate transfers in the system.

One very important thing to understand from the diagram is that the computer's behaviour is controlled by a program inside it. The computer can be made to do other things by changing the program. It is this that distinguishes a modern computer from an 'ordinary' machine which is only designed to do certain preordained tasks. There are, however, computers that are intended to perform only one particular task, in other words, to run only one particular program. These are known as dedicated computers. One example is the computer found in a computer or video game. However, this still does not contradict the principle that a computer is always controlled by a program and that the program is replaceable.

Computers compared with ordinary machines

A computer differs from an ordinary machine in that its actions are controlled by a *program*.

Figure 1.2 shows the central parts of a computer in a little more detail. The computer's 'brain' consists of a **central processing unit** (CPU). In the CPU there is a **control unit** (CU) that controls and coordinates all the computer's activities. Decisions are made in the control unit regarding the operations to be executed and the order in which these should be undertaken. The control unit also sends out control signals which regulate all the other units of the computer. In the CPU there is also an **arithmetic logic unit** (ALU) containing electronic circuits that can carry out various operations on the data being manipulated, such as addition, subtraction, multiplication and division.

Another very important unit in the computer is the **primary memory**, which stores, among other things, the program that the computer is running or executing, at any given time. Various data and temporary storage spaces needed for the executing program to function properly are also found in the primary memory.

Execution

When a program is run in a computer, it is said to be *executed*.

Primary memory can be thought of as a series of **memory cells**, sometimes called **words** (although they have nothing to do with ordinary spoken words). Each cell has a certain **address** determined by its position in the memory. The number of memory cells in a computer varies, depending on the type and model; but it is usually a question of hundreds of thousands, or even millions. Each memory cell consists of a certain number of **bits**, usually 8, 16, 32 or 64. Each bit can contain a **binary digit**, in other words either zero or one.

A group of eight bits is usually called a **byte**. The size of memory is usually expressed in the unit **kilobyte**, shortened to KB. One kilobyte is 1024 (2^{10}) bytes. Memory size can also be given in the units **megabytes** (millions of bytes) and **gigabytes** (billions, that is, thousands of millions, of bytes).

A program that is being executed, and is therefore in primary memory, occupies a number of connected memory cells. A memory cell, or a group of cells, contains one **instruction** from the program. Different instructions can be represented by different combinations of bits in the memory cells. Thus a program consists of a series of instructions. An instruction tells the computer that it should perform a particular task, for example, move the contents of a memory cell from primary memory to the CPU, or add two numbers in the ALU. When a program is executed, the control unit reads the instructions one by one from primary memory and makes sure that they are carried out in the same order.

An instruction can thus be thought of as a particular combination

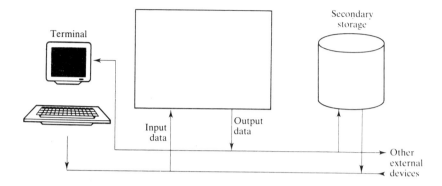

Figure 1.3

of zeros and ones. These combinations look different for different models of computer. The program must be stored in primary memory in this form so that it can be executed in the computer, and then it is said to be in the form of **machine code**. Machine code is very 'unfriendly' in the sense that it is difficult to read and write. In the early days of computers, when the principle of a stored program was first applied, programs had to be written directly in machine code. Fortunately, this area has developed and today the programmer does not generally need to worry about the computer's machine code. As we will see, programs are written in what are known as **high-level languages** (for example, Ada and Pascal), which are much more 'friendly'. Special translator programs are used to translate from high-level language to the machine code, so that the program can be run in the computer.

In Figure 1.3 our computer system is extended with some very common units. To be able to communicate with its environment a computer must have one or more **input and output units**. Figure 1.3 shows the most common input/output unit for communication with people, a **video terminal**. Note that such a terminal actually comprises two separate units: the **keyboard** which is an input unit and the **screen** which is an output unit. Apart from the video terminal there are computer terminals of many kinds, for example, printer terminals, graphics terminals and terminals that are connected to a light-pen or a mouse. There are also other common input and output units, such as line-printers and plotters.

We saw that the primary memory is used partly to store the program being executed, but in general a computer must also be able to store programs that are not being executed. The various data used as input to different programs must also be stored. Such data, which will be saved more permanently, are stored in **secondary storage**. Common types of secondary storage include the **disk** and **magnetic tape**. (Figure 1.3 shows a disk). As a rule, secondary storage has considerably greater capacity than primary memory.

The data in secondary storage is usually organized into **files**. A file is a collection of data that belong together in some way; it might contain, for example, a program or the input data for a particular program. A file can be thought of as an envelope into which related data can be put. Each file is given its own name so that it can easily be referred to. It is possible to create new files, remove files and make changes in files.

The units in a computer that do not belong to the central parts are usually called **external units** or **peripherals**.

Important units of a computer

- *Central processing unit* (CPU) controls the computer and processes data.

- In *primary memory*, the program being executed and the data needed by that program are stored.

- *Peripheral units* are used for reading and writing data (input and output units) or for storing data more permanently (secondary storage).

1.3 How the program gets into the computer

In a programming language such as Ada or Pascal, what form does a computer program take? Because the program is written by an ordinary person, it has the form of normal written text. The program can even be written on ordinary paper. In this section we shall see what happens when this original **program text**, or **source code**, is translated into the machine's own machine code and loaded into the computer.

Since the program is an ordinary text, it can be written using the terminal keyboard. All computer systems are normally supplied with a set of utility programs, written by the supplier. One such program is a **text-editing program** or **text-editor**. Figure 1.4 shows what happens when this program is run in the computer.

Using the text-editor, any text can be fed into the computer or stored as a file in secondary storage. A file containing text is called a **text file**. With the editor's help it is also easy to revise, erase, change, rearrange or add to text. To do this, special commands are given to the editor, using the keyboard. A text-editor that is oriented towards use with

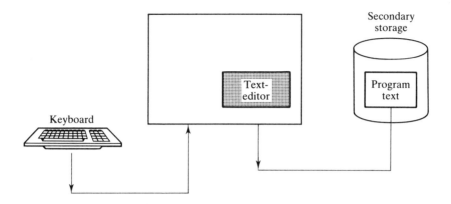

Figure 1.4

a video monitor is particularly convenient to use. A large piece of the text is generally displayed on the screen and it is possible to choose the parts that need revision with the aid of the keyboard, light-pen or mouse. Exactly how the text editor works and which commands it understands vary a great deal from system to system. Note that the text-editor does not normally take any account of what the actual text contains; it is all the same whether it is a program in Ada or a chapter of a book.

The next stage is to translate the program text from normal text to machine code. This is accomplished, as shown in Figure 1.5, using a special program, a **compiler**. Each compiler is designed to deal with a particular programming language. To translate an Ada program requires access to an Ada compiler; likewise to translate a Pascal program requires a Pascal compiler. A computer system normally has compilers for several different languages.

Every programming language has special rules regarding the form of different program constructions; this can be likened to the rules for sentence structure in natural languages. It is said that each language has a certain **syntax**. The compiler reads the program from the text file created earlier and checks first that it obeys the rules of the language, i.e. that it is syntactically correct. If the compiler discovers faults it displays an error message on the screen. Sometimes the compiler attempts to correct errors if they are not too serious, but normally compilation stops when errors are found. The programmer then has to go back a stage and use the text-editor to revise the program and correct the errors. A new attempt to compile the program can then be made. Sometimes this process has to be repeated several times before the program is free of syntax errors.

If no errors are found in this first stage, the compiler goes on to translate the program from text to machine code. The machine code so

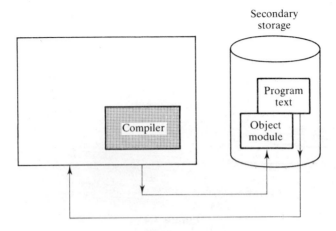

Figure 1.5

produced is generally called the **object module** and it is saved in a file in secondary storage.

Note that, because different models of computer have different machine codes, a compiler designed for one computer will not work on another. Different compilers are needed for different computers. This is no problem for the Ada programmer, because an Ada compiler always requires an Ada program as input, irrespective of the computer being used. The text of an Ada program that is developed for a particular computer can thus easily be transferred to another computer and run there. Thus the programs are said to be **portable**. One of the advantages of high-level languages is the possibility of writing portable programs, which is not possible using machine code.

The compilation of a fairly simple program may give rise to an object module that can be loaded directly into the primary memory and executed, but normally a **linking** stage is needed before this. Figure 1.6 illustrates this stage. A special link program must be run. When a large program is designed it is usually divided into different parts that are written, developed and compiled separately. The link program gathers together the different object modules from these separate compilations into a single entity called the **load module**. This is saved in a file in secondary storage. Even if the program has not been divided, linking might still be necessary because the program needs access to existing system routines, for example, routines for input and output or mathematical routines.

Only the final stage now remains – to get the load module into the primary memory so that the program can be run. This brings us to the

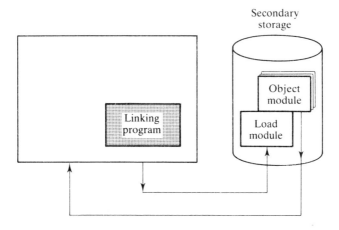

Figure 1.6

question: how does the computer know which program it should run? For the answer to this, study Figure 1.7.

In the earlier figures we have only shown one program at a time in the primary memory – the program that is currently being run. In actual fact there is always one more program permanently stored in the primary memory. That is the **operating system**, abbreviated to OS. The operating system is the program that is always running when no 'ordinary' program is being run. It operates automatically when the ordinary program has finished or stopped for some reason. The computer is also designed to put the operating system directly into operation when the computer starts.

The operating system usually communicates with the user via the terminal. The user writes commands at the keyboard. One common command is the instruction to load and execute a particular program. The operating system then searches after the required load module in secondary storage and copies it into the primary memory, as indicated in Figure 1.7. Control is then passed to the loaded program, which can run until it finishes or stops.

The operating system performs many other tasks in a computer. For example, it checks that the computer's contacts with the peripherals are working and keeps track of all the files stored in secondary storage. The operating system is often a very advanced program and computer manufacturers generally provide one when a computer is delivered.

Now we have seen how a program is written, how it is loaded and run. This process can often be simplified so that the programmer does not need to be aware of the separate stages, by using, for example, a program that combines the compiling and linking stages.

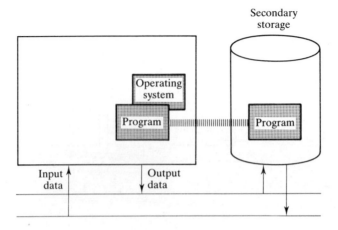

Figure 1.7

The stages of making a working program

- The program text (source code) is created using the text-editor.
- The compiler translates the program text into an object module.
- The linker puts several object modules together to form an executable load module.
- The operating system puts the load module into primary memory and the program is executed.

There is another way of running programs written in a high-level language, distinctly different from the one just described. Instead of a compiler, a special program, called an **interpreter**, is used. This is shown in Figure 1.8.

The program text is created using the text-editor, exactly as before. The interpreter is then run with the program text in secondary storage as input data. Just like the compiler, the interpreter reads the text and checks that the program has no syntax errors. The difference is that the interpreter never translates the program into machine code. Instead, it interprets the program step by step and carries out the tasks of the program. From the user's point of view, it appears as if the program he or

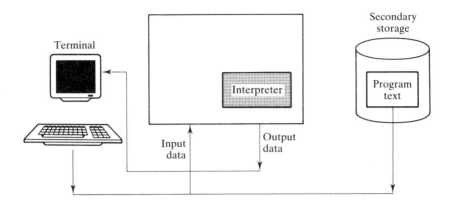

Figure 1.8

she has written is being executed. This often provides a faster and easier way of test running small and simple programs. The disadvantage is that the program runs much more slowly. It is thus not a method to be used in the everyday running of working programs.

In some systems even the text-editor and the interpreter have been combined in one program; most Basic systems work in this way, for example. Then, using just one program, a user's program can be both edited and run.

This section closes with a look at another common picture of a computer, the so-called onion model, illustrated in Figure 1.9. Speaking purely physically, a computer consists only of a mass of electronic and mechanical components, usually called **hardware**. You could think of these components being surrounded by several skins of program, called **software**. Without these programs a computer would be useless. The innermost of these skins is the operating system which deals with all contact with the hardware. This normally comes from the manufacturer, so the purchaser does not need to worry exactly how the hardware is controlled. The next skin consists of the text-editors, compilers and interpreters (tools), which make it possible for us to program in high-level languages and avoid thinking about machine code. The outermost skin is made up of various user programs. Most of the people who use computers never write programs of their own but run ready-written user programs. This is true of users such as bank employees and people who use word processing. The picture one then gets of the computer is simply the program's interface with the user, and this requires no knowledge of the operating system or different programming languages.

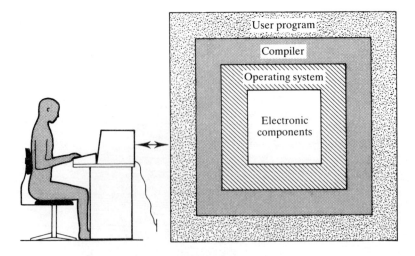

Figure 1.9

1.4 Programming languages

As mentioned earlier, the earliest computers had to be programmed in machine code. Part of such a program may have looked like this:

```
0111000100001111
1001110110110001
1110000100111110
```

It is easy to understand that it was seen as a tremendous advance when **assembler languages** started to be used. Then the above fragment of program may have been rewritten as:

```
LOAD   A
ADD    B
STORE  C
```

In the assembler language each line of the program corresponds to one instruction in machine code. Thus the little program above has three instructions. For a program written in assembler language to be run in the computer, a translating program is required – an **assembler** – that translates the program into machine code. Such a translator does not have to be too complicated because the assembler language lies so close to the structure of the machine code.

In spite of the considerable advance provided by assembler languages, they still have enormous disadvantages. One disadvantage is that each model of computer has its own unique assembler language, naturally enough, because the language is so close to the machine code. An assembler programmer is thus forced to learn many different assembler languages which can differ considerably in their details. Another disadvantage is that the assembler language is extremely detailed. Each individual instruction must be given to the computer, which means it is time-consuming to use an assembler language. Furthermore, the error risk is high, so a program may contain many errors that may be difficult to detect.

With the development of high-level languages in the 1950s, programming changed radically. A program written in a high-level language is more adapted to human modes of expression than to the computer's set of instructions. Programs are expressed in 'half-English' and arithmetic calculations are written in a way familiar from mathematics. The above fragment of program may now be written as:

C := A + B

The programmer can concentrate on the problem to be solved rather than a mass of detail about how the computer works. In principle, it is also possible to write a program in a high-level language with the intention of running it on different computers. There is no need to learn a new language for each computer.

The first high-level language was **Fortran** (FORmula TRANslator), introduced in 1954. It was originally intended to simplify writing programs that made calculations using arithmetic expressions. Fortran became a very popular language among people working in engineering and scientific programming. The language's great weakness, however, is its poor structure, which means that Fortran programs often become muddled and difficult to see as a whole. In addition, the language has poor facilities for describing data and for handling input and output. Fortran had something of a facelift with the more recent version, Fortran 77, but it must be admitted that today the language is out-of-date. Even so, it is still one of the most common programming languages, largely because of the great capital investment in Fortran programs and the training of Fortran programmers.

In 1959 a new programming language, **COBOL** (COmmon Business Oriented Language), was introduced. This was designed for programming in the areas of finance and administration. A few years later the language was standardized and it has become, and still is, one of the most common languages. COBOL programs are very readable; they resemble ordinary English. The disadvantage of this is that the language is sometimes considered 'chatty' and awkward. What was new about COBOL was its better way of describing the data the program had to handle, compared with FORTRAN.

A language that came to be very significant for subsequent

developments was **Algol** (ALGOrithmic Language), which appeared in 1960. The big advantage of the language was its good program structure: tasks such as the selection of alternatives in a program and the iteration of certain parts of a program could be expressed very clearly. In addition, programs could be written in a freer format than in either Fortran or COBOL. For example, lines were not restricted to starting in a particular column, thereby enabling programs to be written such that the way in which they worked was reflected in their appearance. Despite these advances, Algol never had any great commercial success. A completely new version, Algol68, was presented in 1968 but even that never made any real breakthrough.

Algol was a forerunner of **PL/I** which was launched by IBM in 1964. PL/I was intended for use in technical and scientific programming as well as in commerce and administration. Like Algol, the language is structured and there are facilities for describing data that resemble COBOL. However, PL/I never gained popularity outside the IBM world. This may be because it is a large language that requires a big compiler. Also, the language is highly influenced by the fact that it was designed for an IBM environment.

In 1965 the language **Basic** was introduced. At the start it was intended to be used for teaching but it has since become very common. It is a small language that is easy to learn even for those with no previous experience. And it does not need large computer resources, which means that it has become very common on personal computers and even programmable calculators. If its advantage lies in its simplicity, then its disadvantage lies in its lack of structure. It is easy to end up with badly structured programs that are hard to comprehend. This makes Basic most suitable for developing smaller one-off programs.

A language that became significant for later language developments was **Simula**, the first version of which appeared in 1967; it is a direct extension of Algol. In Simula, data can be described in an interesting way, that is, close to the idea of a 'package' in Ada. The language is used mostly, as the name implies, for writing simulation programs.

The language **Pascal** was designed by Niklaus Wirth and presented in 1971. The aim was for Pascal to be a simple language, suitable for use in teaching, and it has achieved wide usage in this field. The reason is that it has a good program structure. This makes it easier for beginners to acquire good 'programming style'. Pascal has also, thanks to its simplicity, become a common language in the world of personal computing, and a rival to Basic. Pascal is built directly on Algol and Algol68, and on ideas from Simula, but several constructs have been deliberately simplified. An important feature of the language is that data can be well described and new **data types** can be introduced by the programmer.

Pascal is standardized, both as an American standard (ANSI) and as an international standard (ISO). Even so, variants of the language have appeared in which certain additions have been made, for example, **UCSD Pascal** and **Turbo Pascal**. The greatest weakness of the language is that it is deficient in the text handling and input–output handling areas. It also has limitations that make it hard to write general mathematical programs.

Remarkably fast developments in the field of electronics, in that more and more powerful components can be produced more and more cheaply, led many to believe that it would similarly be possible to construct ever larger and more complex programs. In the event, this assumption was quite wrong. All too many programs either failed to be ready on time, greatly exceeded their budget, contained many errors or did not fulfil the customers' specifications. This phenomenon became known as the **software crisis**. Among the reasons for this crisis was poor project management, and the fact that the programmer often considered the program to be his or her own property. Many individual and curious programming styles developed and it proved difficult to create error-free programs. In order to remedy this, the concept of **structured programming** was introduced, with the aim that a program should be written in such a way that it is both easily understood and free from errors. Structured programming can be said to be a set of rules and recommendations for how 'good' programs should be written. Such programming needs the support of a suitable programming language and it was this need for well-structured programs that was behind the development of what became known as structured languages, like Pascal.

During the 1970s it became clear that even well-structured programs were not enough for mastering the complexity involved in developing a large program system. It was also recognized that it was necessary to support the division of the program into well defined parts, or **modules**, that could be developed and tested independently of one another, so that several people could work together within one large programming project.

This was recognized by the American Department of Defense, an important customer for systems of programs that were often supplied by many independent companies. These systems were written in a whole range of languages, making the development and maintenance of such programs more expensive. In 1975, in response to the software crisis, the Defense Department published a list of requirements that should be met by any programming language before it would be allowed for use. It turned out that none of the existing languages fulfilled these requirements and a competition was then announced for the design of a modern, general, programming language. Four teams took part in the competition which was won by the European team from Honeywell Bull in Paris. After the winning proposal was chosen in 1978, it was distributed to institutions all over the world for comment, and after subsequent amendment it was accepted as a standard in the USA. The new language was named **Ada**, a name that is registered as a trademark. The official definition of the language is published in a special *Ada Reference Manual*. Thus there can be no variants of Ada; all must keep to the standard and every compiler must go through a special validation test before it can be called an Ada compiler. Ada has received great support, not only from the American Defense Department but also from several major computer manufacturers and international organizations, including support as an industry standard by the Commission of the European Communities. It was accepted as an international ISO standard in 1987.

In addition to being well-structured, Ada also supports the modular development of programs. The concept of a **package** has been introduced and it is possible to build up a library of packages that can be combined into larger programs.

In terms of the basic constructions of the language, Ada is very similar to Pascal, but Ada is more general and has many facilities that are lacking in Pascal. One big difference is that **parallel programs** can be written using Ada. These are programs that are executed simultaneously and interact with the one another. Applications of such programs occur in computer control of various systems.

Some common programming languages

- Fortran: first high-level language (1954).
- COBOL: administrative data processing (1959).
- Algol: first language with structure (1960).
- PL/I: combined technical–administrative, IBM.
- Basic: easy-to-learn beginner's language, poor structure.
- Simula: simulation programs, interesting ideas.
- Pascal: teaching language (1971), types are new.
- Ada: standard 1983, remedy for the software crisis?
- LISP: used in artificial intelligence.
- APL: mathematical applications, special terminal.

Finally, we should mention a couple of computer languages that are partly founded on different principles from those discussed so far, **LISP** and **APL**. LISP was developed as long ago as 1958. It is designed to manipulate symbols of various sorts, such as characters and words. Programs are built up of lists of symbols and have a very distinctive appearance. LISP has found many uses, particularly in the area usually called **artificial intelligence**.

APL was introduced in 1968. It is peculiar in that it is specially suited to manipulating mathematical structures. In order to run APL, a special terminal is required with a special set of symbols.

Chapter 2
Program design

2.1 Specifications and algorithms
2.2 Top-down design

2.3 Simple programming
examples
Exercises

This chapter introduces basic programming methods. Important concepts such as specification and algorithms are discussed, and the technique of top-down design is introduced. A few simple examples of programs are presented so that the reader can become familiar with Ada programs. Only general descriptions of the different programming constructs are given in this chapter; greater detail is saved for later chapters.

2.1   Specifications and algorithms

Writing a computer program, or programming, really means solving a problem – such as a complicated calculation – with the help of a computer. The key feature of all problem solving is that the problem to be solved is clearly understood; in other words, there must be a **specification** of the problem. This may seem self-evident, but unfortunately it is all too common for a programmer to start writing a program too soon, before he or she really knows what the program should do.

There are two items that must be included in a specification of a program:

(1)   A description of what the program should do. There are no established formal methods for making such a description, but various informal methods are commonly used. The most common is to write an explanation in natural language, trying to make it as clear as possible. For example:

> The program takes the integer N, where $N > 0$, as input. The program computes the sum $1 + 2 + 3 + 4 + \ldots + N$ and gives this sum as the result.

(2)   A description of how the program communicates with the outside world. Here it should be stated, for example, what commands are expected from the terminal and what output should be given.

As we shall see, it is common for programs to be divided into **subprograms**, and in this case, the modes of communication between the various subprograms must also be specified. In Ada, such specifications are an integral part of the language. Furthermore, it is possible to develop the different subprograms individually, independently of one another. Use is then made of separate specifications that are distinct from the subprogram itself.

Note that the specification provides adequate information for the user of a program (or subprogram). There is no need to know what the program looks like in detail in order to solve the problem in hand. (After all, when you want to listen to a radio you do not need to know what it looks like inside – it is enough to know that it is a radio and that each knob has a particular function). The program can be considered as a 'black box' as in Figure 2.1. The programming problems in this introductory course are simple in nature, and the specifications are generally given.

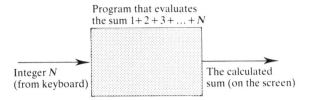

Figure 2.1

Program specification

(1) Description of what the program should do.

(2) Description of how the program communicates with the outside world (for subprograms, how the subprogram communicates with other subprograms).

When the specification is established, the next stage is to decide on a suitable method of solving the given problem. A description of how a particular problem is solved is called an **algorithm**. An algorithm consists of a number of elementary operations and instructions about the order in which they should be carried out. There are certain demands made of an algorithm:

- it should solve the given problem;
- it should be unambiguous;
- if the program has an end in view, such as computing a certain value, then the algorithm should terminate after a finite number of steps.

Note: Not all algorithms have to terminate. For instance, the algorithm that describes the control program for a nuclear power plant should certainly not terminate.

We come across algorithms every day. One example is a recipe; the problem is to prepare a particular dish and the algorithm gives us the solution. Another example is the assembly instructions we get when we buy furniture in kit form; and then there are all the different kinds of instruction manuals. And knitters will recognize that a knitting pattern is nothing other than an algorithm.

Algorithms can be expressed in many different ways. One common way is in natural language. Pictures and symbols can also be used, as in a knitting pattern, so can formal languages like mathematical notation. Flow charts have also been popular. Here we are dealing with programming, so it is naturally of interest to us that algorithms can be expressed in programming languages. The programming language Algol, which lies at the roots of most of today's conventional programming languages, was designed specifically so that it could be made to express algorithms, hence the name.

Algorithms

Description of how a particular problem should be solved.

Let us look at an example. We shall describe an algorithm that shows how the sum $1 + 2 + 3 + ... + N$ can be evaluated, if N is a given whole number > 0. One way of describing the algorithm in natural language is:

(1) Set SUM equal to 0 and the counter K equal to 1.
(2) Repeat the following steps until K is greater than N:
    (2.1) Calculate the sum of SUM and K and save the result in SUM.
    (2.2) Increase the value of K by 1.
(3) The result required is now the number in SUM.

A flow chart that describes the algorithm can be seen in Figure 2.2. Expressed as an Ada program, the algorithm looks like this:

```
GET (N);
SUM := 0;
K := 1;
while K <= N loop
   SUM := SUM + K;
   K := K + 1;
end loop;
PUT (SUM);
```

These lines of program read in the number N from the terminal keyboard and display the required result at the terminal.

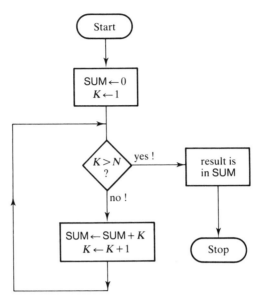

Figure 2.2

To describe general algorithms the description method must be able to express the following three constructs:

(1) **Sequence** A sequence is a series of steps that are carried out sequentially in the order in which they are written. Each step is carried out only once. An example is the assembly instructions for bookshelves:

　　(1) Put the side pieces in position.
　　(2) Screw the back piece onto the sides.
　　(3) Put the shelves into the frame.

(2) **Selection** Selection means that one of two or more alternatives should be chosen. Calculating the absolute value of a number T can be taken as an example:

　　If $T > 0$ then the result is T, otherwise the result is $-T$.

(3) **Iteration** Part of the algorithm should be capable of repetition, either a defined number of times or until a certain condition has been met. An example of the latter repetition could be:

　　Whisk the egg whites vigorously, until they become fluffy.

The most important algorithmic constructs

- Sequence: series of steps.
- Selection: choice between alternative paths.
- Iteration: repetition.

Another kind of construct that is commonly used in algorithms, and which can sometimes replace iteration, is **recursion**. This construct seldom occurs in 'everyday' algorithms and may therefore feel a little strange. The principle is to break down the original problem into smaller, but structurally similar, problems. The smaller problems can then be solved by reapplying the same algorithm. The previous example, calculating the sum of the first N positive integers can be solved with recursion in the following manner:

(1) If $N = 0$ set the result to 0.
(2) Otherwise:
    (2.1) Compute the sum $1 + 2 + 3 + ... + (N - 1)$ using this algorithm.
    (2.2) The required result is obtained by adding N to the result from step (2.1).

Problem solving with computers

(1) Specify the problem.
(2) Design an algorithm for solving the problem.
(3) Express the algorithm as a program in a programming language.
(4) Compile and run the program on the computer.

2.2 Top-down design

When a complicated problem has to be solved it is helpful to split it into smaller subproblems and solve them separately. The subproblems can then be split into further subproblems, and so on. This is a very important technique in algorithm and program design and is known as top-down design, or step-wise refinement. We shall use it extensively in the rest of the book. Let us look at a real-world algorithm that describes how to wash a car. A first, rough algorithm may be simply:

(1) Wash the car.

This can quickly be expanded to:

(1.1) If you are feeling lazy:
  (1.1.1) Wash it at a car wash.
(1.2) Otherwise:
  (1.2.1) Wash it by hand.

Step (1.1.1) can be refined to:

(1.1.1.1) Drive to the nearest car wash.
(1.1.1.2) Buy a token.
(1.1.1.3) Wait in line.
(1.1.1.4) Have the car washed.

Step (1.1.1.4) can be refined further:

(1.1.1.4.1) Drive into the car wash.
(1.1.1.4.2) Check that all the doors and windows are closed.
(1.1.1.4.3) Get out of the car.
(1.1.1.4.4) Put the token into the machine.
(1.1.1.4.5) Wait until the car wash is finished.
(1.1.1.4.6) Get into the car.
(1.1.1.4.7) Drive away.

In this way, different parts of an algorithm can be refined until a level is reached where the solution is trivially simple.

Top-down design
- Divide a problem into subproblems.
- Solve the subproblems individually.
- Divide the subproblems into further sub-problems.
- Continue in this way until all the subproblems are easily solvable.

Let us look at another example where iteration is also involved. Imagine the following situation. In your bookcase you have a cassette holder for ordinary music cassettes. You keep your cassettes there, neatly arranged alphabetically according to the name of the composer. (For simplicity, assume that you only have classical music). The holder is made of small slots, each large enough for one cassette, so that they cannot move sideways. We assume that the cassettes are kept in the left part of the holder, so there are no gaps or empty slots on the left, but at least five empty ones on the right.

Now suppose you have bought five new cassettes that need to be put in the holder in their correct positions, so that alphabetical order is maintained. Assume also that the bookshelves are so full that there is nowhere to put the cassettes, so you have to hold them in your hands while you shift them around. To avoid the risk of dropping any, you cannot have more than one cassette in your hand at a time. The five new cassettes are on the floor and you pick them up one after the other and position them in the holder.

We can make up a crude algorithm:

(1)   Sort the new cassettes into the holder.

The first refinement is:

(1.1)   For each new cassette:
    (1.1.1)   Lift the cassette from the floor in your left hand.
    (1.1.2)   Sort it into its correct place.

The way we have written points (1.1.1) and (1.1.2) inset on the line shows that they have to be repeated several times (once per new cassette). Thus iteration has been introduced into the algorithm. Point (1.1.1) needs no further refinement so we can expand point (1.1.2):

(1.1.2.1)   Locate the slot in the holder where the new cassette should be placed.
(1.1.2.2)   Shift all the cassettes to the right of (and including) the located slot one place to the right, so that the located one becomes empty.
(1.1.2.3)   Put the new cassette into the empty slot.

Refining point (1.1.2.1) gives:

(1.1.2.1.1)   Place your left index finger on the leftmost slot of the cassette holder. (You can do this even though you have the new cassette in that hand.)
(1.1.2.1.2)   Repeat the following point until the located slot is empty or

the composer's name on the cassette in the located slot comes alphabetically after the composer's name on the new cassette.

(1.1.2.1.2.1)   Move the left index finger one place to the right.

(1.1.2.1.3)   The left index finger has now located the slot where the new cassette should be inserted.

Point (1.1.2.2) becomes:

(1.1.2.2.1)   Place your right hand on the cassette on the extreme right hand side and repeat the following steps until the slot pointed to by your left index finger is empty:

(1.1.2.2.1.1)   Move the cassette held in your right hand one place to the right.

(1.1.2.2.1.2)   Move your right hand to the nearest cassette on the left.

If we now put all the expanded steps together, we get the following complete algorithm:

For each of the newly bought cassettes:
Lift the cassette from the floor with your left hand.
Put your left index finger on the slot on the extreme left of the holder.
(You can do this even though you are holding the new cassette.)
Repeat the following step until the slot pointed to is either empty or contains a cassette with a composer whose name comes alphabetically after the name of the composer of the new cassette.
Move your left index finger one slot to the right.
Your left index finger has now located the slot where the new cassette should be placed.
Put your right hand on the rightmost cassette and repeat the following steps until the located slot is empty.
Move the cassette held in your right hand one place to the right.
Move your right hand to the nearest cassette on the left.
Put the new cassette in the located slot.

The numbering has been removed to make it look neater. Note that the lines that are inset are repeated a number of times.

We have just seen an example of what is known as a **sort algorithm**. This is not the only algorithm that could be used for sorting the cassettes into position. You can think of several other ways of doing it. Sort algorithms often occur in programming and many computers are used extensively for sorting different kinds of data.

There are usually several alternative algorithms for solving a particular problem. In general, it is sensible to design an algorithm that is as simple and easily understood as possible because there is a better chance that it will work as it was intended.

2.3   Simple programming examples

We shall now look at some simple examples of programs and become familiar with a number of the constructs of Ada. As mentioned previously, a more thorough treatment of the different constructs will be given in later chapters. Therefore there is no need to pay attention to all the details at this first reading.

2.3.1   Simple output

The first program looks like this:

```
with TEXT_IO;
use  TEXT_IO;
procedure HELLO is
begin
    PUT ("Hello! This is your computer speaking.");
end HELLO;
```

When the program is run, it prints the text:

Hello! This is your computer speaking.

at the terminal. In the program, certain words are written in bold type. These are called **reserved words**, words that have special meanings. When writing a program, it is not necessary to emphasize different words in this way. It will only be done here so that the programs are clearer. If desired, everything can be written with ordinary small or capital letters.

An Ada program consists of a **procedure**. The procedure in the program above starts on the third line and has been given the name HELLO. The name is repeated on the last line so that it is easy to see where the procedure ends.

In the program there is a printout of text (the line starting PUT). Ada is designed for use in many different working environments, so it cannot always be taken for granted that a program should write to a terminal as this one does. If we want to read or write to a terminal, this must be stated, as seen here in the first line. The line says that the program needs the help of a **package** called TEXT_IO that is accessible on all Ada implementations. The package contains several tools, including

PUT, which enable us to read and write text at a terminal. (A complete specification of the package is given in Appendix A.)

When we want to use PUT in our program we must inform the compiler that PUT is to be found in the package TEXT_IO. We can do this by writing TEXT_IO.PUT in the program. This is a bit cumbersome to write, especially if we want to use PUT many times. There is a more convenient way, as shown in our example. On the second line we have written:

use TEXT_IO;

This causes the compiler automatically to search in the package TEXT_IO. Therefore we can continue by writing only PUT instead of TEXT_IO.PUT.

In fact, PUT is a procedure just like HELLO. The line:

PUT ("Hello! This is your computer speaking.");

means that our program calls PUT. This means that the procedure PUT will be carried out, or **executed**. The text in brackets is a **parameter** to PUT. We can say that this parameter is input data to PUT. This parameter is a **text string**, seen from the quotation marks around it. The procedure PUT is designed so that it expects a text string as input. When it is called it will write out the text between the quotation marks, but not the quotation marks themselves.

Printing text

PUT ("the text to be printed");

2.3.2   Reading and writing numbers

The next example shows a program that both reads from and writes to a terminal.

```
with TEXT_IO, BASIC_NUM_IO;
use  TEXT_IO, BASIC_NUM_IO;
procedure SUM_AND_PROD is
  NUMBER1, NUMBER2 : INTEGER;
begin
  PUT_LINE ("Give two whole numbers!");
  GET (NUMBER1);
  GET (NUMBER2);
```

```
        PUT ("The sum of the numbers is:");
        PUT (NUMBER1+NUMBER2); NEW_LINE;
        PUT ("The product of the numbers is:");
        PUT (NUMBER1*NUMBER2); NEW_LINE;
    end SUM_AND_PROD;
```

When the program is run the output looks like this:

```
Give two whole numbers!
4
12
The sum of the numbers is:      16
The product of the numbers is:      48
```

The second and third lines were written by the user and the rest by the program.

Another package has been introduced in this example, BASIC_NUM_IO. This package contains all the facilities needed for reading and writing numbers at the terminal. In Ada, as will be shown later, it is possible to work with many different kinds of numbers, and there is a general mechanism for creating packages of facilities for reading and writing them. The non-standard package BASIC_NUM_IO has been used here instead, to avoid complicating things unnecessarily, even though it is not available on all implementations of Ada. (Appendix B shows how to create this package using TEXT_IO.) The resources in BASIC_NUM_IO are called in exactly the same way as those in Ada's standardized, general packages. Therefore it will look exactly the same as if we had used such packages.[†]

To put it simply, an Ada program can be thought of as a cake recipe. First comes the name of the cake, then the list of ingredients to be used. Finally there is the part stating how the ingredients should be mixed. First in an Ada procedure comes the procedure specification, giving, among other things, the name of the procedure. The procedure's name in the example above is SUM_AND_PROD. This is followed by a part

---

[†] If you do not have access to a package like BASIC_NUM_IO you can start your program as follows (see Chapter 5.5):

```
with TEXT_IO;
use  TEXT_IO;
procedure program_name is
    package INTEGER_INOUT is new INTEGER_IO(INTEGER);
    package FLOAT_INOUT is new FLOAT_IO(FLOAT);
    use INTEGER_INOUT, FLOAT_INOUT;

    : the rest of the program
```

Figure 2.3

of the procedure where **declarations** can be made. In our example, two objects are declared, the variables NUMBER1 and NUMBER2:

NUMBER1, NUMBER2 : INTEGER;

A variable can be thought of as a storage box into which values may be placed. Each box, or store, can only contain values of a certain type. The word INTEGER states that the variables NUMBER1 and NUMBER2 can contain only whole numbers, in mathematics called integers. They are said to have type INTEGER. This can be illustrated as in Figure 2.3. The contents of the stores are not yet defined. Last in the procedure, between the words **begin** and **end**, is the part that describes what it does when it is executed. This part contains a series of **statements**. Each statement is terminated by a semicolon. It is useful to write one statement per line.

Program structure

with ... ;

use ... ;

procedure *program name* **is**

    declarations (including variables)

begin

    statements

end *program name*;

The first statement in the program:

PUT_LINE ("Give two whole numbers!");

makes the program begin by printing at the terminal:

Give two whole numbers!

NUMBER1

GET(NUMBER1): ⇒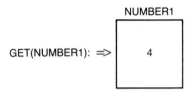

Figure 2.4

when it is run. The procedure PUT_LINE in TEXT_IO has been used here. This works in exactly the same way as PUT in the previous example, but with the difference that a new line is automatically started *after* the text has been printed.

When the program comes to the statement:

GET(NUMBER1);

which contains a call to the procedure GET in BASIC_NUM_IO, it will stop and wait until the user has entered a whole number at the terminal. Assume the user types the number 4, as shown in the example output. Then the procedure GET places the value 4 in the variable NUMBER1, as illustrated in Figure 2.4.

The next statement:

GET(NUMBER2);

works in the same way, but this time the number read is placed in the variable NUMBER2. If we assume that the user has written 12, then the variable NUMBER2 will contain the value 12.

Input of numbers

GET (*variable name*);

The following lines:

PUT ("The sum of the numbers is:");
PUT (NUMBER1+NUMBER2); NEW_LINE;

contain three statements which together produce a line of output at the terminal. First comes a call to the procedure PUT in the package TEXT_IO. This call causes the text:

> The sum of the numbers is:

to be written out. Then comes a fresh call to the procedure PUT, but this time it is not PUT in TEXT_IO that is called but the procedure with the same name in the package BASIC_NUM_IO. This procedure expects a whole number as parameter. The parameter is the expression:

> NUMBER1+NUMBER2

The value of this expression is computed. In our example it has the value 4 + 12, thus PUT gets the value 16 as parameter and writes out this value at the terminal. The compiler sees to it that the correct version of the procedure PUT is chosen. When an integer is given as parameter, it is 'understood' that we mean PUT in BASIC_NUM_IO, and when a text string is given as parameter, it is 'understood' that we mean PUT in TEXT_IO to be used.

The procedure NEW_LINE, called in the last line, causes a new line to be started in the output at the terminal. Why is PUT_LINE not used here as well? The answer is that PUT_LINE only exists for text strings, not for numbers.

Getting new lines in output

> NEW_LINE;

or:

> PUT_LINE ("the text that is to be written");

The new line is generated after the text is written.

The output:

> The sum of the numbers is: 16
> The product of the numbers is: 48

may not look so neat. If we want the output to look as follows:

> The sum of the numbers is: 16
> The product of the numbers is: 48

then we can change the program:

```
PUT ("The sum of the numbers is:");
PUT (NUMBER1+NUMBER2, WIDTH => 7); NEW_LINE;

PUT ("The product of the numbers is:");
PUT (NUMBER1*NUMBER2, WIDTH => 3); NEW_LINE;
```

The parameter WIDTH tells PUT how many positions are to be used in the output, the width of the output field. If the number to be written requires fewer positions than stated (as in our example), PUT fills the field in with spaces to the left of the number. When the width of the field is decided, one position should be allowed for a possible minus sign if the number could be negative.

If the number requires more positions than stated, then it is not an error but the number is output using as many positions as needed. If we had written for example:

```
PUT ("The sum of the numbers is:");
PUT (NUMBER1+NUMBER2, WIDTH => 1); NEW_LINE;
```

and the sum had been 16, then the output would have been:

```
The sum of the numbers is:16
```

If no WIDTH parameter is specified in PUT, then the number of positions needed to write out the greatest whole number that can be stored in the computer is assumed. This is the reason for the original appearance of the output in our example.

Output of whole numbers

> PUT (the value to be output);

or:

> PUT (the value to be output, WIDTH => N);

where N specifies the width of the output field.

2.3.3 Writing an invoice

Now we shall look at an example in which the technique of top-down design will be used in designing and writing a program. Our program will be used in general sales situations and we can imagine that it is intended for use as follows. A customer buys a number of items of the same kind and should receive an invoice stating their product code, the number of items bought, the price per item excluding value added tax (VAT) and the total price for all the goods, including VAT. The invoice should also state what part of the total cost is VAT.

Our task is to write a program to produce such an invoice. Input to the program should be the product code (comprising six letters and numerals), the number of items sold, and the item price, excluding VAT. We assume that the VAT rate is a known percentage that is fixed.

First we write a very rough algorithm:

(1) Read input data.
(2) Make the computations.
(3) Print the invoice.

Step (1) can be split into substeps:

(1.1) Read in the product code.
(1.2) Read in the number of items sold.
(1.3) Read in the unit price (excluding VAT).

For simplicity we shall start with step (1.2) and expand it:

(1.2.1) Ask the operator to enter the number of items sold.
(1.2.2) Read what the operator has written.

Step (1.2.1) can be written in Ada as follows:

```
PUT_LINE ("Enter number of items sold");
```

Step (1.2.2) becomes in Ada:

```
GET (NUMBER_OF_ITEMS);
```

Now we have introduced a variable NUMBER_OF_ITEMS which must be declared:

```
NUMBER_OF_ITEMS : INTEGER;
```

We can continue with step (1.3), 'Read in the unit price', and expand it:

(1.3.1) Ask the operator to enter the price per unit.
(1.3.2) Read what the operator has written.

Step (1.3.1) is in Ada:

```
PUT_LINE ("Enter price per unit");
```

ITEM_PRICE

13.0

Figure 2.5

and step (1.3.2) becomes:

GET (ITEM_PRICE);

We have introduced a second variable, ITEM_PRICE. Obviously, this cannot be an integer variable, that is, have type INTEGER. It is unlikely that the items cost a whole number of monetary units, whether pounds sterling, US dollars or Swiss francs. What we need is another kind of store that can contain real numbers. If we imagine that the user writes 13.0 at the terminal we can picture the situation after the GET call has been executed as in Figure 2.5.

In Ada there is a standard type called FLOAT, and this can be used to declare variables that have to hold real numbers, that is, numbers that are not integers. We let the variable ITEM_PRICE have this type. The declaration is then:

ITEM_PRICE : FLOAT;

In the package BASIC_NUM_IO there is a version of GET that can be used for reading in variables of type FLOAT. There is also a version of PUT for output of numbers of type FLOAT.

Now we can deal with step (1.1), 'Read in the product code'. We can start by subdividing:

(1.1.1)   Ask the operator to enter the product code.
(1.1.2)   Read what the operator has written.

Step (1.1.1) is easy:

PUT_LINE ("Enter product code (6 characters)")

Step (1.1.2) is then:

GET (PRODUCT_CODE);

How should the variable PRODUCT_CODE be declared? It is neither an integer nor a real number, so neither INTEGER nor FLOAT, as used

PRODUCT_CODE

| a | 1 | b | X | 6 | 7 |

Figure 2.6

earlier, will do. In fact the variable PRODUCT_CODE is a text string, exactly the same as the text strings we have written in several places. It must be possible to store an arbitrary code of six characters in the variable, so we need yet another kind of store. If we assume that the user writes the code a1bX67 at the terminal, after the call to GET, we have the situation illustrated in Figure 2.6. Ada has a standard type STRING that can be used. The declaration is:

PRODUCT_CODE : STRING(1..6);

The expression in brackets states that the text string will consist of six characters, numbered from 1 to 6.

Now we can go on to step (2), 'Make the computations', which can be subdivided directly:

(2.1)   Calculate the total price (excluding VAT).
(2.2)   Calculate the total VAT.
(2.3)   Calculate the net price (including VAT).

For step (2.1) we can immediately write the Ada statement:

PRICE := ITEM_PRICE * FLOAT (NUMBER_OF_ITEMS);

This statement contains a few new things. The expression:

ITEM_PRICE * FLOAT (NUMBER_OF_ITEMS)

means that the values of the variables ITEM_PRICE and NUMBER_OF_ITEMS should be multiplied together. Ada does not permit different types to be mixed in expressions of this kind. Since ITEM_PRICE has type FLOAT and NUMBER_OF_ITEMS has type INTEGER, they cannot be mixed without doing something first. We want the final result of the expression to have type FLOAT and therefore we take the value of NUMBER_OF_ITEMS and convert it to a value of type FLOAT. This is achieved with the construct:

FLOAT (NUMBER_OF_ITEMS)

NUMBER_OF_ITEMS

100   FLOAT(NUMBER_OF_ITEMS) =>

Temporary storage

100.0

Figure 2.7

We then get a temporary store containing a real number. If, for example, NUMBER_OF_ITEMS has value 100, then the temporary store will hold the value 100.0. This is shown in Figure 2.7. Note that the variable NUMBER_OF_ITEMS and the value it holds are in no way changed by this.

Mixing types

It is *not* allowed to mix different types (for example INTEGER and FLOAT) in expressions.

It might seem clumsy that all this is necessary, but one of the advantages of Ada, as will be shown later, is that different types are carefully watched and kept apart. It is not possible to mix apples and pears by accident, so to speak.

The effect of the expression:

ITEM_PRICE * FLOAT (NUMBER_OF_ITEMS)

is that we get a new temporary store to hold the result of the multiplication.

Step (2.1) also introduced a new variable PRICE with the type FLOAT. This variable should therefore be declared as:

PRICE : FLOAT;

We shall save the result of the calculation in this variable. This is achieved using an **assignment**. The compound symbol := is called the assignment symbol and is used to denote assignment. Assignment means that whatever is on the right-hand side of the assignment symbol is placed in the variable on the left-hand side. The variable must be of the same type as whatever is on the right of the symbol. Note that any variables that may appear on the right-hand side are not affected by the assignment. Their values are unchanged.

> **Assignment**
>
> *variable_name* := expression;
>
> - The value of the right-hand side is evaluated first.
> - This value is placed in the variable that appears on the left-hand side.
> - The previous value of the variable will be destroyed.
> - The expression on the right-hand side must be of the same type as the variable on the left.

We can now continue with step (2.2), 'Calculate the total VAT'. We make the assumption that the rate of VAT is a known and constant percentage. Clearly it has to be of type FLOAT because it does not necessarily have to have an integral value. It is possible to declare constants in Ada, using a declaration that looks like a variable declaration. If we assume that the VAT rate is 15.0%, we can declare a constant VAT_PERCENT:

    VAT_PERCENT : **constant** := 15.0;

We can then use this to calculate the total VAT due:

    VAT := PRICE * VAT_PERCENT / 100.0;

The statement simply means that the values of PRICE and VAT_PERCENT are multiplied together and the result is then divided by 100. Note that 100 must be written as a real number, 100.0. If we had written 100 it would have been interpreted as an integer. The final result is saved in a new variable VAT which should be declared:

    VAT : FLOAT;

Step (2.3), 'Calculate the net price (including VAT)' is now easy:

    NET_PRICE := PRICE + VAT;

where the variable NET_PRICE has the following declaration:

    NET_PRICE : FLOAT;

INVOICE

Product code: a1bX67
Number of items: 100
Price per item: 13.00
Total price (incl. VAT): 1495.00
Of which VAT is: 195.00

Figure 2.8

We finish with step (3), 'Print the invoice', which we can split into the following steps:

(3.1) Print a heading.
(3.2) Print the product's code.
(3.3) Print the number of items sold.
(3.4) Print the unit price.
(3.5) Print the net price (including VAT).
(3.6) Print the VAT.

We assume that the program will be run from a terminal with printer output. We want the invoice to look like Figure 2.8.

We can deal with step (3.1), 'Write a heading'. For simplicity we will split it into smaller steps:

(3.1.1) Start a new page.
(3.1.2) Set the output position so that the heading starts in column 20 of the page.
(3.1.3) Print the word "INVOICE".
(3.1.4) Skip the next two lines.

Two useful output facilities

NEW_PAGE;

The next output starts on a new page (useful when the terminal output is to paper).

SET_COL(N);

The next output starts in position N on the current line. (If output is already beyond position N, a new line is started.)

We make use of the facilities offered by TEXT_IO. The four steps become the four corresponding statements:

```
NEW_PAGE;
SET_COL (20); PUT ("INVOICE"); NEW_LINE (2);
```

The next step, 'Print the product's code', can be split further:

(3.2.1) Set the output position so that the text starts at column 10.
(3.2.2) Print the text "Product code:".
(3.2.3) Print the product code.
(3.2.4) Move on one line.

We have the corresponding Ada statements:

```
SET_COL (10);
PUT ("Product code:          ");
PUT (PRODUCT_CODE); NEW_LINE;
```

Note the six extra spaces at the end of the text in the second statement. These have been added to provide adequate space between the colon and the code.

Similarly, the next step, 'Print the number of items sold', is:

```
SET_COL (10);
PUT ("Number of items:");
PUT (NUMBER_OF_ITEMS, WIDTH => 9); NEW_LINE;
```

Here the WIDTH parameter to PUT is used to get the right edge of NUMBER_OF_ITEMS directly under the right edge of the product code on the line above.

The step 'Print the unit price' is:

```
SET_COL (10);
PUT ("Price per item:");
PUT (ITEM_PRICE, FORE => 7, AFT => 2, EXP => 0);
NEW_LINE;
```

The variable ITEM_PRICE contains a real number. There are two alternative forms for writing out real numbers. The number 125.7, for example, can be written either:

125.7

or:

1.257E+02

The latter is called **exponent form** and should be read as 1.257 times 10 to the power 2. If we had had the simple statement:

    PUT (ITEM_PRICE);

in the program, PUT would have written ITEM_PRICE in exponent form. But we do not want this, so we make use of the possibility of assigning further parameters to PUT when real numbers are to be output. Instead, we write:

    PUT (ITEM_PRICE, FORE => 7, AFT => 2, EXP => 0);

The parameters FORE and AFT state the number of positions required in the output before and after the decimal point, respectively. Allowance should be made for a possible minus sign among the positions before the decimal point. If the number that is printed does not fill all the positions before the decimal point (as in our example), PUT will place blanks there instead. The parameter EXP gives the number of positions that we want the exponent to be given. Since we have decided not to have an exponent at all, we set EXP to 0.

   If we were to give FORE a smaller value than the number of positions actually needed, no error would result, but PUT would use as many positions before the point as required. If, for example, the variable ITEM_PRICE had the value 13.00 and we had the statements:

    PUT ("Price per item:");
    PUT (ITEM_PRICE, FORE => 1, AFT => 2, EXP => 0);

in the program, then the output would be:

    Price per item:13.00

   Now we can go on to the next step, 'Print the net price'. This is analogous to the previous steps and so are the statements:

    SET_COL (10);
    PUT ("Total price (incl. VAT):");
    PUT (NET_PRICE, FORE => 7, AFT => 2, EXP => 0);
    NEW_LINE;

Output of real numbers

PUT (real value);

or:

PUT (real value, FORE => N, AFT => M, EXP => 0);

where N and M give the number of figures before and after the decimal point, respectively.

The last step, 'Print the VAT', is:

```
SET_COL (10);
PUT ("Of which VAT is:");
PUT (VAT, FORE => 6, AFT => 2, EXP => 0);
```

We finish this example by putting the whole program together. We have several variables of type FLOAT, and their declarations can be put together as shown in the program.

```
with TEXT_IO, BASIC_NUM_IO;
use  TEXT_IO, BASIC_NUM_IO;
procedure WRITE_INVOICE is
    NUMBER_OF_ITEMS : INTEGER;
    ITEM_PRICE, PRICE, VAT, NET_PRICE : FLOAT;
    VAT_PERCENT    : constant := 15.0;
    PRODUCT_CODE : STRING (1..6);

begin
    PUT_LINE("Enter product code (6 characters)");
    GET(PRODUCT_CODE);

    PUT_LINE("Enter number of items sold");
    GET(NUMBER_OF_ITEMS);

    PUT_LINE("Enter price per unit");
    GET(ITEM_PRICE);

    PRICE := ITEM_PRICE * FLOAT (NUMBER_OF_ITEMS);
    VAT := PRICE * VAT_PERCENT / 100.0;
    NET_PRICE := PRICE + VAT;
```

```
NEW_PAGE;
SET_COL(20); PUT("INVOICE"); NEW_LINE(2);

SET_COL(10); PUT("Product code:        ");
PUT(PRODUCT_CODE); NEW_LINE;

SET_COL(10); PUT("Number of items:");
PUT(NUMBER_OF_ITEMS, WIDTH => 9); NEW_LINE;

SET_COL(10); PUT("Price per item:");
PUT(ITEM_PRICE, FORE => 7, AFT => 2, EXP => 0);
NEW_LINE;

SET_COL(10); PUT("Total price (incl. VAT):");
PUT(NET_PRICE, FORE => 7, AFT => 2, EXP => 0);
NEW_LINE;

SET_COL(10); PUT("Of which VAT is:");
PUT(VAT, FORE => 6, AFT => 2, EXP => 0);
NEW_LINE;

end WRITE_INVOICE;
```

2.3.4 Drawing outsize letters

By displaying the character ∗ appropriately at the terminal an outsize letter can be written. A giant A, for example, can be written thus:

```
        *
      *   *
    *       *
    *********
  *             *
*                 *
```

Now we shall write a (slightly useless) program to draw the three letters A D A, under each other, in this giant format. So the program should produce the output shown in Figure 2.9.

The capability of making **comments** will be made use of in this program. The compound symbol -- (double hyphen) introduces a comment and everything written after it on a line will be interpreted as a comment, which means that the compiler does not try to translate it.

Comments are used to make a program clearer to understand and to provide support in writing a program.

Comments

   -- *this is a comment*

- Makes a program clearer.
- Simplifies program design and writing.

Figure 2.9

Using the top-down design technique we make a first sketch of the program using comments:

```
procedure GIANT_ADA is
begin
    -- draw a giant A
    -- draw a giant D
    -- draw a giant A
end GIANT_ADA;
```

Drawing on our experience from earlier examples, we can refine the three steps directly and come up with a first version of the program:

```
with TEXT_IO;
use  TEXT_IO;
procedure GIANT_ADA is
begin
    -- draw a giant A
    NEW_LINE;
    PUT_LINE("      *");
    PUT_LINE("     * *");
    PUT_LINE("    *   *");
    PUT_LINE("   *******");
    PUT_LINE("  *       *");
    PUT_LINE(" *         *");
    NEW_LINE;
```

```
-- draw a giant D
NEW_LINE;
PUT_LINE(" *******");
PUT_LINE(" *      *");
PUT_LINE(" *       *");
PUT_LINE(" *       *");
PUT_LINE(" *      *");
PUT_LINE(" *******");
NEW_LINE;

-- draw a giant A
NEW_LINE;
PUT_LINE("     *");
PUT_LINE("    * *");
PUT_LINE("   *   *");
PUT_LINE("  *******");
PUT_LINE(" *       *");
PUT_LINE("*         *");
NEW_LINE;

end GIANT_ADA;
```

Each giant letter starts and ends with an empty line so that the letters are not too crowded. Since PUT and NEW_LINE are needed from the package TEXT_IO, we have organized access to this package, as before. The comments can remain in the program because they make it clearer.

Note that the step 'draw a giant A' in our program has been repeated and all the statements in it have been written out twice. This is clumsy and makes the program unnecessarily long – imagine what it would be like if we wanted to write DADDA instead of ADA. To set this right we shall create a new procedure DRAW_GIANT_A:

```
procedure DRAW_GIANT_A is
-- this procedure draws a giant A
begin
   NEW_LINE;
   PUT_LINE("     *");
   PUT_LINE("    * *");
   PUT_LINE("   *   *");
   PUT_LINE("  *******");
   PUT_LINE(" *       *");
   PUT_LINE("*         *");
   NEW_LINE;
end DRAW_GIANT_A;
```

We have placed an explanatory comment at the start of the procedure. For the sake of symmetry we will write a corresponding procedure DRAW_GIANT_D, in the same way:

```
procedure DRAW_GIANT_D is
-- this procedure draws a giant D
begin
    NEW_LINE;
    PUT_LINE(" *******");
    PUT_LINE(" *      *");
    PUT_LINE(" *       *");
    PUT_LINE(" *       *");
    PUT_LINE(" *      *");
    PUT_LINE(" *******");
    NEW_LINE;
end DRAW_GIANT_D;
```

Now we can change our program so that the outsize letters are drawn by making **calls** to the new procedures. The central part of the program then becomes:

```
DRAW_GIANT_A;

DRAW_GIANT_D;

DRAW_GIANT_A;
```

Note that the calls to our procedures DRAW_GIANT_A and DRAW_GIANT_D look exactly like calls to the built-in procedures in Ada's standard packages. Compare them with the call to, for example, the procedure NEW_LINE in the package TEXT_IO.

It is worth noting that by choosing good names for our procedures we have made the program so clear that the comments are superfluous. It is always important to choose good names for everything in a program. You should not be concerned about using long names, even if it seems a bit tedious while you are actually writing the program – in the long run there is much to be gained. After all, the program is only written once but it is read many times during development, debugging and maintenance.

Choosing names

- Use clear names within your program.
- Do not be afraid of using long names.

Now comes the question: where should our procedures be placed in the program? We can picture our procedures as 'ingredients' in the program (recall the earlier comparison with the cake recipe) in the same way as variables are 'ingredients'. So our procedures must be declared in the program, just like the variables. In fact, the procedures texts are declarations and we can place them in the declarative part of the program. We then get a new version of our program:

```
with TEXT_IO;
use  TEXT_IO;
procedure GIANT_ADA is

    procedure DRAW_GIANT_A is
    -- this procedure draws a giant A
    begin
      NEW_LINE;
      PUT_LINE("     *");
      PUT_LINE("    * *");
      PUT_LINE("   *   *");
      PUT_LINE("  *******");
      PUT_LINE(" *       *");
      PUT_LINE("*         *");
      NEW_LINE;
    end DRAW_GIANT_A;

    procedure DRAW_GIANT_D is
    -- this procedure draws a giant D
    begin
      NEW_LINE;
      PUT_LINE(" *******");
      PUT_LINE(" *     *");
      PUT_LINE(" *      *");
      PUT_LINE(" *      *");
      PUT_LINE(" *     *");
      PUT_LINE(" *******");
      NEW_LINE;
    end DRAW_GIANT_D;

begin
    DRAW_GIANT_A;        --execution begins here
    DRAW_GIANT_D;
    DRAW_GIANT_A;
end GIANT_ADA;
```

The procedures DRAW_GIANT_A and DRAW_GIANT_D have been declared in the procedure DRAW_GIANT_ADA. So that this is seen clearly, their text is written a little further to the right on the line. This method of organizing the appearance of a program by shifting parts of the text over is called **indentation**. It is very important that you indent your programs properly, a skill that will be developed by studying the various example programs as they are presented.

Indentation

- A program is made much easier to read if the text is indented in such a way that it reflects the structure of the program.
- A well-structured program is always indented.
- Indenting should be used in all program writing.

When the program (the procedure DRAW_GIANT_ADA) is run, the three statements between **begin** and **end**, namely:

```
DRAW_GIANT_A;
DRAW_GIANT_D;
DRAW_GIANT_A;
```

will be executed in order. The first line in the program:

```
DRAW_GIANT_A;
```

for example, means that the statements in the procedure DRAW_GIANT_A are executed. These statements cause a big A to be drawn at the terminal. When this is done and we have reached the line:

```
end DRAW_GIANT_A;
```

we return to the end of the first line in the procedure DRAW_GIANT_ADA. The first statement in that procedure has now been executed and execution can continue with the next statement:

```
DRAW_GIANT_D;
```

This statement is also a call to a procedure and is executed in the same way.

What we have actually done is to divide our original program into a main program and two subprograms. We have broken down the problem of writing the outsize text ADA into two simpler problems: writing an outsize A and writing an outsize D. What has been gained is an increase in the overall clarity of the program and avoidance of the need to repeat identical sequences of statements. This technique of refining problems, breaking them down into subproblems and then using subprograms, is very important. There will be much work with subprograms in the chapters to come.

Suppose we have been given the task of writing another similar program that will print out the giant text DADDA at the terminal. We realize that we should be able to make use of the procedures DRAW_GIANT_A and DRAW_GIANT_D here as well. But these procedures exist only as internal 'ingredients' in the procedure DRAW_GIANT_ADA and are not available to other programs (unless we write them again). Compare this with using the procedure NEW_LINE – a useful procedure that finds uses in many different programs. This is possible because it has been put into a package, TEXT_IO. As we have seen, this package can be accessed so that NEW_LINE can be used without the need to write it out and declare it in every program.

Let us now make the procedures DRAW_GIANT_A and DRAW_GIANT_D generally accessible by placing them in a package. We will create a package called GIANT_LETTER.

A package in Ada can be compared to a meal in a restaurant. The guest sees brief descriptions on the menu. This is all the guest needs to be able to decide whether he or she will order a dish. To prepare the dish, however, a more detailed description is needed – a recipe – but this is needed only by the cook. The guest is not normally interested in the recipe, and even if he or she wanted to see it, it is possible that the restaurant would not agree to it.

Similarly, a package in Ada consists of two parts:

(1)   A **specification** (menu) to inform the programs that want to use it what resources are to be found in the package, for example, procedures, and how they are used.

(2)   A **body** (recipes) where the resources are described in detail. The programs that use the package do not see this part of the package. It can be thought of as the contents of the package's 'black box' and only concerns its designer.

Packages

Two parts:

(1)   *Specification*: gives the user information about the resources contained and how they are used.

(2)   *Package body*: details the resources. Not visible to the user.

We shall start by writing the specification of the new package, GIANT_LETTER:

(not Ada)

```
package GIANT_LETTER is

    procedure DRAW_GIANT_A;
    -- this procedure draws a giant A

    procedure DRAW_GIANT_D;
    -- this procedure draws a giant D

end GIANT_LETTER;
```

This specification informs the program that is going to use the package that the package is called GIANT_LETTER and that it contains two procedures DRAW_GIANT_A and DRAW_GIANT_D (neither of which have parameters). To make this clearer we have put in a comment for each procedure. This specification can now be used by the program that will write the outsize text DADDA:

```
with GIANT_LETTER;
procedure GIANT_DADDA is
begin
    GIANT_LETTER.DRAW_GIANT_D;
    GIANT_LETTER.DRAW_GIANT_A;
    GIANT_LETTER.DRAW_GIANT_D;
    GIANT_LETTER.DRAW_GIANT_D;
    GIANT_LETTER.DRAW_GIANT_A;
end GIANT_DADDA;
```

As before, we can insert a **use** clause and get:

```
with GIANT_LETTER;
use  GIANT_LETTER;
procedure GIANT_DADDA is
begin
    DRAW_GIANT_D;
    DRAW_GIANT_A;
    DRAW_GIANT_D;
    DRAW_GIANT_D;
    DRAW_GIANT_A;
end GIANT_DADDA;
```

The first version is often preferred for packages other than Ada's standard packages, because it states specifically what procedures are meant.

The first line means that the procedure DRAW_GIANT_DADDA gets access to the package GIANT_LETTER. Note that since DRAW_GIANT_

DADDA does not use the facilities in TEXT_IO directly, TEXT_IO does not need to be included in the first line.

Now we can rewrite DRAW_GIANT_ADA in a similar manner. The internal procedures are no longer needed and so the procedure becomes very simple:

```
with GIANT_LETTER;
procedure GIANT_ADA is
begin
    GIANT_LETTER.DRAW_GIANT_A;
    GIANT_LETTER.DRAW_GIANT_D;
    GIANT_LETTER.DRAW_GIANT_A;
end GIANT_ADA;
```

It only remains to write the body of the package GIANT_LETTER:

```
with TEXT_IO;              do you need 'body'?
use  TEXT_IO;
package body GIANT_LETTER is

    procedure DRAW_GIANT_A is
    begin
        NEW_LINE;
        PUT_LINE("     *");
        PUT_LINE("    * *");
        PUT_LINE("   *   *");
        PUT_LINE("  *******");
        PUT_LINE(" *       *");
        PUT_LINE("*         *");
        NEW_LINE;
    end DRAW_GIANT_A;

    procedure DRAW_GIANT_D is
    begin
        NEW_LINE;
        PUT_LINE(" *******");
        PUT_LINE(" *       *");
        PUT_LINE(" *       *");
        PUT_LINE(" *       *");
        PUT_LINE(" *       *");
        PUT_LINE(" *******");
        NEW_LINE;
    end DRAW_GIANT_D;

end GIANT_LETTER;
```

Access to TEXT_IO is needed here because the procedures PUT and NEW_LINE are used in the package body.

By creating a package we have thus made our routines generally accessible as resources for other programs. It would be natural now to extend the package with procedures for drawing large versions of all the letters, not only A and D. The use of packages is one of the fundamental concepts in Ada.

Advantages of packages

- The use of packages provides convenient access to resources that the programmer (or another) has written.

- Programming becomes more efficient and the quality of programs improves.

2.3.5 Comparing numbers

In foregoing example programs we have looked at sequential algorithms – algorithms consisting of a number of stages executed one after the other. Now we shall study a program where there is a choice between different possible actions:

```
with TEXT_IO, BASIC_NUM_IO;
use  TEXT_IO, BASIC_NUM_IO;
procedure BIGGER_NUMBER is
    FIRST_NUMBER, SECOND_NUMBER : INTEGER;
begin
    PUT("Give the first whole number:    ");
    GET(FIRST_NUMBER);
    PUT("Give the second whole number: ");
    GET(SECOND_NUMBER);

    if FIRST_NUMBER > SECOND_NUMBER then
        PUT("The first number is bigger.");
    else
        PUT("The second number is bigger.");
    end if;
end BIGGER_NUMBER;
```

The program asks for two whole numbers. When the user has entered them from the terminal, the program states which is the larger. An example of output from the program is:

```
Give the first whole number:    12300
Give the second whole number: 13200
The second number is bigger.
```

One small detail in the output from the program that might puzzle us is how the second and third lines manage to start on new lines, despite the fact that neither PUT_LINE nor NEW_LINE have been used in the program? The answer is simple. The two numbers, 12300 and 13200, are written by the user at the terminal. When input is written to a program, a number is usually terminated by pressing the terminal's RETURN key. This means that the output at the terminal moves on a line. So the answer to the question is that in this case it is the user who has made the output move on a line and not the program.

The more interesting part of the program is a construct that we have not met before – the **if** statement which starts with the word **if** and ends with **end if**. The first line of the statement:

if FIRST_NUMBER > SECOND_NUMBER **then**

means that the values of the variables FIRST_NUMBER and SECOND_NUMBER will be compared when the program is executed. If the expression:

FIRST_NUMBER > SECOND_NUMBER

is true, that is, that FIRST_NUMBER is larger than SECOND_NUMBER, then the statements that appear after the word **then** will be executed. In this case, the statement:

PUT("The first number is bigger.");

will be executed. If, instead, the expression:

FIRST_NUMBER > SECOND_NUMBER

is false, that is, the SECOND_NUMBER is greater than (or equal to) the FIRST_NUMBER, then the statements following **else** will be executed, in this case the statement:

PUT("The second number is bigger.");

Observe that *either* the statements following **then** *or* those following **else** are carried out. Only one alternative is chosen when the **if** statement is executed. The use of the **if** statement in Ada is one way to formulate algorithms where a choice has to be made.

Note that several statements may appear after the words **then** and **else**. For example, we can alter the program a little:

```
with TEXT_IO, BASIC_NUM_IO;
use  TEXT_IO, BASIC_NUM_IO;
procedure BIGGER_NUMBER is
    FIRST_NUMBER, SECOND_NUMBER : INTEGER;
begin
    PUT("Give the first whole number:      ");
    GET(FIRST_NUMBER);
    PUT("Give the second whole number: ");
    GET(SECOND_NUMBER);

    if FIRST_NUMBER > SECOND_NUMBER then
      PUT("The first number, ");
      PUT(FIRST_NUMBER, WIDTH => 1);
      PUT ("', is bigger.");
    else
      PUT("The second number, ");
      PUT (SECOND_NUMBER, WIDTH => 1);
      PUT("', is bigger.");
    end if;
end BIGGER_NUMBER;
```

When this program is run, the following output is typical of what may appear at the terminal:

```
Give the first whole number:    12300
Give the second whole number: 13200
The second number, 13200, is bigger.
```

The last line has been obtained using three statements in the program. In the second of these the WIDTH parameter has deliberately been given a value that is too small. This means that the compiler chooses to allow exactly as many positions as needed and we get the output of the bigger number exactly as we want it, without unnecessary blanks in front of it. The single blank results from the blank after the comma in the text string that precedes the number.

We need to make one more change to the program. What would happen if the user entered the same number twice? Since the expression

```
FIRST_NUMBER > SECOND_NUMBER
```

is then false, our original program would carry out the statements following **else** and say:

```
The second number is bigger.
```

This, of course, is wrong.

We can make use of another option of the **if** statement, and rewrite our program thus:

```
with TEXT_IO, BASIC_NUM_IO;
use  TEXT_IO, BASIC_NUM_IO;
procedure BIGGER_NUMBER is
   FIRST_NUMBER, SECOND_NUMBER : INTEGER;
begin
   PUT("Give the first whole number:    ");
   GET(FIRST_NUMBER);
   PUT("Give the second whole number: ");
   GET(SECOND_NUMBER);

   if FIRST_NUMBER > SECOND_NUMBER then
      PUT("The first number is bigger.");
   elsif SECOND_NUMBER > FIRST_NUMBER then
      PUT("The second number is bigger.");
   else
      PUT("The numbers are equal.");
   end if;
end BIGGER_NUMBER;
```

Now the **if** statement has been augmented; there is a new part starting with the word **elsif**. When the program is executed the following will occur. If the expression after **if**, that is:

```
FIRST_NUMBER > SECOND_NUMBER
```

is true, then the statement:

```
PUT("The first number is bigger.");
```

will be executed, as before. If the expression is not true then the expression that comes after **elsif**:

```
SECOND_NUMBER > FIRST_NUMBER
```

will be examined. If this second expression is true, then the statement:

```
PUT("The second number is bigger.");
```

will be carried out. If this is also false, as when the two numbers are the same, then the statement that follows **else** will be carried out, namely:

```
PUT("The numbers are equal.");
```

Just as in the simpler type of **if** statement, only *one* alternative is chosen when the statement is executed.

In fact, the **if** statement can be generalized even further; there can be as many **elsif** alternatives as necessary.

Selection

- Can be made by using an **if** statement.
- Only one alternative can be chosen.

2.3.6 Calculating a selling price

We can look at another program that uses selection:

```
with TEXT_IO, BASIC_NUM_IO;
use  TEXT_IO, BASIC_NUM_IO;
procedure CALCULATE_PRICE is
    DISCOUNT_PERCENT : constant := 10.0;
    DISCOUNT_LIMIT      : constant := 1000.0;
    NUMBER_OF_ITEMS   : INTEGER;
    ITEM_PRICE, PRICE, DISCOUNT : FLOAT;
begin
    -- read input data
    PUT("Enter the number of items sold: ");
    GET(NUMBER_OF_ITEMS);
    PUT("Enter the cost per item: ");
    GET(ITEM_PRICE);

    -- do calculations
    PRICE := ITEM_PRICE * FLOAT(NUMBER_OF_ITEMS);
    if PRICE > DISCOUNT_LIMIT then
       DISCOUNT := PRICE * DISCOUNT_PERCENT/100.0;
       PRICE := PRICE - DISCOUNT;
    end if;

    -- print result
    PUT("Final price is ");
    PUT(PRICE, FORE => 1, AFT => 2, EXP => 0);
end CALCULATE_PRICE;
```

The program is designed for calculating a selling price. The input required is the number of items sold and the price per item. The program calculates and displays the total price to the customer. If the total price is above a certain amount, in this case £1000, the customer gets a quantity discount of 10%. In this example, for the sake of simplicity, we shall ignore the problems of VAT and sales tax – they can be assumed to be included in the price from the start. When the program is executed the output may look like this:

```
Enter the number of items sold: 25
Enter the cost per item: 45.50
Final price is 1023.75
```

There is an **if** statement in the program, but note that it has no **else** part. This is quite legal. What happens is that the statements following **then** are carried out if the expression in the **if** statement is true. If the expression is false then nothing is done. In our example, therefore, the two statements:

```
DISCOUNT := PRICE * DISCOUNT_PERCENT/100.0;
PRICE := PRICE - DISCOUNT;
```

are executed only if PRICE is greater than 1000.

Two constants, DISCOUNT_PERCENT and DISCOUNT_LIMIT, have been used. In the statements in the program these have then been used instead of the corresponding numerical values. For example, instead of writing:

```
if PRICE > 1000.0 then
```

we have written:

```
if PRICE > DISCOUNT_LIMIT then
```

It is sensible to try and avoid numerical values in the statements of a program. Suppose at a later date, the discount is lowered to 8% and the minimum discount sale is lowered to £900. Then the only things to be changed are the constant declarations in the program. If the numerical values 10 and 1000 had been written, maybe in several places, it may have been difficult to find all the places requiring change, and something could well have been changed by mistake. Another important reason for using constant declarations is that the program gains clarity. The name DISCOUNT_PERCENT used in the program tells us much more than the number 10.

Using constants

- Avoid numerical values in a program.
- Declare and use constants instead.

2.3.7 Producing tables

Now we have seen examples of programs that use sequences of statements and selection. The third important algorithmic construct is iteration, or the repetition of groups of statements. A couple of programs that use iteration are now presented. The first will produce a table of integers and their squares. Output from the program should look like that in Figure 2.10. It can be seen from this figure that when the program is run the user has to enter the size of the table, that is, how many numbers starting from 1 are to be squared. In the example the user has written 12.

```
with TEXT_IO, BASIC_NUM_IO;
use  TEXT_IO, BASIC_NUM_IO;
procedure TABLE_OF_SQUARES is
    TABLE_SIZE : INTEGER;
begin
    PUT_LINE("Give the size of the table:");
    GET(TABLE_SIZE);
    NEW_LINE;

    PUT_LINE("Number          Square"); NEW_LINE;
    for NUMBER in 1..TABLE_SIZE loop
        PUT(NUMBER, WIDTH => 4);
        PUT(NUMBER * NUMBER, WIDTH => 10); NEW_LINE;
    end loop;
end TABLE_OF_SQUARES;
```

```
Give the size of the table:
12
        Number   Square

           1        1
           2        4
           3        9
           4       16
           5       25
           6       36
           7       49
           8       64
           9       81
          10      100
          11      121
          12      144
```

Figure 2.10

There is an iteration statement in the program that starts with the word **for**. The statements that appear between the words **loop** and **end loop** will be repeated a certain number of times. Note that these lines have been indented. The line:

for NUMBER **in** 1..TABLE_SIZE **loop**

states the number of times the repetition should occur, in this case the number of times given by TABLE_SIZE, which has been given the value 12 in our example. The variable NUMBER introduced on this line is the loop parameter; it counts the number of iterations made. The first time through the loop, NUMBER automatically gets the value 1, on the second loop it becomes 2, the third 3, and so on, until it finally becomes 12. Note that the variable NUMBER should not be declared explicitly. It is declared automatically because it appears after **for**. In this case it is of type INTEGER.

Each time through the loop the program will write one line at the terminal.

Iteration a known number of times

When the number of times an iteration should occur is known before it starts, a construct using **for** is used.

2.3.8   How long before I'm a millionaire?

In the final example in this chapter we will look at what may be unrealistic conditions of employment. Imagine you have been offered a very dangerous job, filled with all sorts of risks. If you take the job, the chances of surviving long are slight. The pay is a bit unusual. On the first day you will receive £0.01, £0.02 for the second day, £0.04 for the third, and so on. The pay is doubled daily. Although you are anxious about your health and safety, you are still prepared to consider taking a few risks if it means riches, so you decide to see what the offer really means. The question you want an answer to is simply: how many days must you work in order to become a millionaire? To get an answer you could use this program:

```
with TEXT_IO, BASIC_NUM_IO;
use  TEXT_IO, BASIC_NUM_IO;
```

```
procedure RICH is
    NUMBER_OF_DAYS   : INTEGER := 1;
    DAYS_WAGE        : FLOAT := 0.01;
    TOTAL_EARNINGS   : FLOAT := 0.01;
    DESIRED_EARNINGS : constant := 1000000.0;
begin

    while TOTAL_EARNINGS < DESIRED_EARNINGS loop
        NUMBER_OF_DAYS := NUMBER_OF_DAYS + 1;
        DAYS_WAGE := DAYS_WAGE * 2.0;
        TOTAL_EARNINGS := TOTAL_EARNINGS+DAYS_WAGE;
    end loop;

    PUT("You will be a millionaire in ");
    PUT(NUMBER_OF_DAYS, WIDTH => 1);
    PUT_LINE(" days.");
end RICH;
```

Three variables are used in this program: NUMBER_OF_DAYS, DAYS_WAGE and TOTAL_EARNINGS. In the declarations we have made use of the option to **initialize** the variables. The declaration:

```
NUMBER_OF_DAYS : INTEGER := 1;
```

for example, means that the variable NUMBER_OF_DAYS automatically gets the initial value 1 when the program is run. (If a variable is not initialized, as in our previous examples, the variable's value is normally undefined when the program starts. This means that the variable contains 'garbage' and should not be used until it has been given a proper value.)

The three variables in our program have been given initial values that represent the situation after one day's work, namely that NUMBER_OF_DAYS is 1, DAYS_WAGE is 0.01, and TOTAL_EARNINGS is also 0.01. DESIRED_EARNINGS contains the amount you want to earn to be rich, in this case £1000000.

The iteration statement in this program starts with **while**. The three statements:

```
NUMBER_OF_DAYS := NUMBER_OF_DAYS + 1;
DAYS_WAGE := DAYS_WAGE * 2.0;
TOTAL_EARNINGS := TOTAL_EARNINGS + DAYS_WAGE;
```

will be repeated a certain number of times, actually once for every day worked except the first day. We see that every day we increase the day counter NUMBER_OF_DAYS by 1; work out DAYS_WAGE, the current day's wage (which is double the previous one); and add the latter quantity to the running total, TOTAL_EARNINGS. After two days (after the first time through the loop) NUMBER_OF_DAYS will thus be 2, DAYS_WAGE will be 0.02, and TOTAL_EARNINGS will be 0.03. After three days (after the second loop) they will be 3, 0.04, and 0.07, respectively.

How many iterations are needed? We do not know. Each iteration represents one day worked, and it is precisely the number of days to be worked that the program is intended to find out. To control the iteration therefore we do not use the construct with **for** as in the previous example, but a version of the **loop** statement where **while** is used. This works as follows. Each time a new iteration begins, the expression after **while** is investigated first. If this expression is true then one iteration of the three statements in the loop is carried out. If it is not true, then the **loop** statement terminates; the loop is not repeated and the program continues with the statement after **end loop**. When the **loop** statement is finished, the program will display the number of days you must work to become a millionaire. The output will be:

You will be a millionaire in 27 days.

Iteration an undetermined number of times

When the number of times an iteration should be carried out is not known in advance, but a condition is known for the iteration to terminate, a construct with **while** is used.

The difference between using constructs with **if** and **while** should be noted. The lines of program:

```
N := 0;
if N < 10 then
  PUT(N, WIDTH => 1); NEW_LINE;
  N := N + 1;
end if;
```

assuming that the variable N has type INTEGER, would give the output:

0

when run. The statements between **then** and **end if** would therefore be executed once only. This can be compared with the lines:

```
N := 0;
while N < 10 loop
   PUT(N, WIDTH => 1); NEW_LINE;
   N := N + 1;
end loop;
```

which would give the output:

```
0
1
2
3
4
5
6
7
8
9
```

Here, then, the corresponding statements are executed 10 times.

EXERCISES

2.1 Give an algorithm for evaluating the sum:

$$\sum_{i=1}^{n} i^2$$

2.2 Specify an algorithm, using any method, to calculate:

$$N! = 1 \times 2 \times 3 \times \dots \times N \quad (N > 0)$$

2.3 A table contains N different numbers. Design an algorithm that looks through the table to find the smallest number. The algorithm should give the position of the smallest number in the table as its result (an index between 1 and N).

2.4 A table contains N different numbers. Design an algorithm that changes the table so that the numbers are in order, from smallest to largest. Use a method that starts by putting the smallest number in the first position, then puts the second smallest in the second position, and so on. (*Hint*: Use the algorithm developed in the previous question.)

2.5   Write an Ada program that will write your name and address at the terminal.

2.6   Write a program that works out and displays the number of miles a car has been driven over the past year. When the program is run it should request the current mileometer reading and that of a year ago. The two mileages should be given as whole numbers of miles.

2.7   Add to the program in Exercise 2.6 so that it will also calculate the car's average petrol consumption in litres per mile. In addition to the two mileages, the program should read in from the terminal the number of litres of petrol used during the year (stated as a real number). The program should also read in the car's registration number so that it can produce output in the following format:

Registration number: ABC123X
Total mileage: 9290
Total petrol consumption in litres: 1234.5
Consumption in litres per mile: 0.13

2.8   When a car is to be insured it is common to choose 'full cover' in the case of a new car (less than 5 years old, say). If the car is older it is often thought that 'third party' insurance is adequate.

(a)   Write a program that tells you whether to choose full or third party insurance. The program should receive as input data the current year and the car's year of manufacture. One of the messages:

Choose full cover
Choose third party insurance

should be displayed, depending on whether the car is less than or more than 5 years old.

(b)   A number of insurance companies offer special insurance policies for veteran cars, that is, cars more than 25 years old. Add to the program so that it can also display the message:

Choose a veteran car policy

if the car is at least 25 years old.

2.9   Write a program that produces a table for all the integers in the interval n_1 to n_2. For each integer k, k^2 and k^3 should be written. The two integers n_1 and n_2 should be read from the terminal.

2.10 A bank gives interest at a rate of 9.25% on money deposited in a deposit account. Suppose you put in £X at the start of a year. Write a program to calculate how many years it will take before the balance in the deposit account exceeds £100000 if no deposits or withdrawals are made. The amount deposited, X, should be read in from the terminal.

2.11 (a) Write a program that draws two circles and two triangles at the terminal.

   (b) Rewrite the program so that the circle and triangle are drawn using separate subprograms.

   (c) Construct a package containing the two subprograms that draw a circle and a triangle.

   (d) Show what the program from part (a) would look like if the package from part (c) is used.

Chapter 3
The basics of Ada

3.1 Standard types

3.2 Identifiers

3.3 Literals

3.4 Expressions

3.5 Variables and constants

3.6 Errors in programs

Exercises

This chapter presents some of the basic concepts behind Ada. The built-in standard types, **INTEGER**, **FLOAT**, **CHARACTER**, **STRING** and **BOOLEAN** are described. A brief discussion is also presented about how data is stored in a computer using binary code.

The rules for stating different values and expressions are given, and Ada's standard operators are described. Finally, the various errors that can occur in the programming process are discussed.

3.1 Standard types

The task of a computer program is to manipulate data objects of various kinds. A data object in a program often represents something that occurs in the real world. In Chapter 2, for example, we saw how a variable, ITEM_PRICE, could represent a real selling price, and how another variable, PRODUCT_CODE, could represent the product's actual code.

Different objects have different properties. For example, the value of the variable ITEM_PRICE could be increased by 10%, but it would be meaningless to talk about increasing PRODUCT_CODE by 10%. Conversely, you can imagine changing all the upper case letters in PRODUCT_CODE to lower case, while trying to change a letter in a selling price would be nonsense. In Ada, we say that objects that have different properties have different **types**. Each object that is to be used in a program must be declared before it is used and its type is stated in the declaration. For example, the variables ITEM_PRICE and PRODUCT_CODE were declared in the following way:

```
ITEM_PRICE : FLOAT;
PRODUCT_CODE : STRING(1 .. 6);
```

Data objects

- A program manipulates data objects.
- An object represents something that occurs in the real world.
- Objects with different properties have different *types*.

A type is characterized by:

(1)   the **values** that can be taken by objects belonging to the type; and

(2)   the **operations** that can be performed on them.

For example, for the type FLOAT the possible values are, in principle, all the real numbers, and the operations are the normal mathematical operations such as addition and multiplication. (In reality, for each implementation of Ada the values possible are limited by the way in which the computer stores numbers in its memory).

Types

Are characterized by:

(1) the values that can be taken by objects of the type; and

(2) the operations that can be carried out on objects of the type.

Ada is a language that keeps careful check on the types of different objects, that is, objects of a certain type can only take values that are acceptable for that type. For example, it would be impossible to store a product code in the variable ITEM_PRICE. One great advantage of keeping different types separate in this way is that it leads to better and more reliable programs. If you try to mix different types in a program, it is often a sign that there is an error in the logic of the program design. The compiler detects forbidden confusion of types and gives an error message; this can be helpful in finding certain logic faults.

In Ada, as we shall see later, there is enormous scope for the programmer to construct types of varying complexity to represent real phenomena. For example, a type can be created to describe a car in a car-hire company's file, or a line of customers in a bank. In Ada there are some basic standard types that can be used to describe objects or to build up more complex types; we shall study some of these in this chapter. The standard types are defined in a special package STANDARD that is included in all implementations of Ada. A listing of the specification of this package is given in Appendix C. All Ada programs automatically have access to the STANDARD packages; thus **with** and **use** clauses are not used to access it.

3.1.1 The numeric types *INTEGER* and *FLOAT*

In earlier programs we have seen the standard types INTEGER and FLOAT. The type INTEGER can be used to describe objects that can take only integral values, such as counters and numbers of things. The type FLOAT can be used for other numerical values, for example, physical properties such as temperature and length. The standard types INTEGER and FLOAT exist in all implementations of Ada.

> ### INTEGER and FLOAT
>
> - INTEGER represents the mathematical concept 'integer', that is, only whole numbers are possible.
> - FLOAT represents the mathematical concept 'real number'.

To the question 'Would it be enough just to have the standard type FLOAT, which could then be used for all numerical quantities?' the answer is 'Yes, in principle.' The reason why INTEGER is still included is that most computers handle integers more quickly and more simply than real numbers. Moreover, integers can always be stored exactly in the computer whereas real numbers often can be stored only in an approximate form.

To help with understanding the properties of the types INTEGER and FLOAT there follows a short description of the principles of storing numerical values in a computer. It is not absolutely essential for the programmer to know this in detail, so those who want to can leave this section for later reading.

■

The computer's memory comprises a number of memory cells, as mentioned in Chapter 1. Each cell consists of a certain number of bits and each bit can contain one binary digit (a zero or a one). This means that numbers are naturally stored in binary form in memory and we shall therefore start by looking at the **binary number system**.

In our culture the decimal system dominates completely (presumably because we have ten fingers). So if we write a number, such as 158.32, we assume automatically that it is expressed in the decimal system where the base is 10. This means that we interpret 158.32 as:

$$1 \times 10^2 + 5 \times 10^1 + 8 \times 10^0 + 3 \times 10^{-1} + 2 \times 10^{-2}$$

Expressing this more generally, we can say that a decimal number:

$$a_n a_{n-1} \ldots a_1 a_0 . d_1 d_2 \ldots d_m$$

(where the as denote the integral part and the ds the decimal part) really means:

$$a_n \times 10^n + a_{n-1} \times 10^{n-1} + \ldots + a_1 \times 10^1 + a_0 \times 10^0 + d_1 \times 10^{-1}$$
$$+ d_2 \times 10^{-2} + \ldots + d_m \times 10^{-m}$$

Using base 2 instead of base 10, the binary number:

$$b_n b_{n-1} \ldots b_1 b_0.c_1 c_2 \ldots c_m$$

is interpreted as:

$$b_n \times 2^n + b_{n-1} \times 2^{n-1} + \ldots + b_1 \times 2^1 + b_0 \times 2^0 + c_1 \times 2^{-1} + c_2$$
$$\times 2^{-2} + \ldots + c_m \times 2^{-m}$$

Here, the bs denote the integral part and the cs denote what is sometimes called the bicimal part. For example, the binary number 10111.101 can be interpreted as:

$$1 \times 2^4 + 0 \times 2^3 + 1 \times 2^2 + 1 \times 2^1 + 1 \times 2^0 + 1 \times 2^{-1} + 0 \times 2^{-2}$$
$$+ 1 \times 2^{-3}$$

or:

$$16 + 0 + 4 + 2 + 1 + 0.5 + 0 + 0.125 = 23.625$$

When an integer is stored in a computer a certain number of bits are used. The actual number of bits varies from computer to computer but it is commonly either 16 or 32. If, for example, the integer 23 has to be stored in 16 bits, we get the binary pattern:

0000000000010111

The bit on the extreme left usually gives the number's sign, zero and one indicating a positive and a negative number, respectively. The greatest positive number that can be stored in 16 bits is therefore:

0111111111111111

This is actually $2^{15} - 1 = 32767$. For storing negative numbers it is usual to employ a form known as **two's complement**. In this, the number -1 is stored in 16 bits as:

1111111111111111

The number -2 is obtained by subtracting 1 from this, thus getting:

1111111111111110

The number −3 is:

1111111111111101

By continuing to subtract one at a time we see that the least number (that is, the most negative number) that can be stored in 16 bits is:

1000000000000000

This has the value $-2^{15} = -32768$. In general, it can be stated that if integers are stored in N bits, the least number that can be stored is -2^{N-1}, and the greatest is $2^{N-1}-1$.

Variables of type INTEGER will be stored in this, or some similar, way in the computer. The programmer does not need to know exactly how the storage works; the compiler takes care of this.

□

There is a certain risk attached to using the type INTEGER. Because the size of the numbers that can be stored depends on the design of the particular computer being used, the type INTEGER will not have the same properties in all implementations of Ada. Suppose we develop a program in a computer that uses 32 bits for storing integers of the type INTEGER. Now suppose a variable of type INTEGER at some point in the program takes the value 100000. This is fine because there is room in 32 bits to store 100000. But if we want to transfer our program to another computer that uses 16 bits to store integers we shall have a problem. When it is run, the program will be terminated because there is not enough space for the value 100000.

To determine the least and greatest numbers of the type INTEGER that can be stored in the computer, another feature of Ada can be used – an **attribute**. For each type there are a number of attributes that give information about particular properties of the type. For INTEGER, for example, there are the two attributes:

INTEGER'FIRST
INTEGER'LAST

These give, respectively, the least and greatest numbers (that is, the most negative and the most positive numbers) of type INTEGER that can be stored. A test program could be written to see which numbers can be stored in the computer in use including the statements:

```
PUT(" The least INTEGER is:    ");  PUT(INTEGER'FIRST);
PUT(" The greatest INTEGER is: ");  PUT(INTEGER'LAST);
```

Attributes for the type INTEGER

INTEGER'FIRST
  gives the least possible integer that can be stored
  (the most negative number).

INTEGER'LAST
  gives the greatest possible integer that can be
  stored.

To be on the safe side and to ensure that programs are portable, i.e. that they can be used on any computer, do not use the type INTEGER, but declare a new integer type where it is explicitly stated how big and how small the numbers involved will be. How to do this will be dealt with later.

In addition to the standard type INTEGER, an Ada implementation may also have the standard types SHORT_INTEGER and LONG_INTEGER. SHORT_INTEGER is then used to store only small integers while LONG_INTEGER is used for integers that cannot be stored as INTEGER. The attributes FIRST and LAST can also be used for these types.

■

In science and engineering, to avoid using too many zeros in a number, standard notation is often used for writing very large and very small numbers. In standard notation the numbers 350 000 000 and 0.000 000 73, for example, are written as:

$$0.35 \times 10^9 \qquad 0.73 \times 10^{-6}$$

The same technique is used for storing real numbers in a computer, but the base 2 is used instead of 10. The decimal number 10.5 can first be translated into binary form, giving the binary number 1010.1, and this can be written as:

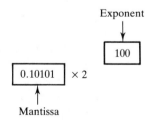

The first part, 0.10101, is usually called the mantissa and the second part, 100, the exponent. Both the mantissa and exponent are written as binary numbers (the exponent 100 meaning 4 in base 10).

When a real number is stored in a computer its mantissa and exponent can each use a certain number of bits, the numbers varying from computer to computer. In addition, one bit is used to store the sign of the number.

The principle of storing real numbers is demonstrated in the following example where we assume that the decimal number 10.5 is stored in a computer that uses 32 bits to store real numbers; the first of the 32 bits holds the sign (0 for plus, 1 for minus), the next 8 bits are used for the exponent, and the remaining 23 bits are used to store the mantissa. The integral part of the mantissa does not need to be stored because it is always 0. (Sometimes, the first digit in the mantissa is not stored either because it is always possible to adjust the number so that this digit is 1).

```
s exponent        mantissa
0 00000100 10101000000000000000000
```

It must be noted that the details of storing real numbers vary considerably from computer to computer. This example merely shows the general principles.

Note that the exponent can also be negative, when a small number is stored. For example, the number 0.06125 (= 1/16) would be stored as follows, using the same format as the previous example:

```
0 11111101 10000000000000000000000
```

Here, the value of the exponent (−3) is expressed in the two's complement form.

This method of storing real numbers means that some numbers, such as the example of 10.5 above, can be stored exactly, whereas others, such as 0.6, cannot. If the number −0.6 is to be stored in the computer using the form outlined above, the pattern of bits would look like:

```
1 00000000 10011001100110011001100
```

The bit pattern 1001 in the mantissa should be repeated infinitely many times, but only 23 bits are available.

The number of significant decimal figures obtained depends on the number of bits used to store the mantissa. (It takes, on average, 3.32 bits per decimal figure). The number of bits used for the exponent determines the largest and smallest numbers (excluding zero) that can be stored. The number zero is usually handled specially and stored exactly using a particular pattern of bits.

□

The type FLOAT uses the foregoing technique to store real numbers. This means that the number of significant figures is the same over the whole range of possible numbers, and that the position of the decimal point 'floats'. It is said the numbers are stored as **floating point numbers** and that FLOAT is a **floating point type**. (Note there is also another technique for storing real numbers in Ada, using a fixed decimal point. 'Fixed point types' are used in this latter situation, but we shall not study these here).

There are also a number of attributes for the type FLOAT that can be used to determine the properties of the type in the computer being used. The most common attributes are FLOAT'DIGITS, FLOAT'SMALL, and FLOAT'LARGE. An Ada implementation may also have the standard types SHORT_FLOAT and LONG_FLOAT which are, respectively, less and more accurate than the type FLOAT. The attributes described above can also be used for these types.

Attributes for the type FLOAT

FLOAT'DIGITS
  gives the number of significant figures one has.

FLOAT'SMALL
  gives the smallest positive number (apart from zero) that can be stored.

FLOAT'LARGE
  gives the largest positive number that can be stored.

Storing real numbers is therefore complicated, but it is reassuring to know that a programmer does not need to worry about the details of what is happening. However, the programmer should be aware of the accuracy that the decimal numbers retain. Furthermore, the programmer should remember that real numbers are not always stored in their exact form, that is, care must be taken when determining whether two real numbers are equal. Even if they are equal in principle, they can still differ by one bit in their mantissas and the computer will then see them as unequal. Such problems do not arise with numbers of the type INTEGER because all numbers are stored exactly.

Comparing real numbers

Avoid comparisons such as:

$$X = Y \quad \text{or} \quad X = 2.37$$

The numbers may be 'equal' but they can still be considered unequal by the computer.

3.1.2 The type *CHARACTER*

Most of the data handled by computers is probably not numerical at all, but text, characters and symbols. In the programs studied earlier we saw how to read in and print out a product code using the type STRING. We shall start by describing a more basic standard type, namely the type CHARACTER. This type is used for handling only single characters, such as letters, digits, special symbols (for example, question mark, full stop or colon), or nonprinting control characters. Nonprinting control characters can be used for communication tasks when the computer needs to make a terminal do certain things, for example, begin a new line, clear the screen or make a bell ring.

Let us write a short program to read a character from the terminal keyboard and write it on the screen.

```
with TEXT_IO;
use  TEXT_IO;
procedure CHARACTER_DEMO is
    CHAR : CHARACTER;
begin
    PUT_LINE("Type any character!");
    GET(CHAR);
    PUT(CHAR);
end CHARACTER_DEMO;
```

In the program we have declared a variable CHAR of type CHARACTER. The package TEXT_IO contains versions of the procedures PUT and GET which can be used to read and write values of type CHARACTER. The statement:

```
GET(CHAR);
```

results in the character that the user types at the keyboard occupying the variable CHAR. We can think of CHAR as a storage box, or store, for characters. If, for instance, the user types a percentage sign, the situation

CHARACTER

Figure 3.1

after the GET statement has been executed could be illustrated by
Figure 3.1. Observe that CHAR can contain only *one* character; if the user
types in several characters at the keyboard only the first one will land in
CHAR.

Values of characters are written enclosed by apostrophes. If, for
example, we want to put a plus sign in CHAR we can write the assignment
statement:

CHAR := '+';

If we want to put an apostrophe in CHAR instead, we would write:

CHAR := '''';

The nonprinting characters have special names that are defined in a
package called ASCII which is included in the STANDARD package. For
example, the character that means line feed at the terminal can be put
into CHAR as follows:

CHAR := ASCII.LF;

There is a generally accepted standard for determining which characters
are allowed. It is called the **ASCII standard** and contains 128 different
characters. Of these, 95 can be printed and the rest are nonprinting
control characters. Among the printable characters are the upper and
lower case letters, numerals and various special symbols.

To store a character in a computer, a group of 8 bits – a **byte** – is
most often used. The ASCII standard defines exactly how the different
characters should be represented for storage. Because there are only 128
ASCII characters, 7 bits are enough for their representation. (Seven zeros
and ones can be arranged in 128 different ways). For each and every one
of the 128 characters there is a unique 7-bit pattern defined in the
standard. The first bit of the 8-bit group is not needed for the
representation but it is sometimes used for control purposes instead. (We

' '	'!'	'"'	'#'	'$'	'%'	'&'	'''
'('	')'	'*'	'+'	','	'-'	'.'	'/'
'0'	'1'	'2'	'3'	'4'	'5'	'6'	'7'
'8'	'9'	':'	';'	'<'	'='	'>'	'?'
'@'	'A'	'B'	'C'	'D'	'E'	'F'	'G'
'H'	'I'	'J'	'K'	'L'	'M'	'N'	'O'
'P'	'Q'	'R'	'S'	'T'	'U'	'V'	'W'
'X'	'Y'	'Z'	'['	'\'	']'	'^'	'_'
'`'	'a'	'b'	'c'	'd'	'e'	'f'	'g'
'h'	'i'	'j'	'k'	'l'	'm'	'n'	'o'
'p'	'q'	'r'	's'	't'	'u'	'v'	'w'
'x'	'y'	'z'	'{'	'|'	'}'	'~'	

Figure 3.2

shall assume it is zero in the examples below). As examples, we show how '%', '9' and 'A' are represented.

```
0 0100101
0 0111001
0 1000001
```

In Ada the type CHARACTER is defined so that it conforms to the ASCII standard. This means that:

(1)   a variable of type CHARACTER can contain any of the 128 characters of the ASCII standard; and

(2)   the different characters are represented in the computer by exactly the bit-pattern defined by the standard.

In our example above, the store CHAR will contain the bit-pattern 0 0100101 if the user types a percentage sign at the terminal.

The type CHARACTER is an **enumeration type**. It is defined by all 128 values that a variable of type CHARACTER can take as listed in the STANDARD package. Later we shall see how programmers can define new enumeration types for themselves.

In an enumeration type there is a relative ordering defined between the different values. The order is decided by how the values are listed in the definition; of two values, the one listed first is considered the lesser. An order is thus defined for values of type CHARACTER. First come 32 nonprinting characters, and then the 95 printable characters in the order given in Figure 3.2. Note that the first printable character is a blank, which corresponds to 'space' on the terminal keyboard.

Below we have amended our earlier program so that it reads in two characters and prints them out in order (as defined in the ASCII standard).

```
with TEXT_IO;
use  TEXT_IO;
procedure CHARACTER_DEMO2 is
    CHAR1, CHAR2 : CHARACTER;
begin
    PUT_LINE("Type two characters!");
    GET(CHAR1);
    GET(CHAR2);
    if CHAR1 < CHAR2 then
      PUT(CHAR1);
      PUT(CHAR2);
    else
      PUT(CHAR2);
      PUT(CHAR1);
    end if;
end CHARACTER_DEMO2;
```

We see that the two variables CHAR1 and CHAR2 can simply be compared by using an **if** statement.

There is an attribute for the type CHARACTER that allows the position of a particular character in the ASCII standard to be determined. For example:

CHARACTER'POS('A')

gives the position of the letter 'A' in the ASCII standard, which is actually 65. The positions are in the range 0 to 127 because the ASCII standard starts numbering from 0.

The parameter in brackets can also be a variable. For example, writing:

CHARACTER'POS(CHAR)

gives the position of the character stored in the variable CHAR.

There is a second attribute for working in the other direction:

CHARACTER'VAL(65)

gives the 65th ASCII character, which is 'A'. Note this attribute returns a result of type CHARACTER and the parameter must be between 0 and 127.

Attributes for CHARACTER

CHARACTER'POS(C)
    gives the position of C in the ASCII standard
    (where C has type CHARACTER).

CHARACTER'VAL(N)
    gives the character that has position N.

3.1.3 The text type *STRING*

The standard type CHARACTER can only be used to describe one character at a time. For an object that contains several characters, the standard type STRING must be used instead. We saw an example of this in the invoicing program of Chapter 2. A declaration of a variable of type STRING, a **text string variable**, might appear as follows:

    NAME : STRING(1 .. 5);

The number of characters to be stored in the variable and how they are to be numbered are stated in the brackets. In this case, NAME will hold five characters, numbered from 1 to 5.

    A text string variable can, just like other sorts of variable, be given a value by assignment. If the statement:

    NAME := "Tommy";

appears in the program, then after execution, NAME will be as in Figure 3.3. Note that the text string on the right-hand side of the statement must contain the same number of characters as the variable on the left-hand side has space for; in Figure 3.3 this is five. To write "Thomas" or "Tom" on the right, for example, is not allowed, but 'padding out' with blanks and writing "Tom " is permitted. Also note that double quotation marks are used to enclose text strings in a program. In the example in Chapter 2, we saw that it is also possible to give a value

NAME

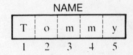

Figure 3.3

Figure 3.4

to a text string variable by reading it in from the terminal using the GET procedure. The situation in Figure 3.3 could also be achieved if the program contained the statements:

```
PUT_LINE("Give a name with 5 letters!");
GET(NAME);
```

and if the user typed the name Tommy at the terminal keyboard.

When a text string variable is declared, the two quantities in the brackets do not need to be constants. It is possible to use simple expressions that may themselves contain variables. What is essential is that the expressions should have integer values and the first expression is greater than zero.

```
MY_WORD : STRING(2 .. 10*N);
ADDRESS  : STRING(K .. K+10);
```

The type STRING is called a **composite type**. An object of type STRING is actually composed of a number of objects of type CHARACTER. The variable NAME, for example, consists of a collection of five CHARACTER objects, numbered from 1 to 5. It is possible to access the individual parts of a variable of type STRING. If, for example, the content of the variable NAME is to be changed to Tammy, the statement:

```
NAME(2) := 'a';
```

can be written. The expression NAME(2) is an example of **indexing**. The 2 specifies that it is the second element of the variable NAME that is meant. This element has type CHARACTER, not type STRING. This is the reason for the apostrophes around the letter a on the right-hand side of the statement; they are used, as we saw earlier, for the type CHARACTER. Figure 3.4 shows the state of NAME after this assignment statement has been executed.

In the following example, indexing is used to print out the last character in the variable NAME:

```
PUT( NAME(5) );
```

With indexing, the expression in brackets need not have a constant value. The index for a text string can be any expression at all, provided it has type INTEGER and its value lies within the declared range, as shown in the following examples:

```
NAME(2+3)
NAME(J+1)    -- correct if 0 <= J <= 4
NAME(2*K)    -- correct if 1 <= K <= 2
```

Indexing in a variable of type STRING

   S(*integer expression*)

where S has type STRING and the value of the integer expression must lie within the index range for S.

The result of indexing is a single component of type CHARACTER.

Using indexing it is thus possible to select a particular element of a text string. It is also possible to choose a number of contiguous elements simultaneously, by creating a **slice** – a part of a string. For example, the variable NAME can be changed so that it contains the name Jimmy instead of Tammy:

```
NAME(1 .. 2) := "Ji";
```

A slice has type STRING and therefore quotation marks are needed on the right-hand side (even if the slice that is cut consists of a single element). The following statement will print the second, third and fourth elements of NAME:

```
PUT( NAME(2 .. 4) );
```

As with indexing, more general expressions are allowed as index limits. When a slice of a text string is taken, the two indexes must have type INTEGER and they must lie within the index range of the text string. An exception is made of the **empty slice** – a slice whose second index number is lower than the first. The index is then allowed to fall outside the range of the text string's index. Here are some examples of slices of the text string NAME:

```
NAME(2 .. 2+1)
NAME(J−3 .. J) -- OK if J has, for example, the value 4
NAME(1 .. 0)    -- empty slice
NAME(3 .. K)    -- slice if 2 < K < 6, empty slice if K < 3, error if K > 5
```

Slices of text strings

   S(N1 .. N2)

where S has type STRING. N1 and N2 are integer expressions.

- If N2 < N1 we get an empty slice.
- Otherwise, N1 and N2 must lie within the index range of S.
- The result has type STRING.

It is possible to join strings together in sequence, to **catenate** strings, using an operator denoted by the symbol &. Here are a few examples:

```
NAME := "Tom" & "my";        -- result is "Tommy"
NAME := "Ji" & NAME(3 .. 5); -- result is "Jimmy"
PUT( NAME & " Johnson");      -- "Jimmy Johnson" is printed
NAME := NAME(1 .. 4) & 'o';   -- result is "Jimmo"
SYMB := 'A'                   -- SYMB has type CHARACTER
PUT( SYMB & "−team");         -- "A-team" is printed
```

The last three lines show that it is also possible to add a CHARACTER onto a text string (either at the beginning or the end).

Catenation of text strings

   S1 & S2

where S1 and S2 can be either variables of type STRING or constant text strings.

- It is also possible for one (or both) of S1 and S2 to have type CHARACTER.
- The result has type STRING.

The next example program shows how catenation and slices can be used. The method used to write the date is different in different countries and can sometimes be a little confusing. For example, the American way of writing 26th March 1987 is 03/26/87, whereas in Britain it would be written 26/03/87. The day and the month have swapped places. According to the ISO standard, the same date should be written 1987-03-26. Let us look at a program that can read in a date in the American format and translate it into the equivalent British and ISO formats. When the program is run the conversation at the terminal would appear:

```
Give the date in the form mm/dd/yy
03/26/87
The British form of the date is:
26/03/87
The ISO form of the date is:
1987-03-26
```

Our first version of the program looks like this:

```
with TEXT_IO;
use  TEXT_IO;
procedure TRANSLATE_DATE is
    AMERICAN_DATE : STRING(1 .. 8);
    BRITISH_DATE   : STRING(1 .. 8)  := " /  /  ";
    ISO_DATE       : STRING(1 .. 10) := "19 - - ";
begin
    PUT_LINE("Give the date in the form mm/dd/yy");
    GET(AMERICAN_DATE);

    BRITISH_DATE(1 .. 2) := AMERICAN_DATE(4 .. 5);
    BRITISH_DATE(4 .. 5) := AMERICAN_DATE(1 .. 2);
    BRITISH_DATE(7 .. 8) := AMERICAN_DATE(7 .. 8);
    PUT_LINE("The British form of the date is:");
    PUT_LINE(BRITISH_DATE);

    ISO_DATE(3 .. 4)  := AMERICAN_DATE(7 .. 8);
    ISO_DATE(6 .. 7)  := AMERICAN_DATE(1 .. 2);
    ISO_DATE(9 .. 10) := AMERICAN_DATE(4 .. 5);
    PUT_LINE("The ISO form of the date is:");
    PUT_LINE(ISO_DATE);
end TRANSLATE_DATE;
```

In the program, the variables BRITISH_DATE and ISO_DATE have been initialized at the same time as being declared. The spaces for the year, month and day numbers have been filled with blanks that are changed later in the program.

We can write a more compact version of the program by

constructing the text string for printing directly in the output statement. We then need only one variable, DATE:

```
with TEXT_IO;
use  TEXT_IO;
procedure TRANSLATE_DATE is
    DATE : STRING(1 .. 8);
begin
    PUT_LINE("Give the date in the form mm/dd/yy");
    GET(DATE);
    PUT_LINE("The British form of the date is:");
    PUT_LINE(DATE(4 .. 5) & "/" & DATE(1 .. 2) & "/" & DATE(7 .. 8));
    PUT_LINE("The ISO form of the date is:");
    PUT_LINE("19" & DATE(7 .. 8) & "-" & DATE(1 .. 2) & "-" &
             DATE(4 .. 5));
end TRANSLATE_DATE;
```

Comparing text strings

- There are normal comparing operations.
- Text strings of different lengths can be compared.
- Ordinary alphabetical order is used.
- Upper and lower case letters are considered to be different.

Text strings can easily be compared with one another:

```
if NAME = "Clare" then
    PUT("Hi Clare");
end if;
```

The text 'Hi Clare' will be printed out only if the variable NAME contains the text string 'Clare'. It is also possible to compare alphabetically, and compare strings of different lengths:

```
NAME < "Diana"
"Betty" < "Peter"      -- True
"Jill" > "Jack"        -- True
"Liz" > "Elizabeth"    -- True
```

```
"Adam" < "Eve"        -- True
"Victor" /= "Victoria"    -- True (/= "not equal to")
"Victor" < "Victoria"     -- True
"Rose" < "rose"        -- True
```

Comparisons are made using ordinary alphabetical order. Note that upper and lower case letters are considered to be different; paradoxically, upper case letters are smaller than the big letters. (See Figure 3.2).

This section concludes with a useful method for reading text of variable length from the terminal. We have seen that it is possible to read text into a variable of type STRING, using GET. For example, in the date program above we had the line:

```
GET(DATE);
```

The disadvantage of GET, however, is that the text typed at the keyboard must contain exactly the same number of characters as there are places in the variable. Since the variable DATE has eight places, in this example, the user must type in eight characters at the terminal. This poses no problem when reading in a date because we know that it always has exactly eight characters; in many other cases, however, it is not possible to decide in advance just how many characters to expect.

As an example, we can look at a program that reads in two lines from the terminal. Each line ends when the user presses the end-of-line key, the RETURN-key in most systems. Assume that each line contains a name, and the program's job is to sort them into alphabetical order.

```
with TEXT_IO;
use  TEXT_IO;
procedure DEMONSTRATE_LINE is
    LINE1, LINE2 : STRING(1 .. 100);
    L1, L2        : INTEGER;
begin
    PUT_LINE("Enter first name");
    GET_LINE(LINE1, L1);
    PUT_LINE("Enter second name");
    GET_LINE(LINE2, L2);
    if LINE1(1 .. L1) < LINE2(1 .. L2) then
        PUT_LINE( LINE1(1 .. L1) );
        PUT_LINE( LINE2(1 .. L2) );
    else
        PUT_LINE( LINE2(1 .. L2) );
        PUT_LINE( LINE1(1 .. L1) );
    end if;
end DEMONSTRATE_LINE;
```

In the program we have declared two text string variables LINE1 and LINE2 where the two lines will be placed. We assume that no line will be more than 100 characters long and, therefore, we let both variables have room for 100 characters. The integer variables L1 and L2 will be used to keep track of how many characters the user writes in the two respective lines.

For the actual reading we use a procedure GET_LINE from the package TEXT_IO. The first line is read with:

```
GET_LINE(LINE1, L1);
```

What happens here is that the characters the user writes at the terminal for the first line are read in and placed in the variable LINE1, from left to right, starting at position 1. The variable L1 will get as its value the number of characters read in the first line. To return to an earlier example, if the user writes 'Tommy' for the first line, the text 'Tommy' will appear in elements 1 to 5 of LINE1 and L1 will automatically get the value 5. The remaining elements of LINE1 (elements 6 to 100) are not defined.

The second line is read in in the same way:

```
GET_LINE(LINE2, L2);
```

If the user should write 'Catherine' for the second line, the text 'Catherine' would appear in elements 1 to 9 of the variable LINE2 and the variable L2 would have the value 9.

Reading in text of variable length

(1) Declare a variable S of type STRING that is long enough to hold a text of the maximum length.

(2) Declare an integer variable N.

(3) Read a line at the terminal using:

```
GET_LINE(S,N);
```

(The user ends a line by pressing the end-of-line key).

The variable N will contain the number of characters in the line read, and the characters themselves will be in elements 1 to N of S.

The two names can now be compared easily. We cut two slices that contain only the two names and write:

if LINE1(1 .. L1) < LINE2(1 .. L2) **then**

If the user writes 'Tommy' and 'Catherine' for the two lines, the text strings 'Tommy' and 'Catherine' will thus be compared with one another. (The remaining elements of LINE1 and LINE2 are of no significance).

The name is then written out using PUT_LINE, and here we also cut out the slice that contains the name read in.

3.1.4 The logical type *BOOLEAN*

In Ada, the comparison:

NUMBER_OF_ITEMS > 0

is considered as much an expression as:

NUMBER_OF_ITEMS + 1

The second expression has type INTEGER, but what type does the first one have?

If you make the claim:

NUMBER_OF_ITEMS > 0

it can either be true or false. In other words, we can say that the expression can take **the value true** or **the value false**. It is quite normal to think of values as numerical, for example, 14 or 68.24. When we discussed the types CHARACTER and STRING, we saw that characters could also be seen as values, but of another kind. Now we have met a third sort of value, logical values, known as **Boolean values** after the mathematician Boole. In Ada there is a standard type BOOLEAN that can be used for handling such values. For example, variables of the type BOOLEAN can be declared:

ACTIVE : BOOLEAN;

The variable ACTIVE can only contain the values TRUE or FALSE. We can make an assignment:

ACTIVE := TRUE;

Figure 3.5

and then we have the situation depicted in Figure 3.5.

In the same way as other variables, we have thought of ACTIVE as a storage box, but now a store that can only contain the values FALSE or TRUE. If we want to, we can assign the result of a comparison to a BOOLEAN variable:

    ACTIVE := NAME = "Tommy";

This may look a little strange to start with, but note the difference between := and =. The assignment symbol := means that what is on its right, that is, the logical expression:

    NAME = "Tommy"

should be evaluated first and then the result should be placed in the variable ACTIVE. In the expression on the right-hand side the operator = appears; this is an operator concerned with comparing and has nothing to do with assignment.

The type BOOLEAN

- The only values allowed are FALSE and TRUE.
- Expressions of type BOOLEAN are called Boolean expressions.

If in a program we want to test the value of a BOOLEAN variable, we could do so as follows:

```
if ACTIVE = TRUE then
    PUT("In action!");
end if;
```

Since ACTIVE already contains a value of type BOOLEAN, it is more elegant to write simply:

```
if ACTIVE then
   PUT("In action!");
end if;
```

BOOLEAN is actually an enumeration type, like the type CHARACTER. It is also defined in the STANDARD package where the two possible values, FALSE and TRUE, have been listed (such that FALSE < TRUE, but this is not normally significant).

3.2 Identifiers

The concept of an **identifier** is found in most programming languages, and Ada is no exception. An identifier can be used as a **name** for different components in a program, such as a procedure or variable. Identifiers are also used to denote **reserved words**. GIANT_ADA, PUT, **begin**, and **if** are all examples of identifiers. There are strict rules governing the appearance of identifiers. In Ada, the rules are as follows:

- An identifier consists of a series of one or more characters. The number of characters permitted in an identifier is, in principle, limitless and all characters are significant. This differs from a number of other languages where only a defined number of characters at the beginning are counted.
- The first character must be one of the letters A, B, C, ..., X, Y, Z.
- The remaining characters may be one of the letters A, B, C, ..., X, Y, Z, or the underline symbol _, or one of the numerals 0, 1, ..., 8, 9. The underline symbol is significant, which means that, for example, NR_1 and NR1 are interpreted as two different identifiers. More than one underline symbol in sequence is not allowed, nor is an underline symbol at the end of an identifier. Blank characters (spaces) are not allowed in an identifier, so that, for example, NUMBER NR1 is interpreted as two identifiers.
- Lower case letters are also permitted. They are interpreted in the same way as the corresponding upper case letter, so that, for example, PUT and puT are taken to be the same.

Here are some examples of identifiers:

```
TOMMY            Smallest_Number     x      P_1
NUMBER_NR1       PageNumber          x1     procedure
THE_LEAST_TEMPERATURE_CALCULATED
```

Some examples of illegal identifiers are:

1X	-- the first character may not be a numeral
_post	-- the first character may not be _
ID−NUMBER	-- the minus sign may not be used
ID number	-- interpreted as two identifiers
km/hr	-- / symbol not allowed

Identifiers

- Used as the names of various items, or as reserved words.
- Arbitrary length.
- First character letter A–Z.
- Remaining characters letter A–Z, numeral, or _ (but not several _ in a row, or _ as the last character).
- Lower case letters can also be used.

The reserved words have special meanings and, therefore, they may not be used as names in a program. For example, there may be no variable called END. To show the reserved words clearly, they are always shown in our examples in bold print. (When writing programs, there is no need to mark the reserved words in any special way). A list of all the reserved words in Ada is presented in Figure 3.6.

3.3 Literals

Sometimes, actual values are needed in a program, such as 12, 34.5 or 'Hello'. In programming, actual values such as these are called **literals**.

Numeric literals are used to give numeric values and can be either integer literals or real literals. It is most common to give numeric literals as decimal numbers, as in the following examples:

13	0	4598	-- integer literals
1E7	15e5	1E0	-- integer literals
13.0	0.0	0.379	-- real literals
1.0e7	43.2E−12	3.2E+8	-- reai literals

The exponent form is interpreted as the number before the 'e' multiplied by 10 to the power of the integer after the 'e'. (Both upper and lower case

abort	abs	accept	access
all	and	array	at
begin	body	case	constant
declare	delay	delta	digits
do	else	elsif	end
entry	exception	exit	for
function	generic	goto	if
in	is	limited	loop
mod	new	not	null
of	or	others	out
package	pragma	private	procedure
raise	range	record	rem
renames	return	reverse	select
separate	subtype	task	terminate
then	type	use	when
while	with	xor	

Figure 3.6

e can be used). 1.234e2 is therefore interpreted as 123.4 while 1.4E−3 is 0.0014. The integer after e can be preceded by a plus or a minus sign.

Zeros can be written at the start if desired, for example, 0028 or 002.35. There must be at least one figure before the decimal point in a real number, for example, .34 is illegal and should be written 0.34. Spaces are not allowed in a literal, so that 1.4e −3 is not allowed, but underline symbols may be inserted for grouping digits. For example, 1_245_000 would be interpreted as 1245000, and 1.356_491 is taken as 1.356491.

These format rules for numeric literals also apply when numbers are read into a program using the procedure GET. This means that the user must follow the same rules at the terminal. Note that if an integer is to be read in, the rules for integers apply; if a real number is to be read in then the rules for real numbers apply. For example, if the variable TEMPERATURE has the type FLOAT and the statements:

```
PUT_LINE("Enter the temperature!");
GET(TEMPERATURE);
```

are in the program, then the user must type a real literal at the terminal. This could be 12.0 or 1.2e1, for example. If the user only types 12, then this is an error because 12 is an integer literal, not a real literal. In Ada, the user will be given a DATA_ERROR. If the statements:

```
PUT_LINE("Give the number of items!");
GET(NUMBER_OF_ITEMS);
```

appear in a program and the variable NUMBER_OF_ITEMS is declared as an INTEGER, then the user must type an integer literal at the terminal, for example, 123, 25_000 or 1e3. The program will malfunction if the user types a real literal such as 1.0e3 or 123.0.

We saw character literals when we discussed the type CHARACTER. A character literal comprises any one of the 95 printable characters enclosed in apostrophes. Some examples are

'z'   'B'   '7'   '?'   '('   ' '   '.'   ''''

The last of these shows how the apostrophe is given as a character literal.

We have also seen several examples of text string literals. These comprise a number of printable characters (which can be zero) enclosed in quotation marks, for example:

```
"This is a text string literal"
"       "
"abx'+%"
" "
```

The quotation marks do not form part of the text string, they only act as delimiters. If a quotation mark must be part of a string, it has to be written twice, as in the following example:

```
"Americans call a " "lift" " an " "elevator" "."
```

This is interpreted as a single text string literal, not as five. A text string literal must appear on a single line in a program. If it is too long for one line, then the catenation operator can be used:

```
"This is a text string literal that is so long that " &
"we shall have to write it on two lines."
```

When the user has to type in a value for a variable of type CHARACTER or STRING from the terminal, then the apostrophes or quotation marks should not be typed. Suppose the variable NAME is declared as a STRING(1 .. 5) and the following two statements are in a program:

```
PUT_LINE("Enter a name with 5 letters!");
GET(NAME);
```

If the user now types the word Tommy (without quotation marks), the variable NAME will take the value 'Tommy'.

The final type of literal we have met is the literal of type BOOLEAN.

Since there are only two values in the type BOOLEAN, there are only two literals:

FALSE   TRUE

It is also possible to read in values to BOOLEAN variables, and then these literals are used. We shall return to this in a later chapter.

Literals

- Constant values, such as numeric values.
- Exist for all types.

3.4 Expressions

Expressions can be constructed in a program to calculate new values from literals and the names of objects. NUMBER_OF_ITEMS * 2 is an example of an expression. Note that every expression is of a particular type that is determined by how it is constructed and the components included in it. The expression NUMBER_OF_ITEMS * 2 has type INTEGER if NUMBER_OF_ITEMS has type INTEGER.

The simplest form of expression comprises only one literal or the name of an object:

```
3.14
ID_NUMBER
VAT_PERCENT
TRUE
"Hello!"
```

More complicated expressions can be built using **operators**. The symbol *, for example, denotes the multiplication operator in the expression NUMBER_OF_ITEMS * 2. A set of basic operators is defined in Ada. (It is also possible for the programmer to define new operators but we shall not do this here). Some operators exist only for certain types, for example, multiplication is defined for two integers but not for two text strings.

> **Expressions**
>
> - Simplest form: literal or name of an object.
> - More complicated expressions are constructed using operators and simpler expressions.

3.4.1 Numeric expressions

Expressions that calculate with ordinary numbers are called **numeric** or **arithmetic expressions**. In arithmetic expressions the normal operations of mathematics can be used: addition, subtraction, multiplication and division. In addition, there are operators to find the remainder after integer division; to find the absolute value of a number; and to carry out exponentiation.

Ada is careful to separate the different types. As we have seen, different types may not be mixed in an arithmetic expression at will. We shall see later that it is possible for the programmer to define new numeric types other than the standard types INTEGER and FLOAT. Therefore, when the term 'integer type' is used in future it will refer not only to the type INTEGER but also to all other integer types; for example, SHORT_INTEGER and integer types defined by the programmer. In the same way, the term 'floating number type' refers not only to FLOAT, but also to SHORT_FLOAT and all other defined types that are related to the type FLOAT. 'Numeric type' means any integer type or float type at all.

> **Numeric expressions**
>
> - Expressions constructed of ordinary mathematical numbers.
> - Different types, for example, INTEGER and FLOAT, may not be mixed at will in an expression.

We begin with a discussion of the types of numeric literals. Each expression has a particular resulting type depending on how it is put together. As we saw above, a numeric literal is the simplest form of expression, but what is its type? What are the types of the expressions 28 and 25.84? If 28 has the type INTEGER and the variable SMALL_NUMBER has the type SHORT_INTEGER, then the assignment:

```
SMALL_NUMBER := 28;
```

would not be permitted, because the two sides have different types. This would be impracticable. Clearly an integer literal does not have the type INTEGER. This problem, and all similar problems, have been solved in Ada by introducing an anonymous type called *universal_integer*, and all integer literals are said to be of this type. A value of the type *universal_integer* is converted automatically to a suitable integer type when it is used. In the assignment statement above, therefore, the value 28 is converted automatically into type SHORT_INTEGER in connection with the assignment. If instead we have the statement:

```
BIG_NUMBER := 28;
```

where BIG_NUMBER has type LONG_INTEGER, then 28 is converted automatically into type LONG_INTEGER. This means that an integer literal can always be regarded as having the 'right' integer type and there is no need to worry about converting it to a particular type.

In a similar way, there is also an anonymous real type called *universal_real* and all real literals can be regarded as having this type and being converted automatically into the 'right' float type.

Literals in numeric expressions

- Integer literals may be used anywhere an integer type is required.
- Conversion to the right integer type occurs automatically.
- Real literals may be used anywhere a real type is required.
- Conversion to the right real type occurs automatically.

Let us examine the different operations that can be performed in an arithmetic expression. Addition, subtraction, multiplication and division can be performed with the operators +, −, * and /. For example:

```
NUMBER + 1          NO_1 + VALUE        3.8 + MEAN_TEMP
SALARY − 378.50     34.8 − 185.3        NUMBER − 8
5 * NUMBER          NO_1 * NO_2         VALUE * 1.3E3
NUMBER / 3          12 / 5              VALUE / 3.76
```

The quantities before and after the operator are called the **operands**. It is essential that both operands have the same type. For example, if NO_1 has type INTEGER, then so must VALUE; if VALUE had another type, such as SHORT_INTEGER or FLOAT, the expression would be faulty. The whole expression has the same type as the operands involved. If NUMBER has type INTEGER, the whole expression NUMBER + 1 also has type INTEGER. The expression 34.8 − 185.3 has the type *universal_real* and the expression 12 / 5 the type *universal_integer*.

There are also **unary** variants of the plus and minus operators. These variants have an operand on the right but none on the left. The unary minus is of use in constructs such as:

K := −1;   K * (−3) PUT(−K);   K := −K;

Division requires a little more explanation. If the operands are of floating point type, there is no problem; ordinary division takes place and the result is of the same type as the operands. If, however, the operands are of integer type, the result is also of integer type; so-called integer division takes place. This means that we see how many times the right-hand operand 'goes into' the left-hand operand. For example, the expression 12 / 5 gives the result 2 because there are 2 whole 5s in 12. The result is *not* 2.4. As a further example, the expression (−7) / 4 gives the result −1, 12 / (−3) gives −4, and (−12) / (−5) gives 2.

The operator **rem** (remainder) can be used to find the remainder after integer division. This needs two integer parameters of the same type. The expression:

12 rem 5

for example, gives the result 2, the remainder when 12 is divided by 5. There is another operator **mod** (modulus operator) that works in almost the same way. The expression:

12 mod 5

also gives the value 2. If one of the operands to **rem** or **mod** is less than zero, then it is a little more complicated. The next few lines can be omitted by readers who are not interested in the details.

■

A mathematical definition is necessary. A and B below denote arbitrary integers. Integer division and the operator **rem** are defined by:

A = (A/B)*B + (A **rem** B)
(−A)/B = −(A/B) = A/(−B)

A	B	A/B	A rem B	A mod B
10	5	2	0	0
12	5	2	2	2
14	5	2	4	4
10	−5	−2	0	0
12	−5	−2	2	−3
14	−5	−2	4	−1
−10	5	−2	0	0
−12	5	−2	−2	3
−14	5	−2	−4	1
−10	−5	2	0	0
−12	−5	2	−2	−2
−14	−5	2	−4	−4

Figure 3.7

where (A **rem** B) has the same sign as A and an absolute value less than the absolute value of B.

For the operator **mod**:

$$A = B*N + (A \textbf{ mod } B) \quad \text{for some integer N.}$$

(A **mod** B) has the same sign as B and an absolute value less than B.

The table in Figure 3.7 illustrates the similarities and differences. If the second operand to one of the operators /, **rem** or **mod** is 0, an error occurs in the program. In Ada, the user is given a NUMERIC_ERROR.

☐

There is an **exponentiation operator** denoted by **∗∗**. Its first operand can either be integer or floating point type. The second operand is the exponent and must always be of integer type. If the first operand is of integer type, the result will also be of integer type; if the first operand is a floating point type then so will the result. Here are a few examples:

```
NUMBER ∗∗ 2      2 ∗∗ NUMBER       5 ∗∗ 4
VALUE ∗∗ 3       MAX_TEMP ∗∗ K     5.78 ∗∗ 7
VALUE ∗∗ (−3)    MAX_TEMP ∗∗ 0
```

The operation that takes place is ordinary exponentiation. The expression N ∗∗ 5, for example, is interpreted as N ∗ N ∗ N ∗ N ∗ N. If the second operand is 0, the result is always 1. If the first operand has floating point type, then a negative exponent is also permitted. The expression X ∗∗ (−4), for example, is interpreted as 1/(X ∗ X ∗ X ∗ X).

The final standard numeric operator is **abs**. This operator has only one operand and that can be of arbitrary numeric type. The operator calculates the absolute value of the operand, in other words the operand itself if it is positive and the negated operand if it is negative. The result is of the same type as the operand.

abs K   **abs** MEAN_VALUE   **abs** (−23.4)

More complicated expressions can be created by combining several operators. For example, expressions such as the following are possible:

NUMBER * 5 + 37
VALUE / FACTOR + 14.3 − CORR
NUMBER **rem** 8 − K
abs VALUE / 5.78 * FACTOR
TEMPERATURE ** 3 * PRESSURE + CORR

The result of one operation is a value that, in turn, is one operand in a new operation. The question of ordering the different operations arises in a complicated expression. In the expression:

2 + 4 / 2 * 3

the result could be completely different, depending on the order of addition, division and multiplication.

Each operator in Ada has a certain **precedence**. The evaluation of a complicated expression occurs in such a way that the operator with the highest precedence is the first to be executed, followed by the one with next highest precedence, and so on, until finally the operator with lowest precedence is executed. If several operators have the same precedence, they are executed from left to right. Of the operators we have seen, **abs** and ** have the highest precedence; next are *, / and **mod**; and then the unary operators + and −. The ordinary + and − operators have the lowest precedence.

If we apply these evaluation rules to the expression above, we see that the operators / and * have higher precedence than + and should therefore be performed first. Since / and * have the same precedence they are carried out from left to right, so that the division 4 / 2 is carried out first. The result of this division, 2, then becomes the left operand to the operator *, which is now executed. The result of the multiplication is 6 and this makes the right operand to the operator +, which is carried out last. Thus, the result of the whole expression is 8.

It is possible to control the order of execution of the various operators using parentheses. The expression:

    (2 + 4) / 2 * 3

has the value 9, for example, and:

    (2 + 4) / (2 * 3)

has the value 1.

Order of evaluation in expressions

- Is determined by the precedence of the operators.
- Can be controlled by the use of parentheses.

In the invoice example of Chapter 2, we saw that sometimes we are forced to mix types. We wanted to multiply a FLOAT variable, ITEM_PRICE with an INTEGER, NUMBER_OF_ITEMS. It is illegal to write ITEM_PRICE * NUMBER_OF_ITEMS because the two operands are of different types. We must use **type conversion** and write:

    ITEM_PRICE * FLOAT(NUMBER_OF_ITEMS)

The value of the variable NUMBER_OF_ITEMS is converted to a value of type FLOAT and this converted value becomes the right-hand operand to the operator *. Conversion between all the numeric types is allowed, and is achieved simply by writing the required type followed by a numeric expression in brackets. The numeric expression is then converted to the type requested. If a real expression is converted to an integer expression, then **rounding** to the nearest whole number occurs. Here are a few examples:

    MEAN_VALUE := SUM / FLOAT(NUMBER_OF_MEASUREMENTS);
    5 * SHORT_INTEGER(2.85)   -- Result is 15
    X * SHORT_FLOAT(N1 + N2)

Type conversion

- This can be used when different numeric types must be mixed in an expression. It has the following form:

    T(*expression*)

    where T is the name of a numeric type and *expression* has another numeric type.

- The result is of type T.

- Rounding occurs if T is an integer type and *expression* has a real type.

The following program can be used for converting a weight in pounds (lb) and ounces (oz) to the equivalent in kilograms (kg) (1 lb = 0.4536 kg and there are 16 oz in 1 lb). Output from the program may look like:

```
Give weight in pounds and ounces
(integers, separated by spaces)
11 9
This is 5.245 kg.
```

The program is as follows:

```
with TEXT_IO, BASIC_NUM_IO;
use  TEXT_IO, BASIC_NUM_IO;
procedure WEIGHT_CONVERSION is
    OZ_PER_LB      : constant := 16.0;
    KG_PER_LB      : constant := 0.4536;
    NO_LBS, NO_OZ : INTEGER;
    WEIGHT         : FLOAT;    -- expressed in kg
begin
    PUT_LINE("Give weight in pounds and ounces");
    PUT_LINE("(integers, separated by spaces)");
    GET(NO_LBS);
    GET(NO_OZ);
    WEIGHT := (FLOAT(NO_LBS)+FLOAT(NO_OZ)/OZ_PER_LB)
                                    * KG_PER_LB;
    PUT("This is ");
    PUT(WEIGHT, FORE => 1, AFT => 3, EXP => 0);
    PUT_LINE(" kg.");
end WEIGHT_CONVERSION;
```

The variables NO_LBS and NO_OZ are declared as INTEGER, so that the user can enter the data in a simple way and not have to type in real numbers. The weight in kg will be a real number and therefore NO_LBS and NO_OZ must be converted to the type FLOAT in the arithmetic expression.

The result of an expression that only contains operands of the type *universal_integer* (or *universal_real*) has the type *universal_integer* (or *universal_real*), depending on the operands involved. The types *universal_integer* and *universal_real* may actually be mixed in multiplication. Also, an operand of type *universal_real* may be divided by an operand of type *universal_integer*. In both cases the result is *universal_real*. Here are a few examples:

```
1 + 2          -- has type universal_integer
1.2 + 5.3      -- has type universal_real
2 ** 8         -- has type universal_integer
2.0 ** 8       -- has type universal_real
5 * 2.8        --  has  type  universal_real
4 / 9          -- has type universal_integer
3.74 / 9       -- has type universal_real
```

On an ordinary calculator there are often several mathematical functions, for evaluating logarithms and trigonometric functions, for example. Which mathematical functions are accessible with Ada, and how do you use them?

As noted earlier, Ada is a language designed for many applications. Not all programs need to use mathematical functions. This type of mathematical function has not been included in the basic definition, so that the language does not become unnecessarily large and complicated. In most implementations of Ada, however, there is a package that contains various useful mathematical functions. This package is not standardized, so its name and content may differ between implementations. If mathematical functions need to be used in a program, the program must have access to the mathematical package. This is achieved by a **with** clause at the start of the program, giving the name of the package. The **with** clause can be combined with a **use** clause to simplify the names of the mathematical functions in the program.

For example, study the following program that reads in the lengths of the shorter sides of a right-angled triangle and calculates and prints the length of the hypotenuse. We assume that the mathematical package in our Ada implementation has the name BASIC_MATH.

```
with TEXT_IO, BASIC_NUM_IO, BASIC_MATH;
use  TEXT_IO, BASIC_NUM_IO, BASIC_MATH;
procedure HYPOTENUSE is
   A, B : FLOAT;
```

```
begin
    PUT_LINE ("Enter the lengths of the shorter sides");
    GET(A);
    GET(B);
    PUT("The hypotenuse has length: ");
    PUT( SQRT(A**2 + B**2), FORE => 1, AFT => 2, EXP => 0 );
    NEW_LINE;
end HYPOTENUSE;
```

The expression:

```
SQRT(A ** 2 + B ** 2)
```

is evaluated in the program. The function SQRT has been called to calculate a square root. The expression in brackets is a parameter to the function. This expression is evaluated first and then passed as input to the function. In Ada, a function call is considered to be an expression. The function call, therefore, has a particular value and type; that is, the function returns output of a certain value and type. Here, the result from the function SQRT has the type FLOAT and the value depends, naturally, on the value of the parameter. If, for example, the parameter has value 25.0, the result is 5.0. We do not need to worry about how the square root is actually evaluated in SQRT; that is something that only the designers of the BASIC_MATH package need to know.

Standard mathematical functions

- Are found in a special package.
- **With** and **use** clauses are used to access the standard functions.

Figure 3.8 lists the common mathematical functions that are usually found in a mathematical package. Note that this is not standardized, so the names can differ from implementation to implementation. The parameter X should be a float type. In the case of trigonometric functions, radians rather than degrees are usually used. In addition, there are usually a number of useful constants in the mathematics package, for example pi. Many packages also contain a further version of the exponentiation operator ** – a version that allows the second operand to be a real number.

```
EXP(X)      -- evaluates e to the power x
LN(X)       -- evaluates natural logarithms
LOG(X)      -- evaluates ordinary (base 10) logarithms
SIN(X)
COS(X)
TAN(X)
ARCSIN(X)
ARCCOS(X)
ARCTAN(X)
SINH(X)
COSH(x)
TANH(X)
```

Figure 3.8

3.4.2 Boolean expressions

Section 3.1.4 showed how to assign values and declare variables of the type BOOLEAN. It is also possible to build an expression whose value has the type BOOLEAN; that is, the result of the expression can have either the value TRUE or FALSE. We call such an expression a **Boolean expression**. In fact, we have already met several examples of Boolean expressions, most often in **if** statements, such as:

```
if K > 5 then
   PUT(K);
end if;
```

The expression K > 5 can either be false or true, it can have the value either FALSE or TRUE. Thus the expression has the type BOOLEAN. The operator > has been used and the integer expressions K and 5 are its operands.

In Ada there is a set of **relational operators** that can be used for making a comparison, for example, in **if** statements. The two operands of a relational operator must be of the same type. For example, the expressions TEMPERATURE < 5 and CHAR = 78 are wrong if we assume that TEMPERATURE has type FLOAT and CHAR has type CHARACTER. The two operands may be expressions, such as:

```
5 * N > K ** 3 + N
3.45 * SIN(ALPHA) / FACTOR <= 0.35
NAME1 & NAME2 = ''PeggySue''
```

Relational operators

=	-- equal to
/=	-- not equal to
<	-- less than
<=	-- less than or equal to
>	-- greater than
>=	-- greater than or equal to

Note that real numbers should be compared with caution because they are not always stored in an exact form. Expressions such as:

```
X = Y
Z = 0.87
```

are dangerous and should be avoided. The variables X and Y may be 'virtually' equal but the computer still interprets them as unequal if they are not stored in exactly the same way. Z might be 'virtually' equal to 0.87 but the two operands may still be seen as unequal by the computer. It is safer to use comparisons such as:

```
abs(X − Y) < 1.0e−9
abs(Z − 0.87) < 0.5e−4
```

The small quantity that should be used on the right-hand side is a matter of judgement; it depends on the order of magnitude of the operands on the left-hand side. Comparing integers, however, is straightforward because they are always stored in an exact form.

The operators **in** and **not in** can be used to test whether a value lies in a given interval:

```
K in 1 .. N
TEMPERATURE not in MIN_TEMP .. MAX_TEMP
CHAR in 'a' .. 'z'
5 in 3 .. 5              -- true!
3.75 not in 1.5 .. 3.5 -- true!
'H' in 'D' .. 'J'        -- true!
```

The second operand has to be an interval defined by its first and last value. The left-hand operand and the limits of the interval should be of the same type. The operators **in** and **not in** exist for all types.

A	B	A **and** B	A **or** B	A **xor** B
TRUE	TRUE	TRUE	TRUE	FALSE
TRUE	FALSE	FALSE	TRUE	TRUE
FALSE	TRUE	FALSE	TRUE	TRUE
FALSE	FALSE	FALSE	FALSE	FALSE

Figure 3.9

A set of operators exist for which both the operands and the result are of the type BOOLEAN. These operators are:

not
and
or
xor
and then
or else

The operator **not** is the simplest. It takes only one operand and performs logical negation, that is, it changes TRUE to FALSE and vice versa.

not ACTIVE
not K > 74
not TRUE   -- gives the value FALSE

The remaining operators are called Boolean operators and all have two operands. Figure 3.9 shows how they work.

The operators **and** and **or** have their natural logical meanings. The operator **xor** is generally called 'exclusive or' and is not used very often. Here are two examples:

ACTIVE **or** TEMPERATURE > 17.6
100 < K **and** K < 500

Note the way of writing the second example. To write the expression:

100 < K < 500   -- MISTAKE

is not allowed.

The operators **and then** and **or else** give exactly the same results as **and** and **or**, respectively. The difference is in the way the operands are evaluated. In expressions such as:

expression1 **and** *expression2*

expression1 **or** *expression2*

there is no way of telling whether *expression1* or *expression2* is evaluated first. Normally it makes no difference, but under certain circumstances it is essential to determine the order of evaluation. In particular, it is sometimes necessary to avoid the evaluation of *expression2*; this is when the operators **and then** and **or else** are valuable. If we look at how the operator **and** works, we notice that it is not necessary to evaluate the second operand if the first operand is FALSE. The result of the **and** will be FALSE regardless of the value of the second operand. In the same way, it is unnecessary to evaluate the second operand of an **or** operator if the first operand is TRUE. The result will be TRUE anyway, regardless of the value of the second operand.

The operator **and then** is defined so that the left operand is evaluated first. If this is FALSE then the right operand is *not* evaluated, and the result of the **and then** operator is FALSE. If the left operand is TRUE the right operand is also evaluated. The result obtained is then the same as using the **and** operator.

For the operator **or else**, the left operator is also evaluated first. If this is TRUE the right operand is *not* evaluated and the result of the **or else** operator is TRUE. If the left operand is FALSE, the right operand is evaluated, and the same result is obtained as if the **or** operator had been used.

For example, the program fragment below determines whether a variable of type STRING(1 .. 10) contains any space characters. If it has no spaces, the message:

No spaces

is printed. Otherwise, the message:

First space is in position X

is printed, where X is in the interval 1 to 10. We assume that the variable K has type INTEGER. The section of program is:

```
K := 1;
while K <= 10 and then TEXT(K) /= ' ' loop
   K := K + 1;
end loop;

if K = 11 then
  PUT("No spaces");
```

```
    else
        PUT("First space is in position ");
        PUT(K, WIDTH => 1);
    end if;
```

In the Boolean expression:

```
    K <= 10 and then TEXT(K) /= ' '
```

it is essential that the operator **and then** is used rather than **and**. If TEXT does not contain any spaces, then after 10 iterations of the loop, the variable K takes the value 11. If the **and** operator had been used, there would have been an attempt to evaluate TEXT(11). This would be an illegal index because TEXT has only 10 elements, and the program would stop with an error message. Using the operator **and then** ensures that this cannot happen.

3.4.3 Operator precedence

We have now seen all the standard operators in Ada, namely: numeric operators; operators that are used in Boolean expressions; and the operator & that is used to catenate strings. Complex expressions containing several of these expressions may be constructed:

```
    N - J < 100 and K ** 2 < 50 or I = 10
    SIN(X) > 0.0 or abs COS(Y) + DELTA < 0.5
    TEMPERATURE > 25.3 or PRESSURE > 2.6 and not ACTIVE
    NAME & "Smith" & "25 Elm Terrace" & "Newtown"
            = PERSONAL_DATA
```

When complicated expressions such as these are constructed, it is important to know the order in which component expressions will be evaluated.

Earlier we saw that operators with the highest precedence were evaluated first and those with equal precedence were evaluated from left to right. We have also seen that control over the order of evaluation in a complicated expression can be achieved by using brackets. For example, the Boolean operators **and** and **or** have the same precedence and it may sometimes be necessary to use brackets to evaluate an expression in the correct order, such as:

```
    not (A and (B or C))
```

Operator precedence

- Operators on the same line have the same precedence.

- The top line has the highest precedence; the bottom has the lowest.

**	abs	not						
*	/	mod	rem					
+	−			(unary + and −)				
&	+	−		(ordinary + and −)				
=	/=	<	<=	>	>=	in	not in	
and	or	xor	and then	or else				

3.5   Variables and constants

In Ada, variables and constants are called **objects**. Objects have a name and a value. In the case of variables, we illustrated this with our storage boxes, or stores. Before a variable or constant can be used in a program it must be declared.

Objects

- Variables and constants.
- Have a name and value.
- Must be declared.

In our programs we have already seen several examples of how variables and constants are declared. We have seen how such declarations are made in the declaration section of a procedure; as we shall see later, they can also be made in a similar way in functions and packages that we write ourselves. The simplest form of variable declaration is:

```
NUMBER_OF_ITEMS     : INTEGER;
TEMPERATURE         : FLOAT;
WEIGHT_PER_PERSON : SHORT_FLOAT;
ADDRESS             : STRING(1 .. 30);
ACTIVE              : BOOLEAN;
SYMBOL              : CHARACTER;
```

First, the name of the variable is given and then its type. If there are several variables of the same type they can be declared in a shortened form:

```
MEAN_TEMP, MAX_TEMP, MIN_TEMP : FLOAT;
```

This is equivalent to:

```
MEAN_TEMP : FLOAT;
MAX_TEMP  : FLOAT;
MIN_TEMP  : FLOAT;
```

Variable declarations

>   variable_name : type;

or:

>   variable_name1, variable_name2, ... : type;

(all the variables listed are given the same type).

What value does a variable have when it is declared like this? Normally, a variable's value is undefined. Certain compilers set numerical variables to zero, but this cannot be relied on absolutely. In most cases, the value of a variable is undefined until it is given a value in the program. In Ada it is possible to initialize variables, give them a starting value at the same time as they are declared:

```
BALANCE  : FLOAT := 0.0;
SYMB     : CHARACTER := '%';
PRESSURE : FLOAT := 1.5;
K, N, M  : INTEGER := 0;
```

The last of these is equivalent to:

```
K : INTEGER := 0;
N : INTEGER := 0;
M : INTEGER := 0;
```

The initial value can be a complex expression but it must be of the same type as the variable:

```
VOLUME    : FLOAT := 37.9;
COEFF     : FLOAT := SQRT(LOG(VOLUME));
MIN_TEMP  : FLOAT := 10.0;
MAX_TEMP  : FLOAT := 100.0;
MEAN_TEMP : FLOAT := (MIN_TEMP + MAX_TEMP) / 2.0;
```

Note that the order of declaration is important here. In the example above, the variable VOLUME had to be declared and initialized before it could be used on the second line.

Initializing variables

> *variable_name* : *type* := *expression*;

or:

> *variable_name1, variable_name2, ...* : *type* := *expression*;

(all the variables listed are given the same initial value).

Constants can also be declared. As with variables, constants can be regarded as storage boxes of a certain type that contain a certain value. The difference is that the value received by the constant at the time of declaration cannot be changed later in the program. Constant declarations look like variable declarations, but the word **constant** is added. In the declaration, the constant must be given a value.

```
END_CHAR    : constant CHARACTER := '*';
MAX_NO      : constant INTEGER := 500;
START_TEMP  : constant FLOAT := MIN_TEMP − 5.0;
```

For constants of type STRING, no index limits need be given in the declaration:

HEADING : **constant** STRING := ''Report for first quarter'';

In addition to the sorts of constants discussed so far, there is a special form of constant declaration in Ada called a **number declaration**. A number declaration looks much like an ordinary constant declaration, but no type is stated:

PI   : **constant** := 3.1415926536;
TWO_PI : **constant** := 2 * PI;
MIN   : **constant** := 5;
TWO_16 : **constant** := 2 ** 16;

Number declarations can only be made for numeric values. A constant takes one of the types *universal_integer* or *universal_real*, depending on the initialization. The initializing value must be of one of these types, that is, it can only be an expression containing numeric literals and other constants that have been declared in number declarations. It can be an advantage to use this type of constant instead of an ordinary constant when the object to be declared is a mathematical constant that should be usable in association with several numeric types.

Constant declarations

    constant_name : **constant** *type* := *expression*;

or:

    constant_name : **constant** := *numeric expression*;

(in the second case, the constant takes the type *universal_integer* or *universal_real*).

3.6 Errors in programs

Writing a computer program is not a trivial task and it is normal to make a number of mistakes. Even an experienced programmer falls into traps of various kinds. It is therefore important when learning to program, that we also learn how to find and correct errors in the program. This can only be learnt by designing and writing programs, running tests and correcting any errors found, which is why practical work is necessary.

When writing a computer program, three kinds of error can occur:

(1)   **Compile-time error** This is an error indicating that the rules of the

language have not been followed. This type of error is detected by the compiler during compilation of the program. A printed listing of the program is usually provided in which the mistake is marked. Examples of compile-time errors are misspelling a variable name, forgetting an **end**, losing a semicolon, or pressing a wrong key when typing the program. ·

(2)   **Run-time error**   Such errors do not occur until the program is run. The program may be syntactically correct – the language rules have been obeyed – but it still contains mistakes which prevent it from continuing normally when executed. Examples of such mistakes are trying to index outside the limits in a STRING variable, and attempting to enter a value of the wrong type from the terminal. A common error is 'overflow', when a value is calculated that is too large for the intended variable. This can happen, for example, if an attempt is made to divide by 0 or some other extremely small number. Normally the program halts when an error occurs and an error message is given. Errors can be trapped by the programmer, however, and as we shall see in Chapter 10, this facility allows the program to continue in execution.

(3)   **Errors of logic**   Such errors are caused simply by faulty thinking when the program was written. A faulty algorithm has been used. It is difficult to find this kind of error because it is possible to compile and run the program without getting any error messages. An error in the logic of a program only shows when a test is run and the result obtained. If there is no verified data available for testing the program, it can be hard to be quite certain that the program is free from logic errors. Even if the program works correctly for a particular set of input data, it can be faulty for another set.

Different kinds of error

- *Compile-time error*
  Rules of the language have been broken. Detected during compilation.

- *Run-time error*
  Illegal values occur when the program is run, for example, incorrect indexing. Detected during execution.

- *Errors of logic*
  Algorithm is incorrect. The program works out wrong values. Detected (hopefully) during test runs.

We shall demonstrate the different types of error by looking at an example. The program that will be written is to evaluate N!, that is, the product:

```
1 * 2 * 3 * 4 * ... * N
```

We start by writing the program with the help of the text-editor:

```
with TEXT_IO, BASIC_NUM_IO;
use  TEXT_IO, BASIC_NUM_IO;
procedure FACTORIAL is
    PRODUCT : INTEGER := 0;
    N_VALUE  : INTEGER;
begin
    PUT("Enter value of N: ");
    GET(N_VALU);
    for I in 1 .. N_VALUE loop
        PRODUCT := PRODUCT * I;
    end loop;
    PUT("Result is: "); PUT_LINE(PRODUCT);
end FACTORIAL;
```

The next step is to try and compile the program using the Ada compiler. We then get the listing:

```
with TEXT_IO, BASIC_NUM_IO;
use  TEXT_IO, BASIC_NUM_IO;
procedure FACTORIAL is
    PRODUCT : INTEGER := 0;
    N_VALUE
begin
    PUT("Enter value of N: ");
    GET(N_VALU);
    _____/\
-- error: identifier undefined
    for I in 1 .. N_VALUE loop
    _____/\
-- warning: high bound may not yet have a value
        PRODUCT := PRODUCT * I;
    end loop;
    PUT("Result is: "); PUT_LINE(PRODUCT);
    _____/\
-- error: types of formal and actual parameter do not match
    end FACTORIAL;
```

Here we see that the compiler has marked certain lines in the program and written error messages. For each error, the compiler tries to point out the line where the error occurs. The first faulty line is:

GET(N_VALU);

The message from the compiler points to the identifier N_VALU and says that this identifier is undefined. We see that we have left off the last letter of the identifier – it should be N_VALUE.

The next line marked is:

for I **in** 1 .. N_VALUE **loop**

The compiler has not found any real error here, but just a line that may be incorrect; it gives us a warning that we should watch out for this line. What may lead to problems is that the upper limit in the expression:

1 .. N_VALUE

in other words N_VALUE might not be given a value when the program is run later on. This would mean a run-time error. The reason for this potential error is that earlier in the program we wrote:

GET(N_VALU);

If this had been correct, the variable N_VALUE would always be given a value and we would not have had a warning from the compiler. Therefore we do not need to change the line:

for I **in** 1 .. N_VALUE **loop**

It is correct and the warning is only the result of our earlier error.

The final line to be marked faulty is:

PUT("Result is: "); PUT_LINE(PRODUCT);

Here the compiler is complaining that the parameter to the procedure PUT_LINE does not have the type that it should have formally. The variable PRODUCT has type INTEGER. If we look at the package TEXT_IO we see that the procedure PUT_LINE is only specified in one place in the package and that it requires a parameter of type STRING. We have mistakenly assumed that the procedure PUT_LINE, just like PUT, also exists for the type INTEGER. The solution is to use PUT and NEW_LINE instead:

PUT("Result is: "); PUT(PRODUCT); NEW_LINE;

Now we use the text-editor again to corrrect the mistakes in the program, and we get:

```ada
with TEXT_IO, BASIC_NUM_IO;
use  TEXT_IO, BASIC_NUM_IO;
procedure FACTORIAL is
    PRODUCT : INTEGER := 0;
    N_VALUE  : INTEGER;
begin
    PUT("Enter value of N: ");
    GET(N_VALUE);
    for I in 1 .. N_VALUE loop
        PRODUCT := PRODUCT * I;
    end loop;
    PUT("Result is: "); PUT(PRODUCT); NEW_LINE;
end FACTORIAL;
```

This program compiles well; no error messages this time. We shall go on to run some tests on it. The program prints the message:

Enter value of N:

We shall try to calculate 4! which we know should be 24; therefore we type a 4 at the terminal. The program answers, to our surprise:

Result is: 0

We run another test, this time giving another value of N as input. Whatever value of N we give, we find that we always get the answer 0. Of course, this is wrong. There is an error of logic in the program.

Now we must look carefully at the program to find out where the fault lies. In the program we have a counter I which counts from 1 to the value of N, and at each count PRODUCT is multiplied by I. At the first count we multiply by 1, at the second by 2, and so on. This seems right, but what was the value of PRODUCT at the start? The declaration shows that at the start PRODUCT had the value 0. That is the mistake! When any number is multiplied by 0 the result is 0. Of course, the variable PRODUCT should be initialized to 1. The text-editor enables us to correct this so that PRODUCT is initialized properly:

PRODUCT : INTEGER := 1;

We compile the program again. (This must be done; it is not enough to make corrections only in the text). A fresh test run shows that we now get the result 24 if we enter the number 4. The program appears to be working correctly. If, for example, we enter 12, we get the result 479001600. We can try with 13, but then we get the following strange output:

Enter value of N: 13
** EXCEPTION "numeric_error" RAISED, line 10.

We have got an execution error. A numeric error has occurred on line 10. On this line we have the statement:

```
PRODUCT := PRODUCT * I;
```

The result of the expression on the right-hand side has become so great that it is bigger than the greatest whole number that can be stored in a variable of type INTEGER in our system. The program cannot continue in the normal way and so it stops running.

If we want our program to calculate N! for values of N greater than 12 we must change the program. The best way is to change PRODUCT to a variable of type FLOAT. Such a variable can hold considerably larger numbers than an integer variable. We now use the text-editor to make the necessary changes:

```
with TEXT_IO, BASIC_NUM_IO;
use  TEXT_IO, BASIC_NUM_IO;
procedure FACTORIAL is
    PRODUCT : FLOAT := 1.0;
    N_VALUE  : INTEGER;
begin
    PUT("Enter value of N: ");
    GET(N_VALUE);
    for I in 1 .. N_VALUE loop
        PRODUCT := PRODUCT * FLOAT(I);
    end loop;
    PUT("Result is: "); PUT(PRODUCT); NEW_LINE;
end FACTORIAL;
```

In addition to changing the declaration of PRODUCT we must also make a change so that I is converted to a floating number on each multiplication:

```
PRODUCT := PRODUCT * FLOAT(I);
```

We may not mix INTEGER and FLOAT in a multiplication. After a further compilation we can run a test of the corrected program. If we now try to calculate 13! we get:

```
Enter value of N: 13
Result is: 6.22702080E+09
```

Looking for errors in a program and correcting them has come to be known, lightheartedly, as 'debugging' the program. In some systems there are excellent aids for debugging. For example, it may be possible to test run a program step by step, or stop at particular points in the program, study the values of the various variables and change them. Such debugging aids are very valuable when errors have to be found in more complicated programs.

If there is no access to such debugging aids, the values of the variables can still be studied at given points in the program by inserting temporary test printouts, and using them to find possible errors.

In general, if a program is well-written from the start, is well-structured and has suitable names for variables, types, subprograms and packages, and if it uses clear and well-thought-out algorithms, it will contain fewer errors and be easier to debug than a less well-written program. Well-written programs, therefore, are also more reliable and require less maintenance than programs that are poorly conceived from the start. Therefore, with program design, the rule is to think first and write later.

Testing programs

- Use debuggers or insert temporary test printing routines in the program.
- Well-written and well-structured programs are easier to rid of errors.

EXERCISES

3.1 Which of the following are allowed as identifiers in Ada? Which are allowed as the names of variables, types and constants?

MY_CAR	CAR_3	"Tommy"
NUMBER1	number1	ADAM&EVE
IN	%VAT	Number_5
3_DIGIT	car-number	identifier

3.2 State for each of the following whether it is an integer literal, a real literal, a text string literal, a character literal or a literal of type BOOLEAN.

167	167.0	'x'
"true"	16.4e3	16e5
7	'7'	"7"
false	1_000	0.000_005

What type do the integer and real literals really have?

3.3 Assume the following declarations have been made:

> I : INTEGER := 2;
>
> J : INTEGER := 3;
>
> X: FLOAT := 4.0;
>
> Y: FLOAT := 5.0;

Evaluate the following expressions and state the type for each value.

(a)	I + J	(b)	I + 5	(c)	2 + 3		
(d)	X − 1.5	(e)	2.0 * 2.5	(f)	Y / X		
(g)	J / I	(h)	14 **rem** 4	(i)	J **mod** I		
(j)	X ** I	(k)	Y ** (−1)	(l)	I ** J		
(m)	I + J * 2	(n)	X * Y ** 2	(o)	**abs** X−Y		
(p)	X / Y * 2.0	(q)	2.0 * FLOAT(J)				

3.4 Make a suitable variable declaration to describe the following:

- the number of goals scored in a football match
- winning time in the 110 m hurdles
- an identity number
- a shoe size
- the size of fine for a parking offence
- the information relating to whether a person has a driving licence
- an address
- a type of vitamin (A, B, C, D or E)

3.5 Write a program to calculate the volume and area of a sphere. The radius of the sphere is to be given as input. The following formulae are given:

$$V = \frac{4\pi r^3}{3} \qquad A = 4\pi r^2$$

3.6 In Europe, a car's fuel consumption is usually given in litres per kilometre. Write a program to read in petrol consumption in this format and translate it into the form more common in Britain, miles per gallon. The following conversion factors apply:

$$1 \text{ mile} = 1.609 \text{ km} \qquad 1 \text{ gallon} = 3.785 \text{ litres}$$

3.7 A car-hire firm takes £30 per day plus a fee of £0.55 per mile for a particular car. In addition there is the cost of the fuel. Assume the car does, on average, 26 miles per gallon and that the price of fuel is £1.75 per gallon.

Write a program to calculate the total cost of hiring the car. The input should be the distance driven and the number of days' hire.

3.8 A running competition consists of two separate races. The winner of the competition is the one with the shortest total time for the two races. Write a program to calculate the total time for a competitor. The input should be the times for the two separate races. These times are given in hours, minutes and seconds in the format hh mm ss and the result is given in the same format.

3.9 Write a program to calculate how much change should be received after making a purchase, and in which notes and coins the change should be given. Input to the program should be the price to be paid and the amount given in payment. For the sake of simplicity, assume that no transactions involve coins smaller than 10 p or notes greater than £20. For example, if a person bought goods for £62.10 and paid with four £20 notes, the program should print out that the change should be one £10 note, one £5 note, two £1 coins, one 50p coin, and four 10p coins.

3.10 The distance between two points (x_1, y_1) and (x_2, y_2) in a coordinate system is given by the formula:

$$s = \sqrt{(x_1 - x_2)^2 + (y_1 - y_2)^2}$$

Write a program to read in the coordinates of two points and write out the distance between them.

3.11 For radioactive decomposition, the amount of radioactive material, n, remaining after a certain time, t, can be calculated using the formula:

$$n = n_0 \, e^{-\lambda t}$$

where n_0 is the amount of radioactive material at time $t=0$. λ is a constant for the material. This is usually given as a half-life (the time taken for half the radioactive material to decompose). If the half-life is denoted by T, it is easy to calculate that:

$$\lambda = \frac{0.693}{T}$$

The half-life for the isotope ^{14}C is 5730 years. Write a program to print out what percentage of this isotope is left after S years. S is the input to the program.

3.12 Write a program that reads in an angle (given in degrees) and prints out the sine and cosine values for the angle. The functions sin and cos that are in the system's maths package require a parameter in radians. The conversion between degrees and radians uses the formula:

$$\text{radians} = \text{degrees} * \frac{2\pi}{360}$$

3.13 Evaluate the following Boolean expressions:

(a)   TRUE **and** 10 > 8
(b)   5.0 >= 10.3 **or** 'a' > 'b'
(c)   3 **not in** 1 .. 7
(d)   I /= 0 **and then** 14 / I > 3   -- assume I = 3
(e)   3 > 3 **or else** "hello" /= "HELLO"

3.14 Evaluate the following expressions:

(a)   CHARACTER'POS('~')
(b)   CHARACTER'VAL(32)

3.15 Assume the CHARACTER variable C contains one of the lower case letters 'a' to 'z'. Write a statement that changes C to hold the corresponding upper case letter instead.

3.16 Assume the CHARACTER variable T has a value in the interval '0' to '9'. Write a statement to convert T's value to an integer in the interval 0 to 9 and which assigns the integer to the variable I of type INTEGER.

3.17 In Sweden, every resident has a personal identification number made up of a six-figure date of birth followed by a four-figure code. The last but one figure is odd for a male and even for a female.

Write a program to read in a Swedish identification number and determine if the person concerned is male or female.

Chapter 4
Control statements

4.1 Sequential program structure
4.2 Assignment statements
4.3 Selection: the **if** statement
4.4 Selection: the **case** statement
4.5 Iteration: the **loop** statement

4.6 **Exit** statement
4.7 Nested **loop** statements
4.8 Interactive input
    Exercises

Chapter 3 dealt with the basic building blocks of Ada. It showed how to use the standard types in expressions and in declarations of data objects. This chapter concentrates on the part of an Ada program that describes what the program does, in other words, the part of the program that describes algorithms.

The chapter deals with the most common statements that can be used to control the behaviour of a program. It shows how to put statements together into a program sequence and how alternative paths through a program can be achieved in various ways. Programming iterative sequences, that is, making certain parts of a program execute repeatedly, is also covered.

In an interactive program – a program that, while running, communicates with a user via a terminal – the user often wants to feed data to the program in stages and decide how long the program should run. Iteration is used in this kind of program; Section 4.8 deals with iteration in the context of interactive programs.

4.1   Sequential program structure

In simple terms, an Ada program or subprogram consists of a specification part, a declarative part and a statement part.

Program and subprogram structure

```
subprogram_specification is
   declarative part
begin
    statement1;
    statement2;

         ⋮

    statementN;
end subprogram_name;
```

The specification of a subprogram contains its name and a description of possible parameters to the subprogram. We shall come back to this in Chapter 6. In the declarative part, variables, constants and other parameters can be declared. It is possible also to make other declarations. For example, declarations of internal subprograms, as seen in one of the example programs in Chapter 2. In Chapter 5 we shall see that programmers can also declare their own types in the declarative part of the program.

Here we shall concentrate on the part of the program between **begin** and **end**. This part of the program should contain a sequence of one or more **statements**. When the program is executed, these statements are executed one at a time, from top to bottom. Each statement is executed once.

Every statement ends with a semicolon. The rules of the language do not specify that statements should be written on special lines or that they should start in particular positions on the line. To write well-structured programs, however, it is important to apply certain rules. Each statement should start on a fresh line. (Exceptions can be made if a number of statements together produce output at a terminal; in this case these statements can be written on the same line). The statements should be indented on the line; statements which belong to the same sequence (such as statement1, statement2, ... , statementN above) should be indented by the same amount.

There are two kinds of statement, **simple statements** and **compound statements**. The most common simple statements are **assignment statements** and **procedure calls**; we have already seen examples of these. Here is another example showing a sequence of simple statements. The sequence reads in two real numbers and calculates their mean.

```
PUT_LINE("Enter two real numbers");
GET(X1);
GET(X2);
MEAN_VALUE := (X1 + X2) / 2.0;
PUT("The mean is: ");
PUT(MEAN_VALUE);
```

The statement:

```
MEAN_VALUE := (X1 + X2) / 2.0;
```

is an assignment statement and the others are procedure calls. Procedure calls will be discussed more fully in Chapter 6.

There is a very simple statement which is written as follows:

null;

This is called a **null** statement. When this statement is executed nothing at all happens. This statement exists because the syntax sometimes demands that a statement should be found at a particular place in a program. If there is nothing to do at this place, a **null** statement can be used.

The most common compound statements are **if** and **loop** statements. A compound statement can contain several statements. Using these, statements can be structured hierarchically.

4.2   Assignment statements

An assignment statement consists of two parts. On the left-hand side (the term on the left of the assignment symbol, :=) there can be the name of a variable while to the right there should be an expression. The expression and variable must be of the same type. When an assignment statement is executed the expression on the right is evaluated and that value is given to the variable on the left, replacing its previous value. There may only be *one* variable on the left-hand side. If the same value is to be given to several variables, several assignment statements must be written. Here are a few examples:

```
K := I + 15;
X1 := 23.8;
ALARM := TEMP > 200.0; -- ALARM has type BOOLEAN
HEAD := "INVOICE";      -- HEAD has type STRING(1 .. 7)
```

If the variable is of type STRING as in the last example, both sides must have the same number of components. However, the components do not need to be numbered in the same way. A slice may also appear in the left-hand side. In the following examples, we start by assuming that S has type STRING(1 .. 15) and that T has type STRING(26 .. 40);

```
S := T;                     -- same number of components
S(7 .. 11) := "HELLO";
T(31 .. 33) := S(4 .. 6);
```

The left- and right-hand sides may even overlap as shown in the following example:

```
S(1 .. 3) := "Ada";
S(3 .. 5) := S(1 .. 3);     -- S(1 .. 5) becomes "AdAda"
```

4.3   Selection: the *if* statement

The most common way of achieving selection in a program, that is, a choice between two or more different paths in a program, is to use an **if** statement. An **if** statement starts with the reserved word **if** and terminates with the reserved words **end if**. An **if** statement comprises a **then** part followed by a number (possibly zero) of **elsif** parts, ending possibly with an **else** part.

The if statement, the simplest form

if *Boolean expression* **then**
    sequence_of_statements
end if;

The sequences of statements within the **then**, **elsif** and **else** parts of an **if** statement should be inset a little on the line, to show clearly where the **if** statement begins and ends, and which parts belong to it.

When the statement is executed, the Boolean expressions that follow the words **if** and **elsif** are evaluated in order from the top down. If any of these Boolean expressions are true, the sequence of statements in the corresponding part of the **if** statement is executed, and then control passes to the first statement after the words **end if**.

The if statement, complete form

if *Boolean expression* **then**
   sequence_of_statements
elsif *Boolean expression* **then**
   sequence_of_statements

     ⋮

elsif *Boolean expression* **then**
   sequence_of_statements
else
   sequence_of_statements
end if;

The Boolean expressions following the first true expression will not be evaluated. If all the Boolean expressions are false, but there is an **else** part, then the sequence of statements contained therein will be executed. If all the Boolean expressions are false and there is no **else** part, then the **if** statement terminates without any of the sequences of statements being executed. Observe that, at most, *one* sequence in an **if** statement is executed.

Some examples of **if** statements are:

```
if K > 5 or J < 4 then
    K := K + J;
    J := J + 1;
end if;

-- ACTIVE, CLOSED, and PASSIVE have type BOOLEAN
if ACTIVE and not CLOSED then
    PUT_LINE("System is in operation");
else
    PUT_LINE("System is down");
    PASSIVE := TRUE;
end if;

if TEMPERATURE < 15.0 then
    PUT_LINE("Emergency!");
    RAD_SET := RAD_SET + 5.0;
elsif TEMPERATURE < 18.0 then
    PUT_LINE("Too cold.");
    RAD_SET := RAD_SET + 1.0;
elsif TEMPERATURE < 21.0 then
    PUT_LINE("OK.");
```

```
      else
         PUT_LINE("Too hot.");
         RAD_SET := RAD_SET - 1.0;
      end if;
```

Any statements are allowed in a sequence of statements, even compound statements as in:

```
   if TEMPERATURE < 15.0 then
      PUT_LINE("Emergency!");
      RAD_SET := RAD_SET + 5.0;
   elsif TEMPERATURE < 18.0 then
      if NIGHT then
         PUT_LINE("OK.");
      else
         PUT_LINE("Too cold.");
         RAD_SET := RAD_SET + 1.0;
      end if;
   end if;
```

Here, the **elsif** part consists of a single statement – a new **if** statement. When one **if** statement is contained within another, they are usually said to be nested. Note that it is particularly important to indent the text clearly in the case of nested statements. It is essential to see the structure underlying the statements.

We can now look at a couple of variants of a program that reads in three (different) integers from the terminal and writes them out in order of increasing size. The first version is:

```
   with TEXT_IO, BASIC_NUM_IO;
   use  TEXT_IO, BASIC_NUM_IO;
   procedure SORT_3 is
      A, B, C : INTEGER;
   begin
      PUT_LINE("Enter three different integers");
      GET(A); GET(B); GET(C);
      if A < B then
        if B < C then
          PUT(A); PUT(B); PUT(C);
        elsif A < C then
          PUT(A); PUT(C); PUT(B);
        else
          PUT(C); PUT(A); PUT(B);
        end if;
      else
        if A < C then
          PUT(B); PUT(A); PUT(C);
```

```
    elsif B < C then
        PUT(B); PUT(C); PUT(A);
    else
        PUT(C); PUT(B); PUT(A);
    end if;
  end if;
end SORT_3;
```

In this version of the program there are two levels of **if** statement. We obtain a somewhat simpler program structure if we employ more complex Boolean expressions.

```
with TEXT_IO, BASIC_NUM_IO;
use  TEXT_IO, BASIC_NUM_IO;
procedure SORT_3 is
    A, B, C : INTEGER;
begin
    PUT_LINE("Enter three different integers");
    GET(A); GET(B); GET(C);
    if A < B and B < C then
        PUT(A); PUT(B); PUT(C);
    elsif A < C and C < B then
        PUT(A); PUT(C); PUT(B);
    elsif C < A and A < B then
        PUT(C); PUT(A); PUT(B);
    elsif B < A and A < C then
        PUT(B); PUT(A); PUT(C);
    elsif B < C and C < A then
        PUT(B); PUT(C); PUT(A);
    else
        PUT(C); PUT(B); PUT(A);
    end if;
end SORT_3;
```

4.4 Selection: the *case* statement

We have seen how the **if** statement can be used to make a selection. In Ada there is also a **case** statement that can be used if a choice has to be made between several different paths in a program. If there are several alternatives, a **case** statement is often preferable to an **if** statement because it gives a clearer program.

A **case** statement starts with the reserved word **case** and ends with the reserved words **end case**. After the word **case** appears an expression whose value determines the choice of one of several alternatives.

Case statement

    case *selector* **is**
      when *list_of_alternatives* =>
        sequence_of_statements
      when *list_of_alternatives* =>
        sequence_of_statements

            ⋮

      when *list_of_alternatives* =>
        sequence_of_statements
    end case;

where *selector* is a discrete expression (integer type or enumeration type) and *list_of_alternatives* is a list with one or more static (constant) expressions.

The selector should be a **discrete expression**. In Ada, the notion **discrete type** covers integer types and enumeration types. A discrete expression is an expression whose value is of a discrete type, that is, the expression is either an integer type (for example, INTEGER) or some enumeration type (for example, CHARACTER). Examples of discrete expressions are:

NUMBER_OF_ITEMS   N + 8   I ** 3   CHAR

Note that the selector may not be a real type.

    A list of alternatives following the word **when** in a **case** statement is a list of one or several possible discrete values that the selector can assume. (Since the selector is a discrete expression, it is possible to name all possible values). When the **case** statement is executed, the selector is evaluated. If the value found appears among the values enumerated in a particular list of alternatives, then the sequence of statements following the list is executed. Note that only *one* sequence of statements is executed.

    In the following example the simplest form of list of alternatives is used, that has only one possible value. The variable MONTH_NUMBER is assumed to have the type INTEGER.

```
case MONTH_NUMBER is
    when 1 =>
      PUT("January");
    when 2 =>
      PUT("February");
```

```
  when 3 =>
     PUT("March");
  when 4 =>
     PUT("April");
  when 5 =>
     PUT("May");
  when 6 =>
     PUT("June");
  when 7 =>
     PUT("July");
  when 8 =>
     PUT("August");
  when 9 =>
     PUT("September");
  when 10 =>
     PUT("October");
  when 11 =>
     PUT("November");
  when 12 =>
     PUT("December");
  when others =>
     PUT("Error in month number");
end case;
```

This **case** statement writes out the name of a month. The particular name written depends on the value of a variable MONTH_NUMBER. If it has value 1, 'January' is written, if 2 then 'February' is written, and so on. If MONTH_NUMBER has a value that lies outside the interval 1 to 12, then the message 'Error in month number' is written.

The values in a list of alternatives must be **static expressions** – expressions made only of constant parts. Often the values in a list of alternatives are simply constant values (literals) as in this example.

If any possible values are omitted from the lists of alternatives, there must be a special **others** alternative. (In our example, INTEGER can take values other than 1 to 12, of course). The **others** alternative must come last in the **case** statement, so that when the **case** statement is executed, the **others** alternative is reached only if the selector has a value other than those already enumerated in the earlier alternatives.

The example is now changed a little to show how it appears when several possible alternatives are enumerated in one list of alternatives:

```
case MONTH_NUMBER is
  when 1 | 2 | 12 =>
     PUT("Winter");
  when 3 | 4 | 5 =>
     PUT("Spring");
```

```
    when 6 | 7 | 8 =>
      PUT("Summer");
    when 9 | 10 | 11 =>
      PUT("Autumn");
    when others =>
      PUT("Error in month number");
  end case;
```

This **case** statement writes the season of the year according to the value of the variable MONTH_NUMBER. If MONTH_NUMBER has one of the values 1, 2 or 12, the text 'Winter' is written; if it has one of the values, 3, 4 or 5, 'Spring' is written; if it is 6, 7 or 8, 'Summer' is written; and if MONTH_NUMBER is 9, 10 or 11, then 'Autumn' is written. As before, the **others** alternative has to appear, to trap illegal month numbers. The different alternatives in the list of alternatives are enumerated with a vertical line (|) or an exclamation mark (!) between them. To avoid enumerating all alternatives in a list, the interval containing them may be stated. We can rewrite our last example to take advantage of this option:

```
case MONTH_NUMBER is
    when 1 .. 2 | 12 =>
      PUT("Winter");
    when 3 .. 5 =>
      PUT("Spring");
    when 6 .. 8 =>
      PUT("Summer");
    when 9 .. 11 =>
      PUT("Autumn");
    when others =>
      PUT("Error in month number");
end case;
```

Alternative list in a case statement

- Examples of different forms:

```
    when 5 =>
    when 5 | 8 | 23 =>
    when 100 .. 125 =>
    when 50 | 60 | 70 .. 75 | 80 .. 85 =>
    when others =>
```

- Reference must be made to all possible values.

- If there is an **others** alternative, it must come last.

The selector can also be an expression of an enumeration type. The following example is a section of program designed to read in a character C of type CHARACTER from the terminal and determine whether it is a letter, figure or some other symbol. We assume that we have already declared three integer variables, .LETTER_COUNT, FIGURE_COUNT and OTHERS_COUNT. If the character is a letter, the variable LETTER_COUNT is increased by one and the text 'Letter' is displayed at the terminal; similar actions are taken if the character is a figure or one of the remaining symbols.

```
GET(C);
case C is
   when 'a' .. 'z' ¦ 'A' .. 'Z' =>
      LETTER_COUNT := LETTER_COUNT + 1;
      PUT_LINE("Letter");
   when '0' .. '9' =>
      FIGURE_COUNT := FIGURE_COUNT + 1;
      PUT_LINE("Figure");
   when others =>
      OTHERS_COUNT := OTHERS_COUNT + 1;
      PUT_LINE("Other");
end case;
```

We shall show one further example of the use of a **case** statement, in a program that simulates a simple calculator. When the program is run it expects the user to type at the terminal a simple arithmetic expression, such as:

63∗35

The program calculates the value of the expression and displays it at the terminal. To simplify matters, we shall allow the user to write the expression only in the form:

NoM

where the operands N and M are whole numbers and ∘ is one of the operators +, −, ∗ or /. We shall not allow spaces between the operands and the operator. Here is the program:

```
with TEXT_IO, BASIC_NUM_IO;
use  TEXT_IO, BASIC_NUM_IO;
procedure CALCULATOR is
   OPERAND_1, OPERAND_2 : INTEGER;
   OPERATOR : CHARACTER;
```

```
begin
   PUT_LINE("Write a simple arithmetic expression");
   GET(OPERAND_1);
   GET(OPERATOR);
   GET(OPERAND_2);
   case OPERATOR is
     when '+' =>
         PUT(OPERAND_1 + OPERAND_2, WIDTH => 1);
     when '-' =>
         PUT(OPERAND_1 - OPERAND_2, WIDTH => 1);
     when '*' =>
         PUT(OPERAND_1 * OPERAND_2, WIDTH => 1);
     when '/' =>
        if OPERAND_2 /= 0 then
           PUT(OPERAND_1 / OPERAND_2, WIDTH => 1);
        else
           PUT("Division by zero not allowed");
        end if;
     when others =>
         PUT("Faulty operator");
   end case;
end CALCULATOR;
```

In the program, checks are made for division by zero, and attempts to use an undefined operator. An appropriate error message is sent to the user in either case. The following display shows the output from four separate runs of the program:

```
Write a simple arithmetic expression
63*35
2205

Write a simple arithmetic expression
17/6
2

Write a simple arithmetic expression
17/0
Division by zero not allowed

Write a simple arithmetic expression
3%67
Faulty operator
```

4.5   Iteration: the *loop* statement

To perform iteration in Ada, that is, to execute one or several statements a number of times, a **loop** statement is used. There are three variants of this:

(1)   a simple **loop** statement for writing part of a program that is to be
        executed an infinite number of times;

(2)   a **loop** statement with **for** for writing part of a program that is to be
        executed a fixed number of times;

(3)   a **loop** statement with **while** for writing part of a program that is to
        be executed until a certain condition is met.

4.5.1   Simple *loop* statement

We shall start with the simple **loop** statement.

Simple loop statement

loop
    sequence_of_statements
end loop;

Between the reserved words **loop** and **end loop** there is a sequence of
statements that is executed endlessly, repeated time after time. (The **loop**
statement can be stopped using the operating system to stop it 'by force'.
This can usually be done by pressing a **break** key or a **delete** key at the
terminal). For example:

```
loop
    PUT_LINE("HELP! I can't stop");
end loop;
```

Figure 4.1 shows the output from the **loop** statement. The program has to
be stopped 'by force'.

   In the next program, the intention is really that the program should
run without interruption. It is part of a simple supervision program
ensuring that a temperature is kept within certain permitted values.
We assume that TAKE_TEMPERATURE, INCREASE_TEMPERATURE and
DECREASE_TEMPERATURE are procedures that we have already written
and that MIN_TEMPERATURE and MAX_TEMPERATURE are two constants.

```
loop
    TAKE_TEMPERATURE(TEMPERATURE);
    if TEMPERATURE < MIN_TEMPERATURE then
       INCREASE_TEMPERATURE;
    elsif TEMPERATURE > MAX_TEMPERATURE then
       DECREASE_TEMPERATURE;
    end if;
end loop;
```

HELP! I can't stop
HELP! I can't stop
HELP! I can't stop
HELP! I can't stop
HELP! I can't stop
HELP! I can't stop
HELP! I can't stop
HELP! I can't stop
HELP! I can't stop
HELP! I can't stop
HELP! I can't stop
.
.
.
etc.

Figure 4.1

4.5.2   The *loop* statement with *for*

Here is an example of the second variant of the **loop** statement, where the repetition occurs a specified number of times. The statements in the example write out the 12 times table, from 1×12 to 12×12.

```
for I in 1 .. 12 loop
    PUT(I * 12); NEW_LINE;
end loop;
```

Loop statement with *for*

```
for loop_parameter in start_value .. end_value loop
    sequence_of_statements
end loop;
```

- *start_value* and *end_value* should be discrete expressions (integer type or enumeration type).

- *loop_parameter* is an identifier that is declared automatically (treated as a constant in the sequence of statements). Its type depends on *start_value* and *end_value*.

There must be start and end values for the iteration after the word **in** (1 and 12 in the foregoing example). These should be discrete expressions, that is, expressions of an integer type or enumeration type.

Note that floating point types are not allowed. The start and end values must be of the same type, except that one may be of integer type and the other of type *universal_integer* (for example, a constant numeric value).

The loop parameter can be seen as a constant that is declared automatically because it occurs in a **for** construct. Thus it should not be declared in the program's declarative part with the other declarations. (In the foregoing example the loop parameter is called I.)

The type of the loop parameter depends on the type of *start_value* and *end_value*. (The rules are a little complicated, so it may not be necessary to go into these in detail at first reading.)

■

If both *start_value* and *end_value* have the same type, the loop parameter also takes that type, provided they do not both have the same type *universal_integer*. In this case, the loop parameter takes the type INTEGER. If *start_value* is an integer type and *end_value* is of type *universal_integer*, then the loop parameter takes the same type as *start_value*. If *start_value* is of type *universal_integer* and *end_value* is an integer type, then the loop parameter takes the same type as *end_value*. We shall see a few examples, where it is assumed that the variable N has type INTEGER and S has type SHORT_INTEGER.

for I **in** 1 .. 10 **loop**	-- I takes type INTEGER
for J **in** 1 .. N **loop**	-- J takes type INTEGER
for K **in** S .. 15 **loop**	-- K takes type SHORT_INTEGER
for L **in** S + 10 .. 2 * S **loop**	-- L takes type SHORT_INTEGER
for T **in** 'A' .. 'C' **loop**	-- T takes type CHARACTER
for B **in** FALSE .. TRUE **loop**	-- B takes type BOOLEAN

It is possible to control the type of the loop parameter by stating it explicitly. If, for example, the loop parameter in the first example above should have type SHORT_INTEGER, it could be rewritten:

for I **in** SHORT_INTEGER **range** 1 .. 10 **loop**

If the loop parameter is intended to run through all possible values for a certain type, the **range** expression can be omitted and only the name of the type stated. In the following example the loop parameter will run through all possible values of the type CHARACTER:

for C **in** CHARACTER **loop**

□

When the **loop** statement is executed, the *start_value* and *end_value* are evaluated first. If *start_value* is greater than *end_value* the **loop** statement terminates immediately; the sequence of statements is not executed. If *start_value* is less than or equal to *end_value*, the loop parameter is initialized to *start_value*. The sequence of statements is then executed once. The loop parameter may be used as a constant within the sequence of statements in the normal way, in expressions for example. To attempt to change the value of the loop parameter by assignment or in any other way is not allowed – it is, after all, a constant.

When the sequence of statements has been executed once, the value of the loop parameter is automatically changed. If it has an integer type it is increased by one; if it has an enumeration type it takes the next value in the series. Then the loop parameter is compared with *end_value*. (Note that *end_value* is not evaluated again; the program 'remembers' the value that it found the first time through the **loop** statement). If the loop parameter is less than or equal to *end_value*, the sequence is executed once again, otherwise the loop statement terminates. This process is repeated until the loop statement terminates. The number of times the sequence of statements is repeated depends, therefore, on the *start_value* and *end_value*.

It should be noted that the loop parameter is only defined within the **loop** statement; it cannot be used either before or after the **loop** statement.

Consider a few more examples. The first is part of a program that reads in an integer N and then displays N * N lines at the terminal with a plus sign on every line. If, for example, the user gives the number 4 at the terminal, 16 lines will be displayed with a plus sign on every line.

```
GET(N);
for LINE_NUMBER in 1 .. N * N loop
  PUT_LINE("+");
end loop;
```

The next example involves a loop parameter that is not an integer type but an enumeration type. In the **loop** statement, the alphabet is written out in small letters.

```
for CHAR in 'a' .. 'z' loop
  PUT(CHAR);
end loop;
```

Here *start_value* and *end_value* have the enumeration type CHARACTER and the loop parameter CHAR also takes this type. The first time through, CHAR has value 'a', the second time 'b', the third time 'c', and so on, until the final time it has the value 'z'. (This is because the lower case letters 'a' to 'z' are next to each other in the ASCII code, as we saw earlier). The display appears:

abcdefghijklmnopqrstuvwxyz

The repetition can be made to go backwards, that is, the loop parameter can count down instead of up, if the word **reverse** is added. For example, the statement:

```
for NUMBER in reverse 1 .. 5 loop
    PUT(NUMBER);
end loop;
```

gives the output:

5 4 3 2 1

Reverse

In a **loop** statement with **for**, the loop parameter can run through its values backwards if the word **reverse** is added.

Note that a loop parameter of integer type will always increase (or decrease) by one, each time it goes through the loop. If another step length is required, it can be achieved as shown in the next example. First two integers, FIRST_NUMBER and LAST_NUMBER are read from the terminal. Then every tenth number in the interval between FIRST_NUMBER and LAST_NUMBER is displayed at the terminal.

```
GET(FIRST_NUMBER);
GET(LAST_NUMBER);
for I in 0 .. (LAST_NUMBER − FIRST_NUMBER) / 10 loop
    PUT(FIRST_NUMBER + I * 10);
end loop;
```

If the user types in 200 and 250, for example, the output is:

200   210   220   230   240   250

4.5.3   The *loop* statement with *while*

The third variant of the **loop** statement can be used when the number of times the repetition will be made is not known in advance. What is known, however, is that it will be obeyed provided a certain condition is true. When the condition becomes false, the repetition stops.

Loop statement with while

while *Boolean expression* **loop**
   sequence_of_statements
end loop;

The statement is executed as follows. First the Boolean expression following the word **while** is evaluated. If this expression is false nothing more is done; the **loop** statement has been executed. If, however, the Boolean expression is true, the sequence of statements within the **loop** statement is executed once. After that, the Boolean expression is evaluated anew. If it is false, the **loop** statement terminates; if it is true it is executed once more, and so on.

Thus, execution continues until the Boolean expression finally becomes false. If the expression never becomes false, the sequence of statements will be executed endlessly, or until the program is terminated 'by force'. It is very common for an error to be made during programming such that the Boolean expression never becomes false; the program is said to have gone into a loop, meaning an endless loop. It is therefore important to ensure that the values used in the Boolean expression that follow **while** are changed by the statements between **loop** and **end loop**.

Here are a couple of simple examples. The lines of program:

```
J := 0;
while J < 6 loop
   PUT(J);
   J := J + 2;
end loop;
```

give the output:

   0   2   4

Before the first time through, J has the value 0 and the Boolean expression J < 6 is therefore true. This means that the two statements between the words **loop** and **end loop** will be executed once; the number 0 is written and J's value is increased to 2. The expression $J < 6$ is evaluated a second time and this time it is also true. The sequence of statements is executed again. The number 2 is written, and J is increased to 4. The expression $J < 6$ is still true and so the statements are executed a third time. The number 4 is written and J is increased to 6. When the Boolean expression $J < 6$ is evaluated this time it is false, which means that the **loop** statement terminates. Execution continues with the next statement after the **loop** statement. Note that the variable J in this example is an ordinary integer variable that is declared in the normal way. It should not be confused with a loop parameter that is used in a **loop** statement with **for**. Such a loop parameter may not be used outside the **loop** statement.

In the next example, it is presumed that the variable X has type FLOAT. The lines of program:

```
X := 10.0;
while X > 1.0 loop
   PUT(X, FORE => 6, AFT => 2, EXP => 0);
   X := X / 2.0;
end loop;
```

give, when executed, the output:

```
10.00    5.00    2.50    1.25
```

After the **loop** statement has been executed the variable X has value 0.625.

We shall now look at a more complicated example. We shall write a program to calculate the sum of the mathematical series:

$$\frac{1}{1 \times 1} - \frac{1}{2 \times 2} + \frac{1}{3 \times 3} - \frac{1}{4 \times 4} + \frac{1}{5 \times 5} - \frac{1}{6 \times 6} \cdots$$

The series has an infinite number of terms, so it is impossible to take account of them all in the program. The signs of the terms alternate between plus and minus and the absolute value of the terms decreases with each new term. The sum of the series therefore approaches a certain limit; the series is said to be convergent. We take the decision to ignore terms that are insignificantly small with respect to. the final result. If the result is to be written with 5 decimal figures, terms with absolute value less than 0.000001 can be ignored without any effect.

We make up an algorithm:

(1) Initialize the sum to 0 and the first term to 1.
(2) If the absolute value of the next term $>= 0.000001$, carry out the following two steps:
    (2.1) Add the next term to the sum.
    (2.2) Evaluate a new next term.
(3) Write out the sum.

We can refine step (1):

```
SUM := 0.0;
NEXT_TERM := 1.0;
```

Here we have introduced two variables, SUM and NEXT_TERM. They are both real types since the sum and its terms are real numbers. The second variable is called NEXT_TERM, even if it gives the value of the first term at this stage, because it can then be used in the rest of the program when calculating the values of the remaining terms. (And anyway, before starting, the first term is the same as the next term). We can initialize the variables directly, at the same time as declaring them:

```
SUM : FLOAT := 0.0;
NEXT_TERM : FLOAT := 1.0;
```

Then the assignment statements above are not needed.
Step (2) becomes a **loop** statement:

```
while abs(NEXT_TERM) >= EPSILON loop
   -- (2.1) Add the next term to the sum
   -- (2.2) Evaluate a new next term
end loop;
```

We have introduced a constant EPSILON here to avoid having a constant value within the program. EPSILON is declared as follows:

```
EPSILON : constant := 10.0 ** (−DEC_FIGS − 1);
```

We have initialized EPSILON in terms of another constant DEC_FIGS which is declared:

```
DEC_FIGS : constant := 5;
```

This is practical. If another time we want to have another number of figures after the decimal point we only need to change the constant DEC_FIGS. EPSILON does not need changing.
Step (2.1) becomes quite simply:

```
SUM := SUM + NEXT_TERM;
```

Step (2.2), 'Evaluate a new next term', requires some thought. A particular term in the series, let us call it the kth term, should have the form:

```
1.0/FLOAT(K * K)
```

To work out its value, therefore, we need a counter K to keep track of the number of the term. It is best to make this counter an integer initialized to 1 and then increase it by 1 each time a new term is calculated. Thus we have the declaration:

```
K : INTEGER := 1;
```

and the statement:

```
K := K + 1;
```

which will be executed first in step (2.2).

Having alternate terms that are positive and negative present a complication. It can be resolved by introducing a variable SIGN which takes alternate values + and −. If the calculated terms are multiplied by SIGN, they will become alternately positive and negative. For simplicity, we shall let SIGN be a real variable. Since term number 1 should be positive, we initialize SIGN to +1, using the declaration:

```
SIGN : FLOAT := 1.0;
```

By including the statement:

```
SIGN := − SIGN;
```

in step (2.2), we make SIGN alternate between +1 and −1 each time a new term is calculated. The actual calculation of the next term is then:

```
NEXT_TERM := SIGN / FLOAT (K * K);
```

NEXT_TERM has type FLOAT, so the right-hand side must also have this type for the assignment to be made. SIGN has type FLOAT but because K has type INTEGER the expression K * K also has type INTEGER. This expression must therefore be converted to type FLOAT before the division can be performed. Note that if we had declared SIGN to be an integer, then the expression SIGN / (K * K) would have been allowed. However, that would have meant integer division, the result of which would always have been an integer and that would be incorrect. NEXT_TERM should not be an integer.

If we put the three statements in step (2.2) together we get:

```
K := K + 1;
SIGN := - SIGN;
NEXT_TERM := SIGN / FLOAT (K * K);
```

Step (3), 'Write out the sum', becomes:

```
PUT("The sum of the series is: ");
PUT(SUM, FORE => 1, AFT => DEC_FIGS, EXP => 0);
```

Now we can assemble all the steps into a complete program:

```
with TEXT_IO, BASIC_NUM_IO;
use  TEXT_IO, BASIC_NUM_IO;
procedure SUM_SERIES is
   SUM                : FLOAT := 0.0;
   NEXT_TERM, SIGN : FLOAT := 1.0;
   K                      : INTEGER := 1;
   DEC_FIGS : constant := 5;
   EPSILON   : constant := 10.0 ** (-DEC_FIGS - 1);
begin
   while abs(NEXT_TERM) >= EPSILON loop
      -- Add the next term to the sum
      SUM := SUM + NEXT_TERM;
      -- Evaluate a new next term
      K := K + 1;
      SIGN := - SIGN;
      NEXT_TERM := SIGN / FLOAT(K * K);
   end loop;
   PUT("The sum of the series is: ");
   PUT(SUM, FORE => 1, AFT => DEC_FIGS, EXP => 0);
end SUM_SERIES;
```

When the program is run, the output:

```
The sum of the series is: 0.82247
```

is obtained.

4.6 *Exit* statement

There is a special **exit** statement that can be used in conjunction with the **loop** statement. There are two variants, the first of which is simply:

exit;

This statement must lie within a **loop** statement. When it is executed the iteration is terminated and control passes out of the **loop** statement to the first statement after **end loop**.

The second variant of the **exit** statement is conditional:

exit when *Boolean_expression*;

On execution, the Boolean expression is evaluated first. If this is true, then a jump out of the **loop** statement takes place, just as in the simple **exit** described above. If the Boolean statement is not true, execution continues with the next statement within the **loop** statement; no jump takes place.

For example:

```
loop
   PUT("Enter data");
   GET(X);
   exit when X < 0.0;
   -- Do calculations
      ⋮
   -- Display result
      ⋮
end loop;
-- This is where you come if a number < 0 is entered.
      ⋮
```

Exit statement

Two forms:

(1)   **exit**;
(2)   **exit when** *Boolean_expression*;

Care must be taken when **exit** statements are used because they can easily lead to a program that is unclear and difficult to understand. Normally, a **loop** statement with **while** can be used instead, with the advantage that the condition for termination is stated at the start. If an **exit** statement is used, this condition is hidden within the **loop** statement and it can be difficult to see it. However, it is sometimes practical to use the **exit** statement in connection with interactive data input, as in the foregoing example, and as we shall see later.

4.7   Nested *loop* statements

Since the sequence of statements within a **loop** statement can be built up of arbitrary statements, there may well be one **loop** statement within another. Such program constructs are common.

Let us look at a simple example. We shall write a few lines of program to print N rows of plus signs at the terminal. On the first row there will be one +, two +s on the second, and so on. The number N will be read as input from the terminal. If, for example, the number 5 is entered, these lines of program will produce the following output:

```
+
++
+++
++++
+++++
```

Using the top-down method we get:

(1)   Read in number N.
(2)   Repeat the following step for each number K from 1 to N.
    (2.1)   Print a row of K plus signs.

Step (1) is simple:

```
PUT_LINE("Enter the number of rows to be printed.");
GET(N);
```

Step (2) is:

```
for K in 1 .. N loop
    -- (2.1) Print a row of K plus signs.
end loop;
```

Finally we have step (2.1):

```
for J in 1 .. K loop
  PUT('+');
end loop;
NEW_LINE;
```

If we put them all together we get:

```
PUT_LINE("Enter the number of rows to be printed");
GET(N);
for K in 1 .. N loop
  for J in 1 .. K loop
    PUT('+');
  end loop;
  NEW_LINE;
end loop;
```

If we want the following output instead:

```
+++++
++++
+++
++
+
```

we only need to add the word **reverse** to the outer loop statement:

for K **in reverse** 1 .. N **loop**

As a further example, let us write a program that reads in 10 lines and counts the number of lower case letters they contain. The 10 lines can be of different length but we shall assume that no line is longer than 100 characters.

We can use the algorithm:

(1)   Set N_SMALL_LETTERS to 0.
(2)   Repeat the following for each of the ten lines.
      (2.1)   Read in the current line.
      (2.2)   Repeat the following for each character in the line.
              (2.2.1)   If the current character is between 'a' and 'z',
                        increase the value of N_SMALL_LETTERS by one.
(3)   Print N_SMALL_LETTERS.

This algorithm can be translated into the Ada program:

```
with TEXT_IO, BASIC_NUM_IO;
use  TEXT_IO, BASIC_NUM_IO;
procedure COUNT_SMALL_LETTERS is
   CURRENT_LINE      : STRING(1 .. 100);
   LENGTH            : INTEGER;
   N_SMALL_LETTERS : INTEGER := 0;
begin
   PUT_LINE("Write 10 lines");
   for LINE_NUMBER in 1 .. 10 loop
      GET_LINE(CURRENT_LINE, LENGTH);
      for CHAR_NUMBER in 1 .. LENGTH loop
         if CURRENT_LINE(CHAR_NUMBER) in 'a' .. 'z' then
            N_SMALL_LETTERS := N_SMALL_LETTERS + 1;
         end if;
      end loop;
   end loop;
   PUT("There are ");
   PUT(N_SMALL_LETTERS, WIDTH => 1);
   PUT(" small letters");
end COUNT_SMALL_LETTERS;
```

Here the procedure GET_LINE is used to read in the current line.

4.8 Interactive input

Programs that communicate with a user at a terminal while being executed are called **interactive programs**. Such programs ask the user for input data, and compute the output data, which is then displayed to the user at the terminal. Interactive programs are very common so we shall make a special study of how such programs can be written.

All the examples shown so far have been interactive programs. We have seen that it is important that there is a message telling the user what data he or she should write before each input of data. A program halts when it comes to an input statement and will not continue until the user has entered data. If there is no message before the input statement, the user will not notice that the program is waiting for input.

Interactive programs

Programs that communicate with the user at the terminal.

Input from the terminal to the program should be preceded by a request for the user to input data.

A computation of any sort has the following general form:

- Read input data.
- Perform computations.
- Write out the result.

Frequently, a program should be able to carry out a computation several times in a row without having to be restarted each time. The program should then act according to the following model:

- Repeat the following three steps time after time until the user wants to stop.

    - Read input data.
    - Carry out computations.
    - Write out result.

This clearly involves iteration. We shall now look at some different ways of producing this type of program.

As an example, we shall use a program that was shown in Section 3.4.1 to calculate the length of the hypotenuse in a right-angled triangle. The input data required are the lengths of the two shorter sides. The program in Section 3.4.1 does only one calculation. We shall now modify the program so that it can be used to carry out several calculations in a row, as in the foregoing model.

In the first version, we make it easy for ourselves as programmers. We simply ask the user to state how many calculations are required at the beginning of the program. Thus we use a **loop** statement with **for** and get the program:

```
-- VERSION 1

with TEXT_IO, BASIC_NUM_IO, BASIC_MATH;
use  TEXT_IO, BASIC_NUM_IO, BASIC_MATH;
procedure HYPOTENUSE is
   A, B : FLOAT;
   N_CALCULATIONS : INTEGER;
begin
   PUT_LINE ("How many calculations do you want to make?");
   GET(N_CALCULATIONS);
   for I in 1 .. N_CALCULATIONS loop
     PUT_LINE ("Enter lengths of the two shorter sides:");
     GET(A); GET(B);
     PUT("The hypotenuse has length: ");
     PUT(SQRT(A**2 + B**2), FORE => 1, AFT => 2, EXP => 0);
     NEW_LINE;
   end loop;
end HYPOTENUSE;
```

Of course, this is inconvenient for the user, who often wants to try out different input data and see how the results vary. In this case the number of times the calculation should be repeated is generally not known in advance.

What the user wants is to be able to terminate the program at any time. This can be achieved by the program asking the user if further calculations are to be made each time a calculation is completed:

```
-- VERSION 2
with TEXT_IO, BASIC_NUM_IO, BASIC_MATH;
use  TEXT_IO, BASIC_NUM_IO, BASIC_MATH;
procedure HYPOTENUSE is
   A, B      : FLOAT;
   ANSWER : CHARACTER := 'y';
begin
   while ANSWER = 'y' loop
      PUT_LINE ("Enter lengths of the two shorter sides:");
      GET(A); GET(B);
      PUT("The hypotenuse has length: ");
      PUT(SQRT(A**2 + B**2), FORE => 1, AFT => 2, EXP => 0);
      NEW_LINE;
      PUT_LINE("Are there more calculations?");
      PUT_LINE("Enter y or n");
      GET(ANSWER);
   end loop;
end HYPOTENUSE;
```

In this version we have introduced a character variable ANSWER. The user is asked if the program should continue, and then the first character entered in reply (a 'y' or an 'n') is read to the variable ANSWER. We have assumed that the user will want to carry out the calculation at least once, and have initialized ANSWER to 'y'. This makes the expression after **while** always true the first time through.

The disadvantage of this second version is that the user must answer a question after each calculation. There is a common trick that can be used to avoid this: a particular value of input can be taken to mean that the program should terminate. This should be a value that would not normally occur. It is not always possible to find such a value. Consider, for example, a program that reads in and adds together an arbitrary number of real numbers. There is no particular real number that may not appear in such a sum and therefore the method cannot be used.

In our hypotenuse example, the input data are the lengths of the shorter sides, which must be greater than 0. We can therefore use a value <= 0 to denote that the program should terminate. If we use a **loop** statement with **while** we get the following program:

```
-- VERSION 3

with TEXT_IO, BASIC_NUM_IO, BASIC_MATH;
use  TEXT_IO, BASIC_NUM_IO, BASIC_MATH;
procedure HYPOTENUSE is
   A, B : FLOAT;
begin
   PUT_LINE ("Enter lengths of the two shorter sides:");
   PUT_LINE ("Terminate by giving a negative length.");
   GET(A); GET(B);
   while A > 0.0 and B > 0.0 loop
      PUT("The hypotenuse has length: ");
      PUT( SQRT(A**2 + B**2), FORE => 1, AFT => 2, EXP => 0);
      NEW_LINE;
      PUT_LINE ("Enter lengths of the two shorter sides:");
      PUT_LINE ("Terminate by giving a negative length.");
      GET(A); GET(B);
   end loop;
end HYPOTENUSE;
```

In this method, the calculation must come first in the loop and the input last (because on the final go through, the negative values are read into variables A and B. If we had the input first, as before, the program would try to carry out the calculation using the negative values, which, of course, it should not do). We must put the first input outside the **loop** statement. This is a bit clumsy because the same statements have to be written in two places in the program.

To make the program less clumsy we can use an **exit** statement. Then the input does not need to be written in several places and the **loop** statement becomes:

```
-- VERSION 4

loop
   PUT_LINE ("Enter lengths of the two shorter sides:");
   PUT_LINE ("Terminate by giving a negative length.");
   GET(A); GET(B);
   exit when A <= 0.0 or B <= 0.0;
   PUT("The hypotenuse has length: ");
   PUT( SQRT(A**2 + B**2), FORE => 1, AFT => 2, EXP => 0);
   NEW_LINE;
end loop;
```

Here the statements appear in an order that might be closer to the natural way of thinking.

In the two final versions of the hypotenuse program we shall use a function in the TEXT_IO package that we have not seen before, called END_OF_FILE. When the function END_OF_FILE is called in a program, a value of type BOOLEAN is returned, in other words a value that is either TRUE or FALSE. The value TRUE is obtained if the user states that he or she does not intend to give more data to the program, and the value FALSE is obtained if the user continues to input data in the normal way.

How does the user state that he does not intend to input more data? If, for example, the program requests:

Enter lengths of the two shorter sides

and the user wants the program to continue, he writes in data in the normal way, for example:

25.7 11.3

If, on the other hand, there is no further input data, a special combination of keys should be pressed at the terminal. The combination varies from system to system, but it is common to use the key that says CTRL on it together with another key. (The D key or the Z key is used in some common systems). In future, we shall assume that the CTRL key and the D key should be pressed simultaneously.

If we use a **loop** statement with **while**, the statements in the program appear:

```
-- VERSION 5

PUT_LINE("Enter lengths of the two shorter sides:");
PUT_LINE("Terminate by typing CTRL-D.");
while not END_OF_FILE loop
   GET(A); GET(B);
   PUT("The hypotenuse has length: ");
   PUT( SQRT(A**2 + B**2), FORE => 1, AFT => 2, EXP => 0);
   NEW_LINE;
   PUT_LINE("Enter lengths of the two shorter sides:");
   PUT_LINE("Terminate by typing CTRL-D.");
end loop;
```

As we already know, there should be an expression of type BOOLEAN after the word **while**. The program can be written as it is because a call to the function END_OF_FILE gives just such a BOOLEAN value as result. As in version 3 of the program, we have been forced to change the order of the reading and calculation within the loop. On the final go through, after the user has pressed the CTRL and D keys, no calculation should be made. Note that the call to END_OF_FILE should occur after the user has been asked to give the input data and before the program tries to read in what the user has written.

In the last version we use an **exit** statement and avoid turning round the order of the statements in the loop and repeating statements before the first **loop** statement. This gives the most compact solution:

```
-- VERSION 6

loop
    PUT_LINE("Enter the lengths of the two shorter sides:");
    PUT_LINE("Terminate by typing CTRL-D.");
    exit when END_OF_FILE;
    GET(A); GET(B);
    PUT("The hypotenuse has length: ");
    PUT( SQRT(A**2 + B**2), FORE => 1, AFT => 2, EXP => 0);
    NEW_LINE;
end loop;
```

The question arises: 'Which of these methods is best?' This depends partly on the application. If it is known that a definite number of input data will be read (for example, that the results from a fixed number of measurements will be input), the first method with a **for** statement might be preferable.

The second version, in which the user is asked if further calculations are to be made, is a bit clumsy, and the user may find it tedious to answer the question over and over. This version may be useful if written for an inexperienced user who needs accurate and easily understood instructions.

Version 3 has the advantage that the condition for continuing with the calculations is seen at the very beginning of the **loop** statement. The disadvantages are clearly that certain lines of program must be repeated and that the statements come in an unnatural order. In this respect, version 4 with its **exit** statement is preferable. This version avoids repeating part of the program and the statements come in a natural order. It can be disadvantageous that the program contains a jump out of a loop. It is usually said that no jumps should occur in a well-structured program. Even so, the jump brought about by this **exit** statement can be said to be well-controlled and, therefore, does not offend the principles of structured programming.

In certain computer systems it may be standard to terminate the input data to certain types of program using END_OF_FILE. Also, if there is no natural 'end value' for input, END_OF_FILE is useful. Then versions 5 or 6 could be used. If these two versions are compared, version 6 might be preferred, for the same reasons as version 4 was preferred to version 3.

EXERCISES

4.1 In an examination it is possible to get a maximum of 60 points. To pass requires 28 points and to get honours requires at least 48 points. Write a program that reads in the marks obtained by a student and writes out one of the comments: *fail*, *pass* or *honours*.

(a) Use an **if** statement.

(b) Use a **case** statement.

4.2 The sides of a triangle can be denoted a, b and c. If the lengths of sides a and b, and the size of the angle γ between them are known then the length of the third side c can be calculated using the formula:

$$c = \sqrt{a^2 + b^2 - 2ab \cos \gamma}$$

Write a program that reads in the lengths of two sides of a triangle and the angle between them (in radians) and determines if the triangle is equilateral (all sides equal length), isosceles (two sides equal), or scalene (no sides equal). The program should print one of the comments: *equilateral*, *isosceles* or *scalene*. Remember to be careful when comparing real numbers.

4.3 In Sweden, everyone has a personal identification number of 10 digits. The first six denote the person's date of birth in the format *yymmdd*, and the last four are a code (described in Exercise 4.9).

Write a program that reads in the day's date in international ISO format, namely *19yy–mm–dd*, including the dashes. The program then reads in a person's 10-digit identification number (no dashes) and prints the message:

Congratulations!

if it is his or her birthday.

4.4 A Swedish postal code consists of five digits; the first two denote the district to which the code belongs. If these digits lie in the range 20 to 62 inclusive, or are 65 or 66, then the code belongs somewhere in the southern part of Sweden (Götaland). If the digits are greater than or equal to 80, the code refers to somewhere in northern Sweden (Norrland), and all others denote central areas (Svealand).

Write a program that reads in an address consisting of two lines: street (number and street name) and town (postal code and town name). Each line can be up to 20 characters long and will be padded with spaces when read in. The program should output one of the messages:

> To southern Sweden
> To central Sweden
> To northern Sweden

depending on the postal code in the first five characters in the second line of the address.

4.5 Write a program that draws up a neat table of values for the following function:

$$f(x) = 3x^3 - 5x^2 + 2x - 20$$

(a) Make the program write out values of $f(x)$ for all integers in the interval -10 to $+10$.

(b) Make the program write out values of $f(x)$ for all x-values in the interval -2 to $+2$ in steps of 0.1, that is, for the values $-2.0, -1.9, -1.8, ..., 1.9, 2.0$.

4.6 A borough has made the following prognosis for the changes in population over the next few years:

- At the start of 1988 there were 26 000 inhabitants.
- The rates of births and deaths are estimated at 0.7% and 0.6% of the population, respectively.
- The number of people moving in and out of the borough annually is estimated at 300 and 325, respectively.

Write a program to calculate the borough's estimated number of inhabitants at the beginning of a particular year. The year in question is to be read in as input.

4.7 Write a program that will print out all the printable ASCII characters and their corresponding ASCII codes.

4.8 A Caesar cipher is a very simple coding method in which each letter in the message to be coded is replaced by the letter a fixed number of places further on in the alphabet. If, for example, a displacement of two places is chosen, then A is replaced by C, B by D, C by E, ..., X by Z, Y by A, and Z by B. The message:

> SEND MORE MONEY

is thus coded to:

> UGPF OQTG OQPGA

(a) Write a program that reads in a message (maximum 80 characters), codes the message and prints it out. Use a displacement of three for coding. Assume that only upper case letters are used. If any character other than an upper case letter appears in the message, do not replace it.

(b) Write a program that will read in a secret message, coded with a displacement of three, and translate the message back to a readable form.

(c) Write a program that will read in a secret coded message where the displacement used is unknown. The program should write out all possible solutions, so that the original message can be found among them.

4.9 Referring again to the Swedish 10-digit identification number (see Exercise 4.3) write a program to check that a given number is correct. If it is incorrect, the text:

Incorrect identification number

should be output.

(a) Make the program check that all characters are numerals.

(b) Make the program also check that the control figure (the final digit) is correct. The control figure is calculated as follows:

    (1) Add digits in positions 2, 4, 6 and 8.

    (2) Multiply the digits in positions 1, 3, 5, 7 and 9 in the identification number by 2 and add the *digits* in the result.

    (3) Add the results of steps 1 and 2.

    (4) The control figure can now be determined because the sum of the control figure and the sum from step (3) should be exactly divisible by 10.

4.10 A palindrome is a text that reads the same forwards as backwards. For example, '*Ada*' and '*Able was I ere I saw Elba*'. Write a program that reads in a word (no more than 20 characters) and decides whether the word is a palindrome.

4.11 Write a program to write out a multiplication table as in the following example:

1	2	3	4	5
2	4	6	8	10
3	6	9	12	15
4	8	12	16	20
5	10	15	20	25

The upper limit of the table should be read in as input.

4.12 Write a program to compute the least integer k such that:

$$\sum_{i=1}^{k} i^2 > n$$

The number n should be read in from the terminal.

4.13 If there is no accessible package with mathematical functions, Maclaurin series can be used to calculate the values of certain common functions. For example, the function 'sin' can be evaluated with the following series:

$$\sin x = x - \frac{x^3}{3!} + \frac{x^5}{5!} - \frac{x^7}{7!} + \frac{x^9}{9!} \cdots$$

Write a program that reads in a value of x and writes out $\sin x$ using this series. The result should be written correct to four decimal places. Neglect any terms in the series that are less than 10^{-5}.

4.14 Write a program that reads in a certain number of real numbers and writes out at the terminal:

- The largest number.
- The smallest number.
- Their mean value.

Formulate the reading in of input data in a suitable way for the following cases:

(a) The number of numbers to be read in is always known (for example, 100).

(b) The number of numbers is arbitrary but it is known that all the numbers are greater than zero.

(c) The number of numbers is arbitrary and any real number can occur.

4.15 Write a program that calculates the value of the sum:

$$H_n = \sum_{i=1}^{n} \frac{1}{i}$$

for different values of n. The program should be designed so that it repeatedly writes out the text:

Enter the value of n

and calculates and writes out the value of H_n. There should be some suitable way of indicating that no further calculations are to be made.

4.16 Write a program that reads a line from the terminal comprising a number of words separated by one or more spaces (80 characters maximum). The program should write out the line of text such that only one space comes between each pair of words.

Chapter 5
Types

5.1 Data abstraction

5.2 Integer types

5.3 Real types

5.4 Enumeration types

5.5 The tools for input and output

5.6 Subtypes

5.7 Array types

5.8 Searching and sorting

Exercises

In earlier chapters use has been made of Ada's predefined types as declared in the package **STANDARD**. This chapter will show how it is possible to declare new types. The concepts of abstraction and representation will be discussed, that is, how types can be introduced in order to describe and represent phenomena from the real world. The ways of declaring new numeric types will also be reviewed. The use of enumeration types to describe the kind of real phenomena that cannot be expressed as numerical quantities will be studied further.

So far a non-standard package, **BASIC_NUM_IO**, has been used to access the tools for input and output of values of the types **INTEGER** and **FLOAT**. In Ada there is a general mechanism for creating new input/output packages for all numeric types and enumeration types, even those declared by the programmer. In Section 5.5 the use of this mechanism is explained.

The use of so-called subtypes in Ada will also be described, showing how these can be used to describe objects that belong to a subgroup of a larger, more general, group. Sections 5.7 and 5.8 deal with types that consist of several components of the same sort and which can be used to represent tables, texts and other data.

161

5.1 Data abstraction

In Chapter 3 we discussed the concept that the task of a computer
program is to manipulate data, and that data objects in a program often
represent some phenomenon in the real world. When we talk about
phenomena in the real world, we nearly always use a technique known as
abstraction. Abstraction means creating a concept of something so that it
can be talked about and described. The word 'truck', for example, is an
abstraction for a vehicle that can be used for transporting things. We can
talk about a truck and say that it has certain properties, such as capacity,
length, running cost and so on.

The abstraction can be made at different levels. For a maintenance
mechanic it is natural to think of a truck as consisting of many
components, such as a gear box, brake system and so on. To go down
another level, it can be said that the gear box is made up of many parts,
axles, gear wheels, etc. This level is appropriate for the design or repair
of a gear box. The level of abstraction chosen, therefore, depends on the
context in which the phenomenon is to be studied.

The advantage of deliberately choosing an abstraction is that it
allows inessential details to be ignored in favour of those properties
important for the study in hand. The driver of a truck is not interested in
how the different gear wheels inside the gear box are moving. He or she
only needs to know how to use the gear lever.

Abstraction

- A 'model' or 'concept' of a real-world phenomenon is created.
- Abstraction is made at such a level that
  inessential details can be ignored.

Because the data objects in a program should represent a
phenomenon in the real world, we must also be able to use abstractions
when we create different data objects. This is possible in Ada. Using
types and packages that we declare ourselves, we can build up
complicated types with particular properties. It can actually be said that
we have already met abstraction of data. A variable of the built-in type
INTEGER, for example, is a representation of a mathematical whole
number. If we prefer, we do not need to study the underlying level of

abstraction that describes how an INTEGER is represented in binary form with ones and zeros. We only need to know which operations can be performed on an object of the type INTEGER.

There are several advantages to be gained by setting up new types that specifically represent the properties of a phenomenon. The program becomes clearer because it is more closely linked with reality. The program also becomes safer; the compiler checks that we are not illegally mixing different types and that we are not giving variables illegal values. The program becomes less complex because we can choose a suitable level of abstraction and ignore unnecessary details.

There is a distinction in Ada between **scalar types** and **composite types**. (There are also types called 'access types' and 'private types', but we shall not consider these yet). Scalar types are used to describe things that can be expressed in a single value, for example, a temperature, a printable character, or the score in a test. Earlier we illustrated scalar data objects as storage boxes containing only a single value. The **numeric types** (integer and real types) and **enumeration types** are among the scalar types.

The composite types are used to build up more complex descriptions of data objects. Descriptions can be built up that contain several component elements of the same sort, for example, text strings or tables, or descriptions that contain component elements of different kinds, for example, the description of a person in a hospital register.

Scalar types

The object can be expressed as **one** single value (for example, a number or a character).

Composite types

The objects are composed of several individual values (for example, a text).

The declarations of types should be placed alongside other declarations in an Ada program. It is the ways of defining different types that will be discussed in the rest of this chapter.

Type declaration

> **type** *typename* **is** *type definition*;

where *type definition* depends on the type being declared.

- A type declaration is placed among the other declarations in the program.
- No objects of the type are created by the type declaration; they are created when an object declaration is given.

The name of a type can be used in the same way as the names of Ada's standard types. This includes being able to declare objects (variables and constants) using the name. If we have the following type declaration, without worrying how the declaration itself continues:

type TEMPERATURE **is** ... ;

then the following object declarations can be made:

MEAN_TEMPERATURE : TEMPERATURE;
LIMITING_TEMPERATURE : **constant** TEMPERATURE := 100.0;

Note that no objects are created when the type is declared. The type (or the idea of) TEMPERATURE is only introduced so that it can be used later. It is only when an object declaration is made that an object is created. Type declarations and object declarations may appear in arbitrary order in the declaration section of a program, but a type must be declared before it is used in another declaration.

When both types and objects are declared in a program it can be a problem to find suitable names. It is all too easy to decide on names in a program that make it difficult to tell types and objects apart, making the program both confusing and hard to understand. It can, therefore, be useful to devise a principle for allocating names. One common principle for differentiating between the names of types and other quantities is to let all type names end in TYPE, for example, TEMPERATURE_TYPE and PERSON_TYPE.

5.2 Integer types

When an integer type is declared, the least and greatest possible integer values that objects of the type can take are stated. A few examples to illustrate this are:

> **type** LINE_NUMBER **is range** 1 .. 72;
>
> **type** SCORE **is range** 0 .. 100;
>
> **type** NEGATIVE_INTEGER **is range** −100_000 .. −1;

Declaration of integer types

> **type** *typename* **is range** *min_value .. max_value*;

where *min_value* and *max_value* are static (constant) integer expressions.

Condition: *min_value* <= *max_value*

Here LINE_NUMBER, for example, describes a type whose possible values are whole numbers in the interval 1 to 72. The permissible limits depend on how integers are stored in the particular Ada implementation. If limits are requested that the Ada implementation cannot cope with, the compiler will give an error message. In the majority of implementations, it would probably not be permitted to declare the following type, for instance:

> **type** GIANT_INTEGER **is range** 0 .. 100_000_000_000_000_000;

In every Ada implementation, as we know, there is a predefined type INTEGER which is declared in the package STANDARD. The declaration of INTEGER can be considered as:

> **type** INTEGER **is range** *least_integer .. greatest_integer*;

where the limits *least_integer* and *greatest_integer* can be different for different implementations of Ada.

The standard type INTEGER

- The least possible and greatest possible values can be different in different implementations of Ada.
- To include all desired values, the programmer should declare a new specific integer type.

The two limits in a declaration of an integer type do not necessarily have to be simple literals as above. Static expressions, that is, expressions consisting of constant components, are also allowed:

```
MAX_LINE : constant := 72;
MAX_COL : constant := 17;
type ELEMENT_NUMBER is range 1 .. (MAX_LINE * MAX_COL);
```

Facts from the real world can be represented using specifically declared integer types. For example, a variable MY_SCORE can be created by making the object declaration:

```
MY_SCORE : SCORE;
```

The variable is thus an object that can only take integral values between 0 and 100. It represents a genuine score in, for example, a test. If an attempt is made to assign a value to MY_SCORE that lies outside the limits 0 and 100, there is a run-time error and an error message is output. This gives valuable assistance in tracing errors of logic in a program. If MY_SCORE were simply declared as an INTEGER, this help would not be available; all the integers included in the type INTEGER would then be allowed. The type INTEGER can be considered as representing the concept of whole numbers in a general mathematical sense, that is, having no connection with any particular real object, but this is too vague a model for a real test score.

All the operations that can be performed on objects of type INTEGER (for example, assignment, addition, comparison) can also be performed with other integer types, but mixing different types is not allowed. Assume, for example, we have the following object declarations:

```
CURRENT_LINE, NEXT_LINE : LINE_NUMBER;
MY_SCORE : SCORE;
K : INTEGER;
```

Then the following assignments are not permitted:

```
CURRENT_LINE := MY_SCORE;    -- Error!
K := NEXT_LINE;              -- Error!
MY_SCORE := K;               -- Error!
```

Nor is it permitted to mix types in expressions:

```
CURRENT_LINE + K    -- Error!
MY_SCORE * K        -- Error!
```

However, the following are allowed:

```
CURRENT_LINE := NEXT_LINE;        -- Same type
CURRENT_LINE := LINE_NUMBER(K)    -- Type conversion
MY_SCORE * SCORE(K)               -- Type conversion
```

In the second example we have used explicit type conversion and converted the value of K, which is of type INTEGER, into a value of type LINE_NUMBER. In the expression in the third example, K's value has been turned into the type SCORE. Type conversion is allowed between all numeric types.

If we have the following declarations:

```
type PAGE_NUMBER  is range 1 .. 500;
type INDEX        is range 1 .. 500;
PAGE : PAGE_NUMBER;
I    : INDEX;
```

then PAGE_NUMBER and INDEX are different types in spite of being declared in the same way. Therefore the variables PAGE and I have different types and may not be mixed.

Operations on integer types

- The normal operations that exist for INTEGER (for example, +, −) also exist for other integer types.
- Different integer types may not be mixed.
- Explicit type conversion is permitted.

As discussed earlier integer literals have the type *universal_integer* and are automatically converted into the 'right' integer type. Therefore, the following, for example, are allowed:

```
CURRENT_LINE := 1;
MY_SCORE + 5
K * 27
```

■

We saw earlier how for the type INTEGER the attributes INTEGER'FIRST and INTEGER'LAST can be used to determine the least and greatest numbers, respectively, in the type INTEGER. FIRST and LAST can be used in the same way for all other integer types. For example, the least possible number in the type LINE_NUMBER can be found by writing LINE_NUMBER'FIRST. The expression LINE_NUMBER'FIRST has the type LINE_NUMBER. If we want to determine the number of possible values for the type LINE_NUMBER we can write the expression:

```
INTEGER(LINE_NUMBER'LAST − LINE_NUMBER'FIRST + 1)
```

The expression within brackets has type LINE_NUMBER. Because the number of possible values should be a whole number in the general mathematical sense, the result has been converted to type INTEGER.

Attributes for integer type

- T'FIRST − states the least possible value for an object of integer type T.
- T'LAST − states the greatest possible value for an object of integer type T.

□

5.3 Real types

In Ada there are two categories of real types, namely floating point types and fixed point types, as mentioned in Section 3.1.1. Only floating point types will be treated here. Floating point types are used to represent real values with a certain precision, that is, with an accuracy of a certain number of digits after the decimal point. As we saw earlier, an Ada implementation uses a binary representation to store floating point numbers internally. Therefore only certain real numbers can be stored exactly. The rest are stored in an approximate form.

Declaration of floating point types

   type *typename* **is digits** *number_of_sig_figs*;

where *number_of_sig_figs* expresses the accuracy as the number of significant figures following the decimal point, and is a static (constant) expression.

· When a floating point type is declared, the accuracy required is simply stated in terms of the number of figures following the decimal point. The compiler then chooses a suitable form of binary representation, namely, how many bits should be used to store the mantissa and the exponent. The number of digits accuracy varies from implementation to implementation. If the number of digits accuracy requested is greater than can be stored in the implementation in use, the compiler will give an error message. (It should be noted that when the compiler accepts a declaration of a floating point type, it also guarantees that a minimum number of bits will be used to store the exponent, which determines the range of numbers that can be stored. The greater the accuracy requested, the greater the number of bits devoted to storing the exponent). Some examples are:

   type TEMPERATURE **is digits** 4;
   type PRECISION_MEASUREMENT **is digits** 15;

Following the word **digits** there must be a static integer expression. An integer literal is most often used, as in these examples.

   We have already met the standard type FLOAT, which can be thought of as being declared in the following manner in the package STANDARD:

   type FLOAT **is digits** *figure_dependent_on_implementation*;

Thus the number of digits' accuracy obtained when the type FLOAT is used can vary from implementation to implementation. It can, therefore, be dangerous to use this type when writing a program that is intended to be portable (usable on all Ada implementations), because it is not possible to be sure of the accuracy of the results computed by the program. It is thus recommended that the programmer declares his or her own floating point types so that he or she can state the desired precision. If it is not possible to obtain that precision, the compiler will detect it as an error, output an error message and the program will not be compiled. Thus the programmer can be assured of getting the desired accuracy if a program can be compiled without error.

The standard type FLOAT

- The number of digits accuracy can be different in different implementations of Ada.
- To be sure of obtaining a certain number of digits accuracy, the programmer should declare a specific floating point type.

It is possible to state the bounds within which the numbers belonging to the type may lie:

type PERCENTAGE **is digits** 4 **range** 0.0 .. 100.0;
type ERROR_PROBABILITY **is digits** 6 **range** 0.0 .. 1.0;

This ensures a check that while the program is running, variables of the particular type never assume values that lie outside its limits. It also offers assistance with tracking down possible errors in the program's logic. The limits that appear after the word **range** must be static real expressions.

In the same way as for integer types, all the operations that exist for the type FLOAT also exist for programmer-declared floating point types, but again, mixing different floating point types in an expression is not allowed. If this is necessary, type conversion can be used. Real literals present no problem because they have the type *universal_real* and automatically take the 'right' type. If, for example, we have the declarations:

MAX_PERCENT : PERCENTAGE;
MAX_PROB   : ERROR PROBABILITY;

the following assignment is incorrect:

MAX_PROB := MAX_PERCENT / 100.0;   -- Error!

because the expression on the right of the assignment has type PERCENTAGE and that on the left has type ERROR_PROBABILITY. However, the following is correct:

MAX_PROB := ERROR_PROBABILITY(MAX_PERCENT / 100.0);

Operations on floating point types

- The normal operations that exist for FLOAT (for example, +, −) also exist for other floating point types.
- Different floating point types may not be mixed.
- Explicit type conversion is allowed.

■

In Chapter 3 it was shown that the attributes FLOAT'DIGITS, FLOAT'LARGE and FLOAT'SMALL could be used for the standard type FLOAT. They give, respectively, the number of digits' accuracy, the biggest number (in magnitude) that can be safely stored and the smallest number (in magnitude), other than zero, that can be safely stored. Corresponding attributes also exist for other floating point types. If, for example, we want to find the biggest number of the type TEMPERATURE that can safely be stored, we can use the attribute TEMPERATURE'LARGE. The attribute DIGITS has type *universal_integer* and the attributes LARGE and SMALL have type *universal_real*. For example, a statement is shown here that writes out the value of the variable MAX_PROB with as many digits' accuracy as is suitable:

PUT(MAX_PROB, FORE => 1,
       AFT => ERROR_PROBABILITY'DIGITS, EXP => 0);

Attributes for floating point types

- T'DIGITS – gives the number of significant figures for floating point type T.
- T'SMALL – gives the smallest number (in magnitude), other than zero, that can be stored as floating point type T.
- T'LARGE – gives the largest number (in magnitude) that can be stored as floating point type T.

☐

5.4 Enumeration types

There are many phenomena in the real world that are described in words rather than numbers, for example, the days of the week. The second day of the week is usually called Tuesday rather than day number 2. In the same way, the suits in a pack of cards are not numbered but have names: hearts, clubs, diamonds and spades. To describe the state of something it is also common to use different terms rather than numbers, such as the state of an elevator being 'going up', 'going down' or 'stationary'. If phenomena like these are to be represented in a program, numeric types will not suffice. Instead, there is the opportunity to use **enumeration types**. When an enumeration type is declared, the possible values are simply enumerated or listed.

Let us look at the three examples already mentioned, the days of the week, the suits in a pack of cards and the state of an elevator. We can make the following type declarations:

```
type DAY_OF_THE_WEEK is (MONDAY, TUESDAY, WEDNESDAY,
                         THURSDAY, FRIDAY, SATURDAY,
                         SUNDAY);
type SUIT is (CLUBS, DIAMONDS, HEARTS, SPADES);
type ELEVATOR_STATUS_TYPE is (GOING_UP, GOING_DOWN,
                              STATIONARY);
```

We can then declare variables of these types:

```
TODAY, TOMORROW : DAY_OF_THE_WEEK;
CURRENT_TRUMP_SUIT, SUIT_PLAYED : SUIT;
ELEVATOR_1_STATUS : ELEVATOR_STATUS_TYPE;
```

The variable CURRENT_TRUMP_SUIT can then take any of the values CLUBS, DIAMONDS, HEARTS or SPADES, but no other value. Although values are usually considered numeric, CLUBS must also be thought of as a *value* of type SUIT in the same way as 257 is a value of type INTEGER. Here are a few examples of permitted statements:

```
SUIT_PLAYED := DIAMONDS;
CURRENT_TRUMP_SUIT := SUIT_PLAYED;
if ELEVATOR_1_STATUS = STATIONARY then
  PUT_LINE("Elevator is free");
end if;
```

It is also possible to initialize variables of enumeration types when they are declared, as in:

ELEVATOR_1_STATUS : ELEVATOR_STATUS_TYPE := STATIONARY;

Of course, to mix types is not allowed. The following are incorrect:

```
CURRENT_TRUMP_SUIT := FRIDAY;          -- Error!
TODAY := 2;                            -- Error!
if CURRENT_TRUMP_SUIT = TOMORROW then  -- Error!
```

The values that are listed when an enumeration type is declared can, as in the example above, be identifiers like TUESDAY, but it is also possible to use character literals as in the following example:

```
type HEX_DIGITS is ('0', '1', '2', '3', '4', '5', '6', '7',
                    '8', '9', 'A', 'B', 'C', 'D', 'E', 'F');
```

Identifiers and character literals can be mixed in the same type declaration if necessary. This has been done in the declaration of the enumeration type CHARACTER in the package STANDARD.

Declaration of enumeration types

- **type** *typename* **is** (*value_1, value_2, ... value_N*);
  where *value_1, value_2,* etc. are either identifiers or character literals (can be mixed in the same declaration).
- The values in the type are ordered in such a way that *value_1 < value_2 < value_3* etc.

The values in an enumeration type are **ordered** so that the value listed first is least and the one that is listed last is greatest. The following logic expressions, therefore, have the value TRUE:

```
TUESDAY < SUNDAY
CLUBS <= HEARTS
STATIONARY > GOING_UP
```

This can be used in constructs such as:

```
if TODAY >= SATURDAY then
   PUT_LINE("Free day");
end if;

if ELEVATOR_1_STATUS in GOING_UP .. GOING_DOWN then
   PUT_LINE("Elevator in motion");
end if;
```

There are some useful attributes for enumeration types. Exactly as for integer types, FIRST and LAST can be used to find out the first and last values. For example, DAY_OF_THE_WEEK'FIRST gives the value MONDAY, and SUIT'LAST gives the value SPADES. The attributes PRED and SUCC can be used to get the predecessor and successor, respectively, of a particular value in an enumeration type:

```
DAY_OF_THE_WEEK'PRED(FRIDAY) -- gives the value THURSDAY
SUIT'SUCC(HEARTS)              -- gives the value SPADES
TOMORROW := DAY_OF_THE_WEEK'SUCC(TODAY);
```

In the last example, we saw that the quantity in brackets does not have to be a constant. The first value in an enumeration type (for example, MONDAY) has no predecessor and the last value (for example, SPADES) has no successor. If an attempt is made to compute such values, a run-time error will occur when the program is executed.

Attributes for enumeration types

- T'FIRST – gives the first value for enumeration type T.
- T'LAST – gives the last value for enumeration type T.
- T'PRED(*value_i*) – gives the predecessor for *value_i* in type T. The parameter *value_i* must be a permitted value for type T and a run-time error occurs if it is the first value.
- T'SUCC(*value_i*) – gives the successor to *value_i* in type T. The parameter *value_i* must be a permitted value for type T and a run-time error occurs if it is the last value.

It is common to use the **case** statement in conjunction with enumeration types, often leading to readable programs as in the following example:

```
case TODAY is
  when MONDAY .. THURSDAY =>
    PUT("Only work");
  when FRIDAY =>
    PUT("Out on the town tonight");
  when SATURDAY .. SUNDAY =>
    PUT("Free day");
end case;
```

No **others** alternative is needed here because all the possible values are listed.

It is also very useful to use enumeration types to control the iteration in a **loop** statement with **for**. The total number of hours worked in a week is calculated in the following program. When the program is run, the operator gives for each day of the week how many hours have been worked.

```
with TEXT_IO, BASIC_NUM_IO;
use  TEXT_IO, BASIC_NUM_IO;
procedure COMPUTE_HOURS_WORKED is
  type DAY_OF_THE_WEEK is (MONDAY, TUESDAY,
                           WEDNESDAY, THURSDAY,
                           FRIDAY, SATURDAY, SUNDAY);
  TOTAL_HOURS      : INTEGER := 0;
  NUMBER_OF_HOURS : INTEGER;
begin
  PUT_LINE("Enter hours worked on each day of the week");
  for DAY in MONDAY .. SUNDAY loop
    GET(NUMBER_OF_HOURS);
    TOTAL_HOURS := TOTAL_HOURS + NUMBER_OF_HOURS;
  end loop;
  PUT("The total number of hours worked is: ");
  PUT(TOTAL_HOURS, WIDTH => 1);
end COMPUTE_HOURS_WORKED;
```

The loop parameter here automatically takes the type DAY_OF_THE_WEEK. The first time through the loop, DAY will have the value MONDAY, the second time it will have TUESDAY, and so on, until, on the final time through, DAY has the value SUNDAY.

In general, using enumeration types increases the clarity of programs. Therefore one should try to use enumeration types and avoid 'coding' information in programs, such as representing a Wednesday by the number 3.

Using enumeration types

- Makes programs clear.
- Avoids 'coding' information with numbers.
- Combines well with **case** statements.

5.5   The tools for input and output

In our programs we have used the resources in the standardized package
TEXT_IO to access read and write values of the types STRING and
CHARACTER. To read and write values of the types INTEGER and FLOAT
we have so far used a 'home-made' package BASIC_NUM_IO that is not
standardized. We have used it to simplify input and output in the early
stages of learning Ada. If we have numeric types other than INTEGER and
FLOAT, the package BASIC_NUM_IO will not do. We shall, therefore, look
at how to use a general, standardized method to create the resources
needed for reading and writing any sort of numeric type. We shall also
look at how to read and write values of enumeration types.

Contained in TEXT_IO as well as the procedures for reading and
writing text, there are some templates that can be used to create new
input/output packages. One template is called INTEGER_IO, and with its
help, new packages containing procedures for reading and writing integer
types can be created. The way this is used in a program is illustrated by
the following example, where a package is created enabling values of the
type INTEGER to be read and written without using BASIC_NUM_IO.

```
with TEXT_IO;
use  TEXT_IO;
procedure INOUT_DEMO_1 is
   package INTEGER_INOUT is new INTEGER_IO(INTEGER);
   use INTEGER_INOUT;

   N : INTEGER;
begin
   GET(N);
   PUT(N);
   NEW_LINE;
end INOUT_DEMO_1;
```

The first **with** statement gives access to the package TEXT_IO and all its
resources. The first **use** statement makes it easy to refer to the contents of
the package TEXT_IO. For example, we can write NEW_LINE, avoiding

writing the longer form TEXT_IO.NEW_LINE as we would have to if the **use** statement were not there.

Within the procedure we use the template INTEGER_IO (which is in the package TEXT_IO) to create a new package that we name INTEGER_INOUT. Since we want our package to contain the resources to enable values of the type INTEGER to be read and written, we write this type name in brackets after the template's name. (The template INTEGER_IO has all that is needed for a complete package to be created; the only thing missing is the name of the type and we must therefore state this).

The second **use** statement makes it easy for us to refer to the routines in the new package INTEGER_INOUT. For example, we can write PUT instead of INTEGER_INOUT.PUT.

Input and output of integer types

- The following must be placed among the program's declarations:

    package *package_name* **is new** INTEGER_IO(T);
    use *package_name*;

  where T is the name of an integer type.
- The procedures PUT and GET can then be used.

If we also want to be able to read and write values of the integer type LINE_NUMBER, we can create another package of routines:

```
with TEXT_IO;
use  TEXT_IO;
procedure INOUT_DEMO_2 is
   type LINE_NUMBER is range 1 .. 72;
   package LINE_NO_INOUT is new INTEGER_IO(LINE_NUMBER);
   package INTEGER_INOUT is new INTEGER_IO(INTEGER);
   use INTEGER_INOUT, LINE_NO_INOUT;

   N    : INTEGER;
   LINE : LINE_NUMBER;
begin
   GET(N);
   PUT(N);
   NEW_LINE;
   GET(LINE);
   PUT(LINE);
end INOUT_DEMO_2;
```

The new package is called LINE_NO_INOUT and is created in the same way as the package INTEGER_INOUT. Both of these packages thus contain exactly the same resources for their respective types. The procedures GET and PUT will be found in two versions, one for the type INTEGER and one for the type LINE_NUMBER.

The template FLOAT_IO in the package TEXT_IO can be used in the same way to create new packages for input and output of floating point values. If we want to be able to read and write values of type FLOAT without using the package BASIC_NUM_IO, we can write in our program:

```
package FLOAT_INOUT is new FLOAT_IO(FLOAT);
use FLOAT_INOUT;
```

Then we get direct access to procedures, including PUT and GET, in versions which can handle values of the type FLOAT.

Input and output packages for other floating point types can be created in an analogous way. If we want to be able to read and write values of the type TEMPERATURE directly, we can add the following lines to a program:

```
type TEMPERATURE is digits 4;
package TEMPERATURE_INOUT is new FLOAT_IO(TEMPERATURE);
use TEMPERATURE_INOUT;
```

Input and output of floating point types

- The following must be placed among the program's declarations:

  ```
  package package_name is new FLOAT_IO(T);
  use package_name;
  ```

  where T is the name of a floating point type.
- The procedures PUT and GET can then be used.

As shown previously, it is good to use enumeration types because they make a program clearer to understand. But to be really useful, there has to be a simple way of reading and writing their values. In TEXT_IO there is a template ENUMERATION_IO that can be used to achieve this. The following program illustrates how a package of resources for reading and writing values of the type SUIT is created.

```
with TEXT_IO;
use  TEXT_IO;
procedure INOUT_DEMO_3 is
   type SUIT is (CLUBS, DIAMONDS, HEARTS, SPADES);
   package SUIT_INOUT is new ENUMERATION_IO(SUIT);
   use SUIT_INOUT;
   TRUMP : SUIT;
begin
   GET(TRUMP);
   PUT(TRUMP);
end INOUT_DEMO_3;
```

The template ENUMERATION_IO is used to create a new package
SUIT_INOUT. Writing SUIT in brackets states that the new package will
contain resources tailored for the type SUIT. In the package there are new
versions of the procedures PUT and GET that can be used as in the
program above. The statement:

```
GET(TRUMP);
```

makes the program halt and wait for the operator to write a value of the
type SUIT at the terminal. The operator can then type one of the words
CLUBS, DIAMONDS, HEARTS or SPADES. (Both upper and lower case
letters are acceptable). Anything else is wrong and gives a run-time error.
   The statement:

```
PUT(TRUMP);
```

means that one of the words CLUBS, DIAMONDS, HEARTS or SPADES will
be displayed at the terminal, depending on the value of the variable
TRUMP.

■

It is possible for the programmer to control whether the output is in
upper or lower case letters. If lower case letters are wanted, the
statement:

```
SUIT_INOUT.DEFAULT_SETTING := LOWER_CASE;
```

can be inserted near the start of the program. If upper case letters are
wanted, then the statement:

```
SUIT_INOUT.DEFAULT_SETTING := UPPER_CASE;
```

should be inserted instead. If no such statement is made, output will be in upper case letters.

□

Input and output of enumeration types

- The following must be placed among the program's declarations:

    package *package_name* **is new**
            ENUMERATION_IO(T);
    use *package_name*;

    where T is the name of an enumeration type.

- The procedures GET and PUT can then be used to write and read values of type T.

The standard type BOOLEAN is an enumeration type and thus values of type BOOLEAN can be read in and written if a new package is declared:

    package BOOLEAN_INOUT **is new** ENUMERATION_IO(BOOLEAN);
    use BOOLEAN_INOUT;

This makes it possible to use PUT and GET as in the following examples:

    GET(ACTIVE);   -- ACTIVE is a variable of type BOOLEAN
    PUT(ACTIVE);
    PUT(A > B);

In the first example, the operator must type one of the words TRUE or FALSE at the terminal, while in the other two examples either TRUE or FALSE is displayed at the terminal.

This section ends by studying a program that reads in a date in the form:

    28 FEBRUARY 1987

and computes the number of the day in the year, the day number. The program will take leap years into account. A year is a leap year if it is exactly divisible by four but not by 100, or if it is exactly divisible by 400.

We introduce three types of our own into the program. We let the numbers of the days have type DAY_NUMBER_TYPE, years have type YEAR_TYPE, and the months have the type MONTH_TYPE. We will confine our interest to the years between 2000 BC and 2100 AD. To be able to read and write values of these types, we shall create new input and output packages using the templates in TEXT_IO. The program looks like this:

```
with TEXT_IO;
use  TEXT_IO;
procedure COMPUTE_DAY_NUMBER is
   type YEAR_TYPE is range −2000 .. 2100;
   type MONTH_TYPE is (JANUARY, FEBRUARY, MARCH,
                       APRIL, MAY, JUNE, JULY,
                       AUGUST, SEPTEMBER, OCTOBER,
                       NOVEMBER, DECEMBER);
   type DAY_NUMBER_TYPE is range 1 .. 366;
   package YEAR_INOUT is new INTEGER_IO(YEAR_TYPE);
   package MONTH_INOUT is new ENUMERATION_IO(MONTH_TYPE);
   package DAY_NUMBER_INOUT is new
                    INTEGER_IO(DAY_NUMBER_TYPE);
   use YEAR_INOUT, MONTH_INOUT, DAY_NUMBER_INOUT;

   YEAR         : YEAR_TYPE;
   MONTH        : MONTH_TYPE;
   DAY, DAY_NO : DAY_NUMBER_TYPE;
begin
   PUT_LINE("Enter date in form: day month year,");
   PUT_LINE("          e.g., 28 FEBRUARY 1987");
   GET(DAY); GET(MONTH); GET(YEAR);

   case MONTH is
     when JANUARY   => DAY_NO := DAY;
     when FEBRUARY  => DAY_NO := 31  + DAY;
     when MARCH     => DAY_NO := 59  + DAY;
     when APRIL     => DAY_NO := 90  + DAY;
     when MAY       => DAY_NO := 121 + DAY;
     when JUNE      => DAY_NO := 151 + DAY;
     when JULY      => DAY_NO := 182 + DAY;
     when AUGUST    => DAY_NO := 212 + DAY;
     when SEPTEMBER => DAY_NO := 242 + DAY;
     when OCTOBER   => DAY_NO := 273 + DAY;
     when NOVEMBER  => DAY_NO := 303 + DAY;
     when DECEMBER  => DAY_NO := 334 + DAY;
   end case;
   if (YEAR mod 4 = 0 and YEAR mod 100 /= 0)
      or YEAR mod 400 = 0 then
      -- leap year
      if MONTH >= MARCH then
        DAY_NO := DAY_NO + 1;
```

```
      end if;
    end if;

    PUT("The day's number in the year is ");
    PUT(DAY_NO, WIDTH => 1);
  end COMPUTE_DAY_NUMBER;
```

The program should contain a check that DAY is not greater than the number of days in MONTH, but to simplify the program we shall ignore this potential problem. However, there is no risk of the program accepting incorrect years or months. If incorrect data is typed in for these, a run-time error will result.

Ada's input/output mechanism may at first appear a little complicated. This is only because it is so general and works for all possible numeric types and enumeration types. There can be much to write in a program if you are working with several types. Sometimes it is tempting to avoid declaring your own types and adhere to the standard types INTEGER and FLOAT. Then access is only needed to the input/output packages for these two types. In spite of this, an attempt should still be made to use Ada's facilities for working with different types. It increases the clarity and reliability of the program. Ada's facilities are better equipped to represent the phenomena required, and these are automatically checked so that variables contain only permitted values. Furthermore, the program is made more easily transferable from one implementation of Ada to another.

Using your own types

- Clearer and more reliable programs.
- Better representation of reality.
- Automatic checks on values.
- Easier to transfer programs.

5.6 Subtypes

When a real-world phenomenon is described, it is sometimes useful to introduce a concept that denotes a subset of a more general concept. For example, 'workday' denotes a subset of the concept 'days of the week', and 'positive integers' is a subset of the concept 'integers'. In Ada, such subsets of concepts can be represented by using **subtypes**. Declarations of subtypes appear much like the ordinary type declarations and are placed in the same part of the program. A declaration of a subtype begins with the reserved word **subtype**.

For example, suppose we have already declared the enumeration type DAY_OF_THE_WEEK:

type DAY_OF_THE_WEEK **is** (MONDAY, TUESDAY, WEDNESDAY,
    THURSDAY, FRIDAY,
    SATURDAY, SUNDAY);

Now we can declare a subtype of DAY_OF_THE_WEEK that we shall call WORKDAY:

subtype WORKDAY **is** DAY_OF_THE_WEEK **range** MONDAY .. FRIDAY;

In the declaration of the subtype we state that the base type is DAY_OF_THE_WEEK and that the permitted values for the new subtype should lie in the interval MONDAY to FRIDAY. Now it is possible to declare objects of either the type DAY_OF_THE_WEEK or the subtype WORKDAY:

TODAY   : DAY_OF_THE_WEEK;
NEXT_WORKDAY : WORKDAY;

The declaration of a subtype does *not* mean that a new type has been created. It simply means that a name has been introduced for a subset of a base type. In our example we can express it thus: the variables TODAY and NEXT_WORKDAY belong to the same type, namely DAY_OF_THE_WEEK, but NEXT_WORKDAY is specified further in that it belongs to the subtype WORKDAY. This means that the following assignment is permitted:

TODAY := NEXT_WORKDAY;

Both variables are simply of the same type. The assignment may also be turned round:

NEXT_WORKDAY := TODAY;

However, this assignment could lead to a run-time error when the program is executed; this would happen if TODAY contained some value outside the interval MONDAY .. FRIDAY (that is, either of the values SATURDAY or SUNDAY).

The good thing about using subtypes, then, is that they provide extra support in finding errors in the logic of a program. Furthermore, they allow a better representation of the facts, which again increases the clarity of a program.

The limits stated in a declaration do not need to be static. Arbitrary expressions may be used:

```
START : INTEGER := ... ;
N     : INTEGER := ... ;
type NUMBER_TYPE is range 1 .. 1000;
subtype CERTAIN_NUMBERS is NUMBER_TYPE
                    range START .. START + N − 1;
```

Here we assume the variables START and N are initialized to some values. If the values are such that one of the limits lies outside the interval 1 to 1000, or if the second limit is lower than the first, we shall get a run-time error.

In the package STANDARD two subtypes of the type INTEGER are declared:

```
subtype NATURAL is INTEGER range 0 .. INTEGER'LAST;
subtype POSITIVE is INTEGER range 1 .. INTEGER'LAST;
```

These represent the mathematical concepts of 'natural numbers' and 'positive integers' and it is appropriate to use them instead of INTEGER for work with general integral values that are known to be $\geqslant 0$ or $\geqslant 1$, respectively.

If we have the following object declarations:

```
N : NATURAL;
P : POSITIVE;
I : INTEGER;
```

then the following statements are allowed because all the variables actually have the same type, INTEGER:

```
P := N + P;
I := P − N;
```

Types other than enumeration and integer types may have subtypes. For example, subtypes of floating point types can be constructed:

```
type MEASUREMENT is digits 10;
subtype PRESSURE is MEASUREMENT range 0.0 .. 3.0;
```

If a numeric object has to be described, then either a completely new type can be declared, as we did earlier, or a subtype of a numeric type already in existence, such as FLOAT or INTEGER, can be used. When is one better than the other? The choice of method should be guided by the actual objects to be represented. To represent things that have nothing to do with one another, use completely new types and not subtypes. Then, of course, it is possible to check that they are not mixed by mistake in the program. Otherwise, subtypes can be used. This can be particularly practical when carrying out many computations with closely related objects, because then it is not necessary to make explicit type conversions throughout the computations.

Declaring subtypes

subtype U **is** T **range** *min_value .. max_value*;

where U is the name of the subtype and T is the name of a type. T can be a numeric type or an enumeration type. The smallest and greatest possible values for objects of subtype U are given by *min_value* and *max_value*.

- U becomes a subtype of T. No new type is created.
- Objects of subtype U will have type T.

Using subtypes

- When closely related objects are in use and many computations are to be made using them.
- Good representation of reality.
- Provide help with tracing errors of logic.
- For real objects that are not closely related, completely new types should be used in preference to subtypes.

Let us look at a program where it is natural to use subtypes. The program asks the user to choose two of the colours red, yellow and blue, and then it writes out the name of the colour obtained by mixing them. A type COLOUR is introduced that describes all possible colours and mixtures. We then let the three primary colours make up a subtype of COLOUR, called PRIMARY_COLOUR.

```
with TEXT_IO;
use  TEXT_IO;
procedure MIX_COLOURS is
  type COLOUR is  (RED, YELLOW, BLUE,
                        ORANGE, GREEN, PURPLE);
  subtype PRIMARY_COLOUR is COLOUR range RED .. BLUE;
  package COLOUR_INOUT is new ENUMERATION_IO(COLOUR);
  use COLOUR_INOUT;

  COLOUR1, COLOUR2 : PRIMARY_COLOUR;
  COLOUR_MIX        : COLOUR;

begin
  PUT_LINE("Welcome to the colour mixing program!");
  PUT_LINE("The primary colours are RED, YELLOW and BLUE");
  PUT_LINE("The colour mixes are ORANGE, GREEN and PURPLE");
  PUT_LINE("Terminate the run with CTRL-D.");

  loop
    NEW_LINE;      -- extra blank line
    PUT_LINE("Enter two of the primary colours");
    exit when END_OF_FILE;
    GET(COLOUR1); GET(COLOUR2);

    if (COLOUR1 = RED and COLOUR2 = YELLOW) or
       (COLOUR2 = RED and COLOUR1 = YELLOW) then
       COLOUR_MIX := ORANGE;
    elsif (COLOUR1 = YELLOW and COLOUR2 = BLUE) or
          (COLOUR2 = YELLOW and COLOUR1 = BLUE) then
       COLOUR_MIX := GREEN;
    elsif (COLOUR1 = RED and COLOUR2 = BLUE) or
          (COLOUR2 = RED and COLOUR1 = BLUE) then
       COLOUR_MIX := PURPLE;
    else -- same colours
       COLOUR_MIX := COLOUR1;
    end if;

    PUT("The colour mixture will be ");
    PUT(COLOUR_MIX); NEW_LINE;
  end loop;
end MIX_COLOURS;
```

The two input colours are of the subtype PRIMARY_COLOUR, thus
automatically checking that no values other than the permitted ones,
RED, YELLOW and BLUE, are input. We can use the same input/output
package, COLOUR_INOUT, for reading and writing all the colours, both
primary colours and mixtures, because they all belong to the same type,
COLOUR.

The program is designed so that it repeatedly reads in the primary
colours and displays the name of the mixture, until the user wants to stop.

The termination variant with END_OF_FILE and an **exit** statement is used in the program, as described in Section 4.8. Below is shown the output from the program:

```
Welcome to the colour mixing program!
The primary colours are RED, YELLOW and BLUE
The colour mixes are ORANGE, GREEN and PURPLE
Terminate the run with CTRL-D.

Enter two of the primary colours
yellow blue
The colour mix will be GREEN

Enter two of the primary colours
blue red
The colour mix will be PURPLE

Enter two of the primary colours
yellow yellow
The colour mix will be YELLOW

Enter two of the primary colours
Now the user types CTRL-D at the terminal
```

5.7 Array types

The scalar types we have declared so far have been simple types where each object of the type assumes only one single value. Now we shall study **array types**. In an array type, an object consists of a numbered collection of similar components. It can also be said that an object of an array type is a kind of table in which each element has a particular number associated with it.

5.7.1 Constrained array types

We shall start by looking at **constrained array types**. When a constrained array type is declared, both the numbering of the components and the types of the individual components must be specified. Let us look at an example:

type SERIES_OF_MEASUREMENTS **is array** (1 .. 10) **of** FLOAT;

The idea is that the type SERIES_OF_MEASUREMENTS should represent a series of 10 measurements of some sort, in which each single measurement is represented by a real number. The reserved word **array** states that the declaration involves an array type. After this word, the

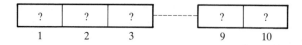

Figure 5.1

numbering of the components is specified. In this example, they will be numbered using the integers 1 to 10, inclusive. Finally, the type of the individual components is given, here FLOAT because each measurement consists of a real number. We can declare variables of this new type:

SERIES_A, SERIES_B : SERIES_OF_MEASUREMENTS;

Figure 5.1 illustrates the variable SERIES_A. The variable can be likened to 10 'compartments', each holding a value of the type FLOAT. The first compartment is numbered 1, the second is 2 and so on. The contents of the compartments are not yet defined; the value of a variable is normally undefined after declaration unless deliberately initialized. (It is possible to initialize array variables at the same time as they are declared in exactly the same way as simple variables. We will return to this soon).

To enable access to a particular component of an array, **indexing** is used; we have already seen this in operation in connection with the type STRING. For example, to give the second component of the variable SERIES_A the value 1.5, we can write:

SERIES_A(2) := 1.5;

Then we get the SERIES_A shown in Figure 5.2. A component that is selected by indexing can be used in the same way as a normal scalar variable, as in the expression:

SERIES_B(1) := 2.0 * SERIES_A(7);

When the type SERIES_OF_MEASUREMENTS was declared, the interval:

(1 .. 10)

was specified as the way in which the individual components should be numbered. What this really means is that the component numbers should have type INTEGER and lie in the interval 1 to 10. When an individual component is selected by indexing, the index expression in the brackets can be a normal expression. It does not need to be a constant value as in the example above. However, the expression must have the same type as the numbers of the components of the array and its value must lie in the specified interval. Thus for the variables SERIES_A and SERIES_B, index

Figure 5.2

expressions must have the type INTEGER and be in the interval 1 to 10.

We shall look at a simple example of a program that uses an array. The program will read from the terminal 10 real numbers that make up a series of measurements. Then it will calculate the mean value of the measurements and display it. Finally, the program will write out all the measurements that are larger than the calculated mean. We shall use the type SERIES_OF_MEASUREMENTS, but in the declaration we have used a constant SERIES_LENGTH instead of writing the literal 10. This constant is also used in the program itself, so the program can be changed easily if the size of the series should change. It is a good rule to use constants in this way. The program is:

```
with TEXT_IO, BASIC_NUM_IO;
use  TEXT_IO, BASIC_NUM_IO;
procedure INVESTIGATE_MEASUREMENTS is
    SERIES_LENGTH : constant := 10;
    type SERIES_OF_MEASUREMENTS is array
                 (1 .. SERIES_LENGTH) of FLOAT;

    SERIES : SERIES_OF_MEASUREMENTS;
    SUM    : FLOAT := 0.0;
    MEAN   : FLOAT;

begin
    PUT_LINE("Enter the measurements");
    for I in 1 .. SERIES_LENGTH loop
      GET(SERIES(I));
      SUM := SUM + SERIES(I);
    end loop;

    MEAN := SUM / FLOAT(SERIES_LENGTH);
    PUT("The mean is "); PUT(MEAN); NEW_LINE;

    PUT_LINE("Measurements greater than the mean: ");
    for I in 1 .. SERIES_LENGTH loop
      if SERIES(I) > MEAN then
        PUT("Measurement no. ");
        PUT(I, WIDTH => 2);
        PUT(" is ");
        PUT(SERIES(I)); NEW_LINE;
      end if;
    end loop;
end INVESTIGATE_MEASUREMENTS;
```

Enter the measurements
4.3 6.5 3.8 3.9 5.2 5.0 3.9 4.4 6.1 5.5
The mean is 4.86000000E+00
Measurements greater than the mean:
Measurement no. 2 is 6.50000000E+00
Measurement no. 5 is 5.20000000E+00
Measurement no. 6 is 5.00000000E+00
Measurement no. 9 is 6.10000000E+00
Measurement no. 10 is 5.50000000E+00

Figure 5.3

It is very common to use **loop** statements with **for** when arrays are involved. In the first **loop** statement we make the loop parameter run from 1 to 10, that is, through all the components of the array SERIES. Each time, one measurement is read and stored in one of the components of the array SERIES. The statement:

    GET(SERIES(I));

causes one measurement to be stored in the component numbered I. Thus, the first time round a value is read to component 1, the second time to component 2, and so on.

While measurements are being read in, the program also calculates the sum of all the components. The mean is obtained by dividing this sum by the length of the series. The constant SERIES_LENGTH has type *universal_integer* and must therefore be converted to type FLOAT in the calculation.

The second **loop** statement runs, again, through all the components in the array SERIES. Each component now holds the result of one measurement. If a measurement is larger than the mean, the number of the measurement and the measurement itself are displayed at the terminal. Figure 5.3 shows the output for one run of this program.

There is much freedom in specifying how the individual components should be indexed when an array type is declared. They do not have to be numbered with integers starting from 1, as we did when we declared the type SERIES_OF_MEASUREMENTS. For example, we can choose to start the numbering with −100:

    type LIST **is array** (−100 .. 100) **of** INTEGER;

Here we have declared a list type in which each component is a whole number of type INTEGER. A list is indexed with integers −100 to 100, so that the first component is numbered −100, the second −99, and so on.

In fact, values of any discrete type (integer type or enumeration

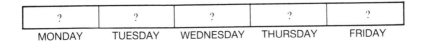

?	?	?	?	?
MONDAY	TUESDAY	WEDNESDAY	THURSDAY	FRIDAY

Figure 5.4

type) can be used for indexing. Here are a few examples where enumeration types are used:

> **type** WORKING_HOURS   **is array** (MONDAY .. FRIDAY) **of** FLOAT;
>
> **type** COLOUR_NUMBER   **is array** (RED .. PURPLE) **of** INTEGER;
>
> **type** NO_OF_DAYS   **is array** (JANUARY .. DECEMBER) **of** INTEGER;

We have assumed that the types DAY_OF_THE_WEEK, COLOUR and MONTH_TYPE have been declared as earlier in the chapter, namely:

> **type** DAY_OF_THE_WEEK **is** (MONDAY, TUESDAY, WEDNESDAY, THURSDAY, FRIDAY, SATURDAY, SUNDAY);
>
> **type** COLOUR **is** (RED, YELLOW, BLUE, ORANGE, GREEN, PURPLE);
>
> **type** MONTH_TYPE **is** (JANUARY, FEBRUARY, MARCH, APRIL, MAY, JUNE, JULY, AUGUST, SEPTEMBER, OCTOBER, NOVEMBER, DECEMBER);

If we declare the variables:

> MY_WORKING_HOURS : WORKING_HOURS;
>
> NO_OF_DAYS_1   : NO_OF_DAYS;

then the first components of the variable MY_WORKING_HOURS has the index 'number' MONDAY, and the first component in the variable NO_OF_DAYS_1 has the index 'number' JANUARY. To illustrate this, we can represent the variable MY_WORKING_HOURS as in Figure 5.4.

In the program, if a particular component is to be chosen by using indexing, then the enumeration values are used as 'numbers':

> MY_WORKING_HOURS(WEDNESDAY) := 8.5;
>
> GET(MY_WORKING_HOURS(FRIDAY));
>
> NO_OF_DAYS_1(MARCH) := 31;
>
> **if** NO_OF_DAYS_1(FEBRUARY) = 29 **then**
>   PUT("Leap year");
> **end if**;

> **Indexing in arrays**
>
> A(N)
>
> where N is an expression of the same type as the index type of A.
>
> N's value must lie within the index constraints of A.

The type of the index expressions and the constraints on their values depend on the index specification in the declaration. To make the type of the index obvious, it is recommended that the following alternative form of array declaration is used.

```
type SERIES_OF_MEASUREMENTS is array
                    (INTEGER range 1 ..10) of FLOAT;
type WORKING_HOURS is array
                    (DAY_OF_THE_WEEK range MONDAY .. FRIDAY)
          of FLOAT;
type LETTER_COUNT is array (CHARACTER range 'a' .. 'z')
                                    of INTEGER;
type COLOUR_NUMBER is array (COLOUR range RED .. PURPLE)
                    of INTEGER;
```

In this alternative, the type of the index is stated in the brackets as well as the interval to be used. In the third example we have used CHARACTER as index type, CHARACTER being an enumeration type which can therefore also be used. The first element in an object of type LETTER_COUNTS is 'numbered' 'a' and the last element is 'numbered' 'z'.

The range expression in the brackets may be left out, meaning that all the values of the given type should be used as index values. The declaration of COLOUR_NUMBER and NO_OF_DAYS can thus be written as follows:

```
type COLOUR_NUMBER is array (COLOUR) of INTEGER;
type NO_OF_DAYS      is array (MONTH_TYPE) of INTEGER;
```

It is often appropriate to introduce a new type or subtype for the index using a special declaration. This often makes the program clearer and, in addition, it is then possible to declare variables of the index type. These variables can then be used for indexing purposes. For example:

```
type LINE_NUMBER        is range 1 .. 72;
type LINE_TABLE         is array (LINE_NUMBER) of INTEGER;
subtype LC_LETTER       is CHARACTER range 'a' .. 'z';
type LC_LETTER_COUNT is array (LC_LETTER) of INTEGER;
```

Ordinary expressions may be used for stating the index constraints in a declaration of an array type; it is not necessary to use constant values as in the examples so far. An expression that specifies a constraint on an index may thus contain variables whose values are unknown until the program is run. The size of the array, therefore, does not need to be known when the program is compiled; this applies irrespective of the form chosen for stating the constraints:

```
type TABLE is array (N .. 2 * N) of FLOAT;
type VECTOR is array (INTEGER range 1 .. N) of FLOAT;
subtype LIST_INDEX is INTEGER range 100 .. 100 + N;
type LIST is array (LIST_INDEX) of CHARACTER;
```

N is assumed to be an integer variable. If the first index expression takes a value which is greater than the second, the declaration is of an array with no components. If such an object is declared, it is called an **empty array**.

Declaring constrained array types

> **type** T **is array** (*index_definition*)
> **of** *component_type*;

where T is the name of the constrained array type and *component_type* is any (constrained) type.

- *Index_definition* can have any of the following forms:

  > (*first_index* .. *last_index*)
  > (*index_type* **range** *first_index* .. *last_index*)
  > (*index_type*)

- *First_index* and *last_index* are expressions (not necessarily constants) of an integer type or an enumeration type.
- *Index_type* should be an integer type or an enumeration type, or a subtype of such a type.

5.7.2   Array aggregates

It has been shown that values can be assigned to the individual components of an array by indexing. If values are to be given to several components in one array, there is a more convenient method than assigning values component by component, and that is by making use of **array aggregates**. Then the values of all components are given at once. A few examples will explain what this means. The following statement means that the first, second and third components of array SERIES_A (declared earlier) are assigned the value 1.0, the fourth is assigned the value 0.5 and the rest of the elements in the array (that is, components 5 to 10) are assigned the value 0.0.

```
SERIES_A := (1.0, 1.0, 1.0, 0.5, 0.0,
             0.0, 0.0, 0.0, 0.0, 0.0);
```

When there is a large array where several components are to be given the same value the reserved word **others** can be used. The statement above can be written:

```
SERIES_A := (1.0, 1.0, 1.0, 0.5, others => 0.0);
```

It is very common to set all the components of an array to zero. Then we write:

```
SERIES_B := (others => 0.0);
```

Using aggregates, array variables can be initialized when they are declared. The variable DAYS_IN_MONTH can, for example, be declared in the following way:

```
DAYS_IN_MONTH : NO_OF_DAYS := (31, 28, 31, 30, 31, 30,
                               31, 31, 30, 31, 30, 31);
```

There is an alternative form of aggregate that has some similarities with the **case** statement. One example is:

```
SERIES_A := SERIES_OF_MEASUREMENTS'(1 .. 3 => 1.0,
                                    4 => 0.5,
                                    others => 0.0);
```

Before the apostrophe the type of the aggregate is given. In some cases when the reserved word **others** is used it is difficult for the compiler to decide the length of the aggregate. In those cases a **qualified expression** including the type name must be given, as in this example. Another example of the alternative form of an aggregate is:

DAYS_IN_MONTH : NO_OF_DAYS :=
    NO_OF_DAYS'(APRIL | JUNE | SEPTEMBER | NOVEMBER => 30,
        FEBRUARY => 28, **others** => 31);

In an aggregate there must be exactly one value for each component. This is most easily arranged using an **others** alternative. If **others** is used it must come last.

Array aggregates

- A list where the values of all the components of an array are stated at the same time.
- Can be used, for example, in assignments and comparisons.
- Alternative forms:

    (value_1, value_2, ..., value_N)
    (index_i => value_i, index_j => value_j, ...)
    (index_k | index_m => value, ...)
    (index_a .. index_b => value, ...)
    *(... **others** => value)*

Value can be a general expression.

In the following example program, all the components of an array are set to zero when the array is declared. The program's task is to read a text from the terminal and count how many times each of the lower case letters 'a' to 'z' occurs in the text. To keep count of the different letters, an array COUNT is used whose components have the standardized subtype NATURAL, that is, they are integers ≥ 0. In the array COUNT there is a component for each of the lower case letters 'a' to 'z' and so the components of the array are 'numbered' with the lower case letters. COUNT has type COUNT_TABLE in the declaration of which the subtype LC_LETTER has been used as index type. LC_LETTER is a subtype of CHARACTER in which the only permitted values are the letters 'a' to 'z'.

In the program, one character at a time is read from the terminal to the variable CHAR. This continues until the user says that the text is finished by typing CTRL-D. If the character read is one of the lower case letters, the corresponding component in the array COUNT is increased by one. The program ends by printing the contents of the array COUNT.

```
with TEXT_IO, BASIC_NUM_IO;
use  TEXT_IO, BASIC_NUM_IO;
procedure LC_LETTER_FREQUENCY is
   subtype LC_LETTER is CHARACTER range 'a' .. 'z';
   type COUNT_TABLE is array (LC_LETTER) of NATURAL;

   COUNT : COUNT_TABLE := (others => 0);
   CHAR  : CHARACTER;
begin
   PUT_LINE("Enter the text; terminate with CTRL-D");
   while not END_OF_FILE loop
     GET(CHAR);
     if CHAR in 'a' .. 'z' then
       COUNT(CHAR) := COUNT(CHAR) + 1;
     end if;
   end loop;

   -- Write how many times each letter has occurred

   NEW_LINE;
   PUT_LINE("Letter       Frequency");
   NEW_LINE;
   for T in 'a' .. 'z' loop
     SET_COL(4); PUT(T); PUT(COUNT(T), WIDTH => 11);
     NEW_LINE;
   end loop;
end LC_LETTER_FREQUENCY;
```

The statement:

```
COUNT(CHAR) := COUNT(CHAR) + 1;
```

means that if the variable CHAR contains, for example, the letter 'g' the component with index 'number' 'g' is increased by one. Figure 5.5 illustrates the output from a run of the program.

5.7.3 Unconstrained array types

The array types we have studied so far have all been **constrained array types**. They are so-called because the index constraints (and hence the number of components) are specified in the type declaration. If we declare objects of such a constrained array type, they will all have the same index constraints and number of components. In certain situations it is undesirable to specify the constraints on the index numbers. If, for instance, a part of a program is to be written that will sort the elements of a list into order of magnitude, or one that will carry out mathematical operations on vectors, then it is desirable that it should work for all lists

Enter the text; terminate with CTRL-D
ada is a registered trademark of the us government
ada joint program office

Letter	Frequency
a	8
b	0
c	1
d	4
e	8
f	3
g	3
h	1
i	4
j	1
k	1
l	0
m	3
n	3
o	5
p	1
q	0
r	7
s	3
t	5
u	1
v	1
w	0
x	0
y	0
z	0

Figure 5.5

or vectors, irrespective of the number of elements in the list or the number of components in the vectors. To cope with such a situation Ada offers the possibility of declaring **unconstrained array types**. When an unconstrained array type is declared, the index type is specified but there is no need to state limits for the index. Instead, the symbol < > is used.

```
type VECTOR       is array (INTEGER range < >) of FLOAT;
type INDEX_TYPE   is range 1 .. 100;
type NUMBER_LIST  is array (INDEX_TYPE range < >) of INTEGER;
type CHAR_COUNT   is array (CHARACTER range < >) of INTEGER;
```

When an object of an unconstrained array type is declared, then the index constraints must be stated:

```
VECTOR_1            : VECTOR(−10 .. 10);
VECTOR_2            : VECTOR(1 .. N);        -- N is a variable
MY_LIST             : NUMBER_LIST(I .. 2 * I); -- expressions OK
YOUR_LIST           : NUMBER_LIST(90 .. 100);
UC_LETTER_COUNT : CHAR_COUNT('A' .. 'Z');
DIGIT_COUNT         : CHAR_COUNT('0' .. '9');
```

In these examples, the variables VECTOR_1 and VECTOR_2 have the same type but different index constraints.

It is also possible to declare subtypes of an unconstrained array type. Then the index constraints are stated in the subtype declaration:

```
subtype LITTLE_VECTOR is VECTOR(1 .. 3);
POINT : LITTLE_VECTOR;
```

Unconstrained array types

```
type T is array (index_type range <>)
                        of component_type;
```

where *index_type* is an integer type or an enumeration type.

The index constraints must be stated when an object of type T, or a subtype of T, is declared.

With unconstrained array types, as with constrained array types, it is possible to give the value of an entire array at once, by assignment or at initialization, using aggregates:

```
VECTOR_1 := (0.0, 0.0, 0.0, others => 1.0);
VECTOR_2 := (others => 0.0);
```

In fact, we have already used an unconstrained array type on several occasions − the standard type STRING that is defined in the package STANDARD:

```
type STRING is array (POSITIVE range < >) of CHARACTER;
```

The declarations of variables of type STRING that we have used, for
example:

    PRODUCT_CODE : STRING(1 .. 6);

are thus nothing more than declarations of variables of an unconstrained
array type. For the type STRING there is, as we have seen, a special short
way of writing an aggregate, namely by enclosing the values of the
components in quotation marks:

    PRODUCT_CODE := "xWy98k";

5.7.4 Assignment and comparison

When assigning values to an array, instead of an aggregate on the right-
hand side, it is possible to have another array of the same type and with
the same number of components as that on the left-hand side. (Two
arrays that belong to the same constrained array type always fulfil these
demands). We can, for example, make the assignments:

    SERIES_A   :=   SERIES_B;   -- constrained array types, always OK
    VECTOR_1   :=   VECTOR_2;   -- OK if same number of components

---

Array assignments

    A1 := A2;

where A1 and A2 have the same type and an equal
number of components.

It is not necessary for the components to have the
same numbering.

It is also possible to compare two entire arrays if they have the
same type. (They may even have different numbers of components if they
belong to the same unconstrained array type).

    if SERIES_A = SERIES_B **then**
    while SERIES_A /= SERIES_B **then**

Aggregates can also be used in comparisons:

    if SERIES_A = SERIES_OF_MEASUREMENTS'(**others** => 0.0) **then**

For making comparisons, the operators = and /= are defined for all array types. Two arrays are equal if they have the same number of components and all their corresponding components are equal. Otherwise, they are unequal. The bounds of the array do not have to be the same. If, for example, A has an index range 1 .. 5 and B an index range 0 .. 4, then A(1) and B(0) are corresponding components, as well as A(2) and B(1), etc. For array types where the individual components are of a discrete type (that is, integer type or enumeration type) the comparison operators <, >, <= and >= are also defined. It is thus possible to write:

if MY_LIST > YOUR_LIST **then**

In such a case the comparison occurs in the same way as it does for alphabetical order: if the first element in MY_LIST is greater than the first element of YOUR_LIST (element number 90) then MY_LIST is considered to be bigger and the Boolean expression above is true. If, however, the first element of MY_LIST is less than the first element of YOUR_LIST, then YOUR_LIST is the bigger and the expression is false. If the two first elements are equal, then the comparison continues to the two second elements. If the arrays have the same number of elements and all corresponding elements turn out to be equal, then the two arrays are equal and the Boolean expression above is false. If the arrays have different numbers of components and all the elements in the shorter array are the same as the corresponding elements in the longer array, then the shorter one is determined to be the lesser of the two.

Comparing arrays

- The operators = and /= exist for all arrays which have the same type (even if the numbers of components are not the same).

- The operators <, <=, > and >= also exist if the components are of an integer type or an enumeration type. Comparison is made on the same principles as sorting into alphabetical order.

In assignments and comparisons, **slices** can be used, in the same way as they were earlier for the type STRING.

```
VECTOR_1 := VECTOR_2(N - 20 .. N); -- N is a variable
VECTOR_1(0 .. 5) := VECTOR_2(1 .. 6);
if VECTOR_1(-10 .. N - 11) = VECTOR_2 then
```

Slices of arrays

A(N1 .. N2)

where A is an array type. N1 and N2 are expressions whose type is the same as the index type for A.

- If N2 < N1, the result is an empty slice.
- Otherwise N1 and N2 must lie within the index constraints for A.
- The result has the same type as A.

5.7.5   Attributes

We have seen that when an array is declared there are many possible ways of indexing it. The index constraints do not even need to be known at compilation time, but they can be determined by expressions that are only evaluated when the program is run. It is sometimes impossible to use constant values in a program to refer to different values of an index, for example, to state the first and last index numbers for an array. Then some of the attributes that are defined for array types can be used. The most useful are FIRST, LAST, RANGE and LENGTH.

FIRST and LAST are used to find the first and last index numbers in an array. VECTOR_1'FIRST, for example, gives the first index value for the array VECTOR_1. FIRST and LAST can be used, for instance, to make a loop run through all the index values for an array:

> **for** I **in** VECTOR_1'FIRST .. VECTOR_1'LAST **loop**
>
>   ...
> **end loop**;

It is more elegant, maybe, to make use of the RANGE attribute instead, giving the index interval for the array. Using RANGE we can rewrite the above **loop** statement:

> **for** I **in** VECTOR_1'RANGE **loop**
>
>   ...
> **end loop**;

Here the loop parameter will run through all the index values for the array VECTOR_1.

The attribute LENGTH is used to find the number of components in an array:

```
PUT("Number of components in the vector: ");
PUT(VECTOR_1'LENGTH);
```

In front of the apostrophe can appear either a name of an array object (variable or constant) or a type name, but not the name of an unconstrained array type. Here are a few further examples:

```
NO_OF_DAYS'LAST        -- gives the value DECEMBER
NO_OF_DAYS_1'FIRST     -- gives the value JANUARY
NO_OF_DAYS_1'LENGTH    -- gives the value 12
NO_OF_DAYS'RANGE       -- gives JANUARY .. DECEMBER
```

Attributes for array types

T'FIRST   – gives first index value for array type T

T'LAST   – gives last index value for array type T

T'LENGTH – gives number of components in array type T

T'RANGE – gives the index interval for array type T

where T is the name of a constrained array type.

Instead of a type name, the name of an object of an array type can be used:

A'FIRST   – gives first index value for array A

A'LAST   – gives last index value for array A

A'LENGTH – gives number of components in array A

A'RANGE – gives the index interval for array A

It is a good habit to try and use these attributes instead of stating index limits as constant values in programs, for example, in **loop** statements. Programs then become much more general and can more easily be changed if the constraints on an array are changed.

5.7.6 Catenating arrays

■

Just as for text strings, the operator & can be used for **catenating** arrays. If the type VECTOR has been declared, as earlier, to be:

type VECTOR **is array** (INTEGER **range** < >) **of** FLOAT;

and we have the variables:

```
V2 : VECTOR(1 .. 2);
V3 : VECTOR(101 .. 103);
V5 : VECTOR(0 .. 4);
```

then we can join V2 and V3 together:

```
V5 := V2 & V3;
```

It is also possible to join a component onto an array as in the following examples:

```
V3 := 27.0 & V2;
V3 := V2 & 8.0;
```

☐

5.8 Searching and sorting

To be able to search for a piece of information in tables or lists is a very common requirement of a computer program. Arrays are naturally used in such programs. As an example of searching we shall study a program that produces the selling price of an article from a catalogue. As input, the user types in the article number at the terminal when the program is run. Assume that there are only seven different articles with the numbers and selling prices shown in Figure 5.6. The program should work like this: if the user types, for example, article number 123 at the terminal, then the program should write out the price £9.15. If the user gives an article number that is not in the table, the program should print out the message "Price details missing". We use two constant arrays in the program, ART_NUMBER_TABLE and ART_PRICE_TABLE,

Article number	Price
56	3.50
81	1.75
123	9.15
379	20.00
505	0.50
811	31.45
944	5.95

Figure 5.6

56	81	123	379	505	811	944
1	2	3	4	5	6	7

Figure 5.7

both with seven components. In ART_NUMBER_TABLE the seven article numbers are stored, one number to each component. The first component, ART_NUMBER_TABLE(1), thus holds the number 56, ART_NUMBER_TABLE(2) holds 81, and so on (see Figure 5.7).

If we want to make it easy we can let the components of array ART_NUMBER_TABLE have type INTEGER. If, however, we want to write a program that more closely represents reality, we should declare an integer type of our own, ARTICLE_NUMBER, and let the components have this type. We can assume that the article numbers lie between 1 and 999.

In the array ART_PRICE_TABLE are stored, in the same way, 3.50 in the first component, ART_PRICE_TABLE(1), 1.75 in the second, ART_PRICE_TABLE(2), and so on. We shall declare a floating point type ARTICLE_PRICE and let the components of ART_PRICE_TABLE have this type, assuming that no prices are higher than £99.99.

Both arrays are initialized when they are declared. Note that the arrays are declared as constants. A constant has been introduced into the program, called TAB_SIZE, with the value 7, which is made use of both in the declarations of the array types and in the program itself. It is a good idea to use a constant in this way because the size of the tables can then easily be changed.

There are several methods available for searching in arrays, and these methods have varying degrees of efficiency. In this program the simplest form of searching, **linear searching**, is employed. This involves going through the array ART_NUMBER_TABLE from the beginning until the component containing the required article number is found, or until the whole array has been searched unsuccessfully. To indicate whether the article number has been found, a variable FOUND of type BOOLEAN is used. This is given the initial value FALSE. Another variable I, initialized to 1, is used to run through all possible values of the index of the array ART_NUMBER_TABLE. The first version of the program looks like this:

```
with TEXT_IO;
use  TEXT_IO;
procedure LOOK_UP_PRICE is
   type ARTICLE_NUMBER is range 1 .. 999;
   type ARTICLE_PRICE    is digits 4 range 0.00 .. 99.99;

   package ART_NO_INOUT is new INTEGER_IO(ARTICLE_NUMBER);
   package ART_PRICE_INOUT is new FLOAT_IO(ARTICLE_PRICE);
   use ART_NO_INOUT, ART_PRICE_INOUT;
```

```
TAB_SIZE : constant := 7;
type ART_NO_TAB_TYPE      is array(1 .. TAB_SIZE)
                          of ARTICLE_NUMBER;
type ART_PRICE_TAB_TYPE is array(1 .. TAB_SIZE)
                          of ARTICLE_PRICE;

ART_NUMBER_TABLE :   constant ART_NO_TAB_TYPE :=
                     (56, 81, 123, 379, 505, 811, 944);
ART_PRICE_TABLE    : constant ART_PRICE_TAB_TYPE :=
                     (3.50, 1.75, 9.15, 20.00,
                      0.50, 31.45, 5.95);

I : INTEGER := 1;
FOUND : BOOLEAN := FALSE;
WANTED_ART_NO : ARTICLE_NUMBER;

begin
  PUT_LINE("Enter the article number");
  GET(WANTED_ART_NO);

  while I < TAB_SIZE and not FOUND loop
    if ART_NUMBER_TABLE(I) = WANTED_ART_NO then
      FOUND := TRUE;
    else
      I := I + 1;
    end if;
  end loop;

  if FOUND then
    PUT("Its price is ");
    PUT(ART_PRICE_TABLE(I),
              EXP => 0, FORE => 1, AFT => 2);
  else
    PUT("Price details missing");
  end if;
end LOOK_UP_PRICE;
```

First we shall comment on the declarations of the constant arrays
ART_NUMBER_TABLE and ART_PRICE_TABLE. These have been given the
types ART_NO_TAB_TYPE and ART_PRICE_TAB_TYPE. When an array is
to be declared, it sometimes seems clumsy to have to declare its type
explicitly before the array itself can be declared, especially if the array
type is not used elsewhere in the program. For such cases, there is a
shorter way of writing a declaration. The array's type can be declared
directly in the object declaration instead. In our program, the declarations of ART_NUMBER_TABLE and ART_PRICE_TABLE could look like this:

```
ART_NUMBER_TABLE : constant array(1 .. TAB_SIZE)
                                of ARTICLE_NUMBER
                := (56, 81, 123, 379, 505, 811, 944);
```

```
ART_PRICE_TABLE      : constant array(1 .. TAB_SIZE)
                                of ARTICLE_PRICE
                     := (3.50, 1.75, 9.15, 20.00, 0.50, 31.45, 5.95);
```

and the declarations of the types ART_NO_TAB_TYPE and ART_PRICE_TAB_TYPE could be omitted.

We have created our own input/output packages in the program for the types ARTICLE_NUMBER and ARTICLE_PRICE. The search itself takes place in the **loop** statement. Each time through, one component of the array ART_NUMBER_TABLE is looked at, and if it is the same as the required article number the variable FOUND is set to TRUE. Otherwise, I is increased by 1 so that the next component will be examined the next time through. This is repeated until I has become greater than the size of the table or until the required article number is found.

When the loop ends, if the required article number has been found in ART_NUMBER_TABLE the variable FOUND has the value TRUE and the variable I contains the number of the relevant component. The corresponding component in the array ART_PRICE_TABLE contains the price of the required article and this is printed in the **if** statement's **then** part. If, however, FOUND has the value FALSE, the message "Price details missing" is printed.

If we make the Boolean expressions after **while** a little more complicated we can manage without the variable FOUND and we can simplify what is written in the **loop** statement. The last part of the program could be written:

```
while I <= TAB_SIZE
    and then ART_NUMBER_TABLE(I) /= WANTED_ART_NO loop
  I := I + 1;
end loop;

if I <= TAB_SIZE then
  PUT("The price is ");
  PUT(ART_PRICE_TABLE(I), EXP => 0, FORE => 1, AFT => 2);
else
  PUT("Price details missing");
end if;
```

The condition for the search to continue another time is that I is not too large and that the component that I points to does not contain the required article number. That is, the **loop** statement is terminated if I is greater than TAB_SIZE or if the required article number has been found. Note that the **and then** operator must be used here instead of **and**. Otherwise there would be an error on the last time through the loop if the required article number is not found in the array because the program would attempt to evaluate ART_NUMBER_TABLE(8), which does not exist. (Compare this with the argument presented in Section 3.4.2).

The variable I can be used in the **if** statement to determine whether the article number sought has been found. If I has a value that is less than or equal to TAB_SIZE then the **loop** statement must have terminated because the Boolean expression after **and then** was false, that is, because the article number has been found in the table, and I points to the component holding it.

If we look at the table of article numbers we see that it is organized in numerical order. This can be exploited to make the program more efficient. If we look for an article number that is not in the table, for example, 250, we can stop looking when we reach a number greater than it, 379 in this case. We then know that all the remaining entries in the table are greater than 250 and hence 250 is not in the table. We can change the program thus:

```
while I <= TAB_SIZE
      and then ART_NUMBER_TABLE(I) < WANTED_ART_NO loop
   I := I + 1;
end loop;

if I <= TAB_SIZE
   and then ART_NUMBER_TABLE(I) = WANTED_ART_NO then
   PUT("The price is ");
   PUT(ART_PRICE_TABLE(I), EXP => 0, FORE => 1, AFT => 2);
else
   PUT("Price details missing");
end if;
```

In the **loop** statement we have changed only the second Boolean expression so that the search is only continued if the article number we are looking at is less than the one required. Thus the loop terminates as soon as we find a component that is greater than or equal to the one we are looking for. A test is made in the **if** statement to see if the required article number has been found in the table. If it has, I must be less than or equal to TAB_SIZE and, in addition, the **loop** statement must have stopped because the article number pointed to is the same as the one required. Note that we must have the **and then** operator here as well, so that there is no error if I has the value 8.

Because ART_NUMBER_TABLE was sorted into order, we were able to make the search more efficient. For work with sorted arrays, there are, in fact, much more efficient methods of searching than the linear method used in this example. (No one looking for a name in a telephone directory, starts from the beginning and works through until he or she finds the name required!) So it is worthwhile having arrays sorted if they have to be searched. Therefore, in addition to searching arrays, it is important to be able to sort them if so required. There are many common algorithms to describe ways of sorting. We have already met one in Section 2.2 when we put cassettes into a cassette holder. We now shall study another algorithm for sorting arrays of integers.

We shall write a program which first reads in a maximum of 100 integers and puts them into an array. Input ends by the user typing CTRL-D at the terminal. Then the program sorts the array into numerical order so that the smallest integer comes first and the largest comes last. Finally, the program prints out the numbers in the array. To do the sort we shall use an algorithm based on the following principle: the smallest number is found first and swapped into the array's first 'compartment', then the next smallest element is found and swapped into the second 'compartment', and so on. The sort algorithm can be described as follows:

(1)   Set K to 1.
(2)   While K is less than the number of elements in the array:
    (2.1)   Search for the smallest element in that part of the array that starts at the Kth position and ends with the last element in the array.
    (2.2)   Swap the smallest element (from step (2.1)) and the element in position K.
    (2.3)   Increase K by 1.

Step (2.1) can be expanded to:

    (2.1.1)   Set M to K.
    (2.1.2)   Let I run from $K + 1$ to the number of the last element in the array:
        (2.1.2.1)   If the Ith element is less than the Mth element, then set M to I.
    (2.1.3)   The smallest element is now the Mth element.

Step (2.2) can be expanded to:

    (2.2.1)   Move the Kth element to a temporary store.
    (2.2.2)   Move the Mth element to position K.
    (2.2.3)   Move the element in the temporary store to position M.

Using this we can now put the program together and also include reading in the numbers to the array and printing out the array.

```
with TEXT_IO, BASIC_NUM_IO;
use TEXT_IO, BASIC_NUM_IO;
```

```
procedure SORT is
  MAX_NO_OF_ELTS : constant := 100;
  subtype INDEX is INTEGER range
                          1 .. MAX_NO_OF_ELTS;
  type INTEGER_ARRAY is array (INDEX) of INTEGER;

  A            : INTEGER_ARRAY;
  NO_OF_ELTS : NATURAL := 0;
  M            : INDEX;
  TEMP         : INTEGER;

begin
  -- Read numbers into the array
  PUT_LINE("Enter at most 100 whole numbers");
  PUT_LINE("Terminate by typing CTRL-D");

  while not END_OF_FILE and
                  NO_OF_ELTS < MAX_NO_OF_ELTS loop
    NO_OF_ELTS := NO_OF_ELTS + 1;
    GET(A(NO_OF_ELTS));
  end loop;

  -- Sort array
  for K in 1 .. NO_OF_ELTS loop
    -- Find the smallest element between
    -- the (K + 1)th and the last, inclusive
    M := K;
    for I in K + 1 .. NO_OF_ELTS loop
      if A(I) < A(M) then
        M := I;
      end if;
    end loop;

    -- Swap Kth and Mth elements
    TEMP := A(K);
    A(K) := A(M);
    A(M) := TEMP;
  end loop;

  -- Write out the sorted array
  NEW_LINE;
  for K in 1 .. NO_OF_ELTS loop
    PUT(A(K));
  end loop;
end SORT;
```

The output from a run of the program is as follows:

```
Enter at most 100 whole numbers
Terminate by typing CTRL-D
16 −8 34 0 −500
        −500    −8    0    16    34
```

EXERCISES

5.1 Write type declarations for the following:

(a) A measurement of numbers of traffic accidents.

(b) The average hourly pay of an industrial worker.

(c) A bank's rate of interest, expressed as a percentage.

(d) A type of bank account. (Assume that there are *current account*, *savings account*, *capital account*, *checking account* and *house account*).

(e) A table of information about the rates of interest on these different bank accounts.

(f) The countries of the European Economic Community (EEC).

(g) A table of the average hourly wage of industrial workers in the countries of the EEC.

5.2 A department store has five different departments numbered 1 to 5. Write a program that reads in the takings of each department for the past week. The output from the program should be a table that shows the percentage share of the total sales that each department is responsible for.

What changes would have to be made to the program if the departments, instead of being numbered, had the names *women*, *men*, *children*, *sport* and *perfume*?

5.3 Write a program to read in a maximum of 1000 integers from the terminal and print them out in the same order, but any given integer should only be printed once. If it has already been printed it should not be printed again.

For example, if the following numbers are read from the terminal:

        45   77   −22   3   45   0   21   −1   3

the program should output the following:

        45   77   −22   3   0   21   −1

5.4 Assume that the enumeration type DAY_OF_THE_WEEK is declared as earlier in the chapter. Declare a table TOMORROW that can be used to find out which day comes after a particular given day. For example, TOMORROW(TUESDAY) should have the value WEDNESDAY, and the value of TOMORROW(SUNDAY) should be MONDAY.

5.5 The Swedish administrative counties are denoted for many purposes by the set of letter codes: *AB, C, D, E, F, G, H, I, K, L, M, N, O, P, R, S, T, U, W, X, Y, Z, AC* and *BD.*

Statistics for all traffic accidents that occurred in each county in a particular year have been examined. Additional information is available on how many cars are registered in each county. Write a program to read in the information about the accidents and the numbers of registered cars, county by county. The program should print out which county had the greatest number of accidents, which county had the most registered cars and which county had the highest accident frequency in terms of accidents per registered car.

5.6 The Roman numerals are indicated by the letters I, V, X, L, C, D and M, standing for 1, 5, 10, 50, 100, 500 and 1000, respectively.

(a) Declare a table that can be used for translating a Roman numeral into an ordinary number (for example, L to 50). Use an enumeration type to describe the Roman numerals.

(b) Write a program to read in a Roman number and translate it into an integer. The Roman number is to be read as input to the program. Terminate input by using the character combination for END_OF_FILE. For simplicity, it can be assumed that when a Roman number is input at least one space is left between the numerals. The user can write, for instance, *M C M L X X X V I I* at the terminal. The program should then print out: 1987.

In a Roman number, if the Roman numeral *P* stands immediately to the left of another Roman numeral *Q* and if *P* denotes a smaller number than *Q*, then the value of *P* is subtracted from the total number (for example, LIX means 59), otherwise *P* is added to the total number (for example, LXI means 61).

5.7 A number can be shown to be a prime number if it is not exactly divisible by any smaller prime number. Use this fact to write a program that computes the first 50 prime numbers and puts them into a table. (When you want to determine whether a certain number *k* is a prime, you can thus find out if *k* is exactly divisible by one of those already saved in the table). The program should end when the table of 50 prime numbers has been printed.

5.8 A travel agency at a tourist resort organizes bus tours. There is one tour on each day of the week, and each tour has 40 places. Customers are able to reserve places on a tour no more than one week in advance.

Write a program for the agency to look after the reservation of places. The program should repeatedly read in the name of a day and one of the following commands: *book*, *cancel* or *new*.

When the command *book* is given the program should see if there is a place free for the given day. If there is, the program should 'remember' that one more place has been reserved for that day. Otherwise the program should print the message *No places left*.

If the command *cancel* is given, the program should cancel one reservation for the given day and 'remember' that there is one more place free. If no places were reserved for that day, an error message should be printed.

The command *new* is given when there is one week until a tour should take place. Then, the program should note that there are 40 free places.

5.9 Write a program to read in a maximum of 100 integers and place them in an array, sorted into ascending numerical order. The program should be designed so that one number at a time is read in and placed in the array. Before each new number is read, the numbers read in so far should be sorted.

5.10 Statistics of the rainfall for a certain location have been collected over the last 20 years. Write a program that reads in the information for the 20 years and presents the results in the form of a histogram. Assume the annual rainfall lies in the interval 0 to 3000 mm.

(a)   Present the result as a horizontal histogram in the format:

```
            0      1      2      3   (× 1000 mm)
                                      rainfall

Year

 1         ***************
 2         ************************
 3         ************
 :             :
 :             :
```

(b)   Present the result as a vertical histogram in the format:

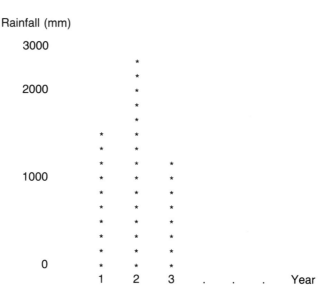

Rainfall (mm)

5.11 Write a program that first reads in an integer k from the terminal. Then the program should read in a maximum of 500 integers from the terminal and place them in an array. The numbers in the array should then be rearranged to form two groups in the array. The left-hand group should contain all the numbers $\leq k$ and the right-hand group all the numbers $> k$ (The number of numbers in each group and where the boundary between the two groups lies depends on the numbers read into the array and the value of k).

For example, if k is 20 and the array consists of the numbers:

23   16   27   3   11   34   25   20   8

then one permissible rearrangement of the array is:

8   16   20   3   11   34   25   27   23

Several other arrangements would be allowed. Note that it is not necessary to sort the array (even if it is a possible way of solving the problem).

Chapter 6
Subprograms

6.1 Functions
6.2 Procedures
6.3 Parameter association
6.4 Top-down design with
subprograms
6.5 The scope of a declaration

6.6 Overloaded subprograms
6.7 Named parameter association
6.8 Recursive subprograms
6.9 Functions as operators
Exercises

It has been shown that a program consists of two parts: a declarative part where the data objects used in the program are described, and a statement section where the actions that the program will perform are described. The statement section describes the algorithm that the program will carry out. Algorithms have been expressed using the statements available in Ada (assignment statements, **if** statements, **loop** statements, etc.). In constructing an algorithm, it is often useful to express certain steps on a 'higher level' than is possible with Ada's basic statements. Steps at such a higher level include, for example, 'calculate the logarithm of X', 'sort the table T', 'print a heading at the terminal' and 'calculate the mean of the measurements'. As we have seen, higher level steps in an algorithm occur naturally when the technique of top-down design is applied to a programming problem. The advantage of using this higher level is that inessential details can be ignored while the algorithm is made the focus of attention.

In Ada it is possible to define **subprograms** that are made up of several basic Ada statements. Calls to subprograms can be used as higher-level algorithmic steps when an algorithm is under construction.

The use of subprograms is a very important technique when mastering the complexity of program design. A program should normally be assembled from several sub-programs, each of which describes a particular calculation or stage of the program. Subprograms can be thought of as building blocks that are used to construct a whole program. It is because of the support given by subprograms that the top-down design method can be used.

In Ada there are two kinds of subprogram: **functions** and **procedures**. A function is used to describe the com-putation of a particular value (for example, the calculation of the mean of a series of measurements) and a procedure is used to describe an action that the program has to perform but that does not result in a direct value (for example, print-ing a heading at the terminal).

Examples have already been given of the use of both functions and procedures that have come in ready-written packages, mostly in connection with input and output. This chapter will deal with how to design subprograms and how to use them.

6.1 Functions

A function can be regarded as a 'black box' into which one or more values can be placed. Out of the box comes a result, whose value depends on the input values. We have used functions before. In the example for calculating the hypotenuse we used the supplied function SQRT which, as its name suggests, calculates the square root of a number. The SQRT black box is illustrated in Figure 6.1. When a supplied function is used, there is no need to worry about its internal looks. Suffice to know how it should be used.

Now we shall look at how to write new functions. As the first simple example, we shall study a function MEAN_VALUE that calculates the mean of two floating point numbers. From the point of view of the programmer who will use it, the function will look like Figure 6.2.

In Ada, the function MEAN_VALUE appears as:

```
function MEAN_VALUE (X1, X2 : FLOAT) return FLOAT is
begin
   return (X1 + X2) / 2.0;
end MEAN_VALUE;
```

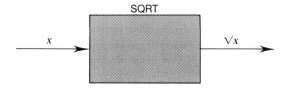

Figure 6.1

This is called a **function body**.

> **Function body**
>
> **function** *function_name* (*parameter_list*)
>   **return** *result_type* **is**
>
> declarative part
>
> **begin**
>   statement_1;
>   statement_2;
>   ⋮
>   statement_N;
> **end** *function_name*;

After the function's name, the data that has to be entered to the function is specified by writing a list of the function's **formal parameters**. Two values of type FLOAT will be entered to the function MEAN_VALUE, so we have written in brackets:

X1, X2 : FLOAT

We have given the function two formal parameters, called X1 and X2, both with type FLOAT. This is very similar to the declaration of two variables. When the function is called, X1 and X2 will contain the two values that are entered to the function.

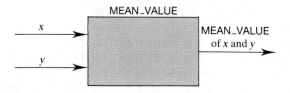

Figure 6.2

Formal parameters to functions

- Contain the values to be entered to the function.
- Exist only within the function.
- Are treated as constants in the function.

After the reserved word **return**, the type of the result that will be returned by the function is specified. We have stated that the value returned by the function MEAN_VALUE will have type FLOAT.

Thus the first line of the function, usually called the function's **specification**, tells the programmer how to use it.

Function specification

- First part of the function body.
- Contains the function name, its formal parameters and the type of its result.

The rest of the function body describes what is inside the 'black box', and the user of the function does not normally need to bother with this. This part of the function looks like the programs we have seen already; first comes a declarative part and then a sequence of statements. The body of our 'box' is only one statement:

```
return (X1 + X2) / 2.0;
```

This is a new sort of statement that we have not met before, a **return** statement, in which an expression follows the word **return**. This expression should have the same type as specified after the word **return** in the function specification. In the function MEAN_VALUE, therefore, the expression must have the type FLOAT. When the **return** statement is executed, the expression will be evaluated. Then execution of the function terminates and the result of the function will be the value of the expression. That is, when the **return** statement is executed, the computations in the 'box' terminate and what comes out of the 'box' is the value of the expression in the **return** statement. There can be several **return** statements in a function, but it is most common to have only one and for that to be the last statement in the function.

> **Return statement**
>
> **return** *expression*;
>
> The type of the expression should be the same as the type of the function's result.

A function is only a description of how a particular computation works, telling us what we can put into the 'box' and what we will get out as a result. To invoke a computation, we have to put something into the 'box'; we must **call** the function. In the example that follows, we have put our function MEAN_VALUE into a complete program that reads in two numbers from the terminal, calculates their mean and displays it at the terminal:

```
with TEXT_IO, BASIC_NUM_IO;
use  TEXT_IO, BASIC_NUM_IO;
procedure EVALUATE_MEAN is
   NUMBER1, NUMBER2, MEAN : FLOAT;

   function MEAN_VALUE (X1, X2 : FLOAT) return FLOAT is
   begin
       return (X1 + X2) / 2.0;
   end MEAN_VALUE;

begin
   PUT_LINE("Enter two real numbers");
   GET(NUMBER1); GET(NUMBER2);
   MEAN := MEAN_VALUE(NUMBER1, NUMBER2);
   PUT("The mean is:"); PUT(MEAN);
end EVALUATE_MEAN;
```

Note that the function body has been placed in the program's declarative part. In general, subprogram bodies should be placed *after* any declarations of types, subtypes, variables and constants.

> **Order of declaration**
>
> A simple rule of thumb:
> - Put subprogram bodies last in the declarations.
> - Put all other declarations first (in arbitrary order).

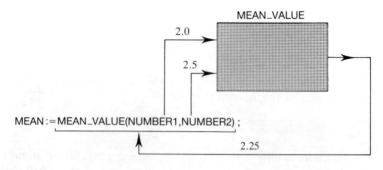

Figure 6.3

When the program is executed, the first statement in the program's statement part is carried out as usual, in this case the first input statement. Suppose the user types the values 2.0 and 2.5 at the terminal. After the program has read these values into the variables NUMBER1 and NUMBER2, there follows, on the third line of the statement part, a call to the function MEAN_VALUE. What happens is illustrated in Figure 6.3.

The expression:

MEAN_VALUE(NUMBER1, NUMBER2)

is the actual function call. First there is the name of the function being called, and then, in brackets, there is a list of the **actual parameters** to the function. When the call is executed, the values of the actual parameters are calculated first. (In this case, no calculation is necessary because the values are already in the variables NUMBER1 and NUMBER2). The values of the actual parameters are then passed to the function. Thus, here the values 2.0 and 2.5 are entered to the function MEAN_VALUE. Figure 6.4 illustrates the function.

The two formal parameters X1 and X2 can be thought of as 'temporary storage boxes' that are created in connection with the call to MEAN_VALUE and which only exist while the function call is in operation. When the function is called, the values of the first and second actual parameters are stored 'in' X1 and X2, respectively. Thus here, X1 takes the value 2.0 and X2 takes the value 2.5. Note that neither NUMBER1 nor NUMBER2 is affected by this; their values are only copied into X1 and X2, respectively.

When the actual parameters have been copied, execution of the program EVALUATE_MEAN stops temporarily, while the statements in the function MEAN_VALUE are executed. In this case the only statement, the **return** statement, is executed. The expression:

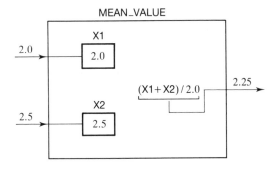

Figure 6.4

(X1 + X2) / 2.0

means that the values in X1 and X2 are added and the result is divided by 2. Thus we get the result 2.25, the same result we would have got if we had calculated the mean of NUMBER1 and NUMBER2 directly. The value calculated in the **return** statement becomes the value which leaves the function. The function call:

MEAN_VALUE(NUMBER1, NUMBER2)

will thus take the value 2.25.

When execution of the statements in the function MEAN_VALUE is finished, the call to the function MEAN_VALUE terminates and normal execution of the program EVALUATE_MEAN is resumed. The value of the function call is assigned to the variable MEAN, thus here MEAN takes the value 2.25. Note that when the function call terminates, the 'storage boxes' X1 and X2 no longer exist. They are only temporary for the duration of the call to MEAN_VALUE.

Within a function, the formal parameters are considered to be constants that are initialized at the time of the call. They can be used as ordinary constants within the statement section of the function. In the function MEAN_VALUE, for example, they are used in an expression. Just as the value of a constant may not be changed, it is not permitted for a function to try and change the value of a formal parameter.

A call to a function is considered to be an expression. The type of the expression is the same as the type given after the word **return** in the function specification. Thus a call to the function MEAN_VALUE is considered as an expression of type FLOAT. This means that a function call can be used in the same way as other expressions in a program. In the program EVALUATE_MEAN, for example, a call to MEAN_VALUE was placed on the right-hand side of an assignment. We could also use a function call in a bigger expression, such as:

MEAN_VALUE(NUMBER1, NUMBER2) / NUMBER1 * 100.0

Since a function call is an expression, it can also be used as a parameter to the output statement PUT. If we make use of this, we can manage without the variable MEAN in our program:

```
begin
    PUT_LINE("Enter two real numbers");
    GET(NUMBER1); GET(NUMBER2);
    PUT("The mean is:"); PUT( MEAN_VALUE(NUMBER1, NUMBER2) );
end EVALUATE_MEAN;
```

In this version, the execution of the last statement is such that the function MEAN_VALUE is called first. It returns a value of type FLOAT and the procedure PUT is then called with this value as parameter.

The **actual** parameters to a function can be expressions; they do not have to be simple variables of the kind used so far. What is essential is that an actual parameter has the same type as the corresponding **formal** parameter in the function specification. For example, the following function call would be permissible:

MEAN_VALUE(NUMBER1 * NUMBER2, NUMBER1 + 10.0)

The first actual parameter is the expression:

NUMBER1 * NUMBER2

and the second is the expression:

NUMBER1 + 10.0

When a function call is executed, first the values of the actual parameters are evaluated. If we assume the same values for NUMBER1 and NUMBER2 as before, 2.0 and 2.5, respectively, then the first actual parameter has the value 5.0 and the second has the value 12.0.

Function calls

function_name(*a1, a2, ... an*)

a1, a2, ... an are *actual* parameters

- They may be expressions.
- Their types must agree with those of the corresponding formal parameters.
- A function call is considered to be an *expression*.

The following occur:

(1) The values of *a1, a2, ... an* are computed.

(2) The value of *a1* is copied to the first formal parameter, that of *a2* to the second, and so on.

(3) The statements in the function are executed.

(4) The function terminates on execution of a return statement.

(5) The value of the function call is the value in the return statement.

(6) Execution continues after the function call.

A common misunderstanding regarding functions is that the values that are entered to and returned by a function should be read from or written to the terminal. Note that a function does not need to have anything at all to do with terminal input and output. The values that enter the function come from the calling program and are entered via the formal parameters (thus the values are not read from the terminal), and the result of the function is returned to the calling program using the return statement (it is not written at the terminal).

Let us look at another example. This time we shall write a function MAX that finds the larger of two integers. Two values of type INTEGER are entered to the function, and the function returns one value, also of type INTEGER. Here is the function:

```
function MAX (X, Y : INTEGER) return INTEGER is
begin
  if X > Y then
    return X;
```

```
    else
      return Y;
    end if;
  end MAX;
```

The function's statement part consists of a single **if** statement, but we have used two **return** statements. If the formal parameter X contains the bigger of the two values, that is returned as the resulting value; otherwise the result is the other formal parameter, Y.

The following program is an example of the use of the function MAX:

```
with TEXT_IO, BASIC_NUM_IO;
use  TEXT_IO, BASIC_NUM_IO;
procedure MAX_DEMO is
  A, B, C, M : INTEGER;

  function MAX (X, Y : INTEGER) return INTEGER is
  begin
    if X > Y then
      return X;
    else
      return Y;
    end if;
  end MAX;

begin
  loop
    PUT_LINE("Enter three whole numbers");
    exit when END_OF_FILE;
    GET(A); GET(B); GET(C);
    M := MAX(A, B);
    M := MAX(M, C);
    PUT("The biggest of them is");
    PUT(M); NEW_LINE;
  end loop;
end MAX_DEMO;
```

Note that the function MAX is called in two places in the program. It is quite permissible to call the same function from several places in one program and use different parameters for different calls. Note also that when the program is executed, the function will be repeated many times because the calls are both in a **loop** statement. In the statement:

```
M := MAX(A, B);
```

the values of the variables A and B are used as actual parameters in the function call. When the call is executed, 'temporary stores' X and Y will be created and the values of A and B will be copied into them. If, say, A has the value 6 and B the value 2, then X and Y will contain the values 6 and 2, respectively. This means that the **then** part of the **if** statement will be carried out. The statement:

return X;

is thus carried out and this means that the value of X is given as the result of the function. In our case, it means that the function call has the value 6 and this value is assigned to the variable M.

In the next statement:

M := MAX(M, C);

The values of M and C are used as actual parameters. New 'temporary stores' X and Y are created, the previous ones no longer exist. If C has the value 9, then the values 6 and 9 will be copied to X and Y. This time, the **else** part of the **if** statement will be executed, and the function returns the value of C, 9, as its result. This becomes the right-hand side of the assignment statement, and the value 9 is assigned to the variable M. (Thus the value of M changes from 6 to 9). Now M contains the biggest of the three numbers.

We can manage without the variable M if we write a more complicated expression as parameter to the last PUT statement:

```
loop
    PUT_LINE("Enter three whole numbers");
    exit when END_OF_FILE;
    GET(A); GET(B); GET(C);
    PUT("The biggest of them is");
    PUT(MAX( MAX(A,B), C)); NEW_LINE;
end loop;
```

The statement:

PUT(MAX(MAX(A,B), C));

means that the procedure PUT is called with the expression:

MAX(MAX(A,B), C)

as parameter. This expression consists of a call of the function MAX with the two actual parameters MAX(A,B) and C. The first of these is in turn a call of the function MAX with the actual parameters A and B. When the statement is executed, the expressions are evaluated from the innermost level, that is, the expressions A and B are evaluated first (which is easy since they are simple variables). Then the expression MAX(A,B) is evaluated (which will take the larger of the two values of A and B) and the expression C. When that is done, the expression:

MAX(MAX(A,B), C)

is evaluated, which thus gives the largest of the three values as a result. This value is passed to the procedure PUT and will be printed.

A function can contain calls to further functions. For example, let us write a function EXPONENTIATE that calculates the value of an expression of the form:

$$p^q$$

where both p and q are real numbers. (The standard operator ** cannot be used because it requires q to be an integer). We shall assume that in our implementation of Ada there is a package with the basic mathematical functions, including the function LN that is called with:

LN(X)

where X is an expression of the type FLOAT. This function gives as its result the natural logarithm of X, ln X. We also assume that the package contains a function EXP that is called by:

EXP(X)

where X is an expression of type FLOAT. As a result, the function EXP returns the mathematical constant e (the number 2.718 28...) raised to the power X.

Applying the ordinary mathematical formulae for logarithms, we get:

$$p^q = e^{q \ln(p)}$$

Since the function ln is only defined for positive numbers, we can only use this formula when p is greater than 0. We use the formula to write our function EXPONENTIATE as follows:

```
function EXPONENTIATE (P : POS; Q : FLOAT) return FLOAT is
begin
   return EXP(Q * LN(P));
end EXPONENTIATE;
```

The function has two formal parameters P and Q. The parameter P has subtype POS which we declare as:

subtype POS **is** FLOAT **range** FLOAT'SMALL .. FLOAT'LARGE;

The values that belong to this subtype are thus all the values of the type FLOAT which lie in the interval FLOAT'SMALL to FLOAT'LARGE. (FLOAT'SMALL is the smallest positive value that is bigger than 0 and FLOAT'LARGE is the largest positive value that can be stored in the current implementation of Ada). By giving P the subtype POS, we guarantee that P is always greater than 0. If EXPONENTIATE is called from a program and the first parameter is less than or equal to 0, then a run-time error will occur.

In the function specification we see how to specify the formal parameters when they are of different types or subtypes; the different parameters are given with semicolons between. If there are several parameters of the same type then they can be written in the shorter way, as in the previous example; by listing the parameters, separated by commas, and only writing the type name once. Thus the rules for writing the formal parameters are like the rules that apply for writing several variable declarations one after another in a program.

Specifying formal parameters

Similar rules as for variable declaration.

For example:

    (X1, X2, ... Xn : *type1*; Y1, Y2, ... Yn : *type2*)

The function EXPONENTIATE can be called from a program that repeatedly reads two real numbers, A and B, from the terminal and calculates A raised to the power B:

```
with TEXT_IO, BASIC_NUM_IO, BASIC_MATH;
use  TEXT_IO, BASIC_NUM_IO, BASIC_MATH;
procedure EXP_DEMO is
  subtype POS is FLOAT range FLOAT'SMALL .. FLOAT'LARGE;
  A : POS;
  B : FLOAT;

  function EXPONENTIATE (P : POS; Q : FLOAT)
                                    return FLOAT is
  begin
    return EXP(Q * LN(P));
  end EXPONENTIATE;
```

```
begin
  loop
    PUT_LINE("Enter two real numbers, the first > 0");
    exit when END_OF_FILE;
    GET(A); GET(B);
    PUT(A); PUT(" raised to the power "); PUT(B);
    PUT(" is equal to ");
    PUT(EXPONENTIATE(A,B));
    NEW_LINE;
  end loop;
end EXP_DEMO;
```

We assumed that the functions LN and EXP were in a package
BASIC_MATH that the program must, therefore, have access to.

The functions we have studied so far have all had parameters and
have returned values of numeric types. Such functions are very common.
However, a function can have parameters and return results of any type.
We shall look at some functions that have parameters and results of types
other than numeric. The first example shows a function LETTER that
determines whether a particular character (of type CHARACTER) is a
letter. The character for investigation is a parameter to the function and
as a result the function returns a BOOLEAN value. The result of the
function can be either FALSE or TRUE. The function can be written:

```
function LETTER (CHAR : CHARACTER) return BOOLEAN is
begin
  case CHAR is
    when 'a' .. 'z' | 'A' .. 'Z' =>
      return TRUE;
    when others =>
      return FALSE;
  end case;
end LETTER;
```

In the function specification we can see that the formal parameter CHAR
has type CHARACTER and that the result type is BOOLEAN. The statement
part of the program consists of only one **case** statement. If CHAR contains
a lower or upper case letter the statement:

```
return TRUE;
```

will be executed. Otherwise the statement:

```
return FALSE;
```

will be executed.

The function can be called as in the following example, assuming the variable C has type CHARACTER:

```
GET(C);
if LETTER(C) then
  PUT_LINE("letter");
else
  PUT_LINE("not a letter");
end if;
```

In an **if** statement, an expression of type BOOLEAN should appear immediately after the reserved word **if**, and the call of the function LETTER is just such an expression.

We can make the function LETTER a little more elegant if we write an expression of type BOOLEAN directly after **return** instead of using a **case** statement:

```
function LETTER(CHAR : CHARACTER) return BOOLEAN is
begin
  return CHAR in 'a' .. 'z' or CHAR in 'A' .. 'Z';
end LETTER;
```

The way of calling the function is not affected by this, since we have not changed the function specification.

Result type

A function may return results of any type.

The next example is a function that calculates the sum of the components of a vector. A vector can be regarded as a list of numbers, such as:

$$(2.0, \ 1.5, \ -1.0)$$

In an Ada program we can represent a vector by an array. A vector with three components can be described by the type:

```
type THREE_VECTOR is array (1 .. 3) of FLOAT;
```

We can now write a function SUM that has a parameter of type THREE_VECTOR and which returns a result of type FLOAT:

```
function SUM(V : THREE_VECTOR) return FLOAT is
  S : FLOAT := 0.0;
begin
  for I in 1 .. 3 loop
    S := S + V(I);
  end loop;
  return S;
end SUM;
```

Within the function the formal parameter can be treated as an ordinary constant array. For example, we can pick out the individual components of V by indexing.

There is something else new in this function. We use a variable S to calculate the sum, and this variable is declared in a declarative part of the function. A variable that is declared within a subprogram like this is usually called a **local variable** because it can only be used locally, within the subprogram. A local variable can be regarded in exactly the same way as a formal parameter, that is, as a 'temporary store', which is created when the function is called and only exists while the call is in operation. After a function has finished execution, the local variables no longer exist. A local variable is something that exists only within the 'black box' of the function. It is one of the things that a programmer who is going to use the function need never know about.

Local variables

- Are declared within a subprogram.
- Exist only within the subprogram.

Let us see how a call to SUM may appear. If we assume that a program has the following variable declaration:

```
A : THREE_VECTOR := (2.0, 1.5, −1.0);
```

then our new function could be called, for example, like this:

```
PUT( SUM(A) );
```

The value 2.5 would be written out.

The function SUM as we have written it so far has one great weakness. It can only be used for calculating the sum of the components of a three-dimensional vector in which the components are numbered from 1 to 3. If on another occasion we want to calculate the sum of the components of, say, a four-dimensional vector, this function cannot be used. We shall now see how, with a few small changes, the function can be made so general that it can be used for vectors of arbitrary length and index constraints. To do this we shall use an unconstrained array type. We declare a type VECTOR:

type VECTOR **is array** (INTEGER **range** < >) **of** FLOAT;

We shall now give the function's formal parameters this type instead of the type THREE_VECTOR. This means that the number of components in V is not predetermined. The number of components can change from call to call and is determined by the number of components in the actual parameter.

One more detail of the function must be changed. We can no longer let the loop parameter go from 1 to 3 in the **loop** statement. The number of times through the loop and the indexing now depend on the number of components in V and the index constraints on V. The solution to this problem is to use the attribute V'RANGE, which gives the interval between V's first and last index. With these amendments, the general version of the function SUM is as follows:

```
function SUM(V : VECTOR) return FLOAT is
  S : FLOAT := 0.0;
begin
  for I in V'RANGE loop
    S := S + V(I);
  end loop;
  return S;
end SUM;
```

Let us look at how to call this general function. If we have a variable declaration:

```
A : VECTOR(1 .. 3) := (2.0, 1.5, −1.0);
```

then the function can be called as before, using:

```
PUT( SUM(A) );
```

and we get 2.5 written out. On this call, the formal parameter V takes length 3 and index limits 1 and 3. However, if we also have the following declarations in the same program:

```
X : VECTOR(0 .. 3) := (1.0, 2.0, 6.5, −4.0);
Y : VECTOR(5 .. 6) := (3.5, 2.5);
```

we can also have the statements:

```
PUT( SUM(X) );    -- returns the result 5.5
PUT( SUM(Y) );    -- returns the result 6.0
```

On the first call the formal parameter V will take the length 4 and have index limits of 0 and 3. On the second call V's length will be 2 and it will have index limits 5 and 6.

An array aggregate or a slice is also allowed as actual parameter. For example, we can make the calls:

```
SUM( (1.4, 0.3) )    -- returns the result 1.7
SUM( X(1 .. 2) )     -- returns the result 8.5
```

Writing subprograms that are as general as possible is a worthwhile habit; they can be used in several contexts, and the chance of having to change them when circumstances change is reduced. The use of unconstrained array types, as in this example, is therefore highly recommended. (One of the weaknesses in the language Pascal is that it is not possible to write general subprograms in this way).

Subprograms and unconstrained array types

It is advantageous to make subprograms general by using unconstrained array types for formal parameters and the result.

The next example will show that a function in Ada can return a value of a composite type as its result. We shall write a function ADD that calculates the sum of two vectors, which is a new vector with the same number of components as the original vectors. The first component of the new vector is the sum of the two first components of the original vectors, the second is the sum of the second components, and so on. For example, the sum of the two vectors:

(1.0,   2.5, 4.3)
(3.1, −1.0, 0.0)

is the vector:

(4.1, 1.5, 4.3)

One condition is that the two vectors to be added have the same number of components. First we shall write a version of the function with the limitation that it can only add two vectors of dimension 3. Both the formal parameters of the function and the result have type THREE_VECTOR. This first version looks like this:

```
function ADD(V1, V2 : THREE_VECTOR) return THREE_VECTOR is
  TEMP : THREE_VECTOR;
begin
  for I in 1 .. 3 loop
    TEMP(I) := V1(I) + V2(I);
  end loop;
  return TEMP;
end ADD;
```

In the function we have used a local array variable TEMP which also has type THREE_VECTOR. The three components of TEMP are calculated in the **loop** statement, one component per loop. The statement:

```
return TEMP;
```

means that we return the value of TEMP as result, TEMP having the type THREE_VECTOR.

If we have the declarations:

```
A : THREE_VECTOR := (1.0, 2.5, 4.3);
B : THREE_VECTOR := (3.1, −1.0, 0.0);
C : THREE_VECTOR;
```

in a program, then the following statement is allowed:

```
C := ADD(A,B);
```

The value of the right-hand side of the statement will be (4.1, 1.5, 4.3) and it will have type THREE_VECTOR. The array variable C will thus be assigned the value (4.1, 1.5, 4.3).

Of course, the function ADD should be formulated generally instead, so that it can deal with vectors of arbitrary length, and only a few minor changes are needed. Instead of the type THREE_VECTOR we can let the parameters and result of the function have unconstrained array type VECTOR, as declared earlier. The declaration of the local array variable TEMP must be changed, to have the same number of components as the parameters V1 and V2. (We assume that V1 and V2 have the same lengths.) We can achieve this using the attribute V1'RANGE in the declaration of TEMP:

```
TEMP : VECTOR(V1'RANGE);
```

In the brackets is an interval with the same limits as the index limits for V1. If, for example, V1 is indexed from 1 to 4, then TEMP will also be indexed from 1 to 4. In the **loop** statement we have used V1'RANGE in the same way as in the function SUM, to let the loop parameter I run through the required index values. With these amendments, the following general version of ADD is obtained:

```
function ADD(V1, V2 : VECTOR) return VECTOR is
   TEMP : VECTOR(V1'RANGE);
begin
   for I in V1'RANGE loop
      TEMP(I) := V1(I) + V2(I);
   end loop;
   return TEMP;
end ADD;
```

If we have the following declarations in a program:

```
X : VECTOR(1 .. 4) := (1.0, 1.0, 1.0, 1.0);
Y : VECTOR(1 .. 4) := (2.5, 3.5, 4.5, 5.5);
Z : VECTOR(0 .. 1) := (0.5, 0.5);
```

then the following calls, as examples, are allowed:

```
ADD(X, Y)      -- gives (3.5, 4.5, 5.5, 6.5)
ADD(Z, Z)      -- gives (1.0, 1.0)
ADD( (2.7, 3.8), (1.0, 2.0) )    -- gives (3.7, 5.8)
```

To be able to add two vectors they must have the same length, but it is not necessary for them to be indexed in the same way. For example, it should be possible to add a vector indexed from 0 to 3 to another vector indexed from 1 to 4. This version of ADD cannot manage it. It demands that both vectors are indexed in the same way. If we were to call it with vectors with different indexing we would get a run-time error. (This is because when V2(I) is executed in the **loop** statement, the loop parameter I will sometimes lie outside the range of V2's index values.)

It is possible to make further amendments to the function so that it can cope with vectors with different index limits. (But the lengths of the vectors must always be the same). When the local variable TEMP is declared, it can be initialized so that its components will contain the same values as those of V2. (This is always possible since TEMP and V2 have the same number of components). In the **loop** statement we can then add V1's components to TEMP's components. Since V1 and TEMP have the same index limits we shall not meet problems with indexing. With this final amendment the function ADD becomes:

```
function ADD(V1, V2 : VECTOR) return VECTOR is
  TEMP : VECTOR(V1'RANGE) := V2;
begin
  for I in V1'RANGE loop
    TEMP(I) := TEMP(I) + V1(I);
  end loop;
  return TEMP;
end ADD;
```

There are also functions without parameters. We have already seen an example of these – the function END_OF_FILE in the package TEXT_IO. When such a function is called it is enough to write simply the name of the function without brackets afterwards. One example of the use of the function END_OF_FILE is:

```
exit when END_OF_FILE;
```

Thus a call to a function without parameters looks exactly as if the function were a normal variable.

To write a function without parameters, we leave out the brackets and the list of formal parameters in the function specification:

```
function MY_RANDOM_NO return FLOAT is

end MY_RANDOM_NO;
```

How should we name functions that we write ourselves? It is best to try and make the function name specific, in the same way as ordinary variables. If the function performs some mathematical operation and the parameters can be regarded as operands to the operation, then an appropriate name will describe the operation, for example, EXPONENTIATE and ADD. Functions that return a BOOLEAN result can be given names in the style of a question, for example, END_OF_FILE, END_OF_INPUT and PERMITTED_VALUE. In these cases it helps to imagine a question mark following the function name.

6.2   Procedures

The other subprogram is the **procedure**. A procedure differs from a function in that it does not return a result when it is called. When a procedure is called, its sequence of statements is put into action.

Procedure body

procedure *procedure_name* (*parameter_list*) **is**

declarative part

begin
    statement_1;
    statement_2;
      ⋮
    statement_N;
end *procedure_name*;

A procedure has exactly the same form as a function. The only differences are that the reserved word **procedure** is used instead of **function**, and that no result type is given in the procedure specification, its first line.

Procedure specification

- The first part of the procedure body.
- Contains the name of the procedure and its formal parameters.

Since a procedure does not return any value as a result, there need not be a **return** statement in the procedure. A procedure normally terminates when execution reaches the final **end**.

For example, let us write a procedure HEAD_NEW_PAGE that can be used when a new page of output is to be started with a page number written at the top. The page number should be written in the middle of the top line as follows:

$$- 34 -$$

We shall assume that the terminal produces printed output and a line of output has at most 80 characters. We shall make use of the existing procedures NEW_PAGE and SET_COL in the package TEXT_IO. NEW_PAGE ensures that a new page is fed and SET_COL allows a particular position on the current line of output to be chosen for printing. The procedure is as follows:

```
procedure HEAD_NEW_PAGE (PAGE_NUM : INTEGER) is
begin
  NEW_PAGE;
  SET_COL(38);
  PUT("– "); PUT(PAGE_NUM, WIDTH => 1); PUT(" –");
end HEAD_NEW_PAGE;
```

Procedures, like functions, can take parameters; HEAD_NEW_PAGE has the formal parameter PAGE_NUM with type INTEGER.

We shall now examine this procedure when it is used in a program that writes the page number at the top of three pages, numbers 34, 50 and 51.

```
with TEXT_IO, BASIC_NUM_IO;
use  TEXT_IO, BASIC_NUM_IO;
procedure PAGE_DEMO is
  N : INTEGER := 50;

  procedure HEAD_NEW_PAGE (PAGE_NUM : INTEGER) is
  begin
    NEW_PAGE;
    SET_COL(38);
    PUT("– "); PUT(PAGE_NUM, WIDTH=>1); PUT(" –");
  end HEAD_NEW_PAGE;

begin
  HEAD_NEW_PAGE(34);
  HEAD_NEW_PAGE(N);
  HEAD_NEW_PAGE(N+1);
end PAGE_DEMO;
```

We notice that a procedure body, like a function body, should be located in the declarative part of the program.

The program PAGE_DEMO has three calls to the procedure HEAD_NEW_PAGE. A procedure call works in much the same way as a function call. A 'temporary store' PAGE_NUM is created in the procedure and the value of the actual parameter is copied to it. In this example, the first call copies the value 34 to PAGE_NUM. Then the execution of PAGE_DEMO is halted while the statements in HEAD_NEW_PAGE are carried out. When their execution is complete, the execution of PAGE_DEMO is resumed and the next statement after the procedure call is executed.

Note that the procedure does not return any value to the calling program. This is what distinguishes a procedure from a function. A procedure call is considered to be an entire **statement** in the calling program whereas a function call, as shown in the foregoing section, is considered to be an **expression**. A call to a procedure is written as in the example above. It is terminated with a semicolon. A function call, however, is written in the same places in a program as ordinary expressions, and the calling program must deal with the result. The following subprogram calls are therefore in error:

```
PUT( HEAD_NEW_PAGE(N) );   -- ERROR! HEAD_NEW_PAGE is a
                                      procedure
N := HEAD_NEW_PAGE(45);   -- ERROR! HEAD_NEW_PAGE is a
                                      procedure
SQRT(X);                   -- ERROR! SQRT is a function
END_OF_FILE;               -- ERROR! END_OF_FILE is a function
```

Procedure call

procedure_name(a1, a2, ... an);

a1, a2, ... an are *actual* parameters.

- Their types must agree with those of the corresponding formal parameters.
- A procedure call is considered to be a *statement*.

As the next example, we shall write a procedure PRINT_CENTRED that will print any piece of text in the centre of the line. A procedure, exactly like a function, can have parameters of any types at all. The procedure we shall write now will have a parameter of type STRING that gives the text to be output.

```
procedure PRINT_CENTRED (TEXT : STRING) is
   LINE_LENGTH : constant := 80;
begin
   SET_COL((LINE_LENGTH - TEXT'LENGTH) / 2);
   PUT(TEXT);
end PRINT_CENTRED;
```

For simplicity, we have assumed that the output has room for only 80 characters. To avoid having numbers in the statements, we have declared a local constant LINE_LENGTH in the procedure. The type STRING is an unconstrained array type and, therefore, the procedure's parameter can be text of arbitrary length. To refer to the length of the text within the procedure, we use the attribute TEXT'LENGTH. If the text is 80 characters long or longer, we shall get a run-time error when the program is executed.

We shall look at a program that uses PRINT_CENTRED to print out the text:

>   Hello
>   Ada
>   is my
>   name!

The program looks like this:

```
with TEXT_IO;
use  TEXT_IO;
procedure PRINT_GREETING is

   procedure PRINT_CENTRED (TEXT : STRING) is
     LINE_LENGTH : constant := 80;
   begin
     SET_COL((LINE_LENGTH − TEXT'LENGTH) / 2);
     PUT(TEXT);
   end PRINT_CENTRED;

begin
   NEW_LINE;
   PRINT_CENTRED("Hello");    NEW_LINE;
   PRINT_CENTRED("Ada");      NEW_LINE;
   PRINT_CENTRED("is my");    NEW_LINE;
   PRINT_CENTRED("name!");    NEW_LINE;
end PRINT_GREETING;
```

6.3   Parameter association

The two procedures we have studied so far in this chapter have both been used for special printing. They, too, can be thought of as 'black boxes'; we put values into them but they return no result value to the calling program.

However, procedures can be used in a much more general way. Transferring parameters between the calling program and the procedure can actually be carried out in more ways than we have seen so far. This is best explained from a simple example. We shall write a procedure NONSENSE that does nothing of any use, but illustrates how **parameter association** works.

```
procedure NONSENSE (A : in     INTEGER;
                    B : in out INTEGER;
                    C : out    INTEGER) is
```

```
begin
  B := B + A;
  C := 0;
end NONSENSE;
```

The procedure NONSENSE has three formal parameters, A, B and C, written on separate lines only for the sake of clarity. What is new is that the reserved words **in** and **out** appear in the parameter specifications.

In Ada, a parameter can be either a **parameter of mode in**, a **parameter of mode in out** or a **parameter of mode out**. In the procedure NONSENSE, these are exemplified by A, B and C, respectively. We can say that A is used to put values into the NONSENSE 'box', B is used both to put values in and get them out, and C is used only to get values out of the NONSENSE 'box'.

The parameters we have seen in our earlier examples, both of functions and procedures, have all been **in** parameters. If neither **in** nor **out** are used in a parameter specification, the parameter is automatically an **in** parameter, that is, the specification **in** is assumed.

We shall put NONSENSE into a program that calls the procedure:

```
with TEXT_IO, BASIC_NUM_IO;
use  TEXT_IO, BASIC_NUM_IO;
procedure PARA_DEMO is
  X, Y, Z: INTEGER;

  procedure NONSENSE (A : in      INTEGER;
                      B : in out INTEGER;
                      C : out     INTEGER) is
  begin
    B := B + A;
    C := 0;
  end NONSENSE;

begin
  X := 1; Y := 5; Z := 10;
  PUT(X); PUT(Y); PUT(Z); NEW_LINE;
  NONSENSE(X, Y, Z);
  PUT(X); PUT(Y); PUT(Z); NEW_LINE;
end PARA_DEMO;
```

To see what happens we shall study a couple of diagrams. The variables X, Y and Z in the main program can be illustrated, as usual, by three storage boxes in the program PARA_DEMO. At the start of the call:

```
NONSENSE(X, Y, Z);
```

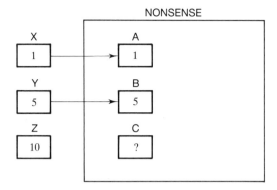

Figure 6.5

three temporary storage boxes, A, B and C, are created in the procedure NONSENSE. They only exist while the call is in progress. At the start of the call the situation is as in Figure 6.5. The formal parameter A is an **in** parameter. The formal parameters we saw in our earlier examples were also **in** parameters, so the result with A is exactly what we are used to. First the value of the corresponding actual parameter is calculated. This is already done here, X already has the value 1. This value is then copied to the formal variable A which thus also gets the value 1. The copying does not affect the variable X at all.

The formal parameter B is an **in out** parameter. As with an **in** parameter, the value of the actual parameter corresponding to an **in out** parameter is copied to the formal parameter at the start of the call. In our example, the value 5 which is in the variable Y is copied to B.

The third formal parameter is an **out** parameter. There is *no* copying for an **out** parameter when the procedure is called. The value in the temporary store C will thus be undefined at the start of the call, as shown in Figure 6.5.

When the temporary stores have been created and those associated with **in** or **in out** parameters have been initialized, execution continues with the procedure's sequence of statements. First, the statement:

    B := B + A;

is executed. This statement means, as usual, that the value in store B is changed to 5 + 1, that is, 6. The next statement:

    C := 0;

means, of course, that the store called C is given the value 0.

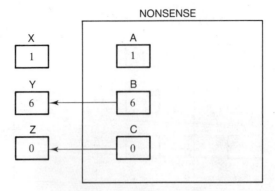

Figure 6.6

Within the procedure NONSENSE the **in** parameter A is considered to be a constant. Therefore no attempt may be made to change its value. If we were to try, for example, to add the statement:

```
A := 0;    -- ERROR!
```

we would get a compile-time error.

An **in out** parameter is considered to be a normal variable within the procedure. Therefore, we can change the value of B and put it into expressions in the normal way.

The value of an **out** parameter is undefined at the start of procedure execution. Therefore it is not possible to refer to the value of an **out** parameter. For example, an **out** parameter may not appear on the right-hand side of an assignment statement. The following statements would lead to compile-time errors:

```
B := C;      -- ERROR!
B := B + C;  -- ERROR!
```

The only thing you can do with **out** parameters is give them values, which is often done with assignment statements, as in NONSENSE.

When the two statements in the procedure NONSENSE have been executed the procedure call terminates. The result is shown in Figure 6.6. The parameter A is an **in** parameter and its value cannot have changed in the procedure. Thus it must still contain the same value as when the procedure was called. *No* copying of the value of an **in** parameter occurs when a procedure terminates. The variable X can thus never be changed by the procedure call.

For an **in out** parameter, the value it has at the end of the procedure call is copied back to the actual parameter. In this case, the value 6 will be copied to the variable Y. Thus Y's value is changed by the procedure call.

For an **out** parameter, its value is also copied to the corresponding actual parameter at the end of the call. The variable Z will thus have been changed by the procedure call and get the value 0.

When the program PARA_DEMO is run, it will give the output:

```
1    5    10
1    6     0
```

We have seen before that an expression can be used as an actual parameter to a call. This is only allowed when the corresponding formal parameter is an **in** parameter. If the corresponding formal parameter is an **in out** parameter or an **out** parameter the actual parameter must be a variable. Otherwise, it would be impossible to copy the value of the formal parameter to the actual parameter at the end of the call – a value cannot be copied to an expression. The calls:

```
NONSENSE(X, 2 * Y, Z);  -- ERROR! The second parameter is an
                        -- in out parameter
NONSENSE(X, Y, Z + 1);  -- ERROR! The third parameter is an
                        -- out parameter
```

are thus in error. However, the following is allowed:

```
NONSENSE(X * 3, Y, Z);  -- CORRECT! The first parameter is an
                        -- in parameter
```

We can now summarize the rules for the different types of parameter. If we look at them first from the point of view of the **calling program**, we can say:

in   The actual parameter can be a variable or an expression and it must have a legal value at the time of the call. If the actual parameter is a variable, its value may never be changed during the call to the subprogram. It will always have the same value after the call as before it.

in out The actual parameter must be a variable and the variable must have a legal value at the time of the call. The value of the variable can change during the procedure call, so that it has a different value at the end.

out   The actual parameter must be a variable. Its value at the time of the call is of no interest, because the procedure ignores it. At the end of the procedure call, the actual parameter will have taken a value other than it had before.

If we look at them from the point of view of the **called subprogram**, the different parameters have the following consequences:

in   When execution of the subprogram begins the formal parameter has a value. In the subprogram the formal parameter is treated as a constant. This value can be used but not changed.

in out When execution of the procedure begins, the formal parameter has a value. In the procedure the formal parameter can be used as an ordinary variable. Its value can both be used and changed. If the value of the formal parameter is changed, then the value of the actual parameter in the calling program will also be changed.

out   When execution of the procedure begins, the value of the parameter is undefined. The value of the formal parameter may not be used in the procedure; it may not be used, for example, in expressions. However, it should be *given* a value, by assignment, for example. The value given to the formal parameter will in turn be given to the corresponding actual parameter in the calling program.

The figures shown earlier in the text illustrate how parameters are copied in a purely logical and abstract way. If there are parameters of compound types, large arrays for example, it might be inefficient to copy values to and fro. The Ada implementation being used may implement parameter association in a more efficient way. However, pay no attention to this, and try not to make use of the fact. A program should always be written so that parameter association occurs as described here.

The three modes of parameter can be used freely in procedures. In functions, however, only **in** parameters may be used. The reason for this limitation is that functions should be clear of **side effects**. A side effect means a subprogram which, during execution, affects a variable that is not local to the subprogram but which occurs in another part of the program. When a function is called the values of actual parameters should not be changed. For example, when the function SQRT is called to calculate the square root of a variable W:

SQRT(W)

it would be very strange if the value of W could be changed by the call. Thanks to the fact that functions only have **in** parameters, there is no risk of this happening; the actual parameters to a function can never be changed by calling the function.

Formal parameters to procedures

- Handle communication between the procedure and other subprograms.
- Exist only within the procedure.
- There are three different types:

  - **in** parameters. Have values at time of call.

    Considered as constants.

    May not be changed in the procedure.

  - **in out** parameters. Have values at time of call.

    Can be both used and changed in the procedure.

  - **out** parameters. Values undefined at time of call.

    May not be used in the procedure but should be *given* values.

The procedures in the previous section had **in** parameters. As a simple example of **in out** parameters we shall look at a procedure that can be used to swap the values of two variables.

```
procedure SWAP (NUMBER1, NUMBER2 : in out INTEGER) is
   TEMP : INTEGER;
begin
   TEMP    := NUMBER1;
   NUMBER1 := NUMBER2;
   NUMBER2 := TEMP;
end SWAP;
```

If we assume that in some program there are two variables P and Q with type INTEGER and values 1 and 2, respectively, then the call:

```
SWAP(P, Q);
```

from the program will result in the variables P and Q swapping values, thus taking values 2 and 1, respectively. It is essential that the formal parameters to SWAP are **in out** parameters; **in** parameters would not have worked, because they may not be changed. Nor would it have been possible to specify **out** parameters, because then it would not have been possible to use the values of P and Q in the procedure.

We can write another procedure ORDER which is similar to SWAP, except that in ORDER the swap will only occur if the second parameter has a smaller value than the first.

```
procedure ORDER (NUMBER1, NUMBER2 : in out INTEGER) is
  TEMP : INTEGER;
begin
  if NUMBER2 < NUMBER1 then
    TEMP    := NUMBER1;
    NUMBER1 := NUMBER2;
    NUMBER2 := TEMP;
  end if;
end ORDER;
```

This procedure can be used to put two numbers into numerical order. If the variables A and B have type INTEGER, then the call

```
ORDER(A, B);
```

causes A and B to exchange values if B had a smaller value than A before the call. If A's value is less than or equal to B's, then no swap takes place. This means that after the call, A is always less than or equal to B.

In Section 4.3 we looked at a couple of versions of a program that read in three integers and wrote them out in numerical order. By using the procedure ORDER we can write a more compact version of this program:

```
with TEXT_IO, BASIC_NUM_IO;
use  TEXT_IO, BASIC_NUM_IO;
procedure SORT_3 is
  A, B, C : INTEGER;

  procedure ORDER (NUMBER1, NUMBER2 : in out INTEGER) is
    TEMP : INTEGER;
  begin
    if NUMBER2 < NUMBER1 then
      TEMP    := NUMBER1;
      NUMBER1 := NUMBER2;
      NUMBER2 := TEMP;
    end if;
  end ORDER;

begin
  PUT_LINE("Give three different integers");
  GET(A); GET(B); GET(C);
```

```
    ORDER(A, B);
    ORDER(A, C);
    ORDER(B, C);

    PUT(A); PUT(B); PUT(C);
end SORT_3;
```

The first two calls to ORDER ensure that A contains the smallest of the three integers and the last call makes sure that B contains the next smallest.

When a subprogram has to be written to compute a certain value dependent on certain input values it is, as we have seen, natural to write it as a function rather than as a procedure. If, for example, we want a subprogram that will search for the smallest element in an array of floating point numbers and return it as the result, we will make the subprogram a function. Sometimes we want more than one result from a subprogram and then a function cannot be used. In our example, if we wanted to know both the smallest element in the array and where in the array it occurred, we would have to write a procedure in which the required results were **out** parameters.

Let us look at such a procedure, for finding details of the smallest element in an array of floating point numbers. Input to the procedure is the array itself, which we will give as an **in** parameter, because the array should not be altered. We have two **out** parameters, the smallest element and its index in the array. We shall formulate the procedure to be general and useful for all arrays of floating point numbers, irrespective of the index constraints. We use the same declaration of the type VECTOR as before:

```
    type VECTOR is array (INTEGER range < >) of FLOAT;
```

The procedure looks like this:

```
procedure FIND_SMALLEST (V                 : in VECTOR;
                         SMALLEST_VALUE : out FLOAT;
                         SMALLEST_PLACE : out INTEGER) is

    SMALLEST_SO_FAR : FLOAT    := V(V'FIRST);
    PLACE           : INTEGER := V'FIRST;

begin
    for I in V'FIRST + 1 .. V'LAST loop
      if V(I) < SMALLEST_SO_FAR then
        SMALLEST_SO_FAR := V(I);
        PLACE := I;
      end if;
    end loop;
```

```
        SMALLEST_VALUE := SMALLEST_SO_FAR;
        SMALLEST_PLACE := PLACE;
    end FIND_SMALLEST;
```

The algorithm we are using is based on looking right through the array, from start to end, and always remembering the least element found so far and its index. At the start we remember the first number and the first index. We use the local variable SMALLEST_SO_FAR to hold the smallest element found so far, and the local variable PLACE to remember its index. When we find in the course of the search an element smaller than the smallest found so far, we have found a new smallest number and we change the variables SMALLEST_SO_FAR and PLACE accordingly. When the whole array has been searched SMALLEST_SO_FAR contains the smallest element of the array and PLACE contains its index. The procedure finishes by assigning these values to the procedure's **out** parameters.

When a subprogram is designed to carry out some particular calculation, it is often the case that the calculation can only be achieved for certain input data; some input data will not work. Then the subprogram should take the form of a procedure, with the calculated value as an **out** parameter, and a further **out** parameter should be introduced with type BOOLEAN. This is given the value TRUE in the subprogram if the calculation can be carried out in the normal way and FALSE if not. The calling program can then, using this parameter, know whether the calculation has been carried out or not.

For example, let us write a procedure COMPUTE_ROOTS that computes the two real roots of a second order equation of the form:

$$x^2 + px + q = 0$$

the roots of which are given by the formula:

$$x = \frac{-p}{2} \pm \sqrt{\left(\frac{p^2}{4} - q\right)}$$

The expression under the square root sign, the discriminant, must be greater than or equal to zero if the equation has real roots. Our procedure can thus only calculate the roots if that is the case.

```
    procedure COMPUTE_ROOTS (P, Q           : in FLOAT;
                             ROOT1, ROOT2 : out FLOAT;
                             REAL_ROOTS    : out BOOLEAN) is
```

```
    D : FLOAT;
begin
    D := P ** 2 / 4.0 - Q;
    if D < 0.0 then
      REAL_ROOTS := FALSE;
    else
      REAL_ROOTS := TRUE;
      ROOT1 := -P / 2.0 + SQRT(D);
      ROOT2 := -P / 2.0 - SQRT(D);
    end if;
end COMPUTE_ROOTS;
```

The procedure takes the two coefficients P and Q as **in** parameters, and it has three **out** parameters, the two calculated roots and a parameter REAL_ROOTS of type BOOLEAN. In the procedure, the parameter REAL_ROOTS is given the value TRUE if the equation has real roots, and otherwise is FALSE. If we assume that the variables A, B, R1 and R2 have type FLOAT and the variable OK has type BOOLEAN, the procedure can be called as follows:

```
PUT_LINE("Enter coefficients P and Q");
GET(A); GET(B);
COMPUTE_ROOTS(A, B, R1, R2, OK);
if OK then
  PUT("The equation has roots ");
  PUT(R1); PUT(" and "); PUT(R2);
else
  PUT("The equation has no real roots");
end if;
```

If OK has the value FALSE after the call, the values of variables R1 and R2 are undefined (they presumably contain rubbish).

What is the best way of naming a procedure? Since a procedure is a program unit that describes how something is done, it is generally appropriate to give them names that specify that something. Suitable names may be, for example, COMPUTE_ROOTS, WRITE_HEADING and CHECK_STATE.

6.4   Top-down design with subprograms

In this section we shall see how subprograms come into use when the technique of top-down design is used. For example we shall design and write a program to calculate and print the binomial coefficients. These are defined for non-negative integers, n and k, as follows:

k	(4:k)
0	1
1	4
2	6
3	4
4	1

Figure 6.7

$$\binom{n}{k} = \frac{n!}{k! \times (n-k)!}$$

where $n!$ is the factorial of n and is given by:

$$n! = \begin{cases} 1 & \text{if } n = 0 \\ 1 \times 2 \times 3 \times \dots \times n & \text{if } n > 0 \end{cases}$$

In future this binomial coefficient will be written in the form $(n{:}k)$.

We can specify that the program should work as follows. Input to the program should be a value of n and the first step is to read this from the terminal. The program should then calculate all the binomial coefficients for this value of n, that is $(n{:}k)$ for all values of k between 0 and n. Finally, the calculated binomial coefficients should be printed as a table. If, for example, the value of n is 4, then the program should print the table in Figure 6.7. The program should be written so that it can be repeated an arbitrary number of times with different values of n.

A first, rough sketch of the program is:

(1)   Repeat the following an arbitrary number of times:
    (1.1)   Read the input (terminate calculations if no more input given).
    (1.2)   Print the table of values.

We shall try to translate this directly into Ada, making use of calls to subprograms. Step (1.1) can be carried out using a procedure READ_INPUT that can have two **out** parameters, the value of n read and a Boolean parameter that says whether data has been input. We will not worry about how to indicate that input is finished when the program is run. To write step (1.1), therefore, we must assume that the procedure READ_INPUT exists, or will exist. Then step (1.1) can be written:

```
READ_INPUT(N_VALUE, INPUT_COMPLETE);
exit when INPUT_COMPLETE;
```

We have introduced two variables that are used as actual parameters in the procedure call. These variables must, of course, be declared in our program. Since the values of *n* must be whole numbers that are greater than or equal to 0, NATURAL is a suitable subtype for N_VALUE. The variable INPUT_COMPLETE is of type BOOLEAN.

In step (1.2) we can introduce another procedure, PRINT_TABLE, that takes the value of *n* as an **in** parameter. This step can be written as:

```
PRINT_TABLE(N_VALUE);
```

Now we can put the algorithm steps into a program where we can include the necessary variable declarations. The specifications of the two procedures we are going to use can also be included, but their details are unimportant for the moment. The program has the following structure:

```
procedure COMPUTE_BINOMIAL_COEFFICIENTS is
   N_VALUE         : NATURAL;
   INPUT_COMPLETE : BOOLEAN;

   procedure READ_INPUT (N_INPUT    : out NATURAL;
                  :        END_INPUT : out BOOLEAN) is

   end READ_INPUT;

   procedure PRINT_TABLE (N : in NATURAL) is

        :

   end PRINT_TABLE;

begin
   loop
      READ_INPUT(N_VALUE, INPUT_COMPLETE);
      exit when INPUT_COMPLETE;
      PRINT_TABLE(N_VALUE);
   end loop;
end COMPUTE_BINOMIAL_COEFFICIENTS;
```

Now we have finished at the top level of the algorithm. By using the top-down technique combined with calls to subprograms, the program has the correct structure right from the start, without any worry about the technical details of reading the input, or about how the calculations or table output should be done. The procedure at the highest level, here the procedure COMPUTE_BINOMIAL_COEFFICIENTS, is usually called the **main program**. It is enough for the main program to have only a few statements, mostly subprogram calls, which outline its main structure. Except for *very* trivial programs, where no subprograms are used, no calculations should be made in the main program. Even in the earlier programs, it would have been better to introduce subprograms and avoid doing everything in the main program.

In the foregoing program we have indicated where to place the body of the subprograms READ_INPUT and PRINT_TABLE, and before the program can be compiled, these procedures must be completed.

The next stage of program development is to write the procedures READ_INPUT and PRINT_TABLE. We shall take them one at a time. It does not matter which we take first; their internal appearance should have nothing to do with the order in which they are written. We can start with READ_INPUT because that should be simpler.

The procedure specification for READ_INPUT is already given:

```
procedure READ_INPUT (N_INPUT    : out NATURAL;
                      END_INPUT : out BOOLEAN)
```

The procedure has to read an integer greater than or equal to 0 from the terminal. This integer will be returned from the procedure as the **out** parameter N_INPUT. In the usual case, when a number is read from the terminal, the second **out** parameter END_INPUT has the value FALSE, but when the operator states that the input is finished it will be given the value TRUE. Now we have to decide how the operator should indicate that the input is over. There are two natural alternatives. One is to make use of the END_OF_FILE, that is, to let the operator note the end of input by writing a special combination of characters, the combination depending on the system, for example, CTRL-D. The other possibility is to let the operator enter a negative number to mark the end of input, because binomial coefficients are not defined for negative values of n. Here we choose the first alternative, END_OF_FILE. The algorithm can be very simple:

(1) Request user to type in data.
(2) If the user indicates END_OF_FILE, then set END_INPUT to TRUE. Otherwise, set the out parameter N_INPUT to the number read and set END_INPUT to FALSE.

If we translate this algorithm to Ada and put it together with the procedure's specification, the whole procedure will be as follows:

```
procedure READ_INPUT (N_INPUT    : out NATURAL;
                      END_INPUT : out BOOLEAN) is
begin
   PUT_LINE("Enter N. Terminate with CTRL-D");
   if END_OF_FILE then
      END_INPUT := TRUE;
```

```
   else
      END_INPUT := FALSE;
      GET(N_INPUT);
   end if;
end READ_INPUT;
```

Now the procedure READ_INPUT is ready and can be put into the program text written earlier.

The next step is to write the procedure PRINT_TABLE. The procedure specification is already written. The procedure takes the current value of n as **in** parameter, and its task is to write out the table in Figure 6.7, with the binomial coefficients $(n:k)$ for all values of k between 0 and n. We start, as usual, with a rough algorithm:

(1)   Write table heading.
(2)   For each value of k in the interval 0 to n:
      (2.1)   Write a line of the table.

Step (2.1) can be refined to:

(2.1.1)   Write the value of k.
(2.1.2)   Calculate $(n:k)$.
(2.1.3)   Write the calculated value.

Should any of these steps be formulated as a subprogram call? The decision as to whether to do this is always a matter for judgement, but here it is obvious that step (2.1.2), 'Calculate $(n:k)$', should be written as a subprogram; the reason is that it is a well-defined calculation. From two input values, n and k, a result is obtained, $(n:k)$. It is always appropriate to carry out a well-defined calculation of this sort in a subprogram, and the subprogram should be a function. Thus we can assume that we have a function BIN_COEFF that is specified as follows:

```
function BIN_COEFF (P, Q : NATURAL) return POSITIVE is

   ⋮

end BIN_COEFF;
```

The function takes two **in** parameters, P and Q, and returns the binary coefficient $(p:q)$.

We choose to translate the other steps in the algorithm directly into Ada without using subprograms. Step (1), 'Write table heading' could well be performed in a subprogram but because the step is not complicated, we have chosen not to do that.

We can translate our algorithm to Ada:

```
-- print table heading
PUT(" k");
PUT("     ("); PUT(N, WIDTH => 1); PUT_LINE(":k)");
NEW_LINE;
for K in 0 .. N loop
  -- print a line of the table
  PUT(K, WIDTH => 3); PUT(BIN_COEFF(N,K), WIDTH => 10);
  NEW_LINE;
end loop;
```

The statements contain a good deal of technical detail to make the output look as we want it to. Step (2.1.2), the calculation of (n:k), is translated as a call to BIN_COEFF. By placing this call inside the call to PUT, we avoid introducing extra variables for saving the calculated values.

If suitable names are chosen for subprograms and an algorithm has steps that are carried out by calls to subprograms, it is often clear what the steps and the algorithm are doing; thus extra comments are not always necessary. If, however, a subprogram is not used to perform a step in the program, it is sensible to add some comments to explain what is happening.

Now we can put together the entire procedure PRINT_TABLE:

```
procedure PRINT_TABLE (N : in NATURAL) is
  function BIN_COEFF (P, Q : NATURAL) return POSITIVE is
    ⋮
  end BIN_COEFF;

begin
  -- print table heading
  PUT(" k");
  PUT("    ("); PUT(N, WIDTH => 1); PUT_LINE(":k)");
  NEW_LINE;

  for K in 0 .. N loop
    -- print a line of the table
    PUT(K, WIDTH => 3); PUT(BIN_COEFF(N,K), WIDTH => 10);
    NEW_LINE;
  end loop;
  NEW_LINE;
end PRINT_TABLE;
```

We have placed the specification of the function BIN_COEFF in the right place in the procedure, but we do not yet need to worry about the inside of the function. Note that we can have several levels of subprogram defined within one another. Here we have three levels because the procedure PRINT_TABLE is defined inside COMPUTE_BINOMIAL_COEFFICIENTS.

Now we can go on and construct the function BIN_COEFF that will take the numbers p and q as **in** parameters and return the value $(p:q)$ as its result. Direct from the definition of the binomial coefficients we can write the following very simple algorithm:

(1)   Calculate and return as result $p!/(q! * (p - q)!)$

We see that three different factorials are calculated, so it makes sense to introduce a special function FACTORIAL to calculate the factorial of a given number. Then we can write the function BIN_COEFF as follows:

```
function BIN_COEFF (P, Q : NATURAL) return POSITIVE is
   function FACTORIAL (NUMBER : NATURAL) return POSITIVE is

      ⋮

   end FACTORIAL;

begin
   return FACTORIAL(P) / ( FACTORIAL(Q) * FACTORIAL(P-Q) );
end BIN_COEFF;
```

The function FACTORIAL is at the fourth level inside BIN_COEFF. The only remaining step is to write the function FACTORIAL. We have already discussed (Section 3.6) how a factorial can be calculated. Using this we get:

```
function FACTORIAL (NUMBER : NATURAL) return POSITIVE is
   RESULT : POSITIVE := 1;
begin
   for J in 2 .. NUMBER loop
      RESULT := RESULT * J;
   end loop;
   return RESULT;
end FACTORIAL;
```

For the sake of clarity, we have given the result the type POSITIVE, but we know that we can have problems with the calculation if the value of n is not relatively small, because there may be insufficient room in an integer type. The solution to the problem, as we saw earlier, would be to let the result have the type FLOAT instead.

Now all the subprograms of the program have been written and we can assemble them together as a complete program:

```
with TEXT_IO, BASIC_NUM_IO;
use  TEXT_IO, BASIC_NUM_IO;
procedure COMPUTE_BINOMIAL_COEFFICIENTS is
   N_VALUE         : NATURAL;
   INPUT_COMPLETE : BOOLEAN;
```

```
procedure READ_INPUT(N_INPUT     : out NATURAL;
                     END_INPUT : out BOOLEAN) is
begin
  PUT_LINE("Enter N. Terminate with CTRL-D");
  if END_OF_FILE then
    END_INPUT := TRUE;
  else
    END_INPUT := FALSE;
    GET(N_INPUT);
  end if;
end READ_INPUT;

procedure PRINT_TABLE (N : in NATURAL) is
  function BIN_COEFF (P, Q : NATURAL) return POSITIVE is
    function FACTORIAL (NUMBER : NATURAL) return POSITIVE is
      RESULT : POSITIVE := 1;
    begin
      for J in 2 .. NUMBER loop
        RESULT := RESULT * J;
      end loop;
      return RESULT;
    end FACTORIAL;

  begin
    return FACTORIAL(P) / ( FACTORIAL(Q) * FACTORIAL(P-Q) );
  end BIN_COEFF;

begin
  -- print table heading
  PUT(" k");
  PUT("      ("); PUT(N, WIDTH => 1);
  PUT_LINE(":k)");
  NEW_LINE;

  for K in 0 .. N loop
    -- print a line of the table
    PUT(K, WIDTH => 3);
    PUT(BIN_COEFF(N,K), WIDTH => 10);
    NEW_LINE;
  end loop;
  NEW_LINE;
end PRINT_TABLE;

begin
  loop
    READ_INPUT(N_VALUE, INPUT_COMPLETE);
    exit when INPUT_COMPLETE;
    PRINT_TABLE(N_VALUE);
  end loop;
end COMPUTE_BINOMIAL_COEFFICIENTS;
```

When we assemble the program we must make sure that we also have access to the packages TEXT_IO and BASIC_NUM_IO, because these are used in READ_INPUT and PRINT_TABLE.

This exercise has shown that using the technique of top-down design with subprograms allows one step to be in focus at a time. In the procedure PRINT_TABLE, for example, we could concentrate on how the table should be printed and not worry about how the input should be read or how the binomial coefficients should be calculated.

Division into subprograms

- A program should always be divided into several subprograms.

- A well-defined calculation or operation (that is, a 'high-level step' of an algorithm) is carried out in a subprogram.

- A subprogram should be no longer than can be easily understood. If it becomes too long it should be divided into further subprograms.

■

In the program above we placed the subprograms that are used by the program within the program. For example, we placed READ_INPUT and PRINT_TABLE in COMPUTE_BINARY_COEFFICIENTS, and the program was not ready until we had written these subprograms. In Ada we have, however, the option of compiling a program before a subprogram is ready. We can tell the Ada compiler that we intend to write and compile a subprogram separately later. We do this by writing the word **separate** after the subprogram specification instead of writing the body of the subprogram. The program COMPUTE_BINOMIAL_COEFFICIENTS could, for example, be written:

```
procedure COMPUTE_BINOMIAL_COEFFICIENTS is
   N_VALUE         : NATURAL;
   INPUT_COMPLETE : BOOLEAN;

   procedure READ_INPUT (N_INPUT    : out NATURAL;
                         END_INPUT  : out BOOLEAN)
                         is separate;

   procedure PRINT_TABLE (N : in NATURAL) is separate;
```

```
begin
  loop
    READ_INPUT(N_VALUE, INPUT_COMPLETE);
    exit when INPUT_COMPLETE;
    PRINT_TABLE(N_VALUE);
  end loop;
end COMPUTE_BINOMIAL_COEFFICIENTS;
```

This program is complete and can be compiled. Of course, it is not possible to run tests on the program until READ_INPUT and PRINT_TABLE are written and compiled. Note that the packages TEXT_IO and BASIC_NUM_IO are not needed. They are not used directly in the procedure COMPUTE_BINOMIAL_COEFFICIENTS.

When the subprograms are compiled separately, the program they are intended for must be specified. The procedure READ_INPUT will, in this case, appear thus:

```
with TEXT_IO, BASIC_NUM_IO;
use  TEXT_IO, BASIC_NUM_IO;

separate (COMPUTE_BINOMIAL_COEFFICIENTS)
procedure READ_INPUT (N_INPUT    : out NATURAL;
                      END_INPUT : out BOOLEAN) is
begin
  PUT_LINE("Enter N. Terminate with CTRL-D");
  if END_OF_FILE then
    END_INPUT := TRUE;
  else
    END_INPUT := FALSE;
    GET(N_INPUT);
  end if;
end READ_INPUT;
```

In front of the procedure READ_INPUT is written the word **separate** followed by, in brackets, the name of the program in which it will be used. The packages TEXT_IO and BASIC_NUM_IO must be accessible because they are used in the procedure READ_INPUT.

There can be advantages to using separate compilation in developing large programs. No program text need then be so big, and a program becomes easier to understand. It is also possible to compile a program before all the subprograms are ready and thus check that it has no compile-time errors. A program can even be tested, if necessary, to see that its main features work correctly. In this case, very simple test versions of the separate subprograms have to be made that can later be replaced by the real versions. The option of writing the different parts of a program separately is of great advantage when several programmers are jointly developing a large program. They do not need to work with the same program texts; the work can be split up so that individual programmers can work independently and develop separate subprograms.

Separate compilation of subprogram bodies

- Where the subprogram body would normally be placed (in another subprogram A, for example) is written instead:

    function *name(parameters)* **return** *result_type*
    is separate;

    or:

    procedure *name(parameters)* **is separate**;

- When the subprogram body is later compiled separately, where it would normally be placed is stated. If the body would normally be in another subprogram A, it is written:

    separate(A)

    subprogram_body

☐

Let us now look at another program using the technique of top-down design with subprograms. We shall write a new version of the sort program in Section 5.8. The program's job was to read a number of integers from the terminal and then print them out in numerical order. A rough algorithm is:

(1) Read in the numbers.
(2) Sort the numbers.
(3) Print the sorted numbers.

This can easily be translated to Ada if we assume that we have three subprograms READ, SORT and WRITE. READ can be a procedure with two **out** parameters: an integer array of the numbers read and an integer which gives the number of numbers read and placed in the array. If we assume that we have the declarations:

```
MAX_NO_ELTS : constant := 100;
subtype INDEX is INTEGER range 1 .. MAX_NO_ELTS;
type INTEGER_ARRAY is array (INDEX range <>) of INTEGER;
```

then the specification of the procedure READ can be written:

```
procedure READ (S    : out INTEGER_ARRAY;
                SIZE : out NATURAL)
```

Now step (1) in the algorithm is:

```
READ (A, N_ELTS);
```

Here we have used two variables, A and N_ELTS, as the actual parameters to READ. They are declared as follows:

```
A       : INTEGER_ARRAY(1 .. MAX_NO_ELTS);
N_ELTS : NATURAL;
```

The variable A is an integer array. The number of places in the array is determined by the constant MAX_NO_ELTS, which has the value 100 in this example. When the procedure READ is called it fills the array A with the numbers that are entered from the terminal. If the user enters fewer numbers than there is room for, then the whole array is not filled. The number of places used is given by the parameter N_ELTS. We assume that the procedure checks that there are no more numbers than the array has room for.

Step (2) in the algorithm is now simple. We start by writing a specification for a subprogram SORT:

```
procedure SORT (S : in out INTEGER_ARRAY)
```

The procedure thus has only one parameter, an **in out** parameter which is an integer array. When the procedure is called the array is sorted so that the elements are in ascending numerical order. Using it, step (2) can be written:

```
SORT (A(1 .. N_ELTS));
```

As parameter, we have not given the entire array, A, but only the part of it that is being used.

Step (3) is also simple. First we specify a procedure WRITE:

```
procedure WRITE(S : in INTEGER_ARRAY)
```

The procedure takes the array to be written as an **in** parameter. Step (3) is:

```
WRITE(A(1 .. N_ELTS));
```

Here, too, we only give the part of the array that is in use.

Now the three steps of the program can be assembled, with the resulting structure:

```
procedure SORT_EXAMPLE is
   MAX_NO_ELTS : constant := 100;
   subtype INDEX is INTEGER range 1 .. MAX_NO_ELTS;
   type INTEGER_ARRAY is array (INDEX range <>) of INTEGER;
   A       : INTEGER_ARRAY(1 .. MAX_NO_ELTS);
   N_ELTS : NATURAL;

   procedure READ (S     : out INTEGER_ARRAY;
                   SIZE : out NATURAL) is

       ⋮

   end READ;

   procedure SORT (S : in out INTEGER_ARRAY) is

       ⋮

   end SORT;

   procedure WRITE(S : in INTEGER_ARRAY) is

       ⋮

   end WRITE;
begin
   READ (A, N_ELTS);
   SORT (A(1 .. N_ELTS));
   WRITE(A(1 .. N_ELTS));
end SORT_EXAMPLE;
```

Now the three subprograms have to be written. We shall start with WRITE which is the simplest and uses the algorithm:

(1) Write heading.
(2) For all the numbers in the array S:
     (2.1) Write out the number.

This is easily translated to Ada:

```
procedure WRITE(S : in INTEGER_ARRAY) is
begin
  NEW_LINE;
  PUT_LINE("The numbers are:");
  for K in S'RANGE loop
    PUT( S(K) );
  end loop;
  NEW_LINE;
end WRITE;
```

Here we have used the attribute S'RANGE to state the index range for S. The algorithm for what should be done in the procedure READ is:

(1) Set the number of elements read to zero and ARRAY_FULL to FALSE.
(2) Request the user to enter the array.
(3) Repeat the following until the user states that nothing more will be entered, or until ARRAY_FULL is TRUE.
    (3.1) If the array is full, output an error message and set ARRAY_FULL to TRUE. Otherwise, read a number into the next vacant place and increase the number of elements read by 1.
(4) Give the number of elements read as result.

We choose to use the END_OF_FILE technique for the user to notify the end of input. The algorithm can be translated to Ada:

```
procedure READ (S    : out INTEGER_ARRAY;
                SIZE : out NATURAL) is
  N_ELTS_READ : NATURAL := 0;
  ARRAY_FULL  : BOOLEAN := FALSE;
begin
  PUT_LINE("Enter the integers to be sorted.");
  PUT_LINE("Terminate input with CTRL-D");
  while not END_OF_FILE and not ARRAY_FULL loop
    if N_ELTS_READ = S'LENGTH then
      PUT_LINE("Too many!");
      ARRAY_FULL := TRUE;
    else
      N_ELTS_READ := N_ELTS_READ + 1;
      GET( S(N_ELTS_READ) );
    end if;
  end loop;
  SIZE := N_ELTS_READ;
end READ;
```

We use a local variable N_ELTS_READ to count the numbers read in. If the entire array is full and another number is input at the terminal, the procedure gives the error message:

Too many!

We have already given the algorithm for the procedure SORT in Section 5.8:

(1) Set K to 1.
(2) While K is less than the number of elements in the array:
     (2.1) Search for the smallest element in that part of the array that starts at the Kth position and ends with the last element in the array.
     (2.2) Swap the smallest element (from step (2.1)) and the element in position K.
     (2.3) Increase K by 1.

To achieve step (2.1) we specify a function SMALLEST as follows:

function SMALLEST (T : INTEGER_ARRAY) **return** INDEX

The function takes an integer array as an **in** parameter. As result it returns the index of the smallest number in the array. Step (2.1) can now be written:

SMALLEST_POSN := SMALLEST(S(K .. S'LAST));

We have introduced the variable SMALLEST_POSN with type INDEX in which we save the result of the call. S is, as we can see in the specification of SORT, the array to be sorted. As parameter to the function SMALLEST we give the part of the array that starts at index K. SMALLEST will thus give the index of the smallest element of that part of the array as result.

Step (2.2) can be carried out using a procedure SWAP which we specify as follows:

procedure SWAP (I, J : **in**   INDEX;
               T   : **in out** INTEGER_ARRAY)

When this procedure is called, elements number I and J in array T will swap places.

The remaining steps in the algorithm can be achieved with a **for** construct. The procedure SORT can then be written:

```
procedure SORT (S : in out INTEGER_ARRAY) is
  SMALLEST_POSN : INDEX;

  function SMALLEST (T : INTEGER_ARRAY) return INDEX is
  -- gives the index number for the smallest element in T

      ⋮

  end SMALLEST;

  procedure SWAP (I, J : in      INDEX;
                  T    : in out INTEGER_ARRAY) is
  -- swap the Ith and Jth elements in array T

      ⋮

  end SWAP;

begin
  for K in S'RANGE loop
    SMALLEST_POSN := SMALLEST(S(K .. S'LAST));
    SWAP(K, SMALLEST_POSN, S);
  end loop;
end SORT;
```

Now it remains to write the subprograms SMALLEST and SWAP. Algorithms for these were given in Section 5.8. The algorithm for SMALLEST can, with some amendment, be written:

(1) Set M to the first index in T.
(2) Let I run from the second to the last index in T.
    (2.1) If element number I is less than element number M then set M to I.
(3) The smallest element is now element number M. Give M as result.

Translation to Ada gives:

```
function SMALLEST (T : INTEGER_ARRAY) return INDEX is
-- gives the index number for the smallest element in T
  M : INDEX := T'FIRST;
begin
  for I in T'FIRST + 1 .. T'LAST loop
    if T(I) < T(M) then
      M := I;
    end if;
  end loop;
  return M;
end SMALLEST;
```

The algorithm for the final procedure, SWAP, was also given in Section 5.8.

(1) Move the *I*th element to a temporary store.
(2) Move the *J*th element to position *I*.
(3) Move the element in the temporary store to position *J*.

The procedure is in Ada:

```
procedure SWAP (I, J : in     INDEX;
                       T   : in out INTEGER_ARRAY) is
-- swap the Ith and Jth elements in array T
   TEMP : INTEGER;
begin
   TEMP := T(I);
   T(I)    := T(J);
   T(J)    := TEMP;
end SWAP;
```

All the different parts can now be assembled to make a complete program, when we also ensure that the packages TEXT_IO and BASIC_NUM_IO are accessible:

```
with TEXT_IO, BASIC_NUM_IO;
use  TEXT_IO, BASIC_NUM_IO;

procedure SORT_EXAMPLE is
   MAX_NO_ELTS : constant := 100;
   subtype INDEX is INTEGER range 1 .. MAX_NO_ELTS;
   type INTEGER_ARRAY is array (INDEX range < >) of INTEGER;

   A     : INTEGER_ARRAY(1 .. MAX_NO_ELTS);
   N_ELTS : NATURAL;

   procedure READ (S     : out INTEGER_ARRAY;
                   SIZE : out NATURAL) is
      N_ELTS_READ : NATURAL := 0;
      ARRAY_FULL  : BOOLEAN := FALSE;
   begin
      PUT_LINE("Enter the integers to be sorted.");
      PUT_LINE("Terminate input with CTRL-D");
      while not END_OF_FILE and not ARRAY_FULL loop
         if N_ELTS_READ = S'LENGTH then
            PUT_LINE("Too many!");
            ARRAY_FULL := TRUE;
         else
            N_ELTS_READ := N_ELTS_READ + 1;
            GET( S(N_ELTS_READ) );
         end if;
      end loop;
      SIZE := N_ELTS_READ;
   end READ;
```

```
    procedure SORT (S : in out INTEGER_ARRAY) is
      SMALLEST_POSN : INDEX;

      function SMALLEST (T : INTEGER_ARRAY) return INDEX is
      -- gives the index number for the smallest element in T
        M : INDEX := T'FIRST;
      begin
        for I in T'FIRST + 1 .. T'LAST loop
          if T(I) < T(M) then
            M := I;
          end if;
        end loop;
        return M;
      end SMALLEST;

      procedure SWAP (I, J : in        INDEX;
                        T    : in out INTEGER_ARRAY) is
      -- swap the Ith and Jth elements in array T
        TEMP : INTEGER;
      begin
        TEMP := T(I);
        T(I)    := T(J);
        T(J)    := TEMP;
      end SWAP;

    begin
      for K in S'RANGE loop
        SMALLEST_POSN := SMALLEST(S(K .. S'LAST));
        SWAP(K, SMALLEST_POSN, S);
      end loop;
    end SORT;

    procedure WRITE(S : in INTEGER_ARRAY) is
    begin
      NEW_LINE;
      PUT_LINE("The numbers are:");
      for K in S'RANGE loop
        PUT( S(K) );
      end loop;
      NEW_LINE;
    end WRITE;

begin
    READ (A, N_ELTS);
    SORT (A(1 .. N_ELTS));
    WRITE(A(1 .. N_ELTS));
end SORT_EXAMPLE;
```

Clearly, this program is longer (with regard to the number of lines) than
the program we wrote in Section 5.8. However, it is not always the case
that a short program is a 'good' program. The clarity of a program is

determined by its structure. In general a program that is developed from the top down with subprograms has a better structure; it does not matter that it is a few lines longer than it would be without subprograms.

6.5   The scope of a declaration

It has been shown that a local variable in a subprogram can be considered as a temporary store that only exists while the subprogram is called. That is, the declaration of the local variable has only a certain **scope**, that extends over the subprogram in which it is declared. It is not only the declarations of variables that have a particular scope; all sorts of declarations, such as those of types, constants and subprograms, have an associated scope so that what has been declared is only known and only used in a certain part of the program; it is said that they are only **visible** in that part of the program. There are well-specified rules in Ada for declaration scope; these are analogous to the corresponding rules in other closely related languages such as Pascal.

To explain the rules we use the outline nonsense program:

```
procedure P1 is
   type T is ... ;
   A : constant INTEGER := 100;
   B : INTEGER := 2 * A;

   procedure P2 (X: INTEGER) is
      A : FLOAT;

      procedure P3 (C : T) is
         X : FLOAT;
      begin
         ⋮
      end P3;

   begin
      ⋮
   end P2;

   procedure P4 (I : INTEGER) is
      Q : T;
   begin
      ⋮
      P2(... , ...);                    -- call of P2
      ⋮
   end P4;

begin
   ⋮
end P1;
```

In the program there are procedures P1, P2, P3 and P4. P1 is the main program and is the outermost procedure. The declarations of P2 and P4 are within P1 and the declaration of P3 is within P2.

The main rule is that the scope of a declaration extends from the place where it is made to the end of the subprogram it is in. This means, in our example, that the variable Q and the formal parameter I are only known in the procedure P4. If attempts are made to use Q or I outside P4 a compile-time error will result. The fact that a declaration's scope begins where the declaration is made means that reference may not be made to something that is declared later in the program, even if it is declared in the same subprogram. In the example, for example, it is important that A's declaration comes before that of B because A is used in the declaration of B.

The scope of a declaration

A declaration applies from the place where it is made to the end of the subprogram in which it is made.

The next rule states that something declared in a subprogram P is also visible in all subprograms declared within P. The type T in our example is thus visible not only in P1 but also in P2 (and therefore also in P3) and in P4, because P2 and P4 are declared within P1. Another example is that P2 is visible in P4 and can be called there, because both P2 and P4 are declared in P1, and P2 is declared before P4.

Global declarations

A declaration that applies in a subprogram P also applies in all the subprograms to P.

The two rules can also be expressed thus: from the outside it is impossible to 'see into' a subprogram and get at the declarations that are made there; it is possible, however, to 'see out from the inside' from a subprogram and get at declarations made outside it.

These rules mean that in a subprogram it is possible to access variables that are declared in an enclosing subprogram. For example, the variable B in P1 is accessible from P4. The variable B is a **global variable** to P4. When programming, it is often very tempting to use global variables in a subprogram and change them thereby avoiding the use of parameters to the subprogram. The use of global variables is, however, contrary to the ideals of good programming style, because using them leads to programs being confused and difficult to understand. Then the risk of errors in the program increases and, at the same time, it becomes more difficult to find the errors in a program. From the calling program it is impossible to see that variables might be changed within a subprogram. Unexpected and elusive side effects can result. The rule is therefore: *never use global variables*. (As with all rules, there have to be exceptions. If subprograms are written in a package, under certain circumstances global variables can be used without offending the rules of good programming style).

Global variables

In a well-structured program, *never*, or virtually never, use global variables.

It is forbidden to declare several items with the same name in a particular subprogram (except for subprograms and enumeration literals). However, the same names may be used in declarations that are in different subprograms. In the foregoing example, the name A appeared in both P1 and P2 and the name X in both P2 and P3. If the same name is used in two declarations in different subprograms the two declared quantities have nothing to do with one another; they only have the same name. The name A, in our example, is used to denote an integer constant in procedure P1 but a floating point variable in P2.

Even if the scope of a declaration extends to the end of the subprogram in which it is declared, the declared quantity can be 'covered' in an enclosed subprogram, if this subprogram contains a declaration where the same name is used. In P2 (and P3), for example, the constant A in P1 cannot be accessed. If the name A is written in P2 or P3 it is the variable A that is declared in P2 that matters. In the same way, P2's formal parameter X cannot be reached within P3 because there it is 'covered' by the floating point variable X.

Using the same names

- Quantities that are declared in the *same* sub-program must have different names (with the exception of subprograms and enumeration literals).
- Quantities that are declared in *different* sub-programs may have the same name.

The rules mean that if global variables are avoided then each subprogram can be considered as a separate 'building block' in the total program. Contact between each 'building block' and its surroundings (that is, the other subprograms) occurs through the subprogram's specification. Within the subprogram, any name can be used for declared quantities; it makes no difference whether the name appears in another subprogram. Subprograms can thus be developed independently of one another.

For example, in the program we wrote to compute the binomial coefficients, we could have used the names N and K for the formal parameters to the function BIN_COEFF; this may have been more natural than calling the parameters P and Q. This would not have been affected by the fact that the names N and K were also used in the procedure PRINT_TABLE. N and K within BIN_COEFF would be considered different from N and K in PRINT_TABLE.

6.6 Overloaded subprograms

■

To declare several quantities with the same name in a subprogram is normally forbidden; but in Ada, to declare several subprograms with the same name in the same sub-program is allowed and they are known as **overloaded subprograms**. To explain when this is allowed, we first need some definitions.

- By **base type** of a subtype we mean the type from which this subtype is derived. (For example, the base type of NATURAL is INTEGER). The base type of an ordinary type that is not a subtype is the type itself. (For example, the base type of INTEGER is INTEGER).

- If two subprograms have the same number of parameters and if the corresponding parameters have the same base types, we say that the two subprograms have the same **parameter type profile**.

- Two subprograms have the same **profile** (parameter and result type profile) if they are both procedures with the same parameter type profile, or if they are both functions with the same parameter type profile and, in addition, their results have the same base type.

If we write the following subprogram specifications, for example:

procedure A (P1 : **in** FLOAT; P2 : **in out** INTEGER)
procedure B (X :   **in out** FLOAT; Y : **out** INTEGER)
function C (U : POSITIVE) **return** CHARACTER
function D (V : INTEGER) **return** CHARACTER

then A has the same profile as B, and C has the same profile as D. Note that the two formal parameters do not need the same names for the two subprograms to have the same profiles. Nor does it matter whether the corresponding parameters are of the same kind in the sense of **in, in out** or **out**.

Several subprograms may have the same name in a subprogram (or a package) if these subprograms have different profiles:

```
type VECTOR is array (INTEGER range < > ) of FLOAT;

function MEAN (X1, X2 : FLOAT) return FLOAT is
begin
   return (X1 + X2) / 2.0;
end MEAN;

function MEAN (V : VECTOR) return FLOAT is
   SUM : FLOAT := 0.0;
begin
   for I in V'RANGE loop
     SUM := SUM + V(I);
   end loop;
   return SUM / FLOAT(V'LENGTH);
end MEAN;
```

Here we have two different functions with the same name; the two functions are overloaded. The functions have different profiles, in that the first takes two parameters of type FLOAT and the second takes one parameter of type VECTOR. If we assume the variables MV, X, Y and W are declared as follows:

```
MV : FLOAT;
X   : FLOAT := 6.5;
Y   : FLOAT := 4.5;
W   : VECTOR (1 .. 3) := (0.5, 3.0, 1.0);
```

then we can call the function MEAN:

```
MV := MEAN(X, Y);        -- MV takes the value 5.5
MV := MEAN(0.0, 1.0);    -- MV takes the value 0.5
MV := MEAN(W);           -- MV takes the value 1.5
MV := MEAN( (1.1, 1.3) );   -- MV takes the value 1.2
```

In the first call there are two actual parameters X and Y which both have type FLOAT. These actual parameters match with the formal parameters for the first function MEAN, but not with the formal parameter of the second. The compiler 'understands' that we intend to call the first of the subroutines MEAN. The second call also matches with the first function but not with the second. The last two calls, however, do not match with the first function. They suit the second instead and that will be called.

Overloaded subprograms

Two subprograms that are in the same subprogram may have the same name (the name may be overloaded) if they have different profiles, that is, different base types for parameters, and for the result in the case of functions.

The reason why overloaded subprograms must have different profiles is that the compiler must be able to choose which subprogram is intended for use every time a call is made. Only one subprogram can be suitable, otherwise the program would be ambiguous. (If none of the subprograms with the same name fit the bill, then the program is in error and an error message will be given during compilation).

We have already called overloaded subprograms many times. In the package TEXT_IO and BASIC_NUM_IO there are several procedures with the name PUT, for example. There are several procedures PUT with different profiles; output of text does not use the same procedure as output of a floating point number, to give one example. In the following statements four different procedures are being called:

```
PUT("Hello!");      -- The parameter has type STRING
PUT('a');           -- The parameter has type CHARACTER
PUT(I);             -- The parameter has type INTEGER
PUT(X);             -- The parameter has type FLOAT
```

Because the compiler has always chosen the correct PUT procedure we have not needed to worry that there are several versions. In the same way, TEXT_IO and BASIC_NUM_IO have several subprograms called GET.

The use of overloaded subprograms is thus a convenient way of carrying out similar operations on objects with different types. It is still possible to use the same name for the operation rather than inventing different names for the subprograms for each type.

☐

6.7   Named parameter association

■

The normal procedure for calling a subprogram is to list all the actual parameters, separated by commas. The first actual parameter is associated with the first formal parameter, the second actual parameter is associated with the second formal parameter and so on. Let us now write a procedure MULTIPLE_WRITE that has the task of writing out a particular character a number of times at the terminal, each time on a new line. As parameters, MULTIPLE_WRITE will have the character to be printed and an integer that specifies the number of times it should be written.

```
procedure MULTIPLE_WRITE (CHAR : CHARACTER;
                          N     : INTEGER) is
begin
   for I in 1 .. N loop
      PUT(CHAR); NEW_LINE;
   end loop;
end MULTIPLE_WRITE;
```

If we want to write the character 'x' 3 times, we would use the procedure call:

```
MULTIPLE_WRITE('x', 3);
```

Then the first actual parameter 'x' will be associated with the formal parameter CHAR and the second actual parameter, 3, will be associated with the second formal parameter N. This can be called **positional parameter association** because the position of an actual parameter in a procedure call determines the formal parameter with which it is associated.

Positional parameter association

- The call appears thus:

  subprogram_name(a1, a2, ... an)

- The actual parameters are listed in the call.
- Normally, all the actual parameters are listed.
- The first actual parameter is associated with the first formal parameter, the second actual parameter with the second formal parameter, etc.

In Ada there is another method of associating the actual parameters with the formal parameters in a subprogram call. It is possible to state the name of the formal parameter the actual parameter is to be associated to. We call this **named parameter association**. How it works is shown in the following call to MULTIPLE_WRITE:

MULTIPLE_WRITE(CHAR => 'x', N => 3);

The term:

CHAR => 'x'

means that the actual parameter 'x' should be associated with the formal parameter CHAR. Similarly,

N => 3

means that the actual parameter 3 should be associated with the formal parameter N. One thing gained by writing a call in this way is that it is clearer (if the formal parameters have good names). Someone reading the program later does not need to know exactly the formal parameters used or the order in which they appear, before being able to understand the significance of the call.

Named parameter association

The call appears thus:

  subprogram_name(name => a1, name => a2,...);

The parameters may be listed in any order.

When named parameter association is used the parameters do not need to be listed in any special order. The previous call could have been written:

  MULTIPLE_WRITE(N => 3, CHAR => 'x');

and this would have been equally correct.

In addition, positional and named parameter association can be mixed. Our call could also be written, for example:

  MULTIPLE_WRITE('x', N => 3);

When the two parameter associations are mixed in a call, the positional associations must be written first in their correct order. Named parameters can then be written in arbitrary order. When one named parameter association has been used in a call, all the remaining parameters in the call must also be named. For example, it is wrong to write:

  MULTIPLE_WRITE(CHAR => 'x', 3);   -- ERROR!

One question that arises is whether all the parameters must be listed in a call and what happens if they are not. First, we can state that in the case of **out** and **in out** parameters they must all be listed in a call. At the end of the call copying to the actual parameters, which must be variables, will occur and this cannot happen if actual parameters are missing.

In the case of **in** parameters, however, it is possible in Ada to omit actual **in** parameters. The condition allowing this to be possible is that a value is given in the subprogram that can be used if no actual parameter is given. To show how this works we can make a simple amendment to the procedure MULTIPLE_WRITE:

  procedure MULTIPLE_WRITE (CHAR : CHARACTER;
                       N   : INTEGER := 2) **is**

```
begin
  for I in 1 .. N loop
    PUT(CHAR); NEW_LINE;
  end loop;
end MULTIPLE_WRITE;
```

Here we have given the formal parameter N a value which is to be used if there is no actual parameter in a call. Such a value, used if no explicit value is stated, is called a **default value**. Thus the formal parameter N has a default value of 2.

Now the actual parameter that is to be associated with the formal parameter N may be omitted. We can write, for example:

```
MULTIPLE_WRITE(CHAR => '+');
```

This call means that two plus signs will be written. The call could also be written:

```
MULTIPLE_WRITE('+');
```

and again two plus signs will be written.

Of course, an actual parameter can still be associated explicitly with N if necessary. The call:

```
MULTIPLE_WRITE(CHAR => '+', N => 10);
```

will write out 10 plus signs and the default value the formal parameter N is of no significance.

Parameters with default values

- An **in** parameter to a subprogram may be given a default value when the formal parameter is specified:

  ```
  (..; parameter_name : in type := default_value; ..)
  ```

- Parameters with default values may be omitted from calls. Then the formal parameter is given the default value.

- **In out** parameters and **out** parameters may *not* have default values.

An **in** parameter may not be omitted from a call if there is no default value for the corresponding formal parameter. For example, it is wrong to write:

MULTIPLE_WRITE(N => 5);   -- ERROR!

When we have called the procedures PUT in the packages TEXT_IO and BASIC_NUM_IO we have made frequent use of named parameter association. We have also made use of the fact that certain **in** parameters to PUT have default values. For example, we have written calls such as:

PUT(I, WIDTH => 5);

where we have used positional parameter association for the first formal parameter and named parameter association for the formal parameter WIDTH. This call could also have been written:

PUT(ITEM => I, WIDTH => 5);

because the first formal parameter to all the PUT procedures is called ITEM.

When we have written a simple call, such as:

PUT(I);

we have made use of the fact that there is a default value of WIDTH in PUT. In the same way, the formal parameters EXP, FORE and AFT also have default values in the version of PUT that is used to write out floating point numbers. When we make a call such as:

PUT(X);

these default values will be used.

☐

6.8 Recursive subprograms

It has been shown that one subprogram can call another. Furthermore, a subprogram can call itself, and such a subprogram is called a **recursive subprogram**.

It is appropriate to use recursive subprograms to solve certain types of problem. The problems for which recursion is most useful are those which are defined from the start in a recursive way; this occurs often in

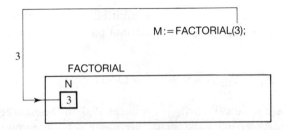

Figure 6.8

mathematical calculations. The most common example of a recursive subprogram – an example that occurs in almost all books about programming – is a function to calculate the factorial of a number n. This is a problem we have studied a couple of times already. We then used iteration to solve the problem but now we shall see how recursion can be used instead. The factorial of a number n, written $n!$, can be defined by:

$$n! = \begin{cases} 1 & \text{if } n = 0 \\ 1 \times 2 \times 3 \times \ldots \times n & \text{if } n > 0 \end{cases}$$

Another way of writing the definition is:

$$n! = \begin{cases} 1 & \text{if } n = 0 \\ n(n - 1)! & \text{if } n > 0 \end{cases}$$

There is one case where the value is given (that is, $0! = 1$) and one case where induction is used to express the solution in terms of values already defined.

This second definition leads naturally to the following Ada function:

```
function FACTORIAL (N : NATURAL) return POSITIVE is
begin
  if N = 0 then
    return 1;
  else
    return N * FACTORIAL(N - 1);
  end if;
end FACTORIAL;
```

The parameter N with subtype NATURAL ensures that the case N < 0 can never occur. If the function is called with an actual parameter that is less than 0, a run-time error will result at the call.

We see that on the sixth line the function calls itself. To see what

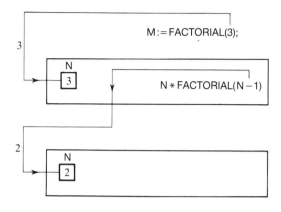

Figure 6.9

happens when the function is called, assume we have a program with the statement:

M := FACTORIAL(3);

where the variable M has type POSITIVE. Figure 6.8 shows the situation at the start of the call. As before, the formal parameter N can be thought of as a temporary store and the value 3 is copied to it.

Because N is not 0, the second of the two **return** statements will be executed. Here a new call to the function FACTORIAL occurs and the actual parameter takes the value 2, as illustrated in Figure 6.9. We get a new instance of the function FACTORIAL and in it a new temporary store is created, also called N. When the new instance of FACTORIAL is called, the value 2 is copied to the new store. Note that we now have two different stores N with different values. When the new instance of FACTORIAL is called, execution of the first instance is temporarily suspended waiting for the new instance to finish execution and return a result. It works like an entirely normal function call.

When the second instance of FACTORIAL is executed it will again be the **else** part of the **if** statement that is executed, because N in the second instance of FACTORIAL has the value 2. This results in a third call to FACTORIAL. A further instance of the function is generated and it creates a third temporary store called N, this time the value 1 being placed in it. When the call occurs, execution in the second instance is temporarily suspended in the normal way, until execution of the third instance is finished and has given a result value. Figure 6.10 illustrates the situation.

Now the third instance of FACTORIAL will be executed. Again, the second of the **return** statements will be executed because N here has the

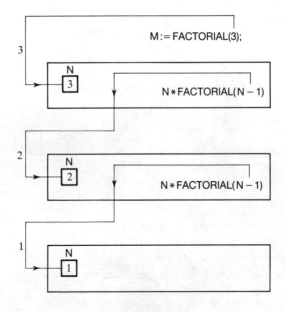

Figure 6.10

value 1. Thus we get a fourth call to FACTORIAL, a fourth instance of the function is made and a fourth temporary store with the name N is created. When the call to the fourth instance of the function occurs the value 0 will be copied into this N. Execution of the third instance will, as the two earlier instances of FACTORIAL, be suspended temporarily.

Execution now continues in the fourth instance of the function FACTORIAL, as illustrated in Figure 6.11. Since the formal parameter N has the value 0, this time the first **return** statement will be executed. As a result the function will give the value 1. This value is returned to the third instance of the function FACTORIAL.

In the third instance of FACTORIAL the function call:

FACTORIAL(N−1)

now has the value 1. Execution of the third instance can continue and the multiplication:

N * FACTORIAL(N−1)

is performed. The result is 1 because N has the value 1 in this instance. Thus the result given by the third instance of FACTORIAL will have the value 1. This value is returned to the calling subprogram, that is, to the second instance of FACTORIAL, as shown in Figure 6.12. Now execution

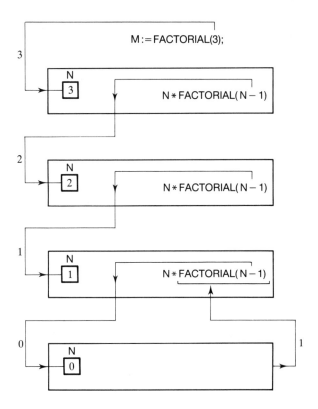

Figure 6.11

of the second instance can be completed. The function call:

FACTORIAL(N−1)

gets the value 1 and the expression:

N ∗ FACTORIAL(N−1)

takes the value 2 since N has the value 2 in the second instance. Thus the second instance of FACTORIAL returns the value 2 to the first instance (see Figure 6.13).

Finally, the first instance of FACTORIAL can be resumed. The function call:

FACTORIAL(N−1)

gets the value 6 since N has the value 3. Thus the first instance of the function FACTORIAL will give the calling program the value 6 as its result.

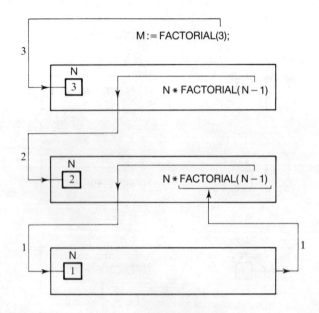

Figure 6.12

This means that the variable M in our original statement:

M := FACTORIAL(3);

takes the value 6, as shown in Figure 6.14.

In this way we are able to visualize what happens in a call to a recursive subprogram. The important thing to note is that several instances of the subprogram will exist and that each instance will have its own temporary stores for its formal parameters and any local variables.

Recursive subprograms

- A subprogram that directly or indirectly calls itself.

- During execution there are as many instances of the subprogram as the number of calls made.

- Each instance has its own unique stores for formal parameters and local variables.

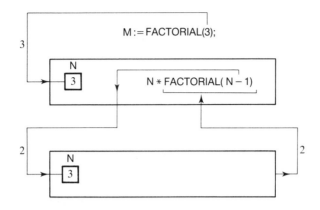

Figure 6.13

We shall now consider a function FIBONACCI that calculates so-called Fibonacci numbers. The Fibonacci numbers are a series of numbers that were originally used in a model to describe the growth of a population of rabbits. The first numbers in the series are 1, 1, 2, 3, 5, 8, 13, 21, 34, ... They are defined as follows:

$$f_n = \begin{cases} 1 & \text{if } n = 1 \text{ or } n = 2 \\ f_{n-2} + f_{n-1} & \text{if } n > 2 \end{cases}$$

It is easy to write a recursive function for calculating the Nth Fibonacci number based on this definition. The number N is given to the function as a parameter.

```
function FIBONACCI (N : POSITIVE) return POSITIVE is
begin
  if N = 1 or N = 2 then
    return 1;
  else
    return FIBONACCI(N−2) + FIBONACCI(N−1);
  end if;
end FIBONACCI;
```

We see that this function contains two recursive calls. If it would help, we could make drawings as before to show what is happening, but even for small values of N there are many instances of the function FIBONACCI and there would be much to draw. This function does not evaluate a Fibonacci number in the most efficient way but it illustrates nicely the fact that a problem specified recursively from the start can easily be solved using a recursive subprogram. Writing the function FIBONACCI is largely a question of rewriting the definition.

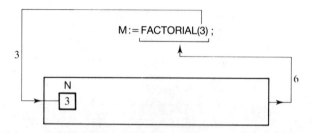

Figure 6.14

Even certain problems that are not initially defined in a recursive way can be solved easily with recursion. But first, the problem has to be reformulated recursively. It can best be demonstrated by the problem of calculating the sum of the components of a vector of floating point numbers. We have already solved this problem using iteration in Section 6.1 where we wrote a function SUM, but here we shall show how the problem can be solved using recursion.

The sum of the components of a vector V with N components can be defined in the following way:

$$\text{sum} = \begin{cases} 0, \text{ if the vector has no components (that is, N = 0)} \\ V(1) + \text{ the sum of the components of the vector } V(2 \ldots N) \end{cases}$$

This definition provides a direct basis for writing the function:

```
function SUM(V : VECTOR) return FLOAT is
begin
    if V'LENGTH = 0 then
        return 0.0;
    else
        return V(V'FIRST) + SUM( V(V'FIRST + 1 .. V'LAST) );
    end if;
end SUM;
```

In the second **return** statement a recursive call to SUM is made. The actual parameter to this call is the vector formed from the components 2 to N, inclusive, of V.

When the function is called we will get N + 1 instances of the function, all in existence at the same time. Each new instance will get as parameter a vector that is one component shorter than that of the previous instance. If we suppose that the original vector had 100 components, for example, we shall get 101 instances of the function SUM. The final instance (number 101) will get an empty vector as its parameter, that is, V will have no components. Instance 101 of SUM will thus return its result, the value 0.0, to instance number 100. Then instance 100 can complete its execution and return as result the sum of component 100 and 0.0, that is, the value of component 100. This result is returned to instance 99 which can then complete its execution. This will give as result the sum of components number 99 and 100, that is, the sum of the two last components. Instance 98 will then give, in an analogous manner, the sum of the last three components. This continues until finally instance 1 is reached, and that will give the sum of all the components as its result.

It is not only functions that can be recursive, recursive procedures can also be written. For example, we shall show a little procedure that reads text from the terminal and writes it out backwards. To solve this problem we use the following recursive idea:

   (1)   If there is any text to read, do the following:
       (1.1)   Read and remember the first character in the text.
       (1.2)   Read in the rest of the text and write it out backwards.
       (1.3)   Write out the first character of the text.

Step (1) is simple. The user can indicate the end of the text by giving an END_OF_FILE sign. Steps (1.1) and (1.3) are also simple. The character read in step (1.1) can be remembered in a variable of type CHARACTER and this variable can then be written out in step (1.3). Step (1.2) is more troublesome. How can we read in the rest of the text and write it out backwards? We observe that it is exactly the same problem as the original one. The only difference is that the text that has to be read in and written out is one character shorter than the original text. Therefore we should be able to use the same algorithm to solve this problem as to solve the whole problem. We can achieve this by placing a recursive call to the procedure which solves the whole problem. Since the first character is already read in, the text that remains to be read from the terminal will consist of the rest of the text, precisely as we want.

It is easy to translate this algorithm into Ada. We get the procedure:

```
procedure BACKWARDS is
   CHAR : CHARACTER;
begin
   if not END_OF_FILE then
      GET(CHAR);
      BACKWARDS;
      PUT(CHAR);
   end if;
end BACKWARDS;
```

The same number of instances of this procedure will exist as there are characters in the text, plus one. The first instance of the procedure reads in the text's first character and saves it in the local variable CHAR. Its execution will then be suspended temporarily while it makes its recursive call. Execution will not be resumed until all the other instances of the procedure have finished being executed.

When execution reaches the last instance of the procedure BACKWARDS, the whole text has been read in. This last instance will observe that there is no more text to read (END_OF_FILE is TRUE) and will therefore do nothing but return immediately to the last but one instance of the procedure. The last but one instance of the procedure has read the final character of the text and writes it out. Thus the last character read in is written out first.

Eventually, control is returned to the first instance of the procedure BACKWARDS which will write out the character that it saved. This means that the first character in the text will always be written out last.

■

In the examples we have looked at, recursion has always occurred because a subprogram called itself. It is also possible to have **indirect recursion**. A subprogram A can call another subprogram B which, in turn, calls A. Then A and B are said to be **mutually recursive**. (It is even possible for recursion to occur through several stages, for example, A calls B which calls C which calls A).

We can illustrate mutual recursion with the example of two subprograms that determine whether a positive number is odd or even. This problem can, of course, easily be solved in Ada by writing the Boolean expression:

N **mod** 2 = 1

which has the value TRUE if the integer variable N is odd. To demonstrate mutual recursion, however, we shall assume that we do not have access to the operators /, **rem** or **mod**. The solution to the problem is then obtained with the algorithm:

(1) If N is equal to 0 then N is not odd.
(2) Otherwise, N is odd if $N - 1$ is even.

If we assume access to a function EVEN that determines whether a number is even or not, we can make a direct translation into Ada:

```
function ODD (NUMBER : NATURAL) return BOOLEAN is
begin
   if NUMBER = 0 then
      return FALSE;
```

```
      else
        return EVEN(NUMBER - 1);
      end if;
    end ODD;
```

The function EVEN is, in structure, like the function ODD and can easily be written:

```
    function EVEN (NUMBER : NATURAL) return BOOLEAN is
    begin
      if NUMBER = 0 then
        return TRUE;
      else
        return ODD(NUMBER - 1);
      end if;
    end EVEN;
```

As we see, this function uses the function ODD. The question remains: 'How should the two functions be placed in relation to one another?' If the function ODD is placed before the function EVEN it is possible to call ODD from EVEN. But then, it is not possible to call EVEN from ODD because ODD has not yet been declared when the call is made. If the functions are written in the other order, the same problem arises but the opposite way round.

The solution lies in first writing a **separate subprogram specification** for one of the functions. If we start by declaring a separate subprogram specification for ODD our declarations will look like this:

```
    function ODD (NUMBER : NATURAL) return BOOLEAN;

    function EVEN (NUMBER : NATURAL) return BOOLEAN is
    begin
      if NUMBER = 0 then
        return TRUE;
      else
        return ODD(NUMBER - 1);
      end if;
    end EVEN;

    function ODD (NUMBER : NATURAL) return BOOLEAN is
    begin
      if NUMBER = 0 then
        return FALSE;
      else
        return EVEN(NUMBER - 1);
      end if;
    end ODD;
```

On the first line the specification for ODD is given. In Ada, this permits the body of a subprogram to be left until later. The complete declaration must be made later, and note that the specification must then be repeated. Since ODD is specified on the first line it is now known by EVEN and can be called from within EVEN.

Separate subprogram specification

>   **procedure** *name*(*parameters*);

or:

>   **function** *name*(*parameters*) **return** *result_type*;

- May appear anywhere among the declarations.
- The complete subprogram body (including the specification) must be written later.

Separate subprogram specifications are always allowed, not only for recursive subprograms. Their specifications can be put anywhere among the declarations.

□

6.9 Functions as operators

■

In Ada, as we have seen, there are many built-in operators. The operator + exists for both integer and floating point types, for example, and the operator = is defined for all types met so far. When we declare our own, more complicated, types we may also like to define operators for them. Let us take, as example, the type VECTOR which we have already used:

   type VECTOR **is array** (INTEGER **range** < >) **of** FLOAT;

We can declare variables of type VECTOR:

   X, Y, Z : VECTOR(1 .. 5);

In Section 6.1 we wrote a function ADD that could be used to add two vectors. The following statement, for example, adds the vectors X and Y and the result is assigned to the vector Z:

```
Z := ADD(X, Y);
```

The meaning is quite clear, but how much more elegant it would be to
write:

```
Z := X + Y;
```

This is not immediately possible because the operator + is not defined for
the type VECTOR, but it is possible in Ada to define operators for any
type. This is achieved using functions that, instead of having ordinary
identifiers as names, are given operator names.

For example, we shall alter the function ADD so that it is called
"+" instead:

```
function "+" (V1, V2 : VECTOR) return VECTOR is
  TEMP : VECTOR(V1'RANGE) := V2;
begin
  for I in V1'RANGE loop
    TEMP(I) := TEMP(I) + V1(I);
  end loop;
  return TEMP;
end "+";
```

The function "+" is now called in the same way as if it were an operator.
Instead of writing, as before:

```
ADD(X, Y)
```

we can now write:

```
X + Y
```

Note that the two parameters are written before and after the function's
name. Here are some examples of different ways in which the function
"+" can be called:

```
Z := X + Y;
Z := X + Y + Z;        -- the function is called twice
X := X + (1.0, 2.0, 3.0, 0.0, 1.5);
Y := (1.3, 3.5, 6.7, 0.8, −3.4) + (0.3, 5.6, 1.2, 0.0, 4.5);
```

The third and fourth examples show that the parameters can also be array
aggregates. The compiler 'understands' that we do not mean the
'ordinary' plus operator but the one we declared ourselves because the
operands have type VECTOR. We can say that we have overloaded

operators in exactly the same sense as the overloaded subprograms we discussed earlier. If we write the expression:

    I + J

where I and J are integer types the compiler would choose the 'ordinary' plus operator in spite of the fact that we have defined another. As many operators as necessary may be declared with the same name, provided their profiles are different (see Section 6.6).

There are only certain operator names that can be used as declared operators, and they are the normal operator names we studied in Chapter 3, namely:

and	**or**	**xor**		
=	<	<=	>	>=
+	−	&		-- normal + and −
+	−			-- unary + and −
*	/	**mod**	**rem**	
**	**abs**	**not**		

The operators that normally have two operands, for example *, **and** and the ordinary + operator, must also have two operands if new versions are declared; that is, the operator functions must have two parameters. The operators **abs**, **not** and the unary versions of + and − should have one operand.

Note that the operator /= is missing from the table above. This operator may not be declared explicitly because it is declared automatically if an equality operator, =, is declared. Since the equality operator exists automatically for all normal types, it may not normally be declared either; it is only allowed for **limited private** types that are used in conjunction with packages (see Section 8.9).

□

EXERCISES

6.1 Write a function to evaluate the sign of an integer in the following way. The function should return as its result the value 1 if the integer is greater than 0, the value 0 if the integer is equal to 0, and the value −1 if the integer is less than 0.

6.2 Write a function that receives a character in the interval 'A'..'Z' as parameter. As its result the function should give the corresponding lower case letter.

6.3 Write a function that uses the following Maclaurin series to calculate the value of e^x.

$$e^x = 1 + \frac{x}{1!} + \frac{x^2}{2!} + \frac{x^3}{3!} + \frac{x^4}{4!} + \ldots$$

Exclude terms that are less than 10^{-7} from the sum.

6.4 (a) **Euclid's algorithm** for evaluating the greatest common divisor of two positive integers m and n can be described as follows:

    (1) Divide m by n and denote the remainder by r.

    (2) If $r = 0$ the evaluation is finished and the result is in n.

    (3) Otherwise, set the value of m to that of n and the value of n to that of r, and return to step 1.

    Use this algorithm to write a function GCD that evaluates the greatest common divisor of two positive integers.

  (b) Write a program that reads in an arbitrary number of pairs of positive integers and writes out the greatest common divisor for each pair. Use the function GCD.

6.5 To calculate the square root of a number x we can use **Newton's method** as follows. Start by guessing a number $g \geqslant 0$. When we guess g, we know that there must be a number h such that $g \times h = x$. (The number h can thus be written as $h = x/g$). If we are very lucky and made a good guess, g and h are approximately equal and we have found the solution. In general, however, guesses are not that good. A new better guess is the mean of g and h:

$$\text{new guess} = \frac{g + \dfrac{x}{g}}{2}$$

Now we can replace g by the new guess and calculate a new value of h. By taking the mean of the new values of g and h we can get a still better guess, and so on.

    Use this method to write a function that evaluates the square root of x. Use $x/2$ for the first guess and let the guesses continue until the difference between two consecutive guesses is less than 10^{-6}.

6.6 The amplitude of a vector $(v_1, v_2, \ldots , v_n)$ can be calculated using the formula:

$$l = \sqrt{v_1^2 + v_2^2 + v_3^2 + \ldots + v_n^2}$$

Write a function that can be used to calculate the amplitude of a vector whose components are real numbers.

(a)   Assume the vector has four components.

(b)   Write the function so that it can calculate the amplitude of a vector with an arbitrary number of components.

6.7 Two vectors $(u_1, u_2, \ldots , u_n)$ and $(v_1, v_2, \ldots , v_n)$ are said to be **orthogonal** if the sum:

$$\sum_{i=1}^{n} u_i v_i$$

is equal to zero. Write a function that determines whether two integer vectors are orthogonal. The function may assume that the vectors have the same number of components, but the actual number should be arbitrary and they need not be numbered in the same way.

6.8 (a)   Write a function that checks that a given text string contains an identifier according to Ada's definition (see Section 3.2). The function should give one of the results TRUE or FALSE.

(b)   Use the function to write a program that reads in a line with a number of words from the terminal and writes out how many of the words are allowed identifiers. The words in the line are separated by one or more spaces.

6.9 Write a function that takes two text strings, T1 and T2, as parameters. The function should determine whether T1 is a substring of T2. If this is true, the function should return as a result the index of the start of the substring in T2. If T1 is not a substring of T2 the function should return the value 0.

Hint: If T1 has the value 'ada' and T2 has the value 'Time enough to be a gadabout when you have finished studying', the function would give the value 22 as its result, assuming that T2 is indexed from 1.

6.10 In an array of integers, 'rotation to the right' can be defined as an operation that moves each element one place to the right and the last element into the first position. Write a subprogram that rotates an array an arbitrary number of places to the right. The subprogram should have two parameters, the array to be rotated and an integer that gives the number of places to be rotated.

6.11 A **list** can be defined as a series of objects all of which are of the same type. A list can have an arbitrary number of objects and can also be a null list, an empty list. Examples of integer lists are:

$$(-1,-8,0,326) \quad (15) \quad ()$$

The last example is of an empty list. A list can be represented in Ada by an unconstrained array type.

(a)   Construct a subprogram that writes out an integer list in the same format as the examples above, that is, enclosed in brackets and with the objects separated by commas. There should be no spaces in the output. The list to be written is given as a parameter to the subprogram.

(b)   The **head** of a list can be defined as the first object in the list, and its **tail** is the list that is formed if the head is removed. The list $(17,-3,8)$, for example, has head 17 and tail $(-3,8)$. Note that the head is a single object and not a list. The head and tail are not defined for an empty list. A list with only one object has the empty list as tail.

Write two functions HEAD and TAIL that return the head and tail of a list, respectively. Both functions should have a list of integers as parameter. If the parameter is the empty list both functions should give a suitable error message.

(c)   Write a function SECOND that gets a list of integers as its parameter and as its result returns the second object in the list. Make use of the functions HEAD and TAIL from part (b).

6.12 When wage statistics are presented, a **median value** is often quoted. The median is the 'central' value of a collection of values; the number of values less than the median is the same as the number of values that are greater. One way to evaluate the median is to sort all the values into numerical order and then select the value in the middle. If there is an even number of values, the median is the mean of the two central values.

Write a program to read in a maximum of 1000 monthly wages and calculate and print their median value.

6.13 A numerically controlled drilling machine drills a large number of holes in a piece to be machined. A large part of the machine's time is spent moving from one hole to another. It is, therefore, desirable to minimize the moving time by making the machine drill holes in an appropriate order. It is practically impossible to find the optimal solution to the problem, even for a small number of holes, but here it is enough to find an 'acceptably' good method rather than the optimal one. One such method is that each time a hole has been drilled the next hole for drilling is the one that is nearest (and still needs to be drilled).

Write a program that reads in the coordinates of the holes to be drilled and then writes them out in the 'acceptable' order, according to the algorithm outlined above. The positions of the holes can be given as points in a two-dimensional coordinate system and can be stored in two arrays, one for each of the x and y coordinates.

Thus the program should start with an arbitrary point and then choose the next point by determining the one that lies closest and has not yet been dealt with, etc. The coordinates of the points should be written out in the order they are to be drilled. The distance between two points (x_1, y_1) and (x_2, y_2) is given by:

$$s = \sqrt{(x_1 - x_2)^2 + (y_1 - y_2)^2}$$

Assume that the coordinates of the points do not exceed a 'reasonable' size, say 100.

Hint: to avoid moving to a hole that has already been drilled, replace the x and y coordinates for each hole visited by a large number, for example, 10^{10}, so that such a point is so far away from the rest that it will not be chosen again.

6.14 A trade union makes the following offer for a long-term wage agreement:

- The first year (year number 1) each employee will receive a monthly wage of £790.

- In the following years (years number 2, 3, 4 and so on) there will be an increase of 4% over the previous year's wage, and an additional general rise of £30 per month.

Write a recursive function that will calculate the monthly wage for a particular year according to the scheme presented above. The only input parameter is to be the year number.

6.15 One way of finding the greatest common divisor of two positive integers is to use the definition:

$$\gcd(m,n) = \begin{cases} m & \text{if } m = n \\ \gcd(m - n, n) & \text{if } m > n \\ \gcd(m, n - m) & \text{otherwise} \end{cases}$$

Write a recursive function GCD that evaluates the greatest common divisor of two positive integers based on this definition.

6.16 The binomial coefficients can be defined in the following way:

$$\binom{n}{0} = 1$$

$$\binom{n}{n} = 1$$

$$\binom{n}{k} = \binom{n-1}{k-1} + \binom{n-1}{k} \qquad 0 < k < n$$

Write a recursive function to evaluate the binomial coefficient $\binom{i}{j}$. Assume that $0 \leqslant j \leqslant i$.

6.17 An efficient way of sorting the elements of an array goes under the name of **quicksort**. The method can be described by the following recursive algorithm:

    (1) If the array has no elements or only one element, then it is sorted. Otherwise, perform the following steps:

    (2) Choose an arbitrary element in the array and call it k.

    (3) Move the elements around in the array so that two groups are formed. The element k should be placed between the two groups. All the elements that are $\leqslant k$ should be placed in the group to the left of k and all the rest in the group to the right.

    (4) Sort the part of the array to the left of k using this algorithm.

    (5) Sort the part of the array to the right of k using this algorithm.

Use the algorithm to write a procedure that sorts an array of integers. (Compare with Exercise 5.11.)

Chapter 7
Data structures

7.1 Multidimensional array types
7.2 Arrays of arrays
7.3 Record types

7.4 Arrays of records
Exercises

In Chapter 5 we saw how Ada's simple types could be used to describe simple data objects – objects that can be represented by a single value, such as a temperature measurement. We also saw that array types can be used to describe a series of simple objects, such as text and lists. This chapter describes two opportunities offered by Ada which enable more complicated data structures to be described. First array types with several dimensions will be used to describe tables and arrays of numbers; then record types will be used to represent objects comprising several different components.

7.1   Multidimensional array types

In the array types studied so far there has been an index that could be used to select particular components from an array. When the array type has been declared the type of the index has also been stated, either integer or enumeration types are allowed. In this section we shall see how array type declarations can be generalized so that an array type can have several indexes.

7.1.1   Constrained array types

Data is often presented in the form of a table. One example is the distance tables found in road atlases, such as the one in Figure 7.1. The types studied so far are not adequate for describing a data structure of this kind. Using an array type, it is possible to describe a row or a column of such a table, but not the whole table.

It is possible to describe this sort of data structure in Ada with a **multidimensional array type**. To illustrate this we shall make a type declaration to describe the table in Figure 7.1. The distance between two cities is expressed as a whole number of kilometres, that can never be negative, so one possibility is to use the type NATURAL to describe a distance. Because this type represents natural numbers in the abstract sense, however, it is rather too general; it is better to declare a new integer type DISTANCE_TYPE:

> **type** DISTANCE_TYPE **is range** 0 .. 40077;   -- expressed in km

(The upper limit for possible distances has been chosen as the equatorial circumference).

The rows and columns of the distance table are named by cities, so we declare an enumeration type CITY that 'numbers' them:

> **type** CITY **is** (AMSTERDAM, BERLIN, LONDON, MADRID,
> PARIS, ROME, STOCKHOLM);

Now the declaration of a type DISTANCE_TABLE can be made:

> **type** DISTANCE_TABLE **is array** (CITY, CITY) **of** DISTANCE_TYPE;

This is a two-dimensional array type. It differs from the one-dimensional array types seen earlier in that two index types have to be stated. The term:

> (CITY, CITY)

	Amster dam	Berlin	London	Madrid	Paris	Rome	Stock holm
Amsterdam	0	648	494	1752	495	1735	1417
Berlin	648	0	1101	2349	1092	1588	1032
London	494	1101	0	1661	404	1870	1807
Madrid	1752	2349	1661	0	1257	2001	3138
Paris	495	1092	404	1257	0	1466	1881
Rome	1735	1588	1870	2001	1466	0	2620
Stockholm	1417	1032	1807	3138	1881	2620	0

Figure 7.1

states that the array will have two indexes, both of type CITY.

Multidimensional array types

> **type** A **is array** (*index1*, *index2*, .. *indexN*)
>   **of** *element_type*;

Index1, *index2*, .. are intervals of the form *first_value .. last_value*, or the names of discrete types.

Element_type is any (constrained) type.

Now a variable of type DISTANCE_TABLE can be declared:

    DISTANCE : DISTANCE_TABLE;

This variable comprises a table, as above, with seven rows and seven columns. Both columns and rows are 'numbered' with the enumeration type CITY. Each element in the table is an integer of type DISTANCE_TYPE. If we make the definitions as above, the contents of the variable DISTANCE are still undefined. Assignment can be used to give a particular value to each element, by indexing, exactly as in a one-dimensional array. For example, to insert the distance from Berlin to Rome in the table, we could write:

    DISTANCE(BERLIN, ROME) := 1588;

If we want to write out this distance we can use the statement:

    PUT((DISTANCE(BERLIN, ROME));

Thus indexing works for multidimensional arrays works in exactly the same way as for one-dimensional arrays, the only difference being that more than one index must be given.

Indexing in multidimensional arrays

A(*value1*, *value2*, ..., *valueN*)

where *value1* has *index_type1*, etc.

In a one-dimensional array it is possible to cut a slice, for example:

```
NAME(2 .. 5)
```

This is not possible in multidimensional arrays. Thus constructs such as:

```
DISTANCE(BERLIN .. ROME, AMSTERDAM)      -- ERROR!
DISTANCE(PARIS, LONDON .. STOCKHOLM)      -- ERROR!
```

are wrong.

It may be practical to give values to the whole distance table at once, and to do this a two-dimensional array aggregate can be used. If the table is to be initialized at the same time as it is declared, we can write:

```
DISTANCE : DISTANCE_TABLE :=
            ((    0,  648,  494, 1752,  495, 1735, 1417),
             (  648,    0, 1101, 2349, 1092, 1588, 1032),
             (  494, 1101,    0, 1661,  404, 1870, 1807),
             (1752, 2349, 1661,    0, 1257, 2001, 3138),
             (  495, 1092,  404, 1257,    0, 1466, 1881),
             (1735, 1588, 1870, 2001, 1466,    0, 2620),
             (1417, 1032, 1807, 3138, 1881, 2620,    0));
```

In the two-dimensional aggregate each row has been stated as an ordinary one-dimensional aggregate. The expression:

```
(  494, 1101,    0, 1661,  404, 1870, 1807)
```

for example, states the value of 'London's' row in the table. The rules for writing aggregates are the same as those we studied earlier. If, for example, we want to set the whole table to zero we can write one of the following alternatives:

```
DISTANCE := ( (0, 0, 0, 0, 0, 0, 0),
              (0, 0, 0, 0, 0, 0, 0),
              (0, 0, 0, 0, 0, 0, 0),
              (0, 0, 0, 0, 0, 0, 0),
              (0, 0, 0, 0, 0, 0, 0),
              (0, 0, 0, 0, 0, 0, 0),
              (0, 0, 0, 0, 0, 0, 0) );

DISTANCE := ( AMSTERDAM => (0, 0, 0, 0, 0, 0, 0),
              BERLIN    => (0, 0, 0, 0, 0, 0, 0),
              LONDON    => (0, 0, 0, 0, 0, 0, 0),
              MADRID    => (0, 0, 0, 0, 0, 0, 0),
              PARIS     => (0, 0, 0, 0, 0, 0, 0),
              ROME      => (0, 0, 0, 0, 0, 0, 0),
              STOCKHOLM => (0, 0, 0, 0, 0, 0, 0));

DISTANCE := ( (others => 0),
              (others => 0),
              (others => 0),
              (others => 0),
              (others => 0),
              (others => 0),
              (others => 0) );

DISTANCE := (others => (others => 0) );
```

As with one-dimensional arrays, sometimes the compiler must be given help in the form of a qualified expression giving the type of the aggregate:

```
DISTANCE := DISTANCE_TABLE'
        (MADRID => (1752, 2349, 1661, 0, 1257, 2001, 3138),
         others    => (0, 0, 0, 0, 0, 0, 0) );
```

It is very common for nested **loop** statements to be used in connection with multidimensional arrays. The following lines of program show how a distance table can be printed at the terminal:

```
-- write out the table
for FROM in AMSTERDAM .. STOCKHOLM loop
  -- write a line of the table
  for TO in AMSTERDAM .. STOCKHOLM loop
    -- write a distance in the current line
    PUT(DISTANCE(FROM, TO), WIDTH => 6);
  end loop;
  NEW_LINE;
end loop;
```

The outer **loop** statement is run through once per row of table. On the first loop the iteration counter FROM has the value AMSTERDAM, on the second it is BERLIN, etc. Each time round, the outer **loop** statement writes out a line at the terminal, the line being terminated by NEW_LINE. The inner **loop** statement is executed once for each time through the outer loop. Each execution of the inner **loop** statement involves seven iterations, the iteration counter TO having the value AMSTERDAM the first time round, BERLIN the second, and so on. This means that the call to PUT will occur for each possible combination of FROM and TO, that is, 49 times.

When a multidimensional array type is declared, in the same way as for one-dimensional arrays, any discrete type, integer or enumeration type can be used as the index types. The same rules apply. It is probably most common to number the rows and columns in a two-dimensional array type with figures. For example, we shall look at the simple game of noughts and crosses, played on a 3 × 3 board. One player has crosses and the other has noughts. They take it in turn to place a piece on the board and the player who gets three of his pieces in a line – a row, a column or a diagonal – is the winner. The game continues until one player wins or the board is full. During the game a square on the board can either be empty or contain a cross or a nought. A square can thus be described by the type declaration:

```
type SQUARE is (EMPTY, X, O);
```

and the board can be described by the two-dimensional array type:

```
type GAMES_BOARD is array (1 .. 3, 1 .. 3) of SQUARE;
```

If we wanted to, we could introduce special index types and write instead:

```
subtype ROW_NUMBER is INTEGER range 1 .. 3;
subtype COL_NUMBER is INTEGER range 1 .. 3;
type GAMES_BOARD is array (ROW_NUMBER, COL_NUMBER) of
                           SQUARE;
```

Now variables of type GAMES_BOARD can be declared, such as:

```
P : GAMES_BOARD := ( others => ( others => EMPTY) );
```

Here P has been initialized so that all the squares are empty when the game starts. Individual elements of P can be selected by indexing. If, for example, we want to put a cross in the centre square we can write:

```
P(2,2) := X;
```

We shall study a function that determines whether the games board is full:

```
function FULL(BOARD : GAMES_BOARD) return BOOLEAN is
begin
    -- find out if board has any empty squares
    for R in 1 .. 3 loop
        -- find out if row R has any empty squares
        for C in 1 .. 3 loop
            if BOARD(R,C) = EMPTY then
                return FALSE;
            end if;
        end loop;
    end loop;
    -- no empty square has been found
    return TRUE;
end FULL;
```

The function gets a board as parameter and returns a BOOLEAN value as its result. If the board is full, that is, all the squares contain either a cross or a nought, the function returns the value TRUE, but otherwise it returns FALSE.

The function contains two nested **loop** statements. The outer one goes through all the rows and the inner one, which is performed once for each row, goes through all the columns. If a square is reached that has the value EMPTY the statement:

```
return FALSE;
```

is executed, which means that execution of the function ceases and the value FALSE is returned. Thus if an empty square is found, the remaining squares are not looked at. If none of the squares are empty then, eventually, the function's last statement:

```
return TRUE;
```

is executed and the function returns the value TRUE.

In a multidimensional array type the index types do not need to be the same, as they have been in the examples seen so far. In the next example we assume that we have measured the temperature of the air every hour for a whole week. We shall write a program that reads in the temperature measurements made and then calculates and writes out the mean hourly temperatures for the week.

We start by declaring an enumeration type DAY:

```
type DAY is (MONDAY, TUESDAY, WEDNESDAY,
             THURSDAY, FRIDAY, SATURDAY, SUNDAY);
```

We can also declare an integer type HOUR to describe the 24 hours of the day:

```
type HOUR is range 1 .. 24;
```

If the temperature measurements have been made with an accuracy of one decimal figure, the following type can be used to describe them:

```
type TEMP is digits 3 range −99.9 .. 99.9;
```

Now we can construct a two-dimensional array type that describes a whole week's measurements:

```
type MEASUREMENT_TABLE is array (DAY, HOUR) of TEMP;
```

The two indexes here are of different types. If we declare a variable of type MEASUREMENT_TABLE:

```
MEASUREMENTS : MEASUREMENT_TABLE;
```

then we can, for example, give the Thursday 7 pm measurement the value 11.3 by writing the statement:

```
MEASUREMENTS(THURSDAY, 19) := 11.3;
```

Now we write a procedure that reads values into a measurement table. The user has to be requested to input 24 hourly measurements for each day. The procedure will have a measurement table as an **out** parameter. When execution of the procedure is complete this table should be filled with the week's measurements.

```
procedure READ_MEASUREMENTS
                (TAB : out MEASUREMENT_TABLE) is
begin

  -- Read values into table
  for D in DAY loop
    PUT("Enter the temperatures for ");
    PUT(D); NEW_LINE;

    -- Read values into a line of the table
    for H in HOUR loop
      GET( TAB(D, H) );
    end loop;
  end loop;
end READ_MEASUREMENTS;
```

hr	mean temp
1	5.0
2	5.0
3	4.9
.	.
.	.
.	.
22	5.7
23	5.3
24	5.2

Figure 7.2

The elements of the table are run through and filled in *row by row*. First the elements in the Monday row get their values in order (for 01.00, 02.00, etc.). Then the elements of the Tuesday row get theirs, then the Wednesday row, and so on. At this point, we assume that packages have been created in the main program to handle reading and writing the types DAY and TEMP.

Note the construct:

for H **in** HOUR **loop**

This ensures that the loop parameter H has the type HOUR and that it will run through all the values of the type HOUR, namely 1 to 24. It would have been wrong to write:

for H **in** 1 .. 24 **loop**   -- ERROR!

because then H would have had type INTEGER and it would not have been possible to use H as index in the array TAB. If we did not want to run through all the hours but only certain ones, for example, 1 to 12 am, we would have to state the type and write:

for H **in** HOUR **range** 1 .. 12 **loop**

The next procedure we shall write receives a completed measurement table as **in** parameter. Its job is to calculate and write out the mean of all the week's measurements for each hour of the day. The output should look like that in Figure 7.2.

We use the algorithm:

(1) Write the heading.
(2) Carry out the following for each hour:

(2.1)   Calculate the mean for the current hour.
(2.2)   Write out the calculated mean.

Step (2.1) can be expanded to:

(2.1.1)   Add all the measurements made during the week for the current hour.
(2.1.2)   Divide the sum obtained by the number of measurements, that is, by 7.

A further refinement can be made for step (2.1.1):

(2.1.1.1)   Set MV to 0.
(2.1.1.2)   Run through all the days of the week and add the temperatures measured to MV.

The algorithm can now be translated to Ada, giving the procedure:

```
procedure WRITE_MEAN (M_TAB : MEASUREMENT_TABLE) is
   MEAN : TEMP;
begin

   -- Write heading
   PUT_LINE("hr        mean temp");
   NEW_LINE;

   for H in HOUR loop

      -- Add all the measurements for this hour
      MEAN := 0.0;
      for D in DAY loop
         MEAN := MEAN + M_TAB(D, H);
      end loop;

      -- Divide by the number of measurements
      MEAN := MEAN / 7.0;

      -- Print the calculated mean value
      PUT(H, WIDTH => 2);
      PUT(MEAN, EXP => 0, FORE => 7, AFT => 1);
      NEW_LINE;
   end loop;
end WRITE_MEAN;
```

In this procedure there is an outer **loop** statement which runs through all the hours. Each time round, this **loop** statement calculates the mean value of the week's measurements at a particular hour of the day. This means that the elements of the table are run through *column by column*.

Compare this with the procedure READ_MEASUREMENTS where the elements were run through row by row.

Running through a table row by row

```
for ROW in first_row_no .. last_row_no loop
    for COL in first_col_no .. last_col_no loop
        ... A(ROW, COL) ...
    end loop;
end loop;
```

Running through a table column by column

```
for COL in first_col_no .. last_col_no loop
    for ROW in first_row_no .. last_row_no loop
        ... A(ROW, COL) ...
    end loop;
end loop;
```

Now we can put these two procedures into a main program where we have also included the necessary type declarations and declared the packages for reading and writing the types DAY, HOUR and TEMP. When the program is run it will first call the procedure READ_MEASUREMENTS to get the week's temperature measurements. Then the procedure WRITE_MEAN is called, to calculate and write out the hourly means of the temperatures.

```
with TEXT_IO;
use  TEXT_IO;
procedure MEASUREMENTS_EXAMPLE is
    type DAY is (MONDAY, TUESDAY, WEDNESDAY,
                 THURSDAY, FRIDAY, SATURDAY, SUNDAY);
    type HOUR is range 1 .. 24;
    type TEMP is digits 3 range −99.9 .. 99.9;
    type MEASUREMENT_TABLE is array (DAY, HOUR) of TEMP;

    package DAY_INOUT is new ENUMERATION_IO(DAY);
    package HOUR_INOUT is new INTEGER_IO(HOUR);
    package TEMP_INOUT is new FLOAT_IO(TEMP);
    use DAY_INOUT, HOUR_INOUT, TEMP_INOUT;

    MEASUREMENTS : MEASUREMENT_TABLE;
```

```
            procedure READ_MEASUREMENTS
                            (TAB : out MEASUREMENT_TABLE) is
        begin

            -- Read values into table
            for D in DAY loop
              PUT("Enter the temperatures for ");
              PUT(D); NEW_LINE;

              -- Read values into a line of the table
              for H in HOUR loop
                GET( TAB(D, H) );
              end loop;
            end loop;
        end READ_MEASUREMENTS;

        procedure WRITE_MEAN (M_TAB : MEASUREMENT_TABLE) is
          MEAN : TEMP;
        begin

            -- Write heading
            PUT_LINE("hr      mean temp");
            NEW_LINE;

            for H in HOUR loop

              -- Add all the measurements for this hour
              MEAN := 0.0;
              for D in DAY loop
                MEAN := MEAN + M_TAB(D, H);
              end loop;

              -- Divide by the number of measurements
              MEAN := MEAN / 7.0;
              -- Print the calculated mean value
              PUT(H, WIDTH => 2);
              PUT(MEAN, EXP => 0, FORE => 7, AFT => 1);
              NEW_LINE;
            end loop;
        end WRITE_MEAN;

    begin
      READ_MEASUREMENTS(MEASUREMENTS);
      WRITE_MEAN(MEASUREMENTS);
    end MEASUREMENTS_EXAMPLE;
```

The examples we have seen so far (distance tables, games boards, tables of measurements) have all been arrays with two dimensions. Even if two-dimensional arrays are the most common among multidimensional arrays, in Ada there are no limits as to the number of dimensions allowed. For example, we can look at the sales of various goods in a supermarket with 10 check-outs. The goods in the store are divided into five categories: food, confectionery, household goods, tobacco and miscellaneous goods. There are statistics concerning the sales for a whole year. For each month the value of the goods sold at each check-out have been collected, classified according to the five categories above. A suitable type for describing the sales statistics is:

type STATISTICS **is array** (MONTH, CHECK_OUT, GOODS) **of** FLOAT;

where the type MONTH, CHECK_OUT and GOODS are declared as follows:

```
type MONTH is (JANUARY, FEBRUARY, MARCH, APRIL,
               MAY, JUNE, JULY, AUGUST,
               SEPTEMBER, OCTOBER, NOVEMBER, DECEMBER);
type CHECK_OUT is range 1 .. 10;
type GOODS is (FOOD, CONFECTIONERY, HOUSEHOLD_GOODS,
               TOBACCO, MISCELLANEOUS);
```

Suppose we want to know which check-out had the best total sales during the year. We write a function BEST_CHECK_OUT to look into it. As **in** parameter to the function we shall give the current year's sales statistics, that is, a multidimensional array of type STATISTICS. As its result the function will return a check-out number, of type CHECK_OUT.

```
function BEST_CHECK_OUT (SALES : STATISTICS)
                                  return CHECK_OUT is
   CURRENT_BIGGEST : FLOAT      := 0.0;
   CURRENT_BEST    : CHECK_OUT := 1;
   SUM : FLOAT;
begin
   -- look for the best check-out
   for C in CHECK_OUT loop

      -- calculate the total sales at check-out C
      SUM := 0.0;
      for M in MONTH loop
        for G in GOODS loop
          SUM := SUM + SALES(M, C, G);
        end loop;
      end loop;
      if SUM > CURRENT_BIGGEST then
         -- check_out C is the best so far
         CURRENT_BIGGEST := SUM;
         CURRENT_BEST    := C;
      end if;
```

```
        end loop;
            return CURRENT_BEST;
      end BEST_CHECK_OUT;
```

In the function there are three nested **loop** statements. The outermost runs through all the check-outs. For each check-out the total sales of all kinds of goods during the year is calculated and placed in the local variable SUM. In order to do this, it must sum over all the months and all the categories of goods. Then it looks as if the current check-out has a better sales result than the best of those already investigated. In that case the variables CURRENT_BIGGEST and CURRENT_BEST are updated. When all the check-outs have been examined, CURRENT_BEST contains the number of the check-out with the largest total sales. This number is returned by the function as its result.

7.1.2 Matrices and unconstrained arrays

In mathematics a set of numbers arranged in M rows and N columns is called an M × N **matrix**. As an example, here is a 3 × 4 matrix:

$$\begin{pmatrix} 11 & 45 & -5 & 0 \\ 4 & 10 & 26 & 32 \\ -1 & 0 & 2 & 16 \end{pmatrix}$$

It is possible to define mathematical operations. For example, addition of two matrices, A and B, can be defined if they have the same numbers of rows and columns. Their sum is then a new matrix in which each element is the sum of the corresponding elements in A and B. Here is an example:

$$\begin{pmatrix} 0 & 3 & 5 & 1 \\ 1 & 2 & 2 & -1 \\ 4 & 8 & 3 & 0 \end{pmatrix} + \begin{pmatrix} 1 & 1 & 1 & 1 \\ 0 & 4 & 5 & 0 \\ 0 & 2 & 1 & 0 \end{pmatrix} = \begin{pmatrix} 1 & 4 & 6 & 2 \\ 1 & 6 & 7 & -1 \\ 4 & 10 & 4 & 0 \end{pmatrix}$$

A matrix is naturally represented in Ada by a two-dimensional array of either integers or real numbers. The indexes are integers and row and column numbering usually starts from 1. For example, a 3 × 4 matrix of integers can be described by this type:

```
type MATRIX34 is array (1 .. 3, 1 .. 4) of INTEGER;
```

Here is a function that adds two 3 × 4 matrices and gives a new 3 × 4 matrix as its result.

```
function ADD (A, B : MATRIX34) return MATRIX34 is
  C : MATRIX34;
begin
  -- Calculate elements of matrix C
  for I in 1 .. 3 loop

    -- Calculate elements of row I of matrix C
    for J in 1 .. 4 loop
      -- Calculate element in column J of row I
      C(I,J) := A(I,J) + B(I,J);
    end loop;
  end loop;
  return C;
end ADD;
```

The function runs through the two matrices, element by element, adding pairs from corresponding positions and placing the result in the local variable C, another 3 × 4 matrix. Then C is returned from the function as its result.

We saw earlier that unconstrained array types may be used to write general subprograms that work for all sizes of array. This is also possible in the case of multidimensional arrays. We can declare a type MATRIX that denotes matrices with arbitrary numbers of rows and columns:

```
type MATRIX is array (POSITIVE range < >,
                      POSITIVE range < >) of INTEGER;
```

The constructs:

```
POSITIVE range < >
```

state that both index types should be of the subtype POSITIVE and that their exact limits can vary. As for a one-dimensional array, the index constraints must be stated when a variable of the type is declared:

```
P35, Q35 : MATRIX(1 .. 3, 1 .. 5);
X24, Y24 : MATRIX(1 .. 2, 1 .. 4);
```

Here P35 and Q35 are 3 × 5 matrices and X24 and Y24 are 2 × 4 matrices.

Unconstrained multidimensional array types

type A **is array** (T1 **range** < >, T2 **range** < >, ...)
                              of *element_type*;

T1, T2 etc. are discrete types.

- Index constraints must be given when an object is declared but unconstrained types may be used in declaring formal parameters to subprograms.

- *Element_type* can be any (constrained) type.

Now we can write a general version of the function ADD that will work for all matrices, irrespective of the numbers of rows and columns. However, the elements must be of the same type and the two matrices must have the same numbers of rows and columns.

```
function ADD(A, B : MATRIX) return MATRIX is
  C : MATRIX(A'RANGE(1), A'RANGE(2));
begin

  -- Calculate elements of matrix C
  for I in A'RANGE(1) loop

    -- Calculate elements in row I
    for J in A'RANGE(2) loop
      -- Calculate element in column J of row I
      C(I,J) := A(I,J) + B(I,J);
    end loop;
  end loop;
  return C;
end ADD;
```

A generalized form of the RANGE attribute, valid for multidimensional arrays, has been used here.

    A'RANGE(1)

gives the interval for the first index of A, and

    A'RANGE(2)

gives the interval for its second index. The declaration:

    C : MATRIX(A'RANGE(1), A'RANGE(2));

thus means that C gets the same numbers of rows and columns as A. For example, if we call the function with:

    ADD(X24, Y24)

then A'RANGE(1) is the equivalent of:

    1 .. 2

and A'RANGE(2) is the equivalent of:

    1 .. 4

If X24 has the value:

    1   3   0   7
    2   4   6   1

and Y24 has the value:

    1   1   2   0
    1   0   1   1

then the function will return:

    2   4   2   7
    3   4   7   2

as the result of being called.

   We could also call ADD in the following way:

    ADD(P35, Q35)

Then it would return the 3 × 5 matrix which is the sum of P35 and Q35.

   The attributes FIRST, LAST, LENGTH and RANGE exist in generalized forms for multidimensional arrays, as is seen from these examples:

    X24'FIRST(1)   gives the value 1
    X24'FIRST(2)   gives the value 1
    X24'LAST(1)   gives the value 2
    X24'LAST(2)   gives the value 4
    X24'LENGTH(1)   gives the value 2
    X24'LENGTH(2)   gives the value 4
    X24'RANGE(2)   gives the range 1 .. 4

Attributes for multidimensional arrays

- FIRST(N) gives the first index value for index number N.
- LAST(N) gives the last index value for index number N.
- LENGTH(N) gives the number of index values for index number N.
- RANGE(N) gives the index interval for index number N.

7.2 Arrays of arrays

When one-dimensional arrays were used earlier we saw that they had components of scalar types, that is, simple objects such as INTEGER or FLOAT. In Ada, however, there is nothing to stop the components being compound types. For example, the components of an array could actually be of array type.

For example, we shall study an alternative way of representing matrices. Instead of considering a matrix as a two-dimensional arrangement of numbers we can see it as a number of rows, each consisting of a number of simple elements. A 4 × 5 matrix can then be described thus:

```
type ROW5 is array (1 .. 5) of INTEGER;
type MATRIX45 is array (1 .. 4) of ROW5;
```

Now variables of type MATRIX45 can be declared, such as:

```
X : MATRIX45;
```

X is a one-dimensional array where each component is in turn a one-dimensional array. To get at individual components in the array, indexing can be used, as normal. The expression:

```
X(2)
```

for example, means that element number 2 in X, that is, the second row, is selected. Since a row is in itself an array, it can also be indexed. To select the third component of the second row we write:

```
X(2) (3)
```

Note that this has a different form to that used to describe a matrix using two-dimensional arrays.

One disadvantage of using arrays of arrays rather than two-dimensional arrays is that unconstrained types may not be used for the rows. When an array is declared its component types must be constrained. Thus it is *not* permitted to make the declarations:

type ROW **is array** (POSITIVE **range** < >) **of** INTEGER;

type MATRIX **is array** (POSITIVE **range** < >) **of** ROW; -- ERROR!

ROW is an unconstrained type and is not allowed to be a component type in the declaration of MATRIX. However, there is nothing against MATRIX being an unconstrained array type. If we amend the row type to be a constrained type, with five components for example, the following declarations are allowed:

type ROW5 **is array** (1 .. 5) **of** INTEGER;

type MATRIX **is array** (POSITIVE **range** < >) **of** ROW5;

The number of rows in the matrix can thus be indeterminate when an array of arrays is used, but the number of columns must be specified.

Arrays of arrays

    type ROW **is array** (*index2*) **of** *element_type*;

    type A **is array** (*index1*) **of** ROW;

- *Index1* and *index2* are intervals of the form *first_value* .. *last_value* or the name of a discrete type.

- *Index1* (but *not index2*) can also be an unconstrained expression of the form:

    discrete_type_name **range** < >

Indexing in arrays of arrays

    A(*value1*) (*value2*)

where *value1* is of *index_type1* and *value2* is of *index_type2*.

One advantage of using an array of arrays instead of a two-dimensional array is that it is possible to cut slices since we have two one-dimensional array types. If the variable X of type MATRIX45 has the value:

```
 1   2   3   4   5
 6   7   8   9  10
11  12  13  14  15
16  17  18  19  20
```

then the expression X(2 .. 4) means rows 2 to 4, that is:

```
 6   7   8   9  10
11  12  13  14  15
16  17  18  19  20
```

Indexing can be used in this part-matrix, or further slices can be cut. The expression X(2 .. 4) (1) thus means:

```
 6  7  8  9  10
```

and the expression X(2 .. 4) (2 .. 3) means:

```
11  12  13  14  15
16  17  18  19  20
```

We can also cut slices from rows. The expression X(4) means the fourth row:

```
16  17  18  19  20
```

and X(4) (2 .. 4) is then the part-row:

```
17  18  19
```

Slices in an array of arrays

- It is permitted to cut out slices.
- F(j .. k) means row j to row k in A.
- A(n) (p .. g) means elements p to g in row n of A.

Whether or not to use a two-dimensional array or an array of arrays to describe a two-dimensional data structure is a matter of judgement. In many cases it is most natural to use a two-dimensional array. Then there is the advantage of being able to use unconstrained arrays. Sometimes it is necessary to be able to cut slices and then an array of arrays should be used, since slices are not permitted in two-dimensional arrays.

As an example of a case when it is appropriate to use an array of arrays we shall study a very simple membership list for a club of some sort. We shall assume that each member has a particular membership number. A register is kept of all the members, an entry consisting of the membership number and the member's surname. There is no fixed upper limit for the number of members the club can have. Each time a new person joins, he or she is allocated the next available membership number and the number and name are entered at the end of the list. This means that the members are not listed in alphabetical order but according to the length of time they have held membership.

A member's name can be described by the type:

```
MAXLENGTH : constant := 20;
subtype NAME is STRING(1 .. MAXLENGTH);
```

Thus we store only the first 20 letters of a member's name and if the name is shorter than that we pad it with blanks.

The membership list can now be described by an unconstrained array type, with room for an arbitrary number of members:

```
type REGISTER_TYPE is array (POSITIVE range < >) of NAME;
```

Since the type NAME is an array type (an array of 20 characters of type CHARACTER) the type REGISTER_TYPE is an array of arrays.

Now we can declare a variable of the type REGISTER_TYPE:

```
MEMBERS : REGISTER_TYPE (1 .. 5);
```

If we want to initialize the variable, we can use a two-dimensional array aggregate:

```
MEMBERS : REGISTER_TYPE := ("Ponsonby      ",
                            "Tomlinson     ",
                            "Donaldson     ",
                            "Ellis         ",
                            "Hall          ");
```

Note that an expression of the form:

```
"Ellis               "
```

is a special aggregate that is used for the array type STRING.

We shall look at a function whose job is to see whether a certain person is in the membership list. The function will have two **in** parameters. The first is the name of the person sought. We shall let this parameter have the unconstrained type STRING. The second parameter is the membership register itself. If the person in question is a member of the club then the function will return the membership number as its result; otherwise it will return the value 0.

```
function FIND_NUMBER (REQUIRED_NAME : STRING;
                     REGISTER : REGISTER_TYPE)
                     return NATURAL is

   LENGTH      : NATURAL;
   TEMP_NAME : NAME := (others => ' ');
begin

   -- Set LENGTH to the lesser of the
   -- required name length and MAXLENGTH
   if REQUIRED_NAME'LENGTH <= MAXLENGTH then
      LENGTH := REQUIRED_NAME'LENGTH;
   else
      LENGTH := MAXLENGTH;
   end if;
   TEMP_NAME (1 .. LENGTH) :=
                 REQUIRED_NAME (1 .. LENGTH);

   -- Look for the name in the register
   for N in REGISTER'RANGE loop
      if REGISTER(N) = TEMP_NAME then
         -- The name is present in the register
         return N;
      end if;
   end loop;
   -- The name is not present
   return 0;
end FIND_NUMBER;
```

If the name sought contains more than 20 characters the local variable LENGTH is set to 20; otherwise it is set to the actual length of the name. Then the number of characters specified by LENGTH are copied from REQUIRED_NAME to the local variable TEMP_NAME. Since TEMP_NAME is initialized to a blank character string it will contain the required name either shortened to 20 characters or padded with blanks. In the **loop** statement the membership register is run through. Each entry in the register is examined for the name required. If it is found the function terminates and the value N – the membership number – is returned as its result. If the whole list is examined without finding the name, the value 0 is returned as result.

The following are examples of ways of calling the function:

```
FIND_NUMBER("Tomlinson", MEMBERS)      -- gives the value 2
FIND_NUMBER("Hall", MEMBERS)           -- gives the value 5
FIND_NUMBER("Ponsonby", MEMBERS)       -- gives the value 1
```

7.3   Record types

We have seen that by using array types we can describe complicated data objects with many components. One limitation of array types is that all the components of an array must be of the same kind. Therefore array types cannot be used to describe compound data objects where the components of an object are of different types. Instead, we use **record** types.

As an example we shall study the description of a car in a hypothetical register of cars. A car can be characterized by many things, such as its registration number, make, year of manufacture, weight and engine capacity. If we have the type declarations:

```
type YEAR_TYPE    is range 1900 .. 2000;
type WEIGHT_TYPE is range 100 .. 10000;      -- measured in kg
type POWER_TYPE  is digits 4;                -- measured in kW
```

the information can be put together using the record type declaration:

```
type CAR_TYPE is
   record
      REG_NUMBER : STRING(1 .. 7);
      MAKE       : STRING(1 .. 20);
      MODEL_YEAR : YEAR_TYPE;
      WEIGHT     : WEIGHT_TYPE;
      POWER      : POWER_TYPE;
   end record;
```

A definition of a record type starts with the reserved word **record** and ends with **end record**. Between these words are declarations of the record type's *components*.

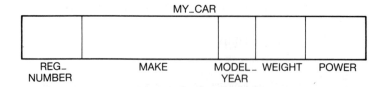

Figure 7.3

Declaration of a record type

    type T **is**
    record
        component_name_1 : *type_1*;
        component_name_2 : *type_2*;

           ⋮

        component_name_N : *type_N*;
    end record;

If there are several components with the same type, it is possible to write instead:

    component_name_i, ... component_name_j : *type_ij*;

Now we can declare variables of type CAR_TYPE:

    MY_CAR : CAR_TYPE;

The variable MY_CAR comprises five different components, as shown in Figure 7.3. (The contents of the different fields are still undefined).

When we worked with arrays we used indexing to get at the individual components in an array. Each component in the array had a unique number (of integer or enumeration type) that could be specified as an index. In a record the components have no numbers, but they do have explicit names. To access a particular component of a record, **selection** is used. A stop is written after the name of the record, followed by the name of the component. If, for example, we want to give the component WEIGHT in the variable MY_CAR the value 920, we can write the assignment:

    MY_CAR.WEIGHT := 920;

The following are some more examples of selection:

```
MY_CAR.POWER := MY_CAR.POWER + 10.0;
if MY_CAR.POWER > 100.0 then
   PUT_LINE("Tuned");
end if;
PUT(MY_CAR.MAKE);
```

A component that is selected in this way can be used in the same way as normal simple variables, in expressions for example.

Selection in record variables

record_variable_name.component_name

The declarations of the components in a record type have exactly the same form as variable declarations but it is important to note that no object is created in connection with the declaration of a record type. As before, a type declaration is only a description of what the objects will look like if some are created later. Objects are only created when there is an object declaration, such as the declaration of the variable MY_CAR.

Selection is thus used for accessing the individual components of a record, but the whole record can also be handled at once. We could declare another variable of type CAR_TYPE:

```
YOUR_CAR : CAR_TYPE;
```

Now we can make assignments and comparisons, as for example:

```
YOUR_CAR := MY_CAR;
if YOUR_CAR = MY_CAR then
```

Only the comparison operators = and /= are defined. Thus it is not possible to see whether one record is 'greater than' or 'less than' another.

Assignment of records

```
R1 := R2;
```

where R1 is a record variable and R2 is a variable or a constant of the same type as R1.

Comparing records

R1 = R2 or R1 /= R2

where R1 and R2 are objects of the same record type.

In the case of arrays, we could use array aggregates to give values to all the components at once. There is a corresponding construct for records, also called an aggregate. If, for example, we want to initialize the variable MY_CAR at the same time as declaring it, we write:

```
MY_CAR : CAR_TYPE := ("C123XYZ", "Ford Fiesta GL    ",
                       1986, 840, 30.0);
```

We can also use record aggregates in assignments and comparisons, such as:

```
YOUR_CAR := ("ABD_544", "Volvo 245 DL    ",
             1982, 1400, 70.0);
if YOUR_CAR = ("12BN123", "Volvo 245 DL    ",
               1982, 1400, 70.0) then
```

In these record aggregates we have simply listed the values of the individual components in their proper order. We have used positional association between the values and the components. Named association can also be used by stating the name of the component and its corresponding value. In that case it is not necessary to give the values of the components in the same order as they appear in the record. For example, we can write:

```
YOUR_CAR := (REG_NUMBER => "ABD_544",
             MODEL_YEAR => 1982,
             MAKE => "Volvo 245 DL    ",
             POWER => 70.0,
             WEIGHT => 1400);
```

> **Record aggregates**
>
> - A specification where the values of all the components of a record can be stated at once.
> - Alternative forms:
>
>   (*value_for_comp_1*, *value_for_comp_2*, ...)
>
>   or:
>
>   (*component_name* => *corresponding_value*,
>   *component_name* => *corresponding_value*,
>
> $\vdots$
>
>   *component_name* => *corresponding_value*)
>
> - The values in a record aggregate can be arbitrary expressions which must have the same types as the corresponding components.

The individual components of a record can have any type. If we declare a new record type PERSON:

```
type PERSON is
   record
      NAME      : STRING(1 .. 20);
      ID_NUMBER : STRING(1 .. 10);
   end record;
```

then we can extend the record type CAR_TYPE with a further component, OWNER:

```
type CAR_TYPE is
   record
      REG_NUMBER : STRING(1 .. 7);
      MAKE       : STRING(1 .. 20);
      MODEL_YEAR : YEAR_TYPE;
      WEIGHT     : WEIGHT_TYPE;
      POWER      : POWER_TYPE;
      OWNER      : PERSON;
   end record;
```

If the owner's identification number has to be found for printing, it can be achieved in two stages:

```
PUT(MY_CAR.OWNER.ID_NUMBER);
```

Using record types it is possible to build up several levels of data description. The type PERSON could well have another component, ADDRESS, which in turn could have a record type, and so on. In this way it is possible to make the kind of data abstraction discussed in Chapter 5. A record type can describe a phenomenon in the real world, as for example, the phenomenon of a 'car'. In studying the concept of a 'car', there is naturally no interest in the detailed description of the 'owner'. Then it becomes natural to introduce a new record type to describe a 'person', and this new record type can then be studied separately if needed.

Since record types can be used to describe phenomena they are commonly used as parameters and results of subprograms. Let us study, as an example, the phenomenon of a 'point' in a two-dimensional coordinate system. A particular point in the system can be defined by an x and a y coordinate. The concept of a point can then be described by the record type:

```
type POINT is
record
   X, Y : FLOAT;
end record;
```

The formula:

$$d = \sqrt{(x_1 - x_2)^2 + (y_1 - y_2)^2}$$

gives the distance d between two points (x_1, y_1) and (x_2, y_2), and this can be used to construct a function DISTANCE. The function will take two points as **in** parameters and give the distance between them, a real quantity, as a result.

```
function DISTANCE (P1, P2 : POINT) return FLOAT is
begin
   return SQRT((P1.X − P2.X) ** 2 + (P1.Y − P2.Y) ** 2);
end DISTANCE;
```

If we declare the variables A and B thus:

```
A : POINT := (1.0, 2.0);
B : POINT := (−3.0, −1.0);
```

then the statement:

```
PUT( DISTANCE(A, B) );
```

will print out the resulting value 5.0.

We can also have record aggregates as parameters to the function. The call:

    DISTANCE((6.0, 8.0), (0.0, 0.0))

for example, will give the result 10.0.

A function can return a result of a record type. A function that finds the mid-point of a line joining two points P1 and P2 could look like this:

```
function MIDPOINT (P1, P2 : POINT) return POINT is
begin
    return ((P1.X + P2.X) / 2.0, (P1.Y + P2.Y) / 2.0);
end MIDPOINT;
```

If we declare a new variable C:

    C : POINT;

and execute the statement:

    C := MIDPOINT(A, B);

then C will get the value $(-1.0, 0.5)$, assuming that A and B still have their earlier values.

The call:

    MIDPOINT((1.0, 1.0), (2.0, 2.0))

returns the point $(1.5, 1.5)$ as result.

■

As discussed earlier, the value of a variable is undefined at the time of declaration unless it is explicitly initialized. Record types have a special feature that does not exist for other types. At the time of type declaration, initial values for the components of the record type can be stated. If this is done, all the variables of that record type that are later declared will automatically be initialized to these values, unless the variable declaration itself gives specific initial values. To illustrate this, let us amend the declaration of the type POINT:

```
type POINT is
    record
        X, Y : FLOAT := 0.0;
    end record;
```

If we now declare a variable START_POINT:

    START_POINT : POINT;

Then this will have the value (0.0, 0.0) after the declaration. If we had not had the initialization expression in the type declaration, the variable START_POINT would have been undefined.

An ordinary initialization when the variable is declared would override the automatic initialization. After the declaration:

    END_POINT : POINT := (10.0, 5.0);

the variable END_POINT will, in the usual way, have the value (10.0, 5.0). It is not necessary to give all the components of a record type the same automatic initialization values, nor do all the components have to have them. As an example, we can rewrite the declaration of CAR_TYPE:

```
type CAR_TYPE is
  record
    REG_NUMBER : STRING(1 .. 7) := "        ";
    MAKE       : STRING(1 .. 20);
    MODEL_YEAR : YEAR_TYPE := CURRENT_YEAR;
    WEIGHT     : WEIGHT_TYPE;
    POWER      : POWER_TYPE;
  end record;
```

where CURRENT_YEAR is a constant:

    CURRENT_YEAR : constant := 1988;

If we now declare a variable NEW_CAR:

    NEW_CAR : CAR_TYPE;

then the component MODEL_YEAR in NEW_CAR will have the value 1988 and REG_NUMBER will have the value "   ". The other components are undefined.

Ordinary scalar variables cannot be automatically initialized on declaration, except by using the trick of enclosing the scalar type in a record type. For example, assume we have a type SCORE_TYPE:

    type SCORE_TYPE is range 0 .. 100;

If we declare a variable S:

```
S : SCORE_TYPE;
```

then S's value is undefined. If, however, we introduce the type SCORE_RECORD_TYPE instead:

```
type SCORE_RECORD_TYPE is
  record
    SR : SCORE_TYPE := 0;
  end record;
```

and make the variable declaration:

```
S : SCORE_RECORD_TYPE;
```

then S will automatically be initialized to the value 0 on declaration. A disadvantage of this is, of course, that every time S is referred to, S.SR must be written instead of S.

Automatic initialization of components of records

- When a record type is declared, initial values can be given for individual components.
- When a variable of the type is later declared, such components will automatically be initialized to these values.
- An initializing value can be a general expression and should have the same type as the record component.

□

7.4 Arrays of records

It is very common in real life to have a number of objects with the same properties. One example is a telephone directory with many subscribers, each entry specifying a telephone number, name, title and address.

Another example is the result list from a sporting event. For each competitor, his or her number, name, club and result are given. The natural data structure to use in Ada to describe such a real thing is an array of records. The result list from the sporting event could be described using the type RESULT_LIST below:

```
type NUMBER is range 1 .. 1000;
type TIME    is digits 7 range 0.0 .. 600.0;
type COMPETITOR is
  record
    ID_NUMBER : NUMBER;
    NAME        : STRING(1 .. 10);
    CLUB        : STRING(1 .. 20);
    RUN_TIME   : TIME;
  end record;

type RESULT_LIST is array (1 .. 500) of COMPETITOR;
```

We have assumed that there are at most 500 competitors but that they can have identifying numbers in the range 1 to 1000, so that not all available numbers are used. We have also assumed that the competition is one where all results are given as times, for example, swimming or cross-country skiing. The times are given in minutes and it is assumed that none are more than 10 hours.

Of course, it is also possible to have an unconstrained array of records, where the number of records is not decided in advance. As an example of this we can take the telephone directory:

```
type TELEPHONE_NUMBER is range 0 .. 9999999;
type SUBSCRIBER is
  record
    NAME     : STRING(1 .. 20);
    TITLE    : STRING(1 .. 15);
    ADDRESS : STRING(1 .. 20);
    NUMBER   : TELEPHONE_NUMBER;
  end record;

type TELEPHONE_CATALOGUE is array (INTEGER range < >)
                                          of SUBSCRIBER;
```

The number of subscribers must then be stated when a variable is declared, such as:

```
NEWTOWN_CATALOGUE : TELEPHONE_CATALOGUE(1 .. 50000);
```

In the rest of this section we shall assume that we have a car hire firm and a list of all its cars. To describe such a list we can use the type CAR_TYPE that we declared earlier:

```
type CAR_TYPE is
  record
    REG_NUMBER : STRING(1 .. 7);
    MAKE        : STRING(1 .. 20);
    MODEL_YEAR  : YEAR_TYPE;
    WEIGHT      : WEIGHT_TYPE;
    POWER       : POWER_TYPE;
    CLIENT      : PERSON;
  end record;
```

We have added a component CLIENT which states who is currently hiring the car in question. The type PERSON is declared as follows:

```
type PERSON is
  record
    NAME          : STRING(1 .. 20);
    CLIENT_NUMBER : STRING(1 .. 10);
    ADDRESS       : STRING(1 .. 30);
  end record;
```

Then we can declare a type CAR_LIST:

```
type CAR_LIST is array (POSITIVE range < >) of CAR_TYPE;
```

If we assume that the firm has at most 100 cars we can declare a variable CARS_OWNED:

```
CARS_OWNED : CAR_LIST(1 .. 100);
```

Data about the firm's cars can now be entered in the array. For example, to give values to car number 23 we can use indexing and write the assignment statement:

```
CARS_OWNED(23) := ("D135ADG", "Volvo 244-411        ",
                   1986, 1320, 70.0,
                   ("Frederick Smith          ", "100121PRIV",
                    "13, High St, Granton               "));
```

Note that the right-hand side contains one record aggregate within another since the component CLIENT in type CAR_TYPE is itself of a record type.

If we want to write out the name of the customer who hired car number 23 we can use indexing and selection:

```
PUT(CARS_OWNED(23).CLIENT.NAME);
```

Assume that values have been assigned to all the components in the array of descriptions of the firm's cars. The following lines of program read in a registration number from the terminal and investigate whether there is a car with that registration number. If there is such a car, the name and address of the client who has hired the car will be written out. If the car is not hired out, the message "The car is not hired out" is written.

```
PUT_LINE("Enter registration number.");
GET(REG_NR);

P := SEARCH(CARS_OWNED, REG_NR);

if P = 0 then
    PUT_LINE("No car with this registration number.");
elsif CARS_OWNED(P).CLIENT.NAME = (others =>' ') then
    PUT_LINE("The car is not hired out");
else
    PUT_LINE("The car is hired out to:");
    PUT_LINE(CARS_OWNED(P).CLIENT.NAME);
    PUT_LINE(CARS_OWNED(P).CLIENT.ADDRESS);
end if;
```

We assume that the variable REG_NUMBER has type STRING(1 .. 7) and that the variable P has the type INTEGER. In these lines we have called a function SEARCH which searches the array for the record containing a particular registration number. As a result, the function returns the index of the record in the array. If it finds no such record, the function returns the value 0. The function SEARCH has two **in** parameters – the array to be searched and the registration number of interest.

Now we have to write the function SEARCH. The simplest way is to use a **linear search** as discussed in connection with arrays in Chapter 5. We simply search through the whole array, either until the array is finished or the record we are looking for is found. The function SEARCH is:

```
-- LINEAR SEARCH

function SEARCH (C : CAR_LIST; REQ_REG_NR : STRING)
                return NATURAL is

    I : POSITIVE := C'FIRST;
```

begin

    -- search until the array is finished or

    -- the required registration number is found

    while I <= C'LAST **and then**

          C(I).REG_NUMBER /= REQ_REG_NR **loop**

      I := I + 1;

    end loop;

    if I <= C'LAST **then**

      -- Required registration number has been found

      return I;

    else

      -- Required registration number not found

      return 0;

    end if;

end SEARCH;

This method of finding something in an array is not particularly efficient. In the worst case, we must search through the whole array. If the array were sorted we would be able to find a more efficient method, so we shall start by sorting the array according to registration number.

We have studied one simple sort method in Section 5.8. Here we shall demonstrate another common and simple (but not particularly efficient) method that is usually called **bubble sort**, which is based on ordering neighbouring pairs. In this method the array is run through time and again. As soon as two neighbouring components of the array are found that are not in correct order, they are swapped. In this way the 'lighter' components (those with smaller values) 'rise up' to the 'surface', while the 'heavier' ones 'sink' to the 'bottom', hence the name.

We can devise a rough algorithm for the bubble sort:

(1)   Repeat the following until the array is sorted, that is, until the array has been run right through without any swap taking place:

    (1.1)   Run through the array and investigate each pair of consecutive components. If the components in a pair are in the wrong order, swap them.

We can refine step (1.1) of the algorithm:

(1.1.1)   Set **SWAP_HAS_OCCURRED** to FALSE.

             (No swap has yet occurred in this run through the array).

(1.1.2)   Let I run from the first to the last but one index in the array.

    (1.1.2.1)   If component I is greater than component I+1:

             (1.1.2.1.1)   Swap components I and I+1.

             (1.1.2.1.2)   Set **SWAP_HAS_OCCURRED** to TRUE.

By making a number of adjustments to this algorithm it can be made more efficient; for example, it is not necessary to run through the whole array each time, since the largest unsorted element ends up in the right place each time. Here we shall not worry about this.

Everything is now ready to translate the algorithm to Ada, and we can write a procedure SORT. Its only parameter is the array to be sorted. The parameter must be an **in out** parameter because the procedure must be able both to read and change components in the array. The array CARS_OWNED can then be sorted by making the call:

```
SORT(CARS_OWNED);
```

We consider component I to be bigger than component J if component I contains a 'bigger' registration number than component J, that is, if I's registration number comes after J's in alphabetical/numerical order.

So that the first run through takes place, we initialize SWAP_HAS_OCCURRED to TRUE. The procedure is as follows:

```
-- BUBBLE SORT

procedure SORT(C : in out CAR_LIST) is
    SWAP_HAS_OCCURRED : BOOLEAN := TRUE;
    TEMP : CAR_TYPE;                    -- used during swap
begin
    while SWAP_HAS_OCCURRED loop
        -- run through array anew
        SWAP_HAS_OCCURRED := FALSE;

        for I in C'FIRST .. C'LAST - 1 loop
            if C(I).REG_NUMBER > C(I+1).REG_NUMBER then
                -- in wrong order - swap places
                TEMP  := C(I);
                C(I)     := C(I+1);
                C(I+1) := TEMP;
                SWAP_HAS_OCCURRED := TRUE;
            end if;
        end loop;
    end loop;
end SORT;
```

This chapter closes by giving a more efficient version of the function SEARCH to find the record in the array that contains a particular registration number. In the new version of SEARCH we shall make use of the fact that the array is sorted to speed up the search. We use the following concept, assuming the array to be sorted into ascending order, from left to right.

First we look at the component in the middle of the array. If this component holds the required registration number then we are lucky and need look no further. If the middle component has a registration number that is greater than the one we want, we know that the required registration number is in the left half of the array, because the array is sorted. Likewise, if the middle component contains a registration number that is less than the one we want, we know that it must be in the right half of the array. When we have looked at the middle component, therefore, we have either found the required component or we know which half we should continue to search.

When we continue the search we can consider the half-array as a new array, smaller than the original. Now we have exactly the same problem as when we started, only this time the new array is smaller. We can thus use the same idea as before, namely, look at the middle component of the new array. If the required component is not the middle component we can determine whether we should continue the search in the left or the right half of the array. We can then apply the same technique once more on the even smaller array left to look in.

This process is continued with decreasingly small arrays until we find the component we are looking for or until the array we are searching is empty. In the latter case the required component is not in the array at all.

What we have discussed here is a recursive search method that is usually known as a **binary search**, that is, the size of the array to be searched is halved at every stage. We can formulate the algorithm, assuming the array ordered from left to right in ascending order:

(1) Evaluate the index of the middle component.
(2) If the array is empty (length is zero) then the required component is not in the array.
(3) If the middle component is the one we want, the algorithm terminates with the index of the middle component as result.
(4) If the middle component is greater than the one we are looking for, we continue our search in the left half of the array, that is, the array that includes the first component up to and including the component to the left of the middle component.
      Use this algorithm to continue the search.
(5) Otherwise the middle component is smaller than the one we are looking for.
      Then continue the search in the right half of the array, that is, the array that includes the component to the right of middle, up to and including the last component.
      Use this algorithm to continue the search.

This search technique is much more efficient than the simple linear search that we looked at before. If, for example, we have an array with 100 elements, the binary search algorithm needs to look at a maximum of seven elements to determine whether a particular element is in the array. If a linear search were used instead, in the worst case we would have to look at all 100 elements. In an array of 1000 elements, binary searching would require in the worst case 10 elements to be investigated while linear searching would, in the worst case, require 1000 elements to be investigated.

The algorithm can be translated directly into a recursive Ada function. Steps (4) and (5) in the algorithm are made up of recursive calls of the function itself with a subarray as parameter.

```
-- BINARY SEARCH

function SEARCH (C : CAR_LIST; REQ_REG_NR : STRING)
                return NATURAL is

   MIDDLE : INTEGER := (C'FIRST + C'LAST) / 2;
begin

   if C'LENGTH = 0 then
     -- required registration number does not exist
     return 0;
   elsif C(MIDDLE).REG_NUMBER = REQ_REG_NR then
     -- we have found the required reg number
     return MIDDLE;
   elsif C(MIDDLE).REG_NUMBER > REQ_REG_NR then
     -- search the left half of the array
     return SEARCH (C(FIRST .. MIDDLE − 1), REQ_REG_NR);
   else
     -- search the right half of the array
     return SEARCH (C(MIDDLE + 1 .. C'LAST), REQ_REG_NR);
   end if;
end SEARCH;
```

EXERCISES

7.1 A table can be drawn to show how different countries border one another. Part of such a table could be:

	Belgium	France	Italy
Belgium	–	yes	no
France	yes	–	yes
Italy	no	yes	–

(a) Make a suitable type declaration in Ada to represent such a table, including some arbitrary countries. Declare the table and initialize it appropriately.

(b) Write a function NUMBER_OF_NEIGHBOURS that takes a country and a table similar to the above as parameters. The function should return the number of countries that border the given country. For an appropriate table, a call NUMBER_OF_NEIGHBOURS(SWEDEN, TABLE), for example, should return the value 2, since its only neighbours joined by land are Norway and Finland.

7.2 A chess board has 64 squares. The columns are usually denoted by the letters a, b, c, d, e, f, g and h, and the rows by the numbers 1 to 8. The different pieces are *king, queen, bishop, knight, rook* and *pawn*, and black pieces and white pieces are used. Write a type declaration that describes the appearance of an arrangement of pieces on the chess board.

7.3 Write a function to determine whether an $n \times n$ matrix is symmetric. In a symmetric matrix A, $a_{ij} = a_{ji}$ for all i and j.

7.4 A magic square is an arrangement of numbers with n rows and n columns. The sums of the values in each row, column and diagonal are the same. The following square is a magic square, for example:

$$\begin{pmatrix} 16 & 9 & 2 & 7 \\ 6 & 3 & 12 & 13 \\ 11 & 14 & 5 & 4 \\ 1 & 8 & 15 & 10 \end{pmatrix}$$

(a) Write a function that takes such an arrangement as parameter and determines whether it is a magic square. The number of rows and columns is arbitrary.

(b) Another condition for an arrangement of numbers with n rows and columns to be a true magic square is that it contains all the integers 1, 2, ... n^2. Amend the function so that it also checks for this condition.

7.5 (a) Write a function that takes an $n \times n$ matrix of integers as parameter. As a result, the function should return the same matrix turned through a quarter-turn anticlockwise. For example, if the function is given the matrix:

$$\begin{pmatrix} 1 & 2 & 3 \\ 4 & 5 & 6 \\ 7 & 8 & 9 \end{pmatrix}$$

as parameter it should return the matrix:

$$\begin{pmatrix} 3 & 6 & 9 \\ 2 & 5 & 8 \\ 1 & 4 & 7 \end{pmatrix}$$

(b)   Use the function in a program to read in a 4 × 4 matrix from the terminal. The matrix is read in row by row. The program should write out the matrix turned first through a quarter-turn anticlockwise and then through a half-turn anticlockwise. In the output, each row of the resulting matrices should be written out as a row at the terminal.

7.6   **Matrix multiplication** can be defined for two matrices A and B with dimensions $m \times n$ and $n \times p$, respectively. (Note that the number of columns in A must be the same as the number of rows in B). The result of the matrix multiplication is a new matrix with dimension $m \times p$. If we call the resulting matrix C, a particular element c_{ij} in C is calculated as the sum:

$$c_{ij} = \sum_{k=1}^{n} a_{ik} \times b_{kj}$$

For example:

$$\begin{pmatrix} 1 & 2 \\ 4 & 7 \\ 8 & 3 \end{pmatrix} \times \begin{pmatrix} 1 & 2 & 0 & 2 \\ 3 & 4 & 3 & 1 \end{pmatrix} = \begin{pmatrix} 7 & 10 & 6 & 4 \\ 25 & 36 & 21 & 15 \\ 17 & 28 & 9 & 19 \end{pmatrix}$$

Use this to construct a function that gets two matrices as parameters. In the result, the function should give the matrix that results from multiplying them together.

7.7   (a)   Write two functions ROW and COL that can be used to select a particular row or column from a matrix. Both should take a matrix as parameter. In addition, ROW should get a row number as parameter and the function COL should get a column number. If matrix M is, for example:

$$\begin{pmatrix} 1 & 4 & 7 & 9 \\ 3 & 0 & 2 & 5 \\ 8 & 7 & 0 & 2 \end{pmatrix}$$

then the call ROW(M,2) should return the vector (3, 0, 2, 5) and the call COL(M,4) should return the vector (9, 5, 2).

(b)   The **scalar product** $u{\cdot}v$ of two vectors $u = (u_1, u_2, ..., u_n)$ and $v = (v_1, v_2, ..., v_n)$ can be defined as the sum:

$$\sum_{i=1}^{n} u_i \times v_i$$

The scalar product of the vectors (1, 2, 3) and (3, 4, 5), for example, is 26. A condition for forming the scalar product is that the two vectors have the same number of elements. Write a function that forms the scalar product of two vectors.

(c)   Multiplication of two matrices A and B with dimensions $m \times n$ and $n \times p$ can now be defined as an operation which gives a new matrix C with dimensions $m \times p$. A particular element c_{ij} of C has as its value the scalar product of row i from A and column j from B. Using this definition, write a function that multiplies two matrices, making use of the functions written in parts (a) and (b) of this question. Compare this function with that of the previous question.

7.8 The morse code for the alphabet is shown in the following table, where dots and dashes are used to represent short and long signals, respectively.

A	$\cdot$ —	H	$\cdot\cdot\cdot\cdot$	O	— — —	U	$\cdot\cdot$ —
B	— $\cdot\cdot\cdot$	I	$\cdot\cdot$	P	$\cdot$ — — $\cdot$	V	$\cdot\cdot\cdot$ —
C	— $\cdot$ — $\cdot$	J	$\cdot$ — — —	Q	— — $\cdot$ —	W	$\cdot$ — —
D	— $\cdot\cdot$	K	— $\cdot$ —	R	$\cdot$ — $\cdot$	X	— $\cdot\cdot$ —
E	$\cdot$	L	$\cdot$ — $\cdot\cdot$	S	$\cdot\cdot\cdot$	Y	— $\cdot$ — —
F	$\cdot\cdot$ — $\cdot$	M	— —	T	—	Z	— — $\cdot\cdot$
G	— — $\cdot$	N	— $\cdot$				

(a)   Write a program that reads in a message and codes it into morse code.

(b)   Write a program that reads in a message in morse code, decodes it and writes out the decoded message. In the morse message letters are separated by one space and words are separated by two spaces.

7.9   Declare a record type that is appropriate for describing a card in an ordinary pack of cards.

7.10   To define a point in a two-dimensional coordinate system it is most common to use the form (x,y), called **rectangular coordinates**. An alternative way of defining it is to use **polar coordinates** (r,θ). r is the distance of the point from the origin and θ is the angle between the straight line joining the point to the origin and the x-axis. Transformation from polar coordinates to ordinary rectangular coordinates can be effected with the formulae:

$$x = r \cos \theta$$
$$y = r \sin \theta$$

Write a function that takes a point described in polar coordinates as input parameter and returns it expressed in rectangular coordinates.

7.11   A rational number can be written as a fraction in which both numerator and denominator are integers.

(a)   Make an appropriate type declaration to describe a rational number.

(b)   Write a function that takes two rational numbers as parameters and returns a new rational number that is the sum of the two parameters.

(c)   Add to the function above so that it always returns a rational number where the numerator and the denominator have no common factor. (Compare with Exercises (6.4) and (6.15).)

7.12   A company has a warehouse where it stores several kinds of articles. There are a number of articles of each kind and a computer program is required to keep track of them all. For each kind of article the following are important:

- The article identification (a code of four characters).
- Article description (a text with at most 30 characters).
- The number of this article in store.
- The selling price.

Write a program that first reads in this information from the terminal for all the kinds of article and saves it using a suitable data structure. Assume that there are no more than 1000 kinds of article in the warehouse. Input can terminate when, for example, the article identification "0000" is given. The program will then repeatedly read commands from the terminal and perform the tasks required. The different commands are, where xxxx stands for an article identification code:

INFO xxxx	Write out all current information about article xxxx.
SOLD xxxx N	Register that N items of article xxxx have been removed from the store.
BOUGHT xxxx N	Register that N items of article xxxx have been put into the store.

7.13 There are a number of chemical elements – for example, carbon, hydrogen, mercury and gold – and for each element there is a symbol comprising one or two letters, in these cases C, H, Hg and Au, respectively. The first letter is always upper case and the second, if there is one, is lower case. Each element has a certain atomic weight.

(a) Declare and initialize a table that contains the symbols for a number of elements and the corresponding atomic weights. Information can be found in any chemistry textbook, but here are some examples:

H	1.0079	O	15.999	F	18.9984
He	4.0026	Na	22.9898	Au	196.9665
Be	9.0122	S	32.06	Hg	200.5
C	12.011	Cl	35.453	Ra	226.0254

(b) A common problem is to calculate a molecular weight. Write a program that reads in a chemical formula and, using the table formulated in part (a), calculates and writes out the corresponding molecular weight. Examples of chemical formulae are:

NaCl H_2O H_2SO_4

The subscript n after an element symbol means that there are n atoms of the corresponding element in the molecule. If no figure is given, it means that there is only one atom of that element. As input to the program a chemical formula can be given in the following format:

NaCl   H2O   H2SO4

Chapter 8
Packages

8.1 Package specification
8.2 The Ada programming
    environment
8.3 Using packages
8.4 Package bodies
8.5 Different categories of
    packages

8.6 Packages of types and
    constants
8.7 Packages with memory
8.8 Abstract data types
8.9 Private types
    Exercises

It has been shown that it is possible to solve problems by breaking them down into smaller subproblems which are then solved one by one. This process can be repeated for each subproblem until all the subproblems are so simple that they can easily be solved. Chapter 6 showed that subprograms helped us to apply this strategy – a call to a subprogram described the solution to a more complicated subproblem, and subprograms could then be written separately, one by one. The advantage of subprograms is that they hide inessential details that the programmer does not need to know, and allows him or her to concentrate on one problem at a time. A subprogram is thus a construction that can be used to bring together a number of statements into a logical unit with a defined interface with the other parts of the program.

In Ada there is another construction for bringing together related parts of a program into a logical unit, and this is called a **package**. Subprograms, types and objects that logically belong together in some way can be brought together in a package. When a package is constructed, its interface with the rest of the program or, in other words, the part of the package that will be visible to the program, has to be specified. Details that are inessential to the user of the package can then be concealed within the package. A package can be developed and compiled alone.

When a complicated product such as a car is being built, it is necessary to make the different parts separately in order to prevent the work from becoming too complex. Eventually, the separate parts are assembled into a complete product. To fit the parts together successfully, a specification of how the parts fit must have been carefully made during the design phase.

Ada is a language that is not only designed to handle small problems, it can also be used in large programming projects where large complicated programs or systems of programs are developed, and where many people are involved. As with building a car, it is necessary that all the parts are written separately and put together later. Ada's package facility allows a program to be built up in the form of several separate modules, each of which forms a logical unit. With the help of a **package specification** it can be stated how a package should be put together with the other parts of the program. Working with large unmanageable programs is thus avoided: one subproblem can be tackled at a time. Most of the common programming languages, such as Pascal and BASIC, lack these features for building up programs in the form of separate packages.

It is also possible to build up a library of general packages that may be used in several contexts within different programs. These could include a package of different mathematical functions or a package of tools for presenting results in a graphic form. These packages may have been written by the individual programmer, or be standard packages in an implementation of Ada, or have been obtained from some other source.

8.1 Package specification

Each package has a **specification**. This can be regarded as the package's 'shop-window' that says what the package has to offer the potential user. The specification specifies the package's interface with other parts of the

program.[†] A package specification is introduced with the reserved word
package followed by the package's name. Within the specification,
declarations of types and objects can be made and subprogram
specifications can be given.

Package specification

    package *package_name* **is**
    declarations
    end *package_name*;

Subprograms can have their specifications but not
their bodies among the declarations.

Let us look at an example. Suppose we want to work with ordinary
two-dimensional geometric figures such as rectangles, circles and
triangles. It may then be appropriate to construct a package containing
the tools for performing various calculations on these figures. We can
call the package PLANIMETRY and write a specification for it. In the
specification we shall declare types LENGTH and AREA that describe,
obviously, lengths and areas associated with the geometric figures. In
addition we declare functions that calculate the areas of rectangles, circles
and triangles. The specification of the package PLANIMETRY is then:

```
package PLANIMETRY is
    type LENGTH is digits 5 range 0.0 .. 1.0E10;
    type AREA    is digits 5 range 0.0 .. 1.0E20;
    function AREA_RECTANGLE (L, H : LENGTH) return AREA;
    function AREA_CIRCLE     (R : LENGTH) return AREA;
    function CIRCUMF_CIRCLE  (R : LENGTH) return LENGTH;
    function AREA_TRIANGLE   (B, H : LENGTH) return AREA;
end PLANIMETRY;
```

[†] Chapter 2 discussed the idea of specification in a general sense. There it was said that a
specification of a part of a program should contain both a description of its interface with
other parts of the program and a description of what it does. A package specification in Ada
contains only the first of these descriptions. If the specification is also required to describe
what the package does, it can be achieved with the help of appropriate names for the
quantities stated in the specification and by using comments.

This is the 'shop-window' for the package PLANIMETRY. Note that we have not yet said anything about what it will look like within the package, that is, what the function bodies will be. We shall state this later by writing a package body.

8.2 The Ada programming environment

Before we go on to see how a package can be used and what a package body looks like, a few words must be said about the programming environment in Ada. When a program or a part of a program is compiled a compiler is used. The compiler reads the program text and gives as a result the program translated into machine code. Compilers of all kinds work in this way, not only the Ada compiler.

An Ada compiler differs from most other language compilers, however, in that it not only produces machine code but also keeps track of all the compilation that is performed. The compiler maintains what is called the **Ada library**. When a compilation is complete, the Ada compiler puts a description of the program (or part of a program) that has been compiled into the Ada library.

This means that it is possible to refer to what has been compiled earlier in a program. The compiler goes into the Ada library and searches for information about the relevant item, making it feasible to build up large complicated programs gradually.

An Ada environment thus contains not only an Ada compiler but also an Ada library. There are also utility programs for creating new Ada libraries and for removing information from a library.

The Ada programming environment

- Ada library with information about all the compilations performed.
- Ada compiler that translates to machine code and places information into the Ada library.
- Utility programs for handling Ada libraries, for example, creating new libraries and removing information from a library.

For compilation, a **compilation unit** is fed into the compiler; or several compilation units can be fed in at once. It is possible for a compilation unit to be made up of a procedure, as seen in our examples so far. However, compilation units other than procedures are allowed. For example, a package specification can be a compilation unit. A package body can also be a compilation unit. Thus the specification and the body of a package can be compiled separately.

In a compilation unit, such as a procedure, a **with** clause can be put first, enabling reference to be made to other compilation units.

With clause

    with *name1, name2, ... , nameN*;

- Put first in a compilation unit.
- States that the current compilation unit needs to have access to compilation units named *name1, name2, ... , nameN*.

If we compile a procedure, for example, we can have the clause:

with Q, R;

on the first line. Here Q and R are the names of other compilation units that are referred to and therefore need to be accessible in P. The Ada compiler then searches the Ada library for information about Q and R. If the compiler cannot find Q and R in the library there is an error and compilation terminates. This means that Q and R need to have been compiled earlier.

The specification of a package must be compiled before the body. However, it is not necessary to compile the body of a package before compiling a procedure that uses the package. Naturally, however, all parts of the program must be compiled before the program can be **executed**.

Compilation order for packages

- Compile the package specification first.
- Then compile, in any order, the package body and the compilation units that refer to the package in question.

If the body of a package is recompiled there is no need to recompile the procedures that use the package. If, however, the specification of a package is recompiled then both the package body and all the programs that use the package must be recompiled. Information is stored in the Ada library stating when each compilation unit was compiled; the Ada compiler can thus monitor that the different parts of a program were compiled in the correct order.

8.3 Using packages

A package whose specification has been compiled can be used in programs, or parts of programs, that are later compiled. If, for example, we write a program COMPUTE_AREAS and we want to use the procedures contained in the package PLANIMETRY, we write at the start of the program:

with PLANIMETRY;

The compiler will search for the package PLANIMETRY in the Ada library and we can use the package in our program. We can use everything that is declared in the package's specification, but what exists within the package body is not known to the procedure COMPUTE_AREAS.

One way to refer to the items declared in the specification of PLANIMETRY is to use selection, or dot notation. For example, we can declare a variable of type AREA:

A : PLANIMETRY.AREA;

Here PLANIMETRY.AREA refers to the type AREA in the package PLANIMETRY. Similarly, we can declare a variable R:

R : PLANIMETRY.LENGTH;

If we now want to read in the radius of a circle in our program and calculate its area, we can write the lines:

PUT_LINE("Enter the radius of the circle");
GET(R);
A := PLANIMETRY.AREA_CIRCLE(R);

The expression on the right of the last line means that we call the function AREA_CIRCLE in the package PLANIMETRY. The variable A will then be assigned the value of the area of the circle requested.

> **Selection**
>
> > P.N
>
> where P is the name of a package and N is the name
> of something that is declared in the specification of
> the package.

This notation, where the name of the package is followed by a dot, is clear. Each time something from a package is used it is obvious which package is being referred to. In one program several different packages may be in use and one name in the declarations of one package may also occur in another package, but under a different name. If selection is used this causes no problems since the intended package is always explicitly stated.

If the contents of a package are used in many places in a program it is clumsy to state the package name every time. In most programs so far, we have used the package TEXT_IO. It would have been inconvenient to write TEXT_IO.PUT every time we wanted to write something out at the terminal. It is more convenient to refer to the items declared in a package specification if a **use** clause is introduced. If we put into our program:

use PLANIMETRY;

for example, the declarations of A and R can simply be written:

A : AREA;
R : LENGTH;

We no longer need to state the name of the package. The call to the function AREA_CIRCLE can be written:

A := AREA_CIRCLE(R);

A **use** clause can either be placed directly after the **with** clause at the start of the compilation unit, or anywhere among the declarations in a subprogram. If the **use** clause is put at the start of the compilation unit, it is valid for the whole compilation unit. Thus it is possible to access the contents of the package everywhere, without using selection. If the **use** clause is placed among the declarations in a subprogram, it is only valid in that subprogram.

Use clause

   use *P1*, *P2*, ... , *PN*;

where *P1*, *P2*, ... , *PN* are names of packages.

Can be placed after **with** clause or among the declarations in a subprogram.

The disadvantage of a **use** clause is that the program can become less clear; names of quantities can occur that are declared in the packages being used. Since these packages have been compiled separately, it is not possible to see from the program how the quantities are declared. Nor is it possible to see the package from which they come. If, for example, we had also used a package SOLID_GEOMETRY and had put the following **use** clause in our program:

   use SOLID_GEOMETRY, PLANIMETRY;

then in the declaration:

   A : AREA;

we would not be able to see if AREA exists in the package SOLID_GEOMETRY or in the package PLANIMETRY.

It is recommended that **use** clauses are employed with caution and are not habitually placed first in compilation units. (This is acceptable in the case of TEXT_IO because it is used so commonly and we know that it contains the procedures GET and PUT). An alternative to using selection, which can be a little clumsy, is to have a local **use** clause for each package and place it within the subprogram where the contents of the package are actually used.

In our examples so far we have seen numerous instances of how packages can be used, in particular TEXT_IO and BASIC_MATH. We have used both **with** and **use** clauses. We have thus assumed that the specifications of these packages have been compiled earlier so that they are in the Ada library. (In the *Ada Reference Manual* it is stipulated that the package TEXT_IO should be present in all implementations of Ada. There is no stipulation regarding the presence of a mathematical package, but one is usually included in most implementations).

If a package is to be used in a program, the same method is used (**with** clause and **use** clause or selection) irrespective of the origin of the package – whether it is written by the individual programmer or by someone else, or whether it is a standard package that has been in the implementation of Ada from the start.

8.4 Package bodies

Now we shall look at how to construct a package body – the part of the package that is concealed from the user. Details that the user does not need to know are placed in the package body, for example, the subprogram bodies and internal data.

A package body is introduced with the reserved words **package body**. The rest of the package body has the same structure as a subprogram body. First comes a declarative part and then a sequence of statements. This latter section can be omitted, and this is most common.

Package bodies

package body *package_name* **is**
   declarations
[**begin**
   statements]
   end *package_name*;

- All kinds of declaration are allowed in the package body.

- The quantities that are declared in the body are not accessible from outside the package.

- The section within square brackets [ ] can be omitted.

- If there is a statement section, the statements are only executed once, when the program using the package starts.

For example, we shall look at how the body of our package PLANIMETRY may appear:

```
package body PLANIMETRY is

    PI : constant := 3.1415926536;

    function AREA_RECTANGLE(L, H : LENGTH) return AREA is
    begin
        return AREA(L) * AREA(H);
    end AREA_RECTANGLE;

    function AREA_CIRCLE (R : LENGTH) return AREA is
    begin
        return PI * AREA(R) ** 2;
    end AREA_CIRCLE;
```

```
    function CIRCUMF_CIRCLE (R : LENGTH) return LENGTH is
    begin
       return 2.0 * PI * R;
    end CIRCUMF_CIRCLE;

    function AREA_TRIANGLE (B, H : LENGTH) return AREA is
    begin
       return AREA(B) * AREA(H) / 2.0;
    end AREA_TRIANGLE;

end PLANIMETRY;
```

Within the package body are the complete function bodies for the functions that were declared in the package specification. There is also a constant PI and this is only known within the package body. Thus in a program that uses the package it is not permitted to write:

```
PLANIMETRY.PI    -- ERROR! PI is only known
                 -- in the package body
```

It is only the items from the package specification that are known outside.

In the functions that calculate areas we have used type conversion so that the results of the functions have type AREA. The expression:

```
B * H
```

would have type LENGTH since both operands have that type. The expression:

```
AREA(B) * AREA(H)
```

however, has the type AREA.

The body of the package PLANIMETRY has no statement section. A section of statements in a package body is used when something has to be initialized within the package body before the package can be used. The constant PI needs to be initialized in the body of PLANIMETRY but we manage with a simple initialization in its declaration and, therefore, no statement part is needed. We shall look at an example of a package with a statement section later.

A package body must be compiled after its specification has been compiled. In the specification we talk about what the package will be able to do and in the body we state how to do what we have promised. It is possible to compile the specification and body separately on separate occasions or, if the texts are to remain together, to compile them as two compilation units but fed to the compiler together. In the latter case the specification should come before the body. It is recommended that the two parts should be compiled separately; since the package body contains whole subprograms it is likely that they will have to be amended and the body recompiled many times during program development. It is then advantageous not to have to recompile the package specification at the same time, since if the specification is recompiled all the programs using the package must also be recompiled.

8.5   Different categories of packages

Packages can be used for different purposes when an Ada program is written. To clarify this concept is may be useful to try and classify the different kinds of package. Generalizing a little, it can be said that there are four different categories of package:

(1)   Packages with a collection of types and constants, for example, a package of mathematical constants.

(2)   Packages with a group of subprograms that logically belong together, for example, a package of standard mathematical functions.

(3)   Packages with 'memory' that can be used to represent complicated objects in different states.

(4)   Packages which construct abstract data types.

We have already seen examples of packages from category (2), our package PLANIMETRY for example. Subprograms in the package belong together logically because they all perform calculations on geometrical figures. The mathematics package BASIC_MATH also belongs to category (2).

8.6   Packages of types and constants

As an example of a package of category (1) we shall study a package ATOMIC_CONSTANTS that contains various constants:

```
package ATOMIC_CONSTANTS is
    ELECTRON_CHARGE : constant := 1.602E-19;     -- coul
    ELECTRON_MASS   : constant := 0.9108E-30;    -- kg
    NEUTRON_MASS    : constant := 1674.7E-30;    -- kg
    PROTON_MASS     : constant := 1672.4E-30;    -- kg
end ATOMIC_CONSTANTS;
```

There are no subprograms in the package, only constants. If the **with** clause:

with ATOMIC_CONSTANTS;

is placed first in a program, then the package can be accessed and the mass of the proton, for example, can be accessed by writing:

ATOMIC_CONSTANTS.PROTON_MASS

Of course, a **use** clause can also be inserted in the program:

use ATOMIC_CONSTANTS;

Then the mass of the proton can simply be referred to by:

PROTON_MASS

The special thing about the packages of category (1) is that they do not need to have a body. Since such a package only contains constants and types, there is no special substance to the package that needs further description.

Packages without bodies

A package whose specification only contains declarations of constants and types does not need to have a body.

8.7 Packages with memory

Now we shall study packages that belong to category (3). This kind of package can be used to build up a description of a complex real object – an object that can be in different states. For example, when a program is written to control an engineering system, for example, an aeroplane, a program design method can be used based on representing each physical component of the system by an Ada package, a package of category (3). For example, it should be possible to represent a fuel valve by an Ada package.

The special thing about packages of category (3) is that they can be in different states. Each time the package is used, its state changes. Therefore the package must be able to 'remember' its state between uses.

The standard package TEXT_IO can be said to belong to category (3). It represents the real object – the 'terminal'. The package must remember how long a line of output can be and how many lines there can be on a page of output. When printing output, between calls to PUT, PUT_LINE and NEW_LINE the package must 'remember' which page is being printed, which line it is on and how much of the output has already been printed.

As another example of a package of category (3) we shall construct a package that can be used to generate random numbers. It will represent a random number generator. In some programs, such as games programs and simulation programs, access to a source of random numbers is necessary.

To obtain random numbers from a computer, the concept used is based on generating a series of numbers that appear to be random. Let us call this series:

$$u_0 \quad u_1 \quad u_2 \quad u_3 \quad \ldots$$

It is most common to use the formula:

$$u_{n+1} = K u_n \bmod M$$

to generate a particular term in the series, where mod means the modulo operator (see Section 3.4.1). If the nth term is known, the $(n+1)$th can be evaluated using the formula. Term number 0 is given a particular start value and thereafter the formula can be applied repeatedly to generate an arbitrary number of terms of the series. The numbers in the series will all lie in the interval 0 to $M - 1$.

For the numbers to appear random, K and M must be chosen in a special way, as must the start value of term number 0. (For example, if we gave K the value 3, M the value 10 and the start value 5, then all terms in the series would be 5 – not particularly random). There are theories that provide suitable values of K and M and the start value. Such suitable values for K and M can be, for example:

$$K = 5^5 \qquad M = 2^{13}$$

Then the start value for the series should be an odd number in the range 1 to $M - 1$.

We shall use the formula above, with the suggested values for K and M, to construct a package for generating random numbers. We want the package to contain a function NEXT_NUMBER that will return a random number when called, and each time it should be a new random number. It is useful if the random numbers obtained lie in a particular fixed interval; the interval 0 to 1 is generally chosen. Thus the random numbers will be real numbers. To be able to generate different series of random numbers the user must be able to specify what start value will be used; if the same start value is always used the same series of random numbers will always be generated. We can solve this by using a procedure INITIALIZE with an **in** parameter that is the start value – known as the seed – to the random number generator.

Now we are in a position to write a specification of the package RANDOM:

```
package RANDOM is

    M : constant := 2 ** 13;

    subtype NUMBER is FLOAT range 0.0 .. 1.0;
    subtype SEED    is INTEGER range 1 .. M − 1;

    procedure INITIALIZE (START_VALUE : in SEED);
    -- initialize random number generator
    -- START_VALUE should be an odd integer

    function NEXT_NUMBER return NUMBER;
    -- gives a random number that is greater
    -- than or equal to 0 and less than 1

end RANDOM;
```

In addition to the subprograms NEXT_NUMBER and INITIALIZE we have declared two subtypes, NUMBER and SEED. The subtype NUMBER describes a floating point number in the interval 0 to 1, a number of the kind that the function NEXT_NUMBER returns as its result. The subtype SEED describes how a start value, the seed, may look. The parameter to the procedure INITIALIZE will be of this subtype. The next step is to construct the body of the package. In the body we must state what the bodies of the subprograms NEXT_NUMBER and INITIALIZE should look like. Let us start with the function NEXT_NUMBER. To evaluate the next number in the series we use the statement:

```
U := U * K mod M;
```

where K and M are constants with values 5^5 and 2^{13}, respectively. U is a variable that we initialize at the start to the first number in the series, the seed. Each time the above statement is executed, U will take the next value in the series. U will take integer values in the interval 1 to $2^{13} − 1$. However, for the result of the function NEXT_NUMBER we want a floating point number in the interval 0 to 1, which can easily be achieved by dividing U by M:

```
return FLOAT(U) / FLOAT(M);
```

(Observe that we must convert U and M to floating point numbers. Had we not done so the result would always have been 0).

The package body is:

```
package body RANDOM is

   U : NATURAL;
   K : constant := 5 ** 5;

   procedure INITIALIZE (START_VALUE : in SEED) is
   begin
     U := START_VALUE;
   end INITIALIZE;

   function NEXT_NUMBER return NUMBER is
   begin
     U := U * K mod M;
     return FLOAT(U) / FLOAT (M);
   end NEXT_NUMBER;
end RANDOM;
```

The important thing to note here is the positioning of the declaration of the variable U. U may not be declared as a local variable in the function NEXT_NUMBER for two reasons:

(1)   U must be accessible to the procedure INITIALIZE, whose job is to give U a starting value. If the declaration had been placed in NEXT_NUMBER, U would not have been known outside NEXT_NUMBER.

(2)   U must 'remember' its value between calls to NEXT_NUMBER. If U had been declared as a local variable inside NEXT_NUMBER it would not have existed between calls. As a consequence, U's value would have been undefined at each new call to NEXT_NUMBER.

The solution to the problem is to place the declaration of U directly in the package body, as above, outside INITIALIZE and NEXT_NUMBER. It is then accessible to both subprograms and, moreover, it will not be spoiled between calls.

Thus U is a global variable to INITIALIZE and NEXT_NUMBER. In normal cases, global variables must not be used, but this is one of the few exceptions, mentioned earlier, where it is allowed. In packages of category (3), global variables are used in the package body to give the package a 'memory'. In the other categories of package, that lack this 'memory', such global variables are not to be used.

Packages with 'memory'

- By using global variables in the package body, a package can be created that has 'memory' so that it can exist in different states.

- The state can be changed by calls to subprograms in the package.

- This is one of the few occasions where it is 'allowed' to use global variables.

Now we shall look at the use of RANDOM in a program. We shall write a short program to test whether the random number generator is 'good'. The program will start with the user entering a start value for the random number generator which will then be used to generate 100 random numbers. These numbers will be written out. Finally the program calculates the mean of the 100 numbers and writes it out. If the mean is not close to 0.5 then either the random number generator is not good or we have chosen an unsuitable start value.[†]

```
with TEXT_IO, BASIC_NUM_IO, RANDOM;
use  TEXT_IO, BASIC_NUM_IO;
procedure TEST_RANDOM is
  S : RANDOM.SEED;
  X : RANDOM.NUMBER;
  SUM : FLOAT := 0.0;
begin
  -- Initialize random number generator
  PUT_LINE("Enter seed for random number generator");
  PUT("An odd integer in the interval ");
  PUT(RANDOM.SEED'FIRST, WIDTH => 1); PUT(" to ");
  PUT(RANDOM.SEED'LAST, WIDTH => 1); NEW_LINE;
  GET(S);
  RANDOM.INITIALIZE(S);
```

[†] To determine whether a random number generator is 'good' in a more correct statistical sense requires more extensive tests. The random number obtained should have an appropriate standard deviation and the periodicity of the series of random numbers, that is, how long it takes before the same sequence of random numbers is repeated, should be adequately large.

```
-- Generate 100 random numbers
for I in 1 .. 100 loop
  X := RANDOM.NEXT_NUMBER;
  PUT(X); NEW_LINE;
  SUM := SUM + X;
end loop;

  -- evaluate and print mean of the random numbers
  PUT("Mean: "); PUT(SUM / 100.0); NEW_LINE;
end TEST_RANDOM;
```

In the program, we have made the random number generator in the package RANDOM accessible by including RANDOM in the **with** clause in the first line of the program. We have no **use** clause for the package RANDOM but use selection with the dot notation for clarity.

The variables S and X are given, respectively, the types SEED and NUMBER which are declared in the specification of RANDOM. In the message that requests a seed from the user, we have used RANDOM.SEED'FIRST and RANDOM.SEED'LAST instead of the numbers 1 and 8191 ($2^{13} - 1$). In this way the program is made more general and would not need to be changed if the value of the constant M, and hence the subtype SEED, were changed in the random number generator. The start value is given to the random number generator by making the procedure call:

```
RANDOM.INITIALIZE(S);
```

The 100 random numbers are generated by 100 calls to the function NEXT_NUMBER:

```
X := RANDOM.NEXT_NUMBER;
```

After each call the variable U in the body of RANDOM will change in value but we do not need to worry about how things are working exactly within the package because this program is only using the facilities. (In fact, we do not even know that there is a variable U).

We see that if the random number generator were initialized automatically our program would be much simpler. We would not need to enter the seed, the variable S would not be necessary and we would not need to know about the subtype SEED.

```
with TEXT_IO, BASIC_NUM_IO, RANDOM;
use  TEXT_IO, BASIC_NUM_IO;
procedure TEST_RANDOM is

  X : RANDOM.NUMBER;
  SUM : FLOAT := 0.0;
```

```
begin

   -- Generate 100 random numbers
   for I in 1 .. 100 loop
     X := RANDOM.NEXT_NUMBER;
     PUT(X); NEW_LINE;
     SUM := SUM + X;
   end loop;

   -- evaluate and print mean of the random numbers
   PUT("Mean: "); PUT(SUM / 100.0); NEW_LINE;
end TEST_RANDOM;
```

Furthermore, we could simplify the specification of the package RANDOM since neither the subtype SEED or the procedure INITIALIZE would be needed.

Instead the specification of RANDOM would be:

```
package RANDOM is

   subtype NUMBER is FLOAT range 0.0 .. 1.0;

   function NEXT_NUMBER return NUMBER;
   -- gives a random number that is greater
   -- than or equal to 0 and less than 1

end RANDOM;
```

How can we get the random number generator to be initialized automatically? One simple way, of course, is that when the variable U is declared in the body of the package RANDOM it is given a suitable initial value. However, this has one big disadvantage. Since U would then always be initialized to the same number, the random number package would generate the same sequence of random numbers each time it is used. This would mean that every time we ran a program that made use of the package RANDOM the program would behave in the same way. The program would not be particularly random.

We shall therefore make use of the possibility offered by having a sequence of statements in the package. Statements can be placed there to read a start value from the terminal. The body of the package RANDOM now looks like this:

```
with TEXT_IO, BASIC_NUM_IO;
use  TEXT_IO, BASIC_NUM_IO;
package body RANDOM is

   U : NATURAL;
   K : constant := 5 * 5;
   M : constant := 2 ** 13;
```

```
function NEXT_NUMBER return NUMBER is
begin
    U := U * K mod M;
    return FLOAT(U) / FLOAT(M);
end NEXT_NUMBER;

begin
    PUT_LINE("Enter seed for random number generator");
    PUT_LINE("An odd number in the interval 1 to ");
    PUT(M − 1, WIDTH => 1); NEW_LINE;
    GET(U);
end RANDOM;
```

Observe that the package now needs access to the packages TEXT_IO and BASIC_NUM_IO. Therefore the **with** and **use** clauses for these are placed first. The main difference from the earlier version is that INITIALIZE is no longer there. Instead, there are statements in the package that read in a start value of the variable U. The question is 'When will these statements be executed?' A package body looks more or less like that of a subprogram. The statements in the body of a subprogram are, as we know, executed each time the subprogram is called. A package body is never called; all that can be called are those subprograms in the package that are declared in the package specification. Therefore a package body must work in a different way from a subprogram body. In fact, the statements in a package body are executed only once and this occurs when the program using the package is started. We can picture it in connection with the program's **with** clause.

This means that if we run the program TEST_RANDOM, the first thing that occurs is that the statements in the statement part of RANDOM will be executed. The program thus begins by writing out at the terminal:

```
Enter seed for random number generator
An odd number in the interval 1 to 8191
```

The user then writes the value at the terminal and this is entered to the variable U in the body of RANDOM. Thereafter execution in RANDOM's body terminates and the statements in the procedure TEST_RANDOM will be executed in the normal way.

8.8 Abstract data types

Earlier, we talked about a data type being characterized by the values that its objects can assume and by the operations that can be carried out on them. The allowed values for a particular type are decided when the type declaration is made, and there are also some standard types, such as CHARACTER and INTEGER, for which the allowed values are specified. As for possible operations, we have seen that for the simple types there are a number of standard operations, such as addition and multiplication. For more complicated types that we construct ourselves, such as array types and record types of various kinds, only comparison operators are normally automatically defined, but we can create new operators for such types by writing subprograms. For example, we have already made functions that add vectors and matrices. It is thus possible, using type declarations and subprograms, to build up whole new types where the permitted values are defined by type declarations and the possible operations are defined by subprograms. Such a type, built up by the programmer, is called an **abstract data type**.

When an abstract data type is constructed, the type declarations and the subprograms that can operate on objects of the type belong together logically; together they define the abstract data type. It is therefore appropriate to combine them into a unit in the program. A package can be constructed containing everything that describes the abstract data type.

As an example of an abstract data type we shall study the complex numbers of mathematics. The quantity under the square root sign is sometimes negative in, for example, the solution to a quadratic equation. To cope with this situation, a quantity, i, has been defined such that:

$$i^2 = -1$$

The number i is no ordinary number. It is usually called an **imaginary number**.

Ordinary numbers can be combined with imaginary numbers to produce a new number system, the **complex numbers**. A complex number has two parts, a real part and an imaginary part. It can be written as:

$$p + qi$$

where p and q are ordinary real numbers. A complex number can also be represented as a point (p,q) in a normal two-dimensional coordinate system, where the x-axis is called the real axis and the y-axis is called the imaginary axis. It is possible to calculate with complex numbers in the normal way. For example, it is possible to add, subtract, multiply and divide complex numbers using the normal laws of arithmetic. The only thing to remember is that the square of i is -1. For example:

$$(5 + 2i)(3 + 4i) = (7 + 26i)$$

When dividing with a complex number the trick of multiplying both the numerator and the denominator by a suitable quantity, so that the denominator is a real number, has to be used. If the denominator is $p + q$i, this multiplier is its complex conjugate $p - q$i. Thus, if we divide the complex number A by the complex number B where:

$$B = p + q\mathrm{i}$$

we get:

$$\frac{A}{B} = \frac{A}{p + q\mathrm{i}} = \frac{A(p - q\mathrm{i})}{(p + q\mathrm{i})\,(p - q\mathrm{i})} = \frac{A(p - q\mathrm{i})}{p^2 + q^2}$$

Now we shall build up an Ada package to describe the abstract data type COMPLEX_NUMBER. Since a complex number consists of a real part and an imaginary part it is natural to use a record type to describe the type COMPLEX_NUMBER:

```
type COMPLEX_NUMBER is
  record
    RE, IM : FLOAT;
  end record;
```

Now we can write a specification of the package that will describe the abstract data type COMPLEX_NUMBER:

```
package COMPLEX is
  type COMPLEX_NUMBER is
    record
      RE, IM : FLOAT;
    end record;

  function MAKE_COMPLEX  (R, I : FLOAT)
                          return COMPLEX_NUMBER;
  function REAL_PART      (A : COMPLEX_NUMBER)
                          return FLOAT;
  function IMAGINARY_PART (A : COMPLEX_NUMBER)
                          return FLOAT;

  -- Operations on numbers of type COMPLEX_NUMBER
  function ADD (A, B : COMPLEX_NUMBER)
                          return COMPLEX_NUMBER;
  function SUB (A, B : COMPLEX_NUMBER)
                          return COMPLEX_NUMBER;
  function MUL (A, B : COMPLEX_NUMBER)
                          return COMPLEX_NUMBER;
  function DIV  (A, B : COMPLEX_NUMBER)
                          return COMPLEX_NUMBER;
```

```
procedure READ (A : out COMPLEX_NUMBER);
-- the real and imaginary parts should be
-- entered as two real numbers

procedure WRITE (A : in COMPLEX_NUMBER);
-- a complex number is printed in the form
-- (real_part, imaginary_part)
end COMPLEX;
```

Here we have declared the type COMPLEX_NUMBER and listed the subprogram specifications for all the subprograms we want. We have chosen to formulate the subprogram READ as a procedure with an **out** parameter because we are used to using the procedure GET and want to be able to call READ in the same way. It would have worked equally well to let READ be a function that gives a complex number as its result. We have used comments to state how we want the reading and writing of complex numbers to appear.

The function MAKE_COMPLEX is used to make a complex number out of two real numbers. If the declaration:

```
C : COMPLEX_NUMBER;
```

is written in a program then C can be given a value by writing, for example:

```
C := MAKE_COMPLEX(1.5, 0.4);
```

Of course, it would also be possible to write a record aggregate on the right-hand side. However, when we work with abstract data types in our program we should avoid utilizing knowledge about how the complex data types are represented in the package. (See Section 8.9.)

Functions that give a value of the abstract type as result are, in this context, sometimes called **constructors** because they can be used to construct a new abstract value.

The functions REAL_PART and IMAGINARY_PART are used to extract the real and imaginary parts, respectively, of the complex number.

```
P := REAL_PART(C);
Q := IMAGINARY_PART(C);
```

We use these functions instead of direct selection with dot notation in the user program. The functions REAL_PART and IMAGINARY_PART are examples of **selectors**. They select parts from an abstract value.

Using the specifications in the package COMPLEX we can now write and compile a program that reads in two complex numbers, one after the other, and then calculates and writes out the sum, difference, product and quotient of the two numbers.

```
with TEXT_IO, BASIC_NUM_IO, COMPLEX;
use  TEXT_IO, BASIC_NUM_IO, COMPLEX;
procedure COMPLEX_DEMO is
  X, Y : COMPLEX_NUMBER;
begin
  PUT_LINE("Terminate with CTRL-D");
  PUT("Enter complex numbers as two real numbers");
  NEW_LINE(2);

  loop
    PUT("Enter the first complex number: ");
    exit when END_OF_FILE;
    READ(X);
    PUT("Enter the second complex number: ");
    READ(Y);

    PUT("The sum is: "); WRITE(ADD (X, Y)); NEW_LINE;
    PUT("The difference is: "); WRITE(SUB (X, Y)); NEW_LINE;
    PUT("The product is: "); WRITE(MUL (X, Y)); NEW_LINE;
    PUT("The quotient is: "); WRITE(DIV (X, Y));
    NEW_LINE(2);
  end loop;
end COMPLEX_DEMO;
```

Before the program can be executed we must, of course, write the body of the package COMPLEX:

```
with TEXT_IO, BASIC_NUM_IO;
use  TEXT_IO, BASIC_NUM_IO;
package body COMPLEX is

  function MAKE_COMPLEX (R, I : FLOAT)
                          return COMPLEX_NUMBER is
  begin
    return (R, I);
  end MAKE_COMPLEX;

  function REAL_PART (A: COMPLEX_NUMBER)
                          return FLOAT is
  begin
    return A.RE;
  end REAL_PART;
```

```
        function IMAGINARY_PART (A : COMPLEX_NUMBER)
                              return FLOAT is
begin
  return A.IM;
end IMAGINARY_PART;

        function ADD (A, B : COMPLEX_NUMBER)
                              return COMPLEX_NUMBER is
begin
  return (A.RE + B.RE, A.IM + B.IM);
end ADD;

        function SUB (A, B : COMPLEX_NUMBER)
                              return COMPLEX_NUMBER is
begin
  return (A.RE − B.RE, A.IM − B.IM);
end SUB;

        function MUL (A, B : COMPLEX_NUMBER)
                              return COMPLEX_NUMBER is
begin
  return (A.RE * B.RE − A.IM * B.IM,
          A.RE * B.IM + A.IM * B.RE);
end MUL;

        function DIV (A, B : COMPLEX_NUMBER)
                              return COMPLEX_NUMBER is
  T : COMPLEX_NUMBER;
  N : FLOAT;
begin
  T := MUL(A, (B.RE, − B.IM) );
  N := B.RE ** 2 + B.IM ** 2;
  return (T.RE / N, T.IM / N);
end DIV;

        procedure READ (A : out COMPLEX_NUMBER) is
begin
  GET(A.RE); GET(A.IM);
end READ;

        procedure WRITE (A : in COMPLEX_NUMBER) is
begin
  PUT("("); PUT(A.RE); PUT(", ");
          PUT(A.IM); PUT(")");
end WRITE;

end COMPLEX;
```

Since the procedures READ and WRITE read from and write to the terminal, the package body needs access to the packages TEXT_IO and BASIC_NUM_IO. In the functions ADD, SUB, MUL and DIV we have used record aggregates in the return statements. In ADD we have simply added

```
Terminate with CTRL-D
Enter complex numbers as two real numbers

Enter the first complex number:    1.0  1.0
Enter the second complex number: 1.0  1.0
The sum is:        (   2.00000000E+00,   2.00000000E+00)
The difference is:(   0.00000000E+00,   0.00000000E+00)
The product is:   (   0.00000000E+00,   2.00000000E+00)
The quotient is:  (   1.00000000E+00,   0.00000000E+00)

Enter the first complex number:    −1.0 2.0
Enter the second complex number:   1.0 2.0
The sum is:        (   0.00000000E+00,   4.00000000E+00)
The difference is:( −2.00000000E+00,   0.00000000E+00)
The product is:   ( −5.00000000E+00,   0.00000000E+00)
The quotient is:  (   6.00000000E−01,   8.00000000E−01)

Enter the first complex number:
The user now types CTRL-D
```

Figure 8.1

the real parts and the imaginary parts of the two parameters; in SUB we have subtracted one real part from the other and one imaginary part from the other. In MUL we have made use of the rule that $i^2 = -1$. In the function DIV, the method explained earlier has been used. To perform the necessary multiplication involved in DIV we have used, of course, MUL.

A test run of the program COMPLEX_DEMO is shown in Figure 8.1.

■

The possibility of naming operators, as discussed in Section 6.9, becomes most useful in the construction of abstract data types. Instead of using the function names ADD, SUB, MUL and DIV in the package COMPLEX we can rename the functions "+", "−", "*" and "/". This makes it possible to call them using the operators. If the variables X and Y are declared in the following way in a program that uses the package COMPLEX:

X, Y : COMPLEX_NUMBER;

we can call the function "+" in the package COMPLEX by writing:

X + Y

The result of this expression will be of type COMPLEX_NUMBER.

Another change we can make in the package COMPLEX is to use the procedure names GET and PUT instead of READ and WRITE. Then, as shown in Section 6.9, we shall have overloaded subprograms, but they have different profiles. Since the procedure names GET and PUT are used for input and output of other numeric types it seems natural to use them for the type COMPLEX_NUMBER as well.

As a result of these changes the specification of the package COMPLEX will now appear as follows:

```
package COMPLEX is

   type COMPLEX_NUMBER is
   record
      RE, IM : FLOAT;
   end record;

   function MAKE_COMPLEX   (R, I : FLOAT)
                                    return COMPLEX_NUMBER;
   function REAL_PART        (A : COMPLEX_NUMBER)
                                    return FLOAT;
   function IMAGINARY_PART (A : COMPLEX_NUMBER)
                                    return FLOAT;

   -- Operations on numbers of type COMPLEX_NUMBER
   function "+" (A, B : COMPLEX_NUMBER)
                                    return COMPLEX_NUMBER;
   function "-" (A, B : COMPLEX_NUMBER)
                                    return COMPLEX_NUMBER;
   function "*" (A, B : COMPLEX_NUMBER)
                                    return COMPLEX_NUMBER;
   function "/" (A, B : COMPLEX_NUMBER)
                                    return COMPLEX_NUMBER;

   procedure GET (A : out COMPLEX_NUMBER);
   -- The real and imaginary parts should be
   -- entered as two real numbers

   procedure PUT (A : in COMPLEX_NUMBER);
   -- A complex number is printed in the form
   -- (real_part, imaginary_part)

end COMPLEX;
```

We also have to amend the program COMPLEX_DEMO so that it fits in with the new specification of the package COMPLEX:

```
loop
   PUT("Enter the first complex number: ");
   exit when END_OF_FILE;
   GET(X);
   PUT("Enter the second complex number: ");
   GET(Y);

   PUT("The sum is:      "); PUT(X + Y); NEW_LINE;
   PUT("The difference is: "); PUT(X - Y); NEW_LINE;
```

```
         PUT("The product is:    "); PUT(X * Y);   NEW_LINE;
         PUT("The quotient is:   "); PUT(X / Y);   NEW_LINE(2);
      end loop;
```

We see that these changes mean that complex numbers can be handled in the program in precisely the same way as ordinary numbers.

☐

In mathematics it is very common to work with sets. As a further example, we shall construct an abstract data type that describes sets of characters. We want to be able to perform the usual set operations, namely, add an element to a set, remove one, form the unions and intersections of two sets, and find out whether one set is a subset of another.

We start by thinking about how to represent a set in Ada. In the sets we shall study, the elements will be characters, that is, have type CHARACTER. If we consider a particular set, then it is true that each character either belongs or does not belong to the set. We can let a set be represented by an array with components of type BOOLEAN. In the array there will be one component for each character, that can be achieved most simply by indexing the array with type CHARACTER. If we call the type SET we can make the declaration:

```
type SET is array (CHARACTER) of BOOLEAN;
```

If we now declare a variable S, for example, of type SET:

```
S : SET;
```

the components of S will state whether the character belongs to the set S. The empty set, the one with no elements, is represented by an array in which all the components have the value FALSE.

Now we can make a specification of the package SET_PACKAGE which describes the abstract data type of sets of characters:

```
package SET_PACKAGE is

   type SET is array (CHARACTER) of BOOLEAN;

   function EMPTY_SET return SET;
   -- gives the empty set

   function ADD (C : CHARACTER; S : SET) return SET;
   -- puts C into the set S

   function SUB (C : CHARACTER; S : SET) return SET;
   -- removes C from the set S
```

```
function MEMBER (C : CHARACTER; S : SET)
                              return BOOLEAN;
-- finds out if C is a member of the set S

function UNION (S1, S2 : SET) return SET;
-- returns the union of the sets S1 and S2

function INTERSECTION (S1, S2 : SET) return SET;
-- returns the intersection of the sets S1 and S2

function SUBSET (S1, S2 : SET) return BOOLEAN;
-- finds out if S1 is a subset of S2

procedure WRITE (S : in SET);
-- prints all the characters in the set S
```

end SET_PACKAGE;

In addition to the operations named above, we have included a function that can be used to create an empty set and a procedure that writes out the characters that belong to a given set. The functions MEMBER and SUBSET give information about how a set looks; such a function that gives a value of type BOOLEAN as result is sometimes called an **informer**.

Let us now look at how to construct the package body. First we note that an empty set can be described as an array in which all the components have the value FALSE. An empty set can thus be expressed using the array aggregate:

(others => FALSE)

To place an element in a set S we have only to make an ordinary assignment. The statement:

S('*') := TRUE;

for example, puts the character '*' into the set S. An element can correspondingly be removed from a set:

S('8') := FALSE;

for example, removes the character '8' from set S.

To find out if a particular character belongs to the set is easy. If, for example:

S('A')

has the value TRUE, then the character 'A' belongs to set S; if it has the value FALSE it does not belong to S.

To form the union and intersection of two sets we make use of the fact that the logic operators **and** and **or** are more general than we showed earlier. These operators do not apply only to simple scalar operands of type BOOLEAN. The two operands can also be arrays in which the components are of type BOOLEAN, provided there are the same number of components in the two arrays. The result of each operation is a new array with components of type BOOLEAN and the same number of components as the two operands. A couple of examples will help to explain how they work. If we have the declarations:

```
type LOGIC_ARRAY is array (1 .. 4) of BOOLEAN;
LA : LOGIC_ARRAY := (TRUE, FALSE, TRUE, FALSE);
LB : LOGIC_ARRAY := (TRUE, TRUE, FALSE, FALSE);
LC, LD : LOGIC_ARRAY;
```

then we can write the statements:

```
LC := LA and LB;    -- LC becomes (TRUE, FALSE, FALSE, FALSE)
LD := LA or LB;     -- LD becomes (TRUE, TRUE, TRUE, FALSE)
```

The logic operators, **not** and **xor**, are also defined for arrays with components of type BOOLEAN.

Now we return to sets of characters. The union of two sets S1 and S2 is a set containing all the elements that are either in S1 or S2. The intersection of S1 and S2 is a set containing all the elements that are in both S1 and S2. If S1 and S2 are of type SET we can easily form their union and intersection:

```
S1 or S2     -- gives a set that is the union of S1 and S2
S1 and S2    -- gives a set that is the intersection of S1 and S2
```

Whether one set S1 is a subset of another, S2, can be investigated by forming their intersection. If this intersection is equal to S1, then S1 contains only elements that are also in S2, that is, S1 is a subset of S2. (S1 could be equal to S2, in which case it would not be a true subset, but here we will accept this).

Now we can write the body of SET_PACKAGE:

```
with TEXT_IO;
use  TEXT_IO;
package body SET_PACKAGE is

  function EMPTY_SET return SET is
  begin
    return (others => FALSE);
  end EMPTY_SET;
```

```
function ADD (C : CHARACTER; S : SET) return SET is
  R : SET := S;
begin
  R(C) := TRUE;  return R;
end ADD;

function SUB (C : CHARACTER; S : SET) return SET is
  R : SET := S;
begin
  R(C) := FALSE; return R;
end SUB;

function MEMBER (C : CHARACTER; S : SET)
                                    return BOOLEAN is
begin
  return S(C);
end MEMBER;

function UNION (S1, S2 : SET) return SET is
begin
  return S1 or S2;
end UNION;

function INTERSECTION (S1, S2 : SET) return SET is
begin
  return S1 and S2;
end INTERSECTION;

function SUBSET (S1, S2 : SET) return BOOLEAN is
begin
  return INTERSECTION(S1, S2) = S1;
end MEMBER;

procedure WRITE (S : in SET) is
begin
  for C in CHARACTER loop
    if S(C) then
      PUT(C);
    end if;
  end loop;
end WRITE;
end SET_PACKAGE;
```

Next we shall look at how the abstract data type can be used in a program. We assume that the following **with** and **use** clauses already exist in the program:

```
with SET_PACKAGE;
use  SET_PACKAGE;
```

We declare the sets LETTER and OP:

```
LETTER, OP : SET := EMPTY_SET;
```

To initialize the sets we have called the function EMPTY_SET in the package SET_PACKAGE. The two variables can be given suitable values with the following statements:

```
for CHAR in 'a' .. 'z' loop
   LETTER := ADD(CHAR, LETTER);
end loop;

for CHAR in 'A' .. 'Z' loop
   LETTER := ADD(CHAR, LETTER);
end loop;

OP := ADD('+', OP); OP := ADD('-', OP);
OP := ADD('*', OP);  OP := ADD('/', OP);
```

Now we can read a character from the terminal and determine whether it is a letter or an operator symbol:

```
GET(C);
if MEMBER(C, LETTER) then
   -- character was a letter
   :

elsif MEMBER(C, OP) then
   -- character was an operator symbol
   :

else
   -- it was some other character
   :

end if;
```

Finally we shall present a program that reads in two lines of text from the terminal. The program writes out all the characters that are in either the first or second line (or both, of course), and all the characters that appear in both lines.

Input occurs via a call to the procedure GET_LINE and the two lines are read to the variables LINE1 and LINE2. We declare two sets, IN_LINE1 and IN_LINE2, in which we place all the characters that are written in the first and second lines, respectively. Then the program forms the union and the intersection of the two sets IN_LINE1 and IN_LINE2. Output takes place via the procedure WRITE in SET_PACKAGE.

```
with TEXT_IO, BASIC_NUM_IO, SET_PACKAGE;
use  TEXT_IO, BASIC_NUM_IO, SET_PACKAGE;
procedure COMPARE_LINES is
  LINE1, LINE2 : STRING(1 .. 200);
  LENGTH1, LENGTH2 : NATURAL;
  IN_LINE1, IN_LINE2 : SET := EMPTY_SET;

begin
  -- Read both lines
  PUT_LINE("Write two lines");
  GET_LINE(LINE1, LENGTH1);
  GET_LINE(LINE2, LENGTH2);

  -- Construct a set of all the characters in line1
  for I in 1 .. LENGTH1 loop
    IN_LINE1 := ADD(LINE1(I), IN_LINE1);
  end loop;

  -- Construct a set of all the characters in line2
  for I in 1 .. LENGTH2 loop
    IN_LINE2 := ADD(LINE2(I), IN_LINE2);
  end loop;

  PUT("These characters appear:            ");
  WRITE( UNION(IN_LINE1, IN_LINE2) );
  NEW_LINE;

  PUT("These characters appear in both lines: ");
  WRITE( INTERSECTION(IN_LINE1, IN_LINE2) );
  NEW_LINE;

end COMPARE_LINES;
```

8.9 Private types

We have seen that it is possible to hide away in the body of a package those details that are of no interest to a user. There is another possible way of concealing the details of an abstract data type in Ada, using so-called **private types**.

In the specification of the package SET_PACKAGE in Section 8.8 the type SET was declared:

```
type SET is array (CHARACTER) of BOOLEAN;
```

Since this declaration is in the package specification, it is known to the user and thus the following declarations could be made in the user program:

```
S1, S2 : SET;
```

The variables could also be used in the normal way, for example, they can be indexed:

```
S1('X') := TRUE;
```

This is not particularly good. The basis of an abstract data type is, of course, to use the operations given as subprograms in the package specification, for example, UNION and INTERSECTION for the type SET. If the user starts to 'poke' into the variables of the abstract type, there is no longer any guarantee that it will work in the intended way.

The designer of a package can prevent the user from treating objects of a type in this way by declaring the type as private in the package specification. The specification of SET_PACKAGE, for example, could be written:

```
package SET_PACKAGE is
    type SET is private;
    function EMPTY_SET return SET;
    -- gives the empty set

        ⋮

    as before

        ⋮

    procedure WRITE (S : in SET);
    -- prints all the characters in the set S
private
    type SET is array (CHARACTER) of BOOLEAN;
end SET_PACKAGE;
```

The type declaration:

```
type SET is private;
```

makes the type SET accessible to the user of a package. Thus a user can declare variables of type SET in his or her program:

```
S1, S2 : SET;
```

and it is also possible to write subprograms that have parameters of type SET.

If the type is private, the user receives no information about what the type looks like; the user is thus not allowed to manipulate objects of type SET himself. Since the user does not know that S1 and S2 are arrays, he or she cannot refer to components by index. All handling of objects of the type will normally occur through calls to the subprograms in the package specification, such as UNION and MEMBER. The only operations the user may utilize on objects of a private type are **assignment** and **comparison** for equality and inequality. Thus the following statement is allowed:

    S1 := S2;

but:

    S1 := (**others** => FALSE);   -- ERROR!

would not be allowed because, of course, we do not know that S1 is an array. If we want to create an empty set we must use the function EMPTY_SET from the package and write instead;

    S1 := EMPTY_SET;

How an empty set is represented has nothing to do with us. It is a detail that only the package designer needs to worry about.

Using private types

- It is possible to declare variables of a private type or to have parameters of a private type to subprograms.

- Outside the body of the package the only operations allowed are assignment and comparison for equality and inequality.

- Within the body of the package the package's private types may be used freely.

In the foregoing package specification we have added a **private part** at the end:

    private
       type SET **is array** (CHARACTER) **of** BOOLEAN;

In this private part, the appearance of the private types is specified. This part of the specification is not visible to the user's program (even if the user can read what is written there). The reason why the private part should appear in the package specification is that the compiler must know what the private type looks like when it comes to compile the user's program. (For example, when a variable of a private type is declared, sufficient space has to be allocated in the computer's memory).

In the body of the package, a private type is known and may be used in all the usual ways.

Declaration of private data types

package P **is**

.

   type T **is private**;

.

private

.

   type T **is** *normal_type_specification*;

.

end P;

The only permitted operations on a private type are, as mentioned, assignment and comparison. There are occasions when the package designer does not want the package user to be able to carry out even these operations on a private type. Then a **limited private type** can be declared. If we want to forbid the user carrying out assignment and comparison of character sets, we could write in the package specification:

type SET **is limited private**;

The reserved word **limited** signifies precisely that assignment and comparison are forbidden. Thus, the statement:

   S1 := S2;   -- ERROR! limited private type

is not allowed.

An object of a limited private type cannot be initialized at the time of declaration because assignment is not allowed. Thus the declaration:

   S1 : SET := EMPTY_SET;   -- ERROR!

is no longer allowed. It is inappropriate to use a limited private type in the package SET_PACKAGE; all the functions in the package that give results of type SET become unusable since it is impossible to do anything with the results in the user program. There are other packages, for example, those concerned with input and output, where the use of limited private types is justified.

Limited private types

> **type** T **is limited private**;

For such a type, neither assignment nor comparison are permitted outside the body of the package.

■

When a package is constructed a limited private type can be given its own equality operator. (Compare this with Section 6.9.) For the type SET we could, for example, have the specification:

> **function** ''='' (SA, SB : SET) **return** BOOLEAN;

The user of the package can then simply call this function:

> **if** S1 = S2 **then**

Note that it is not possible to define a new /= operator. This is declared automatically through the declaration of the operator =, so that:

> **if** S1 /= S2 **then**

can also be written now.

□

EXERCISES

8.1 Write a package that contains the temperature constants:

boiling point of oxygen (at 1 atm)	=	−182.97 °C
boiling point of sulphur (at 1 atm)	=	444.60 °C
melting point of silver (at 1 atm)	=	960.5 °C
melting point of gold (at 1 atm)	=	1063 °C

8.2 Write a package SOLID_GEOMETRY that contains aids for calculating the volumes and areas of a number of common shapes:

$$V = \pi r^2 h$$

volume of a cylinder with radius r and height h

$$A = 2\pi r(r+h)$$

surface area of a cylinder with radius r and height h

$$V = \frac{1}{3}\pi r^2 h$$

volume of a circular cone with base radius r and height h

$$A = \pi r(r + \sqrt{r^2 + h^2}\ )$$

surface area of a circular cone with base radius r and height h

$$V = \frac{4}{3}\pi r^3$$

volume of a sphere with radius r

$$A = 4\pi r^2$$

surface area of a sphere with radius r

8.3 Write a package that contains the ordinary trigonometric functions sin, cos, tan and cot. The following Maclaurin series are given:

$$\sin(x) = x - \frac{x^3}{3!} + \frac{x^5}{5!} - \frac{x^7}{7!} + \ldots$$

$$\cos(x) = 1 - \frac{x^2}{2!} + \frac{x^4}{4!} - \frac{x^6}{6!} + \ldots$$

8.4 Write a package that deals cards randomly from an ordinary pack of cards. In the package there should be a function DEAL that returns a card when called. The package must keep track internally of what cards are dealt out, so that each card in the pack is dealt only once. There should be a procedure SHUFFLE that can be called each time the pack has to be shuffled and a new deal started. Use the package RANDOM from Section 8.7.

Use the package to write a program that lets the user play a hand of 21 with the computer. The game involves the user receiving one card at a time and then deciding whether or not to take another. The aim is to try and get the total value of the cards as close as possible to 21, without going above. An ace can count as either 1 or 14. If the user gets more than 21, he or she goes 'bust' and the computer has won. If the user sticks at less than 21 the computer can also draw one card at a time and decide whether or not to continue after each card. (One strategy the computer can adopt is to continue for as long as its cards total less than 16). If the computer goes bust, the user wins. Otherwise the winner is the one with the higher total. If the user and the computer stick at the same totals, then the computer wins. After each hand the computer writes out the winner and asks the user if he or she would like another game.

8.5 Section 2.3 described a method of writing outsize letters on an ordinary terminal. Write a package that can be used to write such giant letters. It should be possible to write several giant letters on a horizontal line at the terminal. The package should thus keep track internally of each line of letters. The following procedures should be present in the package:

WRITE(C)   Put the character C in the first vacant place in the line of giant letters. If the current line is full it should be written out and C placed at the start of a new line.

WRITE_LINE   Write out the current line of giant letters.

8.6 Many modern terminals and personal computers offer facilities for drawing graphics on the screen, but even on an ordinary screen or printer it is possible to draw simple pictures. A picture is built up as a matrix in which each element is a character. The number of rows in the matrix is set equal to the number of lines on the screen (for a printer the number of rows is arbitrary) and the number of columns is the same as the maximum line length. At the start, all elements in the matrix are set to blanks and then a picture is built up by filling in certain elements as appropriate. When the picture is completely built up, the whole matrix is written out at the terminal.

Write a graphics package that can be used to draw simple pictures in the way described. The following procedures should be present in the package:

INIT(R,C)   Set the number of rows in the picture to R and the number of columns to C. Put blank characters in the whole matrix and set the current position to row 1, column 1.

MOVE(P)   Move the current position to point P without drawing.

LINE(P)   Draw a line from the current position to point P. The new current position is then P.

CHAR(C)   Put character C at the current position.

RECT(H,B)   Draw a rectangle with height H and breadth B with its lower left-hand corner at the current position. The current position does not change.

DRAW   The picture is drawn out at the terminal.

8.7 When a program writes out several pages on a printer it is often desirable to have a title, for example, a chapter name, at the top of each page. A page number may also be required at the bottom of every page. In the package TEXT_IO there are facilities for keeping track of the current page number, but this can also be achieved by writing a package of your own.

Write a package that prints a title at the top of every page and a page number at the bottom. The title and page number should be centred. After the title line and before the page number line there should be two extra blank lines. In the packages should be the procedures:

INIT(L,P)	Set the line length to L characters and the page length to P lines. The current title is set to blank characters and the current page number is set to 1.
TITLE(TEXT)	The current title is set to TEXT.
PAGE_NR(N)	The current page number is set to N.
NU_LINE	If the end of the page has not been reached, NEW_LINE is called. If the end has been reached, the page number is printed at the bottom of the page, a new page is started and the title is printed at the top.

When the package is used in a program the procedures NEW_LINE or PUT_LINE in TEXT_IO should not be called. Instead, the procedure NU_LINE should be called.

8.8 Rational numbers can be written as fractions where both numerator and denominator are integers. Write a package that provides facilities for working with the abstract data type *rational number*. The aim is to create a rational number from two integers, and to extract both the numerator and the denominator from the rational number. In the package there should be functions for adding, subtracting, multiplying and dividing rational numbers, and procedures for reading in and writing out rational numbers.

The package should ensure that the rational numbers given as a result are in their simplest forms; the numerator and denominator should have no common factor. Furthermore, there should never be a negative denominator.

8.9 Section 8.8 showed how the abstract data type set of characters could be built up using a package SET_PACKAGE. Write a package that can be used to build up the abstract data type set of integers instead.

The number of possible numbers in a set of integers is so great that for practical reasons it is not possible to use the technique used in SET_PACKAGE. To represent a set of integers it is possible, for example, to use an integer array in which the integers from the set are placed.

8.10 A **queue** of characters can be regarded as an abstract data type. The following operations can be performed on a queue:

- Empty the queue.
- Place a character last in the queue.
- Take out the first character from the queue.
- Find out whether the queue is empty.

A simple way of representing a queue is to let it consist of a record containing a character array and an integer L that gives the length of the queue. The queue's first element (the one nearest the front) is in the array's first position. When an element is removed from the queue, all the elements in the queue are shifted one place forward. A new element, which is to be placed last, is placed in the (L+1)th position of the array. (A more sophisticated way, that avoids shifting all the elements forward when the first element is removed, is to use the character array as a circular buffer. Then, two integers, FIRST and LAST must be kept up to date, to state where the first and last elements of the queue lie in the array).

Write a package that describes a queue. Then use the package to write a program that reads in 100 characters from the terminal, saves them in a queue, and subsequently writes them out in the order in which they were entered.

Chapter 9
Input and output

9.1 Output at the terminal
9.2 Input from the terminal

9.3 Text files
    Exercises

Large parts of most programs generally consist of statements concerning reading and writing data; to write programs that communicate well with the user, it is therefore important to be aware of the facilities that help with this. In Ada, these facilities are found as subprograms in the standard package TEXT_IO and some of them have been used extensively in previous chapters. A summary of these subprograms will be given in this chapter, to provide a more complete picture of the possibilities available. First, reading and writing via the terminal will be treated in greater detail. Then, **text files** will be introduced as a generalization of input and output, enabling a program to read from and write to other external units and store data permanently in the computer's secondary storage.

9.1 Output at the terminal

We shall start by looking at the facilities for producing output at the terminal. A terminal consists of two separate units: the keyboard, which is an input device, and the screen or printer, which is an output device. All output to a terminal that occurs in a program affects only its output device; all input via a terminal affects only its input device, the keyboard.

When a key is pressed at the keyboard the character is sent to the program and read, but a terminal is usually coupled to the screen or printer in such a way that the character is also output there. For example, if the character A is typed at the terminal keyboard, then A is usually displayed on the screen or printed by the printer. It is important to realize that the character A is not output from the program. It is called an **echo** of what has been typed at the keyboard. What is seen on the screen (or on the printer paper) thus becomes a mixture of what is written out by the program and the echoes of what the user writes at the keyboard.

9.1.1 Page and line structure

The output that occurs at the terminal consists, logically, of a number of pages, irrespective of whether it is displayed on a screen or printed on paper. Each page of output comprises a certain number of lines and each line comprises a certain number of characters. Each page ends with a **page terminator** and each line with a **line terminator**. Neither of these markers is seen in the output itself. They most often consist of unprintable control characters that are sent from the computer to the terminal. When the terminal receives a page terminator, it reacts by shifting the output on to a new page, and when it receives a line terminator it moves the output to a new line. The exact appearance of the different markers depends on the individual computer system, but the Ada programmer need not be concerned with this. Page and line terminators are sent to the terminal by subprograms in TEXT_IO.

A call to the procedure NEW_PAGE causes a page terminator to be sent to the terminal. There are no parameters to the procedure and it is called simply by writing:

```
NEW_PAGE;
```

One way to send a line terminator to the terminal, and thus get a new line in the output, is to use the procedure NEW_LINE, and this is specified in the package TEXT_IO as follows:

procedure NEW_LINE (SPACING : **in** POSITIVE_COUNT := 1);

The procedure has one parameter called SPACING which has type

POSITIVE_COUNT. POSITIVE_COUNT is a subtype of the integer type COUNT. In TEXT_IO there are the declarations:

type COUNT **is range** 0 .. *implementation-dependent_integer*;
subtype POSITIVE_COUNT **is** COUNT **range** 1 .. COUNT'LAST;

COUNT is thus an integer type with permitted values in the interval 0 to an integer that depends on the implementation and which is often large. POSITIVE_COUNT comprises all the integers in COUNT except 0.

The parameter SPACING specifies the number of line terminators to be sent to the terminal, that is, the number of lines that the output should move forward. For example, to move the output on three lines, the call:

NEW_LINE(3);

is used.

If the parameter given is not an integer literal but a variable or an expression, then it must be of the subtype POSITIVE_COUNT. For example, it is possible to declare the variable LINE_STEP:

LINE_STEP : POSITIVE_COUNT;

and use this in the call:

NEW_LINE(LINE_STEP);

Another possibility is to make a specific type conversion:

NEW_LINE(POSITIVE_COUNT(N));   -- where N has the type INTEGER

NEW_LINE can also be called with no parameter. In this case, the parameter SPACING automatically takes the value 1 (as seen from the specification above) and the output is moved on one line.

Page and line changes

NEW_PAGE;

gives a new page in the output.

NEW_LINE(N);

moves the output N lines on.

NEW_LINE;

moves the output on one line.

Another way of sending a line terminator to the terminal and ensuring that a line change occurs, is to use the procedure PUT_LINE when text is written.

The third way of causing a line change is by stating the length of line required and thereafter letting the Ada system start a new line automatically when one line is full. The required line length can be stated by calling the procedure SET_LINE_LENGTH which has the specification:

```
procedure SET_LINE_LENGTH (TO : in COUNT);
```

The call:

```
SET_LINE_LENGTH(60);
```

for example, means that the maximum line length will be 60 characters. The package TEXT_IO always keeps track of how far the current line of output has got along the line. Before each output occurs, TEXT_IO checks whether it will fit into the space remaining left on the line. If there is not room for the output, then a new line is automatically generated before the output is sent. We shall show how this can be utilized in writing out a table:

```
SET_LINE_LENGTH(30);
for I in 1 .. 20 loop
   PUT(I ** 2, WIDTH => 5);
   end loop;
```

These lines of program cause the squares of the numbers from 1 to 20 to be written in a table with 6 numbers on each row and 5 positions for each number. The output is as follows:

```
    1     4     9    16    25    36
   49    64    81   100   121   144
  169   196   225   256   289   324
  361   400
```

We see that the parameter to SET_LINE_LENGTH has type COUNT, not POSITIVE_COUNT. This means that the value 0 is also allowed as a line length. This is a special case that can be interpreted as 'there is no maximum line length'. That is, there is no limit to the length of the lines of output. (Of course, no terminal can cope with this. Some terminals 'stick' at the right-hand side if a line is too long, while others feed a new line automatically. But, from the program's point of view, lines can be indefinitely long). If nothing is specified in the program, then the line length is assumed to be 0, that is, there is no limit to the length of a line.

If it is necessary to determine the current line length in a program, the function LINE_LENGTH can be called. It returns the current line length as its result.

function LINE_LENGTH **return** COUNT;

In an analogous way, a maximum page length can also be set by calling the procedure SET_PAGE_LENGTH.

procedure SET_PAGE_LENGTH (TO : **in** COUNT);

The call:

SET_PAGE_LENGTH(48);

for example, sets the maximum size of page to 48 lines. The package TEXT_IO keeps track of the current line position on the page and if output of more than 48 lines is attempted there is an automatic change to a new page of output.

For page lengths, the special value 0 also means there is no limit to the number of lines on a page. If no other value is given in a program then the value 0 is assumed. The function PAGE_LENGTH:

function PAGE_LENGTH **return** COUNT;

can be called to determine what size of page is currently specified.

Maximum size of line and page

SET_PAGE_LENGTH(N);

set maximum page length to N lines.

SET_LINE_LENGTH(M);

set maximum line length to M columns.

Special case: If N (or M) is 0, then a boundless maximum page (or line) length is assumed.

PAGE_LENGTH

function call that returns the current maximum page length.

LINE_LENGTH

function call that returns the current maximum line length.

There are functions that can be used to find out how far the output has progressed. The function PAGE gives the current page number as its result (numbering starts at 1). The function LINE gives the number of the line to which output is currently being sent and the function COL gives the column number for the next output position on the current line. These functions have the specifications:

```
function COL   return POSITIVE_COUNT;
function LINE  return POSITIVE_COUNT;
function PAGE return POSITIVE_COUNT;
```

It is also possible for the programmer to specify the output position in terms of line and column. The procedure SET_COL can be used to move the output position to a certain column on the line.

```
procedure SET_COL (TO : in POSITIVE_COUNT);
```

To move the output position to column C, where C is assumed to have the subtype POSITIVE_COUNT, we can write:

```
SET_COL(C);
```

If the current column number before the call is less than C, then spaces are output until the current column number becomes C. If the current column number before the call is C, then the call of SET_COL has no effect. If the current column number before the call is greater than C then a new line is started first and then space characters are output until the current column number becomes C.

Similarly, the procedure SET_LINE can be used to move the output forward to a particular line on the page.

```
procedure SET_LINE (TO : in POSITIVE_COUNT);
```

To move the output forward to line L, where L has subtype POSITIVE_COUNT, the call:

```
SET_LINE(L);
```

can be made. If the current line before the call is less than L then repeated calls to the procedure NEW_LINE will be made automatically until the current line number is L. If the current line number is the same as L, then nothing happens. If the current line number is greater than L then first a new page is started and then the output is moved forward to line L using calls to NEW_LINE.

We shall write a procedure NEW_LINE_PLUS that can be called instead of NEW_LINE if automatic page numbering is required. NEW_LINE_PLUS should work as follows. If there is no page size specified (that is, the maximum number of lines has value 0 so that the number of lines on a page is unbounded), then a new line will occur as usual. Each call of NEW_LINE_PLUS will then simply result in a call to NEW_LINE and no page number will be output. If the size of page is specified, by an earlier call to SET_PAGE_LENGTH, then the last line but one on each page will be left blank and the page number will be output on the last line. If a line length is specified the page number will be output in the centre of the line, otherwise it will be written on the left of the last line.

To determine whether the page size is specified, a call to the function PAGE_LENGTH can be made and the result tested for 0. For extra clarity, the value UNBOUNDED can be tested instead, this being a constant of type COUNT, declared in TEXT_IO, with the value 0.

The page number has to be written as part of the procedure NEW_LINE_PLUS, so a package has to be created with the resources for writing integers of type COUNT, here called COUNT_INOUT.

```
procedure NEW_LINE_PLUS is

    package COUNT_INOUT is new INTEGER_IO(COUNT);
    use COUNT_INOUT;
begin
    if LINE < PAGE_LENGTH - 2 or
       PAGE_LENGTH = UNBOUNDED then
        NEW_LINE;     -- make a normal new line
    else

        -- end of page
        -- the next to bottom line should be blank
        NEW_LINE(2);

        if LINE_LENGTH /= UNBOUNDED then
            -- position in middle of the bottom line
            SET_COL(LINE_LENGTH/2);
        end if;

        -- page number on the bottom line
        PUT(PAGE, WIDTH => 1);
        NEW_LINE;     -- automatically gives new page

    end if;
end NEW_LINE_PLUS;
```

Current page, line and column numbers

> PAGE

function call that gives the current page number.

> LINE

function call that gives the current line number.

> COL

function call that gives the current column.

> SET_LINE(L);

move output on to line L. Change of page occurs if necessary.

> SET_COL(C);

moves the output on to column number C. Change of line occurs if necessary.

9.1.2 Output of characters and text

The procedure PUT, of which there are several versions, is used to write out values of various kinds at the terminal. Among these versions is one for the output of characters and one for the output of text.

> **procedure** PUT (ITEM : **in** CHARACTER);
> **procedure** PUT (ITEM : **in** STRING);

Both these versions of PUT have the required output as their only parameter (with the name ITEM). The type STRING is an unconstrained array type and therefore texts of different lengths can be written out. For the type STRING there is a further procedure PUT_LINE:

> **procedure** PUT_LINE (ITEM : **in** STRING);

This works in exactly the same way as PUT with the difference that a new line is started after the output.

Output of characters and text

```
PUT(C);
PUT(S);
PUT_LINE(S);  -- gives new line after the output
```

where C has type CHARACTER and S has type STRING.

9.1.3 Output of integers

The versions of PUT for writing characters and text are always present in the package TEXT_IO. As we saw in Section 5.5, it is not always so simple in the case of numeric and enumeration types. Since it is possible to work with many different integer, floating point and enumeration types, it is not possible for TEXT_IO to contain a version of PUT for every type imaginable. Instead, it has templates for packages for input and output of integer types, floating point types and enumeration types. Such package templates are called **generic packages**, and they are used, as demonstrated in Section 5.5, to generate individual packages. To be able to read and write integers, for example, the following (or similar) must be placed among the declarations in a program (if there is no access to the package BASIC_NUM_IO or the equivalent):

```
package INTEGER_INOUT is new INTEGER_IO(INTEGER);
use INTEGER_INOUT;
```

INTEGER_IO is the name of the generic package in TEXT_IO that contains the facilities for input and output of integers. In INTEGER_IO there is the procedure PUT for integers:

```
procedure PUT (ITEM   : in NUM;
               WIDTH : in FIELD := DEFAULT_WIDTH;
               BASE  : in NUMBER_BASE := DEFAULT_BASE);
```

The first parameter ITEM is the integer that has to be output. This parameter has type NUM, which is not a true type but only a template to be filled in when an individual package is generated. NUM can be thought of as being replaced by the type given when the package is generated. In the package INTEGER_INOUT, for example, NUM is replaced by INTEGER.

We see that the two other parameters WIDTH and BASE are initialized to certain values in the specification. We do not need to include them, therefore, when the procedure is called.

The parameter WIDTH states the number of output positions, or width of the field, that should be used for the output. WIDTH has type FIELD which is a subtype of INTEGER, comprising the integers greater than or equal to 0. If more output positions than needed are specified in a call to PUT, the positions to the left of the number are filled in with blanks. If, however, the number of output positions specified is insufficient for the required output, the output will contain as many positions as needed anyway, even though the value of WIDTH is exceeded. Negative integers are written out with a minus sign in front and this should be borne in mind when the output positions are being counted. The initialization value for WIDTH, DEFAULT_WIDTH, is equal to the number of digits in the largest permitted integer plus one (to allow for a possible minus sign).

Output of integers

        PUT(I);

or:

        PUT(I, WIDTH => W);

where I is an expression of an integer type and W states the number of positions to be allowed for the output, including a possible minus sign. Padding takes place with blanks to the left of the number if W is larger than is needed.

If W is too small, the exact number of required positions are allowed.

The final parameter, BASE, has not yet been discussed. Integers are normally written out in ordinary decimal form, but using the parameter BASE it is possible to state that the output is required in some other form, for example, in binary form (base 2) or hexadecimal form (base 16). BASE has the type NUMBER_BASE:

subtype NUMBER_BASE **is** INTEGER **range** 2 .. 16;

Bases in the interval 2 to 16 may be specified. BASE is initialized to DEFAULT_BASE, which has the value 10, that is, corresponding to decimal numbers. We can write out an integer in binary form:

PUT(I, BASE => 2);

If we assume that I has the value 27, the output will have the following rather strange appearance:

    2#11011#

The first 2 states that the base 2 is in force, and that what is written between the two #-signs is the number 27 in binary form. If we have the call:

    PUT(I, BASE => 8);

instead, we get the output:

    8#33#

The number 33 is 27 in octal form (3 times 8, plus 3). The call:

    PUT(I, BASE => 16);

would give the output:

    16#1B#

The number 1B is 27 written in hexadecimal form (1 times 16, plus 11). The letters A, B, C, D, E and F are used in the hexadecimal number system to denote the values 10 to 15 in the decimal system.

□

9.1.4 Output of floating point numbers

For floating point numbers, as for integers, an individual package must be created for input and output, this time using the generic package FLOAT_IO in TEXT_IO. To create an input and output package for the type FLOAT, for example, write:

```
package FLOAT_INOUT is new FLOAT_IO(FLOAT);
use FLOAT_INOUT;
```

In FLOAT_IO there is a version of PUT:

```
procedure PUT (ITEM : in NUM;
               FORE : in FIELD := DEFAULT_FORE;
               AFT  : in FIELD := DEFAULT_AFT;
               EXP  : in FIELD := DEFAULT_EXP);
```

The first parameter, ITEM, is the floating point value that is to be output. This parameter has the type NUM which is not a true type but a template for a type. NUM takes on the type that is specified when the package is generated. In the case of the package FLOAT_INOUT generated above, we can thus think of FLOAT replacing NUM. The three other parameters state how the output should be presented. All have the type FIELD, a subtype of INTEGER in which the allowed integer values are greater than or equal to 0.

The parameter FORE states how many character positions should be in front of the decimal point in the output. The default value, DEFAULT_FORE, is 2. AFT states how many figures should appear to the right of the decimal point. The default value, DEFAULT_AFT, is equal to the number of figures of accuracy in the current floating point type, less one because it is assumed that one of the figures is output as an integer digit. The parameter EXP states how many character positions are to be used in output of the number's exponent. The default value, DEFAULT_EXP, is 3.

If EXP is given the value 0 in the call then the output will be in the form:

iiiii.ddddd

where the i's denote positions for the integral part and the d's denote the figures in the decimal part. The number of figures before and after the point are determined by FORE and AFT, respectively. If the number of places is greater than needed, the space is padded out with blanks in front of the number. If the number of places is fewer than needed, it is written out in full anyway, with as many figures in the integral part as necessary. One position should be allowed for a possible minus sign in the integral part in case the number is negative.

If EXP is given a value greater than 0, the output is in the form:

ii.dddddEnn

where the i's and the d's, as before, denote figures in the integral part and the decimal part, respectively, and here the n's denote the exponent. This form of output is called **exponent form** and examples are:

−5.73E+1   4.5E−02   0.0E+0

which denote the numbers −57.3, 0.045 and 0.0, respectively. A number output in exponent form always has one figure before the decimal point, preceded by a minus sign if the number is negative. If FORE has a greater value than needed, the space is filled with blanks before the number. The number of figures after the decimal point is determined, as before, by

AFT. The number of positions in the exponent part (including a plus or minus sign) is determined by EXP. If EXP is larger than needed, the space is padded out with zeros.

The number is rounded up to the given number of decimal figures irrespective of the form chosen for output.

Output of floating point numbers

PUT(X);

Gives the exponent form in standard format.

PUT(X, FORE => N, AFT => M, EXP => 0);

Gives the ordinary form without exponent, N positions in front of the decimal point and M positions after it.

PUT(X, FORE => N, AFT => M, EXP => K);

Gives the exponent form with K figures in the exponent, N positions in front of the decimal point and M positions after it.

Padding occurs with spaces if FORE is greater than necessary. If FORE is too small, as many positions as necessary are used.

Let us study a few examples of output. We assume that P and Q are floating point variables with values −123.4 and 0.00567, respectively.

PUT(P);	-- gives:	−1.23400000E+02
PUT(Q);	-- gives:	5.67000000E−03
PUT(P, AFT => 2);	-- gives:	−1.23E+02
PUT(Q, FORE => 5, AFT => 1);	-- gives:	5.7E−03
PUT(P, EXP => 4);	-- gives:	−1.23400000E+002
PUT(Q, EXP => 0);	-- gives:	0.00567000

9.1.5 Output of values of enumeration type

As shown in Section 5.5, it is possible to write out the values of an enumeration type if an input/output package is generated using the generic package ENUMERATION_IO in TEXT_IO. If we have the enumeration type:

type SIGNAL **is** (ON, OFF, NORMAL, ALARM);

we can create a package SIGNAL_INOUT:

package SIGNAL_INOUT **is new** ENUMERATION_IO(SIGNAL);

ENUMERATION_IO includes a procedure PUT:

procedure PUT (ITEM   : **in** ENUM;
                WIDTH : **in** FIELD := DEFAULT_WIDTH;
                SET   : **in** TYPE_SET := DEFAULT_SETTING);

The parameter ITEM is the value of the enumeration type that should be output. The type ENUM is not a true type but a template; when a new package is generated, ENUM is replaced with the specified enumeration type. In the package SIGNAL_INOUT, for example, we can consider ENUM being replaced by SIGNAL. Since the two other parameters have default values they do not have to be present in a call to PUT. If we have the declaration:

S : SIGNAL;

we can write, for example:

PUT(S);

Then one of the words ON, OFF, NORMAL or ALARM will be written out at the terminal.

Exactly as for integers, the second parameter, WIDTH, states how many positions are to be used for the output. The initial value, DEFAULT_WIDTH, has the value 0 and this is therefore the value assumed if no parameter WIDTH is included in the call to PUT. If WIDTH is greater than the value necessary to output the current word, the field is padded out with spaces to the right of the word; if WIDTH is too small then the word is written out in full, anyway.

Output of the values of enumeration types

PUT(E);

The value of E is output, no trailing spaces.

PUT(E, WIDTH => N);

The value of E is output with N positions. If N is too big, the field is padded with spaces to the right of E's value. If N is too small, N is ignored and the whole word is written out anyway.

■

The third parameter SET can be used to control the use of upper or lower case letters in the output. SET is initialized to DEFAULT_SETTING, which is a variable of the type TYPE_SET:

type TYPE_SET **is** (LOWER_CASE, UPPER_CASE);

The default value of SET is UPPER_CASE, and this value is assumed if nothing else is specified; all output will thus be in upper case letters. If some output must be in lower case, then we must write:

PUT(S, SET => LOWER_CASE);   -- gives the output: alarm

assuming that S still has the value ALARM. If all output is to be in lower case letters, it is more convenient to change the default value thus:

SIGNAL_INOUT.DEFAULT_SETTING := LOWER_CASE;

☐

9.2   Input from the terminal

In the package TEXT_IO are facilities for reading data written at the terminal, that is, at the terminal keyboard.

9.2.1   Page and line structure

Imagine all the characters written at the terminal forming a single long stream of characters that can be read by the program. Each key stroke generates one character in the stream. For example, if we write:

Tommy 123

at the keyboard then the sequence of characters illustrated in Figure 9.1 is created and the program that is running can then read it. The blank square denotes a blank character, that is, a space character.

Viewed logically, input from the keyboard, that is, the stream of characters, consists of a number of pages. Each page comprises a number of lines and each line, in turn, comprises a number of characters. The person writing at the keyboard states where the end of lines and pages

Figure 9.1

Figure 9.2

should occur by typing special characters. To indicate where a line should end, for example, it is normal to strike the RETURN key. It is not very common to specify pages in input from the keyboard. In normal cases, therefore, the input can be considered as comprising a single long page.

When an end-of-line character is typed, a **line terminator** is generated in the stream of characters, and if an end-of-page character is typed, then a **page terminator** is generated. If, for example, we type in the following lines:

    line 1
    xyz
    000

from the keyboard, then the sequence of characters illustrated in Figure 9.2 will be generated, where the black squares denote line terminators.

A line or page terminator may consist of one or more characters. The Ada programmer need not be concerned about their exact appearance – it is a detail that depends on the computer in use. When the data is read into a program from the character stream, any terminators present will automatically be skipped, so they can never be read into a program, either deliberately or by accident.

Pages and lines

- Data written at the keyboard forms a long stream of characters that logically consists of a number of pages. Each page comprises a number of lines and each line comprises a number of characters.

- The end of each line is marked in the stream by a line terminator and the end of each page by a page terminator.

- The end of a line is usually caused by striking the RETURN key.

How long is a stream of characters generated by pressing the keys

Figure 9.3

at the terminal? The answer is that it can be of any length. It is always possible to generate new characters in the series by typing them. Sometimes, however, it is useful to be able to indicate that a series of characters is finished, that nothing more is going to be added. This can be achieved by typing a special combination of characters, the exact form depending on the computer being used. We saw earlier that it is usual to use the CTRL key with another key to mark the end of input data. When the end of input of data is indicated, it can be considered, logically, that a special **file terminator** is placed at the end of the generated series of characters. If, for example, we write the lines:

```
12 3
456
78
```

at the keyboard and then type the combination CTRL-D (which we shall assume is used to mark the end of input data) then the series of characters can be depicted as in Figure 9.3. The file terminator is the square at the end. Note that at the end there is both a line terminator and a file terminator. Normally, when data input is finished, the RETURN key has to be pressed so that the data that has been written at the keyboard will be transferred to the computer. This generates a line terminator in the stream of characters. It is therefore natural that the end of data input is marked when a new line has been started (the RETURN key has just been pressed).

It must be noted that even if the stream of characters can be considered logically as terminated by a file terminator, this does not mean that such a marker has to be physically present in the series of characters.

End of input

- Can be regarded as though a file terminator is at the end of the stream of characters.

- Caused by typing a special combination of characters at the keyboard, for example, CTRL-D. It can normally be typed only at the start of a new line, directly after pressing the RETURN key.

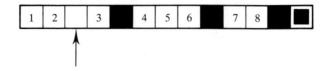

Figure 9.4

In the program, data is read in from the character stream by calls to the procedure GET. Each reading involves a small move along the stream; we can say that each reading consumes a number of characters from the stream. Reading always starts from the start of the stream. Let us assume that we have the variables I, J, K and L of type INTEGER in a program and also the input statements:

```
GET(I);
GET(J);
GET(K);
GET(L);
```

As before, we assume that we typed in the lines:

```
12 3
456
78
```

The first call:

```
GET(I);
```

will mean that the characters '1' and '2' are consumed and that the variable I takes the value 12. Figure 9.4 illustrates this. The arrow shows how far we have come along the character stream and points to the next character waiting to be read.

The next call:

```
GET(J);
```

means that the characters ' ' and '3' are consumed and that J takes the value 3. Blank characters are always skipped automatically when numeric data or data of an enumeration type is read. The situation is now shown in Figure 9.5.

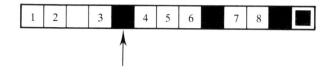

Figure 9.5

Blank characters in input

- Blank characters, that is, spaces, are always automatically skipped when data of numeric or enumeration type is read.

- Blank characters are *not* skipped when data of the type STRING and CHARACTER is read.

The arrow has moved on so that it points to the first line terminator, that is, the first line is now finished. The call:

GET(K);

means that the line terminator and the characters '4', '5' and '6' are consumed. Line and page terminators are always automatically skipped. The next character waiting in line is the line terminator for the second line (see Figure 9.6).

Line and page terminators in input

Line terminators and page terminators are always automatically skipped when data is read. This is true even for data of the type STRING and CHARACTER.

In TEXT_IO there is a function END_OF_LINE that can be used to find out whether the current input line is finished:

function END_OF_LINE **return** BOOLEAN;

The function returns the value TRUE if the next character waiting to be

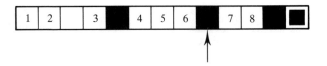

Figure 9.6

input, that is, the character the arrow is pointing to, is a line terminator or a file terminator. If, for example, we call END_OF_LINE after the call:

    GET(K);

the result will be TRUE.

The final call of GET in our example:

    GET(L);

consumes the line terminator for the second line and the characters '7' and '8'. The variable L will take the value 78. The arrow has moved on to the final line terminator, as shown in Figure 9.7. A call to END_OF_LINE would now return the value TRUE.

In TEXT_IO there is another function END_OF_FILE that can be used to determine whether the input series of characters is finished:

    function END_OF_FILE **return** BOOLEAN;

This function gives the result TRUE if a file terminator is next in line to be read, or if a combination of line, page and file terminators is next. A call to END_OF_FILE after the final GET above would thus give the result TRUE.

In TEXT_IO there is also a function END_OF_PAGE that shows whether a page is complete:

    function END_OF_PAGE **return** BOOLEAN;

When called, this gives the value TRUE if the next character in line to be input is a combination of a page and line terminator, or if it is a file terminator. This function is not used much in the case of input from the keyboard.

Figure 9.7

Tests for end of line, page and file

ENDₒOFₒLINE

gives the value TRUE if the next character waiting to be read is a line terminator or a file terminator.

ENDₒOFₒPAGE

gives the value TRUE if the next character waiting to be read is a combination of a line terminator and a page terminator, or a file terminator.

ENDₒOFₒFILE

gives the value TRUE if the next character in line to be read is a file terminator or a combination of line, page and file terminators.

The procedure SKIP_LINE can be used to skip over whole lines in the input data:

procedure SKIP_LINE(SPACING : **in** POSITIVE_COUNT := 1);

The parameter SPACING states the number of lines to be skipped and it can be omitted from a call. If it is absent, one line is skipped. If the call:

SKIP_LINE;

or:

SKIP_LINE(1);

is made, the program skips over all the characters in the stream from the next in line until it finds a line terminator. This is also skipped and if it is followed by a page terminator, this is also skipped. The result is that after the call the next character to be read in will be the first character of the next line. If SKIP_LINE is called with a parameter N greater than one then this process will be carried out N times.

For example, if we write the numbers:

```
12 3
456
```

at the terminal and the program contains the calls:

```
GET(I);
GET(J);
```

then the value 12 is read into I and the value 3 into J, as before. If we insert a call to SKIP_LINE:

```
GET(I);
SKIP_LINE;
GET(J);
```

then the value 456 would be read into J instead, because everything after the character '2' on the first line would be skipped.

There is a function SKIP_PAGE that works in a similar way but skipping pages rather than lines. However, only one page at a time can be skipped.

Skipping to a new line or page

```
SKIP_LINE;
SKIP_LINE(N);
```

skips over everything up to the first character on the next line. If N > 1, it is repeated N times.

```
SKIP_PAGE;
```

skips over everything up to the first character of the next page.

Let us study a program that reads data from the keyboard and writes out the average number of characters in the lines read in. To be able to calculate the average number of characters per line the program must count the total number of lines and characters read. For this, two variables are used, LINE_COUNT and CHAR_COUNT, both initialized to 0. In this program we are not interested in the kind of input; we shall just count the number of lines and the number of characters. Therefore it is simplest to read one character at a time to a variable CHAR of type CHARACTER. We can use the following algorithm:

(1) Set LINE_COUNT and CHAR_COUNT to 0.
(2) Repeat the following until there are no lines left (that is, the input ends):
　　(2.1) Increase LINE_COUNT by 1.
　　(2.2) Read the current line and add the number of characters in it to CHAR_COUNT.
　　(2.3) Skip to the start of the next line.

Step (2.2) can be expanded to:

(2.2) Repeat the following until there are no more characters in the current line:
　　(2.2.1) Read the next character.
　　(2.2.2) Increase CHAR_COUNT by 1.

If we translate this to Ada we get:

```
with TEXT_IO, BASIC_NUM_IO;
use  TEXT_IO, BASIC_NUM_IO;
procedure FIND_LINE_LENGTH is
   LINE_COUNT, CHAR_COUNT : INTEGER := 0;
   CHAR : CHARACTER;
begin
   PUT_LINE("Enter input. Terminate with CTRL-D");

   while not END_OF_FILE loop
     LINE_COUNT := LINE_COUNT + 1;
     while not END_OF_LINE loop
       GET(CHAR);
       CHAR_COUNT := CHAR_COUNT + 1;
     end loop;
     SKIP_LINE;
   end loop;

   PUT("The average line length is");
   PUT( FLOAT(CHAR_COUNT) / FLOAT(LINE_COUNT),
       EXP => 0, FORE => 3, AFT => 2 );
end FIND_LINE_LENGTH;
```

Note that the call to SKIP_LINE is necessary because when the last character on the first line has been read, a line terminator is waiting to be read. If we had not skipped over this, the second loop round the outer loop statement would have started with a line terminator waiting to be read. This would have meant that the inner loop statement would not have been executed at all because the call to END_OF_LINE would have been TRUE at once. Thus no character would have been read from the terminal. Input would have stuck fast at the first line terminator and the program would have gone into an endless loop.

■

As in the case of output, the package TEXT_IO keeps track of the current page, line and column number in the input. Calls to GET, SKIP_LINE and SKIP_PAGE change these numbers automatically. The functions COL, LINE and PAGE, which could be used in connection with output, can also be used to determine the current position in input. If we call the function COL in a program, we get, as seen earlier, the current column in output as a result. To state that we mean the current column, line or page in input rather than output we must therefore use different versions of the functions COL, LINE and PAGE:

```
function COL   (FILE : in FILE_TYPE) return POSITIVE_COUNT;
function LINE  (FILE : in FILE_TYPE) return POSITIVE_COUNT;
function PAGE (FILE : in FILE_TYPE) return POSITIVE_COUNT;
```

These have a single **in** parameter FILE of type FILE_TYPE. To determine the current column in the input we can make the call:

```
COL(CURRENT_INPUT);
```

and to find the current line number we can write:

```
LINE(CURRENT_INPUT);
```

(CURRENT_INPUT is in turn a function call that returns the current input stream. We shall not go into further details here).

It is also possible to call the procedures SET_COL and SET_LINE to move on to a particular position in the input. Again, we must use special forms of the subprograms to indicate that we mean input and not output. The alternative forms of SET_COL and SET_PAGE have the specifications:

```
procedure SET_COL (FILE : in FILE_TYPE;
                   TO   : in POSITIVE_COUNT);
procedure SET_LINE (FILE : in FILE_TYPE;
                   TO   : in POSITIVE_COUNT);
```

For example, we can move on to column N with the call:

```
SET_COL(CURRENT_INPUT, N);
```

Now all the characters and terminators in the input are skipped over until the next character waiting to be read is from column N of a line.

The call:

SET_LINE(CURRENT_INPUT, M);

has the same effect as calling SKIP_LINE repeatedly until the current line number is M.

□

9.2.2   Input of characters and text

To read characters of type CHARACTER, the version of GET that is used is defined as follows in TEXT_IO:

procedure GET (ITEM : **out** CHARACTER);

The only parameter is an **out** parameter of type CHARACTER. If the call:

GET(C);

is made where C is of type CHARACTER, the next character waiting to be read will end up in C. If there is a line or page terminator next, it will be skipped. If there is a space character next in line for reading it is not skipped, but C will have the value ' ' after the call.

To read whole texts into variables of type STRING, another version of GET can be used:

procedure GET (ITEM : **out** STRING);

If the call:

GET(S);

is made where S has the type STRING, the length of S is first determined, that is, how many characters can be held in S. Many calls are then made repeatedly to the first version of GET above. The characters input are placed one by one in S starting on the left. If S has length 0 then nothing happens.

To read a whole line at once to a variable of type STRING there is a special procedure GET_LINE which is sometimes convenient.

procedure GET_LINE(ITEM : **out** STRING;
                              LAST : **out** NATURAL);

We assume that S has type STRING and that the variable N has the type NATURAL. We then make the call:

GET_LINE(S,N);

When the call is made one character after another is read from the input stream and placed in S from left to right. Reading normally ends when a line terminator is met in the input stream. A call to SKIP_LINE is then made automatically; after the call to GET_LINE, the next character waiting to be read is the first character of the next line. Reading can also end if S is too short and there is no room for the current line. If S is longer than the number of characters read, then the positions in S to which nothing has been read will be undefined after the call.

After the call, the **out** parameter LAST (N in our call above), will contain the index number of the last character read in. If the indexing of S starts at 1 this simply means that after the call, N contains the number of characters read. If no characters have been read, LAST will contain a number that is less than S's first index number.

Using GET_LINE we can write another version of the program FIND_LINE_LENGTH:

```
with TEXT_IO, BASIC_NUM_IO;
use  TEXT_IO, BASIC_NUM_IO;
procedure FIND_LINE_LENGTH is
  LINE_COUNT, CHAR_COUNT : INTEGER := 0;
  NR_OF_CHARS_IN_LINE : NATURAL;
  LINE : STRING (1 .. 300);

begin
  PUT_LINE("Enter input. Terminate with CTRL-D");

  while not END_OF_FILE loop
    LINE_COUNT := LINE_COUNT + 1;
    GET_LINE(LINE, NR_OF_CHARS_IN_LINE);
      CHAR_COUNT := CHAR_COUNT
                         + NR_OF_CHARS_IN_LINE;
  end loop;

  PUT("The average line length is");
  PUT( FLOAT(CHAR_COUNT) / FLOAT(LINE_COUNT),
      EXP => 0, FORE => 3, AFT => 2 );
end FIND_LINE_LENGTH;
```

We assume that no line is longer than 300 characters. Note that a call to SKIP_LINE occurs automatically through the call to GET_LINE.

9.2.3 Input of integers

To read in integers, a special input/output package must be created using the generic package INTEGER_IO in TEXT_IO, exactly as for output. If, for example, we have declared a type:

> **type** WHOLE_NUMBER **is range** −1000 .. 1000;

and want to read values into variables of this type, we must create our own package:

> **package** WHOLE_NUMBER_INOUT **is new**
> INTEGER_IO(WHOLE_NUMBER);
> **use** WHOLE_NUMBER_INOUT;

The following version of GET is found in INTEGER_IO:

> **procedure** GET (ITEM   : **out** NUM;
> WIDTH : **in** FIELD := 0);

The first parameter is an **out** parameter corresponding to the integer variable to which input should occur. The type NUM is, as before, a template for a true type that is replaced by the type specified when a package is created. In the package WHOLE_NUMBER_INOUT, for example, we see that NUM stands for WHOLE_NUMBER. The second parameter is not generally used. A call to GET therefore generally resembles:

> GET(W);

where W has the type WHOLE_NUMBER. When the call is made, any line terminators, page terminators and blanks are skipped. Then the procedure GET expects a whole number. In the input this is given as a number of characters, for example, the integer 475 is represented by the three characters '4', '7' and '5' in series.

The exact appearance of an integer to be read is specified strictly. In fact, the rules are the same as those for integer literals discussed in Section 3.3. Input continues for as long as the characters read in can be interpreted as part of an integer. If an incorrect integer is written when data is input to a program, the program usually stops and an error message is given. In Chapter 10 we shall see how to capture this kind of error in a program.

∎

The second parameter, WIDTH, can be used if data are to be read that have been written in a special way, with a particular number of positions in the input. If the parameter WIDTH is given a value N in a call to GET, not equal to 0, then N characters will be read from the keyboard and translated into an integer. This demands that these N characters form a valid integer. Blanks in front of the integer are also counted among the N characters. If we have the call:

    GET(W, WIDTH => 4);

in a program and the following is written at the keyboard:

    −157890

then the variable W will have the value −157 after the call, since only four characters are read by GET. The next character waiting in line to be read after the call is '8'.

□

9.2.4 Input of floating point numbers

To read values into variables of floating point types the generic package FLOAT_IO in TEXT_IO must be used to create an input/output package for the particular floating point type in question. If, for example, we have made the type declaration:

    type TEMPERATURE **is digits** 4;

we can create an input/output package for TEMPERATURE:

    package TEMPERATURE_INOUT **is new** FLOAT_IO(TEMPERATURE);

In FLOAT_IO there is a version of GET:

    procedure GET (ITEM   : **out** NUM;
                   WIDTH : **in** FIELD := 0);

As in the case of input of integers, the second parameter is not generally used. The first parameter corresponds to the floating point variable that is to receive a value. If, for example, we wish to put a value in the variable T of type TEMPERATURE we write the statement:

    GET(T);

Input works in the same way as for integers, except that the format rules for input of a real number differ from those for an integer. A real number for input may look the same as a real literal in a program (see Section 3.3). Data can be input therefore either in the ordinary form, with figures before and after a decimal point, or in exponent form. When the procedure GET is called it can consume all the characters in the input stream that can be part of the real number. Leading blanks, and line and page terminators are skipped. The character in line to be input after a call to GET is the first character that cannot be part of a real number. If the keyboard input does not follow the rules then the program is normally stopped and an error message is given. However, this kind of error can be captured (see Chapter 10).

■

The WIDTH parameter works in the same way as the corresponding parameter when an integer is read. If a value of N is given in a call, that is not equal to 0, then exactly N characters are read from the keyboard and converted into a real number.

□

9.2.5   Input of the values of enumeration type

To read the values of an enumeration type it is first necessary to create an input/output package using the generic package ENUMERATION_IO in TEXT_IO. A package for the type:

> **type** COMMAND **is** (START, FINISH, WRITE, DECREASE, INCREASE);

can be created by writing, for example:

> **package** COMMAND_INOUT **is new** ENUMERATION_IO(COMMAND);
> **use** COMMAND_INOUT;

In ENUMERATION_IO there is a version of GET:

> **procedure** GET (ITEM : **out** ENUM);

The only parameter here is an **out** parameter corresponding to the variable of an enumeration type to which a value will be read. If we assume that C has the type COMMAND we can now make the call:

> GET(C);

When this call is made any line terminators, page terminators and blanks are skipped. Then the word that is typed at the terminal is read. The only words that may be written are the words that a variable of the enumeration type in question can take. In our example, the user must thus write one of the words START, STOP, WRITE, DECREASE or INCREASE. It does not matter whether upper or lower case letters are used. If something is written that is not a permitted value of the enumeration type, the program is stopped and an error message is given, unless the error is captured (see Chapter 10).

9.3 Text files

All the programs we have studied so far have read from or written to the terminal. However, it is often necessary for a program to work with other external devices connected to the computer. For example, output might be required on a line printer or a special high-quality printer instead of the terminal. Another problem is that the variables used in a program only exist while the program is being executed. If the data is to be saved permanently, so that it survives when program execution has finished, it must be stored in the computer's secondary storage, most often on disk. It is therefore important to be able to read and write data to and from secondary storage.

In computer jargon, a sequence of data elements, which can be of arbitrary length, is called a **file**. If the elements in the sequence are characters (type CHARACTER), it is called a **text file**. Programs can be written in Ada to read and write all kinds of files, but in this chapter we shall consider only text files.

Two types of text file can be distinguished:

(1)   text files that correspond to the input or output devices of the computer, such as a line-printer; and

(2)   text files that are stored in secondary storage.

In an Ada program both files are treated in the same way. They are understood logically, by a program, as a series of characters that are either to be read or to be written. Each text file exists physically in the computer system and has a special name. The format of the name depends entirely on the computer system in use. If the text file corresponds to a line-printer it may have a name such as *LPR* or */dev/printer*. A text file that is stored in secondary memory may have a name such as */u/smith/datafile* or *courseregister.text*. The rules for the format of such names do not need to agree (and generally do not agree) with the rules for identifiers in Ada.

In an Ada program all work is performed on **logical** text files. In the package TEXT_IO there is a type FILE_TYPE that can be used to declare such logical text files. If we have the usual lines:

```
with TEXT_IO;
use  TEXT_IO;
```

at the start of a program then we can declare a logical text file (a file variable), for example:

    INFILE : FILE_TYPE;

Thus INFILE has type FILE_TYPE. In the package TEXT_IO, FILE_TYPE is declared as a limited private type. Therefore, the programmer does not get to know what a file variable like INFILE 'really' looks like. The *only* thing that can be done with such a variable is to give it as a parameter to certain subprograms in TEXT_IO. This means that it is not possible, for example, to compare two file variables or to assign one file variable to another.

Henceforth we shall distinguish between a logical file in a program (a file variable) and a physical file in the computer system, by calling the former simply a **file** and the latter an **external file**.

Before reading or writing a file can begin in a program, it must be connected with an external file. This is accomplished by calling one of the procedures CREATE or OPEN in TEXT_IO:

    procedure CREATE (FILE   : **in out** FILE_TYPE;
                      MODE : **in** FILE_MODE := OUT_FILE;
                      NAME : **in** STRING := "";
                      FORM : **in** STRING := "");
    procedure OPEN   (FILE   : **in out** FILE_TYPE;
                      MODE : **in** FILE_MODE;
                      NAME : **in** STRING;
                      FORM : **in** STRING := "");

CREATE is used when a new external file is to be created and OPEN is used when work is to be performed on an existing external file.

The parameter FILE to both procedures should be a file declared as above. The parameter MODE states whether the file is to be written to or read from. In the case of text files it is not possible to both read and write a file at the same time. The type FILE_MODE has the declaration:

    type FILE_MODE **is** (IN_FILE, OUT_FILE);

If the second parameter is not stated when CREATE is called, it is assumed that the intention is to write to the file. (This is reasonable if the file is being created).

The parameter NAME is a text string that should contain the name of the external file. This parameter can be omitted from a call to CREATE. An empty string is then assumed for the name, and the external file created is considered to be a temporary file that will disappear when program execution finishes.

The parameter FORM is not used often. Its appearance depends on the computer system in use. (It can be used, for example, to give a password to protected external files).

If we have the declaration:

```
NEW_FILE : FILE_TYPE;
```

we can create an external file, *my.file* for example, and connect it with the file NEW_FILE using the call:

```
CREATE(NEW_FILE, NAME => "my.file");
```

Now it is possible to write to the file NEW_FILE.

To link the file INFILE, declared earlier, to the external file */u/smith/datafile* so that it can be read, we can write:

```
OPEN(INFILE, IN_FILE, "/u/smith/datafile");
```

If an existing file is opened for writing, then any earlier contents are overwritten and destroyed.

Assume the line-printer in a certain system has the name LPR. If we declare a file:

```
L_PRINTER : FILE_TYPE;
```

we can link it to the line-printer by writing:

```
OPEN(L_PRINTER, MODE => OUT_FILE, NAME => "LPR");
```

If a file is linked to an external file by a call to CREATE or OPEN, it is said to be **open**. When an attempt is made to open a file, errors can occur. For example, the file may already be open, or no external file may exist with the name specified in the call to OPEN. Possible ways of handling this kind of error are described in Chapter 10.

The function IS_OPEN can be used to test whether a particular file is open:

```
function IS_OPEN (FILE : in FILE_TYPE) return BOOLEAN;
```

To determine whether the file NEW_FILE is open, for example, we can write:

```
if IS_OPEN(NEW_FILE) then
```

Opening a file

- First declare a logical file:

    F : FILE_TYPE;

  where F is the name of the logical file.

- Then connect this file with a physical (external) file in one of the following ways. (S is a text string containing the name of the physical file).

    CREATE(F, NAME => S);

  A new external file is created. The file is to be written.

    OPEN(F, MODE => IN_FILE, NAME => S);

  An existing external file is opened. The file is to be read.

    OPEN(F, MODE => OUT_FILE, NAME => S);

  An existing external file is opened. The file is to be written. The earlier contents are destroyed.

The only place in a program where the names of external files are found is in calls to CREATE and OPEN. Everywhere else, logical files are used.

An open file can either be read from or written to, and all the subprograms previously discussed in connection with reading from and writing to the terminal, such as GET, PUT, NEW_LINE, END_OF_FILE, are available. The only difference is that a file has to be given as the first parameter in any call that is not destined for the terminal. For example, to read a character from the file INFILE to a variable C:

    GET(INFILE, C);

can be written, and to write an integer I to the file NEW_FILE PUT can be called thus:

    PUT(NEW_FILE, I);

Text files, in common with input and output to the terminal, can be regarded as logically having line, page and file terminators embedded in the text, as mentioned earlier. To start a new line in the file NEW_FILE we can make the call:

NEW_LINE(NEW_FILE);

and to test whether a line in the file INFILE is finished, the function END_OF_LINE can be called:

if END_OF_LINE (INFILE) **then**

Reading and writing text files

- A text file has line and page structure. The same subprograms can be used as for reading from and writing to the terminal, for example, PUT, GET, NEW_LINE.
- The difference is that in all calls the name of the logical file has to be stated as the first parameter. For example:

    GET(F,N);   -- read an integer from the file F

When reading or writing a file is finished, the file has to be **closed** by calling the procedure CLOSE. To close the file NEW_FILE, for example, the call is made:

CLOSE(NEW_FILE);

If the file has been used for writing, CLOSE takes care that the current line and page are terminated. This is achieved by automatically calling NEW_PAGE before the file is terminated. If we forget to close a file in a program, the result is not well-defined; it varies from system to system. It is probably most common for the system to close the file automatically, but to have control over the files used. The programmer should get into the habit of always closing his or her files after use.

Closing files

> CLOSE(F);

where F is a logical file.

Files should always be closed after use.

We shall study a program that creates a copy of the external file *old.file*. The copy will take the name *copy*. In the program the corresponding logical files are INF and OUTF. One line at a time is read from INF using the procedure GET_LINE and is written to OUTF using PUT_LINE.

```
with TEXT_IO;
use TEXT_IO;
procedure COPY_FILE is
   INF, OUTF    : FILE_TYPE;
   LINE         : STRING (1 .. 200);
   LINE_LENGTH : NATURAL;

begin
   -- open the files
   OPEN(INF, MODE => IN_FILE, NAME => "old.file");
   CREATE(OUTF, NAME => "copy");
   -- copy INF to OUTF
   while not END_OF_FILE(INF) loop
      GET_LINE(INF, LINE, LINE_LENGTH);
      PUT_LINE(OUTF, LINE(1 .. LINE_LENGTH));
   end loop;

   -- close the files
   CLOSE(INF);
   CLOSE(OUTF);
end COPY_FILE;
```

The file OUTF will have exactly the same line structure as the file INF, that is, both files have the same number of lines and a particular line in OUTF is as long as the corresponding line in INF.

Note that INF may not be copied to OUTF using an assignment statement:

```
OUTF := INF     -- ERROR! Assignment is forbidden
```

In the program we have assumed that no line of INF is longer than 200 characters. If the maximum line length in INF is not known, then the copying program should be reformulated so that it can cope with copying a text file with lines of unlimited length. We can solve this problem by reading one character at a time instead of one line at a time, by changing the **loop** statement in the program:

```
while not END_OF_FILE(INF) loop
  while not END_OF_LINE(INF) loop
    GET(INF,   C);
    PUT(OUTF, C);
  end loop;
  SKIP_LINE(INF);
  NEW_LINE(OUTF);
end loop;
```

Here we read one character at a time, assuming the variable C has type CHARACTER, until the current line is finished. When a line in INF is finished we skip the line terminator with a call to SKIP_LINE. Each time a line in INF finishes we have to ensure that the corresponding line of OUTF also finishes. This we do by calling NEW_LINE to write a line terminator.

In the copying program we have assumed that the names of the external files are known when the program is written. We have said that the external file to be copied will have the name *old.file* and the copy will have the name *copy*. It would be better if the program were a little more general so that it could cope with copying any external file, and the copy could be given any name requested. One way of achieving this is to read in the *names* of the external files before reading them. Then the names can be given as parameters to the procedures OPEN and CREATE. To make this change in the program, first we insert the declarations:

```
FILE_NAME    : STRING (1 .. 30);
NAME_LENGTH : NATURAL;
```

Then we amend the part of the program that opens the files:

```
-- open INF
PUT_LINE("Enter name of file to be copied");
GET_LINE(FILE_NAME, NAME_LENGTH);
OPEN(INF, MODE => IN_FILE,
          NAME => FILE_NAME(1 .. NAME_LENGTH));

-- open OUTF
PUT_LINE("Enter the name of the copy");
GET_LINE(FILE_NAME, NAME_LENGTH);
CREATE(OUTF, NAME => FILE_NAME(1 .. NAME_LENGTH));
```

The statement:

```
GET_LINE(FILE_NAME, NAME_LENGTH);
```

indicates, as usual, reading from the terminal. A text string is read in and placed to the left of the variable FILE_NAME. Note that we have cut out the slice of FILE_NAME containing only the name when OPEN and CLOSE are called. If we gave the whole variable FILE_NAME as parameter we could have got 'rubbish' at the end of the file name, and this may have led to trouble for the operating system.

We shall now write another program that copies input from the terminal and stores it as a text file. This program can be used for writing information that is to be stored permanently in a text file. Here is the central portion of the program:

```
-- open OUTF
PUT_LINE("Enter the name of the new file");
GET_LINE(FILE_NAME, NAME_LENGTH);
CREATE(OUTF, NAME => FILE_NAME(1 .. NAME_LENGTH));

-- copy from the terminal to OUTF
PUT_LINE("Enter material to be stored in the file");
while not END_OF_FILE loop
   GET_LINE(LINE, LINE_LENGTH);
   PUT_LINE(OUTF, LINE(1 .. LINE_LENGTH));
end loop;

-- close OUTF
CLOSE(OUTF);
```

This differs from the previous program in that the file INF has disappeared and the parameter INF has been removed from the calls to END_OF_FILE and GET_LINE in the **loop** statement. Input is now from the terminal instead.

Files are often used to save values from calculations or measurements so that they can be analysed or processed further at some later date. In the next example we shall study a program that carries out 1000 computations of some sort and saves the results in a text file DATAFILE. The nature of the computations is of no interest here, so we assume that they take place in the function CALCULATION whose internal workings we can ignore.

In the program real numbers will be written to DATAFILE. We assume, therefore, that we have created a package FLOAT_INOUT containing facilities for writing numbers of type FLOAT. (The home-made package BASIC_NUM_IO is of no use here because it only includes facilities for writing to the terminal). The program has the following statements:

```
-- open DATAFILE

PUT_LINE("Enter the name of the new file");
GET_LINE(FILE_NAME, NAME_LENGTH);
```

```
CREATE(DATAFILE,
          NAME => FILE_NAME(1 .. NAME_LENGTH));
SET_LINE_LENGTH(DATAFILE, 100);

-- do 1000 calculations, save results in DATAFILE
for I in 1 .. 1000 loop
   VALUE := CALCULATION;      -- VALUE has type FLOAT;
   PUT(DATAFILE, VALUE);
end loop;

-- close DATAFILE
CLOSE(DATAFILE);
```

The call in the program:

```
PUT(DATAFILE, VALUE);
```

means that the value of the variable VALUE is written to the file
DATAFILE. Output to DATAFILE will be in standard exponent form. If we
want to have output in some other format, for example, with one figure
before the decimal point and three after, and one blank between each
number written, we can introduce the parameters EXP, FORE and AFT:

```
PUT(DATAFILE, VALUE, EXP => 0, FORE => 2, AFT => 3);
```

In the program we have specified the maximum line length in DATAFILE
to be 100 characters by making the call:

```
SET_LINE_LENGTH(DATAFILE, 100);
```

The procedure PUT automatically starts a new line each time there is
insufficient space to write the next item on the current line. If we had not
specified a maximum line length, all the numbers would have gone on
one, in principle, endless line.

In the next example we shall see part of a program that reads a text
file containing a number of real numbers. (This program could, for
example, read a text file written by the program above). The program
calculates and writes out the mean value of the numbers in the file. We
assume that we have created a package in this program that provides the
facilities for reading and writing values of type FLOAT. Furthermore, we
assume the declarations:

```
VALUE        : FLOAT;
VALUE_COUNT : NATURAL := 0;
SUM          : FLOAT    := 0.0;
```

The reading of the data file and calculations can then be accomplished using the statements:

```
while not END_OF_FILE(DATAFILE) loop
   GET(DATAFILE, VALUE);
   SUM := SUM + VALUE;
   VALUE_COUNT := VALUE_COUNT + 1;
end loop;

PUT("Mean value is: ");
PUT(SUM / FLOAT(VALUE_COUNT));
```

Text files can be used to build up registers of data, or databases, of various kinds. To illustrate this, we shall study a telephone list:

Acklin Gisela
01-345-7654
Booth Roy
021-65-4321
Cooper Sally
096-12-3214

⋮

Thus for each person there are two lines: one line for the name and one for the telephone number. We shall now work on a program that can be used to look up a person's telephone number. The program will read in a name from the terminal and then look for it in the text file *telephone.list*. If the name is present, the program will write out the corresponding telephone number. Otherwise it will give a message saying that the person in question is not on the list. We use the simplest imaginable algorithm: the program starts at the beginning of the list and reads one name at a time until either it finds the name in question, or it comes to the end of the list. To indicate that we have found the person we use the BOOLEAN variable FOUND which has the value FALSE at the start.

Telephone lists are usually sorted alphabetically. If we assume that this telephone list is sorted alphabetically, the search could be made more efficient by stopping when we find a person whose name comes after the sought name. If, for example, we were looking for the name Williams and found the name Wood, we would know that Williams is not present because it should come before Wood. However, here we shall do without this refinement. The program is:

```
with TEXT_IO;
use  TEXT_IO;
procedure FIND_TEL_NO is
   CATALOGUE                : FILE_TYPE;
   REQ_PERS, CURR_PERS      : STRING(1 .. 50);
   TEL_NO                   : STRING(1 .. 15);
   REQ_L, CURR_L, TEL_NO_L: NATURAL;
   FOUND                    : BOOLEAN := FALSE;

begin
   -- read in the name of the required person
   PUT_LINE("What name do you require?");
   GET_LINE(REQ_PERS, REQ_L);

   -- search for the required person in catalogue
   OPEN(CATALOGUE, MODE => IN_FILE,
                    NAME => "telephone.list");

   while not FOUND and not END_OF_FILE(CATALOGUE) loop
      -- read name and telephone number
      GET_LINE(CATALOGUE, CURR_PERS, CURR_L);
      GET_LINE(CATALOGUE, TEL_NO, TEL_NO_L);

      if CURR_PERS(1 .. CURR_L) = REQ_PERS(1 .. REQ_L) then
         PUT_LINE("Telephone number: " & TEL_NO(1 .. TEL_NO_L));
         FOUND := TRUE;
         end if;
      end loop;
   CLOSE(CATALOGUE);

   if not FOUND then
      PUT_LINE("This name is not in the catalogue");
      end if;
end FIND_TEL_NO;
```

We have seen that a text file can either be read or written, but it is not possible to alternate between the two modes. Reading or writing always occurs sequentially from the start of the file; it is not possible to go back to some position in the middle of reading or writing unless certain measures are taken. The only way to go back in a text file, is to go back to the *start* of the file. The procedure RESET is used to do this:

```
procedure RESET (FILE   : in out FILE_TYPE;
                 MODE : in FILE_MODE);
procedure RESET (FILE   : in out FILE_TYPE);
```

There are two versions of this procedure. In the first, apart from stating the name of the file, it is possible to state whether reading or writing is required. Thus when the file is reset it is also possible to reset the mode of the file, so that a file that was previously being written can now be read, and vice versa. In the second version, the file only returns to the start and the mode is not changed. Reading or writing is continued, as before.

If we have created a new file in a program, NEW_FILE, and written to it, we can go back to the start and read from it by writing:

RESET(NEW_FILE, IN_FILE);

If we were reading a file, DATAFILE, earlier and want to go back to the start and read it again, we can make the call:

RESET(DATAFILE);

To go back in a text file

RESET(F, IN_FILE);

go back to the start of F and read it from the beginning.

RESET(F, OUT_FILE);

go back to the start of F and write over it.

RESET(F);

go back to the start of F. If it is open for reading, reading takes place from the start again. If it is open for writing, it is written over.

As an example of an application where files must be reset, we can study a program that can be used to change a number in the telephone list outlined earlier. The program will read in from the terminal the name of a subscriber in the list and his or her new number. The program will then amend the file *telephone.list* so that the new number is inserted. Since both reading from and writing to a text file at the same time is not allowed, the work must be accomplished in two stages. In the first, *telephone.list* is read and a copy is written in a temporary new text file. If the given person is found during this copying process the new telephone number is put into the copy. Both files are then reset and the temporary text file is copied to the file *telephone.list*.

```
      with TEXT_IO;
      use  TEXT_IO;
procedure CHANGE_TEL_NO is
  CATALOGUE, TEMPFILE  : FILE_TYPE;
  REQ_PERS, CURR_PERS : STRING(1 .. 50);
  NEW_NO, TEL_NO       : STRING(1 .. 15);
  REQ_L, CURR_L,
  NEW_NO_L, TEL_NO_L   : NATURAL;
  FOUND                : BOOLEAN := FALSE;
begin
  -- read in the required person's
  -- name and new telephone number
  PUT_LINE("Whose telephone number has changed?");
  GET_LINE(REQ_PERS, REQ_L);
  PUT_LINE("Give the new telephone number");
  GET_LINE(NEW_NO, NEW_NO_L);

  -- open the telephone list for reading
  OPEN(CATALOGUE, MODE => IN_FILE,
                  NAME => "telephone.list");
  -- open a temporary file for writing
  CREATE(TEMPFILE);

  -- copy the telephone list to TEMPFILE
  -- and change the required telephone number
  while not END_OF_FILE(CATALOGUE) loop
    -- read name and tel number
    GET_LINE(CATALOGUE, CURR_PERS, CURR_L);
    GET_LINE(CATALOGUE, TEL_NO, TEL_NO_L);

    -- write name and tel number in TEMPFILE
    PUT_LINE(TEMPFILE, CURR_PERS(1 .. CURR_L));
    if CURR_PERS(1 .. CURR_L) = REQ_PERS(1 .. REQ_L) then
      PUT_LINE(TEMPFILE, NEW_NO(1 .. NEW_NO_L));
      FOUND := TRUE;
    else
      PUT_LINE(TEMPFILE, TEL_NO(1 .. TEL_NO_L));
    end if;
  end loop;

  if FOUND then
    -- return to the start of the files
    RESET(TEMPFILE, IN_FILE);
    RESET(CATALOGUE, OUT_FILE);

    -- copy TEMPFILE to the catalogue
    while not END_OF_FILE(TEMPFILE) loop
      GET_LINE(TEMPFILE, CURR_PERS, CURR_L);
      PUT_LINE(CATALOGUE, CURR_PERS(1 .. CURR_L));
      GET_LINE(TEMPFILE, TEL_NO, TEL_NO_L);
      PUT_LINE(CATALOGUE, TEL_NO(1 .. TEL_NO_L));
    end loop;
```

```
  else
    PUT_LINE("This name is not in the catalogue");
  end if;

  -- close the files
  CLOSE(CATALOGUE);
  CLOSE(TEMPFILE);
end CHANGE_TEL_NO;
```

The file TEMPFILE will only be temporary because no external filename is given when it is created. If the given person is not in the directory, nothing will be changed, so we do not bother to copy TEMPFILE to CATALOGUE.

A file variable, like other variables, can be given as a parameter to subprograms. Let us write a procedure QUICK_OPEN that reads in an external filename from the terminal and opens the corresponding file in the program. The procedure will have two parameters: the logical file to be opened and a parameter of type FILE_MODE which states whether the file should be opened for reading or writing. If the file is to be read, QUICK_OPEN assumes that the file exists and calls OPEN. If the file is to be written, QUICK_OPEN assumes that it is dealing with a new file and calls CREATE. The procedure is easy to write using what we have seen before:

```
procedure QUICK_OPEN (THE_FILE   : in out FILE_TYPE;
                      THE_MODE : in FILE_MODE) is
  FILE_NAME     : STRING(1 .. 30);
  NAME_LENGTH : NATURAL;
begin
  PUT_LINE("Give name of file to be opened");
  GET_LINE(FILE_NAME, NAME_LENGTH);
  if THE_MODE = IN_FILE then
    OPEN(THE_FILE,
         MODE => IN_FILE,
         NAME => FILE_NAME(1 .. NAME_LENGTH));
  else
    CREATE(THE_FILE,
           NAME => FILE_NAME(1 .. NAME_LENGTH));
  end if;
end QUICK_OPEN;
```

Note that the parameter THE_FILE should be an **in out** parameter, because the procedures OPEN and CREATE must be able to both read and change it. If we now have the two files INFILE and OUTFILE in our main program they can easily be opened with the call:

```
QUICK_OPEN(INFILE, IN_FILE);
QUICK_OPEN(OUTFILE, OUT_FILE);
```

In a computer system there are several important programs that work with text files. The text-editor, for example, is dedicated to the task of allowing text files to be edited. Another example is a compiler. The program fed into the compiler is stored as a text file and thus the compiler reads this text file.

■

We have seen that the subprograms in TEXT_IO used to read from and write to the terminal work in the same way as those used for reading and writing text files. If one of these subprograms has no file parameter, it is assumed to refer to the terminal. In fact, the terminal is considered as two text files that are usually called *standard input* and *standard output*. These files are opened automatically when a program is run and are linked to the keyboard and screen (or printing device), respectively. The following functions in TEXT_IO can be used to access these files, returning the logical files as their result:

> **function** STANDARD_INPUT   **return** FILE_TYPE;
> **function** STANDARD_OUTPUT **return** FILE_TYPE;

The package TEXT_IO always takes care of the current input and output files. When a program starts, the current input file is set to *standard input*, that is, the keyboard, and the current output file is set to *standard output*, that is, the screen. If a call is made to one of the input or output subprograms in TEXT_IO (for example, GET or PUT) without specifying a file as the first parameter, it is assumed that the current input file or output file is intended, depending on whether the subprogram refers to reading or writing. This means that reading and writing usually occur via the terminal. However, it is possible to change the current input and output files by calling the procedures:

> **procedure** SET_INPUT   (FILE : **in** FILE_TYPE);
>
> **procedure** SET_OUTPUT (FILE : **in** FILE_TYPE);

For example, if we want the file MY_FILE to be the current input file and the file NEW_FILE to be the current output file, we make the calls:

> SET_INPUT(MY_FILE);
> SET_OUTPUT(NEW_FILE);

Now if we make the call:

> GET(C);

reading will occur from the file MY_FILE instead of from the terminal. In the same way the call:

    PUT_LINE("message");

means that the line will be written to the file NEW_FILE instead of to the terminal.

To determine which files are the current input and output files, the functions:

    function CURRENT_INPUT   **return** FILE_TYPE;
    function CURRENT_OUTPUT **return** FILE_TYPE;

can be used.

We shall finish by mentioning some further subprograms in TEXT_IO that can be of use when handling text files.

An open file is linked to a particular external file and it is open either for reading or writing. This information can be found by calling the functions NAME and MODE. For example, the call:

    NAME(MY_FILE)

returns a text string containing the name of the external file that MY_FILE is linked to, and the call:

    MODE(MY_FILE)

returns the result either IN_FILE or OUT_FILE, depending on whether MY_FILE is open for reading or writing. These functions have the specifications:

    function NAME (FILE : **in** FILE_TYPE) **return** STRING;
    function MODE (FILE : **in** FILE_TYPE) **return** FILE_MODE;

If we want to remove an external file we can use the procedure DELETE:

    procedure DELETE (FILE : **in** FILE_MODE);

For example, the call:

    DELETE(MY_FILE);

means that the external file that is linked to MY_FILE is simply erased.

□

EXERCISES

9.1 Write a program to display the values of log(x) for all values of x between 1.0 and 9.9 inclusive, in steps of 0.1 (that is, 1.0, 1.1, 1.2, ... 9.9). The values should be displayed in tabular form at the terminal. Set 10 values to a line, separated by three blank spaces. Each number should be accurate to five decimal places.

9.2 Write a program to read text from the terminal and save it in a new text file with the name *my.text.file*. The new file should have the same line structure as the text file read from the terminal. In addition, all lower case letters should be translated into upper case in *my.text.file*.

9.3 A secret message is stored in the text file *secret.file*. This has not been stored as straightforward text but in the form of a code message so that it cannot be read easily without authorization. Each letter in the original message has been coded to another using this table:

```
code letter:  g u w y r m q p s a e i c b n o z l f h d k j x t v
original text: a b c d e f g h i j k l m n o p q r s t u v w x y z
```

If the file contains, for example, the lines:

```
lnybrt jgshsbq
jrybrfygt rsqph oc
```

the uncoded message is:

```
rodney waiting
wednesday eight pm
```

Write a program to read the file with the secret message and write it out in plain language. The program should begin by reading in the code (the first line in the table above) from the terminal.

9.4 Write a program to read an existing text file and write out its contents at the terminal. No empty lines (containing only a line terminator) or lines full of blanks should be written out. Otherwise the output should have the same structure as the text file. The program should be applicable to any text file; the text file's name should thus be read from the terminal.

9.5   Write a program to read in two existing text files (FILE1 and FILE2) and form a new one (FILE3). The new file should contain the contents of the first followed by those of the second. The names of the external files corresponding to FILE1, FILE2 and FILE3 should be read in from the terminal.

9.6   Assume a text file contains the text of a program written in an invented programming language XYZ. Assume further that in a program written in XYZ only the following characters may appear: the lower case letters 'a' to 'z'; the digits '0' to '9'; the left and right parentheses '(' and ')', and the space character.

Write a program to read in a text file containing a program in XYZ and write it out at the terminal. In this output any lines in the program containing illegal characters should be marked. This is achieved by writing an extra line in the output under the erroneous line, with an exclamation mark below each erroneous character.

If, for example, the file contains the text:

```
read x read y
Let z x plu? y
write z;
```

then the output at the terminal should appear as follows:

```
read x read y
Let z x plu? y
!          !
write z;
         !
```

9.7   Assume you have equipment for making automatic observations of the weather and that it performs particular measurements and stores the results on magnetic tape. From time to time you have to take the magnetic tape to read it into the computer and analyse the observations statistically.

Assume that the equipment stores data on magnetic tape in the form of a text file. Each line of the file contains the results of one complete observation. It is introduced by text in the format yymmddhhmm, which gives the date in the form year, month, day, and the time in hours and minutes, of the current observation. On the rest of the line there follows the measured values of the temperature, atmospheric pressure, humidity of the atmosphere, wind speed and wind direction. All these values are given as real numbers.

Write a program to read in a text file of weather observations from the computer's magnetic tape unit, and output

the highest and lowest temperatures measured. The output should
have the form:

> Highest temperature: xx.xx deg. Measured xx-xx-19xx, at xx:xx
> Lowest temperature : xx.xx deg. Measured xx-xx-19xx, at xx:xx

Assume that the computer's magnetic tape unit has the external
name *tape0*.

9.8   A text file *member.list* has been used to set up a membership
register for a club. There are three lines of text in the file for each
member: one line for the name, one for the address and one for
the telephone number. The file is sorted so that the members
appear in alphabetical order.

   Write a program to insert a new member in the register. The
program should read from the terminal the name, address and
telephone number of the new member and then insert this
information in the correct place in the file, so that the members
remain in correct alphabetical order. (*Hint*: Use a temporary file.)

9.9   Write a very simple text-editor. The program should read in a text
file, of arbitrary external name, line by line and let the user make
simple changes in the stored text. Each time a line is read from the
text file it should be written at the terminal and then the program
should read an editing command at the terminal. The following
commands can be given:

REMOVE	The current line should be removed. Start editing the next line.
INSERT	Read a line in from the terminal and insert it in the file before the current line.
SWAP *xy*	All occurrences of character *x* on the current line should be replaced by character *y*.
NEXT	Editing the current line is finished. Start editing the next line.

After each line is completely edited it should be written to a
temporary file; when all the lines are ready the program should
then end by copying the temporary file back to the original text
file.

9.10 Write a program that reads a text from a text file and writes it out
in edited form at the terminal. The program should start by reading
in the name of the text file from the terminal. It should also read in

the desired page and line size. Assume that the input text file contains a number of words separated by one or more spaces or by a line terminator. In the output there should be one space between words. The line structure in the output should not be the same as that of the input file. Each line of the output should contain as many words as possible in the given line length, so that the lines are roughly the same length.

Chapter 10
Exceptions

10.1 Predefined exceptions
10.2 Declaring exceptions
10.3 Handling exceptions

10.4 Errors arising during input
and output
Exercises

When a program is executed, unexpected situations sometimes occur. Such a situation is called an **exception**. The
exception may be the result of an error of some kind, for
example, dividing by zero, using an index to an array outside
the allowed constraints, or giving faulty input data to a
program or subprogram. An exception is not necessarily the
result of an error in the program. It may be something that
only happens very rarely when the program is run.

When a program is being written, the algorithm should
be as clear and easy to understand as possible. If checks
were inserted at each stage of the algorithm, however, for
every imaginable error and other abnormal event, the
algorithm would become very clumsy and hard to follow. In
Ada, therefore, there is a mechanism to handle exceptional
events without it showing in the program's ordinary algorithm.

10.1 Predefined exceptions

If an error occurs when a program is executed, it normally leads to the program termination and an error message, such as:

```
** MAIN PROGRAM ABANDONED -- EXCEPTION "constraint_error"
   RAISED
```

What this message is saying is that an exceptional event has occurred, in this case a 'constraint error'.

In Ada there are five predefined exceptions:

CONSTRAINT_ERROR	Occurs, for example, if a variable is assigned an illegal value or indexing is attempted beyond the limits of an array.
NUMERIC_ERROR	Occurs when a numeric operation cannot give a correct result. For example, the result may be larger than it is possible to represent. A common case is trying to divide by 0.
PROGRAM_ERROR	Occurs in unusual circumstances, when part of the program called is not accessible, or when the final **end** in a function is reached, that is, the function has not returned a result. There are also other errors that cause this exception.
STORAGE_ERROR	Occurs if the accessible memory expires, for example, there is a recursive sub-program with a faulty terminating condition so that too many instances of the sub-program are generated.
TASKING_ERROR	Can occur in connection with parallel programs. This will not be discussed here.

These five exceptions are defined in the package STANDARD; thus they are automatically defined in all implementations of Ada.

When an exception occurs, the normal execution of the program ceases immediately. If no special precautions have been taken in the program, it will terminate abnormally with an error message stating the type of exception causing the termination.

These predefined exceptions occur when some error has occurred in the program. However, we can create an exception by placing a special **raise** statement into a program. For example, we can 'raise' the exception NUMERIC_ERROR with the statement:

```
raise NUMERIC_ERROR;
```

When this statement is executed the program will behave as though an error has occurred in the program. The program terminates at once with an error message, unless the exception is treated in some way.

Raise statement

   raise E;

where E is the name of an exception.

Normal execution terminates at once and the exception E occurs.

It is not really of much interest to raise exceptions of one of the predefined types. It is more useful, however, to raise other exceptions, as we shall demonstrate in the following sections.

10.2   Declaring exceptions

In an Ada program it is possible to work with exceptions other than the five predefined ones listed in Section 10.1. It is possible to define our own exceptions. An exception TIME_UP, for example, could be declared as follows:

TIME_UP : **exception**;

This is a declaration and is placed with the other declarations – declarations of variables, for example. In form, it looks like a variable declaration, but TIME_UP is not a variable. It cannot have a value. All the declaration says is that in the program there is an exception, TIME_UP, that may happen. We can make as many declarations as we like of our own exceptions in a program. We can list several in one declaration, for example:

TABLE_EMPTY, TABLE_FULL : **exception**;

The normal rules hold for the scope of the declaration. For example, the name of an exception is not known outside the subprogram in which it is declared. (However, when an exception occurs its effects can spread outside the subprogram in which it was declared).

Declaring exceptions

> *E1, E2, ...* : **exception**;

where *E1, E2, ...* are the names given to the exceptions.

The declarations are placed among the other declarations.

To cause an exception to occur we can use a **raise** statement:

raise TIME_UP;

The same pattern of events occurs as with predefined exceptions. Unless we do something special, normal execution of the program ceases with an error message, in this case:

∗∗ MAIN PROGRAM ABANDONED -- EXCEPTION ''time_up'' RAISED

Such an error message can be much more informative than a message containing one of the five predefined exceptions. A predefined exception could be caused by many different errors in a program, whereas a declared exception can only occur if a **raise** statement has been executed.

10.3 Handling exceptions

So far we have said that an exception interrupts a program so that it stops with an error message. It is, however, possible to trap exceptions in a program and take some appropriate action. If we have a program that controls an industrial process of some sort, it is not acceptable for the program to cease abruptly if an exception occurs. The program must deal with what has happened, by writing a warning message to the operator or closing down a critical process, for example. It is also unacceptable for a program to cease because, for example, an operator has written input data in the wrong format or has entered an integer when the program was expecting a real number.

There are three levels of ambition in dealing with exceptions:

(1)   Take control of the exception, and try and take suitable action to enable the program to continue.

(2)   Trap, identify and pass the exception on to another part of the program.

(3)   Ignore the exception, that is, the program will stop when the exception occurs.

The basic principle should be that the exception is controlled in the part of the program (or outside it if necessary), where its effect can most sensibly be handled. The third level is the one we have seen so far. The exceptions we have seen have been of the predefined sort and have most often occurred because of an error in the logic of our programs. To try and trap such exceptions in the program is not really worthwhile. The correct course of action is to handle what happens from outside the program, that is, correct the program so that the logic error disappears. If the Ada system gives an error message that is too scant when an error of logic occurs (that is, we cannot see where the error occurred), and if we do not have access to a debugging program, then it may be better to trap the logic error in the program ourselves. (A more meaningful error message is then possible).

As an example of the first level of ambition, we shall study a function that calculates the tangent of an angle. We assume that we have access to a mathematical package containing the functions SIN and COS, but not TAN. It is simple to construct the function TAN:


```
function TAN (X : FLOAT) return FLOAT is
begin
   return SIN(X) / COS(X);
end TAN;
```


The problem with this function, however, is that for certain values of X (PI/2, for example), COS(X) has the value 0 and the value of TAN(X) is infinite. (Note that the parameter to TAN must be in radians and not in degrees). If we call our function TAN with the value PI/2 then an attempt is made to divide by 0 and NUMERIC_ERROR occurs. This means that execution terminates with an error message.

We shall now amend the function TAN so that it traps the error and yields a 'sensible' result other than program termination. What constitutes a sensible result is open to discussion. Since we cannot store an infinitely large number we shall let it be represented by the largest possible value that a variable of type FLOAT can assume. Naturally, this is not mathematically correct. If this is unacceptable, we can do it in another way that will be discussed later.

So far we have said that a subprogram consists of a subprogram specification followed by a declarative part and a sequence of statements. In fact, there can be a further section at one end of the subprogram – a section that deals with exceptions. Let us look at TAN if we add such a section:

```
function TAN(X : FLOAT) return FLOAT is
begin
   return SIN(X) / COS(X);

exception
  when NUMERIC_ERROR =>
    if (SIN(X) >= 0.0 and COS(X) >= 0.0) or
       (SIN(X) <  0.0 and COS(X) <  0.0) then
      return FLOAT'LARGE;
    else
      return -FLOAT'LARGE;
    end if;

end TAN;
```

The part we have added starts with the reserved word **exception**. (This should not be confused with the declaration of an exception). The rest of the addition is similar to the structure of a **case** statement. The line:

```
when NUMERIC_ERROR =>
```

means that the statements after this line will be executed if an exception of the type NUMERIC_ERROR occurs. This is called the **exception handler** for the exception NUMERIC_ERROR.

When we execute our function TAN, the NUMERIC_ERROR exception will occur if we try to divide by zero in the statement:

```
return SIN(X) / COS(X);
```

This statement is interrupted and control passes to the statements that are in the appropriate exception handler. In this case, the **if** statement will be carried out. This tests whether the result should be a very large positive or negative number. (Note, the complicated Boolean expression after **if** could be replaced by the somewhat simpler: SIN(X) ∗ COS(X) >= 0.0.) FLOAT'LARGE is, as we have seen, an attribute that gives the largest possible number that can be stored in a variable of type FLOAT. The result from the function will be either FLOAT'LARGE or -FLOAT'LARGE depending on the part of the **if** statement that is chosen.

By trapping the exception NUMERIC_ERROR program termination has been avoided. Control returns to the program that called TAN and execution continues as normal.

It is important to note that control did not return to the statement that was interrupted in the normal statement section of the function. This is not only because we have **return** statements in the exception handler for NUMERIC_ERROR – it is generally true. After the statements in the statement section of the exception handler have been executed the **end** is reached in the part of the program containing the handler. There is never a jump back to the part of the program that was interrupted.

There can be handlers for several exceptions at the end of a subprogram, both predefined and declared. We can have, for example:

```
exception
  when TIME_UP =>
    PUT_LINE("Time to make a move");

  when CONSTRAINT_ERROR =>
    PUT_LINE("Error in index value");

  when TABLE_FULL ¦ TABLE_EMPTY =>
    PUT_LINE("Table error");

  when others =>
    PUT_LINE("Something wrong in package PLAY");
```

We see that it is possible to have common handlers for two or more kinds of exception. In our example, TABLE_FULL and TABLE_EMPTY have a common handler. Thus the message "Table error" is output when exceptions of the kind TABLE_FULL or TABLE_EMPTY occur. We also see that there can be an **others** alternative to handle all other kinds of exception that are not already listed. An **others** alternative must appear at the end if it appears at all.

If an exception of kind E occurs and the current subprogram has no handler for exceptions of this kind (including no **others** alternative), then the exception E will be 'passed on' to the subprogram that called the current subprogram. Thus an exception of kind E will occur in the calling subprogram. If this also has no handler for exception E then the exception will be passed on further, and so on. If an exception occurs in the main program and this too has no handler for E then the program will finally be terminated by the Ada system with an error message.

It should be noted that if an exception occurs in the declarative part of a subprogram, that is, before the statements following **begin** have started to be executed, the exception is passed directly to the calling subprogram. Thus such an exception cannot be trapped in the subprogram where the exception occurs.

Subprograms with exception handlers

subprogram_specification
  declarations
begin
  statements
exception
  one or more exception handlers
end *subprogram_name*;

- When an exception occurs control passes to the handler for the particular exception. When the statements in this have been executed the subprogram terminates and return occurs.

- Control never returns to the place where the interrupt occurred.

- If there is no handler, the subprogram terminates and the exception is passed back to the calling subprogram.

Exception handlers

Different forms:

when *E* =>
  statements;
when *E1* ¦ *E2* ¦ ... ¦ *EN* =>
  statements;
when others =>
  statements;

where *E, E1, E2,* ... are the names of exceptions.

If there is an **others** alternative it must be last.

Let us return to our example with the function TAN. If we consider it unacceptable to use FLOAT'LARGE to approximate infinity, we can approach the problem in another way. If we find that program execution terminates when we try to calculate a value for infinity, we can settle for trapping the error in TAN and giving an appropriate error message so that the programmer can more easily find the error in the program that calls TAN. Thus we find the second level of ambition adequate.

```
function TAN(X : FLOAT) return FLOAT is
begin
  return SIN(X) / COS(X);
exception
  when NUMERIC_ERROR =>
    PUT_LINE("The value of tangent is too big");
    raise;
end TAN;
```

In the handler for NUMERIC_ERROR, instead of trying to work out some reasonable result we have inserted an error message. On the next line we find the statement:

```
raise;
```

Any statements can go into an exception handler, even the **raise** statement. The special form of **raise** statement we have used here, where no exception name is given, is only allowed within a handler. This **raise** statement means that the exception that caused the handler to take control has occurred again, and thus the exception is passed on to the calling program.

Thus in our example, the NUMERIC_ERROR exception will be passed on to the calling program. If there is no handler in this program (or the program that called it, and so on) execution of the program will terminate with an error message "numeric_error". Because we have added the error message:

```
The value of tangent is too big
```

to the function TAN, the logic fault will now be easier to find in the program.

It is not necessarily an error of logic that makes us attempt to calculate the tangent of an angle that gives an incalculable result. Let us study, for example, the following lines of program which read in the values of angles from the terminal and then calculate and write out the tangents of these angles.

```
loop
  PUT("Give a real number, or end with CTRL-D: ");
  exit when END_OF_FILE;
  GET(NUMBER);
  RES := TAN(NUMBER);
  PUT("Tangent is: "); PUT(RES); NEW_LINE;
end loop;
```

We assume that both variables NUMBER and RES have the type FLOAT. There is no direct error in the logic of these lines, but they still do not work if we give a value such as PI/2 as input.

Thanks to the error message in TAN a good error message is sent to the operator. Now we can rewrite these lines so that it traps the exception NUMERIC_ERROR. This then means that the program is not interrupted but can continue by asking for the next value. Our modified form of the loop is:

```
loop
  begin
    PUT("Give a real number, or end with CTRL-D: ");
    exit when END_OF_FILE;
    GET(NUMBER);
    RES := TAN(NUMBER);
    PUT("Tangent is: "); PUT(RES); NEW_LINE;
  exception
    when NUMERIC_ERROR =>
      PUT_LINE("No tangent can be evaluated");
  end;
end loop;
```

Note the addition of the words **begin** and **end** around the contents of the **loop** statement. These words are the start and end of a new statement in Ada that we have not yet met – a **block** statement.

The reason for introducing a block statement here is that an exception handler may be placed at the end of one. When an exception occurs within the block statement, control passes to the appropriate handler (if there is one). When the statements within the handler have been executed, execution of the whole block statement stops and the program continues with the next statement after the block statement.

If the exception NUMERIC_ERROR occurs then the text:

No tangent can be evaluated

is written and execution continues thereafter with a new iteration of the **loop** statement. Thus the whole program is not terminated. If we had not introduced the block statement but had placed the handler for NUMERIC_ERROR at the end of the program instead, the whole program would have terminated because the exception NUMERIC_ERROR had occurred. Using the block statement thus enables us to remain in the program and continue as normal.

It should be noted that the handler can only take care of exceptions that occur within the block statement. If NUMERIC_ERROR occurs elsewhere in the program, control will not pass to this handler.

A block statement is a compound statement that has a structure reminiscent of that of a subprogram. A block statement is considered an ordinary statement and can be placed anywhere an ordinary statement can. It is executed when it is reached in the normal execution sequence of the program (thus it is not called like a subprogram). In a block statement, as in a subprogram, there can be a statement section and a section that contains exception handlers. At its most general, however, the block statement can also contain a declarative part before the statements. In this case the block statement starts with the word **declare**.

Block statement

   [declare
     declarations]
   begin
     statements
   [exception
     one or more exception handlers]
   end;

[...] can be omitted.

- Declarations made are only known inside the block statement.

- When an exception occurs, execution of the whole block terminates and the next statement is carried out.

Let us look at some examples of block statements:

```
begin
  PUT_LINE("This is program XYZ");
  PUT_LINE("Welcome");
end;

declare            -- exchange I and J
  TEMP : INTEGER;
begin
  TEMP : = I;
  I     : = J;
  J     := TEMP;
end;

declare
  I, J : INTEGER;
```

```
begin
  GET(I);
  GET(J);
  PUT(I ** J);
exception
  when CONSTRAINT_ERROR =>
    PUT_LINE("Exponent error");
end;
```

If we return once more to the example of the function TAN, it may be disadvantageous to pass on the exception NUMERIC_ERROR, because it can occur for so many different reasons; it can be difficult for the calling program to identify the error and realize that it occurred in TAN. Moreover, it is not always desirable to have an error message from TAN; the writer of the calling program may prefer to formulate his or her own error messages.

The solution to this dilemma is to declare an exception TAN_ERROR in TAN and to pass this on. But we cannot declare TAN_ERROR in the function TAN, because then it would not be known outside and it would not be possible to write a handler for it in the calling program. Nor is it good to declare TAN_ERROR in the calling program – TAN_ERROR belongs with the function TAN and should therefore be declared in conjunction with it.

If we assume that TAN is included as a function in a mathematical package there is a natural way of solving this problem. We declare TAN_ERROR in the specification of this package. Then TAN_ERROR is known by the program that called TAN but its declaration is still together with TAN. Thus we can have a package MATHEMATICS:

```
package MATHEMATICS is
  function SIN  (X : FLOAT) return FLOAT;
  function COS (X : FLOAT) return FLOAT;
  function TAN  (X : FLOAT) return FLOAT;

     ⋮

  TAN_ERROR : exception;
end MATHEMATICS;
```

The body of the package looks like this:

```
package body MATHEMATICS is

  function SIN (X : FLOAT) return FLOAT is

     ⋮

  end SIN;
```

```
function COS (X : FLOAT) return FLOAT is
    ⋮
end COS;

function TAN (X : FLOAT) return FLOAT is
begin
    return SIN (X) / COS (X);
exception
    when NUMERIC_ERROR =>
        raise TAN_ERROR;
end TAN;

end MATHEMATICS;
```

Now we can write a program that uses the package MATHEMATICS and that makes use of the exception TAN_ERROR;

```
with TEXT_IO, BASIC_NUM_IO, MATHEMATICS;
use  TEXT_IO, BASIC_NUM_IO, MATHEMATICS;
procedure COMPUTE_TAN is
    NUMBER, RES : FLOAT;
begin
    loop
        begin
            PUT("Give a real number, or end with CTRL-D: ");
            exit when END_OF_FILE;
            GET(NUMBER);
            RES := TAN(NUMBER);
            PUT("Tangent is: "); PUT(RES); NEW_LINE;
        exception
            when TAN_ERROR =>
                PUT_LINE("The tangent is too big");
        end;
    end loop;
end COMPUTE_TAN;
```

If the value PI/2 is given as input to this program, the message:

```
The tangent is too big
```

will be output.

It is very common for a package specification to contain declarations of the exceptions that can occur in the package. By trapping problems within the package and passing on well-specified exceptions to the user, the user is given the opportunity to take appropriate action. Errors most often arise during execution of a package because the user has called a subprogram wrongly. Thus, in constructing packages, we generally handle exceptions at the second of our three levels of ambition.

As a further example of packages that use this technique we shall study a package that deals with vectors. Earlier, we wrote functions that can add two vectors. Here we shall build up a small package that offers facilities for adding two vectors and for forming the scalar product of two vectors. As shown in Section 6.1, a vector can be represented by the type:

type VECTOR **is array** (INTEGER **range** < >) **of** FLOAT;

If two vectors are added the result is a new vector in which each component is the sum of their corresponding components. In calculating the scalar product of two vectors, the products of corresponding pairs of components are formed and added together. Thus the result is not a new vector but a single number. One condition governing whether it is possible to add two vectors or form their scalar product is that they both have to have the same number of components.

The specification of a package VECTOR_PACKAGE can be written:

```
package VECTOR_PACKAGE is

    type VECTOR is array (INTEGER range < >) of FLOAT;

    function ADD (V1, V2 : VECTOR) return VECTOR;
    -- add vectors V1 and V2

    function SCALAR_PROD (V1, V2 : VECTOR) return FLOAT;
    -- compute scalar product of vectors V1 and V2

    LENGTH_ERROR : exception;
    -- Occurs if the two parameters to the functions
    -- have different lengths
end VECTOR_PACKAGE;
```

In the specification we have declared an exception LENGTH_ERROR that occurs if the two parameters to ADD or SCALAR_PROD have different numbers of components. The body of VECTOR_PACKAGE can now be assembled:

```
package body VECTOR_PACKAGE is

    function ADD (V1, V2 : VECTOR) return VECTOR is
        TEMP : VECTOR(V1'RANGE);
    begin
        if V1'LENGTH /= V2'LENGTH then
            raise LENGTH_ERROR;
        end if;
        TEMP := V2;
        for I in V1'RANGE loop
            TEMP(I) := TEMP(I) + V1(I);
        end loop;
```

```
      return TEMP;
   end ADD;

   function SCALAR_PROD (V1, V2 : VECTOR) return FLOAT is
      SUM   : FLOAT := 0.0;
      TEMP : VECTOR(V1'RANGE);
   begin
      if V1'LENGTH /= V2'LENGTH then
         raise LENGTH_ERROR;
      end if;
      TEMP := V2;
      for I in V1'RANGE loop
         SUM := SUM + V1(I) * TEMP(I);
      end loop;
      return SUM;
   end SCALAR_PROD;
end VECTOR_PACKAGE;
```

We use one of the concepts raised in Section 6.1. To avoid the problems
that arise when two vectors have different index constraints we declare a
local variable TEMP that is indexed in the same way as V1. Then we make
the assignment:

```
   TEMP := V2;
```

and copy the whole of V2 to TEMP. This is only feasible if V2 and TEMP
(that is, V1) have the same number of components. Therefore we first test
that this is the case. If V1 and V2 have different numbers of components
then we raise the exception LENGTH_ERROR:

```
   raise LENGTH_ERROR;
```

10.4   Errors arising during input and output

In the package TEXT_IO the technique of generating exceptions is used
if something goes wrong. In the specification of TEXT_IO the exceptions STATUS_ERROR, MODE_ERROR, NAME_ERROR, USE_ERROR,
DEVICE_ERROR, END_ERROR, DATA_ERROR and LAYOUT_ERROR are
declared. The names of these exceptions are thus visible to the user of
TEXT_IO who can use them to trap errors that occur during input and
output. The following summary explains when the different exceptions
can occur:

   STATUS_ERROR   Occurs if an attempt is made to read from or write to a file that is not open, or if an attempt is made to open a file that is already open.

MODE_ERROR Occurs if an attempt is made to read from a file that is open for writing or to write to a file that is open for reading.

NAME_ERROR Occurs if an attempt is made to open a file and an incorrect external name is given. The name may be in the wrong form or an external file with that name may not be found.

USE_ERROR Occurs if an attempt is made to open a file for illegal use. This may be, for example, an attempt to open a line-printer file for reading. Another example is if CREATE is called with an external name that already exists and the system will not allow the existing file to be overwritten.

DEVICE_ERROR Occurs if there is a technical failure on an input or output device.

END_ERROR Occurs if an attempt is made to read something from a file and the next thing in line for reading is a file terminator.

DATA_ERROR Occurs if a value of integer, floating point or enumeration type is read in and the input data file contains data in an incorrect form (that is, not following the rules for the type in question).

LAYOUT_ERROR Occurs, for example, if an attempt is made to state a current line or column number for output that exceeds the maximum limits.

We shall study a procedure READ_FLOAT that can be used to read a real number from the terminal. If the user enters the real number wrongly, for example, as an integer, the program will not terminate but the user will be asked to rewrite the number.

The procedure should be 'callable' in the same way as GET in a program. To read a value to a floating point variable X the call:

```
READ_FLOAT(X);
```

should therefore be made. The procedure is:

```
procedure READ_FLOAT (NUMBER : out FLOAT) is
   READY : BOOLEAN := FALSE;
begin
   while not READY loop
```

```
    begin
      GET(NUMBER);
      READY := TRUE;
    exception
      when DATA_ERROR =>
        PUT_LINE("Incorrect number. Please repeat.");
        SKIP_LINE;
    end;
  end loop;
end READ_FLOAT;
```

The procedure consists of a **loop** statement that tries to read a real number from the terminal each time round. Within the **loop** statement there is a block statement. The **loop** statement continues until a real number has been successfully read. The variable READY indicates whether the reading has been successful. At the start READY has the value FALSE. When the call:

```
GET(NUMBER);
```

is executed, the exception DATA_ERROR occurs if the user writes something wrong at the terminal. The normal execution in the **block** statement terminates and control passes to the handler for DATA_ERROR. The statement:

```
READY := TRUE;
```

will thus not be executed before the call to GET has been successful, that is, without a DATA_ERROR.

In the final example we show a procedure that can be used to open an existing text file for reading. The procedure reads in the name of the external file from the terminal and then tries to open it by calling the procedure OPEN in TEXT_IO. If an error occurs during the opening it is trapped and an appropriate error message is output.

```
procedure OWN_OPEN (THE_FILE : in out FILE_TYPE) is
  FILE_NAME     : STRING (1 .. 30);
  NAME_LENGTH : NATURAL;
begin
  PUT_LINE("Give the name of the file to be read");
  GET_LINE(FILE_NAME, NAME_LENGTH);
  OPEN(THE_FILE,
       MODE => IN_FILE,
       NAME => FILE_NAME(1 .. NAME_LENGTH));
exception
  when STATUS_ERROR =>
    PUT_LINE("The file is already open");
```

```
      when NAME_ERROR =>
         PUT_LINE("There is no file with that name");
      when USE_ERROR =>
         PUT_LINE("The file cannot be read");
      when others =>
         PUT_LINE("Unexpected error on opening file");
   end OWN_OPEN;
```

If we assume that we have the declaration:

```
   INFILE : FILE_TYPE;
```

in a program, then we can make the call:

```
   OWN_OPEN(INFILE);
```

to try to open the file. It is possible to test if the opening went well by calling the function IS_OPEN:

```
   if IS_OPEN(INFILE) then
      -- continue as normal
   end if;
```

EXERCISES

10.1 Write a version of the function FACTORIAL that calculates $N!$ for an integer $N >= 0$. The function should give a floating point number as its result and if the result is so great that it cannot be represented in the computer in use, the function should give as its result the largest floating point number that can be represented.

10.2 The procedure COMPUTE_ROOTS in Chapter 6 computed the roots of a quadratic equation. Rewrite this procedure so that it does not have the **out** parameter REAL_ROOTS. If a quadratic equation has no real roots, the procedure should produce the error message:

   Error in COMPUTE_ROOTS. There are no real roots.

and pass the exception NUMERIC_ERROR to the calling program.

10.3 In Exercise 8.10 a package was constructed to describe the abstract data type queue. Add to the package so that it generates the exceptions QUEUE_FULL if an attempt is made to add more elements than the queue can hold, and QUEUE_EMPTY if an attempt is made to remove an element from an empty queue.

10.4 Write a procedure TRY_TO_GET that can be used instead of GET to read an integer from the terminal. The procedure TRY_TO_GET should have two **out** parameters. The first should be an integer parameter to hold the integer read. The second should be of type BOOLEAN. This should be given the value TRUE if the reading is successful (that is, the user writes an integer correctly) or otherwise the value FALSE.

10.5 Write a procedure that can be used to open a new text file. The procedure should read in the name of the new file from the terminal. If the user writes something incorrect, that is, no new file with that name can be opened, the procedure should produce an appropriate error message and ask the user to give another file name. This should be repeated until the new file has been opened successfully.

Chapter 11
Dynamic data structures

11.1 Pointers and dynamic objects
11.2 Linked lists
11.3 Doubly linked lists

11.4 Stacks and queues
11.5 Trees
Exercises

For every ordinary object (variable or constant) we can assume that there is a space in the primary memory of the computer where its value is stored. It could be said that the object's name is the name of that space in memory, or store. The space in the memory is created when the object is declared and it exists during the execution of the program unit in which the object's declaration appears. Such an object is described as **static**. It cannot be created or destroyed during execution of the program unit.

In some applications, the number of objects needed is not known in advance. Then **dynamic data structures** are required, that can grow and shrink during program execution; it must therefore be possible to create new objects during execution. An example of a dynamic data structure is a list where elements can be added and removed dynamically.

This chapter reviews Ada's mechanism for creating dynamic objects. The dynamic data structures – **lists, queues, stacks** and **trees** – will be discussed.

11.1 Pointers and dynamic objects

To create a dynamic object during execution an **allocator** is used. This, in its simplest form, is an expression with the reserved word **new** followed by a type name. To create a dynamic object of type INTEGER, for example, we can write:

> **new** INTEGER

It is most common to work with dynamic objects of record types. If, for example, we have declared the type PERSON:

```
type PERSON is
   record
      NAME    : STRING(1 .. 20);
      HEIGHT : INTEGER;
      WEIGHT : FLOAT;
   end record;
```

then we can create a new object of the type PERSON using the allocator:

> **new** PERSON

When an allocator is used, space is reserved in memory for a new object of the type in question. Each time the allocator is executed a new object is created, or designated.

In the two foregoing examples, the contents of the space in memory is undefined. Therefore the values of the dynamic object are also undefined. It is possible to add an initialization term to the allocator to give a newly created object a value. To create a new object of type INTEGER and, at the same time, give it an initial value 5, we can write:

> **new** INTEGER'(5)

After the type name an apostrophe is written followed by the value in brackets. The value in brackets does not need to be a constant, but it must be an expression with the same type as the new object. If N is a variable of type INTEGER we can thus write:

> **new** INTEGER'(2 * N)

If we want to create a new object of record or array type and initialize the object, an aggregate should be written after the apostrophe. For example, a new PERSON can be created and initialized with the allocator:

> **new** PERSON'("Booth Abigail   ", 170, 55.0)

We know that each expression in Ada has a particular defined type. An allocator is also considered to be an expression, so what type does such an expression have? The result of an allocator is a **reference** or **pointer**, or, as generally called in Ada, an **access value**. We say that this result is of **access type**; in Ada the reserved word **access** is used to denote this pointer type. The result of the expression:

new INTEGER

is thus a pointer to an object of type INTEGER. Similarly, the result of the expression:

new PERSON

is a pointer to an object of type PERSON.

Allocators

    new T

or:

    new T'(*initial_value*)

where T is an arbitrary type. It creates a new object of type T. The result of the allocator is a pointer to an object of type T.

As for other types, it is possible to declare variables of access types. In the following example two access variables are declared, PI and PP:

```
type INT_POINTER    is access INTEGER;
type PERS_POINTER is access PERSON;
PI  : INT_POINTER;
PP : PERS_POINTER;
```

We can now use these variables to save the pointers to the created objects. For example, we can have the statement:

```
PI := new INTEGER'(5);
```

Figure 11.1

The variable PI will now point to an object of type INTEGER. The situation is illustrated in Figure 11.1.

Similarly, we can write the statement:

PP := **new** PERSON'("Booth Abigail   ", 170, 55.0);

and then we have the situation shown in Figure 11.2.

As with other variables, an access variable can be initialized at the same time as it is declared. We could, for example, achieve the same result by declaring PP in the following way:

PP : PERS_POINTER := **new** PERSON'("Booth Abigail   ", 170, 55.0);

If an access variable is not initialized with its declaration it automatically takes the value **null** which means that it is not pointing to anything.

Access variables

    type POINTER **is access** T;
    P : POINTER;

where T is any type.

The variable can be initialized at the same time as it is declared:

    type POINTER **is access** T;
    P : POINTER := **new** T'(*initialization_expression*);

An uninitialized access variable automatically takes the value **null**.

Now PP can be used to get at the new object – it points to it; it provides access to it. To change the new person's weight, for example, we can write:

PP.WEIGHT := 54.0;

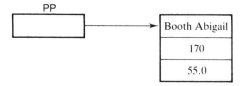

Figure 11.2

and to write out the person's name we can make the call:

PUT(PP.NAME);

If the whole object that PP points to is required, the reserved word **all** can be used. For example, to change the whole record that PP is pointing to we could write:

PP.**all** := ("Booth Russell ", 180, 75.0);

Figure 11.3 illustrates how it would then look.

> **To access an object**
>
>   **P.all**
>
> means the *whole* of an object that is pointed to.
> - If the object is a record type, individual components can be selected by writing:
>
>   P.*component_name*
> - The access variable P is not affected.

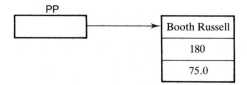

Figure 11.3

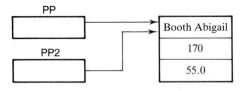

Figure 11.4

Several access variables may point at the same object. If we declare another variable:

    PP2 : PERS_POINTER;

we can now write the statement:

    PP2 := PP;

This means that the access value of PP is assigned to PP2 and, therefore, PP2 will point to the same object as PP. The situation is shown in Figure 11.4.

Assignment of access variables

    P1 := P2;

P1 and P2 must be access variables of the same type.

- The access value of P2 is assigned to P1.
- They point at the same object.
- The value of the object is not affected.

Let us declare yet another access variable:

    PP3 : PERS_POINTER := **new** PERSON;

PP3 has been initialized so that it points at a new object of type PERSON. Thus there are now two objects of type PERSON. Figure 11.5 illustrates the situation. The contents of the record that PP3 is pointing to are still undefined. If we want to copy to it the contents of the record that PP points to we can write the statement:

PP3.**all** := PP.**all**;

Observe that the word **all** must appear on both sides. If it had not been present, the access variable PP3 would have been changed to point to the same object as PP.

A particular access variable can only point to objects of a particular type. For example, PP can only point at objects of the type PERSON, so it would be wrong to try and write:

PP := **new** INTEGER;   -- ERROR! Different types

Note also that an access variable can only point at objects that have been created by the execution of an allocator. An access variable, therefore, can never be made to point at an object that was declared in the normal way.

A dynamic object first ceases to exist when execution leaves the part of the program in which the access type to the object was declared. The Ada system can then automatically re-use the freed space in the memory. The objects of type PERSON in the foregoing example cannot, therefore, exist outside the part of the program where the type PERS_POINTER is declared.

This way of defining the length of time that a dynamic object exists means that there can never be any problems with lingering pointers that point at space in memory that has actually been freed. (However, situations can arise during execution such that there are dynamic objects to which no pointers point).

It should be noted that the normal rules can be abandoned in Ada and the programmer can take more control of when the dynamic objects created should cease to exist. In this case, the programmer takes responsibility for ensuring that there are no pointers that point to memory with undefined contents.

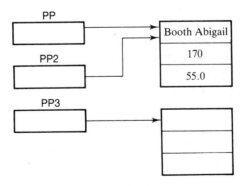

Figure 11.5

11.2   Linked lists

A **linked list**, or simply a **list**, is a dynamic data structure with applications
in many different areas of programming. A list of three integers is
illustrated in Figure 11.6. Each element in the list contains a value (in this
example an integer) and a pointer to the next element in the list.
The first element of a list is usually called its **head** and that element is
pointed to by a special pointer (LIST in the figure).

What is so good about lists is that they can have new elements
added relatively easily – anywhere in the list. (It is most common to put
new elements first or last). It is not necessary to know while programming
how many elements there will be in the list.

11.2.1   Building up a list

It is possible to build up a list in a program using arrays, but the more
natural way is to make use of dynamic objects and pointers. Let us
study the type declarations that have to be made to describe a linked list.
We want each element in the list to consist of two parts: a link to the next
element in the list and a value. An element in a list of integers can, for
example, be described by the record type:

```
type LIST_ELEMENT is
record
   NEXT   : LINK;
   VALUE : INTEGER;
end record;
```

The first part of the list will be a link to the next element in the list, a
pointer. But the type LINK has to be declared. The declaration should be:

```
type LINK is access LIST_ELEMENT;
```

The question is simply: 'Where should it be placed among the
declarations?' If we put it after the declaration of the type LIST_ELEMENT
it is not so good because the type LINK is then undefined when the type
LIST_ELEMENT is declared. If we put the declaration of LINK before that

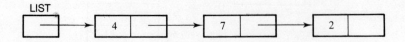

Figure 11.6

of LIST_ELEMENT, then LIST_ELEMENT will be undefined when LINK is declared.

The solution is to start with an **incomplete type declaration** where it is only stated that LIST_ELEMENT is a type:

type LIST_ELEMENT;

When an incomplete type declaration has been made, the type name may then be used in other type declarations. Later (in the same part of the program) a **full type declaration** must be made. Variables of the type may not be declared until the full type declaration has been made.

Using the above, we can now describe our linked list with the declarations:

type LIST_ELEMENT;
type LINK **is access** LIST_ELEMENT;
type LIST_ELEMENT **is**
  record
    NEXT   : LINK;
    VALUE : INTEGER;
  end record;

We shall now look at how a linked list is built up using these type declarations. We start by declaring an access variable:

LIST : LINK;

This variable automatically takes the value **null** on declaration, which describes the fact that the list is empty. We can create a new element and add it to the list:

LIST := **new** LIST_ELEMENT;

LIST will now point at the new list element and we can easily put an integer into the list:

LIST.VALUE := 5;

The first part of the list element, the pointer to the next element in the list, automatically gets the value **null** when the element of the list is created. It now looks like Figure 11.7. It would be easier to achieve this by initializing the new element as soon as it is created:

LIST := **new** LIST_ELEMENT'(**null**, 5);

LIST

Figure 11.7

Assume that we now want to create another element in the list containing the value 3. This element should be placed first in the list. One way of achieving this is to declare a new access variable:

```
NEW_LIST : LINK;
```

and then use the following statements:

```
NEW_LIST          := new LIST_ELEMENT;
NEW_LIST.NEXT   := LIST;
NEW_LIST.VALUE := 3;
LIST              := NEW_LIST;
```

The situation is illustrated in Figure 11.8.

A simpler way of adding the second element is to write:

```
LIST := new LIST_ELEMENT'(LIST, 3);
```

Perhaps the most elegant method of placing a new element into a list is to use the procedure PUT_FIRST:

```
procedure PUT_FIRST (DATA : in INTEGER;
                     L      : in out LINK) is
begin
  L := new LIST_ELEMENT'(L, DATA);
end PUT_FIRST;
```

If we assume that the variable LIST has the value **null** at the start, then we can build up the list in Figure 11.8 by making the calls:

```
PUT_FIRST(5, LIST);
PUT_FIRST(3, LIST);
```

Note that the parameter L in the procedure must be an **in out** parameter because it has to be both read and updated. Using this procedure it is easy to build up a list of arbitrary length by placing new elements first in the list.

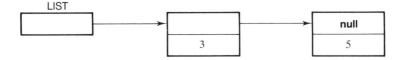

Figure 11.8

11.2.2   Running through a list

If we want to run through all the elements in a list it is easily achieved by starting at the first element and continuing until the last element is reached. The following program construct can be used to write out all the elements in a list of integers:

```
P := LIST;
while P /= null loop
   PUT(P.VALUE);
   P := P.NEXT;
end loop;
```

We have made use of another access variable P of type LINK. This construct works whether the list is empty (LIST has the value **null**) or contains elements. In the latter case, the pointer in the last element will have the value **null**.

In the next example we shall work with a register in which each element contains information about a certain person. The type declaration describes how the register should appear:

```
type PERSON;
type PERSON_LINK is access PERSON;
subtype NAME_TYPE is STRING(1 .. 20);
type PERSON is
   record
      NEXT    : PERSON_LINK;
      NAME    : NAME_TYPE;
      LENGTH : INTEGER;
      WEIGHT : FLOAT;
   end record;
```

We shall study a function that searches for a particular person in such a list. If the person is in the list, the function returns the pointer to the corresponding element in the list, otherwise it will return the value **null**. The function gets the required person's name as parameter and a pointer to the head of the list to be searched.

```
function FIND_PERSON (REQ_NAME : NAME_TYPE;
                      L          : PERSON_LINK)
                      return PERSON_LINK is
   P : PERSON_LINK := L;
begin
   while P /= null and then P.NAME /= REQ_NAME loop
      P := P.NEXT;
   end loop;
   return P;
end FIND_PERSON;
```

In the function, the pointer P is made to run all through the list until it is finished (P has the value **null**) or until the required person is found.

Note that it is important to use **and then** in the Boolean expression in the **loop** statement. If the list runs out then P has the value **null**. If the value of P.NAME were evaluated then, a run-time error would result because P does not point at anything. The use of **and then** ensures that this does not happen.

11.2.3 Putting elements into a list and removing them

We have seen from the above that we can easily put a new element first in a list. To put a new element last in a list is a little more difficult because the whole list has to be run through until the end is reached. The following procedure creates a new element and puts it last in a list of integers. We assume that the types LINK and LIST_ELEMENT are declared in the same way as before.

```
procedure PUT_LAST (DATA : in INTEGER;
                    L     : in out LINK) is
   P1, P2 : LINK;
begin
   if L = null then
      -- Empty list, put in new element first
      L := new LIST_ELEMENT'(null, DATA);
   else
      P1 := L;
      while P1 /= null loop
         P2 := P1;      -- let P2 be one step after P1
         P1 := P1.NEXT;
      end loop;

      -- P2 now points at the last element
      -- Insert new element after P2
      P2.NEXT := new LIST_ELEMENT'(null, DATA);
   end if;
end PUT_LAST;
```

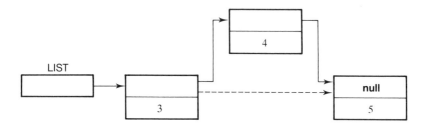

Figure 11.9

The case of the empty list must be treated separately because in that case the pointer L has to be changed. If the list is not empty the pointer P1 is made to run through the whole list until P1 becomes **null** and the end of the list has been reached. The pointer P2 lags one element behind P1. This means that when P1 reaches the end of the list P2 will be pointing at the last element in the list. Therefore the new element has to be placed after the element that P2 is pointing at.

It is sometimes necessary to place a new element in a particular position in a linked list. Suppose, for example, we have an element in a list and a pointer P is pointing at it. Now suppose we want to put a new element with value 4 *after* this. The new element can then be created and placed in the list with a single statement:

    P.NEXT := **new** LIST_ELEMENT'(P.NEXT, 4);

Figure 11.9 illustrates this. The dashed line shows the situation before the statement above is executed. If we wanted to insert a new element *in front of* a particular element that is pointed to, it would be much more trouble. Then we would need to run through the list from the beginning in order to get access to the element in front of the one pointed to.

In certain cases it is simple to remove elements from a list. The first element can be removed with the statement:

    LIST := LIST.NEXT;

This is demonstrated in Figure 11.10.

It is also easy to remove the element coming after one to which there is a pointer. For example, we can remove the element that lies after the one that P points to:

    P.NEXT := P.NEXT.NEXT;

It is a little more trouble to remove the last element, or the one before an

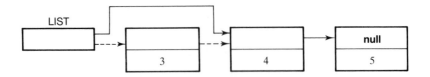

Figure 11.10

element to which there is a pointer. In these cases, as in the procedure PUT_LAST, we would have to use the technique of two pointers, one lagging one step behind the other.

11.2.4   Linked lists and recursion

A list can be seen as a **recursive data type**, and it can be said that a list consists of two components, a **head** and a **tail**. The head is the value in the first element of the list and the tail is a list consisting of all the elements except the first. Thus the tail is a list that is one element shorter than the original. This perspective can be extremely useful in solving certain problems involving list handling.

We saw above that it is possible to write out the contents of a list by going through the elements of the list from start to finish using a **loop** statement. That was easily done. It would have been much harder if we had wanted them written out in reverse order, with the last element written first. But this problem can be solved elegantly using recursion. We shall study a procedure that writes out a list of integers in reverse order:

```
procedure WRITE_REVERSE (LIST : in LINK) is
begin
  if LIST /= null then
    WRITE_REVERSE (LIST.NEXT);
    PUT(LIST.VALUE);
  end if;
end WRITE_REVERSE;
```

This says that a list can be written out in reverse order if we first write out its tail in reverse order and then write out its head. The list's head is accessed by writing LIST.VALUE, and LIST.NEXT is a pointer to the list's tail. An empty list has no elements and there is nothing to write for such a list.

We have already studied the problem of placing a new element at the end of a list, but it can be solved much more simply using recursion. The following algorithm is used:

> If the list is empty then the new element is the list's only element and is thus placed at the start of the list, otherwise the new element should be placed at the end of the tail.

This algorithm is easily translated into this recursive procedure:

```
procedure PUT_LAST (DATA : in INTEGER;
                    LIST  : in out LINK) is
begin
  if LIST = null then
    LIST := new LIST_ELEMENT'(null, DATA);
  else
    PUT_LAST(DATA, LIST.NEXT);
  end if;
end PUT_LAST;
```

11.3 Doubly linked lists

One problem with the lists studied so far is that the whole list has to be run through – using either iteration or recursion – if an element has to be inserted or removed at the end of the list or in front of an element to which there is an access value. If it is necessary to work with a list and these operations, it can therefore be appropriate to construct a **doubly linked list**. In such a list, each element contains two access values apart from the value. One pointer points to the next element in the list, and the other points to the previous element. Figure 11.11 illustrates this concept.

Such a list is often made circular, as in Figure 11.11, by making the forward access value of the last element point to the first element and the first element's backward access value point to the last element. To

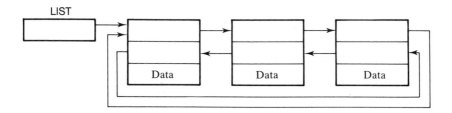

Figure 11.11

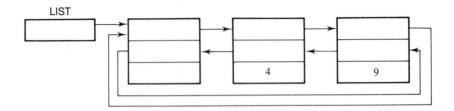

Figure 11.12

describe an element in a doubly linked list of integers we can make the
type declarations:

```
type LIST_ELEMENT;
type LINK is access LIST_ELEMENT;
type LIST_ELEMENT is
  record
     NEXT      : LINK;
     PREVIOUS : LINK;
     VALUE     : INTEGER;
  end record;
```

In work with linked lists, an empty list must be handled in a special way.
This makes the program a little longer and more complicated. To avoid
this problem it is useful to let every list have a special element at the start
of the list, but which does not belong to the list itself. This is particularly
useful when handling doubly linked lists. If, for example, we want to
represent a list of integers that contain two elements, 4 and 9, we can do
this with the list in Figure 11.12. Note that the first element, whose value
is of no importance, does not belong to the logical list. If this technique of
a special first element is used the empty list can be described as in
Figure 11.13.

   If we assume that the variable LIST has type LINK then the structure
in Figure 11.13 can be built up with the statements:

```
LIST          := new LIST_ELEMENT;
LIST.NEXT     := LIST;
LIST.PREVIOUS := LIST;
```

It is even simpler, of course, to use a record aggregate and write instead:

```
LIST   := new LIST_ELEMENT;
LIST.all := (LIST, LIST, 0);
```

LIST

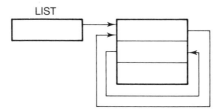

Figure 11.13

The advantage of a doubly linked list is that it is never necessary to run through one in order to make changes. Let us look at the example of removing an arbitrary element from a list. Assume we have a list of integers containing the values 4, 7 and 9, as shown in Figure 11.14. The access value P points at the element to be removed. Now we can write a procedure REMOVE:

```
procedure REMOVE (P : in LINK) is
begin
  P.PREVIOUS.NEXT := P.NEXT;
  P.NEXT.PREVIOUS := P.PREVIOUS;
end REMOVE;
```

and make the call:

```
REMOVE(P);
```

The result is that the element that P is pointing at – the 'target' element – will be 'linked out' of the list. The statement:

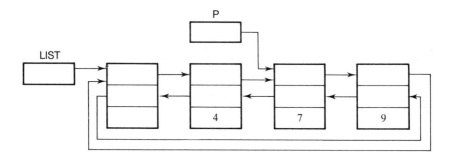

Figure 11.14

```
    P.PREVIOUS.NEXT := P.NEXT;
```

means that the forward access value in the element in front of the target
will point to the one after the target. Correspondingly, the statement;

```
    P.NEXT.PREVIOUS := P.PREVIOUS;
```

means that the backward access value in the element after the target
element will point at the element in front of the target. (We do not need
to worry about changing the access values in the target element. To do a
thorough job, these could be set to **null**).

For the next example we shall take a procedure that creates a new
element and puts it at the end of a doubly linked list:

```
    procedure PUT_LAST (DATA : in INTEGER;
                        L      : in LINK) is
       PNEW : LINK := new LIST_ELEMENT'(L, L.PREVIOUS, DATA);

    begin
       PNEW.PREVIOUS.NEXT := PNEW;
       PNEW.NEXT.PREVIOUS := PNEW;
    end PUT_LAST;
```

The declaration:

```
    PNEW : LINK := new LIST_ELEMENT'(L, L.PREVIOUS, DATA);
```

causes a new element to be created and the access value PNEW to point at
it. The new element is initialized so that its forward access value points at
the list's start element (the element that L points at) and its backward
access value points at the element that was previously last in the list
(pointed at by L.PREVIOUS).

The statement:

```
    PNEW.PREVIOUS.NEXT := PNEW;
```

ensures that the forward access value in the element that was previously
last in the list will point at the new element, and the statement:

```
    PNEW.NEXT.PREVIOUS := PNEW;
```

ensures that the backward access value in the start element points at the
new element.

A further example using doubly linked lists is this procedure that puts a new element first in a list. The new element should be placed after the start element.

```
procedure PUT_FIRST ( DATA : in INTEGER;
                      L     : in   LINK) is
    PNEW : LINK := new LIST_ELEMENT'(L.NEXT, L, DATA);

begin
    PNEW.PREVIOUS.NEXT := PNEW;
    PNEW.NEXT.PREVIOUS := PNEW;
end PUT_FIRST;
```

Note that the use of a special start element in a list means that the access value L does not need to be changed in any of the procedures shown in this section. This has the advantage that we have not had to give special treatment to the insertion or removal of an element first or last in the list.

11.4 Stacks and queues

Two common data structures are **stacks** and **queues**. A queue is a structure that works on the well-known principle 'first in – first out'. Data objects are placed at the end of the queue and taken from the front. A stack is a data structure that uses the principle 'last in – first out'. A stack can be likened to a pile of plates in a self-service cafeteria. When plates are placed on the pile they go on top of those already there, and when you take a plate from the pile you only take the top one. There is often a spring that keeps the top of the pile at a suitable level for customers. There are two operations for stacks, **push** and **pop**, which work on the **top** object in the stack. The operation **push** puts a data element on top of the stack and **pop** removes the top element from the stack. A stack can be illustrated as in Figure 11.15.

A stack can easily be constructed using a singly linked list. The first element in the list is the top of the stack. To demonstrate this we construct a package that describes an abstract data type CHAR_STACK, a stack on which objects of type CHARACTER can be placed. The specification of the package is as follows:

```
package STACK_PACKAGE is
    type CHAR_STACK is limited private;

    procedure PUSH (S : in out CHAR_STACK;
                    C : in CHARACTER);
    procedure POP  (S : in out CHAR_STACK;
                    C : out CHARACTER);
    function EMPTY (S : CHAR_STACK) return BOOLEAN;
```

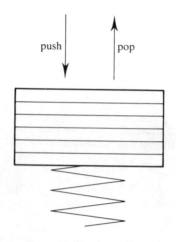

Figure 11.15

```
private
    type STACK_ELEMENT;
    type CHAR_STACK is access STACK_ELEMENT;
end STACK_PACKAGE;
```

The type CHAR_STACK is a limited private type. This means that the user of the package does not know what a stack really looks like – it is not 'visible'. The only thing a user may do is declare objects of the type CHAR_STACK and have parameters of type CHAR_STACK in calls to subprograms.

The concept assumes that the user should only work on a stack through calls to the procedures PUSH and POP as given in the package specification. Both of these have a stack as the first parameter. Since the stack is updated by calls to these procedures, this first parameter is an **in out** parameter. PUSH has as **in** parameter the character that is to be placed on top of the stack; POP has as **out** parameter the character that is removed from the stack. In addition to PUSH and POP, a function EMPTY is defined. The user can call this to find out whether there are any objects stored in the stack.

Finally, the package has a private part that is not visible to the user. First, there is an incomplete type declaration (see Section 11.2.1) stating that STACK_ELEMENT is a type. The private type CHAR_STACK is then declared as access type to an object of type STACK_ELEMENT. The complete declaration of STACK_ELEMENT could have been placed last in the package specification but, since this does not need to be known for a user program to be compiled, it is preferable to place it in the body of the package instead. In this way there are as few details as possible about the internal appearance of a stack in the package specification.

Now we can construct and compile programs that use the specification of STACK_PACKAGE. We shall show the example of a program that reads in text from the terminal and writes it out in reverse order:

```
with TEXT_IO, BASIC_NUM_IO, STACK_PACKAGE;
use  TEXT_IO, BASIC_NUM_IO, STACK_PACKAGE;
procedure STACK_DEMO is
  STACK : CHAR_STACK;
  CHAR  : CHARACTER;
begin
  PUT_LINE("Enter text. Terminate with CTRL-D");

  -- Read in text and put characters on the stack
  while not END_OF_FILE loop
    GET(CHAR);
    PUSH(STACK, CHAR);
  end loop;

  -- Empty the stack and write out the characters
  while not EMPTY(STACK) loop
    POP(STACK, CHAR);
    PUT(CHAR);
  end loop;
end STACK_DEMO;
```

In the program an object STACK of type CHAR_STACK is declared and then the characters from the text are placed on the stack as they are read, one by one. When all the characters in the text have been read in and put on the stack, they are removed from the stack and written out in the same order. Thus the characters are written out in reverse order.

Before the user program using the package can be executed, the body of the package must be compiled. In the body the detailed appearance of the character stack must be given. The complete declaration of the type STACK_ELEMENT is given here, as are the bodies of the subprograms PUSH, POP and EMPTY.

```
package body STACK_PACKAGE is
  type STACK_ELEMENT is
    record
      CHAR : CHARACTER;
      NEXT : CHAR_STACK;
    end record;

  procedure PUSH (S : in out CHAR_STACK;
                  C : in CHARACTER) is
```

```
begin
  S := new STACK_ELEMENT'(C, S);
end PUSH;

procedure POP (S : in out CHAR_STACK;
                C : out CHARACTER) is
begin
  C := S.CHAR;
  S := S.NEXT;
end POP;

function EMPTY (S : CHAR_STACK) return BOOLEAN is
begin
  return S = null;
end EMPTY;
end STACK_PACKAGE;
```

We see that the stack is quite simply a linked list in which each element contains a character, and that the type CHAR_STACK is an access type for such a list. PUSH puts a new element first in the list and POP takes out the first element from the list. If the stack is empty there are no elements in the list and, in this case, the access value to the first element of the list has the value **null**.

Now let us study how to build up a queue that works on the first in–first out principle. A queue, like a stack, can be seen as an abstract data type – a package can be constructed to describe the abstract data type 'queue'. We shall consider the example of a queue in which objects describing people can be placed. The specification may look like this:

```
package QUEUE_PACKAGE is
  type PERSON is
    record
      NAME    : STRING(1 .. 20);
      ADDRESS : STRING(1 .. 30);
    end record;

  type PERSON_QUEUE is limited private;

  procedure INIT  (Q : out PERSON_QUEUE);

  function EMPTY (Q : PERSON_QUEUE) return BOOLEAN;

  procedure PUT_LAST (Q     : in out PERSON_QUEUE;
                      PERS : in PERSON);

  procedure GET_FIRST (Q     : in out PERSON_QUEUE;
                       PERS : out PERSON);

  EMPTY_QUEUE : EXCEPTION
```

```
private
  type QUEUE_ELEMENT;
  type LINK is access QUEUE_ELEMENT;
  type PERSON_QUEUE is
    record
      FIRST : LINK;
      LAST  : LINK;
    end record;
end QUEUE_PACKAGE;
```

First in the specification is a description of what a person looks like; in this case simply a record consisting of a name and address. Then PERSON_QUEUE is declared to be a limited private type. A user of the package can only handle a queue by calling the subprograms given in the specification. The procedure INIT is used to initiate a queue before it can start to be used. This procedure ensures that the queue is empty. INIT can also be used if a queue that has already been used has to be emptied. The function EMPTY states whether there are people in the queue, and the procedures PUT_LAST and GET_FIRST are used to put a person into a queue or take a person away.

In the private part of the specification – in the part not visible to the user – the type PERSON_QUEUE is described. We have chosen to represent a queue by a record containing two access values. The first points to the first element of the queue and the second points to the queue's last element. The compiler does not need to know what an element looks like in order to compile a user program; in the specification, therefore, we give only an incomplete declaration of the type QUEUE_ELEMENT. The complete declaration is given in the body of the package.

In the body of the package are all the details for constructing a queue. We have chosen to use a singly linked list, but in addition to the ordinary access value to the first element of the list we also have an access value to the list's last element. This means that we avoid running through the list every time we want to insert an element at the end. We have collected the access values to the first and last elements into one record. Figure 11.16 shows how this looks.

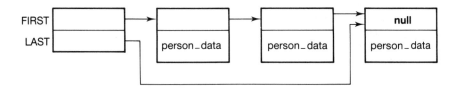

Figure 11.16

The body of the package is as follows:

```
package body QUEUE_PACKAGE is
  type QUEUE_ELEMENT is
    record
      NEXT : LINK;
      DATA : PERSON;
    end record;

  procedure INIT (Q : out PERSON_QUEUE) is
  begin
    Q := (null, null);
  end INIT;

  function EMPTY (Q : PERSON_QUEUE) return BOOLEAN is
  begin
    return Q.FIRST = null;
  end EMPTY;

  procedure PUT_LAST (Q      : in out PERSON_QUEUE;
                      PERS : in PERSON) is
    PNEW : LINK := new QUEUE_ELEMENT' (null, PERS);
  begin
    if Q.FIRST = null then
        -- empty queue, put element first
        Q.FIRST := PNEW;
    else
        -- revise previous last
        Q.LAST.NEXT := PNEW;
    end if;
    Q.LAST := PNEW;
  end PUT_LAST;

  procedure GET_FIRST (Q      : in out PERSON_QUEUE;
                       PERS : out PERSON) is
  begin
    if Q.FIRST /= null then
      PERS := Q.FIRST.DATA;
      Q.FIRST := Q.FIRST.NEXT;
      if Q.FIRST = null then
          -- queue has been emptied
          Q.LAST := null;
      end if;
    else raise EMPTY_QUEUE;
    end if;
  end GET_FIRST;
end QUEUE_PACKAGE;
```

The procedure INIT simply assigns the value **null** to the two pointers
Q.FIRST and Q.LAST. A new element is created in the procedure

PUT_LAST. This should be linked in at the end of the queue, that is, normally after the element that Q.LAST points to. However, we must consider the case of an element that is placed into an empty queue. In this case the new element is placed first in the list. In both cases the access value Q.LAST should point to the new element after the insertion.

In the procedure GET_FIRST it is also necessary, when taking out the first element of the queue, to pay special attention to the case in which the queue becomes empty. In this case the access value Q.LAST should be given the value **null**.

Finally we shall show a program that uses QUEUE_PACKAGE to set up a reservation system. The program reads in people's names and addresses from the terminal. When input is finished, the program writes out a list of the queue in which the people appear in the same order as they were read in.

```
with TEXT_IO, QUEUE_PACKAGE;
use  TEXT_IO, QUEUE_PACKAGE;
procedure MAKE_RESERVATION is
  QUEUE : PERSON_QUEUE;
  P     : PERSON;
  L     : NATURAL;

begin
  INIT(QUEUE);
  PUT_LINE("Terminate input with CTRL-D");

  loop
    PUT("Name: ");
    exit when END_OF_FILE;
    GET_LINE(P.NAME, L);
    -- Pad name with blanks on right
    P.NAME(L+1 .. P.NAME'LAST) := (others => ' ');
    PUT("Address: ");
    GET_LINE(P.ADDRESS, L);
    -- Pad address with blanks on right
    P.ADDRESS(L+1 .. P.ADDRESS'LAST) := (others => ' ');
    PUT_LAST(QUEUE, P);
  end loop;

  NEW_LINE(2);
  PUT_LINE("The queue");
  NEW_LINE;
  while not EMPTY(QUEUE) loop
    GET_FIRST(QUEUE, P);
    PUT_LINE(P.NAME);
    PUT_LINE(P.ADDRESS);
    NEW_LINE;
  end loop;
end MAKE_RESERVATION;
```

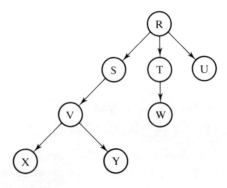

Figure 11.17

11.5 Trees

In Section 11.3 of this chapter dealing with doubly linked lists, we saw that each element could have two pointers. There is naturally no limit on the number of pointers in each element and these pointers do not need to point in such a way as to define a linked list. Using pointers, it is possible to build up data structures with elements that are connected arbitrarily. In this section we shall study **trees** – common data structures in which the elements are connected using pointers. A tree is illustrated in Figure 11.17.

The elements of a tree are usually called **nodes**. The topmost node is called the tree's **root**. (It is usual to draw and think of a tree in an upside-down position compared with the real thing). From the root there can be pointers to other nodes in the tree but there can never be pointers *to* the root from any of the tree's nodes. In general, there are only pointers 'downwards' from each node in the tree. To each node there is only one unique path from the root. (For example, in Figure 11.17 it is only possible to take path R–S–V–Y to get to the node Y). Thus, there may only be one pointer to any one node.

If a node A points to a node B in a tree, the node B is said to be the **child** of A and A is said to be the **parent** of B. The root is the only node that is without a parent. The nodes that have no children, X, Y, W and U in our example, are usually called **leaves** and the pointers in the tree are sometimes called **arcs**.

In the tree in Figure 11.17 the nodes have up to three children. We shall limit ourselves, however, to trees in which a node can have at most two children. Such trees are common in the construction of data structures and they are generally called **binary trees**. An example of a binary tree is shown in Figure 11.18.

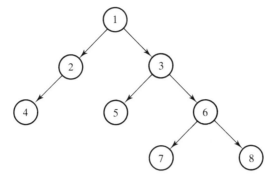

Figure 11.18

Trees

- A *root* is a node that no other node in the tree points to.
- To any one node there is a *unique* path from the root.
- The nodes that do not have pointers to other nodes are called *leaves*.

A node in a binary tree can be described by a record type:

```
type NODE;
type LINK is access NODE;
type NODE is record
  DATA : INTEGER;
  LEFT, RIGHT : LINK;
end record;
```

Each node consists of a data section describing the contents of the node and two access values that point to the node's left and right children, respectively. In our example the data part consists of an integer. If a node is lacking a child the corresponding access value is **null**. In a leaf, both the access values are **null**. The tree in Figure 11.18 can be built up as indicated in Figure 11.19. A special pointer ROOT points at the root of the tree so that the whole tree can be accessed. If we have an empty tree (a tree with no nodes) then ROOT has the value **null**.

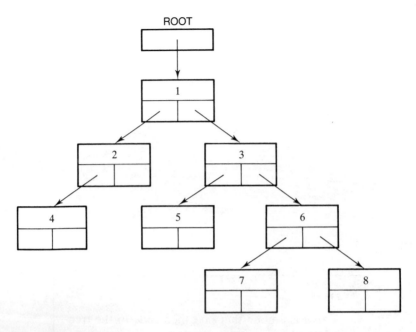

Figure 11.19

If we want to build up a tree according to Figure 11.20 we can use the statements:

```
ROOT              := new NODE;
ROOT.DATA         := 10;
ROOT.LEFT         := new NODE;
ROOT.RIGHT        := new NODE;
ROOT.LEFT.DATA    := 20;
ROOT.RIGHT.DATA   := 30;
```

where we assume that ROOT has an access value of type LINK. Alternatively, this can be achieved in a single statement:

```
ROOT := new NODE' (10, new NODE' (20,null,null),
                       new NODE' (30,null,null) );
```

The nodes that lie to the left of the root can be considered as a new smaller tree with the left child of the root as its root. This tree is said to be the left **subtree** of the original tree. In the same way, the nodes to the right of the root form a right subtree. Figure 11.21 illustrates this. (For example, the left subtree in Figure 11.18 has node 2 as its root and comprises nodes 2 and 4. The right subtree has node 3 as its root and comprises nodes 3, 5, 6, 7 and 8).

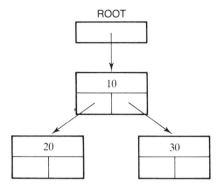

Figure 11.20

With the help of subtrees, a tree can be regarded as a recursive data type and the following definition can be given:

A binary tree is either empty (has no nodes); or consists of a root, a left subtree and a right subtree.

This concept is useful in the design of programs for handling trees. We shall start by studying how to visit all the nodes of a given tree. We assume that we have a pointer ROOT which points at the root of the tree. When we considered linked lists it was natural to visit all the elements starting at the beginning and running through to the end; but it is not that simple with a tree. It is possible to think of several alternative ways of traversing a tree.

If we look at the tree in Figure 11.18, for example, we may think of visiting the nodes in the order, 1–2–3–4–5–6–7–8. However, to write a program for this is rather difficult. It is much simpler and more common to apply the three visiting orders – **preorder**, **inorder** and **postorder** –

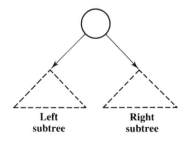

Figure 11.21

Figure 11.22

which are defined recursively. Let us start with the most common, inorder:

If the tree is not empty, then:

(1)   Visit the tree's left subtree.

(2)   Visit the tree's root.

(3)   Visit the tree's right subtree.

We shall now try to apply this visiting order to the tree in Figure 11.18. First we note that the tree is not empty and so the three stages of the algorithm should be carried out. The first stage 'visit the tree's left subtree' means that the tree in Figure 11.22 should be visited. Since this is also a tree, the visiting algorithm (second instance) should be applied. The tree is not empty and so we carry out Stage (1), that is, the subtree in Figure 11.23 is visited.

We now apply a third instance of the algorithm. Since the tree is not empty we carry out the first stage, 'visit the left subtree'; this means that we have to apply a fourth instance of the algorithm. This time the tree to be visited is empty because node 4 has an empty left subtree, and the fourth instance of the algorithm thus does nothing. We return to the third instance of the algorithm and carry out its second stage, 'visit the tree's root'. This means that node 4 is visited. The third stage, 'visit the tree's right subtree', starts a fifth instance of the algorithm which does nothing because the right subtree is empty.

Now all the stages of the third instance of the algorithm have been carried out and we return to the second instance of the algorithm. We carry out the second stage, 'visit the tree's root' for the tree in Figure 11.22. Thus node 2 gets a visit.

Since the tree in Figure 11.22 has an empty right subtree nothing happens when a sixth instance of the algorithm is carried out and we return eventually to the first instance of the algorithm. We carry out the second stage, which means that the root of the original tree, node 1, is visited.

Now we have visited nodes 4, 2 and 1, in that order, and continue by applying the algorithm in the same way to the right subtree. We

Figure 11.23

eventually find that all the nodes in the tree are visited, in the order
4–2–1–5–3–7–6–8.

The following recursive procedure visits and writes out the contents
of the nodes of a binary tree according to the inorder principle. The
procedure needs a pointer to the root of the tree as parameter.

```
procedure IN_ORDER (P : LINK) is
begin
   if P /= null then
      IN_ORDER(P.LEFT);
      PUT(P.DATA);
      IN_ORDER(P.RIGHT);
   end if;
end IN_ORDER;
```

Definitions of the other visiting orders can be made in a similar
way. The only difference is that the three stages in the algorithm already
studied are rearranged. The algorithm for visiting all the nodes of a tree
according to the principle of preorder can be described as follows:

If the tree is not empty, then:

(1)   Visit the tree's root.

(2)   Visit the tree's left subtree.

(3)   Visit the tree's right subtree.

If we visit the nodes in Figure 11.18, for example, we get the visiting
order 1–2–4–3–5–6–7–8 according to this principle. The procedure:

```
procedure PRE_ORDER (P : in LINK) is
begin
   if P /= null then
      PUT(P.DATA);
      PRE_ORDER(P.LEFT);
      PRE_ORDER(P.RIGHT);
   end if;
end PRE_ORDER;
```

writes out the contents of the nodes according to the principle preorder. The definition for the third visiting order, postorder, is:

If the tree is not empty, then:

(1)   Visit the tree's left subtree.

(2)   Visit the tree's right subtree.

(3)   Visit the tree's root.

Applying this principle, the nodes in Figure 11.18 are visited in the order 4–2–5–7–8–6–3–1. The following procedure writes out the contents of the nodes of a tree according to the postorder principle:

```
procedure POST_ORDER (P : in LINK) is
begin
  if P /= null then
    POST_ORDER(P.LEFT);
    POST_ORDER(P.RIGHT);
    PUT(P.DATA);
  end if;
end POST_ORDER;
```

As we see, the algorithms for trees are naturally expressed using recursion. We shall now study a function that evaluates the **depth** of a binary tree. The function takes a pointer to the root of the tree as parameter. The depth of a tree can be defined as the number of nodes on the longest path from the tree's root to a leaf. An empty tree has depth 0 and a tree that consists of only a root has depth 1. We write the function:

```
function DEPTH (P : LINK) return NATURAL is
  L_DEPTH, R_DEPTH : NATURAL;
begin
  if P = null then
    return 0;
  else
    L_DEPTH := DEPTH(P.LEFT);
    R_DEPTH := DEPTH(P.RIGHT);
    if L_DEPTH > R_DEPTH then
      return L_DEPTH + 1;
    else
      return R_DEPTH + 1;
    end if;
  end if;
end DEPTH;
```

The simplest case is if the tree is empty. The function then returns the value 0 as its result. If the tree is not empty, the depths of the left and

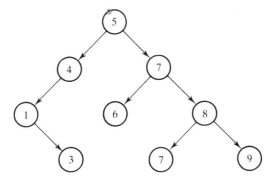

Figure 11.24

right subtrees are evaluated separately and saved in the variables L_DEPTH and R_DEPTH. The function DEPTH is called recursively to evaluate these depths, with access values to the respective subtrees as parameter. The function returns the depth of the deepest subtree plus 1 (the root itself) as its result.

We can now study a special form of binary tree, a **binary search tree**. The value of each node in such a tree is greater than the values of all the nodes in its left subtree and less than or equal to the values of the nodes in its right subtree. The tree in Figure 11.24 is an example of a binary search tree.

A binary search tree has the property that if the principle of inorder is used to traverse the tree, the nodes will be visited in order of size. The nodes in our example, Figure 11.24, will be visited in the order 1–3–4–5–6–7–7–8–9.

A binary search tree can be used when information has to be found quickly. Let us study the example of a binary search tree in which each node contains information about a person. Each node stores a person's name and address. We have the type declarations:

```
subtype NAME_TYPE     is STRING(1 .. 20);
subtype ADDRESS_TYPE is STRING(1 .. 30);

type NODE;

type LINK is access NODE;

type NODE is
  record
    NAME        : NAME_TYPE;
    ADDRESS     : ADDRESS_TYPE;
    LEFT, RIGHT : LINK;
  end record;
```

We can use the following function to find the node in the tree which contains the information about a particular person. The function has two **in** parameters, an access value to the tree and the name of the required person. As its result, the function returns an access value to the node in which the information about the person is stored. If the required person is not found in the tree, the function returns the value **null**.

```
function FIND (ROOT       : in LINK;
                REQ_NAME : in NAME_TYPE) return LINK is
begin
  if ROOT = null then
    return null;
  elsif ROOT.NAME = REQ_NAME then
    return ROOT;
  elsif REQ_NAME < ROOT.NAME then
    return FIND(ROOT.LEFT, REQ_NAME);
  else
    return FIND(ROOT.RIGHT, REQ_NAME);
  end if;
end FIND;
```

The search works as follows. First it checks to see whether the tree is empty and, if so, the result **null** is returned because there are no entries in the tree. If the root contains the required person then the task is easy; the result is simply the access value of the root. In other cases it must look further into one of the subtrees. The particular subtree depends on whether the required name comes alphabetically before or after the name in the root. This further searching is achieved by calling the function FIND recursively with an access value to either the right or left subtree as parameter.

To remove nodes in such a way that the tree remains a binary search tree is somewhat complicated (see Exercise 11.18). However, to insert new nodes is simple and we finish by showing a procedure for placing information about a new person into a binary search tree as described above. As parameters, the procedure takes an access value to the root of the tree and the new person's name and address. The procedure has to create a new node for the new person and insert it in the correct place in the tree so that the tree remains a binary search tree.

```
procedure INSERT (ROOT         : in out LINK;
                  NEW_NAME     : in NAME_TYPE;
                  NEW_ADDRESS : in ADDRESS_TYPE) is
begin
  if ROOT = null then
    ROOT := new NODE'(NEW_NAME, NEW_ADDRESS, null, null);
```

```
    elsif NEW_NAME < ROOT.NAME then
        INSERT(ROOT.LEFT, NEW_NAME, NEW_ADDRESS);
    else
        INSERT(ROOT.RIGHT, NEW_NAME, NEW_ADDRESS);
    end if;
end INSERT;
```

If the tree is empty it is easy to insert the entry in the right place. The new node is then the root of the tree and the access value ROOT is set to point at this node. Note that the parameter ROOT must be an **in out** parameter because it must be both read and updated. If the tree is not empty, a choice must be made as to whether to insert the new node in the left or the right subtree, depending on whether the person's name comes alphabetically before or after the name in the root of the tree.

EXERCISES

11.1 A queue of cars is to be described using a linked list. Write the part of a program that creates a list describing a queue of three cars. For each car the registration number, make and year should be stored.

11.2 Write a function to evaluate the length of a linked list.

11.3 Assume you have a linked list in which the data part of each element contains an integer. Write a function to determine whether the list is sorted.

11.4 A register of club members has been built up in the form of a linked list. Each member is represented by an element in the list, in which the name, address and telephone number are stored. The list is sorted alphabetically according to the member's name.

Write a procedure to insert a new member into the list, so that the list remains sorted.

11.5 Write a function that receives an access value to a singly linked list L as parameter. As its result the function should return the access value to a new list containing copies of all the elements of L but in reverse order.

11.6 A polynomial such as:

$$f(x) = 7.4x^5 + 3.1x^2 - 10.2x + 14.9$$

can be represented as a linked list in which every element corresponds to a term in the polynomial. The corresponding term's coefficient and degree is stored in each element. The polynomial above, for example, can be represented by the list:

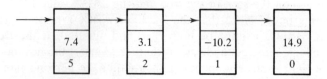

We assume that there is at most one element for any given degree and that the elements are sorted so that the highest degree comes first.

(a) Write a function that calculates the value of a polynomial for a given value of x. As parameters the function receives an access value to the list that represents the polynomial and the given value of x.

(b) Write a function that creates a new list to represent the sum of two polynomials, $P_1(x)$ and $P_2(x)$. As parameters the function gets access values to the two lists representing P_1 and P_2, and as its result it returns the access value to the new list which represents the sum of the two polynomials. The lists representing P_1 and P_2 should not be altered by the function.

(c) The **derivative** of a polynomial:

$$P(x) = a_nx^n + a_{n-1}x^{n-1} + \ldots + a_1x + a_0$$

can be written as:

$$P'(x) = na_nx^{n-1} + (n-1)a_{n-1}x^{n-2} + \ldots + a_1$$

The derivative of the polynomial above, for example, can be written as:

$$f'(x) = 37x^4 + 6.2x - 10.2$$

Write a function that creates a new list representing the derivative of a given polynomial $P(x)$.

11.7 A **sparse matrix** is one in which most of the elements are zero. To save storage space, such a matrix can be represented as a linked list. In the list there is one element for each non-zero matrix element containing its line and column numbers and its value.

Write a function that receives a sparse matrix in the normal format (a two-dimensional array) as a parameter. Assume that all the elements in the matrix are integers. The function should create a list to represent the sparse matrix. The result of the function should be the access value to the list.

11.8 A **graph** is a general data structure in which a number of nodes are connected to one another in an arbitrary manner. A graph in which the nodes contain characters can, for example, be written:

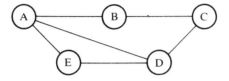

Directed graphs are those in which a particular direction is associated with each link between two nodes. Arrows are usually drawn instead of lines:

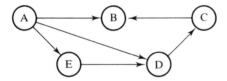

One way of representing a directed graph is to use an **access table**, where each node of the graph is represented by an entry in a table (a one-dimensional array). Each entry stores the data part of the corresponding node (a character in the example above) and an access value to a linked list. The linked list describes the single paths from the given node to other nodes in the graph, and contains one element for each path. The directed graph in the example above can, for example, be represented by:

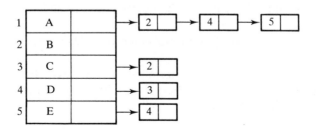

(a)   Write a subprogram that inserts a path between two nodes in a directed graph as represented above. The subprogram takes the access table and two node numbers that state the two nodes that are connected.

(b)   Write a subprogram that removes a connection between one node and another.

(c)   An access table is not very convenient if the number of nodes in a graph must be changed or if nodes must be easily added or removed. In these situations, an access table can be replaced by a linked list in which each element contains the same information as an element of the access table above. Rewrite the subprograms in (a) and (b), representing a directed graph in this way instead.

11.9   Write a package that describes the abstract data type *integer set*. There should be subprograms in the package to carry out all the usual operations on sets. Use a linked list in the body of the package.

11.10   Write a procedure that swaps two neighbouring elements in a doubly linked list. The procedure should take as parameter an access value to the first of the two elements to be swapped.

11.11   An ordinary pack of cards can be represented using a doubly linked list in which every element corresponds to a card and contains the card's suit and colour. Write a program that builds up a list containing all 52 cards in a pack. The program should then deal the pack out randomly to four players so that they each get 13 cards. For each player the program should build up a linked list containing that player's cards. Finally, the program should write out the cards of the four players.

   Assume there is a package RANDOM_PACKAGE containing a function RANDOM_NUMBER (with no parameters) which returns a floating point number x such that $0 \leqslant x < 1$.

11.12   Rewrite the package QUEUE_PACKAGE in Section 11.4 so that a doubly linked list is used to represent the queue.

11.13   Write a function to count the number of leaves in a binary tree.

11.14   Write a function that determines whether two binary trees are equal, that is, whether they contain the same data and have the same structure.

11.15 A binary tree can be used to represent an arithmetic expression. The expression:

$$\frac{2 \times 3}{8 - 4} + 1$$

can, for example, be represented by:

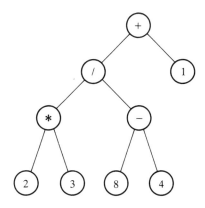

The value of the binary tree can be defined as the value obtained when the corresponding expression is evaluated.

Make the type declarations necessary to describe an arithmetic expression in this way and write a function that calculates the value of a given binary tree.

11.16 Two binary trees can be said to be **reflections** of one another if: (1) both are empty, or (2) both are non-empty, their roots contain the same information, and the right subtree of one is the reflection of the left subtree of the other, and vice versa. Write a function that determines whether two trees are reflections of one another.

11.17 Write a program that reads in a text from a text file and computes how many times different words appear in the text. Use a binary search tree to store the words read together with a counter. Each time a new word has been read from the text file, search to see whether it already appears in the search tree. If it does, increase the word's counter by one. Otherwise, create a new node for the word and insert this node in the correct place in the tree. The program should finish by writing out all the words that have appeared, in alphabetical order, together with the number of times they appeared.

11.18 It is not very difficult to insert a new node into a binary search tree. To remove a node is a little harder. The following algorithm can be applied:

> Call the node to be removed P.
>
> If P is a leaf, set the access value in P's parent that points to P, to null.
>
> If P has a left child but no right child, let P's parent point at P's left child instead of pointing at P.
>
> If P has a right child but no left child, let P's parent point at P's right child instead of pointing at P.
>
> Otherwise, find the node Q in P's right subtree with the smallest value data part. Copy the data part of Q to the node P and remove node Q.

Write a function that removes a given node from a binary search tree.

Chapter 12
Files

12.1 Sequential files
12.2 Sorted files

12.3 Direct files
Exercises

A **file** is an arbitrarily long sequence of data objects where all the objects have the same type (see Figure 12.1). A file can be stored in the computer's secondary storage, for example, on disk, and can therefore be used to store data permanently. Earlier in the book, we discussed text files where the individual objects in a file had the type CHARACTER. In this chapter we review more general files where the data objects are allowed to be of any type. Such general files, where the objects do not have type CHARACTER, are usually called **binary files**. (The objects are actually represented in the same binary form used internally in a program).

In Ada there are two categories of files: **sequential files** where objects must be read and written in their correct order from start to finish; and **direct access files** or **direct files** where an arbitrary object can be accessed without going through the file in a particular order.

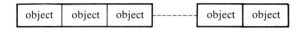

Figure 12.1

12.1 Sequential files

Text files belong to the category of sequential files. Earlier we saw that the package TEXT_IO contains the facilities for handling text files; when we want to work with sequential files other than text files we shall make use of another standard package called SEQUENTIAL_IO (see Appendix D). To gain access to this package the line:

with SEQUENTIAL_IO;

must appear at the start of the program. In a text file the objects are always of type CHARACTER but in the case of other sequential files the objects can be of any type. For this reason SEQUENTIAL_IO is not a 'ready-made' package like TEXT_IO. It is a generic package (a template) that can be used to tailor input/output packages for sequential files in which the objects have exactly the required type.

Other than text files, the most common files to work with are those in which the objects have a record type. Assume we want to collect information about the weight and height of a number of people. We can store the data in a file in which each object is a record containing the person's name, weight and height. There is a record in the file for each person. We have the type declaration:

```
type PERSON is
  record
    NAME   : STRING(1 .. 20);
    WEIGHT : FLOAT;
    HEIGHT : INTEGER;
  end record;
```

The file's structure is made clear in Figure 12.2.

To create a package containing the facilities for handling files in which the objects have type PERSON, we write:

package PERSON_INOUT **is new** SEQUENTIAL_IO(PERSON);

The word PERSON in brackets states that the objects will be of type

Brown	Dodd	Smith		Walton
75.0	90.0	65.0	--------	80.0
180	190	175		183

Figure 12.2

PERSON. The new package will be called PERSON_INOUT. To refer to the package more conveniently, we write:

use PERSON_INOUT;

As in the case of text files, logical files are worked with in a program and file variables are declared to represent the logical files. In TEXT_IO, the type FILE_TYPE could be used to declare logical text files and SEQUENTIAL_IO also had a type called FILE_TYPE. To declare a logical file in which the objects have the type PERSON we can therefore use our new package PERSON_INOUT and write:

PERSON_FILE : PERSON_INOUT.FILE_TYPE;

Note that we have used selector notation and written PERSON_INOUT.FILE_TYPE even though we put in a **use** clause above. The reason is that most programs also use the package TEXT_IO. If we only wrote FILE_TYPE the compiler would not know if we meant the FILE_TYPE specified in TEXT_IO or the FILE_TYPE specified in PERSON_INOUT.

General files have physical names in the computer system. For example, we can imagine that the file described earlier has the physical name person.data. To link a logical file in the program with a physical file, the procedures OPEN and CREATE, also found in the package SEQUENTIAL_IO, are used. These work in exactly the same way for general files as for text files. For example, we can create a new physical file person.data and connect it to the logical file PERSON_FILE by making the call:

CREATE(PERSON_FILE, NAME => "person.data");

Here it is assumed that the file will be used for writing. If the file had already existed, we could have opened it for reading:

OPEN(PERSON_FILE, MODE => IN_FILE, NAME => "person.data");

Reading and writing cannot proceed at the same time in sequential files.

The parameter MODE must be given one of the values IN_FILE or OUT_FILE. There is, however, the possibility of resetting – going back to the beginning of the file and using it in a new way; resetting uses the procedure RESET which also exists for general sequential files. A file is closed with the procedure CLOSE:

CLOSE(PERSON_FILE);

Opening and closing files

- CREATE is used for creating a new file.
- OPEN is used for opening an existing file.
- CLOSE is used for closing a file.
- RESET is used for going back to the start of a file.
- These procedures are specified in the same way as the corresponding procedures for text files.

A file can be erased or deleted by calling the procedure DELETE. In SEQUENTIAL_IO there are also the functions IS_OPEN, MODE, NAME and FORM which can be used to obtain information about a particular file. These subprograms work in the same way as they do for text files.

There is one important difference between text files and general files. In a general sequential file the individual objects may be of any type. Files do not necessarily contain text; therefore it is not possible to talk about pages and lines in a general file. The file only comprises a series of objects. *It is only text files that have page and line structure*, thus everything to do with pages and lines is irrelevant for a general sequential file. It is not possible, for example, to read a line, test whether a line is finished, or write on a new page. The subprograms in TEXT_IO that are concerned with lines and pages (for example, GET_LINE, END_OF_LINE and NEW_PAGE) are not found in the package SEQUENTIAL_IO.

Line and page structure

- Only *text files* have line and page structure.
- There are no lines and pages in general sequential files.
- There are no subprograms concerned with lines and pages.

For reading and writing text files the procedures GET and PUT are used. When numeric values are read and written, these procedures can make the conversion between a sequence of characters and the internal form of representation in the computer. For example, if a variable of type INTEGER is read from a text file, a number of characters are read from the text file and converted into a value of type INTEGER. In some cases, therefore, one reading from or writing to a text file can mean that several characters are read or written.

Reading and writing are in some respects simpler for general sequential files. GET and PUT are not used, but the two procedures READ and WRITE are specified in SEQUENTIAL_IO:

```
procedure READ  (FILE : in FILE_TYPE;
                 ITEM : out ELEMENT_TYPE);

procedure WRITE (FILE : in FILE_TYPE;
                 ITEM : in ELEMENT_TYPE);
```

Here the type ELEMENT_TYPE corresponds to the type of the records in the file. In our package, PERSON_INOUT, ELEMENT_TYPE can be regarded as having been replaced by PERSON.

Assume we have declared a record variable P:

```
P : PERSON;
```

and that we have opened the file PERSON_FILE to read from it. We can then make the call:

```
READ(PERSON_FILE, P);
```

This means that a record in PERSON_FILE is read and copied to P.

Note that a call of READ reads *an entire record* from the file at once. This demands that the types of the objects in the file and the variable being read to are the same. Conversion of data never takes place. Unlike text files, it is not possible to read an individual element of data; it is not possible to read only the name from a record in the file, for example.

When a file is being read the system automatically keeps track of a **current index**. This index states the record in the file that is next in line for reading. When a file is opened (or reset) the current index is set to 1 (the first record in the file). Each time READ is called, the current index increases by 1 after the reading has occurred.

If READ is called and the current index has a value greater than the number of records in the file, then the end of the file has been reached and the exception END_ERROR occurs. To avoid this situation, as for text files, the function END_OF_FILE can be used to test whether the file has any records left to be read.

When READ is called, the exceptions MODE_ERROR and DATA_ERROR can also occur. MODE_ERROR means that an attempt has been made to read from a file that is not open for reading. DATA_ERROR arises if the objects in the file are not of the same type as the variable to which they are to be read. (There is no requirement that an Ada compiler should check for this kind of error.)

Reading sequential files

READ(F, R);

where F is a logical file (file variable) and R is a variable of the same type as the objects in F.

- An *entire* object in the file is read and copied to P.
- The objects are read sequentially from start to finish.
- Each call gives the next object that is waiting in line.

Output works in the corresponding way. If PERSON_FILE were open for writing instead, we could make the call:

WRITE(PERSON_FILE, P);

Writing sequential files

WRITE(F, R);

where F is a logical file (file variable) and R is a variable of the same type as the objects in F.

- A new object is written at the end of the file.
- R's value is copied to the new object.

A new record is placed at the end of the file and the value of P will be copied to this record. As with reading, one *entire* record at a time is copied when writing to a file. It is not possible to write an individual element of data to the file.

When writing, the exception MODE_ERROR can occur if the file given to WRITE is not open for writing. USE_ERROR can occur if the space available to the file in secondary storage is exceeded.

We can now look at a couple of examples. In the first, we have a program that reads in information about the weight and height of a number of people from the terminal and stores it in a new file. This new file will have the physical name *person.data*.

```
with TEXT_IO, BASIC_NUM_IO, SEQUENTIAL_IO;
use  TEXT_IO, BASIC_NUM_IO;
procedure STORE_PERSON_INFO is

  type PERSON is
    record
      NAME   : STRING(1 .. 20);
      WEIGHT : FLOAT;
      HEIGHT : INTEGER;
    end record;

  package PERSON_INOUT is new SEQUENTIAL_IO(PERSON);
  use PERSON_INOUT;

  PERSON_FILE : PERSON_INOUT.FILE_TYPE;
  P : PERSON:
  L : NATURAL;
begin
  CREATE(PERSON_FILE, NAME => ''person.data'');

  PUT_LINE(''Terminate input with CTRL-D'');
  loop
    PUT(''Name: '');
    exit when END_OF_FILE;
    GET_LINE(P.NAME, L);
    -- pad the name with blanks
    P.NAME(L+1 .. P.NAME'LAST) := (others => ' ');
    PUT(''Weight: ''); GET(P.WEIGHT); SKIP_LINE;
    PUT(''Height: ''); GET(P.HEIGHT); SKIP_LINE;
    WRITE(PERSON_FILE, P);
  end loop;
  CLOSE(PERSON_FILE);
end STORE_PERSON_INFO;
```

Note that the information for each person is read in the normal way, element by element from the terminal. When the information is stored in

PERSON_FILE, however, it is written as an entire record at a time. In the new file the weight and height information will be stored in the same binary form as used in the program. They are not stored in the form of text as they would be in a text file, that is, the file cannot be handled by the system programs that are written to work on text files. It is not possible, for example, to edit the file using a text-editor, and if an attempt should be made to write out the contents of the file using a program that lists text files, the result would be a mass of strange and undecipherable characters at the terminal.

If we would like the program to be more general we can arrange to read in the new file's name from the terminal before creating the file:

```
PUT_LINE("Enter the name of the new file.");
GET_LINE(FILE_NAME, L);
CREATE(PERSON_FILE, NAME => FILE_NAME(1 .. L));
```

In the next example we show a program that reads the above file and selects tall people (taller than 2 m). The information about tall people is stored in a new file *tall.data*. The program uses the function END_OF_FILE to see when the register comes to an end.

```
with SEQUENTIAL_IO;
procedure CHOOSE_TALL is
  type PERSON is
    record
      NAME    : STRING(1 .. 20);
      WEIGHT : FLOAT;
      HEIGHT  : INTEGER;
    end record;

  package PERSON_INOUT is new SEQUENTIAL_IO(PERSON);
  use PERSON_INOUT;

  PERSON_FILE, TALL_FILE : PERSON_INOUT.FILE_TYPE;
  P: PERSON;

begin
  OPEN(PERSON_FILE, NAME => "person.data",
                    MODE => IN_FILE);
  CREATE(TALL_FILE,  NAME => "tall.data");
  while not END_OF_FILE(PERSON_FILE) loop
    READ(PERSON_FILE, P);
    if P.HEIGHT > 200 then
      WRITE(TALL_FILE, P);
    end if;
  end loop;
  CLOSE(PERSON_FILE);
  CLOSE(TALL_FILE);
end CHOOSE_TALL;
```

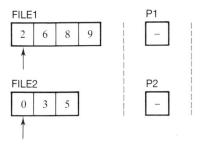

Figure 12.3

12.2 Sorted files

It is very common for files to be sorted in some way, making it easier to obtain required information from the file. We can imagine, for example, that when running the program STORE_PERSON_INFO discussed in Section 12.1, the entries could be in alphabetical order so that the file *person.data* is sorted from the start. The element of the record that defines the sort is called the **key**. If the file *person.data* is sorted in this way, then the element NAME is the key.

To look at methods of handling sorted files, we shall start by considering a common problem – the **merging** of files. Assume we have two sorted files of the same type, that is, the objects in the files have the same type. The task is to merge them together so that a new sorted file, containing all the records from the two files, is obtained.

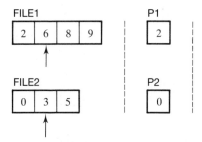

Figure 12.4

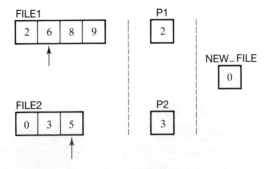

Figure 12.5

We can study some diagrams that will help explain how this works. Assume we have two sorted files, FILE1 and FILE2, and for simplicity, their objects are integers. These two files should be merged into a new file that we shall call NEW_FILE. We shall also assume that we have two variables P1 and P2 to which we can read objects from FILE1 and FILE2, respectively. The initial situation is illustrated in Figure 12.3. An arrow is used in Figure 12.3 to denote the current index in each file, that is, the next object waiting to be read. The variables P1 and P2 do not yet contain any file objects, as indicated by the dashes.

The first step is to read the first object from each file, as shown in Figure 12.4. The first objects from the two files are now in P1 and P2, and the pointers that mark the current indexes have moved on one place.

Now we select which of P1 and P2 contains the smaller value, P2 in this example. The contents of P2 are written to the new file NEW_FILE. This uses up the contents of P2 and we read another element of FILE2 into it. Figure 12.5 illustrates the situation.

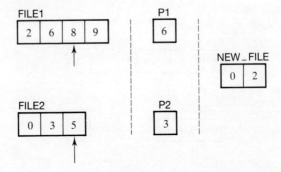

Figure 12.6

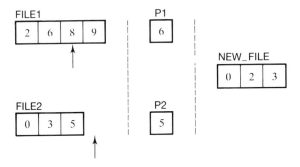

Figure 12.7

Now the smaller of P1 and P2 is chosen again and its contents are written to NEW_FILE. This time P1 is chosen and an object containing the value 2 is written to NEW_FILE. A new object (with value 6) is read from FILE1 to P1. Figure 12.6 shows the current position.

Next time P2 will be chosen and the value 3 written to NEW_FILE, as shown in Figure 12.7. P2 now holds the smaller value (5), so this is written to NEW_FILE. Since FILE2 is now finished we cannot read a new value to P2. Instead we denote that there is nothing in P2, using a dash, as shown in Figure 12.8.

The next time we try and choose the smaller of P1 and P2, we shall see that there is nothing in P2; we shall simply choose P1 and write its contents to NEW_FILE, as shown in Figure 12.9. This action will be repeated until FILE1 is also finished, and we arrive at the situation in Figure 12.9.

We can start to formulate an algorithm to describe how this merge process works:

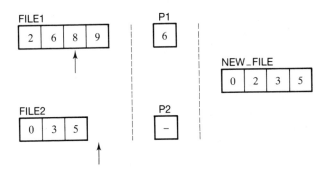

Figure 12.8

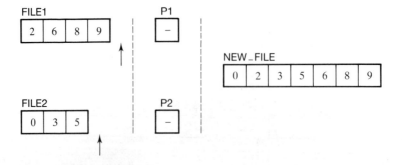

Figure 12.9

(1) Try to get a record from FILE1 and put it into P1.
(2) Try to get a record from FILE2 and put it into P2.
(3) Repeat the following until there is nothing left in either of FILE1 and
     FILE2:
     (3.1) Pick out one of P1 and P2 and write it to NEW_FILE.
     (3.2) Try to get a new record to replace whichever of P1 or P2 was
            chosen.

By the term 'try to get' we mean:

> If the current file is finished, then indicate that there is nothing in
> the variable that belongs to that file; otherwise, read a record from
> the file to the corresponding variable.

We must also clarity step (3.1):

> If there is something in both P1 and P2, then choose the one that
> should come first in a sorted file, otherwise, choose the one that
> contains something.

Note that step (3) guarantees that we shall never reach step (3.1) with
nothing in either P1 or P2.

Using this, we can write a program that merges two registers of
the kind described, *person.data1* and *person.data2*. We can assume that
these files are sorted and were created using the program
STORE_PERSON_INFO from the previous section.

In the program a special procedure FETCH has been written
because 'try to fetch' occurs in several places in the algorithm.

```
with SEQUENTIAL_IO;
procedure MERGE is
  type PERSON is
    record
      NAME   : STRING(1 .. 20);
      WEIGHT : FLOAT;
      HEIGHT : INTEGER;
    end record;

  package PERSON_INOUT is new SEQUENTIAL_IO(PERSON);
  use PERSON_INOUT;

  FILE1, FILE2, NEW_FILE : PERSON_INOUT.FILE_TYPE;
  P1, P2                 : PERSON;
  FOUND1, FOUND2         : BOOLEAN;

  procedure FETCH (F : in out PERSON_INOUT.FILE_TYPE;
                   P : out PERSON;
                   FOUND : out BOOLEAN) is
  begin
    if END_OF_FILE(F) then
      FOUND := FALSE;
    else
      READ(F, P);
      FOUND := TRUE;
    end if;
  end FETCH;

begin
  OPEN(FILE1, NAME => "person.data1",
             MODE => IN_FILE);
  OPEN(FILE2, NAME => "person.data2",
             MODE => IN_FILE);
  CREATE(NEW_FILE, NAME => "person.data.all");

  FETCH(FILE1, P1, FOUND1);
  FETCH(FILE2, P2, FOUND2);

  while FOUND1 or FOUND2 loop
    if ((FOUND1 and FOUND2) and then P1.NAME < P2.NAME)
      or not FOUND2 then
      WRITE(NEW_FILE, P1);
      FETCH(FILE1, P1, FOUND1);
    else
      WRITE(NEW_FILE, P2);
      FETCH(FILE2, P2, FOUND2);
    end if;
  end loop;
  CLOSE(FILE1);
  CLOSE(FILE2);
  CLOSE(NEW_FILE);
end MERGE;
```

We use two Boolean variables FOUND1 and FOUND2 to indicate whether there is anything in P1 and P2, respectively.

A little trick is sometimes used to simplify this type of program. It is easier to recognize the ends of the files if a special record is placed at the end of each file that is to be merged, indicating that the file is finished. In this end record the key is given such a large value that no keys with values greater than or equal to it can arise. (If the key in our example above is a name, the end record might be "zzzzzzzzzzzzzzzzzzzzz").

If we have the constant declaration:

```
END_NAME : constant STRING := "zzzzzzzzzzzzzzzzzzzzz";
```

in the program MERGE, and assume that both FILE1 and FILE2 have such end records, the **while** statement in the program can be simplified somewhat:

```
while P1.NAME < END_NAME or P2.NAME < END_NAME loop
   if P1.NAME < P2.NAME then
      WRITE(NEW_FILE, P1);
      READ(FILE1, P1);
   else
      WRITE(NEW_FILE, P2);
      READ(FILE2, P2);
   end if;
end loop;
```

We do not need the procedure FETCH or the variables FOUND1 and FOUND2. Since we always stop when the end record has been read there is no risk of the files running out.

Even if no special end record is placed in the files, this concept can still be used, by 'imagining' an end record. The procedure FETCH must be retained, but rewritten a little:

```
procedure FETCH (F : in out PERSON_INOUT.FILE_TYPE;
                 P : out PERSON) is
begin
   if END_OF_FILE(F) then
      P.NAME := END_NAME;
   else
      READ(F, P);
   end if;
end FETCH;
```

When the end of the file is reached, like 'imagining' an end record has been read, P.NAME is given the value END_NAME. The **while** statement is then written:

```
while P1.NAME < END_NAME or P2.NAME < END_NAME loop
  if P1.NAME < P2.NAME then
    WRITE(NEW_FILE, P1);
    FETCH(FILE1, P1);
  else
    WRITE(NEW_FILE, P2);
    FETCH(FILE2, P2);
  end if;
end loop;
```

In the second example we shall study another common way of working with sorted files. We assume that a bank has a file *accounts* in which every record contains information about one bank account. In a record there is the account number, balance and information about the account holder:

```
type ACCOUNT_RECORD is
  record
    NO              : ACCOUNT_NO;
    BALANCE         : FLOAT;
    ACCOUNT_HOLDER : PERSON;
  end record;
```

The account file is sorted in order of account number. An account number is assumed to be an eight-digit number:

```
MIN_NO : constant := 10_000_000;
MAX_NO : constant := 99_999_999;
subtype ACCOUNT_NO is INTEGER range MIN_NO .. MAX_NO;
```

Assume that every day all transactions (deposits and withdrawals) to do with the bank's accounts are stored in a special file called *transactions*. This transaction file has one record for each transaction made. A transaction record contains the account number and information about how large an amount has been deposited or withdrawn. (A positive amount means a deposit and a negative amount means a withdrawal).

```
type TRANSACTION_RECORD is
  record
    NO     : ACCOUNT_NO;
    AMOUNT : FLOAT;
  end record;
```

The transaction file is also sorted into account number order.

At the end of each working day, a program is run that reads the transaction file and changes the accounts file so that the information about how much money is in individual accounts is correct after the day's deposits and withdrawals. There may be several transactions on one account, but these follow one another in the transaction file.

Normally, no account number will appear in the transactions file that does not appear in the accounts file, but if it should, the program writes out the error message at the terminal:

Account number nnnnnnnn is missing

If an account is found to have a negative balance after the day's transactions, the program writes:

Negative balance for account nnnnnnnn

The same technique is used here as in the merge program. The two files *accounts* and *transactions* are read and a new file is created. The new file is here a temporary file. Each account record is written to the temporary file after.any transactions concerning the account have been dealt with. The program finishes with the temporary file being copied back to the accounts file.

To simplify the program we use the trick of inserting special end records into the files; we assume that at the end of both the accounts file and the transactions file are records with the account number MAX_NO and that no real account can possibly have this number.

Two input/output packages are used in the program. The package TRANS_INOUT is used for reading the transaction file and the package ACCOUNT_INOUT is used for reading and writing the accounts file and the temporary file. Note that the logical files AC_FILE and TEMP_FILE have the type ACCOUNT_INOUT.FILE_TYPE whereas TR_FILE has type TRANS_INOUT.FILE_TYPE.

When two records are compared – one from the accounts file and the other from the transactions file – one of three things can happen. If the records contain the same account number the transaction should be entered in the current account record and a new transaction record should be fetched. If the account record has a smaller account number than the transaction record there are no (more) transaction records for the current account and a new account record should be fetched. Finally, the account record has a larger account number than the transaction record, the transaction record must refer to an account that is not in the accounts file.

```ada
with TEXT_IO, BASIC_NUM_IO, SEQUENTIAL_IO;
use  TEXT_IO, BASIC_NUM_IO;
procedure PROCESS_TRANSACTIONS is
  type PERSON is
    record
      NAME     : STRING(1 .. 20);
      ADDRESS : STRING(1 .. 30);
    end record;

  MIN_NO  : constant := 10_000_000;
  MAX_NO : constant := 99_999_999;
  subtype ACCOUNT_NO is INTEGER
                          range MIN_NO .. MAX_NO;

  type ACCOUNT_RECORD is
    record
      NO               : ACCOUNT_NO;
      BALANCE          : FLOAT;
      ACCOUNT_HOLDER : PERSON;
    end record;

  type TRANSACTION_RECORD is
    record
      NO      : ACCOUNT_NO;
      AMOUNT : FLOAT;
    end record;

  package ACCOUNT_INOUT is new
              SEQUENTIAL_IO(ACCOUNT_RECORD);
  package TRANS_INOUT is new
              SEQUENTIAL_IO(TRANSACTION_RECORD);
  use ACCOUNT_INOUT, TRANS_INOUT;

  AC_FILE, TEMP_FILE : ACCOUNT_INOUT.FILE_TYPE;
  TR_FILE            : TRANS_INOUT.FILE_TYPE

  A : ACCOUNT_RECORD;
  T : TRANSACTION_RECORD;

begin
  OPEN(AC_FILE, IN_FILE, "accounts");
  OPEN(TR_FILE, IN_FILE, "transactions");
  CREATE (TEMP_FILE);

  READ(AC_FILE, A);
  READ(TR_FILE, T);

  while A.NO < MAX_NO or T.NO < MAX_NO loop
    if A.NO = T.NO then
      A.BALANCE := A.BALANCE + T.AMOUNT;
      READ(TR_FILE, T);
```

```
    elsif A.NO < T.NO then
      WRITE(TEMP_FILE, A);
      if A.BALANCE < 0.0 then
        PUT("Negative balance for account ");
        PUT(A.NO, WIDTH => 9); NEW_LINE;
      end if;
      READ(AC_FILE, A);
    else
      PUT("Account number");
      PUT(T.NO, WIDTH => 9);
      PUT_LINE(" is missing");
      READ(TR_FILE, T);
    end if;
  end loop;
  CLOSE(TR_FILE);

  -- write the temp file as the new account file
  RESET(TEMP_FILE, IN_FILE);
  RESET(AC_FILE, OUT_FILE);
  while not END_OF_FILE(TEMP_FILE) loop
    READ(TEMP_FILE, A);
    WRITE(AC_FILE, A);
  end loop;

  A.NO := MAX_NO;
  WRITE(AC_FILE, A);       -- write a final record
  CLOSE(AC_FILE);
  CLOSE(TEMP_FILE);
end PROCESS_TRANSACTIONS;
```

■

We have seen ways of handling sorted files. The obvious question is 'How do you sort a file?'

One way is to put the records in the file in order from the start. We could create a sorted file by, for example, feeding in the information to the program STORE_PERSON_INFO with the names in alphabetical order, as mentioned earlier.

One efficient way of sorting files that do not contain too many

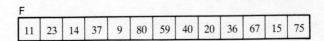

F

| 11 | 23 | 14 | 37 | 9 | 80 | 59 | 40 | 20 | 36 | 67 | 15 | 75 |

Figure 12.10

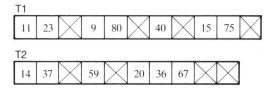

Figure 12.11

records is to read in all the records to an array in a program, sort the array, and then write it back to the file. It is, however, common for files to hold many records and the accessible primary storage is not always sufficient to allow the sorting to take place in an array. Then some file sorting technique must be used, which sorts without reading in all the records to the program at once. This is usually described as **external file sorting**. This is an area of data processing where there are several methods with different degrees of sophistication. To demonstrate the concepts that can be applied, a relatively simple method will be shown here, that is far from the most efficient.

As usual, diagrams best illustrate how things work. We assume that we have to sort the file F in Figure 12.10. For simplicity, we assume that the records contain nothing but an integer key. To carry out the sort we shall use two temporary subsidiary files, T1 and T2. If we look at F, we see that it can be divided into several sequences in each of which the records are sorted. F contains the sequences [11, 23], [14, 37], [9, 80], [59], [40], [20, 36, 67] and [15, 75]. If F had been totally sorted it would have consisted of only one sequence.

The first step in the sort algorithm is that we read F, record by record, and copy alternate sequences to T1 and T2. To indicate the end of each sequence we use a special end record that contains a key value larger than any real record can take. We arrive at the situation shown in Figure 12.11. To enable T1 and T2 to have the same number of sequences, we put an empty sequence at the end of T2.

The next step is to merge pairs of sequences, one from T1 and one from T2, to file F. After this step F will appear as in Figure 12.12. F will thus have half as many sequences as it originally had.

Now we can continue in this manner, sharing the sequences between T1 and T2 and then merging pairs of sequences. This process is

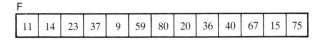

Figure 12.12

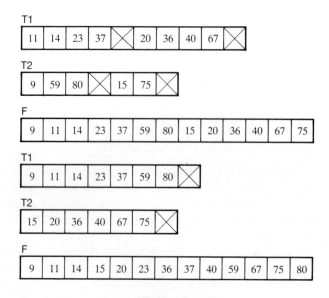

Figure 12.13

repeated until F has only one sequence. Figure 12.13 shows the remaining stages in the process.

We shall present a program that carries out a sort according to this method. The records in the file to be sorted consist of a data part (in this example, a text string) as well as a key.

```
with TEXT_IO, SEQUENTIAL_IO;
use TEXT_IO;
procedure SORT_FILE is
   subtype KEY   is INTEGER;
   subtype DATA is STRING(1 .. 30);
   type FILE_RECORD is
     record
       K : KEY;
       D : DATA;
     end record;

MAX_KEY : constant KEY := INTEGER'LAST;
MIN_KEY : constant KEY := INTEGER'FIRST;

package REC_INOUT is new SEQUENTIAL_IO(FILE_RECORD);
use REC_INOUT;

F, T1, T2        : REC_INOUT.FILE_TYPE;
SORTED           : BOOLEAN := FALSE;
NO_OF_MERGES : NATURAL;
```

```
procedure FETCH (F : in out REC_INOUT.FILE_TYPE;
                    R : out FILE_RECORD) is
begin
  if END_OF_FILE(F) then
    R.K := MAX_KEY;
  else
    READ(F, R);
  end if;
end FETCH;

procedure SPLIT_UP (F, T1, T2 :
                        in out REC_INOUT.FILE_TYPE) is
  R : FILE_RECORD;

  procedure COPY_SEQUENCE
            (F, T : in out REC_INOUT.FILE_TYPE;
             R    : in out FILE_RECORD) is
    PREV_KEY : KEY := MIN_KEY;
    FINAL_REC : FILE_RECORD;
  begin
    while R.K >= PREV_KEY and R.K < MAX_KEY loop
      PREV_KEY := R.K;
      WRITE(T, R);
      FETCH(F, R);
    end loop;
    FINAL_REC.K := MAX_KEY;
    WRITE(T, FINAL_REC);    -- end of sequence
  end COPY_SEQUENCE;

begin
  FETCH(F, R);
  while R.K < MAX_KEY loop
    COPY_SEQUENCE(F, T1, R);
    COPY_SEQUENCE(F, T2, R);
  end loop;
end SPLIT_UP;

procedure MERGE (FILE1, FILE2, FILE3 :
                    in out REC_INOUT.FILE_TYPE) is
  R1, R2 : FILE_RECORD;
begin
  FETCH(FILE1, R1);
  FETCH(FILE2, R2);
  while R1.K < MAX_KEY or R2.K < MAX_KEY loop
    if R1.K < R2.K then
      WRITE(FILE3, R1);
      FETCH(FILE1, R1);
    else
      WRITE(FILE3, R2);
      FETCH(FILE2, R2);
    end if;
```

```
        end loop;
      end MERGE;

  begin
    OPEN(F, IN_FILE, "datafile");
    while not SORTED loop
      -- split up the sequences in F into T1 and T2
      RESET(F, IN_FILE);
      CREATE(T1); CREATE(T2);
      SPLIT_UP(F, T1, T2);

      -- merge the sequences in T1 and T2 into F
      RESET(T1, IN_FILE); RESET(T2, IN_FILE);
      RESET(F, OUT_FILE);
      NO_OF_MERGES := 0;
      while not END_OF_FILE(T1) loop
        MERGE(T1, T2, F);
        NO_OF_MERGES := NO_OF_MERGES + 1;
      end loop;
      SORTED := NO_OF_MERGES = 1;
      CLOSE(T1); CLOSE(T2);
    end loop;
    CLOSE(F);
  end SORT_FILE;
```

We have used a procedure FETCH in the program which reads from F or from one of the temporary files. When F is read, the end of the file is finally reached, and then FETCH 'imagines' that it has read a special end record.

We conclude by mentioning some improvements that could make the program more efficient. The number of times sorting has to be performed can be reduced if the file F has longer sequences from the beginning. This can be achieved by reading N records at a time from F into an array and sorting this array, using some internal sorting method, before writing them to a temporary file. The number N is chosen according to the amount of primary storage available.

Another improvement could be made by using more than two temporary files, so that several sequences could be merged at once.

A further trick is not to put the sequence that results from a merge back into F but into another set of the same number of temporary files. The sequences are placed alternately into the new temporary files. In this way, merging can be carried out 'to and fro' until only one sequence remains.

□

12.3   Direct files

It is not necessary to handle the records in a file sequentially in an Ada program. If instead of using the package SEQUENTIAL_IO another standard package, DIRECT_IO, is used (see Appendix E) it becomes possible to read and write records in arbitrary order.

We have already mentioned that for every open file the Ada system keeps a current index which points at the next record waiting to be read. Work with direct files offers the possibility of controlling the index. In the package DIRECT_IO there are the type declarations:

```
type     COUNT is range 0 .. implementation-dependent integer;
subtype POSITIVE_COUNT is COUNT range 1 .. COUNT'LAST;
```

Current index has type POSITIVE_COUNT.

To set the current index to a particular value the procedure SET_INDEX is used:

```
SET_INDEX(F, 100);        -- F has type DIRECT_IO.FILE_TYPE
SET_INDEX(F, REC_NO);     -- REC_NO has type POSITIVE_COUNT
```

The value of current index can also be read by calling the function INDEX:

```
-- read the first 100 records
while INDEX(F) <= 100 loop
   READ(F, P);
end loop;
```

To determine how many records there are in a file (that is, the index number of the last record) the function SIZE can be used:

```
if SIZE(F) > 100000 then
   PUT("BIG FILE");
end if;
```

The following specifications are found in the package DIRECT_IO:

```
procedure SET_INDEX (FILE : in FILE_TYPE;
                     TO   : in POSITIVE_COUNT);
function INDEX      (FILE : in FILE_TYPE)
                     return POSITIVE_COUNT;
function SIZE       (FILE : in FILE_TYPE)
                     return COUNT;
```

Current index for direct files

- SET_INDEX(F,I) sets the current index in the file F to I.
- INDEX(F) gives the current index for the file F.
- SIZE(F) gives the number of records in the file F.

When a record is to be read or written it is possible to state which record is required. There are two versions of the subprograms READ and WRITE in the package DIRECT_IO:

```
procedure READ  (FILE : in FILE_TYPE;
                 ITEM : out ELEMENT_TYPE);
procedure READ  (FILE : in FILE_TYPE;
                 ITEM : out ELEMENT_TYPE;
                 FROM : in POSITIVE_COUNT);
procedure WRITE (FILE : in FILE_TYPE;
                 ITEM : in ELEMENT_TYPE);
procedure WRITE (FILE : in FILE_TYPE;
                 ITEM : in ELEMENT_TYPE;
                 TO   : in POSITIVE_COUNT);
```

The first of each pair is identical to the READ and WRITE found in SEQUENTIAL_IO. The parameter F gives the file referred to and ITEM is the variable in the program that will be read to or written from. Thus direct files can be treated in exactly the same way as sequential files.

The second version of the two procedures has a third parameter FROM and TO in READ and WRITE, respectively. This third parameter specifies the index in the file for the record that is to be read or written. Before reading or writing starts, the current index is set to the value given. To read record number 100 of file F, for example, we can write:

```
READ(F, R, 100);
```

Another example is:

```
WRITE(F, R, REC_NO);    -- REC_NO has type POSITIVE_COUNT
```

For all versions of READ and WRITE the current index is automatically increased by 1 after reading or writing. For example, after the call:

```
READ(F, R, 100);
```

the current index has value 101.

> **Reading and writing direct files**
>
> READ(F, R);   read the next record in the file F to the variable R.
>
> READ(F, R, I);   read record number I in the file F to the variable R.
>
> WRITE(F, R);   write R to the next record in the file F.
>
> WRITE(F, R, I); write R to record number I in the file F.

Before reading or writing a direct file can begin, the file must be opened using CREATE or OPEN. The difference between direct and sequential files is that a direct file can be opened for *both* reading and writing. The type FILE_MODE has the declaration:

type FILE_MODE **is** (IN_FILE, INOUT_FILE, OUT_FILE);

If it is specified that the file should be of type INOUT_FILE when the file is opened, then the file can be both read and written. After the calls:

```
CREATE (F1, MODE => IN_FILE,    NAME => "file1");
OPEN   (F2, MODE => INOUT_FILE, NAME => "file2");
CREATE (F3, MODE => OUT_FILE,   NAME => "file3");
```

for example, F1 can be read only, F2 can be both read and written, and F3 can be written only.

For the procedure CREATE, the MODE parameter may be omitted, and in this case the file assumes the mode INOUT_FILE.

```
CREATE (F4, NAME => "file4");     -- F4 can be read and written
```

As with sequential files, a direct file can be reset to the beginning and the file's mode can be changed by calling RESET:

```
RESET (F3, INOUT_FILE);     -- now F3 can be read and written
```

the remaining subprograms in SEQUENTIAL_IO, namely CLOSE, DELETE, MODE, NAME, FORM, IS_OPEN and END_OF_FILE are also found in DIRECT_IO and work in exactly the same way.

As an example of the use of direct files we shall return to the file of bank accounts discussed in Section 12.2. We had a file *accounts* that contained a record for every account. In each record there was an account number, the current balance in the account, and information about the account holder's name and address. The file was sorted according to the account number.

Now we shall look at an imaginary program a bank clerk may run when a client wants to make a deposit or withdrawal. The program will read in the account number from the terminal and find the record with this number in the accounts file. If the given account number is missing from the file, the program will give an error message to the clerk.

If the account number is found in the file, the program should read in from the terminal the amount that is to be deposited or withdrawn. A deposit is given as a positive amount and a withdrawal as a negative amount. The record for the account in question should be changed in the file so that the account's balance is correct after the transaction. If the proposed withdrawal is greater than the amount of money held in the account, the program should give an error message and refuse the withdrawal.

We shall use the accounts file as a direct file in this program, and both read from and write to it, that is, we let the file have the mode INOUT_FILE.

To find the required account in the accounts file we use a binary search. The algorithm for a binary search was given in Section 7.4, where we wrote a recursive function to find a particular record in an array. We shall use the same algorithm here but use iteration rather than recursion. The reason for this is that files can sometimes be very large, since they are holding many records. If recursion is used to make a binary search in a very large file, the primary store may run out since too many instances of the recursive function are made.

We use two variables, FIRST and LAST, to define the part of the file where we want to search. These variables are given the type COUNT, so that they can point at records in the file. At the start, FIRST is set to 1 and LAST is set to the index of the file's last record. Then the middle record is looked at. If the required account number is less than the account number in the middle record the search continues in the first half of the file by setting LAST to the index for the record that is one before the middle record. If the required account number is greater than the one in the middle record, the latter half is searched and FIRST is set to the index of the middle record. Now a new middle record is found, in the middle of the chosen half file. This process continues until the required record is found or until the chosen half runs out of records (that is, FIRST > LAST).

We get the program:

```
with TEXT_IO, BASIC_NUM_IO, DIRECT_IO;
use  TEXT_IO, BASIC_NUM_IO;
procedure MAKE_TRANSACTION is
   type PERSON is
```

```
      record
        NAME      : STRING(1 .. 20);
        ADDRESS : STRING(1 .. 30);
      end record;

  MIN_NO : constant := 10_000_000;
  MAX_NO : constant := 99_999_999;
  subtype ACCOUNT_NO is INTEGER
                          range MIN_NO .. MAX_NO;

  type ACCOUNT_RECORD is
      record
        NO                : ACCOUNT_NO;
        BALANCE           : FLOAT;
        ACCOUNT_HOLDER : PERSON;
      end record;

  package ACCOUNT_INOUT is new
                  DIRECT_IO(ACCOUNT_RECORD);
  use ACCOUNT_INOUT;
  AC_FILE            : ACCOUNT_INOUT.FILE_TYPE;
  A                  : ACCOUNT_RECORD;
  REQUIRED_NO        : ACCOUNT_NO;
  AMOUNT             : FLOAT;
  FOUND              : BOOLEAN := FALSE;
  FIRST, LAST, REC_NO : ACCOUNT_INOUT.COUNT;
begin
  PUT("Enter account number: "); GET(REQUIRED_NO);
  OPEN(AC_FILE, INOUT_FILE, "accounts");

  -- find account record
  FIRST := 1;
  LAST  := SIZE(AC_FILE);
  while not FOUND and FIRST <= LAST loop
    REC_NO := (FIRST + LAST) / 2;
    READ(AC_FILE, A, REC_NO);  -- read middle record
    if REQUIRED_NO < A.NO then
      LAST := REC_NO - 1;  -- search in left half
    elsif REQUIRED_NO > A.NO then
      FIRST := REC_NO + 1;  -- search in right half
    else
      FOUND := TRUE;
    end if;
  end loop;

  if FOUND then
    PUT_LINE(A.ACCOUNT_HOLDER.NAME);
    PUT_LINE(A.ACCOUNT_HOLDER.ADDRESS);
    PUT("Balance: ");
    PUT(A.BALANCE, EXP => 0, FORE => 8, AFT => 2);
```

```
     NEW_LINE;
     PUT("Enter amount: "); GET(AMOUNT);
     if AMOUNT < 0.0 and A.BALANCE + AMOUNT < 0.0 then
       PUT_LINE("withdrawal not possible!");
     else
       A.BALANCE := A.BALANCE + AMOUNT;
       WRITE(AC_FILE, A, REC_NO);
       PUT("Balance after transaction: ");
       PUT(A.BALANCE, EXP => 0, FORE => 8, AFT => 2);
       NEW_LINE;
     end if;
   else
     PUT_LINE("Account number not found!");
   end if;

   CLOSE(AC_FILE);
 end MAKE_TRANSACTION;
```

In the program we create a package ACCOUNT_INOUT that provides us with the facilities for accessing directly the accounts file. AC_FILE is the logical file in the program that is linked to the physical accounts file. AC_FILE has the type ACCOUNT_INOUT.FILE_TYPE. We have to use dot notation. If we had only written FILE_TYPE the compiler would not have known whether we meant FILE_TYPE in TEXT_IO or FILE_TYPE in ACCOUNT_INOUT. For the same reason, we must state the type for FIRST, LAST and REC_NO as ACCOUNT_INOUT.COUNT and not only as COUNT, because there is also a type COUNT declared in TEXT_IO.

EXERCISES

12.1 Information about a number of people has been collected into a file *persondata* in order to carry out a statistical investigation. The following information is stored for each individual: name, height, weight, shoe size, age and civil status (married, single or widowed). To analyse the statistics, the sex of the individuals should also be known, but this was forgotten when the file was created.

Write a program that reads the file *persondata* and creates two new files *mandata* and *womandata*. The new files should store the records for all the men and women, respectively. For each person in *persondata* the program should ask the operator if the record read refers to a man or a woman.

12.2 In a scientific experiment many independent series of measurements have been made. Each series comprises 25 real numbers. The measurements are to be stored in a file where each object represents a series of measurements. Write a program that creates a file of measurements. The program should read in the values of the measurements from the terminal, and the values of the measurements from each series should be given sequentially.

12.3 A company has a register of their customers in the form of a data file. There is one record in the file for each customer, containing the customer's name and two lines of address (for example, street address and town, plus postal code). Each of these three items is at most 20 characters in length. To send out information to customers a program is required that can print self-adhesive address labels with the customers' names and addresses. A printing terminal is used loaded with special paper on which the labels are stuck contiguously, three in a row. The total width of the paper is 72 characters and each label is thus 24 characters wide. The height of each label is 5 lines.

Write a program that reads the file of customers and writes out their names and addresses on self-adhesive labels. Use only the three centre lines of each label. The program should work even if the number of customers is not an exact multiple of three.

12.4 The members of a weightlifting club spur one another on to ever greater heights (or weights) by displaying a monthly list of the best results for each member. A computer is used to keep track of the results. There is a record for each member in a file *liftresults*, holding membership number and information about the heaviest weight lifted in the current month.

Write a program that a member can run after each training session. The program should ask for the membership number and how many kilos he (or she) lifted during that session. If the result is better than earlier results the program should update the file *liftresults* so that the new result is put into the file.

(a) Treat *liftresults* as a sequential file.

(b) Let *liftresults* be a direct file.

12.5 A company has set up a list of its employees' rooms and telephone numbers in a computer file. There is a record for each employee and each record contains name, room number and telephone number. The file is sorted alphabetically.

Write a program that can add records for new employees, change existing records and remove records from the file. Name, room number and telephone number are requested. If a name is given that is not found in the file, a new record should be added in the correct place. If the given name is found, then its record should be removed if the room number is said to be zero, otherwise it should be updated. This process is repeated as often as necessary. The records in the file that are not mentioned from the terminal should be left unchanged. It may be assumed that the names are given in alphabetical order.

12.6   Write a program that merges four files into one. The records in the files are of the same type and comprise a key (an integer in the interval 1 to 99 999) and a data array of 100 characters.

12.7   Information about the situation in a football league has been stored in a file *league*. There is one record in the file for each team in the league. A record contains the team's name, number of points, number of goals scored and number of goals let in. The records are in arbitrary order in the file.
    Write a program that sorts the file *league* so that the team with most points comes first and the one with fewest comes last. If two or more teams have the same number of points they should be listed according to goal difference (number of goals scored − number of goals let in). Teams with the same number of points and the same goal difference should be listed alphabetically. (*Hint*: Do the sorting internally in the program).

12.8   Revise the program SORT_FILE from Section 12.2 so that it uses four temporary files instead of two.

12.9   Write a program to sort a file that works on the same principle as the program SORT_FILE but which merges 'to and fro' between four temporary files T1, T2, T3 and T4. When the sequences from the files T1 and T2 are being merged the resulting sequences are placed alternately into T3 and T4. Then T3 and T4 are merged and the resulting sequences placed alternately into T1 and T2, and so on until only one sequence remains.

12.10 A company has a data file *storefile* that is used to keep track of all the articles in its warehouse. There is a record in the file for each type of article. For each article there is a record with a product code (a code of 10 characters), a description (a text of 30 characters), the number of articles in store and the price.

Write a program that can take the following commands from the terminal:

INFO artno   The program displays the information stored for the given article at the terminal.

BOUGHT artno n   The program should save the information in the *storefile* that *n* new articles of type *artno* have been bought for the warehouse stock.

SOLD artno n   The program should place into the file *storefile* the information that *n* articles of type *artno* have been sold from the warehouse stock.

12.11 When large direct files have to be searched, the number of readings made from secondary storage can be reduced if each data file has an **index table**. This table contains one element for each record in the data file. An element holds the key of the corresponding record and its position (index) in the data file. The index table is sorted so that the keys appear in order of size. But the data file does not need to be sorted.

If a record with a particular key has to be found in the data file, the index table is searched first for the index of the record in the file. Then only a single input or output action is necessary on the data file. The index table can be stored as a special file, separately from the data file itself. The program can start by reading in all the index table to an array in the program so that the search can take place internally.

Write a program for the problem formulated in Exercise 12.10, but now use an index table.

Chapter 13
Generic units

13.1 Definitions and instances
13.2 Generic parameters

Exercises

When a program or part of a program is being written it is usually advantageous to try and make it as general as possible. Then, if the conditions for a program should change, fewer changes (or even none) will be required to enable the program to work. Moreover, similar programming problems occur in many different contexts. If a general solution has been designed for one problem, it can often be used on later occasions.

Ada offers the programmer the possibility of writing general programs using **generic units**. Such a program unit can be either a subprogram or a package. A generic unit is not only *one* subprogram or *one* package, but is a description of a whole *family* of similar units. Generic units can be regarded as generalized bits of a puzzle that can be fitted together to develop a new program. Ada libraries of generic units can be built up from different sources, thereby simplifying future program development.

13.1   Definitions and instances

We shall start with a very simple program. In Section 6.3 we constructed a procedure SWAP that could be used for interchanging the values of two variables:

```
procedure SWAP (NUMBER1, NUMBER2 : in out INTEGER) is
   TEMP : INTEGER;
begin
   TEMP    := NUMBER1;
   NUMBER1 := NUMBER2;
   NUMBER2 := TEMP;
end SWAP;
```

The procedure demands that the two parameters have the type INTEGER so it cannot be used for swapping the values of, say, two floating point variables. We shall now rewrite SWAP so that it can be used for all types of parameter. It then gets the new specification:

```
generic
   type ELEMENT is private;
procedure SWAP (A, B : in out ELEMENT);
```

Between the reserved words **generic** and **procedure** is a list of the **formal generic parameters**. In this case there is only one such parameter, the type ELEMENT. (The reason for saying that the type is private will be explained in Section 13.2). The procedure must also have a body:

```
procedure SWAP (A, B : in out ELEMENT) is
   TEMP : ELEMENT;
begin
   TEMP := A; A := B; B := TEMP;
end SWAP;
```

This looks like a perfectly normal procedure, but it is not. It is a template that defines a family of procedures. In the body of SWAP a generic parameter ELEMENT is used. SWAP describes different procedures depending on the 'value' of ELEMENT. If ELEMENT has the 'value' FLOAT, for example, SWAP describes a procedure that can be used to interchange the values of two variables of type FLOAT. It is as though the word 'FLOAT' appeared in all the places that ELEMENT actually appears.

Note that a generic procedure must have a separate specification. The specification and the body may be two separate compilation units. The specification must then be compiled before the body.

> **Definition of a generic unit**
>
> - First make a specification:
>   **generic**
>   declaration of generic parameters
>   *subprogram declaration or package specification*
> - Then give the body of the subprogram or package.
> - The specification and body may be two separate compilation units.

If the procedure SWAP is to be used in a program, the program should begin with:

with SWAP;

So far there is no 'real' procedure SWAP; there is only a template. To get a procedure we have to use the template and **generate** or **create** a version of SWAP. A particular version of a generic unit is called an **instance** of the generic unit, and it is created by making a **generic instantiation**. When an instance of a generic unit is created, the 'value' of the generic parameter has to be specified: the **actual generic parameters** are stated. To instantiate a procedure that can interchange two numbers of the type FLOAT, for example, we make the declaration:

procedure SWAP_FLOAT **is new** SWAP(FLOAT);

Here FLOAT is the actual generic parameter. Now we have a true procedure that can be called in the normal way. If the variables X and Y have the type FLOAT, for example, we make the call:

SWAP_FLOAT(X, Y);

If we also want a procedure that can swap two character variables we can instantiate a further instance of the procedure SWAP:

procedure SWAP_CHAR **is new** SWAP(CHARACTER);

This produces a new procedure that can be called with:

SWAP_CHAR(C1, C2);

where C1 and C2 have the type CHARACTER.

Instantiating generic units

Declaration is made using one of the forms:

- **procedure** *procedure_name* **is new**
  generic_procedure(actual parameters);
- **function** *function_name* **is new**
  generic_function(actual parameters);
- **package** *package_name* **is new**
  generic_package(actual parameters);

It is also possible to have a generic package. To illustrate this we shall first give a simpler version of the character stack discussed in Section 11.4. Instead of describing a stack as an abstract data type, here a package with 'memory' is used. As before, we let the specification contain the subprograms PUSH, POP and EMPTY:

```
package STACK is
  procedure PUSH (E : in CHARACTER);
  procedure POP   (E : out CHARACTER);
  function EMPTY return BOOLEAN;
end STACK;
```

Note that we no longer have a type CHAR_STACK. Instead, we have an array in the body of the package in which we put the characters that are to be placed on the stack. (We assume that there are at most 100 characters on the stack). A variable TOP keeps track of the index of the character that lies on top:

```
package body STACK is
  SIZE : constant := 100;
  A    : array (1 .. SIZE) of CHARACTER;
  TOP : NATURAL := 0;

  procedure PUSH (E : in CHARACTER) is
  begin
    TOP := TOP + 1;
    A(TOP) := E;
  end PUSH;

  procedure POP (E : out CHARACTER) is
  begin
    E := A(TOP);
    TOP := TOP - 1;
  end POP;
```

```
     function EMPTY return BOOLEAN is
     begin
       return TOP = 0;
     end EMPTY;
   end STACK;
```

This stack only works for elements of the type CHARACTER. However, the package can easily be made into a generic package. We start by changing the specification:

```
   generic
     type ELEMENT is private;
   package STACK is
     procedure PUSH (E : in ELEMENT);
     procedure POP   (E : out ELEMENT);
     function EMPTY return BOOLEAN;
   end STACK;
```

We have introduced a generic parameter ELEMENT that we use instead of the type CHARACTER. In the body of the package the only change now remaining is to replace CHARACTER by ELEMENT wherever it occurs.

In any program that wants to use the generic package STACK, the statement:

```
   with STACK;
```

now has to be placed first.

Assume we have a type PERSON:

```
   type PERSON is
     record
       NAME     : STRING(1 .. 20);
       ADDRESS : STRING(1 .. 30);
     end record;
```

If we want to have two stacks, one on which elements of type PERSON can be placed and the other for integers, we can create two instances by writing:

```
   package INT_STACK is new STACK(INTEGER);
   package PERSON_STACK is new STACK(PERSON);
   use INT_STACK, PERSON_STACK;
```

Now we can make the calls:

```
   PUSH(P);    -- P has type PERSON
   PUSH(I);    -- I has type INTEGER
```

Since the procedures PUSH in the two packages have different types of parameters the compiler can determine which of these should be used. If, however, we want to call the function EMPTY, we must use the selector notation for the compiler to know which is intended:

if PERSON_STACK.EMPTY **then**

A generic unit can have any number of parameters. It is also possible to have a generic unit without parameters. We can make use of this when several identical packages with 'memory' have to be created. As an example, we can look again at the package for generating random numbers in Section 8.7. In its final form this had the specification:

```
package RANDOM is
    subtype NUMBER is FLOAT range 0.0 .. 1.0;
    function NEXT_NUMBER return NUMBER;
    -- gives a random number greater than or
    -- equal to 0 and less than 1
end RANDOM;
```

By adding the word **generic** we can convert this into a generic package:

```
generic
package RANDOM is
    subtype NUMBER is FLOAT range 0.0 .. 1.0;
    function NEXT_NUMBER return NUMBER;
    -- gives a random number greater than or
    -- equal to 0 and less than 1
end RANDOM;
```

No changes are necessary in the body of the package. This generic package has no parameters; there is nothing between the words **generic** and **package**. Now we shall present a program that uses the generic random number generator to produce two independent series of random numbers:

```
with TEXT_IO, BASIC_NUM_IO, RANDOM;
use  TEXT_IO, BASIC_NUM_IO;
procedure RANDOM_DEMO is
    package RANDOM1 is new RANDOM;
    package RANDOM2 is new RANDOM;
    X1 : RANDOM1.NUMBER;
    X2 : RANDOM2.NUMBER;
    SUM1, SUM2 : FLOAT := 0.0;
```

```
begin
  for I in 1 .. 100 loop
    X1 := RANDOM1.NEXT_NUMBER;
    X2 := RANDOM2.NEXT_NUMBER;
    SUM1 := SUM1 + X1;
    SUM2 := SUM2 + X2;
  end loop;
  PUT("Mean 1: "); PUT(SUM1 / 100.0); NEW_LINE;
  PUT("Mean 2: "); PUT(SUM2 / 100.0); NEW_LINE;
end RANDOM_DEMO;
```

Two separate random number packages are created in the program, RANDOM1 and RANDOM2, each with its own set of internal variables and each working independently of the other.

13.2 Generic parameters

When an instance of a generic program unit is created, it is as though the generic formal parameters have been replaced by the corresponding actual parameters and the generic unit has then been compiled. (For example, when the package PERSON_STACK was compiled, ELEMENT was replaced by PERSON). The mechanism for generic units is, however, more sophisticated than mere text substitution.

A generic unit can, and should, be compiled before it is used. A kind of partial compilation takes place. The compiler checks that the generic unit is syntactically correct and translates it as far as is possible. When an instance is later created, it is not a complete compilation that occurs – the compiler only fills in the bits that are missing.

So that the compiler will know how a formal parameter will be used in a generic unit, certain information has to be stated at the time of specification. When we generated the generic package STACK, for example, we had to state that the formal parameter ELEMENT would be a type and that the type would be private.

There are three categories of generic parameter: **value and object parameters**, **type parameters** and **subprogram parameters**. We shall examine these sequentially.

13.2.1 Value parameters

Generic parameters can look like ordinary subprogram parameters. They can be of two sorts, **in** parameters and **in out** parameters. **in** parameters are called **value parameters** and **in out** parameters are called **object parameters**. Because **in out** parameters are not so common and can lead to strange global side effects, we shall not discuss them here; instead we shall study value parameters.

Let us look at an example. In the body of the stack package we used an array the size of which was determined by the constant SIZE:

```
SIZE : constant := 100;
A     : array (1 .. SIZE) of CHARACTER;
```

If we want to generate a stack package where we can specify a maximum stack size, we can change SIZE into a generic value parameter. We rewrite the generic package:

```
generic
  type ELEMENT is private;
  SIZE : POSITIVE;
package STACK is
  procedure PUSH (E : in ELEMENT);
  procedure POP   (E : out ELEMENT);
  function EMPTY return BOOLEAN;
end STACK;
```

In the body we simply remove the declaration of SIZE.

When we generate an instance of STACK we can now give a value to the parameter SIZE:

```
package CHAR_STACK is new STACK (CHARACTER, 50);
package PERSON_STACK is new STACK (PERSON, 25);
```

The CHAR_STACK will have room for up to 50 elements and PERSON_STACK for up to 25. The generic package STACK now has two generic parameters. As with calling a subprogram, it is possible to use named parameter association. For example, we could have written:

```
package CHAR_STACK is new STACK(SIZE      => 50,
                                ELEMENT => CHARACTER);
package PERSON_STACK is new STACK(ELEMENT => PERSON,
                                  SIZE      => 25);
```

It is possible to assign a default value to a value parameter:

```
generic
  type ELEMENT is private;
  SIZE : POSITIVE := 100;
package STACK is
  procedure PUSH (E : in ELEMENT);
  procedure POP   (E : out ELEMENT);
  function EMPTY return BOOLEAN;
end STACK;
```

If the corresponding actual parameter is omitted when an instance is created, the parameter will assume the default value. For example, in these two instances:

package INT_STACK1 **is new** STACK(INTEGER, 200);
package INT_STACK2 **is new** STACK(INTEGER);

INT_STACK1 will have room for 200 elements, while INT_STACK2 will have room for 100 elements.

Within the body of the generic unit, a generic value parameter is considered a constant. Its value, therefore, must not be changed.

Generic value parameters

parameter_name : type := default_value;

Default_value may be omitted.

13.2.2   Type parameters

The second category of generic parameter is the type parameter. We have already seen examples of type parameters in the generic procedure SWAP and the generic package STACK. There we wrote in the specifications:

type ELEMENT **is private**;

When a specification of a generic type parameter is given, its properties have to be stated. The reason for this is that the compiler must know how the type will be used in the body of the generic unit. Because ELEMENT has been stated to be private, only the operations of assignment and comparison may be applied to objects of the type ELEMENT in the body of the generic unit.

This way of declaring a type parameter as private is not the same as, and should not be confused with, the private types discussed earlier in connection with packages. If a type is private in a package, the type's exact appearance was known only *within* the package. Outside the package nothing was known of the type's appearance; it was not visible. The type was the private property of the package. A private generic type parameter could be said to be private in the opposite sense. The exact appearance of the type is unknown in the generic unit's body. (The only thing known is that assignment and comparison are allowed). It is outside the generic unit (in the program that creates the instance of the generic program unit) that the appearance of the type is known. If, for example, a package is created:

```
package CHAR_STACK is new STACK(CHARACTER);
```

then it is known that ELEMENT in the package will be the same as CHARACTER.

A generic type parameter can also be specified to be a limited private type, which means that not even the operations of assignment and comparison are allowed.

```
type T is limited private;
```

The next type parameter to be discussed is the discrete type:

```
type T is (< >);    -- T should be a discrete type
```

In the body of the generic unit it may be assumed that T denotes a discrete type, that is, an enumeration type or an integer type. To look at an example, we shall return to the package SET_PACKAGE built up in Section 8.8. This package described the abstract data set set of characters. Now we shall construct a generic package that can be used to describe sets of any discrete type, for example, set of months or set of small integers. The specification of the package takes the form:

```
generic
  type ELEMENT is (< >);
package SET_PACKAGE is

  type SET is private;

  function EMPTY_SET return SET;
  -- gives the empty set

  function ADD (E : ELEMENT; S : SET) return SET;
  -- puts E into the set S

  function SUB (E : ELEMENT; S : SET) return SET;
  -- removes E from the set S

  function MEMBER (E : ELEMENT; S : SET) return BOOLEAN;
  -- finds out if E is a member of the set S

  function UNION (S1, S2 : SET) return SET;
  -- returns the union of the sets S1 and S2

  function INTERSECTION (S1, S2 : SET) return SET;
  -- returns the intersection of the sets S1 and S2

  function SUBSET (S1, S2 : SET) return BOOLEAN;
  -- finds out if S1 is a subset of S2
```

```
private
    type SET is array (ELEMENT) of BOOLEAN;
end SET_PACKAGE;
```

(To simplify things we have removed the procedure WRITE). On the second line we have declared ELEMENT as a generic type parameter that should be a discrete type. In the private part of the package specification we use our knowledge that ELEMENT is a discrete type when we use it as the index type in the declaration of the type SET. This would have been illegal if ELEMENT had been declared as a generic type parameter that was private.

Note that the type SET is a private type in the package in the same way as the private types in earlier chapters. It should not be confused with a generic type parameter.

The body of the package is the same as in Section 8.8, but the elements of the sets are now of type ELEMENT instead of CHARACTER.

Now we can use this generic package in a program to create different kinds of sets. If we have the type declarations:

```
type DAY is (MONDAY, TUESDAY, WEDNESDAY,
                THURSDAY, FRIDAY, SATURDAY, SUNDAY);
type LITTLE_NUMBER is range 0 .. 100;
```

then we can create two instances of the set package:

```
package DAY_PACKAGE is new SET_PACKAGE(DAY);
package NUM_PACKAGE is new SET_PACKAGE(LITTLE_NUMBER);
```

In both these declarations the actual generic parameter is a discrete type. It would be illegal to try and create an instance of the set package and state a type that is not discrete, such as FLOAT. If we insert the line:

```
use DAY_PACKAGE, NUM_PACKAGE;
```

then we can declare the sets:

```
DAY_SET   : DAY_PACKAGE.SET := EMPTY_SET;
NUM_SET1 : NUM_PACKAGE.SET := EMPTY_SET;
NUM_SET2 : NUM_PACKAGE.SET := EMPTY_SET;
```

We must use the selector notation to state which type of set we are referring to because the compiler cannot determine it from the context. However, selector notation is not needed in the initialization expression. There, the compiler 'understands' which of the functions EMPTY_SET should be used. The three sets can be treated in the same way as before. We can have, for example, the statements:

```
DAY_SET := ADD(MONDAY, DAY_SET);
NUM_SET1 := SUB(23, NUM_SET2);
if SUBSET(NUM_SET1, NUM_SET2) then
```

A generic type parameter can also be specified to be a numeric type. A type parameter that will be an integer type is stated by writing:

```
type T is range < >     -- T will be an integer type
```

and a type parameter that will be a floating point type is written:

```
type T is digits < >     -- T will be a floating point type
```

As an example of this we shall study a generic function that can be used to evaluate the largest component in an array of floating point components:

```
generic
  type FLOAT_NR is digits < >;
  type TAB is array (INTEGER range < >) of FLOAT_NR;
function MAX (T : TAB) return FLOAT_NR;
```

Here is something new. There are two generic parameters, FLOAT_NR and TAB. When a generic parameter is declared, generic parameters declared earlier can be used. In the declaration of TAB we have stated that the elements should be of type FLOAT_NR, that is, they can be of any floating point type. The function's body is:

```
function MAX (T : TAB) return FLOAT_NR is
  M : FLOAT_NR := -FLOAT_NR'LARGE;
begin
  for I in T'RANGE loop
    if T(I) > M then
      M := T(I);
    end if;
  end loop;
  return M;
end MAX;
```

Here we have made use of the fact that FLOAT_NR is a floating point type and used the attribute LARGE which exists for all floating point types. We also know that the parameter T is of an array type; we can therefore use the attribute T'RANGE and index T.

In the specification of MAX we have assumed that the type TAB should have an index of type INTEGER. This is an unnecessary limitation. If we want the index type to be any discrete type, we can add a further generic parameter and give the specification:

```
generic
    type INDEX is (< >);
    type FLOAT_NR is digits <>;
    type TAB is array (INDEX range <>) of FLOAT_NR;
function MAX (T : TAB) return FLOAT_NR;
```

Now we can create some instances of MAX. If we make the type declaration:

```
type VECTOR is array (INTEGER range < >) of FLOAT;
```

we can create an instance of MAX that looks for the largest number in an array of type VECTOR:

```
function MAX_NO is new MAX(INTEGER, FLOAT, VECTOR);
```

Thus we state three actual parameters. The function MAX_NO can now be called in the usual way with a parameter of type VECTOR.

Another instance of MAX can be created if we have the type declarations:

```
type TEMP is digits 5;
type DAY   is (MONDAY, TUESDAY, WEDNESDAY,
               THURSDAY, FRIDAY, SATURDAY,
               SUNDAY);
type TEMP_MEASURES is array (DAY range < >) of TEMP;
```

The declaration:

```
function MAX_TEMP is new MAX(DAY, TEMP, TEMP_MEASURES);
```

then produces a function that can find the largest component in an array of the type TEMP_MEASURES.

Finally, it is possible to specify that a generic type parameter will be an access type, by writing, for example:

```
type T is access Q:      -- T will be an access type
```

The type Q can be any type at all, even a generic type parameter previously specified.

Generic type parameters

The following forms are possible:

- **type** T **is private**;
  -- T is any type that allows assignment and comparison

- **type** T **is limited private**;
  -- T is any type
  -- assignment and comparison need not exist

- **type** T **is** (<>);
  -- T is a discrete type (enumeration or integer type)

- **type** T **is range** <>;
  -- T is an integer type

- **type** T **is digits** <>;
  -- T is a floating point type

- **type** T **is array** (*index_type*) **of** *element_type*;
  -- T is an array type

- **type** T **is access** *any_type*;
  -- T is an access type.

13.2.3 Subprogram parameters

■

The third category of generic parameter is the subprogram parameter. As a first example we shall study a problem to do with lists. Assume we have a list L:

$$L = (1_1, 1_2, 1_3, \dots , 1_n)$$

Now assume we have a function f that we want to apply to every element in L. Thus we want a list:

$$(f(1_1), f(1_2), f(1_3), \dots , f(1_n))$$

The elements in the list may be, for example, integers and the function f may be:

$$f(x) = x^2$$

In this case we want to have a list where each element is the square of the corresponding element in the original list. Another example is that we have a list where the elements are single characters. The function may then be a function that translates any upper case letters in the list into lower case.

We shall now give a specification for a generic function APPL which will be applicable to different kinds of lists and different functions f. As its result, APPL gives a new list where the function f has been applied to every element. We assume that a list is represented using an unconstrained array type, each element in the list being stored as a component of the array. The specification of the generic function APPL then appears as follows:

```
generic
  type ELEMENT is private;
  type LIST is array (POSITIVE range < >) of ELEMENT;
  with function F (E : ELEMENT) return ELEMENT;
function APPL (L : LIST) return LIST;
```

We have three generic parameters: ELEMENT, LIST and F.ELEMENT and LIST are type parameters and F is a subprogram parameter. A declaration of a subprogram parameter is introduced by the reserved word **with**. Afterwards a subprogram declaration is written in the normal way, and in it may be used any generic parameters that have been declared previously. In the declaration of F, for example, we have used the type parameter ELEMENT.

The body of APPL is simply:

```
function APPL (L : LIST) return LIST is
  NEW_L : LIST(L'RANGE);
begin
  for I in L'RANGE loop
    NEW_L(I) := F(L(I));
  end loop;
  return NEW_L;
end APPL;
```

Now the generic function APPL can be used in a program. Let us assume we have the type declaration:

```
type NUMBER_LIST is array (POSITIVE range < >) of INTEGER;
```

and the functions:

```
function SQUARE (X : INTEGER) return INTEGER is
begin
  return X ** 2;
end SQUARE;

function TRANSLATE (C : CHARACTER) return CHARACTER is
  DIFF : constant
        := CHARACTER'POS('a') - CHARACTER'POS('A');
begin
  if C in 'A' .. 'Z' then
    return CHARACTER'VAL(CHARACTER'POS(C) + DIFF);
  else
    return C;
  end if;
end TRANSLATE;
```

Then we are able to create two instances of APPL:

```
function QUAD is new
            APPL(INTEGER, NUMBER_LIST, SQUARE);
function LC is new
            APPL(CHARACTER, STRING, TRANSLATE);
```

Thus the function's name is given as an actual parameter. In QUAD the function F will become SQUARE. Every call to F in the body of APPL will mean a call to SQUARE. In LC, in the same way, F will be identified as the function TRANSLATE.

If the variables L1 and L2 have the type NUMBER_LIST, we can now write the statement:

```
L2 := QUAD(L1);
```

L2 will then hold the squares of all the numbers in L1. If S1 and S2 have the type STRING, the corresponding statement can be written:

```
S2 := LC(S1);
```

Then S2 will contain all the characters in S1 but the upper case letters will have been translated into lower case.

Generic subprogram parameters can be used in connection with numeric calculations. In the next example we shall study a generic function FIND_ZERO which finds a zero of a mathematical function, that is, the value of the independent variable for which the function has zero value. We start by writing a specification of FIND_ZERO:

```
generic
   type FLOAT_PT_NO is digits < >;
   with function F (X : FLOAT_PT_NO) return FLOAT_PT_NO;
   EPSILON : FLOAT_PT_NO := 1.0E−5;
function FIND_ZERO (A, B : FLOAT_PT_NO) return FLOAT_PT_NO;
```

FIND_ZERO has three generic parameters: FLOAT_PT_NO, F and EPSILON. FLOAT_PT_NO is a type parameter denoting a floating point type. EPSILON is a value parameter which we have given a default value of 1.0E−5. The generic parameter F is a subprogram parameter. This parameter denotes the mathematical function whose zero we are looking for.

The function FIND_ZERO has two ordinary parameters A and B of type FLOAT_PT_NO, which state the interval in which the zero should be sought. Thus we are looking for a value x in the interval $[a,b]$ such that $f(x) = 0$. We assume that f is a monotonic function and that it has one and only one zero in the given interval.

If $f(x_1) < 0 < f(x_2)$ the following algorithm can be used to evaluate the zero of f. The idea is to close in on the zero by moving the end points x_1 and x_2 nearer and nearer to one another; the condition $f(x_1) < 0 < f(x_2)$ must always hold.

(1) Repeat the following until the interval [X1,X2] becomes sufficiently small:
   (1.1) Let XM be the mid-point of the interval [X1,X2].
   (1.2) Compute the value of the function F(XM).
   (1.3) If F(XM) < 0 then the zero lies to the right of XM. Therefore set X1 to XM.
   (1.4) If F(XM) > 0 then the zero lies to the left of XM. Therefore set X2 to XM.
   (1.5) If F(XM) = 0 then the zero has been found. Terminate the algorithm and return XM as result.
(2) Give the mean of X1 and X2 as result.

Now we can apply the algorithm in the body of the function FIND_ZERO which becomes:

```
function FIND_ZERO (A, B : FLOAT_PT_NO)
                              return FLOAT_PT_NO is
   X1, X2, XM, FM : FLOAT_PT_NO;
begin
   if F(A) < 0.0 and F(B) > 0.0 then
      X1 := A; X2 := B;
   elsif F(A) > 0.0 and F(B) < 0.0 then
      X1 := B; X2 := A;
```

```
   elsif F(A) = 0.0 then
      return A;
   elsif F(B) = 0.0 then
      return B;
   else
      raise ZERO_NOT_FOUND;      -- declared outside the function
   end if;
   -- it is now known that F(X1) < 0 < F(X2)
   while abs (X1 − X2) > EPSILON loop
      XM := (X1 + X2) / 2.0;      -- find midpoint
      FM := F(XM);
      if FM < 0.0 then
         X1 := XM;
      elsif FM > 0.0 then
         X2 := XM;
      else
         return XM;      -- we have found a zero of F
      end if;
   end loop;
   return (X1 + X2) / 2.0;
end FIND_ZERO;
```

In the first part of the function we make sure that the condition
$F(X1) < 0 < F(X2)$ is true. If $F(A) < 0$ and $F(B) > 0$, then we simply set X1
to A and X2 to B. If it is the other way round, then we interchange A and
B. If one of the endpoints A or B is zero, then we return this result
directly. If, finally, F(A) and F(B) are both either less than or greater than
0, then there is no zero in the interval and we raise an exception.

Now we can use the generic function FIND_ZERO to find the zeros
of different functions. If, for example, we have two functions:

```
function F1 (X : FLOAT) return FLOAT is
begin
   return X − 1.0;
end F1;

function F2 (X : FLOAT) return FLOAT is
begin
   return 2.0*X**3 − 3.0*X**2 − 18.0*X − 8.0;
end F2;
```

then we can create two instances of FIND_ZERO:

```
function F1_ZERO is new FIND_ZERO(FLOAT, F1, 1.0E−8);
function F2_ZERO is new FIND_ZERO(FLOAT, F2);
```

The zero of the function F1 can be written out with the statement:

    PUT(F1_ZERO(−10.0, 10.0));

and the zero of F2 which lies in the interval −1 to 1 can be written out with:

    PUT(F2_ZERO(−1.0, 1.0));

Generic subprogram parameters can be given default values. If, for example, we have a generic procedure parameter P (without parameters) and we want to give it the default value PDEF, we write:

    procedure P **is** PDEF;

This means that the procedure PDEF will be used in the body of the generic unit if no actual parameter is given for P.

It may not be of much use to give a special subprogram as default value. The following way of assigning a default value is more useful:

    function "+" (E1, E2 : ELEMENT) **return** ELEMENT **is** < >;

First, note that a subprogram parameter can have an operator name. Here we have used the name "+". The symbol < > denotes that if no actual parameter is given when an instance of the generic unit is created then the function "+" for the type ELEMENT should automatically be used. If ELEMENT is given the type INTEGER, for example, then "+" is, of course, defined for that type and this normal "+" operator is to be used.

As a final example we shall write a generic procedure that can be used to sort all kinds of arrays, with any component type and index type. We make the specification:

•   **generic**
        type INDEX **is** (< >);
        type ELEMENT **is private**;
        type ARRAY_TYPE **is array** (INDEX **range** < >) **of** ELEMENT;
        with function "<" (E1, E2 : ELEMENT) **return** BOOLEAN **is** < >;
    procedure SORT (A : **in out** ARRAY_TYPE);

We have four generic parameters: the index type, the component type, the type of the array and a subprogram parameter "<" which is used to denote the function that compares two components in an array.

In the body of SORT we use the sort algorithm described in Section 5.8. The body is then:

```
procedure SORT (A : in out ARRAY_TYPE) is
  M : INDEX;
  T : ELEMENT;
begin
  for K in A'RANGE loop
    -- find smallest element between K and A'LAST
    M := K;
    for I in INDEX'SUCC(K) .. A'LAST loop
      if A(I) < A(M) then
        M := I;
      end if;
    end loop;

    -- swap elements in Kth and Mth positions
    T := A(K); A(K) := A(M); A(M) := T;
  end loop;
end SORT;
```

Note that we have written:

```
INDEX'SUCC(K)
```

instead of:

```
K + 1
```

The reason for this is that INDEX does not need to be an integer type and an addition operator may not be defined.

The comparison operator "<" which is used in the expression:

```
F(I) < F(M)
```

is the function that is described in the subprogram parameter "<" in the specification.

We can show some examples of the use of SORT. Assume we have the type declarations:

```
type NO_ARRAY is array (NATURAL range < >) of INTEGER;
type PERSON is
  record
    NAME    : STRING(1 .. 20);
    ADDRESS : STRING(1 .. 30);
  end record;
```

```
type NAME_TAB is array (POSITIVE range < >) of PERSON;
type DAY is (MONDAY, TUESDAY, WEDNESDAY,
                THURSDAY, FRIDAY, SATURDAY, SUNDAY);
type TIME is digits 4;
type WEEK_TAB is array (DAY range < >) of TIME;
```

and that we have declared the variables N, P and W:

```
N : NO_ARRAY(1 .. 50);
P : NAME_TAB(1 .. 200);
W : WEEK_TAB(MONDAY .. FRIDAY);
```

Two people can be compared with the function:

```
function BEFORE (P1, P2 : PERSON) return BOOLEAN is
begin
  return P1.NAME < P2.NAME;
end BEFORE;
```

Now we are ready to create three different instances of SORT:

```
procedure NO_SORT is new SORT
                (NATURAL, INTEGER, NO_ARRAY, "<");
procedure PERS_SORT is new SORT
                (POSITIVE, PERSON, NAME_TAB, BEFORE);
procedure TIME_SORT is new SORT
                (DAY, TIME, WEEK_TAB);
```

In the declaration of NO_SORT we have given the subprogram parameter the value "<". Here "<" denotes the normal comparison operator for integers. Since the subprogram parameter had the default value < > in the specification, we could have left out the actual parameter, thus:

```
procedure NO_SORT is new SORT(NATURAL, INTEGER, NO_ARRAY);
```

Then the normal comparison operator for integers would be automatically assumed. In the declaration of TIME_SORT we have used this simpler form. There is no standard "<" for the type PERSON, so we have had to give the function BEFORE as an actual parameter.

The three arrays N, P and W can now easily be sorted with the calls:

```
NO_SORT(N);
PERS_SORT(P);
TIME_SORT(W);
```

> **Generic subprogram parameters**
>
>   **with** *subprogram_declaration*;
>
> Default values can be given using one of the forms:
>
>   **with** *subprogram_declaration* **is**
>   *subprogram_name*;
>   **with** *subprogram_declaration* **is** < >;

☐

EXERCISES

13.1 Write a generic procedure ORDER that has two parameters A and B
of unspecified type. After calling an instance of the procedure, A
must be less than B. (Assume that A and B are of types where the
operator < is defined). Create two instances of the procedure
ORDER, one to order two integers and the other to order two text
strings.

13.2 Make a specification of the package RANDOM_PACKAGE so that the
two constants K and M that are used in the random number
generation can be stated as generic value parameters. (See
Section 8.7).

13.3 Rewrite the package STACK_PACKAGE in Section 11.4 so that it
describes an abstract data type STACK where the elements can be
of arbitrary type. Create instances of the package that describe the
abstract data types *floating point stack* and *person stack*. Then
declare two floating point stacks and one person stack.

13.4 Write a generic queue package that can be used to create queues
with elements of arbitrary type.

    (a)   Use a package with 'memory' and place the elements in an
array within the package. Let the size of the array be a
generic value parameter.

    (b)   Let the package describe an abstract data type and use the
same technique as in Section 11.4.

(c)   Show how to create a queue of integers. Read in 100 integers from the terminal and then write them out in the same order. Use the generic package from part (a).

(d)   Repeat the task in part (c), but use the package from (b).

13.5   Write a generic function NEXT that can be used for arbitrary enumeration types. The function should have an enumeration value as parameter and return the next value in the type when called. If the function gets the last value as parameter it should return the first value as its result. (If there is an instance of the function for the type DAYS_OF_THE_WEEK, then a call with SUNDAY as parameter should return MONDAY as result).

13.6   Write a generic function FIND that can be used to find a certain element in an array of arbitrary type. FIND should have an array and an element value as parameters and, as result, should give the index value for the place in the array where the sought element is to be found.

13.7   Write a generic function that adds the elements in an array of arbitrary type. The function should have a subprogram parameter '+' as generic parameter, which adds two elements of the component type of the array. Give the subprogram parameter an appropriate default value.

13.8   Write a generic package that handles a binary search tree where the elements are of arbitrary type. The package should contain the subprograms INSERT, REMOVE and FOUND which, respectively, inserts an element in the tree, removes an element from the tree, and investigates whether a certain element is to be found in the tree. The package should have '<' and '=' as generic parameters, where '<' determines if one element is less than another and '=' determines whether two elements are equal.

13.9   The value of the integral:

$$I = \int_a^b f(x) \, dx$$

can be approximated, using the **trapezium rule**, by the formula:

$$I \approx$$
$$h\left(\frac{f(a)}{2} + f(a+h) + f(a+2h) + \ldots + f(a+(n-1)h) + \frac{f(b)}{2} \right)$$

The interval a to b has been divided into n subintervals of length h, so:

$$h = \frac{b - a}{n}$$

Write a generic function INTEGRAL to evaluate the integral of an arbitrary function. In the body of INTEGRAL carry out repeated calculations of the integral until the difference between two evaluations becomes sufficiently small. For each new evaluation, double the value of n, that is, double the number of subintervals.

Use the generic function to evaluate the integral:

$$\int_1^5 x^2 dx$$

APPENDICES

A1
The package TEXT_IO

```
with IO_EXCEPTIONS;
package TEXT_IO is

    type FILE_TYPE  is limited private;
    type FILE_MODE is (IN_FILE, OUT_FILE);

    type COUNT is range 0 .. implementation_defined;
    subtype POSITIVE_COUNT is COUNT range 1 .. COUNT'LAST;
    UNBOUNDED : constant COUNT := 0;     -- line and page length

    subtype FIELD        is INTEGER range 0 .. implementation_defined;
    subtype NUMBER_BASE is INTEGER range 2 .. 16;

    type TYPE_SET is (LOWER_CASE, UPPER_CASE);

    -- File Management

    procedure CREATE (FILE   : in out FILE_TYPE;
                      MODE : in FILE_MODE := OUT_FILE;
                      NAME : in STRING := "";
                      FORM : in STRING := "");

    procedure OPEN (FILE   : in out FILE_TYPE;
                    MODE : in FILE_MODE;
                    NAME : in STRING;
                    FORM : in STRING := "");

    procedure CLOSE  (FILE: in out FILE_TYPE);
    procedure DELETE (FILE: in out FILE_TYPE);
    procedure RESET  (FILE: in out FILE_TYPE; MODE: in FILE_MODE);
    procedure RESET  (FILE: in out FILE_TYPE);

    function MODE (FILE: in FILE_TYPE) return FILE_MODE;
    function NAME (FILE: in FILE_TYPE) return STRING;
    function FORM (FILE: in FILE_TYPE) return STRING;

    function IS_OPEN(FILE: in FILE_TYPE) return BOOLEAN;

    -- Control of default input and output files
```

```
procedure SET_INPUT   (FILE: in FILE_TYPE);
procedure SET_OUTPUT(FILE: in FILE_TYPE);

function STANDARD_INPUT    return FILE_TYPE;
function STANDARD_OUTPUT return FILE_TYPE;

function CURRENT_INPUT    return FILE_TYPE;
function CURRENT_OUTPUT return FILE_TYPE;

-- Specification of line and page lengths

procedure SET_LINE_LENGTH (FILE: in FILE_TYPE; TO: in COUNT);
procedure SET_LINE_LENGTH (TO:  in COUNT);

procedure SET_PAGE_LENGTH (FILE: in FILE_TYPE; TO: in COUNT);
procedure SET_PAGE_LENGTH (TO:   in COUNT);

function LINE_LENGTH(FILE: in FILE_TYPE) return COUNT;
function LINE_LENGTH return COUNT;

function PAGE_LENGTH(FILE: in FILE_TYPE) return COUNT;
function PAGE_LENGTH return COUNT;

-- Column, Line, and Page Control

procedure NEW_LINE (FILE:      in FILE_TYPE;
                         SPACING: in POSITIVE_COUNT := 1);
procedure NEW_LINE (SPACING: in POSITIVE_COUNT := 1);

procedure SKIP_LINE (FILE:      in FILE_TYPE;
                         SPACING: in POSITIVE_COUNT := 1);
procedure SKIP_LINE (SPACING: in POSITIVE_COUNT := 1);

function END_OF_LINE(FILE: in FILE_TYPE) return BOOLEAN;
function END_OF_LINE return BOOLEAN;

procedure NEW_PAGE (FILE: in FILE_TYPE);
procedure NEW_PAGE;

procedure SKIP_PAGE (FILE: in FILE_TYPE);
procedure SKIP_PAGE;

function END_OF_PAGE(FILE: in FILE_TYPE) return BOOLEAN;
function END_OF_PAGE return BOOLEAN;

function END_OF_FILE(FILE: in FILE_TYPE) return BOOLEAN;
function END_OF_FILE return BOOLEAN;

procedure SET_COL (FILE: in FILE_TYPE; TO: in POSITIVE_COUNT);
procedure SET_COL (TO:   in POSITIVE_COUNT);

procedure SET_LINE (FILE: in FILE_TYPE; TO: in POSITIVE_COUNT);
procedure SET_LINE (TO:   in POSITIVE_COUNT);

function COL (FILE: in FILE_TYPE) return POSITIVE_COUNT;
function COL  return POSITIVE_COUNT;
function LINE  (FILE: in FILE_TYPE) return POSITIVE_COUNT;
function LINE   return POSITIVE_COUNT;
```

```
function PAGE (FILE: in FILE_TYPE) return POSITIVE_COUNT;
function PAGE return POSITIVE_COUNT;

-- Character Input-Output

procedure GET (FILE: in FILE_TYPE; ITEM: out CHARACTER);
procedure GET (ITEM: out CHARACTER);
procedure PUT (FILE: in FILE_TYPE; ITEM: in CHARACTER);
procedure PUT (ITEM: in CHARACTER);

-- String Input-Output

procedure GET (FILE: in FILE_TYPE; ITEM: out STRING);
procedure GET (ITEM: out STRING);
procedure PUT (FILE: in FILE_TYPE; ITEM: in STRING);
procedure PUT (ITEM: in STRING);

procedure GET_LINE (FILE:  in FILE_TYPE; ITEM: out STRING;
                    LAST: out NATURAL);
procedure GET_LINE (ITEM: out STRING; LAST: out NATURAL);
procedure PUT_LINE (FILE: in FILE_TYPE; ITEM: in STRING);
procedure PUT_LINE (ITEM: in STRING);

-- Generic package for Input-Output of Integer Types

generic
  type NUM is range < >;
package INTEGER_IO is
  DEFAULT_WIDTH: FIELD := NUM'WIDTH;
  DEFAULT_BASE: NUMBER_BASE := 10;

  procedure GET (FILE:   in FILE_TYPE;
                 ITEM:   out NUM;
                 WIDTH: in FIELD := 0);
  procedure GET (ITEM:   out NUM; WIDTH: in FIELD := 0);

  procedure PUT (FILE:   in FILE_TYPE;
                 ITEM:   in NUM;
                 WIDTH: in FIELD := DEFAULT_WIDTH;
                 BASE:  in NUMBER_BASE := DEFAULT_BASE);
  procedure PUT (ITEM:   in NUM;
                 WIDTH: in FIELD := DEFAULT_WIDTH;
                 BASE:  in NUMBER_BASE := DEFAULT_BASE);

  procedure GET (FROM:  in STRING;
                 ITEM:   out NUM;
                 LAST:   out POSITIVE);
  procedure PUT (TO:     out STRING;
                 ITEM:   in NUM;
                 BASE:  in NUMBER_BASE := DEFAULT_BASE);
end INTEGER_IO;
```

contd. overleaf

-- Generic package for Input-Output of Real Types

```
generic
  type NUM is digits < >;
package FLOAT_IO is
  DEFAULT_FORE: FIELD := 2;
  DEFAULT_AFT:  FIELD := NUM'DIGITS − 1;
  DEFAULT_EXP:  FIELD := 3;

  procedure GET (FILE:  in FILE_TYPE;
                 ITEM:  out NUM;
                 WIDTH: in FIELD := 0);
  procedure GET (ITEM:  out NUM; WIDTH: in FIELD := 0);

  procedure PUT (FILE:  in FILE_TYPE;
                 ITEM:  in NUM;
                 FORE:  in FIELD := DEFAULT_FORE;
                 AFT:   in FIELD := DEFAULT_AFT;
                 EXP:   in FIELD := DEFAULT_EXP);
  procedure PUT (ITEM:  in NUM;
                 FORE:  in FIELD := DEFAULT_FORE;
                 AFT:   in FIELD := DEFAULT_AFT;
                 EXP:   in FIELD := DEFAULT_EXP);

  procedure GET (FROM:  in STRING;
                 ITEM:  out NUM;
                 LAST:  out POSITIVE);
  procedure PUT (TO:    out STRING;
                 ITEM:  in NUM;
                 AFT:   in FIELD := DEFAULT_AFT;
                 EXP:   in FIELD := DEFAULT_EXP);
end FLOAT_IO;

generic
  type NUM is delta < >;
package FIXED_IO is
  DEFAULT_FORE: FIELD := NUM'FORE;
  DEFAULT_AFT:  FIELD := NUM'AFT;
  DEFAULT_EXP:  FIELD := 0;

  procedure GET (FILE:  in FILE_TYPE;
                 ITEM:  out NUM;
                 WIDTH: in FIELD := 0);
  procedure GET (ITEM:  out NUM; WIDTH: in FIELD := 0);

  procedure PUT (FILE:  in FILE_TYPE;
                 ITEM:  in NUM;
                 FORE:  in FIELD := DEFAULT_FORE;
                 AFT:   in FIELD := DEFAULT_AFT;
                 EXP:   in FIELD := DEFAULT_EXP);
```

```
    procedure PUT (ITEM:    in NUM;
                   FORE:    in FIELD := DEFAULT_FORE;
                   AFT:     in FIELD := DEFAULT_AFT;
                   EXP:     in FIELD := DEFAULT_EXP);
    procedure GET (FROM:    in STRING;
                   ITEM:    out NUM;
                   LAST:    out POSITIVE);
    procedure PUT (TO:      out STRING;
                   ITEM:    in NUM;
                   AFT:     in FIELD := DEFAULT_AFT;
                   EXP:     in FIELD := DEFAULT_EXP);
end FIXED_IO;


-- Generic package for Input-Output of Enumeration Types

generic
    type ENUM is (< >);
package ENUMERATION_IO is
    DEFAULT_WIDTH:    FIELD := 0;
    DEFAULT_SETTING: TYPE_SET := UPPER_CASE;

    procedure GET (FILE:    in FILE_TYPE; ITEM: out ENUM);
    procedure GET (ITEM:    out ENUM);

    procedure PUT (FILE:    in FILE_TYPE;
                   ITEM:    in ENUM;
                   WIDTH: in FIELD := DEFAULT_WIDTH;
                   SET:     in TYPE_SET := DEFAULT_SETTING);
    procedure PUT (ITEM:    in ENUM;
                   WIDTH: in FIELD := DEFAULT_WIDTH;
                   SET:     in TYPE_SET := DEFAULT_SETTING);

    procedure GET (FROM:    in STRING;
                   ITEM:    out ENUM;
                   LAST:    out POSITIVE);
    procedure PUT (TO:      out STRING;
                   ITEM:    in ENUM;
                   SET:     in TYPE_SET := DEFAULT_SETTING);
end ENUMERATION_IO;


-- Exceptions

STATUS_ERROR: exception renames IO_EXCEPTIONS.STATUS_ERROR;
MODE_ERROR:   exception renames IO_EXCEPTIONS.MODE_ERROR;
NAME_ERROR:   exception renames IO_EXCEPTIONS.NAME_ERROR;
USE_ERROR:    exception renames IO_EXCEPTIONS.USE_ERROR;
DEVICE_ERROR: exception renames IO_EXCEPTIONS.DEVICE_ERROR;
```

contd. overleaf

```
END_ERROR:     exception renames IO_EXCEPTIONS.END_ERROR;
DATA_ERROR:    exception renames IO_EXCEPTIONS.DATA_ERROR;
LAYOUT_ERROR: exception renames IO_EXCEPTIONS.LAYOUT_ERROR;

private
   -- implementation-dependent
end TEXT_IO;
```

A2
The package BASIC_NUM_IO

Given below is the specification of the package BASIC_NUM_IO which can be used to simplify access to the procedures GET and PUT for the standard types INTEGER and FLOAT. The two packages STANDARD_INTEGER_IO and STANDARD_FLOAT_IO have been created using the generic packages INTEGER_IO and FLOAT_IO which are to be found in TEXT_IO. Using the **renames** construct, the names STANDARD_INTEGER_IO.GET and so on have been renamed so that the user of BASIC_NUM_IO can simply write GET and PUT.

```
with TEXT_IO;
package BASIC_NUM_IO is

   package STANDARD_INTEGER_IO is new
                              TEXT_IO.INTEGER_IO(INTEGER);

   DEFAULT_WIDTH : TEXT_IO.FIELD := INTEGER'WIDTH;
   DEFAULT_BASE  : TEXT_IO.NUMBER_BASE := 10;

   procedure GET (ITEM   : out INTEGER;
                  WIDTH : in TEXT_IO.FIELD := 0)
                  renames STANDARD_INTEGER_IO.GET;

   procedure PUT (ITEM   : in INTEGER;
                  WIDTH : in TEXT_IO.FIELD := DEFAULT_WIDTH;
                  BASE   : in TEXT_IO.NUMBER_BASE := DEFAULT_BASE)
                  renames STANDARD_INTEGER_IO.PUT;

   package STANDARD_FLOAT_IO is new TEXT_IO.FLOAT_IO(FLOAT);
   DEFAULT_FORE : TEXT_IO.FIELD := 2;
   DEFAULT_AFT   : TEXT_IO.FIELD := FLOAT'DIGITS - 1;
   DEFAULT_EXP   : TEXT_IO.FIELD := 3;

   procedure GET (ITEM   : out FLOAT;
                  WIDTH : in TEXT_IO.FIELD := 0)
                  renames STANDARD_FLOAT_IO.GET;
```

```
procedure PUT (ITEM   : in FLOAT;
               FORE  : in TEXT_IO.FIELD := DEFAULT_FORE;
               AFT   : in TEXT_IO.FIELD := DEFAULT_AFT;
               EXP   : in TEXT_IO.FIELD := DEFAULT_EXP)
               renames STANDARD_FLOAT_IO.PUT;
end BASIC_NUM_IO;
```

A3
The package STANDARD

package STANDARD **is**
type BOOLEAN **is** (FALSE, TRUE);

-- The predefined relational operators for this type are as follows:

-- **function** ''=''   (LEFT, RIGHT : BOOLEAN) **return** BOOLEAN;
-- **function** ''/=''   (LEFT, RIGHT : BOOLEAN) **return** BOOLEAN;
-- **function** ''<''   (LEFT, RIGHT : BOOLEAN) **return** BOOLEAN;
-- **function** ''<='' (LEFT, RIGHT : BOOLEAN) **return** BOOLEAN;
-- **function** ''>''   (LEFT, RIGHT : BOOLEAN) **return** BOOLEAN;
-- **function** ''>='' (LEFT, RIGHT : BOOLEAN) **return** BOOLEAN;

-- The predefined logical operators and the predefined logical negation operator
-- are as follows:

-- **function** ''**and**'' (LEFT, RIGHT : BOOLEAN) **return** BOOLEAN;
-- **function** ''**or**''   (LEFT, RIGHT : BOOLEAN) **return** BOOLEAN;
-- **function** ''**xor**'' (LEFT, RIGHT : BOOLEAN) **return** BOOLEAN;

-- **function** ''**not**'' (RIGHT : BOOLEAN) **return** BOOLEAN;

-- The universal type *universal_integer* is predefined.

type INTEGER **is** *implementation_defined*;

-- The predefined operators for this type are as follows:

-- **function** ''=''   (LEFT, RIGHT : INTEGER) **return** BOOLEAN;
-- **function** ''/=''   (LEFT, RIGHT : INTEGER) **return** BOOLEAN;
-- **function** ''<''   (LEFT, RIGHT : INTEGER) **return** BOOLEAN;
-- **function** ''<='' (LEFT, RIGHT : INTEGER) **return** BOOLEAN;
-- **function** ''>''   (LEFT, RIGHT : INTEGER) **return** BOOLEAN;
-- **function** ''>='' (LEFT, RIGHT : INTEGER) **return** BOOLEAN;

-- **function** ''+''   (RIGHT : INTEGER) **return** INTEGER;
-- **function** ''−''   (RIGHT : INTEGER) **return** INTEGER;
-- **function** ''**abs**'' (RIGHT : INTEGER) **return** INTEGER;

-- **function** ''+''   (LEFT, RIGHT : INTEGER) **return** INTEGER;
-- **function** ''−''   (LEFT, RIGHT : INTEGER) **return** INTEGER;

```
-- function "*"     (LEFT, RIGHT : INTEGER) return INTEGER;
-- function "/"     (LEFT, RIGHT : INTEGER) return INTEGER;
-- function "rem"  (LEFT, RIGHT : INTEGER) return INTEGER;
-- function "mod" (LEFT, RIGHT : INTEGER) return INTEGER;

-- function "**"    (LEFT: INTEGER; RIGHT: INTEGER) return INTEGER;
```

-- An implementation may provide additional predefined integer types. It is
-- recommended that the names of such additional types end with INTEGER as
-- in SHORT_INTEGER or LONG_INTEGER. The specification of each operator
-- for the type *universal_integer*, or for any additional predefined integer type, is
-- obtained by replacing INTEGER by the name of the type in the specification of
-- the corresponding operator of the type INTEGER, except for the right operand
-- of the exponentiating operator.

-- The universal type *universal_real* is predefined.

type FLOAT **is** *implementation_defined*;

-- The predefined operators for this type are as follows:

```
-- function "="     (LEFT, RIGHT : FLOAT) return BOOLEAN;
-- function "/="    (LEFT, RIGHT : FLOAT) return BOOLEAN;
-- function "<"     (LEFT, RIGHT : FLOAT) return BOOLEAN;
-- function "<="  (LEFT, RIGHT : FLOAT) return BOOLEAN;
-- function ">"     (LEFT, RIGHT : FLOAT) return BOOLEAN;
-- function ">="   (LEFT, RIGHT : FLOAT) return BOOLEAN;

-- function "+"    (RIGHT : FLOAT) return FLOAT;
-- function "−"    (RIGHT : FLOAT) return FLOAT;
-- function "abs"  (RIGHT : FLOAT) return FLOAT;

-- function "+"    (LEFT, RIGHT : FLOAT) return FLOAT;
-- function "−"    (LEFT, RIGHT : FLOAT) return FLOAT;
-- function "*"    (LEFT, RIGHT : FLOAT) return FLOAT;
-- function "/"    (LEFT, RIGHT : FLOAT) return FLOAT;

-- function "**"    (LEFT : FLOAT; RIGHT : INTEGER) return FLOAT;
```

-- An implementation may provide additional predefined floating point types. It is
-- recommended that the names of such additional types end with FLOAT as in
-- SHORT_FLOAT or LONG_FLOAT. The specification of each operator for the
-- type *universal_real*, or for any additional predefined floating point type, is
-- obtained by replacing FLOAT by the name of the type in the specification of
-- the corresponding operator of the type FLOAT.

-- In addition, the following operators are predefined for the universal types.

```
-- function "*"(LEFT : universal_integer;RIGHT : universal_real)
--                                         return universal_real;
-- function "*"(LEFT : universal_real;    RIGHT : universal_integer)
--                                         return universal_real;
-- function "/"(LEFT : universal_real;    RIGHT : universal_integer)
--                                         return universal_real;
```

-- The type *universal_fixed* is predefined. The only operators declared for this
-- type are

-- **function** "*.*"(LEFT : *any_fixed_point_type*; RIGHT : *any_fixed_point_type*)
--   **return** *universal_fixed*;
-- **function** "*/*"(LEFT : *any_fixed_point_type*; RIGHT : *any_fixed_point_type*)
--   **return** *universal_fixed*;

-- The following characters form the standard ASCII character set. Character
-- literals corresponding to control characters are not identifiers; they are
-- indicated in italics in this definition.

type CHARACTER **is**

(	*nul,*	*soh,*	*stx,*	*etx,*	*eot,*	*enq,*	*ack,*	*bel,*
	bs,	*ht,*	*lf,*	*vt,*	*ff,*	*cr,*	*so,*	*si,*
	dle,	*dc1,*	*dc2,*	*dc3,*	*dc4,*	*nak,*	*syn,*	*etb,*
	can,	*em,*	*sub,*	*esc,*	*fs,*	*gs,*	*rs,*	*us,*
	' ',	'!',	'"',	'#',	'$',	'%',	'&',	''',
	'(',	')',	'*',	'+',	',',	'-',	'.',	'/',
	'0',	'1',	'2',	'3',	'4',	'5',	'6',	'7',
	'8',	'9',	':',	';',	'<',	'=',	'>',	'?',
	'@',	'A',	'B',	'C',	'D',	'E',	'F',	'G',
	'H',	'I',	'J',	'K',	'L',	'M',	'N',	'O',
	'P',	'Q',	'R',	'S',	'T',	'U',	'V',	'W',
	'X',	'Y',	'Z',	'[',	'\',	']',	'^',	'_',
	'`',	'a',	'b',	'c',	'd',	'e',	'f',	'g',
	'h',	'i',	'j',	'k',	'l',	'm',	'n',	'o',
	'p',	'q',	'r',	's',	't',	'u',	'v',	'w',
	'x',	'y',	'z',	'{',	'|',	'}',	'~',	*del*);

for CHARACTER **use** -- 128 ASCII character set without holes
   (0, 1, 2, 3, 4, 5, ..., 125, 126, 127);

-- The predefined operators for the type CHARACTER are the same as for any
-- enumeration type.

package ASCII **is**
   -- Control characters:
   NUL : **constant** CHARACTER := *nul*;
   STX : **constant** CHARACTER := *stx*;
   EOT : **constant** CHARACTER := *eot*;
   ACK : **constant** CHARACTER := *ack*;
   BS   : **constant** CHARACTER := *bs*;
   LF   : **constant** CHARACTER := *lf*;
   FF   : **constant** CHARACTER := *ff*;
   SO   : **constant** CHARACTER := *so*;
   DLE : **constant** CHARACTER := *dle*;
   DC2 : **constant** CHARACTER := *dc2*;

contd. overleaf

```
DC4 : constant CHARACTER := dc4;
SYN : constant CHARACTER := syn;
CAN : constant CHARACTER := can;
SUB : constant CHARACTER := sub;
FS  : constant CHARACTER := fs;
RS  : constant CHARACTER := rs;
DEL : constant CHARACTER := del;
SOH : constant CHARACTER := soh;
ETX : constant CHARACTER := etx;
ENQ : constant CHARACTER := enq;
BEL : constant CHARACTER := bel;
HT  : constant CHARACTER := ht;
VT  : constant CHARACTER := vt;
CR  : constant CHARACTER := cr;
SI  : constant CHARACTER := si;
DC1 : constant CHARACTER := dc1;
DC3 : constant CHARACTER := dc3;
NAK : constant CHARACTER := nak;
ETB : constant CHARACTER := etb;
EM  : constant CHARACTER := em;
ESC : constant CHARACTER := esc;
GS  : constant CHARACTER := gs;
US  : constant CHARACTER := us;
```

-- Other characters:

```
EXCLAM      : constant CHARACTER :='!' ;
SHARP       : constant CHARACTER :='#' ;
PERCENT     : constant CHARACTER :='%' ;
COLON       : constant CHARACTER :=':' ;
QUERY       : constant CHARACTER :='?' ;
QUOTATION   : constant CHARACTER :='"' ;
DOLLAR      : constant CHARACTER :='$' ;
AMPERSAND   : constant CHARACTER :='&' ;
SEMICOLON   : constant CHARACTER :=';' ;
AT_SIGN     : constant CHARACTER :='@';
L_BRACKET   : constant CHARACTER :='[' ;
R_BRACKET   : constant CHARACTER :=']' ;
UNDERLINE   : constant CHARACTER :='_' ;
L_BRACE     : constant CHARACTER :='{' ;
R_BRACE     : constant CHARACTER :='}' ;
BACK_SLASH  : constant CHARACTER :='\' ;
CIRCUMFLEX  : constant CHARACTER :='^' ;
GRAVE       : constant CHARACTER :='`' ;
BAR         : constant CHARACTER :='|' ;
TILDE       : constant CHARACTER :='~' ;
```

```
-- Lower case letters:

LC_A : constant CHARACTER := 'a' ;
...
LC_Z : constant CHARACTER := 'z' ;

end ASCII;
```

-- Predefined subtypes:

```
subtype NATURAL is INTEGER range 0 .. INTEGER'LAST;
subtype POSITIVE is INTEGER range 1 .. INTEGER'LAST;
```

-- Predefined string type:

```
type STRING is array (POSITIVE range < >) of CHARACTER;

pragma PACK(STRING);
```

-- The predefined operators for this type are as follows:

```
-- function ''='' (LEFT, RIGHT : STRING) return BOOLEAN;
-- function ''/='' (LEFT, RIGHT : STRING) return BOOLEAN;
-- function ''<'' (LEFT, RIGHT : STRING) return BOOLEAN;
-- function ''<='' (LEFT, RIGHT : STRING) return BOOLEAN;
-- function ''>'' (LEFT, RIGHT : STRING) return BOOLEAN;
-- function ''>='' (LEFT, RIGHT : STRING) return BOOLEAN;

-- function ''&'' (LEFT : STRING;    RIGHT : STRING)    return STRING;
-- function ''&'' (LEFT : CHARACTER; RIGHT : STRING)    return STRING;
-- function ''&'' (LEFT : STRING;    RIGHT : CHARACTER) return STRING;
-- function ''&'' (LEFT : CHARACTER; RIGHT : CHARACTER) return STRING;
```

```
type DURATION is delta implementation_defined range
                       implementation_defined;
```

-- The predefined operators for the type DURATION are the same as for any
-- fixed point type.

-- The predefined exceptions:

```
CONSTRAINT_ERROR : exception;
NUMERIC_ERROR    : exception;
PROGRAM_ERROR    : exception;
STORAGE_ERROR    : exception;
TASKING_ERROR    : exception;

end STANDARD;
```

A4
The package SEQUENTIAL_IO

---

with IO_EXCEPTIONS;
generic
  type ELEMENT_TYPE **is private**;
package SEQUENTIAL_IO **is**

  type FILE_TYPE **is limited private**;

  type FILE_MODE **is** (IN_FILE, OUT_FILE);

  -- File management

  procedure CREATE (FILE : **in out** FILE_TYPE;
                        MODE: **in** FILE_MODE := OUT_FILE;
                        NAME : **in** STRING := "";
                        FORM : **in** STRING := "");

  procedure OPEN   (FILE : **in out** FILE_TYPE;
                        MODE: **in** FILE_MODE;
                        NAME : **in** STRING;
                        FORM : **in** STRING := "");

  procedure CLOSE (FILE : **in out** FILE_TYPE);
  procedure DELETE (FILE : **in out** FILE_TYPE);
  procedure RESET (FILE : **in out** FILE_TYPE; MODE: **in** FILE_MODE);
  procedure RESET (FILE : **in out** FILE_TYPE);

  function MODE   (FILE : **in** FILE_TYPE) **return** FILE_MODE;
  function NAME   (FILE : **in** FILE_TYPE) **return** STRING;
  function FORM   (FILE : **in** FILE_TYPE) **return** STRING;

  function IS_OPEN (FILE : **in** FILE_TYPE) **return** BOOLEAN;

  -- Input and output operations

  procedure READ (FILE: **in** FILE_TYPE; ITEM: **out** ELEMENT_TYPE);
  procedure WRITE (FILE: **in** FILE_TYPE; ITEM: **in** ELEMENT_TYPE);

  function END_OF_FILE(FILE: **in** FILE_TYPE) **return** BOOLEAN;

-- Exceptions

```
STATUS_ERROR: exception renames IO_EXCEPTIONS.STATUS_ERROR;
MODE_ERROR:   exception renames IO_EXCEPTIONS.MODE_ERROR;
NAME_ERROR:   exception renames IO_EXCEPTIONS.NAME_ERROR;
USE_ERROR:    exception renames IO_EXCEPTIONS.USE_ERROR;
DEVICE_ERROR: exception renames IO_EXCEPTIONS.DEVICE_ERROR;
END_ERROR:    exception renames IO_EXCEPTIONS.END_ERROR;
DATA_ERROR:   exception renames IO_EXCEPTIONS.DATA_ERROR;

private
  -- implementation-dependent
end SEQUENTIAL_IO;
```

A5
The package DIRECT_IO

```
with IO_EXCEPTIONS;
generic
  type ELEMENT_TYPE is private;
package DIRECT_IO is

  type FILE_TYPE is limited private;

  type FILE_MODE is (IN_FILE, INOUT_FILE, OUT_FILE);
  type COUNT       is range 0 .. implementation_defined;
  subtype POSITIVE_COUNT is COUNT range 1 .. COUNT'LAST;

  -- File management

  procedure CREATE (FILE:  in out FILE_TYPE,
                    MODE: in FILE_MODE := INOUT_FILE;
                    NAME: in STRING := "";
                    FORM: in STRING := "");

  procedure OPEN    (FILE:  in out FILE_TYPE;
                    MODE: in FILE_MODE;
                    NAME: in STRING;
                    FORM: in STRING := "");

  procedure CLOSE  (FILE:  in out FILE_TYPE);
  procedure DELETE (FILE:  in out FILE_TYPE);
  procedure RESET  (FILE:  in out FILE_TYPE; MODE: in FILE_MODE);
  procedure RESET  (FILE:  in out FILE_TYPE);

  function MODE    (FILE:  in FILE_TYPE) return FILE_MODE;
  function NAME    (FILE:  in FILE_TYPE) return STRING;
  function FORM    (FILE:  in FILE_TYPE) return STRING;

  function IS_OPEN (FILE:  in FILE_TYPE) return BOOLEAN;

  -- Input and output operations

  procedure READ   (FILE:  in FILE_TYPE;
                    ITEM:  out ELEMENT_TYPE;
                    FORM: in POSITIVE_COUNT);
```

564

```
procedure READ  (FILE:   in FILE_TYPE; ITEM: out ELEMENT_TYPE);

procedure WRITE (FILE:   in FILE_TYPE;
                 ITEM:   in ELEMENT_TYPE;
                 TO:     in POSITIVE_COUNT);

procedure WRITE (FILE:   in FILE_TYPE; ITEM: in ELEMENT_TYPE);

procedure SET_INDEX (FILE: in FILE_TYPE; TO: in POSITIVE_COUNT);

function INDEX (FILE: in FILE_TYPE) return POSITIVE_COUNT;
function SIZE   (FILE: in FILE_TYPE) return COUNT;

function END_OF_FILE (FILE: in FILE_TYPE) return BOOLEAN;

-- Exceptions

STATUS_ERROR: exception renames IO_EXCEPTIONS.STATUS_ERROR;
MODE_ERROR:   exception renames IO_EXCEPTIONS.MODE_ERROR;
NAME_ERROR:   exception renames IO_EXCEPTIONS.NAME_ERROR;
USE_ERROR:    exception renames IO_EXCEPTIONS.USE_ERROR;
DEVICE_ERROR: exception renames IO_EXCEPTIONS.DEVICE_ERROR;
END_ERROR:    exception renames IO_EXCEPTIONS.END_ERROR;
DATA_ERROR:   exception renames IO_EXCEPTIONS.DATA_ERROR;
private
    -- implementation-dependent
end DIRECT_IO;
```

Solutions to selected exercises

2.3 Set SMALLEST equal to the first number in the table.
Set POSITION equal to 1.
Repeat the following for each of the numbers in the table:
If the current number is smaller than SMALLEST then set SMALLEST equal to the current number and POSITION equal to the current index in the table.
The index required is now the number in POSITION.

2.4 1. Set FIRST equal to 1.
2. Repeat the following steps until FIRST=N.
    2.1 Find the index for the smallest number in that part of the table that starts with index FIRST. (Use the algorithm in Exercise 2.3). The index obtained is called K.
    2.2 If K is not equal to FIRST then swap the numbers with index K and FIRST.
    2.3 Increase the value of FIRST by 1.

2.10
```
with TEXT_IO, BASIC_NUM_IO;
use  TEXT_IO, BASIC_NUM_IO;
procedure BANK is
   BALANCE          : FLOAT;
   DESIRED_BALANCE : constant := 100000.0;
   INTEREST_RATE    : constant := 9.25;
   NO_OF_YEARS      : INTEGER := 0;
begin
   PUT("Amount deposited? "); GET(BALANCE);
   while BALANCE < DESIRED_BALANCE loop
      NO_OF_YEARS := NO_OF_YEARS + 1;
      BALANCE := BALANCE * (1.0 + INTEREST_RATE / 100.0);
   end loop;
   PUT("Number of years: "); PUT(NO_OF_YEARS, WIDTH => 1);
end BANK;
```

3.5   **with** TEXT_IO, BASIC_NUM_IO;
   use TEXT_IO, BASIC_NUM_IO;
   procedure SPHERE **is**
    R : FLOAT;
    PI : **constant** := 3.14159_26535_89793_23846_26433_83279_50288;
   begin
    PUT("Radius? "); GET(R);
    PUT("Volume: "); PUT(4.0 / 3.0 ∗ PI ∗ R ∗∗ 3); NEW_LINE;
    PUT("Area: "); PUT(4.0 ∗ P1 ∗ R ∗∗ 2); NEW_LINE;
   end SPHERE;

If we assume that there is a mathematical package BASIC_MATH in our Ada implementation including the constant PI we can write:

with TEXT_IO, BASIC_NUM_IO, BASIC_MATH;
use TEXT_IO, BASIC_NUM_IO, BASIC_MATH;
procedure SPHERE **is**
  R : FLOAT;
begin
  etc.

3.7   **with** TEXT_IO, BASIC_NUM_IO;
   use TEXT_IO, BASIC_NUM_IO;
   procedure CAR_HIRING **is**
    FEE_PER_DAY   : **constant** := 30;
    FEE_PER_MILE   : **constant** := 0.55;
    MILES_PER_GALLON   : **constant** := 26.0;
    FUEL_PRICE   : **constant** := 1.75;
    DISTANCE, NO_OF_DAYS : INTEGER;
   begin
    PUT("Distance driven? "); GET(DISTANCE);
    PUT("Number of days? "); GET(NO_OF_DAYS);
    PUT("The total cost is: ");
    PUT(FLOAT(FEE_PER_DAY ∗ NO_OF_DAYS) +
        FLOAT(DISTANCE) ∗ (FEE_PER_MILE + FUEL_PRICE /
                MILES_PER_GALLON),
      EXP => 0, FORE => 1, AFT => 2); NEW_LINE;
   end CAR_HIRING;

3.9   **with** TEXT_IO, BASIC_NUM_IO;
   use TEXT_IO, BASIC_NUM_IO;
   procedure PURCHASE **is**
    PRICE, PAID, CHANGE : INTEGER;
   begin
    PUT("Price? "); GET(PRICE);
    PUT("Amount paid? "); GET(PAID);
    CHANGE := (PAID − PRICE) ∗ 100; -- expressed in p
    PUT_LINE("Change:");
    PUT(CHANGE / 2000, WIDTH => 1); PUT_LINE(" £20 notes");

```
    CHANGE := CHANGE rem 2000;
    PUT(CHANGE / 1000, WIDTH => 1); PUT_LINE(" £10 notes");
    CHANGE := CHANGE rem 1000;
    PUT(CHANGE / 500, WIDTH => 1); PUT_LINE(" £5 notes");
    CHANGE := CHANGE rem 10;
    PUT(CHANGE / 100, WIDTH => 1); PUT_LINE(" £1 coins");
    CHANGE := CHANGE rem 100;
    PUT(CHANGE / 50, WIDTH => 1); PUT_LINE(" 50p coins");
    CHANGE := CHANGE rem 50;
    PUT(CHANGE / 10, WIDTH => 1); PUT_LINE(" 10p coins");
  end PURCHASE;
```

3.11
```
  with TEXT_IO, BASIC_NUM_IO, BASIC_MATH;
  use  TEXT_IO, BASIC_NUM_IO, BASIC_MATH;
  procedure DECOMPOSITION is
    LAMBDA : constant := 0.693 / 5730;
    S : INTEGER; .
  begin
    PUT("Number of years? "); GET(S);
    PUT("Amount left: ");
    PUT(EXP(-LAMBDA * FLOAT(S)) * 100.0,
        EXP => 0, FORE => 1, AFT => 1);
    PUT_LINE(" %");
  end DECOMPOSITION;
```

3.15
```
  C := CHARACTER'VAL(CHARACTER'POS(C) - CHARACTER'POS('a')
                  + CHARACTER'POS('A'));
```

3.16
```
  I := CHARACTER'POS(T) - CHARACTER'POS('0');
```

3.17
```
  with TEXT_IO, BASIC_NUM_IO;
  use  TEXT_IO, BASIC_NUM_IO;
  procedure ID_TEST is
    ID_NO : STRING(1 .. 10);
  begin
    PUT("Identification number? "); GET(ID_NO);
    if PUT(CHARACTER'POS(ID_NO(9)) - CHARACTER'POS('0')) rem 2
                                = 0 then
        PUT_LINE("female");
    else
        PUT_LINE("male");
    end if;
  end ID_TEST;
```

4.2
```
  with TEXT_IO, BASIC_NUM_IO, BASIC_MATH;
  use  TEXT_IO, BASIC_NUM_IO, BASIC_MATH;
```

```
procedure TRIANGLE_TEST is
  A, B, C, GAMMA : FLOAT;
  EPS : constant := 1.0E-6;
begin
  PUT_LINE("Enter the lengths of two sides");
  GET(A); GET(B);
  PUT_LINE("Enter the angle between the sides (in radians)");
  GET(GAMMA);
  C := SQRT(A ** 2 + B ** 2 - 2.0 * A * B * COS(GAMMA));
  if abs(A - B) < EPS and abs(A - C) < EPS
                      and abs(B - C) < EPS then
    PUT_LINE("equilateral");
  elsif abs(A - B) < EPS or abs(A - C) < EPS
                      or abs(B - C) < EPS then
    PUT_LINE("isosceles");
  else
    PUT_LINE("scalene");
  end if;
end TRIANGLE_TEST;
```

4.4   ```
with TEXT_IO;
use TEXT_IO;
procedure LETTER is
  STREET, TOWN : STRING(1 .. 20);
  DISTRICT   : STRING(1 .. 2);
begin
  PUT("Street? "); GET(STREET);
  PUT("Postal code and town? "); GET(TOWN);
  DISTRICT := TOWN(1 .. 2);
  if DISTRICT >= "80" then
    PUT_LINE("To northern Sweden");
  elsif (DISTRICT >= "20" and DISTRICT <= "62") or
      DISTRICT =   "65" or   DISTRICT =   "66" then
    PUT_LINE("To southern Sweden");
  else
    PUT_LINE("To central Sweden");
  end if;
end LETTER;
```

4.8   (a)   ```
with TEXT_IO;
use  TEXT_IO;
procedure CAESAR is
  NUMBER  : constant := 26;
  STEP    : constant := 3;
  CHAR_NO : INTEGER;
  LINE    : STRING(1 .. 80);
  N       : INTEGER;
```

```
    begin
      GET_LINE(LINE, N);
      for I in 1 .. N loop
        if LINE(I) in 'A' .. 'Z' then
          CHAR_NO := CHARACTER'POS(LINE(I))
                     - CHARACTER'POS('A');
          CHAR_NO := (CHAR_NO + STEP) mod NUMBER;
          LINE(I)    := CHARACTER'VAL(CHAR_NO
                       + CHARACTER'POS('A'));
        end if;
      end loop;
      PUT_LINE(LINE(1 .. N));
    end CAESAR;
```

(b) The same program as in part (a) can be used. The declaration
     of the constant STEP must be changed:

```
STEP : constant := -3;
```

(c) ```
     with TEXT_IO;
     use TEXT_IO;
     procedure CAESAR is
       NUMBER   : constant := 26;
       CHAR_NO, N   : INTEGER;
       IN_LINE, OUT_LINE : STRING(1 .. 80);
     begin
       GET_LINE(IN_LINE, N);
       for STE! n 1 .. NUMBER loop
         OUT_LINE := IN_LINE;
         for I in 1 .. N loop
           if OUT_LINE(I) in 'A' .. 'Z' then
             CHAR_NO   := CHARACTER'POS(OUT_LINE(I))
                          - CHARACTER'POS('A');
             CHAR_NO   := (CHAR_NO + STEP) mod NUMBER;
             OUT_LINE(I) := CHARACTER'VAL(CHAR_NO
                            + CHARACTER'POS('A'));
           end if;
         end loop;
         PUT_LINE(OUT_LINE(1 .. N));
       end loop;
     end CAESAR;
     ```

```
4.13 with TEXT_IO, BASIC_NUM_IO;
     use TEXT_IO, BASIC_NUM_IO;
     procedure CALCULATE_SIN is
       DEC_NO : constant := 4;
       EPSILON : constant := 1.0E-5;
       SUM   : FLOAT   := 0.0;
       X, TERM : FLOAT;
       K   : INTEGER := 1;
```
```

```
    begin
      PUT("Enter x: "); GET(X);
      TERM := X;
      while abs TERM >= EPSILON loop
        SUM := SUM + TERM;
        K := K + 2;
        TERM := - TERM * X ** 2 / FLOAT((K - 1) * K);
      end loop;
      PUT("sin(x) = "); PUT(SUM, EXP => 0, FORE => 1,
                                AFT => DEC_NO); NEW_LINE;
    end CALCULATE_SIN;
```

4.16
```
    with TEXT_IO;
    use TEXT_IO;
    procedure REMOVE_SPACES is
      LINE1, LINE2 : STRING(1 .. 80);
      N1, N2, I1, I2 : INTEGER;
    begin
      PUT_LINE("Enter a line");
      GET_LINE(LINE1, N1);
      I1 := 1;
      N2 := 0;
      while I1 <= N1 loop
        -- find the start position of the next word
        while I1 <= N1 and then LINE1(I1) = ' ' loop
          I1 := I1 + 1;
        end loop;
        if I1 <= N1 then
          -- find the last position of the word
          I2 := I1;
          while I2 <= N1 and then LINE1(I2) /= ' ' loop
            I2 := I2 + 1;
          end loop;
          I2 := I2 - 1;
          -- copy the word to LINE2
          LINE2(N2+1 .. N2+1+I2-I1) := LINE1(I1 .. I2);
          N2 := N2 + I2 - I1 + 2;
          LINE2(N2) := ' '; -- put a space after the word
          I1 := I2 + 1;
        end if;
      end loop;
      PUT_LINE(LINE2(1 .. N2 - 1)); -- exclude the last space
    end REMOVE_SPACES;
```

5.4
```
    type WEEK_TAB is array(DAY_OF_THE_WEEK) of
                          DAY_OF_THE_WEEK;
    TOMORROW : constant WEEK_TAB
                  := (TUESDAY, WEDNESDAY, THURSDAY,
                      FRIDAY, SATURDAY, SUNDAY, MONDAY);
```

-- or simpler: --

```
TOMORROW : constant array(DAY_OF_THE_WEEK) of
                 DAY_OF_THE_WEEK
           := (TUESDAY, WEDNESDAY, THURSDAY,
               FRIDAY, SATURDAY, SUNDAY, MONDAY);
```

5.6 (a) ```
type ROMAN_NUMERAL is (I, V, X, L, C, D, M);
TRANSL_TAB : constant array (ROMAN_NUMERAL) of POSITIVE
                 := (1, 5, 10, 50, 100, 500, 1000);
```

(b)  ```
with TEXT_IO, BASIC_NUM_IO;
use  TEXT_IO, BASIC_NUM_IO;
procedure ROMAN is
  type ROMAN_NUMERAL is (I, V, X, L, C, D, M);
  MAX_NO : constant := 100;
  type ROMAN_NUMBER is array (1 .. MAX_NO) of
                              ROMAN_NUMERAL;
  package ROMAN_INOUT is new
          ENUMERATION_IO(ROMAN_NUMERAL);
  use ROMAN_INOUT;
  TRANSL_TAB : constant array (ROMAN_NUMERAL) of
                      POSITIVE := (1, 5, 10, 50, 100, 1000);
  NUMERAL_READ : ROMAN_NUMBER;
  LENGTH         : NATURAL := 0;
  SUM            : INTEGER := 0;
begin
  PUT_LINE("Give a roman number");
  while not END_OF_FILE loop
    LENGTH := LENGTH + 1;
    GET(NUMERAL_READ(LENGTH));
  end loop;
  for K in 1 .. LENGTH − 1 loop
    if NUMERAL_READ(K) < NUMERAL_READ(K+1) then
      SUM := SUM − TRANSL_TAB(NUMERAL_READ(K));
    else
      SUM := SUM + TRANSL_TAB(NUMERAL_READ(K));
    end if;
  end loop;
  SUM := SUM + TRANSL_TAB(NUMERAL_READ(LENGTH));
  PUT("The number is: "); PUT(SUM, WIDTH => 1); NEW_LINE;
end ROMAN;
```

5.8 ```
with TEXT_IO;
use TEXT_IO;
procedure TRAVEL_AGENCY is
  type DAY is (MONDAY, TUESDAY, WEDNESDAY, THURSDAY,
               FRIDAY, SATURDAY, SUNDAY);
```
```

```
        type COMMAND is (BOOK, CANCEL, NEW);
        RESERVATION_TAB : array (DAY) of NATURAL := (others => 0);
        MAX_NO : constant := 40;
        C        : COMMAND;
        D        : DAY;
        package DAY_INOUT is new ENUMERATION_IO(DAY);
        package COMMAND_INOUT is new
                        ENUMERATION_IO(COMMAND);
        use DAY_INOUT, COMMAND_INOUT;
    begin
        loop
            PUT("Day of the week: "); GET(D);
            PUT("book, cancel or new? "); GET(C);
            case C is
                when BOOK =>
                    if RESERVATION_TAB(D) < MAX_NO then
                        RESERVATION_TAB(D) := RESERVATION_TAB(D) + 1;
                    else
                        PUT_LINE("No places left");
                    end if;
                when CANCEL =>
                    if RESERVATION_TAB(D) > 0 then
                        RESERVATION_TAB(D) := RESERVATION_TAB(D) - 1;
                    else
                        PUT_LINE("No places reserved");
                    end if;
                when NEW =>
                    RESERVATION_TAB(D) := 0;
            end case;
        end loop;
    end TRAVEL_AGENCY;
```

5.9 ```
     with TEXT_IO, BASIC_NUM_IO;
     use TEXT_IO, BASIC_NUM_IO;
     procedure SORT is
        MAX : constant := 100;
        A   : array (1 .. MAX) of INTEGER;
        I   : INTEGER;
        N   : NATURAL := 0;
        POS : POSITIVE;
     begin
        PUT_LINE("Enter a number of integers. Give CTRL-D to finish.");
        while not END_OF_FILE loop
            -- read the next number
            N := N + 1;
            GET(I);
            -- find the position for the new number
            POS := 1;
```
```

```
    while I > A(POS) and POS < N loop
       POS := POS + 1;
    end loop;
    -- move all numbers to the right of the position one step to the right
    for I in reverse POS .. N−1 loop
       A(I+1) := A(I);
    end loop;
    -- place the new number in the array
    A(POS) := I;
  end loop;
  for I in 1 .. N loop
     PUT(A(I)); NEW_LINE;
  end loop;
end SORT;
```

The program can be made more efficient. When we look for the
position for the new number we can also move all numbers greater
than the new number one step to the right. The central part of the
program becomes:

```
while not END_OF_FILE loop
  -- read the next number
  N := N + 1;
  GET(I);
  -- move to the right until the correct position is found
  POS := N;
  while POS > 1 and then I < A(POS−1) loop
    A(POS) := A(POS−1);
    POS := POS − 1;
  end loop;
  -- place the new number in the array
  A(POS) := I;
end loop;
```

6.4 (a)
```
      function GCD (I1, I2 : POSITIVE) return POSITIVE is
             M : POSITIVE := I1;
             N : POSITIVE := I2;
             R : NATURAL := M rem N;
      begin
        while R > 0 loop
           M := N;
           N := R;
           R := M rem N;
        end loop;
        return N;
      end GCD;
```

   (b)   **with** TEXT_IO, BASIC_NUM_IO;
       use TEXT_IO, BASIC_NUM_IO;

```
        with TEXT_IO, BASIC_NUM_IO;
        use  TEXT_IO, BASIC_NUM_IO;
        procedure DIVISOR is
          NUM1, NUM2 : POSITIVE;
          function GCD (I1, I2 : POSITIVE) return POSITIVE is
            as above
          end GCD;
        begin
          PUT_LINE("Enter pair of positive integers. ");
          while not END_OF_FILE loop
            GET(NUM1); GET(NUM2);
            PUT("The greatest common divisor is: ");
            PUT(GCD(NUM1, NUM2), WIDTH => 1); NEW_LINE;
          end loop;
        end DIVISOR;
```

6.7
```
    type VECTOR is array (INTEGER range < >) of FLOAT;
    function ORTHOGONAL (U, V : VECTOR) return BOOLEAN is
      TEMP : VECTOR(U'RANGE) := V;
      S     : FLOAT := 0.0;
      EPS   : constant := 1.0E−10;
    begin
      for I in U'RANGE loop
        S := S + U(I) * TEMP(I);
      end loop;
      return abs S < EPS;
    end ORTHOGONAL;
```

6.9
```
    function SUBSTRING (T1, T2 : STRING) return NATURAL is
    begin
      for I in T2'FIRST .. T2'LAST − T1'LENGTH + 1 loop
        if T2(I .. I + T1'LENGTH − 1) = T1 then
          return I;
        end if;
      end loop;
      return 0;
    end SUBSTRING;
```

6.13
```
    with TEXT_IO, BASIC_NUM_IO, MATH;
    use  TEXT_IO, BASIC_NUM_IO, MATH;
    procedure DRILL is
      MAX : constant := 500;
      type FLOAT_ARRAY is array (INTEGER range < >) of FLOAT;
      X, Y           : FLOAT_ARRAY(1 .. MAX);
      NO_OF_HOLES : NATURAL;

      procedure READ_COORDINATES(X, Y : out FLOAT_ARRAY;
                                 NUMBER : out NATURAL) is
        N : NATURAL := 0;
```

```ada
begin
  PUT_LINE("Enter the coordinates of the holes. ");
  while not END_OF_FILE loop
    N := N + 1;
    GET(X(N)); GET(Y(N));
  end loop;
  NUMBER := N;
end READ_COORDINATES;

procedure WRITE_ORDER(U, V : FLOAT_ARRAY) is
  FROM, TO      : INTEGER;
  BIG_NUMBER : constant := 1.0E10;
  X                 : FLOAT_ARRAY(U'RANGE) := U;
  Y                 : FLOAT_ARRAY(V'RANGE) := V;

  function CLOSEST_HOLE(X, Y : FLOAT_ARRAY;
                FROM : INTEGER) return INTEGER is
    SMALLEST_DISTANCE : FLOAT := FLOAT'LARGE;
    THIS_DISTANCE        : FLOAT;
    WANTED_HOLE        : INTEGER;
  begin
    for I in X'RANGE loop
      if I /= FROM then
        THIS_DISTANCE := SQRT((X(I) − X(FROM)) ** 2 +
                            (Y(I) − Y(FROM)) ** 2);
        if THIS_DISTANCE < SMALLEST_DISTANCE then
          SMALLEST_DISTANCE := THIS_DISTANCE;
          WANTED_HOLE := I;
        end if;
      end if;
    end loop;
    return WANTED_HOLE;
  end CLOSEST_HOLE;

begin
  PUT_LINE("Acceptable order: ");
  TO := X'FIRST; -- start with the first hole
  for I in 1 .. X'LENGTH loop
    PUT(X(TO), EXP => 0, FORE => 5, AFT => 2);
    PUT(Y(TO), EXP => 0, FORE => 5, AFT => 2); NEW_LINE;
    FROM := TO;
    TO := CLOSEST_HOLE(X, Y, FROM);
    X(FROM) := BIG_NUMBER; Y(FROM) := BIG_NUMBER;
  end loop;
end WRITE_ORDER;

begin
  READ_COORDINATES(X, Y, NO_OF_HOLES);
  WRITE_ORDER(X(1 .. NO_OF_HOLES), Y(1 .. NO_OF_HOLES));
end DRILL;
```

6.16 **function** BIN_COEFF (N, K : NATURAL) **return** POSITIVE **is**
begin
    if K = 0 **or** N = K **then**
      return 1;
    else -- assume that K < N
      return BIN_COEFF(N − 1, K − 1) + BIN_COEFF(N − 1, K);
    end if;
end BIN_COEFF;

6.17 **type** INDEX **is range** 1 .. INTEGER'LAST;
    type INTEGER_ARRAY **is array** (INDEX **range** < >) **of** INTEGER;
    procedure QUICKSORT (F : **in out** INTEGER_ARRAY) **is**
    POINT : INDEX;

    procedure SWAP(A, B : **in out** INTEGER) **is**
    T : INTEGER;
    begin
      T := A; A := B; B := T;
    end SWAP;

    procedure REARRANGE (F : **in out** INTEGER_ARRAY;
                             K : **in** INTEGER; LIMIT : **out** INDEX) **is**
    -- On return: F(I) <= K if I <= LIMIT and F(I) > K if I > LIMIT
    LOWER, UPPER : INDEX;
    begin
      LOWER := F'FIRST; UPPER := F'LAST;
      while LOWER < UPPER **loop**
        while LOWER < UPPER **and then** F(LOWER) <= K **loop**
          LOWER := LOWER + 1;
        end loop;
        while LOWER < UPPER **and then** F(UPPER) > K **loop**
          UPPER := UPPER − 1;
        end loop;
        if LOWER < UPPER **then**
          SWAP(F(LOWER), F(UPPER));
        end if;
      end loop;
      if F(LOWER) > K **then**
        LIMIT := LOWER − 1;
      else
        LIMIT := LOWER;
      end if;
    end REARRANGE;

    begin
    if F'LENGTH > 1 **then**
      -- choose F(F'FIRST) as K
      REARRANGE(F(F'FIRST+1 .. F'LAST), F(F'FIRST), POINT);
      SWAP(F(F'FIRST), F(POINT)); -- insert K between the two parts

```
      QUICKSORT(F(F'FIRST .. POINT - 1));
      QUICKSORT(F(POINT + 1 .. F'LAST));
    end if;
  end QUICKSORT;
```

7.5   (a)   **function** TURN (M : MATRIX) **return** MATRIX **is**
```
              T : MATRIX(M'RANGE(1), M'RANGE(1));
            begin
              if M'FIRST(1) = M'FIRST(2) and M'LAST(1) = M'LAST(2) then
                -- assume that rows and columns are indexed in the same way
                for I in M'RANGE loop -- M'RANGE means M'RANGE(1) etc.
                  for J in M'RANGE loop
                    T(M'LAST - J + M'FIRST, I) := M(I, J);
                  end loop;
                end loop;
              else
                PUT_LINE("Rows and columns must be "&
                         "indexed in the same way");
              end if;
              return T;
            end TURN;
```

       (b)   **with** TEXT_IO, BASIC_NUM_IO;
```
              use  TEXT_IO, BASIC_NUM_IO;
            procedure TURN_MATRIX is
              type MATRIX is array (POSITIVE range < >,
                                    POSITIVE range <>) of INTEGER;
              M4 : MATRIX (1 .. 4, 1 .. 4);

              function TURN (M : MATRIX) return MATRIX is
                as above
              end TURN;

              procedure READ (M : out MATRIX) is
              begin
                for I in M'RANGE(1) loop
                  for J in M'RANGE(2) loop
                    GET(M(I,J));
                  end loop;
                end loop;
              end READ;

              procedure WRITE (M : in MATRIX) is
              begin
                for I in M'RANGE(1) loop
                  for J in M'RANGE(2) loop
                    PUT(M(I,J), WIDTH => 5);
                  end loop;
                  NEW_LINE;
                end loop;
              end WRITE;
```

```
            begin
              PUT_LINE("Enter a 4 x 4 matrix");
              READ(M4);
              M4 := TURN(M4);
              NEW_LINE; PUT_LINE("A quarter turn anticlockwise:");
              WRITE(M4);
              M4 := TURN(M4);
              NEW_LINE; PUT_LINE("A half turn anticlockwise:");
              WRITE(M4);
            end TURN_MATRIX;
```

7.6   **function** MULT (A, B : MATRIX) **return** MATRIX **is**
```
       C    : MATRIX (A'RANGE(1), B'RANGE(2));
       SUM : INTEGER;
```
       begin
```
         if A'FIRST(2) = B'FIRST(1) and A'LAST(2) = B'LAST(1) then
           -- step through C and calculate all its elements
           for I in C'RANGE(1) loop
             for J in C'RANGE(2) loop
               SUM := 0;
               for K in A'RANGE(2) loop
                 SUM := SUM + A(I,K) * B(K,J);
               end loop;
               C(I,J) := SUM;
             end loop;
           end loop;
         else
           PUT_LINE("The matrices have illegal dimensions");
         end if;
         return C;
       end MULT;
```

7.8   (a)   **with** TEXT_IO;
```
              use  TEXT_IO;
              procedure TO_MORSE is
                MESS : STRING(1 .. 100);
                N    : NATURAL;

                function CODE (C : CHARACTER) return STRING is
                  subtype MORSE_CODE is STRING(1 .. 5);
                  TAB : constant array('a' .. 'z') of MORSE_CODE :=
                            (".-   ", "-... ", "-.-. ", "-..  ", ".    ", "..-. ",
                             "--.  ", ".... ", "..   ", ".--- ", "-.-  ", ".-.. ",
                             "--   ", "-.   ", "---  ", ".--. ", "--.- ", ".-.  ",
                             "...  ", "-    ", "..-  ", "...- ", ".--  ", "-..- ",
                             "-.-- ", "--.. ");
```

```
CODE_LENGTH : constant array('a' .. 'z') of
                POSITIVE :=
                (2, 4, 4, 3, 1,
                 4, 3, 4, 2, 4,
                 3, 4, 2, 2, 3,
                 4, 4, 3, 3, 1,
                 3, 4, 3, 4, 4,
                 4);
    begin
      if C in TAB'RANGE then
        return TAB(C) (1 .. CODE_LENGTH(C)) & " ";
      else
        return " ";
      end if;
    end CODE;

  begin
    PUT_LINE("Write a message"); GET_LINE(MESS,N);
    for I in 1 .. N loop
      PUT(CODE(MESS(I)));
    end loop;
    NEW_LINE;
  end TO_MORSE;
```

(b)
```
  with TEXT_IO;
  use TEXT_IO;
  procedure FROM_MORSE is
  MESS : STRING (1 .. 500);
  N    : NATURAL;

    function LETTER (S : STRING) return CHARACTER is
      -- translates a morse code into a letter
      subtype MORSE_CODE is STRING(1 .. 5);
      TAB : constant array ('a' .. 'z') of MORSE_CODE :=
          as before
      CODE_LENGTH : constant array ('a' .. 'z') of POSITIVE :=
          as before
    begin
      for C in TAB'RANGE loop
        if S = TAB(C) (1 .. CODE_LENGTH(C)) then
          return C;
        end if;
      end loop;
      return '*'; -- indicates an illegal morse code
    end LETTER;

    procedure DECODE (S : STRING) is
    I, J : NATURAL;
```

```
        begin
          I := S'FIRST;
          while I <= S'LAST loop
            -- find the beginning of a letter
            while I <= S'LAST and then S(I) = ' ' loop
              I := I + 1;
            end loop;
            if I > S'LAST then
              I := S'LAST;
            end if;
            -- find the end of a letter
            J := I + 1;
            while J <= S'LAST and then S(J) /= ' ' loop
              J := J + 1;
            end loop;
            J := J - 1;
            -- write a letter
            PUT(LETTER(S(I .. J)));
            I := J + 2;
            if I <= S'LAST and then S(I) = ' ' then
              PUT(' '); -- end of word
              I := I + 1;
            end if;
          end loop;
        end DECODE;

      begin
        PUT_LINE("Enter a message in morse code");
        GET_LINE(MESS,N);
        DECODE(MESS(1 .. N)); NEW_LINE;
      end FROM_MORSE;
```

7.13 (a)   **type** WEIGHT_TYPE **is digits** 8;
            subtype SYMBOL_TYPE **is** STRING(1 .. 2);
            type TAB_ELEMENT **is**
              record
                SYMBOL : SYMBOL_TYPE;
                WEIGHT : WEIGHT_TYPE;
              end record;
            type WEIGHT_TAB **is array** (POSITIVE **range** < >) **of**
                                  TAB_ELEMENT;
            T : **constant** WEIGHT_TAB :=
                    (("H ", 1.0079),   ("He", 4.0026),   ("Be", 9.0122),
                     ("C ", 12.011),   ("O ", 15.999),   ("Na", 22.9898),
                     ("S ", 32.06),   ("Cl ", 35.453), ("F ", 18.9984),
                     ("Au", 196.9665), ("Hg", 200.5),   ("Ra", 226.0254));

      (b)   **with** TEXT_IO, BASIC_NUM_IO;
            use TEXT_IO, BASIC_NUM_IO;

```ada
procedure CALCULATE_WEIGHT is
  type WEIGHT_TYPE is digits 8;
  subtype SYMBOL_TYPE is STRING(1 .. 2);
  FORMULA : STRING(1 .. 100);
  MOL_WEIGHT, AT_WEIGHT : WEIGHT_TYPE;
  SYMB: SYMBOL_TYPE;
  L     : NATURAL;
  I,N   : POSITIVE;
  OK    : BOOLEAN;

  function ATOMIC_WEIGHT (S : SYMBOL_TYPE) return
                            WEIGHT_TYPE is
    type TAB_ELEMENT is as above
    type WEIGHT_TAB is   as above
    T : constant WEIGHT_TAB := as above
  begin
    for I in T'RANGE loop
      if S = T(I).SYMBOL then
        return T(I).WEIGHT;
      end if;
    end loop;
    PUT_LINE("Weight not known for " & S);
    return 0.0;
  end ATOMIC_WEIGHT;

  function TO_INTEGER (C : CHARACTER) return POSITIVE is
  begin
    return CHARACTER'POS(C) - CHARACTER'POS('0');
  end TO_INTEGER;

  package WEIGHT_INOUT is new FLOAT_IO(WEIGHT_TYPE);
  use WEIGHT_INOUT;
begin
  PUT_LINE("Give a chemical formula");
  GET_LINE(FORMULA, L);
  I := 1;
  OK := TRUE;
  while I <= L and OK loop
    if FORMULA(I) in 'A' .. 'Z' then
      SYMB(1) := FORMULA(I);
      I := I + 1;
      if I <= L and then FORMULA(I) in 'a' .. 'z' then
        SYMB(2) := FORMULA(I);
        I := I + 1;
      else
        SYMB(2) := ' ';
      end if;
      if I <= L and then FORMULA(I) in '1' .. '9' then
        N := TO_INTEGER(FORMULA(I));
        I := I + 1;
```

```
    else
       N := 1;
    end if;
    AT_WEIGHT := ATOMIC_WEIGHT(SYMB);
    OK := AT_WEIGHT > 0.0;
    MOL_WEIGHT := MOL_WEIGHT + AT_WEIGHT
                       * WEIGHT_TYPE(N);
  else
    PUT_LINE("Illegal formula");
    OK := FALSE;
  end if;
 end loop;
 if OK then
    PUT("The molecular weight is");
    PUT(MOL_WEIGHT, EXP => 0, FORE => 4, AFT => 4);
 end if;
end CALCULATE_WEIGHT;
```

If the following declaration is added:

```
    package INTEGER_INOUT is new INTEGER_IO(NATURAL);
    use INTEGER_INOUT;
```

then an alternative form of GET can be used. This form reads an integer from a text string, not from the terminal (see Appendix A). In the program we make a change:

```
    if I <= L and then FORMULA(I) in '1' .. '9' then
       GET(FORMULA(I .. L), N, I);
       -- I now points to the last character in the number
       I := I + 1;
    else
       N := 1;
    end if;
```

The function TO_INTEGER is no longer needed. This version of the program can also handle chemical formulas with more than 9 atoms of the same kind.

8.4
```
   with RANDOM;
   use RANDOM;
   package CARD_PACKAGE is
      type SUIT   is (CLUBS, DIAMONDS, HEARTS, SPADES);
      type VALUE is (TWO, THREE, FOUR, FIVE, SIX, SEVEN,
                     EIGHT, NINE, TEN, JACK, QUEEN, KING, ACE);
      type CARD  is record
                      S : SUIT;
                      V : VALUE;
                    end record;
```

```
  procedure SHUFFLE;
  function DEAL return CARD;
end CARD_PACKAGE;


with TEXT_IO;
use  TEXT_IO;
package body CARD_PACKAGE is
  PACK : array (1 .. 52) of CARD;
  TOP   : NATURAL := 52;

  procedure SHUFFLE is
    IN_PACK  : array (INTEGER range 0 .. 51) of
                           BOOLEAN := (others => FALSE);
    CARD_NO : NATURAL;
    N          : NATURAL := 0;
  begin
    if TOP /= 0 then -- otherwise the pack is shuffled
      while N < 52 loop
        CARD_NO := INTEGER(NEXT_NUMBER * 52.0 + 0.5) − 1;
                     -- 0 <= CARD_NO <= 51
        if not IN_PACK(CARD_NO) then
          IN_PACK(CARD_NO) := TRUE;
          N := N + 1;
          PACK(N) := (SUIT'VAL(CARD_NO / 13),
                       VALUE'VAL(CARD_NO rem 13));
        end if;
      end loop;
      TOP := 0;
    end if;
  end SHUFFLE;

  function DEAL return CARD is
  begin
    if TOP >= 52 then
      PUT_LINE("No more cards. Using a new pack of cards.");
      SHUFFLE;
    end if;
    TOP := TOP + 1;
    return PACK(TOP);
  end DEAL;

begin
  SHUFFLE;
end CARD_PACKAGE;


with TEXT_IO, CARD_PACKAGE;
use  TEXT_IO, CARD_PACKAGE;
procedure TWENTY_ONE is
  type CARD_VALUE is range 0 .. 34;
  type PLAYER is (YOU, I);
```

```ada
package PLAYER_INOUT is new ENUMERATION_IO(PLAYER);
package CARD_VALUE_INOUT is new INTEGER_IO(CARD_VALUE);
use PLAYER_INOUT, CARD_VALUE_INOUT;
NEW_GAME : BOOLEAN := TRUE;
WINNER    : PLAYER;
YOUR_CARD_VALUE, MY_CARD_VALUE : CARD_VALUE;

function READ_ANSWER return BOOLEAN is
  type ANSWER is (YES, NO);
  package ANSWER_INOUT is new ENUMERATON_IO(ANSWER);
  THE_ANSWER : ANSWER;
begin
  ANSWER_INOUT.GET(THE_ANSWER);
  return THE_ANSWER = YES;
end READ_ANSWER;

function TAKE_CARDS (THE_PLAYER : PLAYER)
                     return CARD_VALUE is
  package SUIT_INOUT is new ENUMERATION_IO(SUIT);
  package VALUE_INOUT is new ENUMERATION_IO(VALUE);
  use SUIT_INOUT, VALUE_INOUT;
  TOTAL       : CARD_VALUE := 0;
  NO_OF_ACES : NATURAL := 0;
  CONTINUE    : BOOLEAN := TRUE;
  CA          : CARD;
begin
  while CONTINUE loop
    CA := DEAL;
    PUT(THE_PLAYER); PUT(" got "); PUT(CA.S); PUT(' ');
    PUT(CA.V);
    if CA.V = ACE then
      NO_OF_ACES := NO_OF_ACES + 1;
    end if;
    TOTAL := TOTAL + VALUE'POS(CA.V) + 2;
    if TOTAL > 21 and NO_OF_ACES > 0 then
      TOTAL := TOTAL - 13;        -- count one ace as 1
      NO_OF_ACES := NO_OF_ACES - 1;
    end if;
    if TOTAL <= 21 then
      PUT(" and have the value "); PUT(TOTAL, WIDTH => 1);
      if THE_PLAYER = YOU and TOTAL < 21 then
        PUT("One more card? ");
        CONTINUE := READ_ANSWER;
      else
        CONTINUE := TOTAL < 16;
      end if;
    else
      PUT_LINE("BUST!");
      CONTINUE := FALSE;
```

```
        end if;
      end loop;
      return TOTAL;
    end TAKE_CARDS;

begin
    PLAYER_INOUT.DEFAULT_SETTING := LOWER_CASE;
    while NEW_GAME loop
      SHUFFLE;
      WINNER := I;
      YOUR_CARD_VALUE := TAKE_CARDS(YOU);
      if YOUR_CARD_VALUE <= 21 then
        MY_CARD_VALUE := TAKE_CARDS(I);
        if MY_CARD_VALUE > 21 or MY_CARD_VALUE
                        < YOUR_CARD_VALUE then
          WINNER := YOU;
        end if;
      end if;
      PUT(WINNER); PUT(" win "); NEW_LINE(2);
      PUT("New game? ");
      NEW_GAME := READ_ANSWER;
    end loop;
end TWENTY_ONE;
```

The random number generator does not work very well in this example. The same sequence of cards is repeated too often. It works better if the constants K and M are changed in the package RANDOM: K = 5 ** 6 and M = 2 ** 13.

8.8 **package** RATIONAL_PACKAGE **is**
    type   RATIONAL_NUMBER **is private**;
    function MAKE_RATIONAL (NU, DE : INTEGER) **return**
                        RATIONAL_NUMBER;
    function NUMERATOR (R : RATIONAL_NUMBER) **return** INTEGER;
    function DENOMINATOR (R : RATIONAL_NUMBER) **return**
                        NATURAL;
    function ADD (R1, R2 : RATIONAL_NUMBER) **return**
                RATIONAL_NUMBER;
    function SUB (R1, R2 : RATIONAL_NUMBER) **return**
                RATIONAL_NUMBER;
    function MUL (R1, R2 : RATIONAL_NUMBER) **return**
                RATIONAL_NUMBER;
    function DIV (R1, R2 : RATIONAL_NUMBER) **return**
                RATIONAL_NUMBER;
    procedure READ (R : **out** RATIONAL_NUMBER);
    -- reads a rational number in the format: N/D
    procedure WRITE (R : **in** RATIONAL_NUMBER);
    -- writes a rational number in the formal: N/D

```
private
  type RATIONAL_NUMBER is
          record
              N : INTEGER;
              D : NATURAL;
          end record;
end RATIONAL_PACKAGE;

with TEXT_IO;
use  TEXT_IO;
package body RATIONAL_PACKAGE is
  package INT_INOUT is new INTEGER_IO(INTEGER);
  use INT_INOUT;

  function MAKE_RATIONAL (NU, DE : INTEGER) return
                          RATIONAL_NUMBER is
    DIV : POSITIVE;
    function GCD (T1, T2 : POSITIVE) return POSITIVE is
      as in Exercise 6.4
    end GCD;
  begin
    if NU = 0 or DE = 0 then
      return (NU, abs DE);
    else
      DIV := GCD(abs NU, abs DE);
      if DE > 0 then
        return (NU / DIV, DE / DIV);
      else
        return (−NU / DIV, −DE / DIV);
      end if;
    end if;
  end MAKE_RATIONAL;

  function NUMERATOR (R : RATIONAL_NUMBER) return
                      INTEGER is
  begin
    return R.N;
  end NUMERATOR;

  function DENOMINATOR (R : RATIONAL_NUMBER) return
                        NATURAL is
  begin
    return R.D;
  end DENOMINATOR;

  function ADD (R1, R2 : RATIONAL_NUMBER) return
              RATIONAL_NUMBER is
  begin
    return MAKE_RATIONAL(R1.N * R2.D + R2.N * R1.D, R1.D * R2.D);
  end ADD;
```

```
function SUB (R1, R2 : RATIONAL_NUMBER) return
                RATIONAL_NUMBER is
begin
  return MAKE_RATIONAL(R1.N * R2.D - R2.N * R1.D, R1.D * R2.D);
end SUB;

function MUL (R1, R2 : RATIONAL_NUMBER) return
                RATIONAL_NUMBER is
begin
  return MAKE_RATIONAL(R1.N * R2.N, R1.D * R2.D);
end MUL;

function DIV (R1, R2 : RATIONAL_NUMBER) return
                RATIONAL_NUMBER is
begin
  return MAKE_RATIONAL(R1.N * R2.D, R1.D * R2.N);
end DIV;

procedure READ (R : out RATIONAL_NUMBER) is
  A, B : INTEGER;
  C    : CHARACTER := ' ';
begin
  GET(A);     -- read the numerator
  while C = ' ' loop
    GET(C);
  end loop;
  if C = '/' then
    GET(B);   -- read the denominator
    R := MAKE_RATIONAL(A, B);
  else
    PUT_LINE("Illegal rational number");
    R := (0, 0);
  end if;
end READ;

procedure WRITE (R : in RATIONAL_NUMBER) is
begin
  PUT(R.N, WIDTH=>1); PUT('/'); PUT(R.D, WIDTH=>1);
end WRITE;

end RATIONAL_PACKAGE;
```

8.10 ```
package QUEUE_PACKAGE is
    type   QUEUE is limited private;
    procedure INIT   (Q : in out QUEUE);
    procedure PUT_LAST (Q : in out QUEUE; C : in CHARACTER);
    procedure TAKE_OUT (Q : in out QUEUE; C : out CHARACTER);
    function   EMPTY   (Q : in QUEUE) return BOOLEAN;
```
```

```
private
  MAX_NO : constant := 200;
  type CHAR_ARRAY is array (POSITIVE range < >) of CHARACTER;
  type QUEUE is
          record
            BUF : CHAR_ARRAY(1 .. MAX_NO);
            L    : NATURAL;
          end record;
end QUEUE_PACKAGE;

with TEXT_IO;
use  TEXT_IO;
package body QUEUE_PACKAGE is
  procedure INIT (Q : in out QUEUE) is
  begin
    Q.L := 0;
  end INIT;
  procedure PUT_LAST (Q : in out QUEUE; C : in CHARACTER) is
  begin
    if Q.L < MAX_NO then
      Q.L := Q.L + 1;
      Q.BUF(Q.L) := C;
    else
      PUT_LINE("The queue is full!");
    end if;
  end PUT_LAST;
  procedure TAKE_OUT (Q : in out QUEUE; C : out CHARACTER) is
  begin
    if Q.L > 0 then
      C := Q.BUF(1);
      Q.BUF(1 .. Q.L - 1) := Q.BUF(2 .. Q.L);
      Q.L := Q.L - 1;
    else
      PUT_LINE("The queue is empty");
    end if ;
  end TAKE_OUT;
  function   EMPTY (Q : in QUEUE) return BOOLEAN is
  begin
    return Q.L = 0;
  end EMPTY;
end QUEUE_PACKAGE;
```

-- The main program

```
with TEXT_IO, QUEUE_PACKAGE;
use  TEXT_IO, QUEUE_PACKAGE;
procedure QUEUE_EXAMPLE is
  QU : QUEUE;
  C  : CHARACTER;
```

```
begin
  INIT(QU);
  for I in 1 .. 100 loop
    GET(C); PUT_LAST(QU, C);
  end loop;
  NEW_LINE(2);
  for I in 1 .. 100 loop
    TAKE_OUT(QU, C); PUT(C);
  end loop;
end QUEUE_EXAMPLE;
```

9.3   ```
      with TEXT_IO;
      use TEXT_IO;
      procedure SECRET is
        MESS   : FILE_TYPE;
        LINE   : STRING(1 .. 100);
        L   : NATURAL;
        CODE_TAB : array ('a' .. 'z') of CHARACTER;
        C   : CHARACTER;
      begin
        for L in 'a' .. 'z' loop
          GET(C);
          CODE_TAB(C) := L;
        end loop;
        OPEN(MESS, MODE => IN_FILE, NAME => "secret.file");
        while not END_OF_FILE(MESS) loop
          GET_LINE(MESS, LINE, L);
          for I in 1 .. L loop
            if LINE(I) in 'a' .. 'z' then
              LINE(I) := CODE_TAB(LINE(I));
            end if;
          end loop;
          PUT_LINE(LINE(1 .. L));
        end loop;
        CLOSE(MESS);
      end SECRET;
      ```

9.5   ```
      with TEXT_IO;
      use TEXT_IO;
      procedure CAT is
        FILE1, FILE2, FILE3 : FILE_TYPE;
        FILE_NAME : STRING(1 .. 30);
        L : NATURAL;

        procedure COPY (FROM, TO : in out FILE_TYPE) is
          LINE : STRING(1 .. 200);
          L     : NATURAL;
      ```

```
    begin
      while not END_OF_FILE(FROM) loop
        GET_LINE(FROM, LINE, L);
        PUT_LINE(TO, LINE(1 .. L));
      end loop;
    end COPY;

  begin
    PUT("file1? "); GET_LINE(FILE_NAME, L);
    OPEN(FILE1, MODE => IN_FILE, NAME => FILE_NAME(1 .. L));
    PUT("file2? "); GET_LINE(FILE_NAME, L);
    OPEN(FILE2, MODE => IN_FILE, NAME => FILE_NAME(1 .. L));
    PUT("file3? "); GET_LINE(FILE_NAME, L);
    CREATE(FILE3, NAME => FILE_NAME(1 .. L));
    COPY(FILE1, FILE3);
    COPY(FILE2, FILE3);
    CLOSE(FILE1); CLOSE(FILE2); CLOSE(FILE3);
  end CAT;
```

9.10
```
    with TEXT_IO;
    use  TEXT_IO;
    procedure EDIT is
      F               : FILE_TYPE;
      FILE_NAME       : STRING(1 .. 30);
      LINE            : STRING(1 .. 200);
      L               : NATURAL;
      PAGESZ, LINESZ : POSITIVE COUNT;
      package SIZE_INOUT is new INTEGER_IO(COUNT);
      use SIZE_INOUT;
      I1, I2, LINEPOS, LINEL : NATURAL;

      procedure NEXT_WORD (S : in STRING;
                                  STARTPOS, STOPPOS : out NATURAL) is
        START, STOP : POSITIVE;
      begin
        -- find the start position of the next word (skip blanks)
        START := S'FIRST;
        while START <= S'LAST and then S(START) = ' ' loop
          START := START + 1;
        end loop;
        STOP := START;
        -- find the next blank or the end of S
        while STOP <= S'LAST and then S(STOP) /= ' ' loop
          STOP := STOP + 1;
        end loop;
        STARTPOS := START;
        STOPPOS  := STOP - 1;
      end NEXT_WORD;
```

```
begin
  PUT("File name? "); GET_LINE(FILE_NAME, L);
  OPEN(F, MODE => IN_FILE, NAME => FILE_NAME(1 .. L));
  PUT("Number of lines per page? "); GET(PAGESZ);
  SET_PAGE_LENGTH(PAGESZ);
  PUT("Number of characters per line? "); GET(LINESZ);
  SET_LINE_LENGTH(LINESZ);
  while not END_OF_FILE(F) loop
    GET_LINE(F, LINE, LINEL);
    LINEPOS := 1;
    loop
      NEXT_WORD(LINE(LINEPOS .. LINEL), I1, I2);
      exit when I1 > I2; -- no more words in the line
      if COL > 1 then
        if INTEGER(LINE_LENGTH - COL) > I2 - I1 then
          PUT(' ');
        else
          NEW_LINE;
        end if;
      end if;
      PUT(LINE(I1 .. I2));
      LINEPOS := I2 + 1;
    end loop;
  end loop;
  NEW_LINE;
end EDIT;
```

10.3 Add the following line to the package specification:

```
QUEUE_FULL, QUEUE_EMPTY : exception;
```

In the package body the statements:

```
PUT_LINE("The queue is full");
PUT_LINE("The queue is empty");
```

should be replaced by:

```
raise QUEUE_FULL;
raise QUEUE_EMPTY;
```

10.4
```
procedure TRY_TO_GET (ITEM : out INTEGER;
                      OK : out BOOLEAN) is
begin
  GET(ITEM)
  OK := TRUE;
exception
  when DATA_ERROR => OK := FALSE;
end TRY_TO_GET;
```

11.4   **type** MEMBER **is**
   record
     NAME : STRING(1 .. 30);
     ADDR : STRING(1 .. 50);
     TEL   : STRING(1 .. 15);
   end record;
  type ELEMENT;
  type POINTER **is access** ELEMENT;
  type ELEMENT **is**
   record
     NEXT : POINTER;
     INFO : MEMBER;
   end record;

  procedure INSERT (NEW_MEMB : **in** POINTER; L : **in out** POINTER) **is**
   P1, P2 : POINTER;
  begin
   if L = **null or else** L.INFO.NAME > NEW_MEMB.INFO.NAME **then**
    -- insert the new member first in the list
    NEW_MEMB.NEXT := L;
    L := NEW_MEMB;
   else
    P1 := L.NEXT;
    P2 := L;
    while P1 /= **null and then** P1.INFO.NAME <
                NEW_MEMB.INFO.NAME **loop**
     P2 := P1;
     P1 := P1.NEXT;
    end loop;
    -- insert the new member after P2
    NEW_MEMB.NEXT := P1;
    P2.NEXT := NEW_MEMB;
   end if;
  end INSERT;

  -- recursive version

  procedure INSERT (NEW_MEMB : **in** POINTER; L : **in out** POINTER) **is**
  begin
   if L = **null or else** L.INFO.NAME > NEW_MEMB.INFO.NAME **then**
    NEW_MEMB.NEXT := L;
    L := NEW_MEMB;
   else
    INSERT(NEW_MEMB, L.NEXT);
   end if;
  end INSERT;

11.6   **type** TERM;
  type POLYNOMIAL **is access** TERM;
  type TERM **is**

```
record
  NEXT  : POLYNOMIAL;
  COEFF : FLOAT;
  DEG   : NATURAL;
end record;
```

(a)
```
function VALUE (P : POLYNOMIAL; X : FLOAT) return FLOAT is
begin
  if P = null then
    return 0.0;
  else
    return P.COEFF * X ** P.DEG + VALUE(P.NEXT, X);
  end if;
end;
```

(b)
```
function SUM (P1, P2 : POLYNOMIAL) return
                    POLYNOMIAL is
begin
  if P1 = null and P2 = null then
    return null;
  elsif (P1 /= null and P2 /= null) and then
                P1.DEG = P2.DEG then
    return new TERM' (SUM(P1.NEXT, P2.NEXT),
                P1.COEFF+P2.COEFF, P1.DEG);
  elsif P2 = null or else (P1 /= null and then
                           P1.DEG > P2.DEG) then
    return new TERM' (SUM(P1.NEXT, P2), P1.COEFF,
                P1.DEG);
  else
    return new TERM' (SUM(P1, P2.NEXT), P2.COEFF,
                P2.DEG);
  end if;
end SUM;
```

(c)
```
function DER (P : POLYNOMIAL) return POLYNOMIAL is
begin
  if P = null or else P.DEG = 0 then
    return null;
  else
    return new TERM' (DER(P.NEXT), FLOAT(P.DEG) * P.COEFF,
                P.DEG-1);
  end if;
end DER;
```

11.9
```
package SET_PACKAGE is
  type SET is limited private;
  procedure ASSIGN (S1 : in SET; S2 : out SET);
  function   EQUAL (S1, S2 : SET) return BOOLEAN;
  procedure CLEAR (S : out SET);
  function   ADD (NUMBER : INTEGER; S : SET) return SET;
```

```
function   SUB (NUMBER : INTEGER; S : SET) return SET;
function   MEMBER (NUMBER : INTEGER; S : SET) return
                  BOOLEAN;
function   UNION (S1, S2 : SET) return SET;
function   INTERSECTION (S1, S2 : SET) return SET;
function   SUBSET (S1, S2 : SET) return BOOLEAN;
procedure WRITE (S : in SET);
private
  type ELEMENT;
  type SET is access ELEMENT;
end SET_PACKAGE;

with TEXT_IO;
use  TEXT_IO;
package body SET_PACKAGE is
  type ELEMENT is
    record
      I      : INTEGER,
      NEXT : SET;
    end record;

  function COPY (S : SET) return SET is
  begin
    if S = null then
      return null;
    else
      return new ELEMENT' (S.I, COPY(S.NEXT));
    end if;
  end COPY;

  procedure ASSIGN (S1 : in SET; S2 : out SET) is
  begin
    S2 := COPY(S1);
  end ASSIGN;

  function EQUAL (S1, S2 : SET) return BOOLEAN is
  begin
    if S1 = null and S2 = null then
      return TRUE;
    elsif (S1 = null or S2 = null) or else S1.I /= S2.I then
      return FALSE;
    else
      return EQUAL(S1.NEXT, S2.NEXT);
    end if;
  end EQUAL;

  procedure CLEAR (S : out SET) is
  begin
    S := null;
  end CLEAR;
```

```
function ADD (NUMBER : INTEGER; S : SET) return SET is
begin
    if S = null then
    return new ELEMENT' (NUMBER, null);
  elsif S.I < NUMBER then
    return new ELEMENT' (S.I, ADD(NUMBER, S.NEXT));
  elsif S.I = NUMBER then
    return COPY(S);
  else
    return new ELEMENT' (NUMBER, COPY(S));
  end if;
end ADD;

function SUB (NUMBER : INTEGER; S : SET) return SET is
begin
  if S = null then
    return null;
  elsif S.I < NUMBER then
    return new ELEMENT' (S.I, SUB(NUMBER, S.NEXT));
  elsif S.I = NUMBER then
    return COPY(S.NEXT);
  else
    return COPY(S);
  end if;
end SUB;

function MEMBER (NUMBER : INTEGER; S : SET)
                                    return BOOLEAN is
begin
  if S = null or else S.I > NUMBER then
    return FALSE;
  elsif S.I = NUMBER then
    return TRUE;
  else
    return MEMBER(NUMBER, S.NEXT);
  end if;
end MEMBER;

function UNION (S1, S2 : SET) return SET is
begin
  if S1 = null then
    return COPY(S2);
  elsif S2 = null then
    return COPY(S1);
  elsif S1.I < S2.I then
    return new ELEMENT' (S1.I UNION(S1.NEXT, S2));
  elsif S1.I > S2.I then
    return new ELEMENT' (S2.I, UNION(S1, S2.NEXT));
```

```
      else
        return new ELEMENT' (S1.I, UNION(S1.NEXT, S2.NEXT));
      end if;
    end UNION;

    function INTERSECTION (S1, S2 : SET) return SET is
    begin
      if S1 = null or S2 = null then
        return null;
      elsif S1.I < S2.I then
        return INTERSECTION(S1.NEXT, S2);
      elsif S1.I > S2.I then
        return INTERSECTION(S1, S2.NEXT);
      else
        return new ELEMENT' (S1.I, INTERSECTION(S1.NEXT,
                             S2.NEXT));
      end if;
    end INTERSECTION;

    function SUBSET (S1, S2 : SET) return BOOLEAN is
    begin
      return EQUAL(INTERSECTION(S1, S2), S1);
    end SUBSET;

    procedure WRITE (S : in SET) is
      package INT_INOUT is new INTEGER_IO(INTEGER);
      use INT_INOUT;
      P : SET;
    begin
      PUT(' (');
      if S /= null then
        PUT(S.I, WIDTH => 1);
        P := S.NEXT;
        while P /= null loop
          PUT(", "); PUT(P.I, WIDTH => 1);
          P := P.NEXT;
        end loop;
      end if;
      PUT(')');
    end WRITE;
  end SET_PACKAGE;


11.14 function EQUAL (T1, T2 : TREE) return BOOLEAN is
     begin
       return (T1 = null and T2 = null)
             or else ((T1 /= null and T2 /= null)
                     and then T1.DATA = T2.DATA
                     and then EQUAL(T1.LEFT, T2.LEFT)
                     and then EQUAL(T1.RIGHT, T2.RIGHT));
     end EQUAL;
```

11.17 **with** TEXT_IO, BASIC_NUM_IO;
      use TEXT_IO, BASIC_NUM_IO;
      procedure COUNT_WORDS **is**
        MAXL : **constant** := 20;
        subtype WORD **is** STRING(1 .. MAXL);
        type NODE;
        type LINK **is access** NODE;
        type NODE **is**
          record
            WO : WORD,
            NUM : POSITIVE;
            LEFT, RIGHT : LINK;
          end record;
        F   : FILE_TYPE;
        TR   : LINK;
        FILE_NAME : STRING(1 .. 30);
        L   : NATURAL;
        W   : WORD;
        procedure READ_WORD (F : **in out** FILE_TYPE; S : **out** STRING;
                               N : **out** NATURAL) **is**
          C : CHARACTER := ' ';
          I : NATURAL := S'FIRST−1;
        begin
          while C = ' ' **and not** END_OF_FILE(F) **loop**
            GET(F, C);
          end loop;
          while C /= ' ' **loop**
            I := I + 1;
            S(I) := C;
            exit when END_OF_LINE(F) **or** I = S'LAST;
            GET(F, C);
          end loop;
          N := I;
        end READ_WORD;

        procedure COUNT (T : **in out** LINK; W : **in** WORD) **is**
        begin
          if T = **null then**
            T := **new** NODE' (W, 1, **null, null**);
          elsif W = T.WO **then**
            T.NUM := T.NUM + 1;
          elsif W < T.WO **then**
            COUNT(T.LEFT, W);
          else
            COUNT(T.RIGHT, W);
          end if;
        end COUNT;

        procedure WRITE_INFO (T : **in** LINK) **is**
        begin

```
      if T /= null then
         WRITE_INFO(T.LEFT);
         PUT(T.WO); PUT(T.NUM, WIDTH => 4); NEW_LINE;
         WRITE_INFO(T.RIGHT);
      end if;
   end WRITE_INFO;
begin
   PUT("File name: "); GET_LINE(FILE_NAME, L);
   OPEN(F, NAME => FILE_NAME(1 .. L), MODE => IN_FILE);
   loop
      READ_WORD(F, W, L);
      exit when L = 0;
      W(L+1 .. MAXL) := (others => ' ');
      COUNT(TR, W);
   end loop;
   WRITE_INFO(TR);
end COUNT_WORDS;
```

11.18 **procedure** REMOVE (T : **in out** LINK; W : **in** WORD) **is**
                      -- See Exercise 11.17
```
   Q : LINK;
   procedure REMOVE_SMALLEST(S : in out LINK; P : out LINK) is
   -- removes the smallest node from the tree S
   -- and lets P point at the removed node
   begin
      if S.LEFT = null then
         -- this is the smallest
         P := S;
         S := S.RIGHT; -- remove the node
      else
         REMOVE_SMALLEST(S.LEFT, P);
      end if;
   end REMOVE_SMALLEST;
begin
   if T /= null then
      if W < T.WO then
         REMOVE(T.LEFT, W);
      elsif W > T.WO then
         REMOVE(T.RIGHT, W);
      else
         -- this node shall be removed
         if T.LEFT = null and T.RIGHT = null then
            T := null;
         elsif T.RIGHT = null then
            T := T.LEFT;
         elsif T.LEFT = null then
            T := T.RIGHT;
```

```
          else
            REMOVE_SMALLEST(T.RIGHT, Q);
            T.WO := Q.WO;
            T.NUM := Q.NUM;
          end if;
        end if;
      end if;
    end REMOVE;
```

12.3
```
    with TEXT_IO, SEQUENTIAL_IO;
    use TEXT_IO;
    procedure PRINT_LABELS is
      type CUSTOMER is
              record
                NAME, STREET, TOWN : STRING(1 .. 20);
              end record;
      package CUSTOMER_INOUT is new SEQUENTIAL_IO(CUSTOMER);
      use CUSTOMER_INOUT;
      CFILE           : CUSTOMER_INOUT.FILE_TYPE;
      CUSTOMER_LINE : array (1 .. 3) of CUSTOMER;
      NO_ON_LINE    : NATURAL;
      FILE_NAME      : STRING(1 .. 30);
      L              : NATURAL;
    begin
      PUT("Customer file? "); GET_LINE(FILE_NAME, L);
      OPEN(CFILE, NAME => FILE_NAME(1 .. L), MODE => IN_FILE);
      while not END_OF_FILE(CFILE) loop
        NO_ON_LINE := 0;
        while NO_ON_LINE < 3 and not END_OF_FILE(CFILE) loop
          NO_ON_LINE := NO_ON_LINE + 1;
          READ(CFILE, CUSTOMER_LINE(NO_ON_LINE));
        end loop;
        NEW_LINE;
        for I in 1 .. NO_ON_LINE loop
          PUT(" " & CUSTOMER_LINE(I).NAME & " ");
        end loop;
        NEW_LINE;
        for I in 1 .. NO_ON_LINE loop
          PUT(" " & CUSTOMER_LINE(I).STREET & " ");
        end loop;
        NEW_LINE;
        for I in 1 .. NO_ON_LINE loop
          PUT(" " & CUSTOMER_LINE(I).TOWN & " ");
        end loop;
        NEW_LINE(2);
      end loop;
      CLOSE(CFILE);
    end PRINT_LABELS;
```

12.10
```
with TEXT_IO, BASIC_NUM_IO, DIRECT_IO;
use TEXT_IO, BASIC_NUM_IO;
procedure STORE is
  subtype PRODUCT_CODE is STRING(1 .. 10);
  type ARTICLE is
    record
      CODE              : PRODUCT_CODE;
      DESCR             : STRING(1 .. 30);
      NUMBER_IN_STORE: NATURAL;
      PRICE             : FLOAT;
    end record;
  type COMMAND is (INFO, BOUGHT, SOLD);
  package ART_INOUT is new DIRECT_IO(ARTICLE);
  package COM_INOUT is new ENUMERATION_IO(COMMAND);
  use ART_INOUT, COM_INOUT;
  AFILE   : ART_INOUT.FILE_TYPE;
  A       : ARTICLE;
  COM     : COMMAND;
  ART_NO : PRODUCT_CODE;
  POS     : ART_INOUT.COUNT;
  N       : NATURAL;
  BLANK   : CHARACTER;

  procedure SEARCH (F             : in out ART_INOUT.FILE_TYPE;
                    CO            : in PRODUCT_CODE;
                    FILE_INDEX: out ART_INOUT.COUNT;
                    ART           : out ARTICLE) is
    P              : ARTICLE;
    I1, I2, INDEX: ART_INOUT.COUNT;
    FOUND        : BOOLEAN := FALSE;
  begin
    I1 := 1;
    I2 := SIZE(F);
    while not FOUND and I1 <= I2 loop
      INDEX := (I1 + I2) / 2;
      READ(F, P, INDEX);
      if CO < P.CODE then
        I2 := INDEX − 1;
      elsif CO > P.CODE then
        I1 := INDEX + 1;
      else
        FOUND := TRUE;
      end if;
    end loop;
    if FOUND then
      FILE_INDEX := INDEX;
      ART := P;
    else
      FILE_INDEX := 0;
```

```
      end if;
   end SEARCH;

   procedure WRITE_INFO (ART : in ARTICLE) is
   begin
      NEW_LINE;
      PUT_LINE("Product code:  " & ART.CODE);
      PUT_LINE("Description:    " & ART.DESCR);
      PUT("Number in store: ");
      PUT(ART.NUMBER_IN_STORE, WIDTH => 1); NEW_LINE;
      PUT("Price:          ");
      PUT(ART.PRICE, EXP => 0, FORE => 1, AFT => 2);
      NEW_LINE(2);
   end WRITE_INFO;

begin
   OPEN(AFILE, INOUT_FILE, "storefile");
   loop
      PUT_LINE("Give command:");
      exit when END_OF_FILE;
      GET(COM); GET(BLANK); GET(ART_NO);
      SEARCH(AFILE, ART_NO, POS, A);
      if POS = 0 then
         PUT_LINE("Article missing");
         SKIP_LINE;
      else
         case COM is
            when INFO    => WRITE_INFO(A);
            when BOUGHT =>
               GET(N);
               A.NUMBER_IN_STORE := A.NUMBER_IN_STORE + N;
               WRITE(AFILE, A, POS);
            when SOLD    =>
               GET(N);
               if A.NUMBER_IN_STORE >= N then
                  A.NUMBER_IN_STORE := A.NUMBER_IN_STORE - N;
                  WRITE(AFILE, A, POS);
               else
                  PUT_LINE("Not that many in store");
               end if;
         end case;
      end if;
   end loop;
   CLOSE(AFILE);
end STORE;
```

12.11 **with** TEXT_IO, BASIC_NUM_IO, DIRECT_IO, SEQUENTIAL_IO;
     use TEXT_IO, BASIC_NUM_IO;
     procedure LARGE_STORE **is**

   ...

declarations as in Exercise 12.10

...

```
type INDEX_RECORD is
  record
    CODE : PRODUCT_CODE;
    IND   : ART_INOUT.COUNT; -- index in the store file
  end record;
type INDEX_TAB is array (POSITIVE range < >) of
                            INDEX_RECORD;
package INDEX_INOUT is new SEQUENTIAL_IO(INDEX_RECORD);
use INDEX_INOUT;
IFILE : INDEX_INOUT.FILE_TYPE;
IR    : INDEX_RECORD;

function SEARCH (T : INDEX_TAB; CO : PRODUCT_CODE)
                        return ART_INOUT.COUNT is
  I1, I2, INDEX : NATURAL;
begin
  I1 := T'FIRST; I2 := T'LAST;
  while I1 <= I2 loop
    INDEX := (I1 + I2) / 2;
    if CO < T(INDEX).CODE then
      I2 := INDEX - 1;
    elsif CO > T(INDEX).CODE then
      I1 := INDEX + 1;
    else -- found
      return T(INDEX).IND;
    end if;
  end loop;
  return 0; -- not found
end SEARCH;

procedure WRITE_INFO (ART : in ARTICLE) is
```
as in Exercise 12.10

```
begin
  OPEN(IFILE, IN_FILE, "indextable");
  -- let IND in the first record in IFILE hold the number of records
  READ(IFILE, IR);
declare
  ITAB : INDEX_TAB(1 .. INTEGER(IR.IND));
begin
  -- read the index table to ITAB
  for K in ITAB'RANGE loop
    READ(IFILE, ITAB(K));
  end loop;
  OPEN(SFILE, INOUT_FILE, "storefile");
  loop
    PUT_LINE("Give command:");
    exit when END_OF_FILE;
```

```
      GET(COM); GET(BLANK); GET(ART_NO);
      POS := SEARCH(ITAB, ART_NO);
      if POS = 0 then
        as in Exercise 12.10
      end if;
    end loop;
  end;
  CLOSE(IFILE); CLOSE(SFILE);
end LARGE_STORE;
```

13.3
```
generic
    type   ELEMENT is private;
package STACK_PACKAGE is
  type   STACK is limited private;
  procedure PUSH   (S : in out STACK; E : in   ELEMENT);
  procedure POP    (S : in out STACK; E : out ELEMENT);
  function   EMPTY (S : STACK) return BOOLEAN;
private
  type STACK_ELEMENT;
  type STACK is access STACK_ELEMENT;
end STACK_PACKAGE;

package body STACK_PACKAGE is
  type STACK_ELEMENT is
    record
      EL    : ELEMENT;
      NEXT : STACK;
    end record;

  procedure PUSH (S : in out STACK; E : in ELEMENT) is
  begin
    S := new STACK_ELEMENT' (E, S);
  end PUSH;

  procedure POP (S : in out STACK; E : out ELEMENT) is
  begin
    E := S.EL;
    S := S.NEXT;
  end POP;

  function EMPTY (S : STACK) return BOOLEAN is
  begin
    return S = null;
  end EMPTY;
end STACK_PACKAGE;

with STACK_PACKAGE;
    ...
```

```
     type PERSON is
       record
         NAME : STRING(1 .. 30);
         ADDR : STRING(1 .. 50);
       end record;
     package FLOATING_POINT_PACK is new
             STACK_PACKAGE(FLOAT);
     package PERSON_PACK is new STACK_PACKAGE(PERSON);
     FP_STACK1, FP_STACK2 : FLOATING_POINT_PACK.STACK;
     P_STACK              : PERSON_PACK.STACK;
```

13.7 ```
      generic
        type ELEMENT is private;
        type INDEX is (< >);
        type ROW is array (INDEX range < >) of ELEMENT;
        with function "+" (E1, E2 : ELEMENT) return ELEMENT is < >;
      function SUM (R : ROW) return ELEMENT;

      function SUM (R : ROW) return ELEMENT is
        S : ELEMENT := R(R'FIRST); -- no "zero value" known
      begin
        if R'LENGTH > 1 then
          for I in INDEX'SUCC(R'FIRST) .. R'LAST loop
            S := S + R(I);
          end loop;
        end if;
        return S;
      end SUM;
      ```

13.9  ```
      generic
        type REAL_NUMBER is digits < >;
        with function F (X : REAL_NUMBER) return REAL_NUMBER;
        EPSILON : REAL_NUMBER := 1.0E-6;
      function INTEGRAL (A, B : REAL_NUMBER) return REAL_NUMBER;

      function INTEGRAL (A, B : REAL_NUMBER) return REAL_NUMBER is
        VALUE, PREVIOUS_VALUE : REAL_NUMBER;
        N : POSITIVE := 10;

        function APPROX (A, B : REAL_NUMBER; N : POSITIVE)
                         return REAL_NUMBER is
          H   : constant REAL_NUMBER := (B - A) / REAL_NUMBER(N);
          SUM : REAL_NUMBER := (F(A) + F(B)) / 2.0;
        begin
          for I in 1 .. N - 1 loop
            SUM := SUM + F(A + REAL_NUMBER(I) * H);
          end loop;
          return SUM * H;
        end APPROX;
      ```

```
begin
  PREVIOUS_VALUE := APPROX(A, B, N);
  loop
    N := N * 2;
    VALUE := APPROX(A, B, N);
    if abs (VALUE - PREVIOUS_VALUE) < EPSILON then
      return VALUE;
    end if;
    PREVIOUS_VALUE := VALUE;
  end loop;
end INTEGRAL;

with BASIC_NUM_IO, INTEGRAL;
use  BASIC_NUM_IO;
procedure INTEGRAL_EX is
  function X2 (X : FLOAT) return FLOAT is
  begin
    return X ** 2;
  end X2;
  function INT_X2 is new INTEGRAL(FLOAT, X2);
begin
  PUT(INT_X2(1.0, 5.0));
end INTEGRAL_EX;
```

Index

abort 94
abs 100
absolute value 100
abstract data type 359, 469
abstraction 162
accept 94
access 453
access table 487
access type 453
access variable 453
  assignment of 455
accuracy 76, 168
actual parameters 220, 239
  generic 525, 529
Ada v, 2, 18
  library 344
  programming environment 344
  Reference Manual vii, 18
addition 98
address 6
AFT 44, 392
aggregate(s) 194, 300, 322
  array 194, 300
  record 322
Algol 16
algorithm 23
all 455
allocator 452
analytical engine 2
and 108, 369
and then 108
ANSI 17, 18
APL 18
ARCCOS 105
ARCSIN 105

ARCTAN 105
arithmetic expression 97
arithmetic-logic unit 6
array 187, 298, 314, 327
array aggregate 194, 300
array of arrays 314
array types 187, 298, 314, 327
  attributes for 201
    multidimensional 312
  constrained 187, 298
  multidimensional 298
  unconstrained 196
  unconstrained multidimensional 310
arrays 187, 298, 314, 327
  to assign 199
  to catenate 202
  to compare 199
ASCII package 79, 559
ASCII standard 79, 80, 559
assembler 14
assembly language 14
assignment 40, 127
  of access variables 456
  of arrays 199
  of records 321
assignment statement 40, 127
at 94
attribute(s)
  for array types 201
  for enumeration types 174
  for floating point types 171
  for integer types 168
  for multidimensional arrays 312
  for the type CHARACTER 81
  for the type FLOAT 77

attribute(s) *contd.*
    for the type INTEGER 74

BASE 390
base type 270
Basic 16
BASIC_NUM_IO 32, 176, 555
begin 33, 126, 217, 236, 359, 440
binary digits 6, 72
binary file 491
binary form 390
binary number system 72
binary search 333, 516
binary search tree 483, 490
binary tree 477
binomial coefficients 249, 295
bit 6, 72
blank character 399
block statement 440
body 349
BOOLEAN 90
    literals of the type 96
Boolean expression 106
Boolean value 90
break 137
bubble sort 331
byte 6

call 31, 49, 219, 237
case selector 132
case statement 131, 175
    list of alternatives 132
categories of packages 351
catenation
    of arrays 208
    of strings 85, 95
central processing unit 5
CHARACTER 78
    attributes for the type 81
character(s) 78
    blank 399
    to read 405
    to write 388
character literals 79, 95
circular list 465
CLOSE 414, 494, 515
closing a file 414, 494, 515
COBOL 15
COL 386, 404

column by column 306
comment 46
comparison 106
    of arrays 199
    of records 321
    of strings 87
compilation 9, 114, 344
compilation order 345, 350
compilation unit 344, 350
compiler 9, 114, 344
compile-time error 114
composite types 83, 163
compound statements 126
constant declaration 113, 205
constant 113, 205
constrained array 187, 298
CONSTRAINT_ERROR 432
constructor 362
control statements 125
control unit 5
COS 105
COSH 105
COUNT 383, 513
CPU 5
CREATE 411, 493, 515
CTRL key 154, 397
current index 495, 513
CURRENT_INPUT 425
CURRENT_OUTPUT 425
current page, line and column numbers
        386, 404

data object 72, 162
data register 421, 497
data structure 297
    dynamic 451
data type 161
    abstract 359
    private 372
    recursive 464, 479
DATA_ERROR 446
debugger 120
debugging 119
declaration(s)
    constant 113, 205
    exception 433
    global 268
    number 114
    order of 219

declarations *contd.*
　scope of 267
　type 162
　variable 111
declare 441
default value 276, 530, 541
DEFAULT_SETTING 179, 395
delay 94
DELETE 425, 494, 515
delta 94
depth, of a tree 482
DEVICE_ERROR 446
difference engine 2
digit, binary 6, 72
DIGITS 77, 171
digits 169, 534
direct access file 513
direct file 513
directed graph 487
DIRECT_IO 513, 564
discrete type 132
　expression of 132
disk 8, 410, 491
disk storage 8, 410, 491
division 98
　integer division 99
do 94
doubly linked lists 465
dynamic data structure 451
dynamic object 452
　lifetime 457

echo 382
editor, text- 8
else 55, 128
elsif 58, 128
empty slice 84, 201
end 33, 126, 128, 131, 137, 217, 236,
　319, 359, 440
END_ERROR 446
endless loop 137, 142
END_OF_FILE 154, 400, 496, 515
END_OF_LINE 399
END_OF_PAGE 400
ENIAC 3
entry 94
enumeration types 172
　to read and write 178, 393, 409
ENUMERATION_IO 178, 393, 409

equality operator 106, 376
error 114, 432, 445
　compile-time 114
　logical 115
　run-time 115
error message 116
Euclid's algorithm 291
EXCEPTION 431
exception 431
exception declaration 433
exception handler 436
exclusive **or** 108, 369
execution 6
exit statement 147
EXP 44, 392
　mathematical function 105
exponent 75
　form 44, 93, 392
exponentiating operator 100
expressions
　arithmetic 97
　Boolean 106
　discrete 132
　numeric 97
　static 133
external file 411, 493

factorial 250, 278
FALSE 90, 96
file 410, 491
　binary 491
　direct 513
　direct access 513
　external 411, 493
　logical 410, 493
　physical 411, 493
　sequential 492
　sorted 499, 516
　temporary 411, 421, 506
　to close a 414, 494, 515
　to open a 411, 493, 515
　to reset a 420, 494, 515
　to sort a 508
　transaction 505, 516
file name 410, 416, 493
file terminator 397
file variable 411, 493
FILE_MODE 411, 494, 515
FILE_TYPE 411, 493

FIRST 75, 168, 174, 201, 313
FLOAT 38, 71, 169
  attributes for the type 77
floating point numbers 77, 168
  to read 178, 408
  to write 178, 391
floating point types 77, 168
FLOAT_IO 178, 391, 408
flow chart 24
for 61, 138
FORE 44, 392
formal parameters 217, 239
  generic 524, 529
Fortran 15
full type declaration 459
function 216
function body 217
function call 219
function specification 218, 287
functions 216
  mathematical 105
  trigonometric 105

generations of computers 3
generic 524
generic actual parameters 525, 529
generic formal parameters 524, 529
generic instantiation 525
generic package 526
generic parameter 529
generic procedure 524
generic subprogram parameter 536
generic type parameter 531
generic unit 523
generic value parameter 529
GET 405, 407, 408, 409
GET_LINE 84, 405
gigabytes 6
global declarations 268
global variable 269
goto 94
graphs 487
  directed 487
greatest common divisor 291, 294

hardware 13
hexadecimal form 396
hexadecimal numbers 396
high-level language 7, 15

histogram 212
Hollerith 2
Honeywell Bull 17

IBM 3
identifier 92
if statement 55, 128
imaginary numbers 360
in 62, 107, 138
in parameter 239
in out parameter 239
incomplete type declaration 458
indentation 50
INDEX 513
index, current 495, 513
index bounds 190, 197, 300, 311
index types 190, 197, 300, 311
indexing 83, 188, 191, 299, 312, 330
indirect recursion 286
IN_FILE 411, 494, 515
informer 368
initialization 63, 112, 194, 322, 454
  of record components 325
initial value 63, 112, 194, 322, 325, 454
inorder 479
INOUT_FILE 515
input, end of 154, 400, 496, 515
input device 7
input termination 154, 400, 496, 515
input/output 381, 491
  of enumeration types 178, 393, 409
  of floating point types 178, 391, 408
  of integer types 176, 389, 407
instance 279, 524
instantiation 524
instruction 6
INTEGER 33, 71, 165
  attributes for the type 74
integer division 99
integer literal 93
integer type 71, 165
INTEGER_IO 176, 389, 407
integers 71, 165
  to read 176, 407
  to write 176, 389
integral 545
interactive data input 150
interactive programs 150
interpreter 12

ISO 17, 18
IS_OPEN 412, 494, 515
iteration 25, 61, 62, 136

KB 6
key
   CTRL 154, 397
   RETURN 56, 88, 396
keyboard 7
kilobyte 6

LARGE 77, 171
large scale integration 3
LAST 75, 168, 174, 201, 313
LAYOUT_ERROR 446
leaves 476
LENGTH 201, 313
library 342, 344
lifetime of dynamic objects 457
limited private 375, 532
LINE 386, 404
line 382, 395
line feed 383
line length 384
line number 386, 404
line terminator 382, 396
LINE_LENGTH 385
linear search 204, 330
lingering pointer 457
linked list 457, 465
linking 10
LISP 18
list 293, 457
   circular 465
   doubly linked 465
   linked 457
literals 93
   BOOLEAN 96
   character 79, 95
   integer 93
   numeric 93
   real 93
   text string 95
LN 105
load module 10
local variable 230
LOG 105
logical error 115
logical file 410, 493

LONG_FLOAT 77
LONG_INTEGER 75
loop, endless 137, 142
loop parameter 62, 138
loop statement(s) 61, 63, 136
   nested 148
LOWER_CASE 179, 395
LSI 3

machine code 7
machine ware 13
Maclaurin series 159, 291, 377
magnetic tape 8
main program 51, 251
mantissa 75
Mark I 3
mathematical standard functions 105
matrix 310, 314
matrix multiplication 336, 337
maximum page and line length 385
median 293
megabyte 6
memory, packages with 352
memory cell 6
merge 499
microprocessor 3
mixing types 40
mod 99
MODE 411, 425, 494, 515
MODE_ERROR 446
module 17, 341, 523
modulus operator 99
multi-choice situation 128, 131
multidimensional array 298
multiplication 98
mutual recursion 286

NAME 411, 425, 494, 515
name 49, 92, 164, 235, 249
   of file 410, 416
   of operator 288, 365
   the same 269, 270
NAME_ERROR 446
named parameter association 273
nested loops 148
new 176, 452, 525
NEW_LINE 32, 382
NEW_PAGE 42, 382
Newton's method 291

node 476
not 108, 369
not in 107
null 127, 454
number declaration 114
NUMERIC_ERROR 432
numeric expressions 97
numeric literals 93
numeric type 71, 165, 168

object 70, 111
    dynamic 452
    static 452
object module 10
object parameters 529
octal form 391
of 187
OPEN 411, 493, 515
operating system 11
operations 70, 359
operator precedence 101, 110
operators 96
    equality 106, 376
    exponentiation 100
    modulus 99
    names of 288, 365
    relational 106
or 108, 369
or else 108
order of evaluation 102, 110
OS 11
others 133, 194, 198, 301, 437
out parameter 239
OUT_FILE 411, 494, 515
output
    of characters 388
    of floating point numbers 391
    of integers 389
    of text 388
    of values of enumeration types 393
    test 120
output device 7
overflow 115, 119, 432
overloaded subprograms 270

PL/I 16
package 53, 176, 343, 349
package bodies 349
    statement part 359

package specification 52, 342
packages 341
    categories of 351
    generic 526
    with memory 352
    without body 352
PAGE 386, 404
page and line length, maximum 385
page number 386, 404
page terminator 382, 396
PAGE_LENGTH 385
pages 382, 395
palindromes 158
parallel programs vi, 18
parameter
    actual 220, 239
    actual generic 525, 529
    formal 217, 239
    formal generic 524, 529
    generic 529
    in 234
    in out 239
    object 529
    out 239
    value 529
parameter association 273
    named 273
    positional 273
parameter type profile 271
Pascal 2, 16
Pascal Turbo 17
Pascal UCSD 17
peripheral device 8
peripheral equipment 8
physical file 411, 493
pointer 453
    lingering 457
polynomial 486
pop 469, 526
portable programs 10
POS 81
positional parameter association 273
POSITIVE_COUNT 383, 513
postorder 479
pragma 94
PRED 174
preorder 479
primary memory 6
prime numbers 211

private 372, 531
private part 374
private type 372
    limited 375
problem solving 23
procedure 235
    generic 524
procedure body 236
procedure call 237
procedure specification 236, 287
profile 271
    parameter and result type 271
    parameter type 271
program 2, 5, 33, 126
program structure 33, 126
program text 8
PROGRAM_ERROR 432
push 469, 526
PUT 388, 389, 391, 393
PUT_LINE 33, 388

qualified expression 194, 301
queue 469
quicksort 295

raise statement 434
random numbers 353, 528
RANGE 201, 312
range 165, 183, 192, 197, 311, 534
rational numbers 338, 379
READ 495, 514
reading
    characters 405
    floating point numbers 408
    integers 407
    text 405
    values of an enumeration type 409
real literals 93
real numbers 77, 168
    to read 178, 408
    to write 178, 391
real types 77, 168
record 319
record, transaction 505
record aggregate 322
record assignment 321
record type 319
records 319
    comparing 321

records *contd.*
    initializing components in 325
recursion 26, 277
    indirect 286
    mutual 286
recursive subprograms 277
recursive type 464, 479
reference 453
relational operator 106
rem 99
remainder on integer division 99
renames 94
reserved words 94
RESET 420, 494, 515
resetting a file 420, 494, 515
RETURN key 56, 88, 396
return statement 218
reverse 141
root 476
rounding 102
row by row 305
run-time error 115

same name 269, 270
scalar product 337
scalar type 163
scope of declaration 267
screen 7
search
    binary 333, 516
    linear 204, 330
secondary storage 7, 410, 491
select 94
selection 25, 128, 131
selection in records 320
selector 362
semicolon 126
separate 257
sequence 25
sequential file 492
sequential program structure 126
SEQUENTIAL_IO 492, 562
SET_COL 386, 404
SET_INDEX 513
SET_INPUT 424
SET_LINE 386, 404
SET_LINE_LENGTH 384
SET_OUTPUT 424
SET_PAGE_LENGTH 385

sets 367, 379, 488, 532
SHORT_FLOAT 77
SHORT_INTEGER 75
side effects 244
simple statement 126
Simula 16
SiN 105
SINH 105
SIZE 513
SKIP_LINE 401
SKIP_PAGE 402
slice 84, 128, 200, 300, 316
SMALL 77, 171
software 13
software crisis 17
sort
  bubble 331
  file 509
sorted files 499, 516
sorting 29, 208, 212, 259, 295, 331, 509,
    520, 541
source code 8
space character 399
sparse matrix 486
specification 22
SQRT 105
stack 469, 526, 544
STANDARD 71, 557
standard functions, mathematical 105
standard input 424
standard output 424
standard types 70
statement(s) 126
  assignment 127
  block 440
  case 131, 175
  compound 126
  control 125
  exit 147
  loop 61, 63, 136
  raise 434
  simple 126
  sequence of, in package body 359
static expressions 133
static objects 452
STATUS_ERROR 445
stepwise refinement 26, 249
storage
  disk 8, 410, 491

storage contd.
  secondary 7, 410, 491
STORAGE_ERROR 432
STRING 39, 82, 198, 388, 405
string literals 95
string variables 82
strings, to compare 87
structured programming 17
subprogram specification 218, 236, 287
subprogram structure 126
subprograms 215
  overloaded 270
  recursive 277
subtraction 98
subtree 478
subtype 182
SUCC 174
syntax 9
system routines 10

table 61, 187, 203, 298
TAN 105
TANH 105
task 94
TASKING_ERROR 432
temporary files 411, 421, 506
terminal 7, 382, 395
terminate 94
terminator
  file 397
  line 382, 396
  page 382, 396
test output 120
text
  to read 405
  to write 388
text files 8, 410
  logical 410
  to read and write 413
text-editor 8
TEXT_IO 30, 176, 381, 549
then 55, 128
top-down design 26, 249
transaction 505, 516
transaction file 505
transaction record 505
trapezium rule 545
tree 476
  binary 477

tree *contd.*
  binary search 483, 490
  depth of a 482
  sub- 478
TRUE 90, 96
Turbo Pascal 17
two's complement form 73
type parameter, generic 531
type conversion 102
types
  abstract 359, 469
  access 453
  array 187, 298, 314, 327
  base 270
  composite 83, 163
  declaration of 162
  discrete 132
  enumeration 172
  floating point 77, 168
  full declaration 459
  incomplete declaration 458
  index 190, 197, 300, 311
  integer 71, 165
  limited private 375, 532
  mixing 40
  numeric 71, 165, 168
  private 372
  real 77, 168
  scalar 163
  sub- 182

UCSD Pascal 17
unconstrained array 196
unconstrained multidimensional array
    310
UNIVAC 3
universal_integer 98, 104, 114, 168

universal_real 98, 104, 114, 170
UPPER_CASE 179, 395
use clause 347
USE_ERROR 446

VAL 81
validation v, 18
value
  absolute 100
  Boolean 90
  default 276, 530, 541
  initial 63, 112, 194, 322, 325, 454
value parameter 529
variable 111
  access 453
  file 411, 493
  global 269
  local 230
variable declaration 111
very large scale integration 3
video terminal 7
visiting order in trees 479
VLSI 3
von Neumann 3

when 132, 436
while 63, 142
whole numbers 33, 71, 165
WIDTH 36, 390, 407
with clause 345
word 6
WRITE 495, 514

xor 108, 369

zero of a function 538